The Armenian Diaspora and Stateless Power

Armenians in the Modern and Early Modern World

Recent decades have seen the expansion of Armenian Studies from insular history to a broader, more interactive field within an inter-regional and global context. This series, *Armenians in the Modern and Early Modern World*, responds to this growth by promoting innovative and interdisciplinary approaches to Armenian history, politics, and culture in the period between 1500-2000. Focusing on the geographies of the Mediterranean, Middle East, and Contemporary Russia [Eastern Armenia], it directs specific attention to imperial and post-imperial frameworks: from the Ottoman Empire to Modern Turkey/Arab Middle East; the Safavid/Qajar Empires to Iran; and the Russian Empire to Soviet Union/Post-Soviet territories.

Series Editor

Bedross Der Matossian, *University of Nebraska, Lincoln, USA*

Advisory Board

Levon Abrahamian, *Yerevan State University, Armenia*
Sylvie Alajaji, *Franklin & Marshal College, USA*
Sebouh Aslanian, *University of California, Los Angeles, USA*
Stephan Astourian, *University of California, Berkley, USA*
Houri Berberian, *University of California, Irvine, USA*
Talar Chahinian, *University of California, Irvine, USA*
Rachel Goshgarian, *Lafayette College, USA*
Ronald Grigor Suny, *University of Michigan, USA*
Sossie Kasbarian, *University of Stirling, UK*
Christina Maranci, *Tufts University, USA*
Tsolin Nalbantian, *Leiden University, the Netherlands*
Anna Ohanyan, *Stonehill College, USA*
Hratch Tchilingirian, *University of Oxford, UK*

Published and Forthcoming Titles

The Politics of Naming the Armenian Genocide: Language, History and 'Medz Yeghern', Vartan Matiossian
Picturing the Ottoman Armenian World: Photography in Erzerum, Kharpert, Van and Beyond, David Low

The Armenian Diaspora and Stateless Power

Collective Identity in the Transnational 20th Century

Edited by
Talar Chahinian, Sossie Kasbarian and
Tsolin Nalbantian

I.B. TAURIS
LONDON • NEW YORK • OXFORD • NEW DELHI • SYDNEY

I.B. TAURIS
Bloomsbury Publishing Plc
50 Bedford Square, London, WC1B 3DP, UK
1385 Broadway, New York, NY 10018, USA
29 Earlsfort Terrace, Dublin 2, Ireland

BLOOMSBURY, I.B. TAURIS and the I.B. Tauris logo are trademarks of Bloomsbury Publishing Plc

First published in Great Britain 2024

Copyright © Talar Chahinian, Sossie Kasbarian, Tsolin Nalbantian, 2024

Talar Chahinian, Sossie Kasbarian, Tsolin Nalbantian and Contributors have asserted their rights under the Copyright, Designs and Patents Act, 1988, to be identified as Authors of this work.

Copyright Individual Chapters © 2023 Boris Adjemian, Sylvia Alajaji, Sebouh Aslanian, Talar Chahinian, Nare Galstyan, Karen Jallatyan, Sossie Kasbarian, Lilit Keshishyan, Hasmik Khalapyan, Gegham Mughnetsyan, Tsolin Nalbantian, Hrag Papazian, Vahe Sahakyan, Christopher Sheklian, Talin Suciyan, Khachig Tölölyan

For legal purposes the Acknowledgements on pp. vii and 163 constitute an extension of this copyright page.

Series design by Adriana Brioso
Cover image © Sako Shahinian

All rights reserved. No part of this publication may be reproduced or transmitted in any form or by any means, electronic or mechanical, including photocopying, recording, or any information storage or retrieval system, without prior permission in writing from the publishers.

Bloomsbury Publishing Plc does not have any control over, or responsibility for, any third-party websites referred to or in this book. All internet addresses given in this book were correct at the time of going to press. The author and publisher regret any inconvenience caused if addresses have changed or sites have ceased to exist, but can accept no responsibility for any such changes.

A catalogue record for this book is available from the British Library.

Library of Congress Cataloging-in-Publication Data
Names: Chahinian, Talar, editor. | Kasbarian, Sossie, editor. | Nalbantian, Tsolin, editor.
Title: The Armenian diaspora and stateless power : collective identity in the transnational 20th century / edited by Talar Chahinian, Sossie Kasbarian, Tsolin Nalbantian.
Description: London ; New York, NY : I.B Tauris, [2023] | Series: Armenians in the modern and early modern world | Includes bibliographical references and index. | Contents: In Lieu of an Introduction / Talar Chahinian, Sossie Kasbarian, Tsolin Nalbantian – In search of the Sedentary : Armenian Diaspora Homelands between Addis Ababa, Jerusalem, Valence and Paris / Boris Adjemian – Armenian Displaced Persons : From Funkerkaserne to Montebello / Gegham Mughnetsyan – Diaspora-Homeland relations Re-examined : The case of Syrian Armenian in the Netherlands / Nare Galstyan – Serialized Struggle for Power in the Armenian Periodical Press of Europe, Late 19th and Early 20th Centuries / Hasmik Khalapyan – Transnational Politics and Governmental Strategies in the Formative Years of the PostGenocide Armenian Diaspora (1920s-1930s) / Vahe Sahakyan – Defiant Adherence : Cultural Critiques in Late Twentieth Century Armenian Diaspora Literature / Lilit Keshishyan – Liturgical Subject of the Armenian Apostolic Church : Recent Waves of Migration / Christopher Sheklian – Sounding Armenian : The Contours of the Diasporic Musical Imaginary / Sylvia Alajaji – "Toward the Diaspora" : The Performative Powers of Vahé Oshagan's Poetry / Karen Jallatyan – "Our good Armenians" : Survival and Denial in Post-Genocide Turkey / Talin Suciyan – Are Istanbul Armenians Diasporic? Unpacking the Famous Debate / Hrag Papazian – Afterword / Khachig Tölölyan – Epilogue / Sebouh Aslanian.
Identifiers: LCCN 2023011387 (print) | LCCN 2023011388 (ebook) | ISBN 9780755648207 (hardback) | ISBN 9780755648214 (paperback) | ISBN 9780755648221 (pdf) | ISBN 9780755648238 (epub) | ISBN 9780755648245
Subjects: LCSH: Armenian diaspora. | Armenians–Civilization. | Armenians–Ethnic identity.
Classification: LCC DS172.2 .A7617 2023 (print) | LCC DS172.2 (ebook) | DDC 305.891/922–dc23/eng/20230321
LC record available at https://lccn.loc.gov/2023011387
LC ebook record available at https://lccn.loc.gov/2023011388

ISBN: HB: 978-0-7556-4820-7
ePDF: 978-0-7556-4822-1
eBook: 978-0-7556-4823-8

Typeset by Deanta Global Publishing Services, Chennai, India
Printed and bound in Great Britain

The publication of this book was supported by the Calouste Gulbenkian Foundation.

To find out more about our authors and books visit www.bloomsbury.com and sign up for our newsletters.

Contents

Acknowledgements	vii
Note on Translation and Transliteration	ix
List of Contributors	x

In Lieu of an Introduction *Talar Chahinian, Sossie Kasbarian and Tsolin Nalbantian*   1

I 'The Logic of the Sedentary': Complicating notions of home and homelands

1 In Search of the Sedentary: Rethinking homelands in the Armenian Diaspora *Boris Adjemian*   27
2 Armenian Displaced Persons: From displacement to a diaspora community *Gegham Mughnetsyan*   45
3 Diaspora–Homeland Relations Re-examined: The case of Syrian Armenians in the Netherlands *Nare Galstyan*   67

II 'Diasporic Social Formation': Leadership elites, institutions and transnational governmentality

4 Forging Diasporic Identity in the *Fin de Siècle* Armenian Periodical Press in Europe *Hasmik Khalapyan*   91
5 Transnational Politics and Governmental Strategies in the Formative Years of the Post-genocide Armenian Diaspora (1920s–1930s) *Vahe Sahakyan*   107
6 Defiant Adherence: Cultural critiques in late twentieth-century Armenian Diaspora literature *Lilit Keshishyan*   135
7 The Liturgical Subject of the Armenian Apostolic Church: Recent waves of migration *Christopher Sheklian*   148

III 'The Social Text of Diaspora': Diasporic becoming and legibility in diaspora's semantic domain

8 Sounding Armenian: The contours of the diasporic musical imaginary *Sylvia Angelique Alajaji*   175
9 'Toward the Diaspora': The performative powers of Vahé Oshagan's poetry *Karen Jallatyan*   194

10 The Armenians in Turkey: From autochthonous people to
   diaspora *Talin Suciyan* 212
11 Are Istanbul Armenians Diasporic? Unpacking the famous debate
   Hrag Papazian 232

Afterword: *Armenian diaspora studies and its transformative supplement, the
study of diasporas* Khachig Tölölyan 250
Epilogue *Sebouh Aslanian* 269

Bibliography 275
Index 301

Acknowledgements

Our gratitude goes to all the authors in this volume for their intellectual camaraderie and especially to Khachig Tölölyan for the Afterword and Sebouh Aslanian for the Epilogue. The intellectual groundwork for this book was shaped and solidified over the conference in honour of Khachig Tölölyan, '"Diaspora and Stateless Power": Social Discipline and Identity Formation Across the Armenian Diaspora during the Long Twentieth Century', organized by the Society of Armenian Studies (SAS) and held at the University of California, Los Angeles (UCLA), in October 2019. It coincided with the marking of the SAS's forty-fifth anniversary. This stimulating and inspiring two-day conference was hosted by Sebouh Aslanian, Professor & Richard Hovannisian Endowed Chair in Modern Armenian History at UCLA and co-sponsored by the Calouste Gulbenkian Foundation, the Richard Hovannisian Endowed Chair in Modern Armenian History (UCLA), the Narekatsi Chair in Armenian Studies (UCLA), the Meghrouni Family Presidential Chair (UC Irvine), the Institute of Armenian Studies (USC), the Armenian Studies Program (California State University, Fresno), the Armenian Studies Program (CSU Northridge) and the National Association for Armenian Studies and Research (NAASR). We are grateful for their vision and support.

We are indebted to Bedross Der Matossian for his unparalleled support throughout and for especially believing in this project and our vision from its inception. We are so grateful to Sako Shahinan, who designed our amazing cover image that we love so much, and we deeply appreciate Cyrus Schayegh's help in making it possible. Rory Gormley, Yasmin Garcha and Paige Harris at I.B. Tauris/Bloomsbury and Raffi Mohammed have been tremendously helpful, and the Leiden Institute for Area Studies at Leiden University provided funds to help index the work. Finally, we must express our gratitude to the Calouste Gulbenkian Foundation, which generously supported this project and financed the simultaneous paperback publication of this volume.

This volume was developed in a protracted period of crises. As such we want to acknowledge the friends, family and colleagues that we lost in this period and recognize that grief and crises have accompanied this project for each one of the contributors in different ways. A few months after the conference that conceived this project, the Covid-19 pandemic struck. And while the Autumn 2020 War in Artsakh/Nagorno-Karabakh was a traumatic period for all of us, some of our contributors felt its pain more acutely. We are in awe that they continued to work through ongoing trauma.

Gratitude and love from Talar to Anto, to Aram and Arene, and to her family; from Sossie to her family and to the virtual global community of Armenian Studies – related friends that coalesced in this period; from Tsolin to Cyrus, and to Rostom and Nazani. Finally, we want to thank one another. Working together has been a source not just of support to bring this volume to publication but also one of comfort, refuge and solidarity throughout our daily experiences and struggles across three countries and multiple time zones.

Finally, we want to once again recognize our debt to Khachig Tölölyan, whose body of work, mentorship, intellectual generosity, sincerity and vision have inspired and guided this volume and the intellectual paths of its editors and contributors. We dedicate this book to him and to his future students.

Note on Translation and Transliteration

Translations from Armenian source material are the authors' own unless otherwise specified. In the case of some key terms, authors present the Armenian word in transliteration and follow with a translation.

All Armenian titles are transliterated using the Library of Congress romanization chart, adopted by the *International Journal of Middle East Studies* and the *Journal of the Society for Armenian Studies*. Authors use both Western Armenian phonetic and Eastern Armenian phonetic values according to preference.

Armenian proper names follow a phonetic romanization pattern, avoiding the diacritic system mentioned above.

Contributors

Boris Adjemian obtained his PhD from École des Hautes Études en Sciences Sociales and Università degli Studi di Napoli 'L'Orientale', and is a historian and the director of the AGBU Nubar Library (Paris). He is the co-editor of the academic journal *Études arméniennes contemporaines* and an editorial board member of *20 & 21: Revue d'histoire*. He is an affiliated researcher to the Centre de recherches historiques (CRH, EHESS) and the Institut Convergences Migrations (ICM).

Sylvia Angelique Alajaji is Professor of Music at Franklin & Marshall College. She is the author of *Music and the Armenian Diaspora: Searching for Home in Exile* (2015).

Sebouh Aslanian is Professor of History and the Richard Hovannisian Endowed Chair of Modern Armenian History at UCLA. He is also Director of the Armenian Studies Center within the UCLA Promise Armenian Institute. He is the author of *From the Indian Ocean to the Mediterranean: The Global Trade Networks of Armenian Merchants from New Julfa* (2011) and *Early Modernity and Mobility: Port Cities and Printers Across the Armenian Diaspora, 1512–1800* (2023).

Talar Chahinian holds a PhD in Comparative Literature from UCLA and lectures in the Program for Armenian Studies at UC Irvine, where she is also a visiting faculty in the Department of Comparative Literature. She is the author of *Stateless: The Politics of the Armenian Language in Exile* (2023) and co-editor of *Diaspora: A Journal of Transnational Studies*.

Nare Galstyan obtained a PhD degree in Sociology and Methodology of Social Research from the University of Milan and the University of Turin. Her dissertation analysed the differences between diaspora engagement practices of the stateless Assyrian and state-linked Armenian diasporas. Currently she works as Senior Research Associate at the Burton Blatt Institute, Syracuse University.

Karen Jallatyan is Lecturer in the Department of Armenian Studies at the Pázmány Péter Catholic University, Budapest, Hungary. When composing the essay in the present volume, he was a Calouste Gulbenkian Foundation Postdoctoral Fellow in the same Department. He obtained a PhD in Comparative Literature from the University of California, Irvine, in 2019 and mainly researches the Armenian diaspora.

Sossie Kasbarian is Senior Lecturer in Politics at the University of Stirling and co-editor of *Diaspora: A Journal of Transnational Studies*. Her research interests and publications broadly span diaspora studies; contemporary Middle East politics and society; nationalism and ethnicity; and refugee, displacement and migration studies. She is the co-editor of *Diasporas of the Modern Middle East: Contextualising Community* (2015).

Lilit Keshishyan is Project Director of the 'California History through Armenian Experiences' oral history project at the USC Institute of Armenian Studies and a lecturer in USC's Writing Program. She holds a PhD in Comparative Literature from UCLA. Her academic work has explored issues of identity, language and place in the literature of the Armenian diaspora.

Hasmik Khalapyan is Assistant Professor at the American University of Armenia. Her original research is on the Armenian women's movement in the Ottoman Empire, 1876–1914. Her research interests include histories of social change in local/global perspective; Ottoman history; women's history in comparative perspective; theories and histories of empires and colonialism; and ideologies and education policies in the early Soviet period.

Gegham Mughnetsyan is the Chitjian Researcher Archivist at the University of Southern California's Dornsife Institute of Armenian Studies, where he manages the Institute's archival collections and coordinates the *Displaced Persons Documentation Project*.

Tsolin Nalbantian is Associate Professor of Modern Middle East History at Leiden University. She is the author of *Armenians Beyond Diaspora: Making Lebanon Their Own* (2020) and co-editor of *Practicing Sectarianism: Archival and Ethnographic Interventions on Lebanon* (2022). She is also the series co-editor of *Critical, Connected Histories*.

Hrag Papazian holds a DPhil in Anthropology from the University of Oxford (2020). When working on the chapter in this volume, he was first a Promise Armenian Institute Postdoctoral Fellow at UCLA's Department of Anthropology, then Kazan Visiting Professor in Armenian Studies at California State University, Fresno.

Vahe Sahakyan (Armenian Research Center, University of Michigan-Dearborn) is an interdisciplinary scholar with doctorates in sociology and Near Eastern studies, whose research and work draw on the methods and theories of sociology, anthropology, history and cultural studies. He is broadly interested in population movements, transnational formations and diasporas with a particular focus on the Armenian diaspora.

Christopher Sheklian is currently a Postdoctoral Researcher in the Department of Comparative Religious Studies at Radboud University in Nijmegen, part of the ERC-funded 'Rewriting Global Orthodoxy' Project. His work explores the sensorial, affective and embodied aspects of religious belonging in minority, migrant and diasporic populations. He is currently preparing a monograph entitled *Liturgical Rights: Armenian Christian Minority Presence in Turkey.*

Talin Suciyan is Associate Professor (Privat Dozentin) of Turkish Studies at Ludwig Maximilian University of Munich. She is the author of the book *The Armenians in Modern Turkey: Post-Genocide Society, History and Politics* (2016). Her second book, *Outcasting Armenians: Tanzimat of the Provinces*, will be published soon.

Khachig Tölölyan (emeritus) was Professor of the Humanities at the College of Letters in Wesleyan University. He is the founding editor of *Diaspora: A Journal of Transnational Studies* and of *Pynchon Notes*. He has published on diaspora studies in general and the Armenian diaspora in particular, as well as studies of American novels and Armenian terrorism.

In Lieu of an Introduction

Talar Chahinian, Sossie Kasbarian and Tsolin Nalbantian

Over the course of the twentieth century, it became impossible to imagine the Armenian experience outside the framework of dispersion. The 1915 Genocide had either killed or displaced the majority of the world's Armenian population, concentrated in the Armenian provinces of the Ottoman Empire. For many Armenians who survived in exiled communities dispersed throughout the Middle East, Europe and the Americas, the process of rebuilding their lives came with an analogous process of reconstructing their identity, according to the demands of their host polity and the allegiances of their Armenian communal belonging. Often hailing from geographically disparate towns, survivors found themselves in a new proximity with fellow Armenians. The inner diversity of these newly instituted exilic communities, compounded by inter-community exchange facilitated by private correspondence and the burgeoning network of Armenian-language periodicals, gave rise to a new form of transnational consciousness among Armenians. Since the post-war political refashioning of the region, the incorporation of eastern Armenian lands into the Soviet Union and the creation of the Republic of Turkey made return impossible for survivors,[1] community leaders in dispersion initiated nation-building projects grounded in their new locales and centred on the concept of diaspora. In other words, the establishment of institutions, organizations, schools, churches and printing presses was guided by the discourse of diasporic identity. In time, as Armenians became visible in host nations around the world, this internal, orchestrated intellectualization of diaspora as the auxiliary facilitator of survival in dispersion also found reflection in international public discourse. The Armenian experience in the twentieth century became known as 'quintessentially' diasporic.

While the narrative that roots the Armenian Diaspora in the twentieth century frames it as a by-product of the genocide, many scholars have argued that Armenians' diasporicity predates 1915.[2] In discussing the post-genocide possibility of literary production outside the validating structures of either land or a state, Hagop Oshagan, for instance, reminds his readers that the Western Armenian literary tradition was cultivated in diasporic centres in the early nineteenth century and in cities like Venice, Paris, Smyrna and Istanbul.[3] Levon Zekiyan goes back even further in time: he breaks what he calls 'the Armenian process of diasporization' into three phases, consisting of the fall of the Bagratid capital Ani (1045), the end of the Cilician Kingdom (1375) and the 1915 Genocide.[4] For Zekiyan, the phenomenon of Armenians living outside their homeland is not distinctively modern but rather a millennium-long experience of cultivating attachments in dispersion.

Even though scholars vary in their dating of Armenians' diasporic experiences, the discursive fashioning of dispersion as diaspora developed over the course of the twentieth century. The word *spʻiwrkʻ* (diaspora) circulated in intellectual debates carried out in the Western Armenian press, often in reaction to Soviet Armenian publications, beginning in the 1940s.[5] By the 1970s, it was clear that a grand narrative of diaspora governed all spaces of communal life, whether through the transnational structure of political parties and organizations, the distribution patterns of literature and textbooks or the subscription configuration of periodicals. Fluid in its definition of homeland, this narrative cultivated the ideas of return and of territorial attachment to host countries, producing ample opportunities for intellectual debate.

No scholar has contributed to theorizing the Armenian Diaspora more than Khachig Tölölyan, a founding figure of diaspora and transnational studies. His theorizations of the Armenian Diaspora, first developed in his Armenian-language essays published in the Parisian newspaper *Ḥaṛach* and the Boston-based *Hayrenikʻ* throughout the 1970s, and later in edited volume chapters and scholarly articles, were unique in their disciplinary scope, for they situated the concept simultaneously within linguistic, literary, historical and sociopolitical contexts.[6] Tölölyan's commitment to interdisciplinary scholarship found a new platform with the launch of *Diaspora: A Journal of Transnational Studies* in 1991. In his capacity as the journal's founding editor, Tölölyan penned several influential articles that not only produced a comparative understanding of the Armenian Diaspora but also turned diaspora into a field of epistemological inquiry beyond case studies. His rigorous and generous editorship also shaped foundational works that defined the emerging field of diaspora studies and led decades of intellectual conversations spanning continents and disciplines.

To honour Khachig Tölölyan's immense contribution to the field of Armenian diaspora studies and to explore the vast range of research it enabled, the Society for Armenian Studies organized an international conference held at the University of California, Los Angeles, on 12–13 October 2019. Titled 'Diaspora and "Stateless Power": Social Discipline and Identity Formation Across the Armenian Diaspora during the Long Twentieth Century', the conference brought together scholars from Mexico, Armenia, the United Kingdom, France, the Netherlands and throughout the United States for two days of presentations and discussions around 'the Armenian transnation', forms of diasporic transnationalism, and the productive and prohibitive attributes of 'stateless power'.

Born of this conference, *The Armenian Diaspora and Stateless Power: Collective Identity in the Transnational 20*[th] *Century* seeks to build on the discussions of Tölölyan's work and its impact on various conceptualizations of the Armenian Diaspora, in all its heterogeneity. Reproducing the multidisciplinary impetus of Tölölyan's scholarship, this volume brings together historians, cultural theorists, literary critics, sociologists, political scientists and anthropologists to explore how Armenian Diaspora elites and their institutions emerged in the post-genocide period and used 'stateless power' to practice forms of social discipline on collective identity, belonging and loyalty among Armenians. Focusing on cultural, religious, political and literary production, as well as community groups and leaders in such far-flung cities of the Armenian Diaspora as Amsterdam, Addis Ababa, Aleppo, Beirut, Detroit, Istanbul, Jerusalem,

Los Angeles and Paris, this collection offers original insight and novel perspectives on the history and experience of the Armenian Diaspora through the long twentieth century. More broadly, this collection shows how diasporic history and practice can help re-conceptualize and illuminate non-state forms of power and governmentality.

The theoretically engaged and empirically grounded chapters in this volume speak to the richness and magnitude of the Armenian experience throughout the twentieth century, from genocide, forced displacement and dispersion to the gradual establishment of sedentary and rooted global communities. This collection builds upon Khachig Tölölyan's insight that a diaspora's statelessness can serve as evidence of its power and that by wielding this 'stateless power', the diaspora can act as an alternative and a complement to the nation-state.

Diaspora studies: The evolution of a field[7]

During the rapid globalization of the 1990s, which transformed social, economic and political interactions and networks across the world, the ancient concept of diaspora resurfaced to encapsulate a wide multidisciplinary engagement with questions of home, migration, belonging and identity. This old notion was revived by its close association with a new concept: transnationalism. The serendipitous resonance of the pre-modern term "diaspora" in a post-modern, global age resulted in a remarkable phoenix-like rise of the term that once meant 'Other of the nation-state', now signifying 'exemplary communities of the transnational moment'.[8] In 1991, the pioneering *Diaspora: A Journal of Transnational Studies*[9] was founded by the Zoryan Institute, with Khachig Tölölyan at the editorial helm, capturing the new decade's zeitgeist. Tölölyan and other notable pioneers[10] set out an intellectual agenda and proceeded to carve out a space for the conceptual and empirical study of diaspora while being mindful of its inherent expansiveness as concept and practice.

In the following three decades, a substantial scholarship developed, founded on the triad of diaspora community, host state and homeland. This basic model has persisted in the social sciences in areas of study ranging from migration and refugee studies to international relations, often taking for granted a clear point of origin and a present site of (permanent) residence. The humanities are arguably less fixated on static sites, recognizing fluidity and context as defining features of both old and new diasporas.

In early discussions in the emerging field, scholars tended to recognize the Jewish case as the 'ideal type'[11] and consequently emphasized forced expulsion, exile and statelessness as key characteristics of diaspora. In this understanding, diaspora had at its centre a violent fracture and featured loss and dispossession, as well as 'the political obligation, or the moral burden, of reconstituting a lost homeland or maintaining an endangered culture'.[12] Writing on the African Diaspora created by the violence of slavery, Gilroy similarly defines diaspora as 'a network of people, scattered in a process of non-voluntary displacement, usually created by violence or under threat of violence or death'.[13]

It soon became apparent that attempts to define diaspora primarily with respect to forced or traumatic dispersion from a place of origin were ill-suited to what became an explosion in diaspora studies and a proliferation of social formations claiming the label. Older iterations of diaspora as an academic concept[14] needed revisiting, and Tölölyan's bold and expansive manifesto in the first issue of *Diaspora* articulated the resulting shift clearly:

> We use 'diaspora' provisionally to indicate our belief that the term once described as Jewish, Greek, and Armenian dispersion now shares meanings with a larger semantic domain that includes words like immigrant, expatriate, refugee, guest-worker, exile, community, overseas community, ethnic community. This is the vocabulary of transnationalism, and any of its terms can usefully be considered under more than one of its rubrics.[15]

Tölölyan's words proved prophetic. Indeed, a defining characteristic of the field has been its expansion, a theme that was debated regularly by Tölölyan and others in the pages of *Diaspora* and beyond. The extraordinarily well-suited marriage of diasporas to globalization[16] offered a new vision for a way of life and held instinctive appeal for a widening constituency, as Tölölyan explained:

> at its best the diaspora is an example, for both the homeland and hostlands' nation-states, of the possibility of living, even thriving in the regimes of multiplicity which are increasingly the global condition, and a proper version of which diasporas may help to construct, given half a chance. The stateless power of diasporas lies in their heightened awareness of both the perils and rewards of multiple belonging, and their sometimes exemplary grappling with the paradoxes of such belonging, which is increasingly the condition that non-diasporan nationals also face in the transnational age.[17]

Another key reason for the expansion of the use of the concept is that it had become elastic enough to accommodate related concepts and adjacent experiences. Speaking of these concepts and experiences that now wished to associate with diaspora or rebrand as diasporan, Tölölyan described 'the move towards re-naming as diasporas the more recent communities of dispersion, those that were formed in the five centuries of the modern era and which were known by other names until the late 1960s: as exile groups, overseas communities, ethnic and racial minorities, and so forth'.[18] This development was twofold, as Tölölyan points out: the 'rapidity of material and discursive change in the past three decades has increased both the number of global diasporas and the range of diversity of the new semantic domain that the term "diaspora" inhabit'.

The second defining feature of diaspora studies is an inherent tension between the fixed and the fluid. Uses of the concept in the social sciences in particular often rely on fixed, seemingly undisputed sites (home of origin, host state), self-evident binaries (state and diaspora) and directions ('return', 'homecoming') that reflect both 'methodological nationalism' and bounded concepts. In contrast, humanities-based uses of diaspora are often more cognisant of mobility and versatility and encompass culture and consciousness. More broadly, this tension is replicated in multiple forms: in studies that celebrate diaspora as emancipatory and exciting versus studies that reveal it to be as disciplining and confining as the power structures of the nation-state; in the view of diaspora as counter-state and subversive versus the view of diaspora as the state's advocate and appendage; and in a diaspora seen as inclusive and progressive versus a diaspora seen as exclusionary, with boundaries that are policed.

Situating the Armenian Diaspora

Historically, scholars have considered the Jewish case the paradigmatic one and the Armenians and Greeks as classical cases. Each of these peoples shared a rich premodern life characterized by the condition of being scattered across empires and sharing defining features of a national collectivity such as language and religion, as well as a sense of exile from a homeland, whether spiritual or geographical. Crucially, the dispersed communities maintained connections, networks and communications with each other. Armstrong deems the Armenians 'a mobilised diaspora' from the early Middle Ages, 'behaving like an archetypal diaspora' in part because 'the compact settlement area had not only been subjugated for centuries by foreign conquerors, but had suffered an equally long period of economic and cultural eclipse compared to the affluence and vitality of the Armenian diaspora'.[19]

Scholars in the early period of diaspora studies were engrossed in defining the concept of diaspora and determining which groups fit the criteria,[20] as well as developing typologies and rubrics. The most influential of these studies is Cohen's seminal *Global Diasporas* (1997), which identifies Armenians as a 'victim diaspora' but also stipulates that groups may fall into more than one category of diaspora and that categories may overlap. Indeed, in the literature, historic Armenian communities are identified historically as a 'trade diaspora',[21] a 'merchant diaspora'[22] and as a set of geographically dispersed communities practising 'transimperial cosmopolitanism' in the seventeenth century.[23]

Within the terrain that became known as diaspora studies, the Armenians, as mentioned above, were considered one of the 'classical' diasporas, for whom living in diaspora was an intrinsic part of their pre-modern identity. For contemporary diaspora theorists, the Armenians met all the criteria for being a diaspora in the original usage: they had undergone a violent and forced displacement to multiple sites. Consequently, the Armenians were conceptualized as a historical 'old' diaspora, enduring and thriving in a global age that was giving rise to an abundance of 'new' diasporas.

The state-centric turn in diaspora studies

The proliferation of diasporas as social formations and the broadening of diaspora studies are attributable in no small part to state policies. Political theorists have long examined the role played by ethnic (and religious) diasporas in international relations, particularly in the areas of political lobbying,[24] in war and peace building[25] and in global civil society and advocacy.[26] Much of this scholarship has been underpinned by the perception that states need to control and curtail the influence of transnational communities as part of a general anxiety about the impending dissolution of the nation-state.[27]

In parallel, scholars have noticed an interesting development. While trying to monitor and discipline diaspora communities within their own borders, states have been working to expand their parameters by constructing and acquiring diasporas of their own. Varadarjan's groundbreaking work[28] looking at how states reconstitute their migrants abroad as 'the domestic abroad' and themselves as 'homelands' is the most significant study of this trend. In this imagining of the nation, the diaspora is a source of resources, opportunities and advocacy and functions as a worthy and important extension of the state. State-generated diasporas are therefore usually its appendage, without a culture and identity that is distinctly 'diasporic'. State-generated diasporas share a dependence on the state, institutionally and emotionally, and in most cases are designed and directed by the state's agenda. In state-sponsored or state-generated diasporas, the diaspora is the object to be harnessed for the benefit of the home state. In this trend of new diaspora-making by states, the state seeks to mould its diaspora into its image and use it for its agenda: diasporas are the object of state power and projection.

In contrast, older, more established diasporas, like the Armenian Diaspora, have an organic identity of their own and have invested in articulating their own histories and culture *as diaspora*. Diasporas with longevity supersede the state as homeland and do not depend on this state for legitimacy or direction. They share a degree of institutionalization and infrastructure that is intrinsically diasporic and located in the diaspora space – not initiated or led by a home state. In older diaspora formation, it is the diaspora itself that is the protagonist, the site of power and agency.

A diaspora of longue durée

Origins and history have an enduring influence on how a diaspora develops as an entity and as a political project and stance. In the Armenian case, the diaspora predates the Republic of Armenia and has a vast and layered history and culture that are both connected to and separate from the state. Various waves of arrivals make up the core of the contemporary diaspora – survivors of massacres and genocide, refugees, the displaced and emigrants – with the result that it is complex and heterogeneous, with competing and complementary projects, affiliations, articulations and orientations, as reflected in the chapters of this volume.

As the Armenian Diaspora has over centuries developed its own culture and traditions that are distinct from those of the modern state, it is not dependent on the state as a source of validation or guidance. This situation makes for a complicated relationship with Armenia as homeland, despite the state's political projects, overtures and policies.[29] The status of a homeland in established diasporas inevitably changes. Tölölyan explains how the shift from 'exilic transnationalism' to 'diasporic transnationalism' has resulted in the homeland becoming 'one of several nodes of interest and loyalty'[30] rather than occupying an elevated position. In this conceptualization, the Republic of Armenia is one of many sites that the diaspora network extends to and is connected to.[31] In this framework, we are moving away from the traditional triadic diaspora caught between homeland and host state and proposing a multi-noded diaspora, which can be viewed as both polycentric[32] and multilocal.[33] As a diaspora of longue durée, the Armenian Diaspora involves a practice of 'diasporic transnationalism' that is both rooted in locality and routed to global networks and connections.

Tölölyan's approach represents a radical shift in thinking about diaspora. It enables a more expansive and fluid vision of living in diaspora: here, the diaspora space is the terrain in which the homeland, the community and other communities are located. It inverts the triad in which homeland and host state are the defining influences on a diaspora, often seen as their subsidiary. In doing so, it repositions and centralizes the diaspora experience. In this framework, the homeland is 'a place to care about and to do good works in, but not the authoritative center that can dictate either political or affective behaviour for long'.[34] Tölölyan offers an important caveat, however: 'the link to the homeland is one of several links, not privileged or subordinate to others' except in so far as survival and security are concerned'.[35] When the 'homeland' is threatened, it takes on far greater significance in the diaspora imagination, mobilizing all the various nodes into action.[36] This phenomenon was evident in the Artsakh War of 2020, which was interpreted and felt as an existential crisis throughout the Armenian Diaspora.[37] In this respect, the homeland has a stronger ability to unite and mobilize than centres in crisis typically possess because, as the Armenian state, it represents the seat and hope for a continued Armenian existence.

Khachig Tölölyan's 'diasporic transnationalism' and studies of Armenians

How does one account for the many ways Armenian institutions and organizations, such as the Armenian Apostolic Church and various Armenian political parties, engage with Armenians across the world? In the intervention that follows, we discuss recent studies of Armenians through the lens of Khachig Tölölyan's 'diasporic transnationalism'.[38] Even in locales where Armenians have lived for generations, such as New Julfa (in Iran) and Crimea (in Eastern Europe), transnational and/or regional Armenian institutions and formal or informal linkages such as trade networks connect to additional nodes and centres with their own dynamics. While we do not consider Armenians to be members of 'one nation that is spread across different states', we, as the editors of this volume, cannot deny the impact of transnational institutions and organizations on local communities and the connections they have forged.[39] At the same time, the presence of transnational actors does not imply that the Armenian experience is foreign or non-local. These connections, whether historic or active, should not be used to separate, and thus isolate, Armenians from their co-inhabitants. How can we study Armenian communities *and* their global connections, while understanding their presence and contributions locally?

To point out the connections among Armenians in multiple locations through networks and institutions is neither to minimize their achievements nor to question their local belonging. And yet non-Armenian histories often ignore Armenians or treat their presence as merely a consequence of violence elsewhere.[40] These myopic views have led some scholars to react by arguing against the diaspora classification for Armenians.[41] This volume brings together diverse voices in Armenian studies to explore the diasporic stances of Armenians. The contributors refuse to portray Armenians as exclusively local or global actors. By examining their agency in both local and global contexts, the authors published in this volume focus on Armenians as historical actors and political agents.

Challenging the dominant paradigm

Recent contributions to Armenian scholarship have shed new light on the issues outlined above. These works challenge the dominant paradigm in which Armenians are viewed solely through the lens of diaspora and, relatedly, as victims of historical injustice or as perpetually connected to a usually unreachable home. Because the works in this volume focus on different geographic regions and even time periods, they allow us, in their diversity, to access the experiences of Armenian institutions, organizations and individuals as historical actors.

Sebouh Aslanian's work on Armenian traders and merchants between New Julfa, India, Europe and the Americas has deeply influenced not only the study of Armenian historiography in the last twenty years but also the study of world history in the pre-modern period. *From the Indian Ocean to the Mediterranean: The Global Trade Networks of Armenian Merchants from New Julfa* argues that in their success, these Armenians were able to connect the Mughul, Ottoman and Safavid empires, Muscovite Russia, Qing China and all of the major European seaborne empires.[42] In this book's introduction, Aslanian also contributes to an important debate on the categorization of Armenians as a trade diaspora. New Julfans, he maintains, may be described as a 'trade diaspora', but analytically, the term falls short of explaining how these merchants communicated with one another and what types of institutional mechanisms they relied upon.[43] Moreover, the identification of a 'trade diaspora' does not automatically reveal whether the members of such a diaspora based their business decisions on information from their networks.[44] Instead, Aslanian calls for the use of the term 'circulation society', which better captures the dynamics between nodal centres and their 'routing stations', or the more sedentary settlements. These arguments are made to both connect the New Julfan network to other networks, such as the Shikarpuri and Hyderabadi merchants of Sind in India, the Multani network, and the Sephardic Jewish network, and to distinguish it from such networks.[45]

Understanding trade communities and exploring what it meant for Armenians to be part of these circulation societies not only opened up these geographic areas to scholars of Armenian studies but also forced scholars of the various regions and time periods involved to do so as well. While Aslanian's intervention ends with the destruction of New Julfa as a nodal centre in 1747, which led to the eventual collapse of the network, its impact on the study of Armenian societies reverberated far beyond the Indian Ocean and the early modern period.[46] To note Aslanian's influence is not to imply that Armenian history had a linear progression. Rather, Aslanian made it possible to recognize that studying the centre and nodes in one time period and space can illuminate other centres and nodes, irrespective of whether the actors involved are Armenian.

In this volume, considering multiple nodes and centres is necessary so that contemporary scholars of Armenians and diaspora studies can move beyond an engagement with the past that fixates on the Armenian Genocide and catastrophe. While this focus is understandable given the denial that defines the Turkish government's discourse and the varying support for an Armenian presence in scholarly works on Ottoman and Turkish studies, centring the Armenian Genocide skews the study of Armenians towards violence and divorces them from their global connections and networks. Scholarship that centres the genocide also tends to misrepresent Armenians' circulation as a unidirectional movement driven exclusively by loss and tragedy.

'Approaching' genocide

Recent historical works that connect Armenians to global networks study the period leading up to the genocide by focusing on unconventional time frames and broadened perspectives. Notable recent works include Richard Antaramian's *Brokers of Faith, Brokers of Empire: Armenians and the Politics of Reform in the Ottoman Empire* and Bedross Der Matossian's *Shattered Dreams of Revolution: From Liberty to Violence in the Late Ottoman Empire*. Antaramian's *Brokers of Faith* uses the study of Armenian religious networks in the late Ottoman Empire to show the limitations of relying on the centre–periphery binary.[47] While this dichotomy is losing popularity in Ottoman and Middle Eastern studies, it continues to be used to distinguish the Ottoman central government from the provinces of Anatolia, the Balkans and the Levant, implying a differentiation between the inhabitants of the two. Antaramian, however, demonstrates that members of both the clergy and the notable classes failed to conform to the geographical distinction and articulated their own agendas within the context of imperial reform throughout the empire.[48] Viewing the Ottoman Empire as a 'tapestry', Antaramian pays homage to the networked Armenian community and contributes to our understanding of the ways Armenians used religion during the Ottoman governance.[49]

Shattered Dreams of Revolution: From Liberty to Violence in the Late Ottoman Empire looks beyond the 'Armenian network'. In this groundbreaking work, Der Matossian uses non-dominant groups in the Ottoman Empire, including Armenians, to demonstrate how the 1908 Ottoman Revolution inspired ethnic religious communities and how they in turn upheld and forwarded the Ottoman constitutional revolution.[50] By considering these groups as actors, rather than solely as reactors, Der Matossian shows how they engaged with the revolution and why their euphoria gave way to ethnic tensions and pessimism.[51] Der Matossian's latest work, *The Horrors of Adana: Revolution and Violence in the Early Twentieth Century*, continues to analyse actors within their historical moments, rescuing them from the homogenization that comes with viewing Armenian history as a singular, lachrymose saga leading to genocide.[52]

Particularizing Armenian historical experiences requires an examination of the relationships between Armenians and their local environments. Studying how individuals worked within their sociopolitical contexts to press for their own causes reveals their agency as historical actors. What is particularly important in both Antaramian's and Der Matossian's works is how they describe the *life* (not merely the death) of Armenians just a few decades before (and in Der Matossian's case, less than a decade before) the start of the Armenian Genocide. In *The Horrors of Adana*, Der Matossian narrows the focus even further by examining the Adana massacres of 1909 and this event's connection to the counter-revolution. His examination of the connections between Armenians in Adana and their local, regional and international contexts de-homogenizes violence against Armenians by demonstrating that the Adana massacres were intended to tame a population, whereas the Armenian Genocide was planned to eradicate one. Without these differentiations, which we can acquire only through a micro-level analysis, we will continue to see Armenians as one-dimensional victims, rather than as subjects of their own history.[53] This scholarship responds to Armenian, Ottoman and Turkish historiographies that view the Armenian presence in the Ottoman Empire in different but consistently limiting ways. Armenian scholarship until the last twenty years or so described the Armenian presence in the Ottoman Empire as a build-up to the cataclysmic era of genocide as if every Armenian experience acted as a tributary that fed into the final destruction of the community. Conversely, Ottoman and Turkish historiography anachronistically begins and ends with the absence of Armenians and therefore fails to adequately study their presence and legacy.

Synthesizing Armenian history

The shifting social, political and economic dynamics that permitted such violence in Adana parallel the transformations that Antaramian's religious networks and Aslanian's trading nodes and centres underwent. Other works that study such transformations in different time periods and geographic locations help us understand how changes were experienced and used by the actors themselves. In this way, they connect us to an Armenian history, though not to a history that has a linear trajectory. This scholarship draws attention to the connections and tensions among historical experiences.

Houri Berberian's *Roving Revolutionaries Armenians and the Connections Revolutions in the Russian, Iranian and Ottoman Worlds* contributes to studying the circulation of Armenians by focusing on Armenians living under three empires.[54] In analysing the movement of ideas, individuals and objects among the Armenian minorities in the Russian, Iranian and Ottoman empires, Berberian systemically synthesizes their moves and motivations. *Roving Revolutionaries* exposes the ties that actors historically made and maintained.[55] In other words, it does not need to artificially make connections between Armenians to construct an Armenian history, because these connections were made by the actors themselves. In this respect, it avoids reproducing the shortcomings of conventional Armenian, Ottoman, Iranian and Russian historical scholarship, which relies on nationalist histories to understand the past and so fails to imagine the trans-spatial movement of people and ideas beyond the construction of the proto-nation-state.

After catastrophe

As mentioned earlier, the Armenian Genocide has traditionally been seen as an epistemological break in the study of Armenians.[56] Nevertheless, just as the destruction and dispersion of a network does not necessitate viewing Armenians solely as victims, recent works on Armenians in the wake of the Armenian Genocide have demonstrated the agency of its survivors.[57] Lerna Ekmekcioglu's *Recovering Armenia: The Limits of Belonging in Post-Genocide Turkey* explores how, in the wake of near extermination, public figures continued their activism and developed a feminism that often but not always participated in 'bettering the nation'.[58] By analysing *Hay Gin* (1913–33), the women's journal edited by Haiganoush Mark, among other publications, Ekmekcioglu argues that the apex of feminism for Armenians counterintuitively occurred in post-genocide Turkey.[59] Her inclusion of the connection of Armenian proponents of feminism in Turkey and those in Soviet Armenia (and beyond) highlights the networks and connections that Armenians were part of, even in the midst of one centre's destruction.[60]

While Ekmekcioglu begins with destruction, Tsolin Nalbantian's *Armenians Beyond Diaspora: Making Lebanon Their Own* argues that in the wake of the Armenian Genocide, Armenians created powerful centres.[61] While focusing on one such centre, Lebanon, she weaves in references to other geographies and time periods. She discusses, for example, the Cilician See, located in Antelias, Lebanon, since 1930, which acted as the spiritual authority of the Cilician Kingdom of Armenia, even though the kingdom collapsed in 1375.[62] The authority that the see had historically enjoyed in Cilicia under diverse sociopolitical circumstances had to be adjusted to the new environment in Lebanon.

In fact, the see gained additional political authority in the sectarian system in Lebanon.[63] As Nalbantian shows, the Cilician See used the Lebanese sectarian political system to expand its power not only within the civil realm of the Armenian population in Lebanon but also vis-à-vis other Armenian institutions – and, accordingly, their congregations – in Istanbul and in Echmiadzin, Armenia. The analysis of these actions helps to support the seemingly incongruent idea that despite, or perhaps even because of, the genocide, Armenians created powerful centres. After all, in the aftermath of the Armenian Genocide and the establishment of the Republic of Turkey, which destroyed Istanbul as an Armenian centre, the Cilician See found refuge in the sectarian system of Lebanon. Together with the Cold War, with its global contestation between left-wing and right-wing politics and ideologies, the Cilician See created the unprecedented opportunity to compete with the 'mother' Echmiadzin See for the spiritual and ideological leadership of the worldwide Armenian community.[64]

Nalbantian's work is not principally concerned with demonstrating how something 'Armenian' was created. Rather, it shows how Armenians in Lebanon experienced politics in everyday life, and what those experiences teach us about interlinked national and global events. Armenian institutions enjoy a trans-spatial component: they use past historical experiences to claim power in completely different environments. This adaptive quality simultaneously changes the new environment. As the Cilician

See innovated, it transformed Lebanon. Armenian experiences informed Lebanese, Middle Eastern and Cold War histories, and vice versa.

In *Stateless: The Politics of the Armenian Language in Exile*,[65] Talar Chahinian similarly examines the making of diasporic centres by looking at the consolidation of literary production in post–First World War Paris and post–Second Word War Beirut. In positioning the Paris intellectuals' de-centred, multilocal model of transnational literary orientation against the attempts of Beirut intellectuals to 'centre' the exiled communities through the nationalization of language, education and literature, she explores both the constructive and the prohibitive limits of stateless power.

Post-genocide works can thus focus on both destruction and construction. Sylvia Alajaji's *Music and the Armenian Diaspora: Searching for a Home in Exile* directs the reader to another node: dispersion. By focusing on music among many possible nodes, she builds upon the work of scholars who have examined how Armenian identity is performed and produced in diasporic communities in the United States, Canada, United Kingdom and Cyprus.[66] Could we have reflected on how music became a space to practice identity without, for example, Anny Bakalian's careful consideration of the process by which Armenians went from 'being' to 'feeling' Armenian?[67] Through Bakalian's detailed account of the Armenian-American community in New York, we learn how, even as traditional institutions 'lose their holding power' over Armenians, Armenian identity survives through formal and informal networks and activities, which Bakalian terms 'Armenian-American subculture'.[68] While Bakalian examines how Armenians practised their identity through social, cultural and economic participation, Alajaji contends that music offers access to political, cultural and social struggles experienced by Armenians in host communities that become their homes.[69] For her, 'musical narratives speak to the complex relationships between diasporas and homelands, between diasporic communities and the countries in which they live, and between and within the diasporic communities themselves'.[70] Even when people do not physically move, music connects Armenians in different geographies and historical experiences. This is not to say that Alajaji is attempting to homogenize these experiences into an Armenian one through music; rather, she painstakingly traces how music exposes Armenian networks that have been created in the wake of trauma and violence.

Some of the most powerful interventions of this type have been in the field of literary studies. In the introduction to a collection of articles on Zabel Yesayan, Talar Chahinian delicately uses the image of Yesayan's floating corpse (a victim of Stalinist purges) to discuss both her 'out of placeness' and 'Western Armenian literature's post-genocide exilic and stateless condition'.[71] This pursuit of Zabel Yesayan, however, results in the revelation of the circulation of her works and their impact on a variety of genres, including literary and memory studies, works of testimony and history. In other words, one notes Yesayan's presence – albeit in her absence – in Istanbul, Bulgaria, Paris, Tbilisi, Yerevan, Baku and a variety of locations in Anatolia.[72]

Marc Nichanian's *Mourning Philology: Art and Religion at the Margins of the Ottoman Empire* engages in a similar activity.[73] Nichanian uses the works of Daniel Varuzhan (1884–1915), the *Mehyan* literary review and the latter's manifesto that appeared in its first issue (of which Varuzhan was one of the five signatories) to demonstrate how central orientalist philology was to this generation of writers and to the literary figures who would survive the Armenian Genocide.[74] In so doing, Nichanian also reveals that the desire to reclaim 'the popular' as art was expressed seventy years prior to the *Mehyan* movement in the works of Khachatur Abovean, as well as in the work of the *Menk* literary collective in Paris in the interwar period.[75] Nichanian's pursuit of the 'recovery' of art through Varuzhan and his generation creates additional nodes through which we can access the experiences of Armenians.

Armenians used historical events, personalities, myths and institutions to pursue their own ends and adapted to a variety of social, political and economic environments. They reoriented authority to benefit their communities and increase their power. By revealing this history, these works of scholarship defy the view of Armenians as perpetual victims of violence and trauma. Only by accounting for these historical social, legal and political changes can we make textured comparisons in time and space.

Diaspora's diasporas[76]

As editors of this volume, we are in no way attempting to romanticize the lives of Armenians following the destruction of communities and networks. Rather, we are invested in furthering the understanding of the lived experiences of Armenians in the wake of trauma and beyond. In addition, we cannot forget those who escaped direct violence and/or survived these experiences and went on to create new networks and connections. What of their histories? Should their experiences be read only through the annihilation of others?

In *The Politics of Armenian Migration to North America, 1885–1915: Migrants, Smugglers and Dubious Citizens*, a history of Armenian migration to North America in the late nineteenth and early twentieth centuries, David Gutman argues that Sultan Abdulhamid II's ban on the migration of Armenians was motivated by the belief that Armenian migration was related to the emergence of political networks and organizations.[77] This, it was thought, would lead Armenians to seek greater autonomy in the Ottoman Empire.[78] In response to the ban, Armenians created an expansive smuggling network that helped Armenians avoid the ban.[79]

This focus on yet another Armenian network continues the trend of pursuing a more nuanced understanding of Armenian experiences in the eastern provinces. Once again, the point is not to minimize the suffering Armenians experienced. But what is particularly useful in studying Armenians – in this case and in others – is how their experiences contribute to our understanding of themes like migration, economic, social and political change, and attempts to overhaul community infrastructure. Research that focuses on Armenians provides an opportunity for fresh readings of these fields. After all, as Gutman demonstrates, it was the presence of an influential elite and the economic stability in the Harput/Mezre region that enabled the migration of thousands of Armenians to North America.[80] It would be inaccurate to simply attach this phenomenon to the Armenian Genocide, which took place some years later. A focus on Armenians also gives scholars the opportunity to study how this circulation of people was considered such a threat to the Ottoman State, while the activity of the New Julfa Armenian merchants posed no such threat to the Saffavid state.

As editors of this volume dedicated to centring Tölölyan's contribution to a myriad of disciplines within Armenian studies and beyond, we find it imperative to make connections among works that focus on the movements and (re)settlements of Armenians. Such connections also demonstrate that the distinctions between the pre-modern, early modern and modern eras are both contrived and limiting. With this in mind, we connect these to another classic work in Armenian studies, Susan Pattie's *Faith in History*, which – though not explicitly about circulation – examines the Armenian community in Cyprus and its subsequent move to London due to unrest and conflict – from the struggle for independence in the 1950s, to the intercommunal violence of 1963–4, which resulted in Armenians losing their homes and businesses in the Armenian quarter, through to the Turkish invasion of the island in 1974. Pattie's insightful work on the 'diaspora of the diaspora', or the movement of Armenian Cypriots first from the mainland of the Ottoman Empire to Cyprus and then to Great Britain, has shown how established networks, partly a legacy of colonial experience, were used by Armenians who did not want to continue living a cycle of uncertainty, vulnerability, loss and dispossession, and sought opportunities and security elsewhere.[81] In certain ways, Pattie mirrors Gutman's and Aslanian's interventions that follow Armenians who used their established nodes and networks to build and nurture communities in different and even disparate geographic settings.

In recent years, scholars examining Armenians have continued to offer textured analyses of connections, centres and nodes, even in the wake of trauma, be it the punitive massacres of the Ottoman period, the Armenian Genocide or the Lebanese Civil War. They have likewise demonstrated how Armenians have formed new and vibrant centres despite their devastating experience of loss, deportation and dispersion. Sossie Kasbarian, drawing from Tölölyan's 'diasporic transnationalism',[82] has taken this work to its logical conclusion, suggesting that even the present-day Republic of Armenia is no different from Beirut or Paris or Los Angeles or Buenos Aires as an Armenian node.[83] This claim illustrates how the Armenian Genocide created new opportunities for surviving institutions to claim power, all the while exposing Armenians as powerful actors capable of articulating their own agency in these newly emergent diasporic spaces. The chapters in this volume build on these themes, each through a particular disciplinary lens and evidence base.

Organization of the volume

The Armenian Diaspora and Stateless Power is divided into three parts, each featuring a set of chapters that engage with one of Khachig Tölölyan's key theoretical contributions to diaspora studies.

Part I, '"The Logic of the Sedentary": Complicating Notions of Home and Homelands', discusses forms of attachment to place in exile, as well as the construction of new homes (and homelands) in diaspora. Boris Adjemian uses Tölölyan's reflections on 'the logic of the sedentary'[84] to bridge the perceived gap between diaspora studies and the history of immigration. In 'In Search of the Sedentary: Rethinking Homelands in the Armenian Diaspora', Adjemian argues that the notion of exile and the dream of 'the promised land' should not lead us to underestimate the role of host lands, which are not only places of refuge but also sites of settlement and attachment. Sedentary approaches, in short, affirm that 'life in the diaspora matters'. Moving between Ethiopia, Jerusalem and France, Adjemian reflects on what sedentary approaches to diasporas might reveal to a historian of Armenian immigration in the long twentieth century, and how they might contribute to our understanding of diaspora experiences and the historical transformation of their host societies.

In his chapter, Gegham Mughnetsyan presents the little-known case of four thousand Soviet Armenian displaced persons who found post-war refuge at the Funkerkaserne camp in Germany and were eventually resettled in Montebello, California. In 'Armenian Displaced Persons: From Displacement to a Diaspora Community', he looks at the camp as 'a midpoint in the leap from dispersion to community', a place where 'a process of identity shaping and nation building facilitated the transformation from an exilic group into a community'. Once its members regrouped in California, this group retained their distinct identity and established an active community in East Los Angeles. In this fascinating story of the transformation of a displaced disparate group into a successful, close-knit group in America years later, the role of community is the key to constructing both transitory and permanent (sedentary) homes in diaspora.

Taking up Tölölyan's call for scholars to exercise caution in locating the 'diasporic's home in the ancestral homeland too easily', Nare Galstyan analyses the case of the Dutch Armenian community, which has been 'replenished' by ethnic Armenian asylum-seekers fleeing the Syrian Civil War. In 'Diaspora–Homeland Relations Re-examined: The Case of Syrian Armenian in the Netherlands', she explores the complexities of diaspora imaginings and perceptions of home and homeland. In this case, Syrian Armenians prefer to construct a new home in another diaspora community, where they feel 'at home', rather than 'return' to (i.e. resettle in) Armenia. More broadly, Galstyan's analysis of this example highlights the multidimensionality and historical complexity of diasporas and situates them within contemporary migration studies.

Part II, '"Diasporic Social Formation": Leadership Elites, Institutions and Transnational Governmentality', examines the dynamics of non-state governance across religious, political, literary and cultural institutions. Hasmik Khalapyan explores the production of knowledge and the imposition of social discipline in an environment where the Armenian state and national institutions are absent. In 'Forging Diasporic Identity in the Fin de Siècle Armenian Periodical Press in Europe', she demonstrates how prominent literary figures used several Armenian periodicals published in Europe to cultivate Armenianness. Using Tölölyan's term 'interstate diaspora', she argues that for these literati, publishing became a tool of social discipline.

Vahe Sakahyan's chapter, 'Transnational Politics and Governmental Strategies in the Formative Years of the Post-Genocide Armenian Diaspora (1920s–1930s)', focuses on the 'governmental efforts' of the Armenian Revolutionary Federation to mobilize their global followers around an anti-Bolshevik discourse and project their power over the dispersed Armenian populations in the 1920s and 1930s. More broadly, Sahakyan demonstrates how the ARF, as the Armenian 'government-in-exile' aspiring to become the 'government of exiles',[85] used social discipline and exclusion to deal with dissenters and consolidate the party's ranks around the anti-Soviet discourse. Drawing from Tölölyan's important discussion[86] of the role that elites and institutions play in the construction of diasporic discourses and cultural production and diaspora social formations, he argues that these strategies consisted of three parallel processes: the discursive construction of Armenian collective need; the creation of spaces of socialization, in which diaspora Armenians would be exposed to these discourses regularly; and the expansion of their governmental efforts to the organized and established Armenian spaces in the diaspora.

Lilit Keshishyan's chapter, 'Defiant Adherence: Cultural Critiques in Late Twentieth-Century Armenian Diaspora Literature', turns to Khachig Tölölyan's understanding of 'leadership elites', which he posits are central to an organized diaspora, to explore the tension between the necessity of institutions and the constraints they impose on diasporic life. Drawing on Tölölyan's distinction between the elites who organize diaspora (activists, political leaders etc.) and those who produce diaspora's discourse (intellectuals), she examines the works of three writers: Vahé Oshagan, Hakob Karapents and Vahe Berberian. Through a close reading of their literary representations of Armenian diasporic life, she shows that while these authors critique diaspora institutions' prohibitive power over artistic production, they also recognize the institutions' enabling power and cannot fully reject them, thus hinting at what she calls 'the paradox of diaspora's intellectuals'.

In 'Liturgical Subject of the Armenian Apostolic Church: Recent Waves of Migration', Christopher Sheklian shows how 'ecclesial governmentality', or a mode of power specific to the institution of the church, helps form a particular type of liturgical subject. This subject, through affective experience and the institutional role of the Armenian Apostolic Church, demonstrates the crisis of belonging of the Armenian Church and delineates the place and power of the church in the diaspora. Using participant ethnographic observation in Turkey, France and the United States, Sheklian takes Tölölyan's work on the Armenian Apostolic Church as an institution as a starting point to explore the role of its ecclesial and non-state governmental power.

Part III, '"The Social Text of Diaspora": Diasporic Becoming and Legibility in Diaspora's Semantic Domain', engages with Tölölyan's discussions of diaspora's discursive fashioning by looking at the performance of Armenian diasporic identity across various disciplinary debates. Sylvia Angelique Alajaji's chapter, 'Sounding Armenian: The Contours of the Diasporic Musical Imaginary', focuses on the life and work of the Armenian composer and folklorist Komitas Vardapet (1869–1935) to ask what it means for diaspora 'to articulate itself sonically'. In other words, Alajaji is interested in exploring the implications of Komitas's centrality in Armenian music of the diaspora in fashioning the diaspora as a legible whole to an outside, and particularly a Western, gaze. Her meditative chapter examines the discourses surrounding Komitas to argue that the notion of 'purification' that leads Armenian diasporans to revere Komitas's music and his place in the Armenian musical tradition is precisely what makes Komitas vulnerable to the European gaze. She demonstrates that this form of legibility is the result of a discursive process that both fashions a collective whole out of a pluralistic diasporic condition and enables that new construction to mandate back the limits of diasporic belonging.

In '"Toward the Diaspora": The Performative Powers of Vahé Oshagan's Poetry', Karen Jallatyan turns to Khachig Tölölyan's discussions of what he has referred to as diaspora's social text to examine and revise the intersection of literary production, critical theory and the politics of identity. He argues that Oshagan's poetry orients Armenian life towards diasporic becoming through performative gestures that have a deterritorializing aesthetic. By 'deterritorializing', Jallatyan means to explore the ways in which Oshagan's poems decode markers of Armenian life in the diaspora such as the political party ARF, the nation-state order, Christian theology and notions of modernist narrativity. Jallatyan makes a case for Oshagan's discursive practices of diasporic becoming, claiming that they elude the essentializing tendencies of a national understanding that generally frames transnational literary production.

Talin Suciyan's chapter, 'Armenian in Turkey: From Autochthonous People to Diaspora', revisits the works of the Istanbul intellectuals Aram Pehlivanian and Zaven Biberyan to argue that Armenians were turned into a diaspora community within Turkey. Using the term 'non-contemporaneous contemporaries', which results from the divergence of experiences among Armenians living in Istanbul but hailing from the provinces, she probes Tölölyan's assertion that Istanbul is not usually thought of as diasporic. For Suciyan, while Istanbul was indeed the only remaining city where Armenians could access Armenian institutional support in what became the Turkish Republic, their presence there also facilitated the Turkish government's surveillance and control.

While Hrag Papazian's contribution, 'Are Istanbul Armenians Diasporic? Unpacking the Famous Debate', does not necessarily disagree, the author tackles the question of the diasporicity of Istanbul Armenians head-on to bring Tölölyan's understandings of emic and etic fields of diaspora studies into conversation with one another. Drawing on print publications that engage in the debate and his own ethnographic observations, Papazian discusses the question of whether Istanbul Armenians are diasporic or not and reveals the methodological problems and inaccuracies inherent in such a debate. It is notable that both Suciyan's and Papazian's contributions in this volume identify the Turkish state as responsible for some elements of diaspora formation, albeit from opposite angles. Suciyan argues that the Turkish state's support of the persecution of Armenians in Anatolia led Armenians to move to Istanbul, and thus drew them into perpetual exile and eventually diaspora. Papazian, in contrast, argues that the Turkish state acted as a reference point for Istanbul Armenians, reinforcing their sense of *not* living in a diaspora.

We conclude this volume with Sebouh Aslanian's brief microhistory of Khachig Tölölyan's life and works that attempts to bridge Tölölyan's intellectual legacy with the conditions of his exilic path, and with an Afterword by Khachig Tölölyan that calls on us to recalibrate our thoughts about the past of the Armenian diaspora and its current practices to engage with the challenging contexts it faces. This volume is our humble attempt to respond to this call.

Notes

1 While the migration of genocide survivors to Soviet Armenia beginning in the 1920s (with the largest waves during the Soviet sponsored worldwide repatriation

drive, or *nerkaght'*, from 1946 to1948) is collectively referred to as a process of repatriation, it did not comprise a strict return to lands lost, rather consisting of a symbolic return to an Armenian 'republic', albeit of a different cultural and linguistic context. For more on *nerkaght'*, or the organized drive to repatriate worldwide Armenians to the Armenian Soviet Socialist Republic (ASSR), see Joanne Laycock, 'The Repatriation of Armenians to Soviet Armenia, 1945–1949', in *Warlands Population Resettlement and State Reconstruction in the Soviet-East European Borderlands, 1945–1950*, ed. Peter Gattrell and Nick Baron (London: Palgrave Macmillan, 2009); Joanne Laycock, 'Armenian Homelands and Homecomings, 1945–1949', *Cultural and Social History* 9, no. 1 (2012): 103–23; and Sevan Nathaniel Yousefian, 'The Postwar Repatriation Movement of Armenians to Soviet Armenia, 1945–1948' (Ph.D. diss., University of California, Los Angeles, 2011).

2 Likewise, there are scholars who have argued against viewing the Armenian Genocide as an epistemological break, all the while as they acknowledge the (ongoing) trauma of genocide. See, for example, Sebouh Aslanian, 'From "Autonomous" to "Interactive" Histories: World History's Challenge to Armenian Studies', in *An Armenian Mediterranean: Words and Worlds in Motion*, ed. Kathryn Babayan and Michael Pifer (London: Palgrave Macmillan, 2018), 81–125; Bedross Der Matossian, 'Explaining the Unexplainable: Recent Trends in the Armenian Genocide Historiography', *Journal of Levantine Studies* 5, no. 2 (winter 2015): 143–66; and Tsolin Nalbantian, *Armenians Beyond Diaspora: Making Lebanon Their Own* (Edinburgh: Edinburgh University Press, 2020), 17–19.

3 Hagop Oshagan, 'Sp'iwrk'i K'raganut'ean Abak'an' (The Future of Diaspora Literature). *Nayiri* 4, no. 1 (1948): 78.

4 Boghos Levon Zekiyan, *The Armenian Way to Modernity* (Venice: Supernova, 1997), 23–6.

5 For Khachig Tölölyan, the discursive turn from exile to diaspora in the Armenian case is formally marked by the 1959 founding of a weekly called *Sp'iwrk'* (Diaspora) by Simon Simonian. Khachig Tölölyan, 'Elites and Institutions in the Armenian Transnation', *Diaspora* 9, no. 1 (2000): 120. Talar Chahinian situates it a bit earlier, within the heated post–Second World War exchange between diaspora and Soviet Armenian intellectuals occasioned by the 1946 Soviet Armenian Writers' Union congress and a rival conference held in Lebanon in 1948. Talar Chahinian, 'The Making of a Diasporic Literary Center: Post WWII Armenian Intellectual Life in Beirut', in *Armenians in Lebanon*, ed. Carla Edde, Levon Nordiguian, and Vahé Tachjian (Beirut: University of Saint Joseph Press, 2017), 284–303.

6 A collection of Tölölyan's Armenian-language essays are included in his publication *Sp'iwrk'i Mēch* (In Diaspora) (Paris: Harach Series, 1980).

7 This section draws from Sossie Kasbarian, *The Armenian Middle East – Diasporic Remnants, Resilience and Reconfigurations* (forthcoming).

8 Khachig Tölölyan, 'The Nation-State and Its Others: In Lieu of a Preface', *Diaspora: A Journal of Transnational Studies* 1, no. 1 (Spring 1991): 3–7.

9 https://www.utpjournals.press/journals/diaspora/scope.

10 Including but not limited to Gabriel Sheffer, ed., *Modern Diasporas in International Politics* (London: Croom Hem, 1986); Stuart Hall, 'Cultural Identity and Diaspora', in *Identity: Community, Culture, Difference*, ed. J. Rutherford (London: Lawrence & Wishart, 1990), 222–37; William Safran, 'Diasporas in Modern Societies: Myths of Homeland and Return', *Diaspora* 1, no. 1 (1991): 83–99; J. Clifford, 'Diasporas',

Cultural Anthropology 9, no. 3 (1994): 302–38; Avtar Brah, *Cartographies of Diaspora: Contesting Identities* (London: Routledge, 1996); Robin Cohen, *Global Diasporas: An Introduction* (London: Routledge, 1997); Glick Schiller Basch and Szanton Blanc, *Nations Unbound: Transnational Projects, Postcolonial Predicaments and De-Territorialized Nation-States* (Langhorne: Gordon and Breach, 1994); Pnina Werbner, 'The Place Which is Diaspora: Citizenship, Religion and Gender in the Making of Chaordic Transnationalism', *Journal of Ethnic and Migration Studies* 28, no. 1 (2002): 119–33.

11 Safran, 'Diasporas in Modern Societies'.
12 Ibid., 85.
13 Paul Gilroy, 'Diaspora and the Detours of Identity', in *Identity and Difference*, ed. K. Woodward (Open University Press: Sage Publications, Inc; 1997), 299–346, p. 328.
14 The first notable academic appearance of diaspora is Simon Dubnow's 1931 entry in *Encyclopaedia of the Social Sciences*, which in the first paragraph (126) explicitly extends the term to the Greeks and Armenians: 'Diaspora is a Greek term for a nation or part of a nation separated from its own state or territory and dispersed among other nations but preserving its own national culture. In a sense, Magna Graecia constituted a Greek diaspora in the ancient Roman Empire, and a typical case of diaspora is presented by the Armenians, many of whom have voluntarily lived outside their small national territory for centuries.' Simon Dubnow, 'Diaspora', in *Encyclopaedia of the Social Sciences,* ed. Edwin R. Seligman and Alvin Johnson (New York: Macmillan, 1931–35), 126–30.
15 Tölölyan, 'The Nation-State and Its Others', 4–5.
16 Cohen, *Global Diasporas.*
17 Khachig Tölölyan, 'Rethinking Diaspora (s): Stateless Power in the Transnational Moment', *Diaspora: A Journal of Transnational Studies* 5, no. 1 (Spring 1996): 7.
18 Ibid., 3.
19 J. A. Armstrong, 'Mobilized and Proletarian Diasporas', *The American Political Science Review* 70, no. 2 (1976): 393–408. https://doi.org/10.2307/1959646.
20 Sheffer, *Modern Diasporas in International Politics*; Safran, 'Diasporas in Modern Societies', 83–99; Michel Bruneau, *Diasporas* (Montpellier: GIP Reclus, 1995).
21 P. Curtin, *Cross-Cultural Trade in World History* (Studies in Comparative World History) (Cambridge: Cambridge University Press, 1984). doi:10.1017/CBO9780511661198.
22 Fernand Braudel, *La Méditerranée et le monde méditerranéen à l'époque de Philippe II*, 3 vols. (Paris: Librairie générale française, 1949).
23 Sebouh Aslanian, *From the Indian Ocean to the Mediterranean: The Global Trade Networks of Armenian Merchants from New Julfa*, (Los Angeles: University of California Press, 2011).
24 Yossi Shain, *Marketing the American Creed Abroad: Diasporas in the U.S. and Their Homelands* (New York: Cambridge University Press, 1999); Gabriel Sheffer, *Diaspora Politics: At Home Abroad* (Cambridge: Cambridge University Press, 2003).
25 Hazel Smith and Paul Stares, eds., *Diasporas in Conflict: Peace-Makers or Peace-Wreckers?* (Tokyo: UNU Press, 2007).
26 M. E. Keck and K. Sikkink, 'Transnational Advocacy Networks in International and Regional Politics', *International Social Science Journal* 51 (1999): 89–101.
27 Shampa Biswas, 'W(h)ither the Nation-State? National and State Identity in the Face of Fragmentation and Globalisation', *Global Society: Journal of Interdisciplinary International Relations* 16, no. 2 (2002): 175–98.

28 Latha Varadarjan, *Constructing the 'Domestic Abroad': Re-examining the Role of Diasporas in International Relations* (Oxford: Oxford University Press, 2010).
29 See Sossie Kasbarian, 'The Myth and Reality of "Return" – Diaspora in the Homeland', *Diaspora: A Journal of Transnational Studies* 18, no. 3 (Fall 2015): 358–81, and Razmik Panossian, 'Between Ambivalence and Intrusion: Politics and Identity in Armenia-Diaspora Relations', *Diaspora: A Journal of Transnational Studies* 7, no. 2 (Fall 1998): 149–96.
30 Khachig Tölölyan, 'Beyond the Homeland: From Exilic Nationalism to Diasporic Transnationalism', in *The Call of the Homeland*, ed. Allon Gal, Athena S. Leoussi, and Anthony D. Smith (Leiden: Brill, 2010), 27–45.
31 Ibid.
32 Aslanian, *From the Indian Ocean to the Mediterranean*.
33 Razmik Panossian, *The Armenians: From Kings and Priests to Merchants and Commissars* (New York: Columbia University Press, 2006).
34 Tölölyan, 'Beyond the Homeland', 40.
35 Ibid., 37.
36 Diaspora-wide mobilization in the form of raising funds, support and visibility is not limited to crises in Armenia but extends to all its communities. Examples in recent years include the Lebanese Civil War (1975–1990) (and currently its continuing political and economic crises); the Syrian Civil War (since 2011), the #SaveKessab and #ArtsakhStrong twitter campaigns, and previous crises in Palestine, Iran and Iraq.
37 See *IJMES Roundtable* 'Fault lines and Fractures in the 2020 Artsakh/ Nagorno Karabakh War - silence, absence and erasure in Middle East Studies' *International Journal of Middle East Studies* 54, no. 3, (August 2022).
38 Tölölyan, 'Beyond the Homeland', 39.
39 'Rethinking Diaspora(s)', 14.
40 See, for example, the corpus on Lebanese nationalist histories that make limited mention of Armenians. Even those works that are celebrated as exceptions to the limitations of Lebanese historiography such as Kamal Salibi's *A House of Many Mansions: The History of Lebanon Reconsidered* (Los Angeles: University of California Press, 1990) and Fawwaz Traboulsi's *A History of Modern Lebanon* (London: Pluto Press, 2012) are inadequate, if they mention Armenians at all. See also Tsolin Nalbantian, 'Going Beyond Overlooked Populations in Lebanese Historiography: The Armenian Case', *History Compass* 11, no. 10 (2013): 821–32.
41 See, for example, Nalbantian, *Armenians Beyond Diaspora*, and also, Hrag Papazian, this volume.
42 Aslanian, *From the Indian Ocean to the Mediterranean*, 3.
43 Ibid., 10–12.
44 Ibid., 12.
45 Ibid., 13.
46 Ibid., 15.
47 For a work that focuses on the eastern provinces of the Ottoman Empire, see Yaşar Tolga Cora, Dzovinar Derderian and Ali Sipahi, eds., *The Ottoman East in the Nineteenth Century: Societies, Identities and Politics* (New York: I.B. Tauris, 2016). For a brief description of the political, social and economic organization of the Istanbul Armenian community in the late Ottoman Empire, see Panossian, *The Armenians*, 83–6. For a more thorough reading of the history of the Armenian community in the Ottoman Empire, see Vartan Artinian, 'A Study of the Historical Development of the

Armenian Constitutional System in the Ottoman Empire, 1839-1863' (PhD Diss., Brandeis University, 1970).
48 Richard Antaramian, *Brokers of Faith, Brokers of Empire: Armenians and the Politics of Reform in the Ottoman Empire* (Stanford: Stanford University Press, 2021), 6.
49 Ibid., 6-7.
50 Bedross Der Matossian, *Shattered Dreams of Revolution: From Liberty to Violence in the Late Ottoman Empire* (Stanford: Stanford University Press, 2011), 5.
51 Ibid.
52 Bedross Der Matossian, *The Horrors of Adana: Revolution and Violence in the Early Twentieth Century* (Stanford: Stanford University Press, 2022).
53 Ibid., 4.
54 Houri Berberian, *Roving Revolutionaries Armenians and the Connected Revolutions in the Russian, Iranian and Ottoman Worlds* (Los Angeles: University of California Press, 2019).
55 A work that singularly profiles Armenians in the Iranian Constitutional Period is Houri Berberian, *Armenians and the Iranian Constitutional Revolution of 1905-1911: 'the Love for Freedom Has No Fatherland'* (Boulder: Westview Press, 2001).
56 Sebouh Aslanian, Tsolin Nalbantian and Bedross Der Matossian have written in different capacities about this reflex. See Aslanian, 'From "Autonomous" to "Interactive" Histories: World History's Challenge to Armenian Studies', in *An Armenian Mediterranean: Words and Worlds in Motion*, ed. Kathryn Babayan and Michael Pifer (London: Palgrave Macmillan, 2018), 81-125; Matossian, 'Explaining the Unexplainable'; and Nalbantian, *Armenians Beyond Diaspora*, 17-19. For historical works on the Armenian Gencoide, see, among others, Raymond H. Kevorkian, *The Armenian Genocide: A Complete History* (London: I.B. Tauris, 2011); Ronald Grigor Suny, *'They Can Live in the Desert but Nowhere Else': A History of the Armenian Genocide* (Princeton: Princeton University Press, 2015); and Ronald Grigor Suny, Fatma Müge Göçek, and Norman M. Naimark, eds., *A Question of Genocide: Armenians and Turks at the End of the Ottoman Empire* (Oxford and New York: Oxford University Press, 2011).
57 In *The Armenians in Modern Turkey: Post Genocide Society, Politics, and History*, 150, Suciyan, also a contributor to this volume, demonstrates the agency of Armenians through their activity in the Armenian press even as she demonstrates the continuation of persecution for Armenians post-genocide.
58 Lerna Ekmekcioglu, *Recovering Armenia: The Limits of Belonging in Post-Genocide Turkey* (Stanford: Stanford University Press, 2016), 1-2.
59 Ibid., 54.
60 Ibid., 59.
61 Another important work on the study of Armenians in Turkey is by Talin Suciyan, one of the contributors of this volume. In her work, *The Armenians in Modern Turkey*, she critically explores life for Armenians in Turkey during its modernization programme and beyond. See also Hratch Tchilingirian, 'The "Other" Citizens: Armenians in Turkey between Isolation and (Dis)integration', *Journal for the Society of Armenian Studies* 25, no. 4 (2017): 123-55.
62 For more on Armenian Orthodox Church and its various sees, see Hratch Tchilingirian, 'The Catholicos and the Hierarchal Sees of the Armenian Church', in *Eastern Christianity: Studies in Modern History, Religion and Politics*, ed. Anthony O'Mahony (London: Melisende, 2004), 140-59. For more specifically on the history of the Catholicosate of Cilicia, see Dickran Kouymjian, 'Cilicia and its Catholicosate

from the Fall of the Armenian Kingdom to 1915', in *Armenian Cilicia*, ed. Richard Hovannisian and Simon Payaslian (Costa Mesa: Mazda, 2008), 297–308. For more on the Jerusalem Patriarchate, see Bedross Der Matossian, 'The Armenians of Jerusalem in the Modern Period: The Rise and Decline of a Community', in *Routledge Handbook on Jerusalem*, ed. Suleiman A. Mourad, Naomi Koltun-Fromm, and Bedross Der Matossian (New York: Routledge, 2019), 396–407.

63 For an important work on the establishment of Armenian political, religious, social and educational life in Syria and Lebanon following the Armenian Genocide, see Nicola Migliorino, *(Re)Constructing Armenia in Lebanon and Syria: Ethno-cultral Diversity and the State in the Aftermath of a Refugee Crisis* (Oxford: Berghahn Books, 2008).

64 See, for example, Nalbantian, *Armenians Beyond Diaspora*, and Nalbantian, 'From Murder in New York to Salvation from Beirut: Armenian Intra-Sectarianism', in *Practicing Sectarianism: Ethnographic and Archival Interventions on Lebanon*, ed. Lara Deeb, Tsolin Nalbantian, and Nadya Sbaiti (Stanford: Stanford University Press, 2022), 116–37.

65 Talar Chahinian, *Stateless: The Politics of the Armenian Language in Exile* (Syracuse: Syracuse University Press, 2023).

66 Lalai Manjikian, 'Collective Memory and Diasporic Articulations of Imagined Homes: Armenian Community Centres in Montréal' (PhD diss., McGill University, 2005); Susan Pattie, *Faith in History: Armenians Rebuilding Community* (Washington, DC: Smithsonian Institution Press, 1997); Sevan Yousefian, 'Picnics for Patriots: The Transnational Activism of an Armenian Hometown Association', *Journal of American Ethnic History* 34, no. 1 (2014): 31–52.

67 Anny Bakalian, *Armenian-Americans: From Being to Feeling Armenian* (New Brunswick: Transaction, 1993).

68 Ibid., 179.

69 Bakalian, *Armenian-Americans*, 179–250; Sylvia Alajaji, *Music and the Armenian Diaspora: Searching for a Home in Exile* (Indianapolis: University of Indiana Press, 2015).

70 Alajaji, *Music and the Armenian Diaspora*, 2.

71 Talar Chahinian, 'Zabel Yesayan: The Myth of the Armenian Transnational Moment', *Journal for the Society of Armenian Studies* 28, no. 2 (2021): 203–11.

72 The three articles Chahinian introduces are: Maral Aktokmakyan, 'So, Did We Really Find Yesayan?', *Journal of the Society for Armenian Studies* 28, no. 2 (2021): 212–19; Meriam Belli, 'Zabel Yesayan, "Chronicle – The Role of the Armenian Woman during the War"', *Journal of the Society for Armenian Studies* 28, no. 2 (2021): 220–34; and Elyse Semerdjian, 'The Liberation of non-Muslim Women and Children in Turkey', *Journal of the Society for Armenian Studies* 28, no. 2 (2021): 235–48.

73 Marc Nichanian, *Mourning Philology: Art and Religion at the Margins of the Ottoman Empire*, trans. Jeff Fort and G. M. Goshgarian (New York: Fordham University Press, 2014).

74 The Mehyan literary review first appeared in Istanbul in 1914. It ran for seven months until the departure of its lead promoter, Constant Zarian. The five signatories were Daniel Varuzhan, Hagop Oshagan, Constant Zarian, Aharon and Kegham Parseghian. It should be noted that Nichanian refrains from using the word "genocide" and uses the term "Great Catastrophe" instead: Nichanian, *Mourning Philology*, 15.

75 Ibid., 16, 28.

76 A play on Rogers Brubaker's 'The "Diaspora" Diaspora', *Ethnic and Racial Studies* 28, no. 1 (2005): 1–19.

77 David Gutman, *The Politics of Armenian Migration to North America, 1885–1915: Migrants, Smugglers and Dubious Citizens* (Edinburgh: University of Edinburgh Press, 2021), 5.
78 Ibid.
79 Ibid.
80 Ibid.
81 Pattie, *Faith in History*, 124–5.
82 Tölölyan, 'Beyond the Homeland'.
83 Sossie Kasbarian, 'The Armenian Middle East – Boundaries, Pathways and Horizons', in *The Routledge Handbook on Middle Eastern Diasporas*, ed. Dalia Abdelhady and Ramy Aly (New York: Routledge, 2022), 405–419.
84 Khachig Tölölyan, 'Restoring the Logic of the Sedentary to Diaspora Studies', in *Les diasporas: 2000 ans d'histoire*, ed. Lisa Anteby-Yemini, William Berthomière, and Gabriel Sheffer (Rennes: Presses Universitaires de Rennes, 2005), 137–48.
85 Tölölyan, 'Elites and Institutions in the Armenian Transnation', 108.
86 Khachig Tölölyan, 'Exile Governments in the Armenian Polity', in *Governments-in-Exile in Contemporary World Politics*, ed. Yossi Shain (New York: Routledge, 1991), 166–85; Tölölyan, *Redefining Diasporas: Old Approaches, New Identities. The Armenian Diaspora in an International Context* (London: Armenian Institute, 2002).

I

'The Logic of the Sedentary'

Complicating notions of home and homelands

1

In Search of the Sedentary

Rethinking homelands in the Armenian Diaspora

Boris Adjemian

As a historian interested in the processes of integration of immigrants and their descendants into local and host societies in the modern period, I have often found it stimulating to situate my work and analysis within diaspora studies, despite the fact that diaspora is rarely an object of study for contemporary history. The necessary engagement with the concept of and literature on diaspora is probably better understood across specialized fields such as Jewish studies and Armenian studies, given the fact that Jews and Armenians have commonly been regarded – rightly or wrongly – as classical if not archetypal diasporas in the scholarly literature that has flourished from the 1990s onwards.[1] Thus, many recent works on the history of Armenian migrations show a willingness to integrate the findings of diaspora studies.[2] However, the literature on diasporas remains largely developed by social scientists rather than historians. While historians of the early modern period who study the mobility of global trading networks and worldwide interconnection of merchant or religious communities, as in the cases of the Julfan Armenian traders, Greek communities abroad or Huguenot emigration[3] engage with diaspora as a historical phenomenon, their contribution to debates and conceptual reflections within diaspora studies of geographers, anthropologists, sociologists, specialists in cultural studies or literature, seems limited.[4] As to the historians of immigration in the modern period – at least for what may be said of the French historiography that has developed since the 1980s – they rarely engage with the notion of diaspora[5] – unless perhaps when it comes to Armenian and/or Jewish immigration[6] – implicitly suggesting that the history of immigration and diaspora studies are two fields somehow hermetically sealed from each other, talking to distinct academic audiences and raising divergent questions.

Khachig Tölölyan's reflection on 'the logic of the sedentary' can help bridge this perceived gap between diaspora studies and the history of immigration. In his writings, he criticizes 'the misconception that because diasporas develop as a result of displacement, attachment to place does not have and could not have a major role in their contemporary self-conception and practice'.[7] Indeed, mainstream literature has long favoured the study of diaspora as an expression of movement, circulations and fluid identities, or as an incarnation of exile for communities intrinsically linked to a desired and sometimes inaccessible place of origin. In contrast, the notion of the sedentary has been developed almost in reaction by authors who considered it necessary to question this circulatory understanding of diaspora. Their new stance was about nuancing a diasporic model in which individuals and communities appeared primarily as agents of de-territorialized networks who would be characterized by some sort of relation – material or spiritual – to remote places. As Tölölyan suggests, the horizon of 'homecoming'[8], the notion of exile and the dream of the promised land should not lead us to underestimate the role of host lands, not only as places of refuge but also of settlement, of personal and collective attachments, and of 'predilection'.[9] In other words, the purpose of sedentary approaches was about affirming that life in the diaspora matters.

The fact that attachment to places and diasporic experiences of rootedness are the results of historical processes in the longue durée might represent a convincing invitation to consider the study of diaspora as a legitimate subject for historians of our contemporary societies. If so, what would a sedentary approach of diasporas bring to the conceptual toolbox of a historian of Armenian immigration in the long twentieth century, confronted with the notions of the nation-state, national identities, uprooting, exile and the legacy of genocide, while aiming to understand and historicize the processes of integration in a given society? How would the study of such processes contribute to our knowledge of the experiences of diasporas and the historical transformation of their host societies? In order to discuss these questions, I will follow the thread of a conversation with Tölölyan's and other diaspora specialists' works, while putting into perspective my own itinerary of research into various sites of fieldwork, as a historian of Armenian immigration between Ethiopia, Jerusalem and France.

Places and off-places in the diaspora

The 'logic of the sedentary', that is the question of how the local (or the host society) affects the experience of immigrants and their descendants lies at the core of my research on Armenians in Ethiopia. The latter is a study of historical interaction and its social effects rather than a mere community history which would be limited to narrowly describe and enumerate the events, names, institutions and achievements of Armenian communal life in Ethiopia. It aims to analyse and understand the making of a situation in which Armenian immigrants to Ethiopia and their descendants belonged fully to the host society while cultivating their own specificity, tending to consider themselves and to appear as insiders as well as outsiders according to the context and to their own interest, thus blurring the lines of identity borders and ready-made categories. Armenian immigration to Ethiopia had started in the last decades of the nineteenth century, after centuries of uninterrupted cross-cultural interactions between Ethiopian and fellow Armenian Christians materialized through long-distance journeys, inter-monastic relations, exchanges of relics, religious items, manuscripts and travel information or news from remote lands and communities.[10] A small Armenian settlement of a handful of men started to develop in Harar from the

1870s, in the wake of a short-lived Egyptian military expansion in the Horn of Africa. This early implantation was later on favoured by the annexation of this old Muslim city by the Christian kingdom of Shäwa, in 1887. These Armenian immigrants were joined by their families, mostly coming from the area of Arapgir (in the Ottoman vilayet of Kharpert), after the massacres and depredations perpetrated against Ottoman Armenians in 1895–6.[11] The small colony moved gradually to Addis Ababa, the newly founded (1886) capital city of the Empire of Ethiopia, benefiting from the protection of the *negusä negest*,[12] Emperor Menelik II (1889–1913).[13] Thus, Armenians became one of the main groups of foreigners in Ethiopia, although their number remained limited. There were probably about 200 Armenians in the country on the eve of the First World War, and no more than 1,200 after a second wave of immigration in the 1920s, with a significant proportion of people coming from Ayntab (in the former Ottoman vilayet of Aleppo) and its surroundings. The total Armenian population had remained more or less the same at the end of the 1960s. However, it decreased drastically after the Ethiopian revolution of 1974. When I was conducting my field research, between 1997 and 2002, there were barely 100 Armenians in the country, all living in Addis Ababa. Today the community numbers less than eighty, yet still perpetuates the existence of its institutions and collective life on a miniaturized scale.

Despite their small number, Ethio-Armenians (*Habeshahay*, or *Etʻovbahay*), as they call themselves, enjoyed a specific position in the local society and in the perceptions of foreignness that existed in the country. They were not considered to be, nor called, *färänj* (i.e. Franks, or White men, or Europeans, or Foreigners in Amhareñña and Tegreñña[14]) by the locals, unlike most Europeans and foreigners in Ethiopia. More than many other 'foreign' groups in the twentieth century, they appeared closely integrated into the society of the *Habäsha*, the Christian peoples of the Abyssinian Highlands.[15] They shared the same food, the same customs, the same languages and, perhaps more importantly, the same stories and memories, the same tastes and references regarding poetry and music. That is why, as far as I was able to discern, they lived somewhere in an undefined place between *färänj* and *habäsha*. It was the sociological and historical making of this very blurred state that my research aimed to analyse.

This shifting reality escapes the patterns usually mobilized in the literature when it comes to identities, belonging, nationhood and diaspora. In the 1990s, the concept of diaspora gave rise to rich discussions in scholarship but also became more diluted in an increasing range of uses. The 'communal' or ethno-national perception of diaspora, well represented in the literature of diaspora studies,[16] has tended to define it as a dispersion from and around a supposed centre usually identified with the country of origin, be it one of the people themselves or of their (sometimes very remote) ancestors. Obviously, this primordialist definition of diasporas does not allow one to contextualize nor to analyse the blurring of identity borders and the processes of rootedness and mixed belongings. On the other hand, diasporas have been more and more celebrated since the 1990s as an incarnation of fluidity and hybridity in a globalized world. The literature on the Afro-Caribbean diaspora has played an important role in this evolution.[17] By the early 2000s, diaspora was often described as the antithesis of nationalism, celebrated as a virtuous model in opposition to the nineteenth and twentieth centuries inherited frame of the nation-state,[18] as in the case of the Greek diaspora, due to its 'galactic organisation'.[19] But this opposite stance to the earlier mentioned 'centred' or communal conception of diaspora leaves aside the question of how people make roots in host societies because it highlights an understanding of diaspora as a de-essentialized and de-territorialized social formation. Further on, studying the attachment to places by people in diaspora reached an impasse when diaspora was characterized as a *non-lieu* (a 'non-place') or an experience of the *hors-lieu* (an 'off-place'),[20] almost simultaneously in the early 2000s in studies about the Armenian and the Chinese diasporas. In the view of Martine Hovanessian, the radicality of the rupture with the ancestral fatherland in the case of the Armenian Diaspora, as a consequence of the genocide, made it difficult to consider the place of residence as something other than a non-place. From a different perspective, for the French geographer Emmanuel Ma Mung, the self-perception of 'exterritoriality' across the Chinese diaspora would announce 'the end of the territories'.[21]

Although many authors in the field focus on the link between the diaspora and their territories, they often interpret the territory as a projection, in the diaspora, of a place of origin whose idealization would be proportional to the suffering caused by its loss or its inaccessibility.[22] The 'territorializing ability' of the diaspora, described by Martine Hovanessian, aims precisely to recreate communal links in these off-places, to initiate 'other ways of "being together" in the dispersion'.[23] Thus, when territoriality is considered, it is often in reference to the fidelity of diasporas to the lands of their ancestors, as for the Pontic Greeks in Greek Macedonia who recreated symbolically the lost fatherland after their forced displacement and their immigration to Northern Greece in the 1920s: their territory was rebuilt in reference or by analogy to the place of origin.[24] The diaspora becomes a 'collective projection in a re-appropriated future', an 'active fictional space', through the materialization of its presence in the local space, as a means to disentangle the knots of exile and mourning.[25] One may observe therefore that diaspora studies not only deals with networks, fluidity and movement but also considers territories, often in reference to the remote country of the ancestors, or by paying attention to its symbolic duplication abroad.

Studying the historical making of a strong yet elusive attachment and self-identification to place *in* the diaspora, such as in the Ethio-Armenian case, also reveals the relationship and interactions within the host society, which are far from being secondary in the diasporic experience, as many other case studies illustrate.[26] This approach aims to objectify a perceptible yet undefined reality that deals with settlement, instead of movement, and with *ancrage*, or *enracinement* (imperfectly rendered by the English 'integration', better by the Armenian *armadats'nel*), instead of exile. Analysing oral sources and interrogating collective memories prove instrumental in this perspective.

Memories of Armenian immigration to Ethiopia have built upon the leitmotiv of the Ethiopian kings' friendship with the Armenians, upon the idea of a collective adoption. This belief is epitomized, in particular, by the story of the *Arba Lejoch* (the 'forty children'), the Amharic name for the forty Armenian pupils from the Araradyan orphanage of Jerusalem who were recruited in 1924 to become the official music band of Crown Prince Täfäri Mäkonnen and the Ethiopian government. At a time when Ethiopia's sovereigns had to show their commitment to defend the independence of their people against the imperialism of colonial powers, the choice of stateless Armenian musicians to play the official music of Ethiopia – and of their director Kevork Nalbandian to create the first Ethiopian anthem – was interpreted as a political stance.[27] The political context, added to the religious proximity between the Ethiopian and Armenian Churches, facilitated a kind of symbolic naturalization of Armenian immigrants in a period of affirmation of Ethiopian national symbols. Although the boys had signed a fixed-term work contract of five years, which was never completely fulfilled by the Crown Prince,[28] the myth of their adoption remained in the collective memory because the image of the Ethiopian King's charity towards the Armenian orphans fit with the idealized narrative, widely shared among the small Armenian community, that had developed earlier, soon after the end of Emperor Menelik's reign.[29] The *Arba Lejoch* became a symbol of the specific status enjoyed by Armenians in Ethiopia, and, to the eyes of Armenian immigrants and their descendants, evidence of their collective acceptance by the Ethiopian people of the unique place that they claimed, somewhere between *färänj* and *habäsha*. Their story epitomized the idea that Armenians – all Armenians – belonged to Ethiopia, and were part of it. Although this hypothesis requires more research, it may be argued that such memorialization of Armenian immigration happened in hindsight, at least partly, especially after the 1960s, when governmental policies of 'ethiopianization' made it more and more necessary for the descendants of Armenian immigration to claim and legitimize their belonging to Ethiopia.

As the Ethio-Armenian case reminds us, diasporas are also rooted in places. Although diasporas have been idealized, as underlined by Khachig Tölölyan, 'as open, porous, circuit-based, cosmopolitan not parochial, deterritorialized, exemplary communities of the transnational moment', their sedentary dimension is, again in Tölölyan's terms, 'the indispensable other of diasporic mobility and porousness'.[30] Thus, they are not only about mobility or exile but also 'a catalyst of the relationship to the Other', a kind of 'social intelligence'[31] able to generate cultural synthesis within the host societies. Therefore, an essential though less visible side of diasporas' reality is left aside if we fail to consider their immobility. Described as paragons of the eternal merchant in the European travel literature of the seventeenth, eighteenth and early nineteenth centuries, Armenians have for long been associated with the study of long-distance trade by specialists of the early modern period.[32] Together with Indians, Lebanese and Greeks in Africa or in the Middle East, they have been categorized as trading diasporas and/or middlemen minorities from the 1970s onwards,[33] and these stereotypes were adopted and confirmed by historians and social scientists. Thus, in the historiography of Ethiopia, Armenians were described for decades as a population of merchants, whose activities were limited to trade and crafts, as if they were disconnected from the real life of the land and its inhabitants. Nevertheless, Armenians had developed strong ties within the host society. Far from being depoliticized and de-territorialized middlemen minorities, they had played a role in the entourage of Ethiopian kings, they had exerted a social and cultural influence, and, whether exaggerated or not, they prided themselves as being, from all the foreigners, the closest to the Ethiopian people.[34] Seemingly, whereas theoreticians beginning in the 1990s tended to categorize the Armenian Diaspora, among others, as a diaspora of victims,[35] Ethio-Armenians did not seem to complain about being uprooted or feeling exiled. Their memories were not built upon the themes of exile, of the uprooting from the fatherland, of the sufferings engendered by the genocide, of its heavy burden. In contrast, they claimed to be part of their country of residence they considered as their *home* or *homeland* (the difference between the two terms that I discuss further on is, I have to admit, still not entirely clear to me). This is not to minimize the centrality of the genocide in the historical formation of the Armenian modern diaspora in the twentieth century, nor the importance of the theme of loss in the relationship of this diaspora to the ancestral homeland. However, the nuances offered by the Ethio-Armenian case study drive me to the observation that the homeland is not necessarily a place that had existed prior to the being of a diaspora. It may also be a place that is constructed by, and/or within the diaspora.

Constructing the homeland

It is particularly revealing that the notion of homeland, as used for example by William Safran,[36] is generally understood as the ancestral fatherland, as if no critical definition of the term was needed. Khachig Tölölyan himself pointed out that 'a terminological problem dogs diaspora studies when "home" is at issue' in a long footnote of his article 'The Contemporary Discourses of Diaspora Studies':

> The actual home of many diasporic peoples may be the United States or Canada, yet scholars continue to speak of such countries as the host land. For the first generation, this is true. But in the case of those born in these and similar receiving countries, where the extension of citizenship to the native-born is very nearly automatic (as it is not, say, for Kurds born in Germany), to speak of the United States or Canada as a host land after the first generation of migration is odd. To address this oddity, in my own work I now refer to the United States as my home and the home of its Armenian diaspora and to Armenia as the homeland (of my ancestors).[37]

I would even go further than this distinction between home and homeland, and use 'homeland' for the host land also, when it is the self-perception of the people that the place where they live is theirs, which was and still is the case for Armenians in Ethiopia, despite 'delusions and disillusionments'.[38] Of course, one should not idealize the feelings towards the so-called 'host' land, whose denomination can be as misleading as the 'home' land or the 'father' land and 'mother' land. Although it appears that Ethiopia has been idealized as a kind of Armenian substitute homeland in the grand narrative forged and transmitted among Armenian immigrants and their descendants,[39] this does not mean that the reality of their life and experience in Ethiopia was idyllic. After the 1960s and the 1970s, and especially after the Ethiopian revolution of 1974, Armenians faced some hostility and were sometimes denied access to Ethiopian citizenship although they were born in the country. A majority of them preferred to leave the country in the years preceding and following the revolution, and those who remained had to keep a low profile, like the rest of the population, in order to survive the 'Red terror' of Mängestu Haylä Maryam's regime (1974–91). Vartkes Nalbandian's recent autobiographical book details many such difficulties. Nevertheless, he still talks about Ethiopia as the homeland: 'Yes, Ethiopia became our motherland with the grace of its people and rulers',[40] the kings of Ethiopia 'who gave a homeland to our ancestors'.[41] That is why he claims that 'Ethiopia is my homeland'.[42] The book shows the 'concerns, convictions and deep-rooted love' of the author 'for a country that I call home'.[43] In doing so, Vartkes Nalbandian situates his personal testimony in the footsteps of some of his elders, like Avedis Terzian (1904–2000), whose narratives I have commented on extensively elsewhere.[44]

The fact that people could consider the place they live as their homeland is not necessarily linked to a generational transition: first-generation immigrants may adopt the host land as their new homeland as well. When, for instance, in Avedis Terzibashian's book *Ergu Dari Adis Abēbayi mēch* ('Two Years in Addis Ababa'), the Van-born former jeweller of the Ethiopian emperor Haylä Sellasē, Hagop Baghdassarian, described the hills and springs of the province of Shäwa around Addis Ababa; he did it with the same emotion that he would have had regarding his native province of Vasbouragan in historic Armenia, and he stressed the physical analogies between the two places.[45] He considered himself a Habeshts'i (an Abyssinian) as well as a Vanets'i (a resident of Van).

Moreover, if we think again of the Ethio-Armenian case, the granting of the citizenship of the country of residence is not an absolute condition for people to feel at home, although it understandably might be in European or Western contexts, or in any other context where political status is an important issue. In France, for example, full access to citizenship became a sine qua non for political and social integration since the late nineteenth and early twentieth centuries, especially after the First World War. However, in Ethiopia, the very notions of nationhood and citizenship remained unclear during the first half of the twentieth century. Thus, in the 1930s, Armenians used to consider and declare themselves as Ethiopian subjects although they were not officially recognized as such. This ambiguity persisted during the five years Fascist Italy occupied the country (1936–41), creating a number of administrative imbroglios.[46] Only from the 1960s on, in the context of a new policy of Ethiopianization, did access to local citizenship prove crucial for individuals aiming to continue living and working in the country their parents or grandparents had immigrated to. As late as in the 1980s–1990s, cases of stateless Ethio-Armenians still applying for Ethiopian citizenship despite their family having lived in the country for three generations and who considered themselves Ethiopians, were not rare. The growing importance of issues of citizenship during the second half of the twentieth century did not prevent Armenian immigrants and their children or grandchildren from integrating deeply into local society. Therefore, one may ask: where was 'home' for those Ethio-Armenians who left Ethiopia after the 1974 revolution and died or lived in exile in Sydney, Montreal or Los Angeles? Was it Arapgir and Ayntab or Addis Ababa, Dire Dawa and Harar? Where is their nostalgia directed towards?

Martine Hovanessian, whose important oeuvre exerts a wide influence in diaspora studies, has placed the loss of the fatherland at the centre of her reflections. Throughout her numerous books and articles, the '*rupture radicale*' of the genocide appears at the core of the process of identity-making and memorialization in the Armenian Diaspora.[47] The precedence granted to the land of the forefathers in the preoccupations of diasporas is widespread in the literature of diaspora studies, and not just to archetypical cases such as the Armenian or the Jewish diasporas. Facing the inflated – and often diluted – uses of the term 'diaspora', of 'the increasing collapse of the distinction between diaspora and dispersion',[48] Khachig Tölölyan, like others, underlined the importance of criteria such as memory, commemoration, mourning, trauma, attachment to the homeland and a rhetoric of restoration and return, in the definition of what a diaspora is. However, he added, defining diaspora as 'that segment of a people living outside the homeland typifies a problem characteristic of much contemporary diaspora discourse',[49] freezing the notion of diaspora in a form of biologism, as if it was a given rather than a process. It is precisely because diaspora needs to be considered as a social and historical process that in my opinion, scholars would be well advised to be more inclusive in their understanding of what a homeland is.

Jerusalem and its Armenian community offer a good illustration of this proposition. Here the self-identification of the people with the place they live in is particularly strong, due to the symbolic centrality that characterizes the holy city in the archipelago of the diaspora and beyond. The first time I visited the city in February 2010, I was particularly struck by the sociological reality of the Armenian Quarter and its inhabitants as it reminded me of the in-between situation experienced by Armenians in Ethiopia four or five decades earlier. That is, a situation characterized by the capacity of Armenians in Jerusalem to become one with the city as to personify its complex cultural, national and linguistic milieu. The difference was that, in Jerusalem, this symbiosis was still visible – despite the sempiternal concern for the demographic decline of the community – whereas in Addis Ababa it had remained only perceptible through fading traces, by those who already knew about the past of Armenian presence in the city.

The genesis of the Armenian Quarter of Jerusalem, a place in the Holy Land marked by centuries-old Armenian ecclesiastical and monastic presence, was also the result of a succession of Armenian migration waves in the modern period. Among the oldest waves, families of *kaghakats'i* (lit. 'the people of the city'), many of them the descendants of pilgrims, settled there in the eighteenth and nineteenth centuries. A second wave was constituted by the massive immigration to Palestine of Armenian refugees after the First World War, some of whose descendants still live in the Armenian Quarter, among whom a significant part resides within the walls of St. James Monastery.[50] Therefore, the important presence of refugees and orphans in the early twentieth century has left traces in a place that had already been durably marked by multiple layers of histories and memories. Consequently, the tracks of a recent past of Armenian immigrations of the twentieth century have converged and merged with older tracks and memories. They contributed to the multilayered construction of a communal space in Jerusalem, linking the present with the long history of pilgrimages and Armenian presence.[51] Such a memory phenomenon resembles the one analysed by the French sociologist Maurice Halbwachs in his seminal book on 'the legendary topography of the Gospels in the Holy Land', where he showed how early Christians tended to locate the (claimed) recollections of Jesus' life in and around Jerusalem in the footsteps of a Jewish memory as a way to legitimize and fortify a Christian memory in the Holy Land. For instance, Halbwachs interpreted the location of Jesus' birthplace in Bethlehem as the expression of a collective will to underscore the genealogical continuity which supposedly linked him and his lineage to King David. Halbwachs argued that it was as though the authors of the Gospels of Matthew and Luke had thought such a link might help convince the Jews that Jesus was the Messiah.[52] Contemporary self-perceptions of the Armenian presence in Jerusalem, where several waves of Armenian immigration converged on and succeeded one another until the mid-twentieth century, are based on a comparable pattern of memory construction. They provide an enlightening example of the making of an Armenian homeland in diaspora, where past layers of Armenian settlements in Palestine are permanently summoned to legitimize the current existence of a community, on a more than ever disputed territory. If the post-genocide Armenian refugees have succeeded to settle in Jerusalem, this is not only due to the endeavours of the Patriarchate and Armenian philanthropic organizations but also partially due to the links they were able to figure out between themselves and the older presence of the *kaghakats'i* families. Similar observations can be made about the successive layers of Armenian immigration to Ethiopia, from the late nineteenth century immigrants coming from Arapgir and surroundings to the post-genocide immigration of Armenians from Ayntab and other places.[53] As in Jerusalem, collective memory has erased the distinctions and antagonisms between the newcomers and their predecessors, merging their diverse experiences of migration into a commonly idealized narrative of the making of an Armenian substitute homeland in Ethiopia.

Rethinking immigrants' experiences

Restoring the logic of the sedentary is the thread that runs through my research into the history of Armenian immigration to France during the long twentieth century. This research began in Valence and the surrounding area and includes cities, towns and regions such as Lyon, Valence, Grenoble, Saint-Martin-d'Hères, Vienne, Romans, Décines and Saint-Étienne. While Armenian communities have been settling along the Rhône valley since the 1920s, one finds Little Armenias here even today. Despite the persistence of identity markers (rather than identity boundaries),[54] the history of Armenian immigrants and their descendants in these towns is telling of their deep integration into the local, where they have made their homes. The following vibrant paragraph in the French sociologist Roger Bastide's pioneering study on Armenian settlement in Valence in the late 1920s may offer, I believe, if not a convincing definition, at least some reflection on what a homeland is:

> When one says that a homeland is first a soil, one does not refer to the bare ground, but to a ground enriched of feelings, habits and ideas, by the tender memories of childhood inextricably mixed with rocks, meadows and woods, the sweetness of love and motherhood united with the stones of the house, the farmyard, the street

of the city. In a word, this soil of which we are talking about is a chain of images and emotions.[55]

In Valence, Lyon and neighbouring '*hayashad*' (Armenian populated) towns of France, this 'chain of images and emotion' is well rendered in autobiographical books and testimonies. Born and raised in Vienne (near Lyon), a former Roman city that became an industrial town in the nineteenth century, Jean Ayanian narrates the life and times of his fellow Armenians who used to live inside the 'Kemp'. Pronounced like 'camp' (with the American pronunciation), as a legacy from the past experience of some of these immigrants in the Near East Relief refugee camps of Syria and Lebanon, the Kemp was an old factory whose residents – who called themselves the '*Kempjis*' – had turned into their home for several decades, between the 1930s and the 1960s. Ayanian remembers how, in his childhood, he and the kids of the compound used to climb on the high chimney of the Kemp which they compared to 'their' Mount Ararat. 'Thus, Vienna the Roman became by the vicissitudes of history, Vienna the Armenian, with all the emotional attachment that it means.'[56] Considering the concentration of Armenian graves in the upper part of the town's old cemetery located on the bucolic hill of Pipet, Ayanian concludes that this is 'the Kemp of the deceased we have not forgotten and whose memory we keep'.[57] In the same vein, Kharpert-born Jean Der Sarkissian, in his book *Les pommes rouges d'Arménie*, describes with emotion the central boulevards of Valence and the neighbouring ruins of the medieval castle of Crussol, a town where he was able to return after his long years as a *nerkaght'ts'i* in Soviet Armenia.[58] Of course, the disillusionment and disappointments the author experienced in Armenia, where he settled at the age of nineteen in 1947 during the second biggest phase of 'repatriation' from the diaspora to Soviet Armenia, could partly explain the homesickness he expresses towards Valence. However, the same nostalgia pervades other autobiographies, such as Jacques Der Alexanian's narratives about the story of his family and Armenian community life, also in Valence.[59]

In citing such examples, my aim is neither to refute the importance of the link that dispersed genocide survivors had to their destroyed homelands in post-Ottoman Turkey nor to downplay the fact they may have dreamt of rebuilding such homelands in Soviet Armenia from the 1920s to the 1940s, and even later on. However, I seek to highlight that in the same period, homelands were also being made on site, '*deghwuyn vray*', through many channels such as labour, school, leisure time, friendship, marriage, wartime hardships, from birthplace to grave. The blossoming of a community life through an Armenian cultural life, Armenian associations, organizations and institutions and so on, was crucial in this collective construction of new diaspora homelands. The typical Armenian compatriotic associations (*hayrenagts'agan miut'iwnner*), based on regional affiliations and solidarities, were not solely looking towards Ararat and repatriation in the 1930s–1950s, although their nominal raison d'être was the reconstruction of the lost fatherland. In reality, they were also a powerful vector of territorialization and integration into the local, like for instance the Education Society of Malatia (*Malat'ioy Grt'asirats' Miut'iwně*), very well established in Saint-Chamond,[60] near Saint-Étienne, and galvanizing the Armenian local community life in most of the towns of the area.

In Search of the Sedentary 37

Here lies what Khachig Tölölyan defines as the existence of a stateless power when he elaborates on the often-overlooked tendency of diasporas to territorialization, that is,

> the emphatic preference of some diasporic individuals and groups for settling in areas where they can be with kin and compatriots; where they can be a substantial minority or a majority; where their religious institutions, schools, shops and restaurants, clubs, and old-age homes can draw on a population base; where geographical but especially cultural borders can be established and symbolically patrolled; and, sometimes, where a power base for electoral and lobbying politics can be developed.[61]

In a particularly enlightening passage of his analysis on the dual nature of diasporic institutions, both local and transnational, Tölölyan holds up as an example the organization of the Armenian Apostolic Church. The non-married priests, the *vartabed*-s, as well as the bishops, operate in a transnational frame and are even supposed to make a career and cultivate their networks in the Middle East or in Northern America if they aspire to the highest functions in the Church. Whereas the *k'ahanay*-s or married priests officiate in the same parish, sometimes their entire life, thus being firmly rooted into the local even though they might originally come from another locale, or even from abroad. From this example, Tölölyan concludes that diasporic organizations are able to affirm their transnational dimension as long as they succeed in cultivating their connections to the local. This is the reason why, most of the time, the self-proclaimed leaders of these diasporic communities are well integrated into the local establishment and can act as go-betweens. Through their voices, the public expression of the community relies simultaneously on its local integration and its belonging to a diasporic or transnational reality.[62] Similar observations could be made about the Armenian General Benevolent Union (AGBU), a diaspora-based organization whose transnational dynamism is firmly rooted thanks to the activities of its local chapters. The archives of the AGBU (one of the rare Armenian diasporic organizations to have constituted and preserved such documentation) vividly show the dual dimension – local and transnational – of its presence and activities in all the Armenian communities of the Rhône valley from the 1920s to the 1980s.[63]

When compared to the rest of France and perhaps Europe, the particularity of the Armenian presence in the Rhône valley is that it is visible through a constellation of local communities, including small- and middle-sized towns whose urban spaces are marked by Armenian symbols (*khach'k'ar*-s, ethnic shops and restaurants, street names etc.) and monuments. In this sociological landscape, the Armenian community is never forgotten in local politics, especially when it comes to commemorating the genocide. The first street of '24 April 1915' in France was inaugurated in Décines (in the suburb of Lyon) in 1965. In the following years, others were inaugurated in Vienne (1973), Chasse-sur-Rhône (1978), Charvieu (1982), Saint-Chamond (1988), Saint-Martin d'Hères (1996), Meyzieu (1999), Bourg-lès-Valence (2005), Vaulx-en-Velin (2007) and so on. A monument to the Armenian Genocide was erected in Décines as early as 1972, followed by many towns of the area in the 1980s and 1990s, thus pioneering the public recognition of the genocide in France. It was also in Vienne, on the occasion of the Armenian Christmas in 1983, that French president François Mitterrand (1981-95) was the first French high-ranking official to talk openly about the Armenian Genocide in a speech. After the mid-1970s and 1980s, the increasing importance and public consideration granted by French politicians and institutions to the Armenian community in these localities started being transcribed into a discourse celebrating its 'exemplary' integration. In a context of tense debates about immigration from Africa and the Middle East, and the supposed incompatibility between Islam and the principles of the French Republic, such positive public discourses about the Armenians generalized as a cliché in France throughout the 2000s and 2010s, in contrast to the negative stereotypes attributed to their parents and grandparents in the interwar period. In many places of the Rhône valley, this evolution of public discourses and collective perceptions paved the way for the institutionalization of the Armenian presence, through the annual – and almost mandatory – participation of mayors, deputies and state representatives (such as prefects) in the gatherings of 24 April, as well as through a number of associations and institutions such as the Maisons de la Culture arménienne founded and funded by the municipalities, from the 1970s onwards, in Décines, Villeurbanne, Vienne, Grenoble, Valence, Romansménien (Centre for Armenian Heritage) created in Valence in 2005.[64] Thus, memory and memorialization are key factors of this process of integration into the local, as illustrated by the space and visibility allocated to the memory of the Armenian Genocide and its monuments. The relations these Armenian diasporic associations and institutions were able to build with local and governmental French representatives are determinative. It is within this memorial frame of a well-integrated community that new waves of Armenian immigration, from Istanbul and Aleppo in the 1960s, from Beirut in the 1970s and from Armenia in the 2000s have managed to settle in France. The pre-existence of deeply sedentarized Armenian communities facilitated the arrival and settlement of newcomers, in a way which, albeit in different contexts, is comparable to what we observed for Armenians in Jerusalem and in Ethiopia.

* * *

In a preliminary report to Boghos Nubar Pasha anticipating the foundation by the AGBU of a library in Paris, in the late 1920s, the former journalist and author from Istanbul, Aram Andonian, argued that this would be a unique opportunity for Armenians in the diaspora to maintain their cultural existence and to strengthen the 'Little Armenias' (*ayn p'ok'rig hayut'iwně*) that already existed here and there. Andonian meaningfully proposed to call this new institution the Armenian National Library of Paris (*P'arizi Haygagan Azkayin Madenatarané*). Furthermore, he insisted on the fact that 'an Armenian library in Paris will not go against the fatherland; on the contrary, it will become a tool of its reinforcement'.[65] The Armenian Library was founded in 1927-8. It was renamed as the Nubar Library after its benefactor's death, in 1930. Together with the famous bookshop Librairie Orientale founded by Hrand Samuel in 1930 (also known as Librairie Samuelian), at the heart of Paris' Quartier Latin, and the daily *Haṛach* published in Paris by Chavarch Missakian from 1925 on, the Nubar Library became iconic in the history and memories of Armenian immigration to France, at a time when Paris appeared as a cultural and intellectual hotspot of the Armenian Diaspora. Undoubtedly, the history of books and cultural institutions such as these open promising fields towards the understanding of the making of sedentariness within national communities living in exile, such as the first generations of Armenians in France.[66]

Discussing attachment to place may seem trivial to the ongoing debates in diaspora studies. The nostalgia for a recreated homeland somewhere in the diaspora may even appear as a simplistic notion. This is nevertheless constitutive of the reality experienced by generations of immigrants and their descendants, as exemplified in Ethiopia, Jerusalem, Valence, Vienne, Paris and so on. However, the phenomenon of *enracinement* – that the English 'integration', once again, fails to translate – is hard to objectify by social scientists and historians because it is a process which is subtle, slow and silent. No one keeps records of the sedentary, because there are no archives of the invisible. Sedentariness does not always materialize in the edification of monuments, the naming of streets or the development of businesses or institutions. It regards above all the many ways immigrants or diasporic people make the place they live their own, through the forging of material as well as invisible links. In a nutshell, this is about their *enracinement*. Therefore, when scholars do care about it – as happens sometimes – they encounter the absence of ready-made documentations and methodologies, even though they may be convinced that making roots in the place one lives plays an eminent role in the very experience of the diaspora.

One may object, from what precedes, that the socio-historical experience of Armenians in Ethiopia is a borderline case of self-identification to the host land and cannot be generalized. The symbolic appropriation of a diasporic homeland is so strong there, as it is in Palestine for other reasons, that it challenges the possibility to generalize its analysis. However, from Valence to Paris, like from Addis Ababa to Jerusalem and many other sites, a history of sedentariness, of attachment to places, would enrich our understanding of a diaspora, as being not only movement and fluidity, nor exile and loss. Furthermore, such approaches would allow us to go beyond the community and ethnic understandings of diasporas, by paying attention and analysing their interactions within local and national contexts, therefore never losing sight of their constructed nature. These would be, I believe, some of the benefits of restoring 'the logic of the sedentary' to diaspora studies.

Notes

1 See Alain Médam, 'Diaspora/Diasporas. Archétype et typologie', *Revue européenne des migrations internationales* 9, no. 1 (1993): 59–66; Robin Cohen, *Global Diasporas: An Introduction* (London: University College of London Press, 2001); Stéphane Dufoix, *Les diasporas* (Paris: Presses Universitaires de France, 2003); Michel Bruneau, *Diasporas et espaces transnationaux* (Paris: Anthropos/Economica, 2004); Richard G. Hovannisian and David N. Myers, eds., *Enlightenment and Diaspora: The Armenian and Jewish Cases* (Atlanta: Scholars Press, 1999).

2   See, for instance, Tsolin Nalbantian, *Armenians beyond Diaspora: Making Lebanon Their Own* (Edinburgh: Edinburgh University Press, 2020); Anouche Kunth, *Exils arméniens: du Caucase à Paris, 1920–1945* (Paris: Belin, 2016); Vahe Sahakyan, 'Between Host-Countries and Homeland: Institutions, Politics and Identities in the Post-Genocide Armenian Diaspora (1920s to 1980s)' (PhD, University of Michigan, 2015); Boris Adjemian, *La fanfare du négus. Les Arméniens en Éthiopie (XIXe-XXe siècles)* (Paris: Éditions de l'EHESS, 2013).

3   See, for instance, Sebouh David Aslanian, *From the Indian Ocean to the Mediterranean: The Global Trade Networks of Armenian Merchants from New Julfa* (Berkeley: University of California Press, 2011); Francesca Trivellato, *The Familiarity of Strangers: The Sephardic Diaspora, Livorno, and Cross-Cultural Trade in the Early Modern Period* (New Haven: Yale University Press, 2009); Mathieu Grenet, *La fabrique communautaire: Les Grecs à Venise, Livourne et Marseille : v. 1770-v. 1840* (Athènes: École française d'Athènes, 2016); Mathieu Grenet, 'Appartenances régionales, expérience diasporique et fabrique communautaire: le cas grec, fin XVIe-début XIXe siècle', *Tracés. Revue de sciences humaines* 23 (2012): 21–40; Natalia Muchnik, 'La terre d'origine dans les diasporas des XVIe-XVIIIe siècles. "S'attacher à des pierres comme à une religion locale . . . "', *Annales. Histoire, Sciences Sociales* 66e année, no. 2 (2011): 481–512.

4   There is a rich literature on the history of diasporas in the early modern period, although it has rarely appeared in a leading publication in the field such as *Diaspora: A Journal of Transnational Studies*. For a recent and stimulating panorama of the historiography, see Mathilde Monge and Natalia Muchnik, *L'Europe des diasporas: XVIe-XVIIIe siècle* (Paris: Presses universitaires de France / Humensis, 2019).

5   Many examples might be quoted here. See, for instance, the pioneer works of Gérard Noiriel, *Le Creuset français. Histoire de l'immigration XIXe - XXe Siècle* (Paris: Gallimard, 2006, first published in 1988). More recently, Gérard Noiriel, *Immigration, antisémitisme et racisme en France, XIXe-XXe siècle: discours publics, humiliations privées* (Paris: Fayard, 2007).

6   See Maud Mandel, *In the Aftermath of Genocide: Armenians and Jews in Twentieth-Century France* (Durham: Duke University Press, 2003); Kunth, *Exils arméniens*.

7   Khachig Tölölyan, 'Restoring the Logic of the Sedentary to Diaspora Studies', in *Les diasporas: 2000 ans d'histoire*, ed. Lisa Anteby-Yemini, William Berthomière, and Gabriel Sheffer (Rennes: Presses universitaires de Rennes, 2005), 137–48.

8   A notion which is interrogated and complexified in Sossie Kasbarian, 'The Myth and Reality of "Return" – Diaspora in the "Homeland"', *Diaspora: A Journal of Transnational Studies* 18, no. 3 (Fall 2009): 358–81; Sossie Kasbarian, 'Refuge in the "Homeland": The Syrians in Armenia', in *Aid to Armenia: Humanitarianism and intervention from the 1890s to the present*, ed. Jo Laycock and Francesca Piana (Manchester: Manchester University Press, 2020); Jo Laycock, 'Armenian Homelands and Homecomings, 1945–9. The Repatriation of Diaspora Armenians to the Soviet Union', *Cultural and Social History* 9, no. 1 (2012): 103–23.

9   Chantal Bordes-Benayoun, 'Revisiter les diasporas', *Diasporas. Histoire et sociétés* 1, no. 1 (2002): 11–21. See also Suzanne Schwalgin, 'Why Locality Matters: Diaspora Consciousness and Sedentariness in the Armenian Diaspora in Greece', in *Diaspora, Identity and Religion*, ed. Waltraud Kokot, Khachig Tölölyan, and Carolin Alfonso (London, New York: Routledge, 2004), 72–92.

10 On this aspect of Ethiopian-Armenian relations, the reference study is Enrico Cerulli, *Etiopi in Palestina: storia della comunità etiopica di Gerusalemme*, 2 vols (Rome:

Libreria dello Stato, 1943). For further references, see Richard Pankhurst, 'The History of Ethiopian-Armenian Relations (I)', *Revue des études arméniennes (nouvelle série)* 12 (1977): 273–345; Richard Pankhurst, 'The History of Ethiopian-Armenian Relations (II)', *Revue des études arméniennes* 13 (1978–79): 259–312. See also Adjemian, *La fanfare du négus*.

11 On this origin from Arapgir and surroundings in the vilayet of Kharpert, there is of course a general context of emigration, especially towards North America. See David Gutman, *The Politics of Armenian Migration to North America, 1885–1915: Sojourners, Smugglers and Dubious Citizens*, Edinburgh Studies on the Ottoman Empire (Edinburgh: Edinburgh University Press, 2019). It should be noted, however, that the percentage of families originally coming from Arapgir was already significant among the Armenians living in Cairo in the mid-nineteenth century. See Anne Kazazian, 'Les Arméniens au Caire dans la première moitié du XIXe siècle: l'implantation d'une communauté en diaspora', in *Arméniens et Grecs en diaspora: approches comparatives*, ed. Michel Bruneau et al. (Athènes: École française d'Athènes, 2007), 133–49.

12 May be translated roughly as 'King of Kings', although there is no direct equivalence between Abyssinian and European titles. In the modern period, from the late nineteenth century on, the title of 'Emperor' was also used in international politics and in official translations of Amharic documents.

13 The first author to document these early developments of an Armenian community – or colony (*kaghout*) – in Ethiopia was Hayg Patapan, *Arti Et'ovbia ew Hay Kaghoutĕ* (Modern Ethiopia and the Armenian Colony) (Venice: Mekhitarist Congregation of St. Lazare, 1930).

14 See Wolf Leslau, *Concise Amharic Dictionary* (Wiesbaden: Harrassowitz, 1976).

15 Abyssinia – *Habeshisdan* in Armenian – was often used indifferently as Ethiopia in former Western publications. In this article, it refers to the populated highlands covering some parts of the neighbouring states of Ethiopia and Eritrea, characterized by the dominance of Christianism and a literary culture derived from the Ge'ez.

16 See Gabriel Sheffer, *Diaspora Politics: At Home Abroad* (New York: Cambridge University Press, 2003) which is strikingly illustrative of this perception of 'ethno-national diasporas' as 'bona fide actual entities' (245–6). Of course the identity presupposition of such approach, and its tendency to 'groupism' and essentialism, has for long been criticized. See, for instance, Rogers Brubaker, 'The "Diaspora" Diaspora', *Ethnic and Racial Studies* 28, no. 1 (2005): 1–19 (10–13); Christine Chivallon, *La diaspora noire des Amériques: Expériences et théories à partir de la Caraïbe* (Paris: CNRS Éditions, 2016), 25–6. Dufoix, *Les diasporas*, 61–4.

17 See Paul Gilroy, *The Black Atlantic: Modernity and Double Consciousness* (London: Verso, 1993). For an analyse of this evolution, see Christine Chivallon, 'Du territoire au réseau: comment penser l'identité antillaise', *Cahiers d'Études africaines* 37, no. 148 (1997): 767–94; Christine Chivallon, 'La diaspora noire des Amériques. Réflexions sur le modèle de l'hybridité de Paul Gilroy', *L'Homme. Revue française d'anthropologie* 161, no. 1 (2002): 51–73, and Chivallon, *La diaspora noire des Amériques*.

18 See, for instance, Georges Prévélakis, 'Les diasporas comme négation de l'"idéologie géographique"', in *Les diasporas: 2000 ans d'histoire*, ed. Lisa Anteby-Yemini, William Berthomière, and Gabriel Sheffer (Rennes: Presses universitaires de Rennes, 2005), 113–24.

19 Georges Prévélakis, ed., Les réseaux des diasporas Nicosia, Paris: KYKEM, L'Harmattan, 1996.

20 Martine Hovanessian, ed., *Diaspora arménienne et territorialités*, Special issue of *Hommes et migrations* no. 1265 (2007): 17–19. All translations are mine.
21 Emmanuel Ma Mung, 'Non-lieu et utopie: la diaspora chinoise et le territoire', in *Les réseaux des diasporas*, ed. Georges Prévélakis (Nicosia, Paris: KYKEM, L'Harmattan, 1996), 205–14.
22 See, for example, Martine Hovanessian, *Le lien communautaire: trois générations d'Arméniens* (Paris: Armand Colin, 1992); Michel Bruneau, *Les Grecs pontiques: diaspora, identité, territoires* (Paris: CNRS éd, 1998); Lisa Anteby-Yemini, *Les juifs éthiopiens en Israël: les paradoxes du paradis* (Paris: CNRS éditions, 2004); Giulia Bonacci, *Exodus !: l'histoire du retour des rastafariens en Ethiopie* (Paris: Scali, 2007).
23 Martine Hovanessian, 'La notion de diaspora', *Journal des anthropologues* 72–73, no. 1 (1998): 11–30.
24 Michel Bruneau, 'Les monastères pontiques de Macédoine, marqueurs territoriaux de la diaspora', in *Les Grecs pontiques: diaspora, identité, territoires*, ed. Michel Bruneau (Paris: CNRS éditions, 1998), 213–28.
25 Martine Hovanessian, 'Diaspora arménienne et patrimonialisation d'une mémoire collective: l'impossible lieu du témoignage ?', *Les Cahiers de Framespa* 3 (2007). See also Martine Hovanessian, 'Le religieux et la reconnaissance: Formes symboliques et diaspora arménienne en France', *Les Annales de la recherche urbaine* 96, no. 1 (2004): 125–34.
26 See, for instance, Sossie Kasbarian, 'Rooted and Routed: The Contemporary Armenian Diaspora in Cyprus and Lebanon' (PhD, School of Oriental and African Studies (University of London), 2006); Susan Paul Pattie, *Faith in History: Armenians Rebuilding Community*, Smithsonian Series in Ethnographic Inquiry (Washington, DC: Smithsonian Institution Press, 1997); Nalbantian, *Armenians beyond Diaspora*. Joanne Nucho, *Everyday Sectarianism in Urban Lebanon: Infrastructures, Public Services, and Power* (Princeton: Princeton University Press, 2016); Joanne Randa Nucho, 'Becoming Armenian in Lebanon', *Middle East Report*, no. 267 (Summer 2013): 32–6.
27 See Boris Adjemian, 'La fanfare arménienne du négus. Représentations des étrangers, usages du passé et politique étrangère des rois d'Éthiopie au début du 20e siècle', *Vingtième Siècle. Revue d'histoire* 119, no. 3 (2013): 85–97.
28 Täfäri was crowned as *negus* in 1928, then *negusä negest* or emperor in 1930 under the name of Haylä Sellasē I.
29 See Boris Adjemian, 'Immigrants and Kings. Foreignness in Ethiopia through the Eye of Armenian Diaspora', *African Diaspora* 8 (2015): 15–33.
30 Khachig Tölölyan, 'Elites and Institutions in the Armenian Transnation', *Diaspora: A Journal of Transnational Studies* 9, no. 1 (2000): 112.
31 Bordes-Benayoun, 'Revisiter les diasporas'.
32 See Fernand Braudel, *Civilisation, économie et capitalisme: XVe-XVIIIe siècle* (Paris: Librairie générale française, 1993); Fernand Braudel, *La Méditerranée et le monde méditerranéen à l'époque de Philippe II* (Paris: Armand Colin, 1990); Philip D. Curtin, *Cross-Cultural Trade in World History*, Studies in Comparative World History (Cambridge; New York: Cambridge University Press, 1984).
33 See Edna Bonacich, 'A Theory of Middleman Minorities', *American Sociological Review* 38, no. 5 (1973): 583–94. For a critic of these categorizations, see H. Laurens Van der Laan, *The Lebanese Traders in Sierra Leone* (The Hague: Mouton & Co., 1975). More recently, Andrew Arsan, *Interlopers of Empire: The Lebanese Diaspora in Colonial French West Africa* (London: Hurst & Company, 2014).

34 See Boris Adjemian, 'Les Arméniens en Éthiopie, une entorse à la "raison diasporique"? Réflexion sur les concepts de diaspora marchande et de minorité intermédiaire', *Revue européenne des migrations internationales* 28, no. 3 (2012): 107–26. The situation of the Armenian community in Egypt offers some parallels with the Ethiopian case, albeit on a different scale, especially regarding the role of Armenian families and agents in the entourage of Egyptian monarchs. See Rouben Adalian, 'The Armenian Colony of Egypt During the Reign of Muhammad Ali (1805–1848)', *Armenian Review* 33 (June 1980): 115–44.
35 See Cohen, *Global Diaspora*.
36 William Safran, 'Diasporas in Modern Societies: Myths of Homeland and Return', *Diaspora: A Journal of Transnational Studies* 1, no. 1 (1991): 83–99.
37 Khachig Tölölyan, 'The Contemporary Discourse of Diaspora Studies', *Comparative Studies of South Asia, Africa and the Middle East* 27, no. 3 (2007): 647–55 (see 649, fn. 9).
38 To quote the words of Vartkes Nalbandian. See note 40. For a recent discussion of these two associated notions, see Yaşar Tolga Cora and Laurent Dissard, ed., *Home(land)s: Place, Loss and Return in Contemporary Turkey*, theme issue of *Études arméniennes contemporaines* 13 (2021).
39 Boris Adjemian, 'Immigrants arméniens, représentations de l'étranger et construction du national en Éthiopie (XIXe - XXe siècle): socio-histoire d'un espace interstitiel de sociabilités' (PhD, École des hautes études en sciences sociales, Università degli studi di Napoli 'L'Orientale', 2011); Adjemian, *La fanfare du négus*.
40 Vartkes Nalbandian, *'I Want to Die with a Flag'. Ethiopia: My Delusions and Disillusionment* (no place (Canada), 2019), 101.
41 Ibid., 108.
42 Ibid., 167.
43 Ibid., 177.
44 Adjemian, *La fanfare du négus*; Adjemian, 'Immigrants arméniens, représentations de l'étranger et construction du national en Éthiopie (XIXe - XXe siècle)'; Adjemian, 'Du récit de soi à l'écriture d'un Grand Récit: une autobiographie collective arménienne en Éthiopie', *Diasporas. Histoire et sociétés* 22 (2013): 139–53.
45 Avedis Terzibashian, *Ergu Dari Adis Abēbayi mēch* (*Two Years in Addis Ababa*) (Paris: Imp. A. Der Agopian, 1944).
46 Boris Adjemian, 'Stateless Armenians in Ethiopia Under Fascist Occupation (1936–1941): Foreignness and Integration, From Local to Colonial Subject', in *Citizens and Subjects of the Italian Colonies: Legal Constructions and Social Practices, 1882–1943*, ed. Simona Berhe and Olindo De Napoli (London: Routledge, 2022), 223–44.
47 Martine Hovanessian, 'Récits de vie et mémoire(s) de l'exil: les enjeux à l'œuvre dans l'histoire orale', *Revue du monde arménien moderne et contemporain* 6 (2001): 75–96; Martine Hovanessian, 'La notion de diaspora: les évolutions d'une conscience de la dispersion à travers l'exemple arménien', in *Les diasporas: 2000 ans d'histoire*, ed. Lisa Anteby-Yemini, William Berthomière and Gabriel Sheffer (Rennes: Presses universitaires de Rennes, 2005), 65–78; Martine Hovanessian, 'Diasporas et identités Collectives', *Hommes et migrations* 1265 (2007): 9–21.
48 Tölölyan, 'The Contemporary Discourse of Diaspora Studies', 648. See also Brubaker, 'The "Diaspora" Diaspora'.
49 Tölölyan, 'The Contemporary Discourse of Diaspora Studies', 649.
50 For a historical overview, see Bedross Der Matossian, 'The Armenians of Palestine 1918–48', *Journal of Palestine Studies* 41, no. 1 (November 2011): 24–44; Der Matossian, 'The

Armenians of Jerusalem in the Modern Period: The Rise and Decline of a Community', in *Routledge Handbook on Jerusalem*, ed. Suleiman A. Mourad, Naomi Koltun-Fromm, and Bedross Der Matossian (London, New York: Routledge, 2019), 396–407. On the Armenian Jerusalemite experience and specificities of the '*kaghakats'i*' cultural context, the reference book is John H. Melkon Rose, *Armenians of Jerusalem: Memories of Life in Palestine* (London: Radcliffe Press, 1993). On Armenian pilgrims to Jerusalem, see Sossie Andézian, 'Des pèlerins sédentaires. Formation d'une diaspora arménienne à Jérusalem', in *Les pèlerinages au Maghreb et au Moyen-Orient*, ed. Sylvia Chiffoleau and Anna Madœuf (Damas: Presses de l'Ifpo, 2010), 47–69.

51 See Boris Adjemian and Talin Suciyan, 'Making Space and Community through Memory: Orphans and Armenian Jerusalem in the Nubar Library's Photographic Archive', *Études arméniennes contemporaines* 9 (2017): 75–113.

52 Maurice Halbwachs, *La topographie légendaire des Évangiles en Terre Sainte. Étude de mémoire collective* (Paris: Gallimard, 1941), 175.

53 Boris Adjemian, 'De l'expérience migratoire au Grand Récit de la migration: le mythe de l'adoption dans la mémoire des Arméniens d'Éthiopie', *L'Homme. Revue française d'anthropologie* 211 (2014): 97–116.

54 Street names, shops' signs referring to Armenian origin, *khach'k'ar*-s and monuments dedicated to the memory of the genocide and so on are among the most visible of these identity markers. However, such markers do not equate to identity boundaries in the sense that Armenian communities and their heritage are nowadays fully integrated to the local urban landscape.

55 Roger Bastide, 'Les Arméniens de Valence', *Revue internationale de sociologie* 1–2 (février 1931): 17–42 (24).

56 Jean Ayanian, *Le Kemp: une enfance intra-muros* (Marseille: Ed. Parenthèses, 2001), 68.

57 Ibid., 99.

58 Jean Der Sarkissian et Lucie Der Sarkissian, *Les pommes rouges d'Arménie* (Paris: Flammarion, 1987), 162.

59 Jacques Der Alexanian, *Les héritiers du pays oublié: 1922–1987* (Paris: R. Laffont, 1991), 140.

60 See, for instance, Arshag Alboyadjian, *Badmut'iwn Malat'ioy Hayots': Deghakragan, badmagan ew azkakragan* (A History of the Armenians of Malatia) (Beirut: Sevan, 1961), 1490–505.

61 Tölölyan, 'Elites and Institutions in the Armenian Transnation', 107–36 (110–11 and 131, fn. 9).

62 Ibid., 114–15.

63 These archives are preserved at the AGBU Nubar Library (Paris). See, for example, AGBU, Correspondences with local committees: 25/5 (Valence, 1928–1943), 25/6 (Saint-Étienne, 1929–1942), 68/1 (Grenoble, 1946–1972), 68/4 (Vienne, 1937–1960), and so on.

64 See Boris Adjemian, *Les Petites Arménies de la vallée du Rhône: histoire et mémoires des immigrations arméniennes en France* (Lyon: Éditions Lieux Dits, 2020).

65 'Haygagan madenataran mě, P'arizi mēch, ayt hayrenik'in tēm ch'bidi ěllay, ěnthagaṛagě anor zōrats'man mich'ots'nerēn mēgě bidi taṛnay.' See Aram Andonian, *Dzrakir* ('Project'), manuscript dated 1927 (f. 15), in AGBU Nubar Library Archives, Bibliothèque, 1, Projet de Bibliothèque arménienne.

66 Since the submission of the first draft of this chapter, I have extensively written on this question in Boris Adjemian, '*Archives, exil et politique: Aram Andonian et la Bibliothèque arménienne de Paris (1927–1951)*', mémoire inédit pour l'habilitation à diriger des recherches (Paris: École normale supérieure, 2022).

2

Armenian Displaced Persons

From displacement to a diaspora community

Gegham Mughnetsyan

Displacement has come to be synonymous with the Armenian experience.[1] A continuous dispersion transformed individual and collective Armenian identities, and communities formed around the shared trauma of collective exodus.[2] The experience of the displaced persons (DPs) is a microcosm of the Armenian ordeal of generational dispersion. Coined by sociologist Eugene Kulischer, 'displaced person' was a classification given to refugees who were forcefully or otherwise displaced as a result of the Second World War.[3] Overall, some 55 million people were displaced between 1939 and 1947.[4] After the war, with the changes in American immigration laws and the passing of the Displaced Persons Act in 1948, the term took on a meaning of status with which refugees could get permission to settle in America. Among these millions of people were a few thousand Armenians from the Soviet Union, stranded mainly in Germany, Austria and Italy, due to displacement, separation of families and uncertainty of the future in the face of the rapidly descending Iron Curtain across the European continent.

However, only two decades after being stranded in post-war Europe, these displaced Armenians had regrouped in California, where they went on to establish a community in East Los Angeles which included one of the first Armenian day schools in the country,[5] the largest monument in the United States dedicated to the victims of the Armenian Genocide, and one of the largest Armenian church complexes.[6] They maintained the Armenian diasporic fixtures ranging from political, athletic, relief organizations to cultural groups. In this leap from a dispersion to diaspora the narratives of the individuals converged and produced a collective story of a community. In this chapter, I will give a background overview of how almost 4,000 Armenians ended up in post-war Germany as displaced persons and how that ordeal created a continued basis for community and identity formation. I will frame the story of the Armenian displaced persons in the exilic, transnational and intercommunal contexts, to show how a group's identity has been shaped by the bouts of being in transit and stateless. Finally, I will argue that the collective DP experience during this arduous journey and settlement had a lasting impact on the evolution of a displaced group into a close-knit diasporic community in America.

Oral histories

A review of the existing literature on displaced persons reveals a number of works exploring the histories of Jewish, Polish, Ukrainian, Belorussian, Baltic, Hungarian, Balkan DPs and displaced Germans (*Volksdeutsche*), while the presence of Armenians in this sea of displacement and the particular experiences of those Armenians in this context have remained unexplored.[7] The historiography of the Second World War has sidestepped the narratives of the displaced persons of Armenian origin due to the layers of identity that classified them under larger descriptors as 'Soviet', 'Ukrainian DPs', 'forced labor' or 'POWs'. Armenian historiography has in its turn only briefly dealt with the story of the Armenian DPs. Due to the scarcity of existing academic sources on the topic, the process of writing the story of the Armenian DPs had to involve the collection of narratives in the form of oral histories from those who had been displaced persons.[8] As part of the Displaced Persons Documentation Project, an oral history initiative from the USC Institute of Armenian Studies, I have conducted interviews with people who had been inhabitants of a displaced persons camp in Germany. Currently there are thirty-two interviews in the collection. The average age of the interviewees was eighty-six, with the youngest seventy-one and the oldest ninety-seven at the time of the interview. The first interview was conducted in February 2018 and the latest interview in September 2021. One of the interviewees, who, due to their displacement, had never managed to get a proper education and conversed in a mix of Russian, Armenian, German and English, said, 'I have never shared my story much because one needs to be fluent in four languages to understand it'. This chapter is in part informed by the accounts of those interviewees.[9]

From post-genocide displacement to life in interbellum Soviet Union

All of the oral history interviewees were either children of Armenian Genocide survivors or from families that had been uprooted in the aftermath of the genocide. This life trajectory was largely representative of the Armenians that eventually became known as displaced persons. During the Armeno-Turkish clashes in the spring of 1918 and during the short-lived period of Armenian independence, thousands of Armenians living along the Eastern Front had gradually retreated towards Erivan (Yerevan) and Tiflis (Tbilisi) and then headed towards the historic Armenian communities in Russia, that is, North Caucasus, Rostov and Crimea, that attracted refugees who wanted to settle and rebuild their lives.[10] After 1921, they had become residents of the newly formed Union of the Soviet Socialist Republics, the Soviet Union. And while there was a titular Soviet republic of the Armenians, these refugees had ended up at what had become Soviet Ukraine and the RSFSR (Soviet Russia). Those who had settled at the Russian Black Sea port of Novorossiysk and then were forced to collectivize had named their collective farm in the rural outskirts of the city *Yerznka*, the Armenian name of Erzincan in Turkey, since the Armenians in Novorossiysk were predominantly from there. This is similar to the description of the post-genocide Armenian refugees in Cyprus described by Susan Pattie: 'The refugees thought of themselves as associated with particular towns, such as Adana, Zelifke, Mersin, Gessaria, Marash – as well as family, church and for many, craft or training.'[11] Those from Artvin who had settled in Kharkov, Ukraine, in order to make a living had started a collective bakery in the long-running tradition of bakers from Artvin. Armenian Catholics from Erzurum who had settled in Kiev had done the same, but once the state had banned private property and taken over the bakery, they had reformed themselves into a cooperative and had started making soap. These trade cooperatives known as *artel*, in a way had served the purpose of compatriotic unions like those of Van-Vaspurakan or Marash that would spring up in Armenian communities around the world and in the absence of a national entity had taken the role of harbouring identity.

While in the case of the older generation whose pre-genocide and pre-displacement Armenian identities found new expressions in the form of trade unions and collective farms, the new generation born in the Soviet Union had a further complication in the identity formation process. Those interviewees who had been old enough to attend schools in the Soviet Union mentioned that initially they had been able to attend Armenian schools. In the 1920s the 'Nationalities Policy' of the newly formed USSR had stressed the importance of native language instruction for all the nationalities.[12] However, gradually the Soviet state policy of *Korenizatsiya* (Indigenization) came to take precedence, intended to give the titular republics of the Soviet Union individual characteristics[13] or as described by Anastas Mikoyan, the USSR was creating and organizing new nations.[14] Most of the Armenian DPs, and the interviewees I worked with, came from Soviet Ukraine.[15] By the 1930s, the Armenian-language schools were closed in Ukraine under the localized version of *Korenizatsiya* known as Ukrainization. This policy was intended to give Ukraine a more homogenic national character. For example, 'on 31 August 1929, the predominantly Russian-speaking residents of Odessa woke up to discover their daily *Izvestia* had been transformed into the Ukrainian-language *Chernomorska Komuna*'.[16] Interviewees originally from Kiev and Kharkov in Ukraine recounted having to attend Russian schools after the closure of the Armenian schools. At the same time, the Armenian church was virtually abolished by the Soviet authorities under the guise of rooting out nationalism and religion because while the practice of national attributes, that is, folklore and food, was encouraged among the minorities, anything deemed nationalistic was discouraged by the state. As a result, Armenian identity within the USSR, but outside of Soviet Armenia, was reduced to familial ties and rituals.

The Soviet policies had gradually eroded the elements of Armenian identity from the Armenians who lived in the USSR, but outside of Soviet Armenia. This was evident in their perceptions of a community or a communal identity. The interviewees, during their oral history interviews, used the word *hayut'yun*, Armen-ity or the collective of Armenians, when asked if there was a population of Armenians in the places where they lived. The terms *hamaynk'*, community, or *gaghut'*, the exilic colony, were not used to describe the life in the Soviet Union. Those Armenians who lived in Crimea or the Donbas were not considered an Armenian Diaspora and did not experience life as such. The concept of internal diaspora officially did not exist within the Soviet Union while examples such as Georgians in Moscow did fit that description.[17] Unlike the

Georgians who were transplants in Moscow from their native Georgia, the Armenians who had settled in different parts of the Soviet Union did not hail from what had become the Armenian Soviet Socialist Republic, the titular home of the Armenians in the USSR. These Armenians largely had never lived in Soviet Armenia. Out of over thirty interviewees with whom I spoke, only one had been born in Yerevan and the parents of three others hailed from localities currently in Armenia. For example, in Crimea and Krasnodar there had been Armenian communities for centuries, and at the inception of the Soviet Union the Armenians in those communities were seen as integral parts of those areas, just like Russian Cossacks in Don or Germans on the banks of the Volga.[18] Comparable to this are also the cases of Armenians in Lebanon and those of Cyprus who were enshrined in the constitutions of the states, affirming their status as 'part of the state fabric'.[19] The relative newcomers, those displaced by genocide, did not originate from Soviet Armenia either. Their birthplaces in the former Ottoman and Russian empires had become parts of Turkey.[20] So, on the eve of 21 June 1941, when the war came to the Soviet Union, the reality of these Armenians was that of local formations around common trade and place of origin, where the people had leveraged their past experiences and communal ethnic ties to make a life for themselves.

In addition, the politics of naturalization and citizenship in the Soviet Union further complicated the layers of identity and belonging for the newly settled Armenians within the western periphery of the Soviet Union. Those interviewed who were born in the Soviet Union had been its citizens, while the generation of their parents, the displaced from the Russo-Turkish borderland, had not been able to receive proper papers during the tumultuous period of the Russian Revolution and the formation of the Soviet Union. Moreover, the 1938 law on USSR Citizenship 'specified that certain people within Soviet territory would formally be considered stateless' and foreign-born individuals and immigrants were gradually stripped of or outright denied Soviet citizenship.[21] Thus, on paper, many of the refugee Armenians were still considered Turkish subjects and, as such, became targets of exile and persecution during the period of the Great Purge. For example, one of the interviewees was born in Ordzhonikidze (current-day Vladikavkaz in North Ossetia), after her parents had settled there when displaced from Yerznka/Erzincan. Then, the family had moved to Novorossiysk on the Black Sea coast to evade prosecution for her father who was classified as a Turkish subject. Later they moved once again to the collective farm away from Novorossiysk. In other words, by the time the Armenians stranded in Germany, Italy and Austria became classified as displaced persons, each of them had already on average been through three rounds of uprooting during the course of their lives. Displacement, whether forced or out of necessity, was well known to all of them.

While trying to gain footing and establish some kind of normalcy of life, a new calamity approached, when as a result of the *blitzkrieg* beginning in the summer of 1941, the German forces rapidly advanced to the outskirts of Moscow, Leningrad (St. Petersburg), and the banks of river Volga. At the height of the invasion of the USSR Germans occupied some 350,000 square miles of territory including present-day Ukraine, Belarus, Moldova, the Baltic states, the entire Crimean Peninsula and parts of North Caucasus.[22] This territory coincided with the regions containing Armenian community centres.[23] The Armenians who had been rebuilding their lives for two decades in the Soviet Ukraine, Crimea and the North Caucasus now fell under German occupation.

Displacement to Germany

In order to maintain wartime production and a growing military force, Germany required a colossal workforce and this demand was met by bringing in populations from the newly conquered territories. In March 1942 the Reich Ministry for the Occupied Eastern Territories ordered the administration of occupied Ukraine to supply farm and industrial workers for German work needs.[24] Subsequently, the Germans uprooted families and moved them to Germany. Among the displaced were the hundreds of Armenians, picked up from Ukraine, the Crimean Peninsula and the North Caucasus, once again being forced to leave behind their livelihood.

In the 1930s, as Nazi Germany was forming its racial doctrine, the Armenians had been classified as people of the Semitic race.[25] This classification meant that Armenians would also face the fate of the Jews in the Nazi plan for the future of the continent. However, the Deutsch-Armenische Gesellschaft, the German-Armenian Society, comprised of German and Armenian academics and intellectuals, with the agenda to safeguard the Armenians from complete annihilation in the event of German and possibly Turkish invasion and occupation of the Caucasus,[26] undertook an effort to make a case in front of the Nazi leadership proving that the Armenians were 'Aryan' instead of Semitic. An instrumental figure in this task was Artashes Abeghian, linguist Manuk Abeghian's nephew and a professor of Armenology at the Berlin University. He was a member of the Armenian National Council, a civilian body that worked with the German government to safeguard Armenian interests in the case of potential invasion of Soviet Armenia during the war. Several interviewees recounted how in train stations during their displacement they were designated to convoys headed to Germany for labour instead of those destined for the concentration camps due to this 'Aryan' classification.[27] The 'Aryan' classification had added a certain degree of self-awareness among the displaced Armenians that they were different from the Poles and the Ukrainians who shared their fate and that their Armenian heritage was special. As a result, 'the Armenian identity' came to play an increasing role in these people's lives who were now embracing it as a survival tactic.

In addition to those Armenians who were forcefully relocated to Germany for labour, there were scores of Armenians who retreated voluntarily with their families. The German occupation, which lasted up to three years in some areas and had allowed for commercial activities, permitted Armenians, who had been small business owners prior to collectivization, to reopen their storefronts and bakeries. Those who had larger houses were forced to offer rooms or at times even the whole house for the purposes of housing invading forces. This resulted in situations where families shared a home with a German officer for a prolonged period. These Armenians, similar to the Ukrainians, Poles, the Baltic people and the *Volksdeutsche*, feared the wrath of the returning Red Army, for the charge of collaboration. However, even those who had managed to voluntarily leave ended up in the same situation as those forced to be labourers. Upon reaching Germany and Austria, the displaced were assigned, based on labour needs, to farms and factories, at times separated from their kin. Children were also put to work. By August 1944, there were 2.8 million Soviet citizens working in the Reich.[28] In total, during the war, the German forces had brought into the Reich 6.5 million civilians in addition to Soviet POWs for labour.[29]

After the victory of the Allies in Europe, Germany was divided into four occupation zones: American, Soviet, British and French. German cities lay in ruin and millions of people were displaced without a clear end in sight to that state of displacement. In other words, displacement was a fundamental feature of life in early post-war Germany.[30] The issue of the displaced was so paramount that when in the last months of the war the Allied leaders convened in Yalta to agree on a post-war settlement, the displaced persons were dealt with in Article One of the signed agreement.[31] According to the Yalta Agreement, 'All Soviet citizens liberated by the forces operating under United States command . . . will, without delay after their liberation, be separated from enemy prisoners of war and will be maintained . . . in camps or points of concentration until they have been handed over to the Soviet . . . authorities.'[32] When the war ended, the USSR demanded the repatriation of its citizens and Soviet officials were granted unprecedented access to and control over Soviet nationals in areas of Germany and Austria occupied by the Western Allies.[33] It was implied that Soviet nationals could be repatriated by force.[34] The Allies reported that 3.2 million refugees had found their way home by the summer of 1945, mainly to the USSR.[35] However, as reports spread that repatriated Soviet citizens were exiled and even executed for suspected collaboration with the Germans during the war, concerns grew among the Allies regarding forced repatriation. As concerns mounted, General Joseph T. McNarney, the military governor of the American Occupation Zone in Germany, issued a policy statement on nonforcible repatriation that no displaced person would be forced to return to their homeland against their will.[36]

In the midst of these displaced masses, there were at least 3,900 displaced persons of Armenian descent in the barracks of Germany and Italy.[37] As late as May 1949 there were close to 1,400 Armenians in Stuttgart, 40 in Frankfurt, 25 in Heidelberg, 20 in Berlin and another 500 scattered between Naples, Rome, Vienna and France.[38] The interviewees also mentioned being in Fellbach, Mannheim, Innsbruck, Reutlingen, Heilbronn and other locations in Germany, Austria, Romania and Poland. Interviewees recalled that due to this separation of families between workplaces, individuals would make the trek on foot or on a bike from one location to another to visit their relatives. These visitations had established an unofficial communication network with fellow Armenians with whom they had shared the hardships of the journey. A visiting reporter from *The New Yorker* remarked, 'The DP grapevine is the best and most alert underground communication system in Western Europe today.'[39] This circulation of information, according to the interviewees, alerted the Armenian DPs to flock to the American zone of occupation in an effort to escape forced repatriation to the USSR, since they feared that their wartime actions amounted to collaboration and that they would be sent to Siberia or, worse, executed.

Many Soviet DPs hid their status, by taking cover under another nationality or by declaring themselves stateless.[40] In the case of the Armenians, since many of them had been denied citizenship and classified as Turkish subjects while in the Soviet Union, they used their original birthplaces, presently in Turkey, on their refugee documentation so as not to appear as individuals who were from the USSR. Those hailing from Kharkov and Kiev turned into Armenians from Artvin and Erzurum. In a 1 January 1949 register containing 1,652 names of Armenians residing in DP camps in American, British and French Occupation Zones in Germany, 656 have Turkey listed as their birthplace while another 337 have listed Iran.[41] In the case of Turkey, most older displaced Armenians from the Soviet Union were actually listing their correct birthplaces and omitting their place of residence. In the case of Iran, as some of the interviewees mentioned, it was a common tactic to list it as a place of origin to conceal Soviet residency or citizenship.[42]

Funkerkaserne: A DP camp turns into a community

Organized by the United Nations Refugee Rehabilitation Authority (UNRRA), displaced persons camps had popped up all over the Allied-occupied territories.[43] At their inception, the DP camps were meant to serve as temporary refuge for people who were in the process of being repatriated to their homelands. However, when it became evident that a number of DPs could neither be repatriated nor stay in Germany, these facilities served as shelters for people for a longer period of time. These were also rehabilitation centres where those who had suffered through the disaster of the war could return to a normal life. Some 1,600 Armenian DPs were housed in the former army barracks, the *Funkerkaserne*, in Bad Cannstatt, Stuttgart, in the American Occupation Zone in Germany. It is important to note that some DPs did live away from the camp, in Wangen, a neighbourhood of Stuttgart, due to the lack of additional living space in *Funkerkaserne* or because they were working in the city and it was more convenient. However, all of them stayed connected to the camp by participating in the activities and gatherings, and by their DP status. *Funkerkaserne* consisted of officers' quarters that resembled apartments, and the rooms in these apartments were assigned to multiple families resulting in communal living that was familiar to some from their previous lives in the Soviet Union. Every DP was entitled to less than fifty square feet of living space which usually housed more than one person.[44] This type of living also resulted in extreme closeness between families, as mentioned by all of the interviewees. One of them, who got married while living in the camp, talked about how the women at the camp made the wedding dress and prepared the food while the roommates of the apartment put up divider curtains and left the room to give the newlyweds privacy.

Funkerkaserne housed predominantly Armenians and became known as the Armenian camp, referred to by its inhabitants as 'camp' or by the German/Russian *Lager*. The interviewees recounted the presence of non-Armenians such as Assyrians, Russians and Ukrainians, who had either been acquaintances from their hometowns or were married to Armenians. As a result, the Armenian populations in the *Funkerkaserne* predominantly interacted only with other Armenians for four to five and in some cases up to seven years during their stay in Stuttgart. At a reunion of DPs in

1997 held at the Armenian community centre in Montebello, 'Zefa Mosikian, the then five-year-old girl who began her frightening odyssey to freedom when the Germans forced her family onto a barge in the mine-filled Black Sea', said, 'Whoever made it there to Stuttgart, had made it through the war. After the war, it was beautiful. We just enjoyed life'.[45] Another interviewee, who had spent five years of her life between the ages of ten and fifteen at the camp said, 'the life in the camp was good because the war was over, people were working somehow, making money, we were eating well and there was hope'.[46] All those interviewed recall their years at the camp as some of the best years of their lives – after all that suffering it was a period of peace, and cultural and communal awakening.

While monitored by UNRRA and later the IRO, the International Refugee Organization, many international religious and humanitarian organizations including the American Jewish Joint Distribution Committee, American Friends Service Committee, the Lutheran World Federation, Catholic Charities, the Red Cross organizations (also, the Armenian Relief Society known to Armenians as the *Haykakan Karmir Khach'* (Armenian Red Cross)), The Polish American Congress and Ukrainian American Relief Committee worked to alleviate the tremendous burden of taking care of these refugees at the camps.[47] Soon enough, the inhabitants who were trained in the UNRRA workshops in various trades began to make a living on their own. One of these UNRRA-taught trade skills was shoemaking. In 1949, after three years of camp life, a fifth of all working-age Armenian DPs in the camps had listed 'shoemaker' as their profession.[48] One of the Armenian DP families, the Magdesians, even carried the shoemaking tradition with them to America and opened a factory in 1952, which is still family owned and in operation today, in the City of Industry, an East Los Angeles suburb.[49]

On the one hand, initially the Soviet agents surveyed the vicinity to detain and deport back to USSR any of their former citizens. On the other hand, on 23 May 1949, the American, British and French Occupation zones were converted into the Federal Republic of Germany.[50] This returned governance to Germans who did not want foreign DP populations in their midst since they needed to rebuild their country and take care of displaced Germans and *Volksdeutsche* estimated to be some 14 million people.[51] The experience of the Armenian DPs confined at *Funkerkaserne* is comparable to the Armenian refugee encampment in Port Said, Egypt, during the First World War where the Armenians, 'having been saved from certain death by French warships' from Jebel Musa (Musa Dagh), were refused entry by the French in Cyprus and the British in Egypt and were confined to a makeshift encampment at the port.[52] The notable difference was that after a four-year displacement in Port Said the Armenians were able to, albeit briefly, return home to Cilicia, only to later be displaced to Lebanon. In Germany the realization among the DPs was that all those at *Funkerkaserne* would not be able to return to their homes in the Soviet Union. With no plans to go back to the Soviet Union, unwanted in Germany, prevented by American quotas to find asylum in America, and with the rest of the continent in ruin, the camp became a safety net for Armenian DPs, a ready support system – one of the 'little Armenias' forming in 'close-knit and compact communities' around the world which 'were also very important in the shaping of identity'.[53]

The camps were largely self-governing with administrations made up of the inhabitants of the camp 'who had been merchants and professors, musicians, poets and artists'.[54] These elites, 'as organizers of the community and middlemen between it and sources of power',[55] were important in the process of community formation at *Funkerkaserne*. The camp government consisted of elected camp councils which appointed a camp executive and coordinated the handing out of aid and organizing the community life.[56] Following the collapse of the first independent Republic of Armenia in 1920, many of its leaders and ideologues had escaped Bolshevik persecution and found refuge in the West as émigrés. Some of these Armenian leaders had been members of the Armenian National Council in Berlin who had been involved in the process of making the case for the 'Aryan' origins of the Armenians. After the capitulation and partition of Germany, when large numbers of Armenian refugees congregated in and around Stuttgart, many of these elites also ended up among the Armenian DPs, to evade Soviet capture. They either lived at the camp or became closely associated with it. As natural leaders and renowned among the older generation of DPs, they took leadership positions at the camp and shaped it into an Armenian community unit.

These elites included the last chief of police of independent Armenia's capital Yerevan, Sedrak Jalalian, former ambassador Davit Davitkhanian, prominent politician and Ottoman parliament member Vahan Papazian a.k.a. *Goms*, General Drastamat (Dro) Kanayan's adjutant Colonel Tigran Baghdasarian, Armenian vigilante Misak Torlakian and others.[57] Also present were Professor Artashes Abeghian and writer Garo Kevorkian, who later published one of diaspora's most important series, *Amenun Darekirk'ĕ*, the Armenian Almanac from 1954 to 1968.[58] In their capacity, best described by Tölölyan's concept of 'government-of-exile', these leaders fostered the 'political organization and cultural production . . . that empower exiles to live on as a collective'.[59] The aforementioned elites were prominent members of the Armenian Revolutionary Federation and as Kevorkian put it, 'there was an ARF contingent numbering some hundred old and new members and the entire public life, camp administration and auxiliary bodies were coordinated by the ARF Committee'.[60] Here it is also important to reiterate that the ARF and its auxiliary bodies such as the Armenian Relief Society played a crucial role in the process of rescuing the DPs and securing resettlement in the United States.[61] The political reawakening was to a degree that Soviet Armenians, while hailing from the Ottoman Empire,[62] and having spent their lives in Ukraine and Russia, were by 1948 celebrating with grandiosity the thirtieth anniversary of the First Armenian Republic's founding in 1918.[63]

A process of identity shaping and nation-building facilitated the transformation from an exilic group into a community at the camp. *Funkerkaserne* was a mid-point in the leap from dispersion to community. This army base that in its containment felt like a sort of an enclave, an island in a volatile sea, 'a neighborhood as a nation-state',[64] was the location where, under the influence of internal and external factors, a group of people from varying backgrounds, who up to that point were connected by a chain of life-altering traumatic experiences, were moulded into a community.[65] This development is along the lines of other community formations in the diaspora, for example in Lebanon, where 'what had been multiple Armenian communities back in the Ottoman Empire's vast lands grew into a single community in Beirut.[66] Similar to the de-Turkification efforts among the Armenian Diaspora in the Middle East,[67] in the case of these displaced Armenians from the Soviet Union the process was the de-assimilation of the Soviet identity back into an Armenian one as a rediscovery after a generation of self-described 'Russification' in Soviet Russia and Ukraine. In that process, language became 'a key cultural marker around which modern Armenian identity could be cemented'.[68] According to the interviewees, school-aged children, who began to receive Armenian-language education, constantly interrupted their elders who conversed in Russian or Turkish and urged them to speak in Armenian 'and parents learnt from their children'.[69] In other words, 'it was made very clear: to be Armenian one had to speak Armenian'.[70] The DPs also established a school, a scout organization, a performing theatre troupe and even a dance group at the camp.[71] There were weekly *Darakir* and *Banber* periodicals printed at the camp.[72] This kind of national awakening was not particular to the Armenian DPs. For example, the Lithuanian DPs originating in Königsberg (present-day Kaliningrad), who eventually ended up in Chicago, described their community formation as 'our native language ... [became] our homeland'.[73]

For the Armenian DPs, this post-war refuge at the *Funkerkaserne* was also a period of a return and rediscovery of church and religion, which had been suppressed in the Soviet Union. As in other places where a diasporic Armenian identity was being formed, in the cases where the Armenian language did not have a stronghold, 'the Apostolic Church ... replaced language as the key cultural marker of Armenianness'.[74] Since the majority of the displaced had nominally been Apostolic Christians or embraced it as a marker of Armenianness, the Armenian Apostolic Church got to have a dominant presence and a makeshift chapel was put together within the campgrounds.[75] Another contributing factor was that one of the DPs, Fr Vahan Askarian, was a priest from Crimea, which meant that the Apostolic Church had a representation at the camp.[76] The Armenian Catholics, who according to one interviewee numbered up to 500, were prevented from organizing services at the chapel on the camp grounds. They held mass in a nearby German church. The Armenian Catholics were supported by the Mekhitarist Congregation of Vienna, the Armenian Catholic monastery. The Mekhitarists through their channels had tried to rescue Armenians from German camps, but only if the captives had been Catholics. This, as the interviewees recalled, had also been a reason why there was antagonism towards the Armenian Catholics from the rest of the Armenian DPs, who had felt overlooked while in labour or POW camps.

America: From displacement to diaspora

George Mardikian, the owner of the popular *Omar Khayyam*'s restaurant in San Francisco, credited with introducing Middle Eastern dishes to America, served as a food supply consultant for the US Army during the war, and as such, got to travel throughout the army bases for inspections. While travelling through the American bases in Europe he was led to *Funkerkaserne*.[77] There he vowed to make efforts to rescue the displaced Armenians. Mardikian was himself a product of dispersion and displacement. Born in Bayburt in the Ottoman Empire, he had lost his family in the genocide before eventually ending up in the United States. He was emotionally moved to assist the Armenians stranded in DP camps after the war. In order to undertake the task of assisting the displaced Armenians in Europe, Mardikian, who had become close friends with many commanders of the American forces in Europe, along with a San Francisco lawyer Suren Saroyan, founded the American National Committee to Aid Homeless Armenians (ANCHA).[78] The objective became to lobby the US government to raise immigration quota numbers and accept more refugees.[79] Supported by the ARF, the organization consisted of Armenians from Armenian-populated localities throughout the United States, who at the beginning raised awareness of the plight of the Armenians in Europe and sent aid, and then after the easing of immigration policies found sponsors for the DPs to guarantee their admission into the United States. President Truman's sympathy towards the plight of the displaced and the resulting Stratton Bill and the DP Act of 1948 cleared the way for more immigrants and the ANCHA got to work to bring the Armenian DPs into the United States.[80] Once the law went into effect, the voluntary agencies launched massive campaigns to locate sponsors in the United States to match them with the DPs in Europe and organize transportation.[81]

Facilitated by the efforts of the ANCHA, the DPs gradually arrived in America in waves between 1948 and 1952. The newcomers were spread throughout the country in places as distant as New Orleans, Louisiana, and Sanger, California. In a few examples existing acquaintances in America found out where their relatives were going to land and went to bring them to reunite with the extended family.[82] The ANCHA also provided initial money and helped with finding housing. It had been the wish of some of the sponsors that the new arrivals would integrate into the pre-existing Armenian communities. In some cases their nationalism came to awaken the spirit among those who had emigrated decades ago.[83] However, while actively trying to integrate into American society and make a living for their families, the primary concern for the new arrivals was finding jobs and places to settle. Since the arrival of the DPs coincided with the post-war decline of the industrial centres on the East Coast, as interviewees described, they gradually relocated to Detroit and then to California where new opportunities, the warm weather and affordable living were plentiful.[84]

The perceptions about these displaced people; however, differed widely within the Armenian world. The official Soviet position was that these people were traitors who had assisted the occupiers and then had defected.[85] Some 25,000 Armenians, POWs and civilians, had voluntarily or forcefully returned to the Soviet Union, and the reluctance of a few thousand Armenians to follow suit was interpreted by the Soviet narrative as admission of collaboration with the Germans.[86] Only in the 1960s, during a thaw in Soviet–American tensions, were some of the Soviet Armenians who had been displaced to Germany and then ended up in the United States able to establish contacts with and travel to visit their families left behind up in the Soviet Union. Two interviewees shared that when their parents had finally returned to visit, they were treated coldly as traitors by their own extended family.

Elsewhere in the diaspora, attitudes were influenced by another phenomenon that was sweeping Armenian communities following the end of the war: repatriation to Soviet Armenia. This state-sponsored initiative was an effort to get those Armenians who were dispersed around the world to settle in Soviet Armenia and participate in the post-war rebuilding. As reported by the Soviet Armenian committee that facilitated the repatriation efforts, 'by January 20, 1948, 86,364 repatriates had arrived in Armenia: 32,238 from Syria/Lebanon, 4,383 from Bulgaria, 20,997 from Iran, 1,783 from Romania, 18,215 from Greece, 5,260 from France, 1,669 from Egypt, 1,250 from Palestine, 856 from Iraq, 151 from the United States (a further 162 left the United States in January 1949) and 16 from China'.[87] On this point Tölölyan elaborates that 'this was not a true repatriation, in the sense that these returnees were in fact born not in the portion of Armenia that had been under Russian/Soviet rule since 1828 but in the part of Armenia ruled by Ottoman Turkey and were survivors or children of survivors, of the Genocide'.[88] To the organizations in the diaspora that were actively promoting the 'repatriation' to the Armenian SSR and preparing segments of the community for the big move, it seemed heretical that there were some 4,000 Armenians from elsewhere in the Soviet Union who had been trapped in the former territory of the German Reich and had not wanted to go back to the Soviet Union. However, the situation was not easy for the DPs. Just like the 'repats' described by Tölölyan, the DPs had not left Armenian SSR and upon return, if not exiled to Siberia then at best would be settled in their old places of habitation in Ukraine and Russia, which lay in ruin. In addition, the Armenian DPs who had changed their documents to reflect place of origin in the Ottoman Empire instead of the USSR, could not possibly be returned to Turkey since a 1927 law in Turkey had stripped the citizenship of those subjects who had 'left' and had not returned.[89] The Armenian publications of the time reveal editorial back-and-forth criticisms between organizations as to how to deal with the plight of displaced Armenians in Germany.[90] This also affected how the DPs saw themselves and their community in relation to the rest of the Armenian communities in the diaspora.

In addition to the mixed perceptions they encountered upon arrival, linguistic and cultural differences further hindered the integration of these new immigrants into the local Armenian communities in America. As with the example of the Armenian communities in the Middle East emerging from the ghettoized neighbourhoods and refugee encampments, Panossian states, 'as social boundaries between host societies and many Armenian communities loosened, paradoxically a strong diasporan national identity emerged'.[91] In the case of the DPs the loosening boundaries were that of leaving the premises of the camp and arriving in the United States. After five years of intense cultural awakening at *Funkerkaserne*, Armenian DPs had a hard time coming to terms with the communities whose members had largely assimilated after decades of life in America. Furthermore, the arrival of the DPs in the United States coincided with the 'red scare' panic investigations by Senator Joseph McCarthy and the House Un-American Activities Committee. The Soviet origins, Russian names and accents of the newcomers attracted prejudice. For example, two interviewees recounted getting into fights because they were called 'Stalin' in school. The harsh reality of making a life in America, pushed the DPs from different corners of the country to revive the connections made during the years at the camp and share information about their respective locations and opportunities. Some DPs had settled in Los Angeles and communicated to others that the weather was good all year around and there was plenty of opportunity and a sizeable Armenian community. Since those DPs who were spread all over the country were not as tightly connected to the communities where they initially settled as they were to their former DP campmates, they usually loaded up the car and moved. By the early 1950s almost all of the *Funkerkaserne* residents who were in America had reached California, predominantly Los Angeles. They settled in East Los Angeles, home to many other immigrant communities because of its affordability. As the families were able to elevate themselves into middle class, they also began to gradually move to the suburbs, the closest one being Montebello. For the DPs, those who had shared their journey and close quarters at *Funkerkaserne* became their community unit. For some, the neighbourly ties carried through all the way to Montebello, California, where the 'homeland' one turned to was the support system created during the internment.[92]

Although where the community chose to settle was for economic reasons, it was more than the job opportunities and affordable housing that kept them near each other. One of the interviewees compared the gathering of Armenians in Montebello to the congregation of the Polish people in Chicago or the Irish in Boston, saying that people wanted to live around others they were familiar with, for comfort. Identifying themselves as *rusahay* (Russian Armenian) they referred to American Armenians as *teghats'is*, the locals.[93] The Soviet, Russian and Caucasian customs in the form of dances and food that they could not find among the established American Armenian hotspots, they recreated in Montebello, shared with and enjoyed by the members of the community. While there was the natural isolation of Montebello as the other Armenian hotspots were in Hollywood and later gradually the San Fernando Valley, the community did not stand as an Armenian island in the San Gabriel Valley. Rather, by establishing the local branches of every existing diasporan organization including the Montebello Dro Chapter of the ARF, the Nairy Chapter of the Armenian Relief Society, the San Gabriel Valley Chapter of the Armenian National Committee of America and the Vahan Cardashian Chapter of the Armenian Youth Federation, it stayed connected with the larger Armenian community of Los Angeles.

The community in Montebello organized cultural programmes and invited artists, performers and composers from Soviet Armenia to perform in Los Angeles and these events also brought out the larger community beyond Montebello. At their weddings the *Lezginka*, the dance of the North Caucasians, was a must, performed by Jora Makarian and his Sevan Armenian Dance Ensemble.[94] The Ukrainian borsch and potato-filled piroshkies were staples on their tables. Russian lacquer boxes decorated with scenes from Russian folk tales were present in all of the houses of interviewees. In a photograph, a known community member, dressed in a Circassian *chokha* and with the tricolour of the First Armenian Republic in the background, poses next to newly elected Jerry Brown, the governor of California. They were very involved in politics when it came to Armenian affairs such as supporting the election of George Deukmejian, the first Armenian-American candidate into the governorship of California in 1983. In 1965, the first Armenian elementary school in the United States, Mesrobian, was established through the efforts of the community members. The school, which now also includes a kindergarten,[95] a middle school and a high school, was where many children and grandchildren of the DPs born in America went to school. Soon after the school, the community, whose elder generation included many survivors of the Armenian Genocide, had an initiative to mark the fiftieth anniversary of the Armenian Genocide[96] and the result was the first monument erected on public land in America commemorating the victims.[97]

Conclusion

'By the Community, For the community'[98] a title of an article dedicated to the fiftieth anniversary of the Armenian Mesrobian School is the most accurate description of this community. Armenia in its modern rendition was not the major formulator of this diasporic community. Under the umbrella of 'Armenian DPs' all these layers as survivors, entrepreneurs, immigrants, as Ottoman, Soviet, Russian, Ukrainian, Armenian, German, American and stateless, have played a role in propagating an identity that one descendant of the DPs described with, 'from the United States to France, Syria to Lebanon, and any other country which boasts an Armenian population; [Displaced] Armenians, such as ones from the Montebello community have come together to prove that Armenia is not just a location on a map, but rather a state of mind'.[99] Identifying as Armenians independent of the state, as diaspora, was also evident in a particular term used by the DPs to describe fellow community members who are really involved in Armenian affairs. Instead of the usual *hayrenaser* (patriot or nationalist) they used *hayaser* (Armenophile), highlighting the centrality of the transnation, the totality of the 'diasporic communities *and* the homeland'[100] rather than the sole nation-state.

For many in the older generation of DPs, their sole visit to Armenia was during the thaw in the Soviet–American relations in the 1960s, while others never managed to visit since by the time Armenia had gained independence in 1991 they were already advanced in age and had difficulties with travel. At the same time, many of them had been back to Stuttgart to visit the premises of their old dwelling, the *Funkerkaserne*, in a sort of a pilgrimage similar to present-day diasporan trips to Western Armenia.[101] While the camp in Stuttgart is not a lost homeland in a way that Western Armenia is for the visiting Armenians, the reason for the pilgrimage is similar in the sense that the visit confirms and preserves the experience.[102] While Western Armenia visits challenge decades of genocide denial, DPs visits address the fact that their story is largely unknown within the Armenian transnation. At the same time, some 150 children were born at the camp during the post-war years and hundreds of others who arrived at the camp as children had it as their only 'Armenia' experience, hence the transformative years lived at the *Funkerkaserne* remain as the 'fundamental element'[103] actively maintained by the community as the uniform '*collective* memory'.

A recent editorial described the community as based on 'a symbiotic triangle of support, with pillars in the form of Armenian Mesrobian School, Holy Cross Armenian Apostolic

Cathedral, and the Armenian Revolutionary Federation.'[104] In a way there were the 'two halves of a single identity – a timeless, unalterable' Armenian self and 'its complementary American half in the mind frame of a people with a powerful sense of the identity of their own and for the future generations'.[105] By firstly leveraging their Armenian identity to avoid Nazi persecution, they then leveraged the Ottoman and subsequent stateless identities to avoid Soviet forced repatriation. In America they first leveraged their DP identity to pull together former campmates and create a community and then leveraged their Soviet identity to forge cultural ties with Soviet Armenia. That 'heightened awareness of both the perils and rewards of multiple belonging'[106] and the ability of repeatedly being able to survive in the most daunting of situations have come to be a cornerstone of the defining myth of this group on its way to becoming a diasporic community. The Russian invasion of Ukraine and the latest iteration of bombardments and warfare have caused another wave of mass displacement of people and have brought to the attention of the world the landscape from which the Armenian DPs were displaced some eighty years ago. Many of them constantly follow the news about their distant birthplaces and try to reach out to old branches of their families who were left behind after the first displacement and who are themselves now the newly displaced. In 2014, Jack Hadjinian, a descendant of DPs, was elected as the first Armenian-American mayor of Montebello. In the end, above all, the connecting glue was the collective story, kept, celebrated and retold at every gathering and reunion, a story of displacement, of resiliency and of a journey that turned a people into a community.

Notes

1 'Armenian nation existed both on a fragment of its homeland and in diaspora'. Khachig Tölölyan, 'Rethinking Diaspora(s): Stateless Power in the Transnational Moment', *Diaspora* 5, no. 1 (1996): 7. 'Writing about Armenia and the Armenians entails writing about dispersion, diaspora . . .' Razmik Panossian, *The Armenians: From Kings and Priests to Merchants and Commissars* (New York: Columbia University Press, 2006), 1.
2 Susan Pattie, 'Refugees and Citizens: The Armenians of Cyprus', *The Cyprus Review* 25, no. 1 (2013): 133–45. As characterized by Susan Pattie, 'Being a survivor, a refugee, a sojourner, displaced person – all these are common identities for many Armenians at one point in their lives', 134.
3 Eugene M. Kulischer, 'Displaced Persons in the Modern World', *The Annals of the American Academy of Political and Social Science* 262 (1949): 166–77.
4 Anna Marta Holian, *Between National Socialism and Soviet Communism: Displaced Persons in Postwar Germany* (Ann Arbor: University of Michigan Press, 2011).
5 'And so it was that Mesrobian became the first daily Armenian elementary school in this country in 1951.' https://mesrobian.org/about/history/
6 The Armenian Genocide Martyrs Monument in Montebello was built in 1968 through the community's grassroots campaign and the Holy Cross Armenian Apostolic Cathedral, consecrated in 1984, has been the cathedral of the Western Prelacy of the Armenian Apostolic Church of America.

7 See Marta Dyczok, *The Grand Alliance and Ukrainian Refugees* (New York: St. Martin's, 2000); Emily Gilbert, *Rebuilding Postwar Britain: Latvian, Lithuanian and Estonian Refugees in Britain, 1946–51* (South Yorkshire: Pen & Sword History, 2017); David Nasaw, *The Last Million: Europe's Displaced Persons from World War to Cold War* (New York: Penguin Press, 2020).
8 Four of the interviewees were born in Germany, two at the displaced persons camp and the other two were German-born Armenians who ended up at the camp because of internal displacement. One interviewee was a German DP from Poland that had married an Armenian DP. Eighteen of the interviewees were born in what is present-day Ukraine, five of them originating from Crimea which at the time of the war was not part of Ukraine but of Russia. Eight came from Russian North Caucasus, mainly Novorossiysk, Rostov and Pyatigorsk. Only one interviewee was born in Armenian Soviet Socialist Republic (ASSR), in Yerevan.
9 A few of the interviewees, even though born in the Ukraine and Russia, spoke Armenian in the dialect of their parents' birthplaces, that is Van, Yerznka/Erzincan; others were partially or completely Russophone. Eight of the interviews were conducted in Armenian, one in Russian, three in a mix of Russian and Armenian and the rest in English.
10 Simon Vratsian, the last prime minister of the First Republic of Armenia, in his *The Republic of Armenia*, 98, gives statistics of Armenians who exited the Armenian-populated areas and headed towards North Caucasus due to the dire situation with famine, disease and the incoming Turkish invasion. Some interviewees proudly displayed at home their parents' passports and travel passes issued by the short-lived independent Republic of Armenia (1918–20).
11 Pattie, 'Refugees and Citizens', 140.
12 Yuri Slezkine, 'The USSR as a Communal Apartment, or How a Socialist State Promoted Ethnic Particularism', *Slavic Review* 53, no. 2 (1994): 414–52 at 432. 'This derived from Lenin and Stalin's firm belief that the ideology could be spread among the nationalities only in their native language and this needed to be stimulated and mandated as state policy'.
13 '*Korenizatsiya* represented elements of the equalization aspect of Soviet nationality policy, which clearly accelerated the pace of nationalization and an emerging "sense of exclusiveness" regarding the indigenes' perceived standing in their own homelands.' Robert J. Kaiser, 'National Consolidation and Territoriality During the Interwar Period', in *The Geography of Nationalism in Russia and the USSR* (Princeton: Princeton University Press, 1994), 95.
14 *Natsionalny vopros i natsionalnaya kultura v Severo-Kavkazskom kraye (Itogi i perspektivy): K predstoyashchemu syezdu gorskikh narodov* (The National Question and Culture in South-Caucasian Region (Outcomes and Perspectives): Ahead of the Congress of Mountain People), Rostov-on-Don, 1926.
15 Fifteen out of thirty-two interviewees were born in Ukraine and four were born in Crimea, which at that time was part of Russia but later became part of Ukraine.
16 Slezkine, 'The USSR as a Communal Apartment', 438. In 1924 there had been ninety-five Russian-language newspapers in Ukraine while only thirty-five newspapers were in Ukrainian. Yelena Borisenok, 'Concepts of Ukrainization and Its Realization in the State Policy in the Westerneuropean Region (1918–1941)' (PhD diss., Russian Academy of Sciences, 2016).
17 Erik Scott, *Familiar Strangers: The Georgian Diaspora and the Evolution of the Soviet Empire* (New York: Oxford University Press, 2016), makes the case that Georgians constituted a powerful 'internal diaspora' within the Soviet Union.

18 For more on Cossacks, see Anton Popov, 'Re-Making a Frontier Community or Defending Ethnic Boundaries? The Caucasus in Cossack Identity', *Europe-Asia Studies* 64, no. 9 (2012): 1739–57; Barbara Skinner, 'Identity Formation in the Russian Cossack Revival', *Europe-Asia Studies* 46, no. 6 (1994): 1017–37. For more on Volga Germans, see Tony Waters, 'Towards a Theory of Ethnic Identity and Migration: The Formation of Ethnic Enclaves by Migrant Germans in Russia and North America', *The International Migration Review* 29, no. 2 (1995): 515–44.
19 Sossie Kasbarian, 'The "Others" Within: The Armenian Community in Cyprus', in *Diasporas of the Modern Middle East: Contextualising Community*, ed. Anthony Gorman and Sossie Kasbarian (Edinburgh: Edinburgh University Press, 2015), 241.
20 During the First World War the Russian armies had reached all the way to Van and conquered some parts of the Ottoman Empire heavily populated by Armenians while other places such as Kars and Artvin had been a part of the Russian Empire since the nineteenth century and were only ceded to the newly emerging Republic of Turkey in the 1920s by the Bolsheviks.
21 For more on the evolution of Soviet policy on citizenship, see Golfo Alexopoulos, 'Soviet Citizenship, More or Less: Rights, Emotions, and States of Civic Belonging', *Kritika: Explorations in Russian and Eurasian History* 7 (2006): 487–528.
22 For the breakdown of German rapid advance into the Soviet Union, see Alexander Dallin, *German Rule in Russia, 1941–1945: A Study of Occupation Policies* (Boulder: Westview Press, 1981).
23 For a breakdown of historic Armenian communities in Russia, see Kolosov, Galkina, Kuybishev, *Geografiya Diaspor na Territorii Byvshego SSSR* (Geography of Diasporas in the former USSR) (1996), 39–45.
24 Dallin, *German Rule in Russia*, 429.
25 'Among the Caucasian Christian nationalities, the Armenians were suspected of being racially inferior because of their alleged proclivity for "parasitic trade practices," said to derive from a presumed kinship with the Semitic race and miscegenation with the Jews.' From Patrick von zur Muhlen *Zwischen Hakenkreuz und Sowjetsern*, quoted in Alex Alexiev, *Soviet Nationalities in German Wartime Strategy, 1941–1945* (Santa Monica: RAND, 1982), 5.
26 Levon Thomassian at length describes the extent of German–Armenian relations in *Summer of '42: A Study of German-Armenian Relations During the Second World War* (Atglen: Schiffer, 2012).
27 One of the interviewees, born in 1930 and displaced from Novorossiysk during the war, recalled their train stopping at a station in Poland, where after a visit by Armenian officials who worked with the Germans they were moved into a different train to be sent to Germany while they believed others were sent to concentration camps.
28 Holian, *Between National Socialism and Soviet Communism*, 228.
29 Ibid.
30 Ibid., 37.
31 'Agreement Relating to Prisoners of War and Civilians Liberated by Forces Operating Under Soviet Command and Forces Operating Under United States of America Command', signed at Yalta by Major General John R. Deane and Lieutenant General Anatoly Alexeyevich Gryzlov, 11 February 1945. Executive Agreement Series No. 505; 59 Stat. (2) 1874 (Foreign Relations, The Conferences at Malta and Yalta, 1945), 985.
32 Ibid.

33 Ibid. 'Soviet and United States repatriation representatives will have the right to immediate access into the camps and points of concentration where their citizens are located and they will have the right to appoint the internal administration and set up internal discipline and management in accordance with the military procedure and laws of their country.'
34 Holian, *Between National Socialism and Soviet Communism*, 38. The French especially in the beginning allowed Soviet agents to roam the French Zone of occupation and take back their citizens.
35 Mark Wyman, *DPs: Europe's Displaced Persons, 1945–1951* (Ithaca: Cornell University Press, 1998), 64. Those forcefully or otherwise repatriated to the Soviet Union from Germany usually had their families there and wanted to return to them. A lot of the DPs usually had their immediate families already with them in Germany.
36 *Letter of The Secretary of War Patterson to the Secretary of State* (U.S. Department of State, 1945), https://history.state.gov/historicaldocuments/frus1945v02/d564.
37 George M. Mardikian, *Song of America* (New York: McGraw-Hill, 1956), 269. 'They were also in occupied Austria, while some former POWs had managed to find refuge in France as well.'
38 John Roy Carlson, 'The Armenian Displaced Persons: A First Hand Report on Conditions in Europe', *Armenian Affairs* 1, no. 1 (1949–50): 26.
39 Janet Flanner, 'Letter from Aschaffenburg', *The New Yorker*, October 22, 1948, 100.
40 Holian, *Between National Socialism and Soviet Communism*, 38. Some Soviet Armenian POWs who had been in the ranks of the Armenian Legion and would otherwise be considered collaborator also managed to evade capture by the Soviet forces and joined the ranks of the DPs by hiding at the camp or marrying DPs.
41 'Armenian Displaced Persons List No. 1', *American National Committee to Aid Homeless Armenians*, printed 1 January 1949. The archives at the USC Institute of Armenian Studies contain a photocopied version of this document sent to the Institute by a community member.
42 Two interviewees, one born in Kiev and one born in the Donbas, shared that they had put Iran as their birthplace when questioned by the American authorities in Germany. In addition, as I cross-referenced the oral history interviews with the names from the aforementioned Armenian Displaced Persons List, it was evident that Moloians from Rostov, Russia, had listed Robertow, Poland, as their birthplace, while Badalians originally from Yerevan and later from Novorossiysk had listed Ploiesti, Romania, as their place of origin.
43 Most notably the ethnic Germans who were cast out of Eastern Europe could not return. Eastern Poles could not return because their homes were now in Ukraine and the Baltic people hesitated to return because their countries had been annexed by the Soviet Union.
44 Flanner, 'Letter from Aschaffenburg', 98.
45 Michael Krikorian, 'A Reunion of the Displaced', *Los Angeles Times*, 15 September 1997.
46 The interviewee, born in Kharkov, Ukraine, had been displaced along with her family when she was eight.
47 A few of the interviewees, especially those who were Armenian Catholics, mentioned that in the end it was the Catholic Charities that brought them to America. Others similarly had been assisted by the Lutheran World Federation.

48 This statistic comes from the 'Armenian Displaced Persons List No. 1'. Around 240 Armenians on the list have shoemaker listed as their profession. In addition, almost all thirty-one of the interviewees I have spoken to have either mentioned having personally been involved in some aspect of the shoemaking trade or having a family member involved in the process.
49 'Magdesians® shoes have been hand made in the beautiful suburbs of Los Angeles, California since 1952 and remains one of the few footwear collections still manufactured in the United States. While most in the footwear industry have completely disappeared, Magdesians shoes have flourished.' https://www.zappos.com/b/magdesians/brand/95.
50 'Trabant and Beetle: 'The Two Germanies, 1949–89', *History Workshop Journal* 68, no. 1 (2009): 1–2.
51 Federal Ministry for Expellees, Refugees and War Victims, *Facts Concerning the Problem of the German Expellees and Refugees* (Bonn, 1967).
52 Described by Armin Kredian in 'The Armenian Community in Egypt: World War 1 and Genocide 1914–19', *Haigazian Armenological Review* 35 (2015): 201–47.
53 Panossian, *The Armenians*, 303.
54 Mardikian, *Song of America*, 250.
55 Khachig Tölölyan, 'Elites and Institutions in the Armenian Transnation', *Diaspora: A Journal of Transnational Studies* 9, no. 1 (2000): 107–36. For the DPs the transformation from exilic nationalism to diasporic transnationalism – a process described by Tölölyan – does take place.
56 Senate Committee on the Judiciary, *Displaced Persons in Europe* (1948), 18.
57 Misak Torlakian, *Ōrerus het* (With My Days) (Beirut: Hamazkayin Vahē Set'ean Press, [1952] 2001).
58 The inaugural issue of *Amenoun Darekirke*, published in 1954, includes a lengthy piece on the history of Armenian DPs in Germany by Kevorkian based on events he witnessed and helped organize. The names and details in this paragraph are from that account.
59 Khachig Tölölyan, 'Exile Government In The Armenian Polity', *Journal of Political Science* 18, no. 1 (1990): 128.
60 Garo Kevorkian, 'Hay Darakirnere Germanio Mej. Yerkrord Ashkharhamarti Entatskin Yev Atke Yetk (Displaced Armenians in Germany during and after the Second World War)', *Amenoun Darekirke* (1954): 139–52. Translated by me from the Armenian original.
61 Mardikian, *Song of America*, 156.
62 This point needs a note in that some of the places where these Armenians relocated from, for example, Artvin, Erzurum and Alashkert, were either temporarily part of the Russian Empire or were under Russian control during the First World War.
63 The documentary footage, shot by Karapet (Carpo) Dilanian, an eighteen-year-old resident of *Funkerkaserne* at the time, exists and is occasionally shown during the gatherings and the reunions of the DPs. Recent illness has left Mr Dilanian unable to talk, which prevented me from recording his oral history and accessing his archives. The footage of the 1948 celebration is accessible on YouTube: https://youtu.be/ga27JbrFpnY 8:45-10:20.
64 Henry Goldschmidt, '"Crown Heights Is the Center of the World": Reterritorializing a Jewish Diaspora', *Diaspora: A Journal of Transnational Studies* 9, no. 1 (2000): 83–106. Goldschmidt's description of the Crown Heights neighbourhood in Brooklyn as the home of Hassidic Jewish communities closely reflects the attitudes of the Armenian DPs with respect to the *Funkerkaserne*.

65 Similar to what Magliorino described in the case of the Armenians in the refugee camps in Lebanon and Syria as 'the new conditions forced to mix together Armenian refugees from different classes, different cultural and religious backgrounds': Nicola Migliorino, *(Re) Constructing Armenia in Lebanon and Syria: Ethno-Cultural Diversity and the State in the Aftermath of a Refugee Crisis* (New York and Oxford: Berghahn Books, 2008), 45.
66 For more on the Armenian community in Lebanon, see Tsolin Nalbantian. *Armenians Beyond Diaspora: Making Lebanon Their Own* (Edinburgh University Press, 2019), 3.
67 'Those who had arrived from Cilicia . . . often used Turkish as their day-to-day language and could not speak Armenian well; some apparently, could not speak Armenian at all': Migliorino, *(Re) Constructing Armenia in Lebanon and Syria*, 74.
68 Panossian, *The Armenians*, 299.
69 Susan Pattie, *Faith in History: Armenians Rebuilding Community* (Washington: Smithsonian Institution, 1997), 52. Pattie's description of the Armenians in Cyprus testifies true to the accounts shared by the interviewees who were school-aged children during their time spent at *Funkerkaserne*.
70 Panossian, *The Armenians*, 299.
71 In the case of the Port Said encampment, too, eventually there came to be a 'a special kitchen, a school and a workshop'. Kredian, 'The Armenian Community in Egypt', 215.
72 *Darakir* had a dozen issues starting in July of 1946. *Banber* was published between 2 August 1948 and 29 October 1949. Kevorkian, 'Hay Darakirnere Germanio Mej', 135–72.
73 As described by Antanas Van Reenan, *Lithuanian Diaspora: Königsberg to Chicago*, 102, 'By sensitizing the young in DP schools, a succeeding generation was to share in the same language and culture. The stress on posterity essentially centered around a communal spirit in which the community was not composed of individual persons but was seen as a corporate body composed of the living, the dead, and those yet to be born'.
74 Panossian, *The Armenians*, 300.
75 'Nominally' because, as mentioned earlier, the Armenian Apostolic Church had been decimated during the initial decades of Soviet rule and in general in the USSR religion had been suppressed due to the atheist inclination of the Bolsheviks. That being said, many of the interviewees mentioned that their elders were still privately very religious.
76 Kevorkian, 'Hay Darakirnere Germanio Mej', 160.
77 Mardikian, *Song of America*, 67.
78 Ibid.
79 'The Immigration Act of 1924 limited the number of immigrants allowed entry into the United States through a national origins quota. The quota provided immigration visas to two percent of the total number of people of each nationality in the United States as of the 1890 national census.' US Department of State, Office of the Historian, *The Immigration Act of 1924 (The Johnson-Reed Act)*.
80 Wyman, *DPs: Europe's Displaced Persons*, 194. 'William C. Stratton of Illinois, introduced the bill by Citizens Committee on Displaced Persons to allow 400,000 DPs into the United States over a four-year span'.
81 Ibid.

82 'The Terdjanians were brought through these efforts and were headed to California. Their cousin in New Britain [Connecticut] met the plane they were on and brought them back to New Britain.' Jennie Garabedian, *New Britain's Armenian Community* (Charleston, NC: Arcadia Publishing, 2008), 45.
83 Rubchak, in '"God made me a Lithuanian": Nationalist Ideology and the Construction of a North American Diaspora', *Diaspora: A Journal of Transnational Studies* 2, no. 1 (1992): 117–30, uses this when talking about Lithuanian DPs who settled in America in a similar fashion, but the description of the community and its practices testifies true to the Armenian DP experience too.
84 One interviewee, originally settled in Philadelphia, described working for a year in a retirement home, but then in East Los Angeles being able to find an apartment for half the rent and buying a gas station with the savings.
85 Tigran Ghanalanyan, 'Transportation of Displaced Armenians to America after the Second World War' (in Armenian). *Etchmiadzin*, No. 12 (2015).
86 Ibid.
87 Statistics from the Armenian National Archive, quoted in: Jo Laycock, 'Survivor or Soviet Stories? Repatriate Narratives in Armenian Histories, Memories and Identities', *History and Memory* 28, no. 2 (2016): 123–51.
88 Tölölyan, 'Elites and Institutions in the Armenian Transnation', 132.
89 'On May 23, 1927 a second law was passed by the government which stated that "Ottoman subjects who during the War of Independence took no part in the National movement, kept out of Turkey and did not return from July 24, 1923 to the date of the publication of this law, have forfeited Turkish nationality."' In addition to this, a subsequent law passed on May 28, 1928 stipulated that 'those who are deprived of their Turkish citizenship shall be expelled if they are in Turkey. The return to Turkey of all persons deprived of their Turkish citizenship is prohibited'. Quoted in Bedross Der Matossian, 'The Taboo within the Taboo: The Fate of "Armenian Capital" at the End of the Ottoman Empire', *European Journal of Turkish Studies* [Online], http://journals.openedition.org/ejts/4411, accessed 24 April 2021.
90 Tigran Ghanalanyan, 'Transportation of Displaced Armenians to America after the Second World War'. This paper gives a detailed account of accusations between AGBU and ARF-affiliated sectors of the Armenian community in America arguing over response and course of action in the context of ARF's anti-Soviet stance and AGBU's championing of repatriation of worldwide Armenian communities into the 'Armenian homeland' in Soviet Armenia.
91 Panossian, *The Armenians*, 304.
92 'It makes more sense to think of diasporan existence as not necessarily involving a physical return but rather a re-turn, a repeated turning to the concept and/or the reality of the homeland and other diasporan kin through memory written and visual texts, travel, gifts and assistance, etc': Tölölyan, 'Rethinking Diaspora(s): Stateless Power in the Transnational Moment', 14.
93 This language is consistent with other classifications such as *akhpar/teghats'i* in Soviet Armenia or the *kaghakats'i*/refugee dynamic in Jerusalem and the *deghats'i*/refugee in Cyprus, explored by Susan Pattie in 'Refugees and Citizens', 137.
94 'Sevan Dance Ensemble at the Music Center, 1990-03-09; Sevan Dance Ensemble performance, Los Angeles, 1986'. *Dance Heritage Video Archive*. University of Southern California, Digital Library. Archival file: Volume116/dhva_arminst_0004.mp4.

95 The kindergarten is named after Ron and Goharik Gabriel. Goharik Mosikian-Gabriel was born in the *Funkerkaserne* displaced persons camp.
96 'The idea of the Armenian Genocide Martyrs Memorial originated following the 50th anniversary of the Armenian Genocide on April 24, 1965, when thousands of Armenians walked through the streets of Los Angeles in a march of solidarity and remembrance.' 'History of the Monument', *Armenianmonument.org*, http://armenianmonument.org/monument-history.html, accessed 25 May 2022.
97 Y. T. Nercessian, *A Short History of Armenian Martyrs Memorial Monument in Montebello, California* (California: Armenian Monument Council, 2007).
98 'By the Community, For the Community', *Asbarez*, 18 February 2016.
99 *Haytoug*, 'Displaced Person Strengthening Communities: The Story of the Montebello DPs', June 2011, https://ayfwest.org/news/displaced-person-strengthening-communities/, accessed 10 May 2022.
100 Tölölyan, 'Elites and Institutions in the Armenian Transnation', 130.
101 For more on diasporan tourism, see Anny Bakalian and Zeynep Turan, 'Diaspora Tourism and Identity: Subversion and Consolation in Armenian Pilgrimages to Eastern Turkey', in *Diasporas of the Modern Middle East*, ed. Sossie Kasbarian and Anthony Gorman (Edinburgh: Edinburgh University Press, 2015), 173–212.
102 Presently *Funkerkaserne* is used as German army facility where the entrance of civilians is prohibited and some interviewees who had been there have shown their photographs of posing in front of the gates and expressed regret that they could not access their former dwelling.
103 Tölölyan, 'Rethinking Diaspora(s): Stateless Power in the Transnational Moment', 13.
104 'By the Community, For the Community'.
105 The example is also drawn from Rubchak's description of the Lithuanian DPs in '"God made me a Lithuanian"'. Tölölyan, 'Rethinking Diaspora(s): Stateless Power in the Transnational Moment', 8.
106 Ibid.

3

Diaspora–Homeland Relations Re-examined

The case of Syrian Armenians in the Netherlands

Nare Galstyan

Introduction

Syrian nationals account for some of the largest number of asylum applications (10,296) in the Netherlands.[1] Notably, religious and ethnic minority groups, such as Armenians, Assyrians, Yezidis and Chaldeans, are among the larger Syrian migrant population fleeing the country due to the civil war that began in 2011. The circumstances Syrian Armenians face differ from the mainstream Syrian refugee population because the Armenian government has offered Syrian Armenians citizenship in order to resettle them in their 'ancestral homeland'. The picture becomes more complex as most Syrian Armenians do not actually have 'ancestral' connections with the current territories of the Republic of Armenia and consist mostly of individuals who are descendants of genocide survivors from the Ottoman Empire.[2] These survivors were separated from the homeland referred to today by Armenians as 'Western Armenia', which consists of territories in Eastern Turkey, while the current Republic of Armenia represents a small territory of the historic Armenian homeland.[3] The existence of an ancestral homeland impacts the settlement of Syrian Armenian migrants in Europe as the Dutch authorities claim that newly arrived ethnic Armenians from Syria obtained Armenian citizenship prior to arriving in the Netherlands.[4] This situation opens a valuable setting for a re-examination of diaspora–homeland relations and the theoretical debates surrounding it.

In the past decade, there has been a growing tendency to look at diasporas as a practice of power driven by the interest of home or host states, or international organizations, without questioning a diaspora's links with the homeland.[5] This has been a major shift in diaspora literature considering that in classical diaspora conceptualizations the 'homeland' was presented as having almost a mythical value for a diaspora population.[6] A number of scholars claim that even when there is a loss of the actual homeland or a change in its existing borders, it continues to be the key feature for diasporic identification.[7] Tölölyan raises the need for careful examination of a diaspora's orientation towards their homeland, rather than taking it for granted.[8]

Tölölyan points out that after generations, the diasporic 'is now a citizen in his or her "new" home country, possesses a hybrid culture and identity or at the very least has developed a comfortable bicultural competence'.[9] Parallel to these debates, migration literature agrees that diaspora institutions and ethnic networks can transform into increasingly visible actors that ease the entrance and settlement of migrants in a new country.[10] However, diasporic support to newcomers has rarely been placed in the context of an examination of diaspora–homeland relations.

Against this background, this chapter attempts to bridge and re-examine this literature based on the qualitative study of newly arrived Syrian Armenians in the Netherlands. The aim of the chapter is twofold: first, it counterbalances recent state-centric approaches of examining diaspora–homeland relations and unpacks the multilayered perception of homeland among Syrian Armenians; second, it points out the role of diasporic networks for newly arrived migrants by placing the study of diasporic experience in recent migration circumstances. The chapter examines the ways in which established Armenian diaspora organizations support or influence the needs of newly arrived Syrian Armenian asylum seekers and refugees to remain in the Netherlands instead of resettling in Armenia. It highlights Dutch Armenian diaspora organizations' positionality towards their ancestral homeland, that is, Armenia, when liaising with the Dutch authorities and their creation of positive grounds for Syrian Armenians to remain in the Netherlands. It also discusses Syrian Armenians' relations with Armenia and Syria by highlighting where they see their new home in practice. This chapter analyses the choices that led Syrian Armenians to choose the Netherlands as a new site of residence instead of 'return' to Armenia. In doing so, this study highlights the multidimensionality and historical complexity of diasporas and situates them within the concerns of contemporary migration studies.

Homeland and diaspora return

The orientation of a diaspora towards its homeland has been considered a defining feature of diasporic identity by scholars who have stressed the importance of having a vision or reminder of an idealized place to which the members of the diaspora may return when possible.[11] For Safran, the Jewish and the Armenian cases of dispersion are 'archetypical' models, where the absence of a physical homeland or statelessness is the most crucial factor in the formation of diaspora.[12] Safran[13] suggests that homeland has a mythical value for ethno-religious diasporas as a site of sacred places, monuments and memories of ancestors.[14] By examining Jewish diasporas, Safran noted that they existed almost exclusively as a diasporic phenomenon: since Jews lacked a 'homeland' for two millennia, their diasporic consciousness was constructed in exile under conditions of minority status and of powerlessness and with a hope of homeland return.[15]

The major change in the literature on diasporic conceptualization of the homeland has been the shift from a primordialist/essentialist approach to a constructivist one.[16] Diaspora formation is discussed as a product of specific processes of mobilization that are ongoing and remain incomplete, as well as a basis of collective mobilization.[17]

Similarly, instead of taking for granted that the idea of a shared homeland produces diasporic identities, it has been argued that homeland is 'imagined' through a mobilization process. Brubaker emphasizes the historical perception of homeland and claims that homeland is an important feature for diaspora invention or mobilization.[18] Diasporas produce homelands by collectively imagining them, even when the homeland itself is contested.[19]

By considering diasporas as a category of mobilization, scholars have been able to study not only how diasporas mobilize themselves, but how they are mobilized by others (e.g. states and other non-state actors). Migrant organizations, home and host governments, and international organizations now routinely refer to migrants as 'diasporas' to facilitate mobilization, construct shared grounds of identity, and pursue social, economic and political projects.[20] In these discussions the historical depth of diasporas is not acknowledged: diasporas are about the collective experience of multiple generations around a shared project, while migrant groups are about the experience of a single generation or two. For example, Gamlen proposes looking at 'diaspora building' mechanisms that cultivate or formally recognize non-residents as members of a diasporic community, and mechanisms of 'diaspora integration' that grant membership responsibilities onto various extraterritorial groups.[21] In doing so, states manage migrants and expect loyalty from diasporas. As a consequence, recent migration literature is evolving in picturing diasporas as descendants of nation-states.[22] A growing number of scholars focus on the transnational governmentality of diasporas by comparing sending states' strategies, institutions, policies and motives for connecting with migrant communities abroad.[23] In these state-centric studies, the diaspora–homeland relationship is examined from the so-called 'Solar System' perspective, where diaspora is viewed as a 'periphery' connected and belonging to one 'centre' (the homeland).[24] Craven calls this 'structure-centrism', meaning that these studies erase the agency of both the diaspora and the various actors tasked with engagement.[25]

Tölölyan warns that this tendency contains a major risk for diaspora studies to become a servant to global political forces.[26] In his discussion of past and present diaspora studies, he counterbalances the usage of homeland and state as interchangeable categories:

> After several generations, the diasporic is no longer committed because of kinship links and personal memories (though both will matter to the extent that they can be revived and invigorated through travel and participation); nor is he or she committed simply because of not being integrated into the host society, as the first and second generations of dispersion often are not.[27]

Similarly, Tölölyan's discussion of the institutional base for diasporic communities challenges the widespread tendency of state-centrism: he goes so far as to metaphorically name diaspora institutions as 'governments-in-exile'.[28] He finds that these so-called 'governments' of migrant communities do considerable work in political and social organization and mobilization, particularly in Middle Eastern states where governments have historically neglected the material and social needs of minorities.[29] This diasporic mobilization can organize, for instance, the material and cultural exchange between the dispersed diasporic community and the homeland. This serves as an empowerment for the 'exiles' to live on as a collective, or at least to represent their situation as such to themselves and others.[30] Tölölyan has rightly called for diaspora scholars to highlight the complexity of diasporas instead of locating the 'diasporic's home in the ancestral homeland too easily'.[31]

The complexity of diaspora–state–homeland relations have a particular resonance in the context of physical return to the homeland. Clifford finds that the contrast between diaspora roots and routes becomes more vivid in the context of home, homeland and diaspora.[32] Authors studying diasporic return to countries of ancestral origin that occur after members have lived outside for generations have pointed out that ancestral homelands often fail to fulfill returnees' expectations.[33] Social and cultural differences as well as economic challenges usually fracture the romanticized image of return. Gilroy designates this experience a 'historical and experiential rift between the locations of residence and the location of belonging'.[34]

In discussing Syrian Armenians' resettlement, scholars agree that historical and cultural connections between the current-day Armenian territory and Syrian Armenians are missing: Della Gatta names Armenia a 'foreign homeland', and Kasbarian a 'step-homeland' for Western diasporans, including Syrian Armenians.[35] Kasbarian's definition highlights that different generations of the diaspora may not perceive Armenia as their historical homeland or as their country of origin.[36] For example, for many of the third or fourth generation of diaspora Armenians, the historical homeland is Western Armenia, from where their ancestors were expelled in 1915, finding refuge in different countries of the world, most notably in the Middle East. Kasbarian notes that 'the older diasporans have to negotiate the gap between mythical homeland and an actual "step-homeland" in the shape of the present Republic of Armenia'.[37]

The tension between diaspora, the 'idealized/historical homeland' and 'state' has also been clearly manifested in the context of diasporic migration to Armenia (also referred to as 'return' migration and 'repatriation'[38]) that took place during the Soviet period (mainly known for the 'Great Repatriation' of 1946–8), and after the independence of Armenia in 1991. During the Soviet period ethnic Armenians immigrated to Armenia from different countries. The diaspora Armenians had very little connection with the territory of Armenia and had major difficulties adapting to Soviet life and culture. Additionally, they faced a harsh socioeconomic situation in Armenia, as there was no adequate housing, food or decent living conditions awaiting them there.[39] This period is also known for heightened tensions between diaspora 'returnees' and local Armenians.[40] As a consequence, many diaspora Armenians used the opportunity to migrate from the Soviet Union to Europe and the United States after Stalin's death (in 1953), in the mid-1960s and the late 1970s.[41] The 'repatriation' that took place after the independence of Armenia in 1991 can be divided into two categories: individual 'repatriation' and 'repatriation' conditioned by conflicts and difficult sociopolitical conditions. Individual 'repatriates' have been mainly composed of highly qualified professionals, business representatives and well-off families that do not need state support to settle in Armenia. Their 'repatriation' is conditioned by a number of reasons, such as patriotism and the possibility of having a relatively higher standard of living in Armenia with their foreign incomes. The 'returnees' have had a change-making role in Armenia by contributing to the development of the homeland: they set up universities, law firms, technology centres, media organizations and so on.[42] According to Fittante, these 'returnees' have a strong connection with the country, but at the same time have a 'separation' from the local population.[43] Thus, some 'repatriate' Armenians remain in a specific social circle communicating mostly with other repatriated diaspora Armenians. The second type of 'repatriation' has been conditioned by the sociopolitical tensions and conflict situations, such as the Iraq War in 2003–11, the war in Donbas (Ukraine) in 2014, the civil war in Syria since 2012 as well as the explosion in Lebanon in 2020. According to various sources most of the 'repatriated' Armenians emigrated to Western countries, as they could not adapt to the economic and sociocultural conditions of Armenia.[44] As in the past, the present territory of the Republic of Armenia is not considered *the* homeland for different generations of Armenians, but potentially *one* 'homeland' among several, based on their identities and orientations. As Pawłowska notes, the distance between a diaspora and the homeland is not only a geographical distance but also a symbolic one, referring to the different perceptions of ancestors and traditions.[45]

Diaspora organizations and newly arrived migrants: State of the art

In this section, I will discuss diaspora organizations' support to newly settled migrants in a wider homeland–diaspora context. I will focus on the role of diaspora organizations in mobilizing assistance in terms of communicating to the host state that it is unacceptable for newly arrived asylum seekers to be deported to a national homeland that offers them citizenship.

Migration literature widely discusses the supporting role of ethnic networks for migrant resettlement in new countries.[46] Flores-Yeffal highlights the role of migration-trust networks (MTNs) by stating that the dependence on networks starts at the very beginning of migrants' journeys.[47] Portes uses the term 'bounded solidarity' to highlight the important role of co-ethnic support in responding to the social needs of recently arrived migrants in the host society.[48] Ambrosini suggests that a reliable contact in the receiving country is more advantageous than a high school diploma for irregular migrants since they assist in the regularization of legal status, provision of services (e.g. health services, language classes), legal advocacy, and moral support (mainly by religious institutions and faith groups).[49] Notably, most of these studies have been based on the examination of individual connections between the newly arrived asylum seekers and their co-ethnics in the host society.

Ambrosini offers a systematic review of actors and actions that mediate the entry of migrants into a new country, such as access to the labour market, provision of accommodation, responses to their social needs and regularization of their legal status.[50] He finds that the role of diasporic institutions is more relevant when discussing the role of supporters and alternative help providers.[51] He highlights the importance of political and cultural activities of ethnic networks/organizations against the criminalization of irregular immigrants and in defence of asylum seekers.[52] By adopting a frame that mainly focuses on the victimization of irregular immigrants, civil society actors often play a role in the cultural struggle on immigration.[53] Diasporas are among the actors who can shape, re-formulate or even drive truth-seeking mechanisms as its members are not only activists but, in the majority of cases, victims and witnesses of a shared experience of loss as well.[54]

However, the role of diaspora institutions in justice and truth-seeking has been mainly discussed with regard to their homeland and transitional justice-seeking mechanisms, while diasporas' efforts in defence of asylum seeker co-ethnics have remained an understudied subject. Similarly, a significant amount of academic literature has been focused on common trauma in producing diasporic attachment, although these attempts have not been reflected in the field of ethnic support to newly arrived asylum seekers. For example, Macdonald uses the term 'past presencing' to analyse how the past is being preserved not only through commemoration but also in continuous and even implicit efforts to re-purpose the past in the present.[55] These notions have been discussed mainly as ways to transmit and maintain diasporic identity for the next generations and cultivate attachments to homeland.[56] The Syrian Armenians' arrival in the Netherlands as well as their relations with local Armenian diaspora organizations opens an opportunity to examine whether the mobilized efforts of diasporic organizations to re-purpose past traumas can also strengthen the victimization framing of newly arrived asylum seekers in the host country. In doing so, this chapter will also analyse whether diaspora organizations' efforts to support newcomers may create a conflict between their interests and the interests of the homeland, and also question common notions of diaspora that imply uprooting from an idealized homeland.

Methodology

This research is based on in-depth interviews with representatives of diaspora organizations, core/'elite' members of the diaspora communities in Amsterdam, The Hague, Utrecht, Maastricht and Almelo, newly arrived Armenians from Syria as well as participant observations of mainstream community events from 2016 to 2018. Fifteen in-depth interviews were conducted with Syrian Armenians residing in the Netherlands as well as thirteen key informant interviews with community leaders and heads of diaspora organizations, to capture the 'official voices' of the diaspora. Among the Syrian Armenians interviewed there were persons who have already gained the legal status of refugees and asylum seekers who were still looking for state protection. Interviewees were identified using snowball sampling, and every possible entry point was accessed to obtain as diverse a representation of respondents as possible. As a result, interviewees vary by age, gender, generation, rural/urban background and home region. Interviews were combined with participative observations to fully understand the dynamics involved in diaspora engagement practices. Diaspora organizational activities, including fundraising events, cultural events, Sunday masses and social gatherings, were observed. Participative observations were also an opportunity to have several informal conversations with people involved in community events and to obtain a broader and more in-depth understanding of community life.

Interviews were audio-recorded in Armenian or English and then transcribed and translated. The interviews usually lasted one hour but, in many cases, turned into informal conversations that could last up to several hours. The goal was to obtain narratives of the interviewees' migration journeys, their interpretations of where they feel they belong, their attachment/detachment to their homelands (both Syria and Armenia) and their personal experiences of displacement in as much illustrative detail as possible. Informal conversations combined with semi-structured interviews were invaluable for developing a broader understanding of Syrian Armenians' experience as well as for comparing beliefs that people reveal during formal interview settings to what people state in less formal circumstances.

Prior to the interviews, the participants were asked for permission to use the information provided by them for publication. Though respondents were open to collaborate and share their stories, the names of interviewees were changed to respect their anonymity. This approach is preferred considering that some Syrian Armenians are still facing legal issues to settle in the Netherlands and there is a risk of 'deductive disclosure'.[57] The risk is exceptionally high when presenting detailed qualitative research about small communities: the research participants cannot be identifiable to the public, while someone, who is familiar with the community, can identify participants based on age and/or affiliation to the organization.

New but connected: Common points of Syrian Armenian and Dutch Armenian diasporic networks

Before the eruption of the Syrian Civil War in 2011, it is estimated that almost 100,000 Armenians lived in Syria, which was once described as 'the largest Armenian center in the Arab World'.[58] Most of the Armenians in Syria were descendants of the victims of the Armenian Genocide of 1915, who found a safe haven in Syria.[59] The community can be considered an example of the 'classical diaspora' that Cohen and Armstrong referred to when naming Armenians as an 'archetypical' case of diaspora.[60] The Syrian Armenian community was a substantial Armenian diasporic community that developed distinct community boundaries in Syria by establishing several cultural, social, religious and political institutions. Syrian Armenians reflecting on their lives in Syria noted that their lives revolved around Armenian social, cultural and religious unions and organizations that had their own infrastructure or branches in all regions with Armenian populations: Aleppo, Damascus, Kessab, Kamishli, Latakia and Homs. Affiliation to diaspora organizations was often not by choice, but received at birth, as parents and family members were organization members. Migliorino described Armenian community life in Syria as 'true islands of Armenianness' (35), where diaspora organizations served as hubs for Syrian Armenians, spaces of socialization and entertainment.[61] Similarly, according to my interviewees, almost every Armenian in Syria was closely related to at least one Armenian organization. 'In 2010 no one could expect that there could be any internal political problem in Syria or terrorists may appear. We had our church, national unions, representatives in the Syrian parliament, social and cultural clubs. Armenians were living prosperously in Syria' (Lusin, Syrian Armenian).

Arriving in the Netherlands, Syrian Armenians found a more heterogeneous and recently developed Armenian community that had emerged as a consequence of migration from different countries beginning in the 1950s. The Armenian community in the Netherlands currently consists of around 20,000 migrants from Iraq, Iran, Syria, Turkey, Lebanon, Greece and Armenia.[62] In 1948 approximately fifty families migrated to the Netherlands from Indonesia, a former Dutch colony. They were the descendants of the first community in Amsterdam that had migrated to Southeast Asia in the nineteenth century to trade. In the 1950s, Armenians from Greece migrated to the Netherlands due to economic and political reasons. A major migration wave from Turkey to the Netherlands occurred due to the guest worker (in Dutch: 'gastarbeiders') agreement in the 1960s: nearly 400 Armenian families from Turkey arrived in the Netherlands. Their relatives and family members would later join them, and they were concentrated mainly in the eastern Twente region. Due to economic crises, sociopolitical reasons and wars, from 1970 to 1980, a number of Armenians living in the Middle East (Lebanon, Iraq, Iran, Syria) arrived in the Netherlands as refugees. Many were descendants of those who had fled from their Ottoman homes in the genocide, finding refuge in the neighbouring emerging Arab states. From 1990 to 2000, a migration wave followed the collapse of the Soviet Union, when many Armenians from Armenia migrated to the Netherlands. According to the representatives of diaspora organizations, the majority of them arrived as asylum seekers due to the conflict between Armenia and Azerbaijan in the 1990s, as well as for socioeconomic reasons. The most recent and ongoing wave of migration is from Syria.

The heterogeneity of the Armenian diaspora in the Netherlands is based not only on the country of origin but also on its linguistic diversity. A notable fact about the Armenian language is that it is divided into Western and Eastern dialects.[63] Language schools usually face the problem of choosing between Western or Eastern Armenian, as, for example, Syrian Armenian children mainly attend Western Armenian classes, while Armenians from Armenia tend to attend Eastern Armenian classes. The decisions made about this issue may not satisfy all Armenians in the community and as a result, parents may choose not to send their children to these schools. In addition to the Eastern and Western Armenian usage, there are also Dutch Armenians who do not know Armenian (mainly those from Turkey). In general, among the younger generation the most common language is Dutch, which plays a unifying role for the diverse Dutch Armenian community.

Dutch Armenians have developed several religious, political, cultural and social organizations in the Netherlands. Some of the Dutch Armenian organizations have a transnational character, meaning that the organizational network operates in multiple countries, including Syria and the Netherlands. These organizations bring coherent diaspora ideologies into the Dutch context and serve as bridges between the Dutch Armenian community and newly arrived Armenians from Syria. Syrian Armenians named two main diaspora organizations that they connected with upon arrival: the Armenian Apostolic Church and the Armenian Revolutionary Federation (ARF).[64] Currently, the churches in Almelo, Amsterdam and Maastricht gather the biggest groups of Armenians living in the Netherlands.

The Armenian Apostolic Church not only reinforces religious ideology but also works to preserve and reproduce national identity and culture, bringing together Armenians 'to prevent the community from complete assimilation into the host society' (interview with a priest). Various organizations targeting different groups of Armenians (e.g. the women's union, youth organizations, Sunday language schools, and dance school) are attached to the church. Importantly, as Armenians were registered as a religious minority group in Syria, the Syrian Armenian community was formally governed by the national-religious authorities (Armenian Apostolic Community) and had judicial and legal functions for community members. Therefore, in the pre-migration context, the Armenian Apostolic Church substituted the role of the state and played a key role for the community in Syria. Even though the structure is different in the Netherlands, it still plays an important role in the diasporic lives of Syrian Armenians. Moreover, most of the Syrian Armenians interviewed stated that locating the Armenian Apostolic churches in the Netherlands was one of the first steps that they took to connect with the local Dutch Armenian community.

Another transnational organization that bridges the Dutch Armenian and Syrian Armenian communities is the political party the Armenian Revolutionary Federation, which has organizations in over thirty countries. As Tölölyan describes, the ARF has been a transnational organization since its inception in 1890 in Tbilisi.[65] After Armenia's incorporation into the Soviet Union, ARF members regarded themselves as the true guardians of Armenian national identity and as a government in exile.[66] Today, ARF branches continue to cooperate closely with each other and still play a central role in the preservation of Armenian culture as well as the political mobilization of the Armenian Diaspora. Armenians from Iraq, who were members of the ARF before migrating to the Netherlands, set up the ARF branch in the Netherlands in 1995. Syrian Armenians that were members of the ARF in Syria also cooperate with the organization in the Netherlands: 'If we even end up in a desert, we will look for an Armenian community and ARF because we have grown up in that way. And when you do not find it, you feel a specific kind of "hunger"'(Syrian Armenian). Similarly, representatives of the ARF claimed that Syrian Armenians in the Netherlands know that the organization exists: 'We don't put in any effort towards recruitment because they have lived in a diasporic environment all their life. They come and find the organization and become members, just as they used to in Syria or Iraq' (ARF representative).

To understand the role that these organizations play for newcomers, a local organization leader suggested I participate in an event organized after the Sunday mass at Surb Karapet Church in Maastricht. This is an informal gathering of Armenians who have fled Syria during the recent war and local Dutch Armenians. This social event usually takes place once a week and lasts three to four hours. Topics of discussion may vary from the situation in Syria to family issues. When asked about the role and importance of these events and organizations, participants underlined that these events are a way to keep in contact with the community and overcome the feeling of being a stranger in the Netherlands. By attending these events, Syrian Armenians get to know the local Dutch Armenian community consisting of Armenians from Iraq, Armenia, Russia, Turkey and other places. Even though these events aim to provide a 'familiar space' and a 'feeling of being at home', diaspora practices of the heterogeneous Dutch Armenian community are often unfamiliar to Syrian Armenians. For example, during one observation of a diaspora activity organized by Iraqi Armenians on Sundays, newly arrived Syrian Armenians expressed their surprise at the local diasporic lifestyle. Iraqi Armenians played games, such as bingo, while having dinner. During informal talks with Syrian Armenians, they revealed that those activities were strange for them because they never played similar games during their gatherings back in Syria. Nevertheless, both newly arrived asylum seekers and Dutch Armenians do not find these differences an obstacle to cooperation:

> When my family migrated from Turkey to the Netherlands in the 1960s, they were completely new to this country. Then they found the Armenian Church, met Armenians, which made this country more familiar for them. I know how valuable it is to have your people around you, it gives you a unique feeling of safety. Of course, later Syrian Armenians will settle here, find jobs and maybe have less time for the community, but during the first years it is important to realize that you have your community here. (Organization leader, Dutch Armenian, male)

With the help of the transnational organizations, newly arrived migrants also connect with local diaspora life. Representatives of the Armenian organizations state that while they help newly arrived asylum seekers and refugees socialize with local Armenians, they also encourage integration. On many occasions, they proudly underlined that they do not encourage isolation of Armenians from Dutch society: 'The first step of integrating into Dutch society is learning the language, that's why we organize Dutch classes. The more integrated the Armenians are, the better the chance they will assist with the development of their homeland (Armenia)' (Organization leader, Dutch Armenian, male). Support provided to newly arrived Syrian Armenians is not a core function of these organizations but rather a complementary activity and an illustration of diasporic solidarity. Diaspora actors assisting newly arrived migrants complement the activities of civil society organizations and other non-diasporic 'formal organizations'. Diaspora representatives believe that they can provide more direct and effective assistance, mainly because they have shared the same challenges and difficulties that make them more aware of the problems that the newly arrived migrants face. The priest of the Armenian Apostolic Church in Amsterdam stated:

> New migrants do not know the Dutch language to communicate properly. We help them solve documentation problems; we show them paths to overcoming problems smoothly. They are Armenians, so we should help each other. We also live in a foreign country and we are also foreigners in this country. Therefore, we find ways to be useful for our newly arrived compatriots. For example, if they experience problems with their legal status, we connect them with Armenian lawyers. We provide them contacts if they, for instance, have accommodation

issues. The church doesn't have such a mission, but we mobilize our personal networks.

In organizing efforts to help migrants stay in the Netherlands, organization leaders stated that newly arrived Syrian Armenians bring a 'new spirit' into the community and guarantee the continuation of diaspora life in the Netherlands. In the Armenian community, Syrian Armenians are considered 'exemplary diaspora members'. Often, the representatives of diaspora organizations compare Syrian Armenians with Armenians from Armenia that arrived in the Netherlands in an earlier migration wave due to the conflict in Nagorno-Karabakh. Armenians who migrated in the 1990s from Armenia state that it was much easier for them to obtain refugee status compared to Syrian Armenians due to less restricted migrant reception policies.[67]

Members of Armenian transnational organizations underline that Armenians from Armenia did not have any experience collaborating with diaspora organizations and as a result, many of them do not connect with diaspora organizations. Armenians from Armenia or other post-Soviet countries mostly rely on informal networks, such as neighbours, relatives, friends and acquaintances rather than joining formal organizational structures. In contrast, diaspora leaders find that Syrian Armenians are an asset to the community and will guarantee that 'traditional' characteristics of the diaspora will not disappear, such as links with diaspora organizations, attendance of community events, preservation of traditional cultural, religious and linguistic values and so on. Community leaders hope that practices and traditions of 'proper diaspora Armenians' brought by Syrian Armenians will take on new forms and localized practices that reflect the particularities of the Dutch context. Syrian Armenians are perceived as 'bearers' of traditional diasporic values by the diasporic leaders interviewed and therefore considered as people who can potentially 'replenish' the Dutch Armenian diasporic community.

'Collective' problems and the response of diaspora organizations

More than 22,000 Syrian Armenians have arrived in Armenia since the start of the Syrian conflict in 2011.[68] As a response to the Syrian crisis, the Armenian government facilitated a straightforward citizenship process for Syrian refugees. Syrian citizens of Armenian origin were able to receive Armenian citizenship at diplomatic representations and consular posts of the Republic of Armenia. The Armenian government did not treat them as refugees, but as ethnic Armenian 'returnees' from Syria to the homeland. Hakobyan described the choice of migration to Armenia as 'ethnic identity together with the idea of motherland play[ing] the important role in selecting a survival strategy'.[69] Moreover, this was the easiest way for Syrian Armenians to leave the country. The choice of Armenia, the acquisition of Armenian citizenship or long-term residence was based on practical reasons rather than diasporic feeling. Syrian Armenians chose to settle in Armenia because obtaining Armenian citizenship/

dual citizenship and an Armenian passport allows them to travel to other countries, ensuring freedom of movement, as well as certain legal and political protection.[70] The Armenian government used the terms 'homecoming' or 'repatriation' for the internal audience when referring to the influx of Syrian Armenians to Armenia; for the external audience, however, this migration wave was named a 'reception of refugees'.[71] Whether this migration wave is repatriation or a continuation of forced migration is contentious within the Syrian Armenian community. Syrian Armenians mostly described this process as displacement and not voluntary migration or repatriation. Moreover, they expressed a shared attachment to Syria by using a common expression: 'Armenia is our motherland, but Syria is our fatherland'.

Although Syrian Armenians would not face security challenges in Armenia, some of them got an Armenian passport as a survival tool to migrate from Armenia to Europe, the United States and Canada. Dutch authorities argue that the Netherlands is one of the countries that Syrian Armenians migrated to and claimed refugee status while ignoring their Armenian citizenship. At the time of fieldwork, Syrian Armenians in the Netherlands faced the danger of deportation after the Dutch government discovered that some already had Armenian citizenship, as the latter was necessary for them to be able to leave Syria in the first place. Diasporic organizations, notably those formed by Armenians from the Middle East, took the lead in supporting the newcomers. Representatives of these organizations stated that there were cases when families migrated directly to the Netherlands, but as there were questions regarding their migration journeys, they were at risk of being deported. As soon as Syrian Armenians received notices about possible deportations in 2016, Armenian organizations addressed a joint statement to the House of Representatives in the Netherlands expressing their concerns.[72] A community leader stated that they had arranged meetings with the necessary authorities. During a visit to an Armenian organization, a leader had gathered Syrian Armenian representatives to discuss the problems they faced and possible ways to overcome them. During the discussion, they linked the legacy of the genocide to this group of migrants in order to create positive grounds for them to remain in the Netherlands. One of the leaders stated:

> They have no one here in the Netherlands. And if not us who else would help them? If the Dutch government may provide support to Syrians, why not to Armenians? These people have faced double genocide and deportation. The first one was in 1915 when they were forced to flee their homeland and take refuge in Syria and now this. (Organization leader, Dutch Armenian, male)

Organization leaders stated that they used their contacts to explain the situation of newly arrived Syrian Armenian migrants to the authorities. In doing so, they emphasized the notion of a 'victim diaspora' and connected the memory of the genocide with the violence generated by ISIS. This discourse is based on the idea of Armenians being 'one of the Christian minorities in the Middle East that has already suffered from persecution', referring to the genocide in 1915: 'If the Dutch government accepts those fleeing the conflict, the Christian minority should also have its place in the Netherlands.

Who else would understand them? For other people it may seem that, yes, why not, they should return. But they need to know that these people have the right to choose where to stay, they have been displaced twice' (Organization leader, Dutch Armenian, male). Moreover, representatives of Assyrian political organizations stated that they had helped Armenians organize meetings with Dutch political parties, such as 'Christen Unie', by constructing a victimized 'Christian' image, taking into account the growing hostile attitudes towards mass migration from Middle Eastern 'Muslim' countries.[73]

The interviewees often told family stories of the genocide to underline the relevance of being a 'survivor of the genocide' to the Syrian Armenian experience:

> I am the third-generation survivor. Why do I say 'survivor'? Because I have that trauma and sadness inside myself. I am the great-grandson of Shushi and Vardges who escaped the genocide in their own homeland and found shelter in Syria. I am the great-grandson of people who went through violence, massacre and hunger. Whatever I do, wherever I go I feel the responsibility in front of their memory. I owe them for my hard-working, patriotic and more importantly, humanist characteristics. (Hovig, Dutch Armenian)

Another interviewee expressed the following: 'We used to live in very good conditions in Syria; we had equal rights as Syrians, we were respected, we had our own businesses, schools, associations and churches. Now we are witnessing a second genocide, they forced us to leave our homes' (Saro, Syrian Armenian). Many interviewees, like Hovig and Saro, whose grandparents were genocide survivors, present themselves as the 'carriers of the memory'. In order to link their memory with the current situation of Syrian Armenians and make the claim more viable, organization leaders refer to difficult social and economic conditions in Armenia that make the country incapable of hosting Syrian Armenians:

> It is not necessary to live in Armenia to be Armenian. These people [referring to Syrian Armenians] can be helpful to our country while also living in diaspora. Of course, we all would have liked to move back to our country if there were sufficient conditions. But we will be useful for our nation by being successful here in diaspora. (Organization leader, Dutch Armenian, male)

For this reason, community leaders invest in financial resources to hire 'the best lawyers in Amsterdam' to assist Syrian Armenians. Although the issue is ongoing, this case makes salient the victimization frame used by the organizations and challenges the state-centred characterization of diasporas.

A new 'home' or a temporary solution?

To have a complete picture about the positionality towards Syria, Armenia and the Netherlands, Syrian Armenians were asked if they foresaw their 'home' or the place worth living and spending their lives in, as based in either Armenia, Syria or the Netherlands. The analyses of this question stress both the emotional and practical aspects of separation from the homeland and settlement in a new country.

Unlike other minority groups in Syria, such as Assyrians, Armenians never had internal secessionist claims in Syria.[74] Reflecting on their lives in Syria, the Syrian Armenians interviewed stated that they had been loyal to the Syrian government, as, according to them, it protected minorities like the Christian population. When remembering their lives in Syria, Syrian Armenians often began their stories with the expression 'living in diaspora'.[75] However, their life narratives were expressions of warm attachment to Syria, as a country where they and their grandparents had established their home. Interestingly, observations of social events among Armenians showed that they highlighted their 'Syrianness' in diaspora: this nostalgia was cultivated by playing Arab music and encouraging Arab dances and cuisine during Armenian parties. The tendency to idealize Syria was also observable during the interviews:

> Two years ago, a friend of mine returned from Syria where I had a vineyard. I was very happy and immediately planted it in our home garden. We dug, gave fertilizers and did everything to protect it from the cold. However, despite our efforts, the grape vines dried day by day. It is the same for people: if you uproot them, later, you cannot expect them to be the same. (Aleq, Syrian Armenian)

This forced exodus has strengthened attachment and developed nostalgic feelings towards Syria, as is expected in conflict-related diasporas, according to my fieldwork. In discussions about Syria, many Armenian interviewees referred to it as a 'prosperous state', to which they would return if the situation normalized. Interviewees who wanted to return to Syria stated that they would go back 'when Syria is a safe country again'. When asked for their reasons for returning specifically to Syria, many answered: 'because I was born there, and it is my country'. One interviewee explained, 'because in Aleppo we had a good life, Syria gave us comfort and security'. The majority of interviewees state that even though they grew up speaking Armenian, going to Armenian schools, dreaming about Armenia and its landscapes, heritage and traditions, they feel lost and without any prospects in Armenia. Syrian Armenians mostly discuss the burden of economic conditions as impacting their desire to 'return' to Armenia:

> The idea of returning to Armenia has always been in our mind. Our little child always asks me why we are here, why we don't go back to Armenia. It is a bit difficult to explain why we are here and why we left Armenia even though we were yearning for it for so many years. But if we rationally think, we don't have anything to do in Armenia for now. Here we are used to the rules, here we feel protected, while in Armenia there is no law, I am not sure if we can find a job. (Lusin, Syrian Armenian)

A common theme was that they would prefer to migrate to Armenia 'with money or when there is a stable situation', considering the difficult socioeconomic situation in Armenia. Some Syrian Armenians also highlighted cultural and social differences between Armenians in Armenia and Syrian Armenians, as well as the difficulties of the Armenian bureaucracy, termed the 'Soviet mentality that is present in Armenia'. The combination of these factors made Syrian Armenians consider the alternative survival strategy of migrating to Western countries, including the Netherlands. Discussions with Syrian Armenians confirmed Kasbarian's observation of the relationship between the diaspora Armenians and the Republic of Armenia as a 'step-homeland': 'two entities that are not related by descent [are] forced into a familial relationship by external forces; that is, it is not a naturally occurring relationship but one that is forged through circumstances'.[76]

The majority of interviewees underlined that they had never thought actively about returning to Syria or Armenia since arriving in the Netherlands. Interviewees mentioned that the violence committed against the Christian population in Syria emptied their villages and towns. They were concerned about unsafe conditions and feared that the Middle East would never again be a safe place for Christians. Interviewees discussed both the socioeconomic conditions and the possibility of living a diaspora life as reasons to stay in the Netherlands. Syrian Armenians state that the existence of a functioning Armenian community ensures that preservation of cultural and social values is possible in the Netherlands: 'I have solved my financial issues and started to look for Armenian social and cultural clubs in the Netherlands. Here we will try to get involved in diaspora activities as much as possible, just like we used to do in Syria' (Shant, Syrian Armenian).

The question of return opened up one of the many different ways in which people experience their home state and homeland belonging. Armenians felt the 'Syrian' part of their 'Syrian Armenian' belonging more strongly. Nevertheless, the return to Armenia or Syria was discussed mainly as an abstract possibility by most of the interviewees, as they found it more realistic and promising to build their new home in the Netherlands. Similar to the Jewish expression 'next year in Jerusalem', discussions about return mostly expressed idealistic wishes, rather than concrete future plans.[77]

Conclusion

This chapter re-examined diaspora–homeland relations based on the case study of Armenian migrants that fled from Syria to the Netherlands (some via Armenia) after the beginning of the Syrian Civil War in 2011. The situation of Syrian Armenians is quite unique within migration and refugee studies as the Armenian government allowed them to gain Armenian citizenship. This caused major legal difficulties for Armenians resettling in the Netherlands as Dutch authorities claimed that they had the alternative option of resettling in Armenia. This situation offers an opportunity to re-examine diaspora–homeland relations and respond to Tölölyan's call for re-examining the role of the homeland for diasporas instead of relying on dominant theories that claim that orientation towards the homeland is an essential feature of diasporic identity.[78] The chapter contributes to the diaspora and migration scholarship in two directions: first, it counterbalances recent state-centric approaches of examining diaspora–homeland relations and unpacks the multilayered perception of homeland among Syrian Armenians; second, it points out the role of diasporic networks for newly arrived migrants by situating the study of diasporic experience in the recent migration circumstances.

The unique case of the Syrian Armenian migration to the Netherlands shows that newly arrived asylum seekers and refugees in countries where there are transnational diaspora institutions have the advantage of relying on these networks. This research confirms the findings of several migration studies on the importance of the role of well-established networks as providers of emotional and cultural support, as well as practical advice on accommodation, social and health services assistance in accessing the labour market to newcomers.[79] The study expands the understanding of the role of migrant networks and identifies the main difference between diaspora organizations and individual ethnic networks: diaspora organizations assist with integration not only within the new host society, but within diaspora settings as well. The organizations, in turn, have a vision of establishing a long-term cooperation model with newcomers, as they see Syrian Armenians as an asset to diaspora communities and a guarantee of the continuity of diaspora life. These findings also provide additional evidence in support of Tölölyan's claim that a defining quality of diasporic people or social formations is that they care about others in diaspora with whom they share an ethnodiasporic origin.[80]

The 'collective problems' of Armenians in the Netherlands offer a new insight into the diaspora's proactive involvement in the protection of recent Syrian Armenians who have fled conflict. The existence of a historical homeland has been one of the core obstacles to newly arrived asylum seekers' attempts to settle in the Netherlands. Diaspora organizations take on the responsibility for their newly arrived co-ethnics and invest human and material resources into solving their problems. The Armenian community uses a victimhood framework and elements of the past when addressing current issues. Diasporas have the advantage of providing support to newcomers based on their emotional commitment in prioritizing areas of help that can be overlooked by other non-diaspora actors. Diaspora organizations help position newly arrived Syrian Armenians in favourable conditions and act as intermediaries to gain the trust of the Dutch authorities in order to overcome the obstacles that they faced themselves as newcomers. Newly arrived migrants find advocacy support from diaspora organizations that claim more rights for them, as diaspora organizations prioritize their common 'traumatic past' as a legacy that justifies helping newly arrived Syrian Armenians to settle in the Netherlands and avoid deportation to Armenia. The 'victim past' is framed as something 'extra' that is added to common notions of asylum request to push back against deportation to Armenia, and position Syrian Armenians as a 'victimized Christian minority group' in the Middle East. Diaspora organizations have been one of the main support providers for Syrian Armenians that may otherwise be neglected by international organizations, host societies, sending country or country of origin.

These findings confirm Tölölyan's call for diaspora scholars not to locate a 'diasporic's home in the ancestral homeland too easily': the study shows that Syrian Armenians experience duality when it comes to notions of attachment to the 'homeland' and 'returning to the homeland'.[81] Syrian Armenians mainly prefer to maintain nostalgic identification with Armenia and Syria, and the existence of ethnic networks and diaspora institutions are considered contributing factors towards choosing the Netherlands as a permanent place to stay, as well as a chance for replenishing and developing life in diaspora. Thanks to long-established transnational diasporic organizations and shared diasporic culture, it is much easier and familiar for Syrian Armenians to move from one diaspora community to another and adapt to it than to settle in Armenia. This research challenges the assumption that displaced persons long for an idealized lost homeland, and instead highlights the struggle of settling in a new 'home'.

In addition to problematizing homeland–diaspora relations, their complexities and characteristics, this chapter also suggests an answer to the question posed by Tölölyan that he qualified as an 'emerging issue': how would Yerevan deal with Syrian Armenian refugees, and would it be able to function as a homeland for them?[82] Based on the case study of Syrian Armenians, the research suggests that diaspora–homeland relations are more complex than a simple link to a certain territory. The findings show that Syrian Armenians prefer to self-identify as diasporans first. Moreover, it is easier for Syrian Armenians to sustain their diasporic transnationalism in a new destination country, and therefore to settle somewhere in the diaspora rather than in Armenia.

Notes

1. IND Naturalisatiedienst, 'Asylum Trends. Language Selection Nederlands', 2020, https://ind.nl/en/about-ind/figures-and-publications/Pages/Asylum-Trends.aspx, accessed 24 April 2020.
2. The Armenian presence in Syria has been recorded long before the Genocide. The number of Armenians in Syria increased during the fall of the Bagratuni kingdom in Armenia (1064), the Seljuk Turks Raids (1064–1220), Mongol-Tatar long-term rule (1220–1468), and later as a result of the fall of Cilician Armenia (1375) (Aaraqs Pashayan and Lilit Harutyunyan, and A. Gasparyan, ed., *The Armenian Community of Syria: Actual Issues* (Yerevan: Institute of Oriental Studies National Academy of Sciences of the Republic of Armenia, 2011).
3. Razmik Panossian, 'Courting a Diaspora: Armenia-Diaspora Relations Since 1998', in *International Migration and Sending Countries*, ed. Eva Østergaard-Nielsen (London: Palgrave Macmillan, 2003), 140–68.
4. Uitspraken.rechtspraak.nl., 2020, https://uitspraken.rechtspraak.nl/inziendocument?id=ECLI%3ANL%3ARBDHA%3A2020%3A8018, accessed 21 August 2020.
5. Alan Gamlen, 'The Emigration State and the Modern Geopolitical Imagination', *Political Geography* 27, no. 8 (2008): 840–56; Wendy Larner, 'Expatriate Experts and Globalising Governmentalities: The New Zealand Diaspora Strategy', *Transactions of the Institute of British Geographers* 32, no. 3 (2017): 331–45; Francesco Ragazzi, 'A Comparative Analysis of Diaspora Policies', *Political Geography* 41, no. 1 (2014): 74–89.
6. John A. Armstrong, 'Mobilized and Proletarian Diasporas', *American Political Science Review* 70, no. 2 (1976): 393–408; Pamela Ann Smith, 'The Palestinian Diaspora, 1948–1985', *Journal of Palestine Studies* 15, no. 3 (1986): 90–108; Steven Vertovec, 'Three Meanings of "Diaspora," Exemplified Among South Asian Religions', *Diaspora: A Journal of Transnational Studies* 6, no. 3 (1997): 277–99; William Safran, 'The Jewish

Diaspora in a Comparative and Theoretical Perspective', *Israel Studies* 10, no. 1 (2005): 36–60; Roger Brubaker, 'The "Diaspora" Diaspora', *Ethnic and Racial Studies* 28, no. 1 (2005): 1–19.

7   John A. Armstrong, 'Mobilized and Proletarian Diasporas'; Smith, 'The Palestinian Diaspora, 1948–1985'; Vertovec, 'Three Meanings of "Diaspora", Exemplified among South Asian Religions'.
8   Khachig Tölölyan, 'Diaspora Studies: Past, Present and Promise', Working Papers, Paper 5 (Oxford: International Migration Institute (IMI), 2012), 11.
9   Ibid.
10 Maurizio Ambrosini, 'Why Irregular Migrants Arrive and Remain: The Role of Intermediaries', *Journal of Ethnic and Migration Studies* 43, no. 11 (2017): 1813–30; Suzanne Wessendorf, 'Pioneer Migrants and Their Social Relations in Super-Diverse London', *Ethnic and Racial Studies* 42, no. 1 (2019): 17–34; Avtar Brah, *Cartographies of Diaspora: Contesting Identities* (New York: Psychology, 1996); Anne-Marie Fortier, *Migrant Belongings: Memory, Space, Identity* (Oxford: Berg, 2000); Nando Sigona, Alan John Gamlen, Giulia Libertore and Helene Neveau-Kringelbach, *Diasporas Re-Imagined: Spaces, Practices and Belonging* (Oxford Diasporas Programme, 2015); Suzanne Wessendorf, 'Pathways of Settlement among Recent Migrants in Super-Diverse Areas', IRiS Working Paper Series (2018), 25; Camilla Orjuela, 'Divides and Dialogue in the Diaspora During Sri Lanka's Civil War', *South Asian Diaspora* 9, no. 1 (2017): 67–82.
11 Armstrong, 'Mobilized and Proletarian Diasporas'; Smith, 'The Palestinian Diaspora, 1948–1985'; Vertovec, 'Three Meanings of "Diaspora," Exemplified among South Asian Religions'.
12 William Safran, 'Diasporas in Modern Societies: Myths of Homeland and Return', *Diaspora: A Journal of Transnational Studies* 1, no. 1 (1991): 83–99.
13 Safran, 'The Jewish Diaspora'.
14 Ibid., 36–60.
15 Ibid., 38.
16 For more on the primordialist/essentialist approach, see van Hans Amersfoort, 'Gabriel Sheffer and the diaspora experience', *Diaspora: A Journal of Transnational Studies* 13, no. 2–3 (2004): 359–73; Gabriel Sheffer, 'Israel Diaspora Relations in Comparative Perspective', in *Israel in Comparative Perspective: Challenging the Conventional Wisdom*, ed. M. Barnette (New York: State University of New York Press, 1996), 53–85. For more on a constructivist one, see Cathy Wilcock, 'Mobilising Towards and Imagining Homelands: Diaspora Formation among UK Sudanese', *Journal of Ethnic and Migration Studies* 44, no. 3 (2018): 363–81.
17 Michelle Reis, 'Theorizing Diaspora: Perspectives on "Classical" and "Contemporary" Diaspora', *International Migration* 42, no. 2 (2004): 41–60; Brubaker, 'The "Diaspora" Diaspora'; Khachig Tölölyan, 'Beyond the Homeland: From Exilic Nationalism to Diasporic Transnationalism', in *The Call of the Homeland*, ed. A Gal, A. Leoussi and Am.Smith (Leiden: Brill, 2010); Östen Wahlbeck, 'The Concept of Diaspora as an Analytical Tool in the Study of Refugee Communities', *Journal of Ethnic and Migration Studies* 28, no. 2 (2002): 221–38.
18 Brubaker, 'The "Diaspora" Diaspora', 1–19.
19 Wahlbeck, 'The Concept of Diaspora as an Analytical Tool in the Study of Refugee Communities', 221–238.
20 Manuel Orozco and Michelle Lapointe, 'Mexican Hometown Associations and Development Opportunities', *Journal of International Affairs* 57 (2004): 31–51; Katrina Burgess, 'Collective Remittances and Migrant-State Collaboration in Mexico and El

Salvador', *Latin American Politics and Society* 54, no. 4 (2012): 119–46; Simona Vezzoli and Thomas Lacroix, 'Building Bonds for Migration and Development: Diaspora Engagement Policies of Ghana, India and Serbia', Eschborn: Deutsche Gesellschaft für technische Zusammenarbeit (GTZ) GmbH, Migration and Development Sector Project, 2010, 58.

21 Gamlen, 'The Emigration State and the Modern Geopolitical Imagination', 840–56.
22 Yehonatan Abramson, 'Making a Homeland, Constructing a Diaspora: The Case of Taglit-Birthright Israel', *Political Geography* 58, no. 1 (2017): 14–23; Wisdom J. Tettey, 'Regenerating Scholarly Capacity Through Diaspora Engagement: The Case of a Ghana Diaspora Knowledge Network', in *Diaspora, Development and Governance*, ed. A. Chikanda, Abel, Jonathan Crush, and Margaret Walton-Roberts (Geneva: Springer International Publishing Switzerland, 2016), 171–86.
23 Eva Østergaard-Nielsen, 'The Democratic Deficit of Diaspora Politics: Turkish Cypriots in Britain and the Cyprus Issue', *Journal of Ethnic and Migration Studies* 29, no. 4 (2003): 683–700; A. Gamlen, 'Diaspora Engagement Policies: What Are They and What Kinds of States Use Them?', Centre on Migration, Policy and Society Working Paper Series 32 (2006); Rahel Kunz, 'The Discovery of the Diaspora', *International Political Sociology* 6, no. 1 (2012): 103–7; Maria Koinova, and Gerasimos Tsourapas, 'How Do Countries of Origin Engage Migrants and Diasporas? Multiple Actors and Comparative Perspectives', *International Political Science Review* 39, no. 3 (2018): 311–32; Ragazzi, 'A Comparative Analysis of Diaspora Policies'; Latha Varadarajan, *The Domestic Abroad: Diasporas in International Relations* (Oxford: Oxford University Press, 2010).
24 André Levy, 'A Community That Is Both a Center and a Diaspora: Jews in Late Twentieth Century Morocco', in *Homelands and Diasporas: Holy Lands and Other Places*, ed. A. Levy and A. Weingord (Stanford: Stanford University Press, 2005), 68–96.
25 Craven, Catherine Ruth 'Critical Realism, Assemblages and Practices Beyond the State: A New Framework for Analysing Global Diaspora Engagement', *The SOAS Journal of Postgraduate Research* 11 (2018): 100–16.
26 Tölölyan, 'Diaspora Studies', 4–14.
27 Ibid.
28 Khachig Tölölyan, 'Exile Government in the Armenian Polity', *Journal of Political Science* 18, no. 1 (1990): 6.
29 Ibid.
30 Tölölyan, 'Beyond the Homeland', 27–45.
31 Tölölyan, 'Diaspora Studies', 4–14.
32 James Clifford, *Routes: Travel and Translation in the Late Twentieth Century* (Cambridge, MA: Harvard University Press, 1997), 251.
33 Takeyuki Tsuda, 'When the Diaspora Returns Home', in *A Companion to Diaspora and Transnationalism*, ed. A. Quayson and G. Daswani (New York: Wiley-Blackwell, 2013), 172–89. Jennifer M. Brinkerhoff, 'Creating an Enabling Environment for Diasporas' Participation in Homeland Development', *International Migration* 50, no. 1 (2012): 75–95; Bahar Baser and MariToivanen, 'Diasporic Homecomings to the Kurdistan Region of Iraq: Pre-and Post-Return Experiences Shaping Motivations to Re-Return', *Ethnicities* 19, no. 5 (2019): 901–24.
34 Paul Gilroy, *Against Race: Imagining Political Culture Beyond the Color Line* (Cambridge, MA: Harvard University Press, 2000), 124.

35 Marisa Della Gatta, 'A "Nation in Exile": The Renewed Diaspora of Syrian Armenian Repatriates', *British Journal of Middle Eastern Studies* 46, no. 3 (2019): 339–57; Sossie Kasbarian, 'The Myth and Reality of "Return" – Diaspora in the "Homeland"', *Diaspora: A Journal of Transnational Studies* 18, no. 3 (2015): 358–81.
36 Kasbarian, 'The Myth and Reality of "Return" – Diaspora in the "Homeland," 358-381'.
37 Ibid., 358.
38 In this chapter I use the words 'repatriation' and 'returnees' in scare quotation marks to show that the word is not being used in its literal sense, as the emigrated diasporic Armenians or their ancestors usually didn't have connections with the Soviet Armenian territories.
39 Armenuhi Stepanyan, *Repatriation of the XX Century in the System of Armenian Identity* (Yerevan: Gitutyun, 2010).
40 Vardan Marashlyan, Nare Galstyan, and Irena Hovhannisyan, *Integration Practices of Repatriates in Armenia* (Yerevan: Ministry of Diaspora of the Republic of Armenia, 2015).
41 Stepanyan, *Repatriation of the XX Century in the System of Armenian Identity*, 164.
42 Tsypylma Darieva, 'Rethinking Homecoming: Diasporic Cosmopolitanism in Post-Soviet Armenia', *Ethnic and Racial Studies* 34, no. 3 (2011): 490–508.
43 Daniel Fittante, 'Connection Without Engagement: Paradoxes of North American Armenian Return Migration', *Diaspora* 19, no. 2–3 (2017): 147–69.
44 See, for example, Mihran Galstyan, Ruben Ohanjanyan, Tamar Zaqaryan, and Gayane Hakobyan, *Contemporary Armenian Family in Transformative Society* (Yerevan: NAS RA, Gitutyun, 2017); Lusine Tanajyan, 'The Experience of Integration of Syrian-Armenian in Armenia. Problem Solving Mechanisms', Report for Open Society Foundation, 2018;Tiran Loqmakeozyan, 'Best in Baghramyan Avenue', *Agos*, 3 July 2015.
45 Karolina Pawłowska, 'Ethnic Return of Armenian Americans: Perspectives', *Anthropological Notebooks* 23, no. 1 (2017): 93–109.
46 Shawn Malia Kanaiaupuni, 'Reframing the Migration Question: An Analysis of Men, Women, and Gender in Mexico', *Social Forces* 78, no. 4 (2000): 1311–47; Janroj Yilmaz Keles Eugenia Markova, and Rebwar Fatah, 'Migrants with Insecure Legal Status and Access to Work: The Role of Ethnic Solidarity Networks', *Equality, Diversity and Inclusion: An International Journal* (2019); Masja Van Meeteren, Peter Mascini, and Devorah van den Berg, 'Trajectories of Economic Integration of Amnestied Immigrants in Rotterdam', *Journal of Ethnic and Migration Studies* 41, no. 3 (2015): 448-69; Alejandro Portes and Julis Sensenbrenner, 'Embeddedness and Immigration: Notes on the Social Determinants of Economic Action', *American Journal of Sociology* 98, no. 6 (2018): 1320–50.
47 Nadia F. Flores-Yeffal, 'Migration-Trust Networks: Unveiling the Social Networks of International Migration', in *Immigration and Categorical Inequality*, ed. E Castañeda (London: Routledge, 2017), 83–98.
48 Alejandro Portes, *Economic Sociology: A Systematic Inquiry* (Princeton: Princeton University Press, 2010), 34.
49 Maurizio Ambrosini, *Irregular Immigration in Southern Europe* (New York: Springer International Publishing, 2018) 42.
50 Ambrosini, 'Why Irregular Migrants Arrive and Remain', 1813–30.
51 Ibid.
52 Ibid.
53 Ibid.

54　Orjuela, 'Divides and Dialogue in the Diaspora During Sri Lanka's Civil War', 67–82.
55　Sharon Macdonald, *Memorylands: Heritage and Identity in Europe Today* (London: Routledge, 2013), 16.
56　Abramson, 'Making a Homeland, Constructing a Diaspora'; T. A. Tami Amanda Jacoby, 'A Theory of Victimhood: Politics, Conflict and the Construction of Victim-Based Identity', *Millennium* 43, no. 2 (2015): 511–30.
57　Martin Tolich, 'Internal Confidentiality: When Confidentiality Assurances Fail Relational Informants', *Qualitative Sociology* 27, no. 1 (2004): 101–6.
58　Richard Hovannisian, 'The Ebb and Flow of the Armenian Minority in the Arab Middle East', *Middle East Journal* 28, no. 1 (1974): 19–32.
59　Della Gatta, 'A "Nation in Exile"', 339.
60　Cohen uses the term 'victim diaspora', in *Global Diasporas: An Introduction* (London: Routledge, 2008), 48–59, while Armstrong uses 'archetypical'. Armstrong, 'Mobilized and Proletarian Diasporas', 393–408.
61　Nicola Migliorino, '"Kulna Suriyyin"? The Armenian Community and the State in Contemporary Syria', *Revue des Mondes Musulmans et de la Méditerranée* no. 115–16 (La Syrie au quotidien) (2006): 97–115.
62　Dutch official sources do not provide data on ethnic belonging. This estimate is provided by the Armenian Embassy in the Netherlands.
63　Western Armenian is based on the dialect of Constantinople, while Eastern Armenian is based on the dialect of Yerevan (usually referred to as Araratian) (Razmik Panossian, *The Armenians: From Kings and Priests to Merchants and Commissars* (New York: University of Columbia Press, 2006). Eastern Armenian is spoken by Armenians from Armenia and Iran, while Western Armenian is spoken mostly by the immigrants of the Middle East (Daniel Douglas and Anny Bakalian, 'Sub-ethnic Diversity: Armenians in the United States', *Journal of the Society of Armenian Studies* 18, no. 2 [2009]: 55–70).
64　The Armenian Revolutionary Federation, also known as Dashnaktsutyun (Armenians: Hay Heghapʻokhakan Dashnaktsʻutyun).
65　Khachig Tölölyan, 'Rethinking Diaspora(s): Stateless Power in the Transnational Moment', *Diaspora: A Journal of Transnational Studies* 5, no. 1 (1996): 3–36.
66　Ibid.
67　Halleh Ghorashi, 'Agents of Change or Passive Victims: The Impact of Welfare States (The Case of the Netherlands) on Refugees', *Journal of Refugee Studies* 18, no. 2 (2005): 181–98.
68　Arsen Hakobyan, 'From Aleppo to Yerevan: The War and Migration from the Window of the Bus', in *Fundamentalism: Ethnographies on Minorities, Discrimination and Transnationalism*, ed. Marcello Mollica (Wien: LIT, 2016), 21–41.
69　Ibid., 22.
70　Ibid., 21–41.
71　Armenpress, 'Our Compatriots That Continue to Live in Syria Are Heroes', *Armenpress.am*, n.d., armenpress.am/arm/news/868647/, accessed 21 March 2022; United Nations High Commissioner for Refugees, 'UNHCR Helps Displaced Syrian-Armenians Facing Hardship Amid Pandemic', *UNHCR*, 2020, www.unhcr.org/news/stories/2020/5/5ecf78874/unhcr-helps-displaced-syrian-armenians-facing-hardship-amid-pandemic.html#:~:text=Around%2022%2C000%20Syrians%20have%20fled, accessed 31 March 2022.
72　This issue had not been resolved at the end of the fieldwork in August, 2018.

73 Nare Galstyan, 'Engaging Stateless and State-Linked Diasporas: Assyrians and Armenians in the Netherlands' (PhD, diss., University of Milan and University of Turin, 2019).
74 Pashaya and Harutyunyan, 'The Armenian Community of Syria'; Migliorino, '"Kulna Suriyyin"? The Armenian Community and the State in Contemporary Syria'.
75 Armenian translation of the phrase is 'abrelov sp'iwṛk'i mēch'.
76 Kasbarian, 'The Myth and Reality of "Return" – Diaspora in the "Homeland," 358-381'.
77 Leonard J. Greenspoon, ed., *Next Year in Jerusalem: Exile and Return in Jewish History* (West Lafayette: Purdue University Press, 2019).
78 Tölölyan, 'Diaspora Studies', 4–14.
79 Jacqueline Maria Hagan, 'Social Networks, Gender, and Immigrant Incorporation: Resources and Constraints', *American Sociological Review* 63 (1998): 55–67. Ambrosini, 'Why Irregular Migrants Arrive and Remain', 1813–30.
80 Tölölyan, 'Diaspora Studies', 4–14.
81 Ibid., 11.
82 Khachig Tölölyan and Taline Papazian, 'Armenian Diasporas and Armenia: Issues of Identity and Mobilization. An Interview with Khachig Tölölyan', *Études arméniennes contemporaines* 3 (2014): 83–101.

II

'Diasporic Social Formation'

Leadership elites, institutions and transnational governmentality

4

Forging Diasporic Identity in the *Fin de Siècle* Armenian Periodical Press in Europe

Hasmik Khalapyan

Introduction

In 1909, Arshak Chobanian (1872–1954), a prominent Ottoman Armenian author and editor of the journal *Anahit* published in Paris, wrote:

> The nation comes into being when a group of people assemble around an ideal and ideology, when [the group] has a collective and unique way of thinking and worldview, and when it develops the divine ability to express this unique way of thinking and worldview in writing. And this expression [in writing] is the proof of [the existence] of the national identity.[1]

Chobanian was one of the many Ottoman Armenian literati who, in the late nineteenth century, had taken refuge in Europe to escape growing economic hardship and political persecution by the Ottoman state. These literati, with Arshak Chobanian, Arpiar Arpiarian, Yervant Otian and Mkrtich Portugalian among them, had already earned themselves fame among the Ottoman Armenians as writers and editors prior to exile. Once in Europe, they founded journals to continue their careers in the new setting. Like Chobanian, these editors believed that writing in the period was a major enterprise towards the establishment of a modern Armenian national identity. The European host countries such as France and England were new opportunities for the literati to continue to 'imagine the community'[2] and forge an Armenian identity in a less restrictive political and cultural setting.

This chapter analyses several influential European Armenian periodicals established in Europe in the late nineteenth and early twentieth centuries[3] to illustrate how a group of literati struggled to create a 'diasporic public sphere' of readers for the consumption of new definitions of the Armenian collective identity in diaspora.[4] It analyses the multilayered pressures, tensions and negotiations that arose in the process: revisitation and re-examination of the past and its relevance for national identity, recognition by the hosting countries and intergenerational transmission of a collective identity.[5] Through an exchange between the known and novel cultures, the periodical press turned into a tool through which prominent literary figures sought to cultivate 'Armenianness' by controlling production of knowledge and imposing social discipline in the absence of the state and national institutions.

Agendas of modernization and the periodical press

By the mid-nineteenth century, a chain of political events, including the 1828 Russian occupation of the eastern Armenian lands; the *Tanzimat*, the Ottoman state-initiated reforms between 1839 and 1856; and the French Revolution in 1848, impacted the Ottoman Armenians.[6] Those who were educated in Europe and inspired by French modernity strove to modernize the Armenian national identity and national institutions. The events in this period were characterized as 'Awakening' (*Zartōnkʻ*) and coincided with progressive thinkers challenging the role of the *amiras*[7] as the elites of the Armenian community. The religious institution of the Patriarchate of Constantinople was likewise challenged by the adoption of the 1863 Constitution, leading to the establishment of a National Assembly. Secular Armenian schools were founded, and the literati made their appearance in publications as agents of modernization. Literature became the means through which the Ottoman Armenian literati communicated their vision for a new Armenian national identity in the newly adopted vernacular language.[8] The transition from Classical Armenian to vernacular helped enlarge the symbolic boundaries of the nation to include all layers of society, both in the urban and provincial spaces.

The periodical press especially played an enormous role in the agenda of modernization. As Benedict Anderson has argued, in nationalist movements, the massive daily circulations of press fostered a national consciousness in unprecedented ways. Through the act of reading the same daily publications, large sections of the population shared the *same message* at the *same time* in an 'unbound and unenumerated seriality'.[9] This daily and almost indiscernible consumption of new national ideals was key to the nationalist and modernizing agendas.[10]

The role of the dissemination of this serialized information in the forging of a new national concept among the Ottoman Armenians cannot be overestimated. According to the twentieth-century poet and literary critic Vahé Oshagan, '[o]f all the elements that made up the Armenian cultural potential at the turn of the century (the Church, elites, schools, language, press and literature), only the press and literature were destined to play an important role in the elaboration of the national hero-models and self-consciousness'.[11] Moreover, since every writer contributed to the press, the distinction between periodical press and literary works was blurred. It was the aim of the writers to influence public opinion while informing and serving the Armenian people. This, Oshagan argues, resulted in 'total coincidence of private and public destines' when under the historical circumstances, the writers and journalists assumed political roles.[12] For years to come, the periodical publications defined, negotiated and attempted to control the discourses leading to the formation of new national ideals in their social and cultural manifestations.

The move from the Ottoman Empire to Europe changed the conditions of the editors' diasporic existence. Back in the Ottoman context, the editors and prominent contributors of periodical press were members of what Khachig Tölölyan defines as an 'intrastate diaspora', a community that was outside the ancestral territory but within the boundaries of the state that ruled and controlled the ancestral territory.[13] In the intrastate diaspora, according to Tölölyan, 'elites struggled for the control of its institutions and contested each other's claim to represent the renascent nation' in the eyes of the rulers and act as 'quasi-governments'.[14] For the literati, publishing in periodicals and newspapers served as powerful tools for control and social discipline. In exile, outside of Turkey, the editors had to find themselves in 'overseas diaspora'[15] and writing had to acquire new meaning. The negotiation of national identity, as will be illustrated in what follows, led to the adoption of a 'dialogical' model between multiple locales and the grander idea of the transnation in the absence of the state and national institutions.

Editors in exile

Towards the end of nineteenth century when many Ottoman Armenian intellectuals and writers took refuge in large cities of Europe in search of more favourable economic conditions and to escape political restrictions and persecutions by Sultan Abdul Hamid's (1876–1909) regime, they had already earned themselves the reputation as prominent national figures and reformers. Moving to Europe, the authors stayed loyal to their 'call' of being the public voice of the Armenian people and acting as its 'quasi-government'. This time, however, the diasporic space offered more challenges. Absent here was not only the state but also the religious and national institutions that supported the political and cultural coexistence of the Armenian *millet* within the Ottoman Empire.[16]

The editors recognized the challenges of the new diasporic space. Arpiar Arpiarian (1851–1908), for example, explained his decision to establish the journal *Nor Keank'* in London with his concern over lack of institutional structures for political leadership:

> The Armenian nation does not have a Ministry that would lead its national politics. The Armenian politics must derive from the Armenian nation, and when a Nation, as a whole, is [deprived of] political education, it can be subjected to great dangers. *Nor Keank'* will do its best to support the political education of the Armenian nation taking the example of leading European publications.[17]

The new setting offered new opportunities too. Tölölyan has argued that '[t]he stateless power of diasporas lies in their heightened awareness of both the perils and rewards of multiple belonging, and in their sometimes exemplary grappling with the paradoxes of such belonging'.[18] As much of a challenge as the lack of national political institutions was to the editors, the politically less restrictive setting offered a unique opportunity for assertion of greater power in the community through controlling the public discourse and establishing social discipline.

The launching of a new periodical was accompanied with statements that had to both demonstrate the responsibility the editors felt towards their compatriots and justify their entry into the field. The inaugural issues of journals included the editors' notes explaining their motives to launch the periodical publication. 'Why this paper?' or 'Our Right for Existence'[19] were among the common headlines. Using almost identical language, first issues justified their decision to step into the field in terms of a void (*parap*) and lack in the field, a gap they felt urged, and considered their duty, to fill. Thus, M. Sivaslian's *Hayastan* (Paris) claimed that their aim was 'to fill the void for an independent newspaper'.[20] *Patani* (London), founded by 'young and proud students' in 1902, clarified that the journal's objective was 'not to compete with other papers by supplying pleasant readings to our subscribers' but rather 'to fill the void' in the sphere of periodical publications.[21] *Azat Khōsk'* (Paris), on the other hand, in its inaugural issue, expressed concern that 'in all the periodical publications in the Armenian centres abroad, there is a lack of a true satirical paper', a gap which it sought to address.[22]

These explanations for publishing initiatives were, in fact, a disclaimer of the competition in the field and an attempt to be spared the rivalry and hostility that the newcomers knew only too well they would be facing. The editors routinely made references to each other, with very few exceptions, negatively and offensively. *Anahit*'s (Paris) Chobanian, who of all the editors had the closest relationships and ties with the local (French) authorities, was sarcastically called 'National Saviour' and 'Achilles of Armenian journalism'[23] by Yervand Otian (1869–1926) and mocked in almost every issue of *Azat Khōsk'*. Chobanian, in turn, published long serial reflections on the Armenian journals on the pages of *Anahit*, harshly criticizing the editors for the content, and sometimes with possible consequences for the authors. For example, *Banasēr*'s Karapet Basmadjian was called a 'brutal Russia-loather' by Chobanian on the eve of Basmadian's trip to Russia for archaeological research.[24] This was interpreted as Chobanian's intent to have Basmadian's 'entry to Russia hampered'.[25] Occasionally, the critiques would turn into more intentional offences. Through derogatory wordplays, Minas Cheraz (1852–1929) referred to Azat Khōsk' (free speech) as Azat Khozk' (free pigs)[26] and Chobanian referred to prominent author Hagop Oshagan (1883–1948) as Ishagan (donkeyish).[27] Even women's magazine *Artemis*, published in Cairo, and almost exclusively covering women's issues, was not spared the attacks and was referred to as 'worshippers of Mammona', the demon of wealth and greed in the New Testament by *Zhamanak*,[28] and 'plague' by *Azat Khōsk'*.[29]

To attract readership, the editors tried to be as multigenre as possible. Often a journal would start with a limited scope and enlarge to survive the competition and appeal to wider audiences. *Banasēr*, for example, started out as a journal of archaeological studies only to become a literary and academic journal later. *Armenia*'s Portugalian was more practical. His journal started out as dedicated to 'National, Political and Literary' topics but became 'National, Political, Et Cetera'. Printing stories or novels in serial form known as *tertōn* was another tactic to keep readers in suspense and engaged over a certain period of time, a practice also exercised by the editors in Constantinople and Tiflis.

Financial sustainability was not easily achieved, and the coverage of multiple, at times, unrelated themes perhaps also served as a solution to the problem. Unable to sustain itself, *Azat Khōsk'* moved from Paris to Alexandria, a less expensive location, after only eight issues printed in Paris.[30] Some journals, such as *Nor Keank'*, turned into the Hnchak political party's organ in order to have the financial backup of the party. *Banasēr* explained its expansion of thematic coverage with the growing financial needs because,[31] as *Zhamanak* sarcastically noted, 'to deal with Armenian archeology in the 20th century is a caprice of a kind'.[32]

Ironically, despite these contestations, the articles did not differ much in their intent *and* content, so much so that Armenia's Portugalian criticized the like-mindness and the tendency of each 'newcomer' to start from a 'new page' rather than continue the discussion that had already been going on:

> How much paper and ink would have been spared . . . had the beginner writers and activists bothered to read what had been discussed and critiqued before them on the matters so enthusiastically addressed by them as if it were for the first time ever![33]

The hostility and harsh critiques were a response to the editors' heightened perception of their role in the new communicative space where new meanings of nation were to be articulated, and cultural and political identities were to be modified and expanded to allow new forms of belonging. These journals served as a platform for an asynchronous dialogue through which a new collective identity was to emerge. As Pnina Werbner argues drawing on Mikhail Bakhtin's notion of dialogism, diasporic public spaces emerge 'dialogically' through 'dialogical encounters' among diasporic actors occupying different positions in their community.[34] In these encounters, three themes were especially of concern to the editors: negotiation of tradition understood as the past, connection with the host culture and country understood as the present and intergenerational transmission of the collective identity understood as the future.

Negotiating tradition: Clearing up the past

The periodical press in diaspora was the means through which new definitions of the nation were communicated with the readers in a continuous dialogue. According to Ronald Suny, the forging of national identity is an 'open-ended process, never fully complete'.[35] The cornerstone of this identity, as theories of nationalism hold, is the past represented in symbols and tradition. These symbols and traditions may be in continuation with the past,[36] or in Eric Hobsbawm's terms, may be invented[37] because 'nations without a past are a contradiction in terms; what makes the nation is a past'.[38]

The past and traditions of homeland are defining elements of diasporic identity too. According to Tölölyan, diaspora renders itself as 'linked to but different from those among whom it has settled . . . [and as] powerfully linked to, but in some ways different from the people in the homeland'.[39] Diasporic identity is shaped by a 'paradoxical combination of localism and transnationalism', which manifests itself through 'fierce aspiration to achieve economic and social success and the willingness to sacrifice for the community and the homeland'.[40] From this perspective, as illustrated in what follows, references to the past allowed for the manifestation of difference, while the (re-) invention and (re-)examination of tradition paved the way for compatible coexistence with the host culture.

One way of solving the 'different-yet-similar' paradox by the editors was to reconfigure and rearticulate the stories of homeland in dialogue with the local context. The journals covered news reports on Armenians in the historic homeland in the Ottoman, Russian and Persian empires and attached a significant role to the periodical press in acting as a medium among the territorially dispersed co-nationals:

> The Armenian nation, being dispersed all over the world, has a considerable presence in Europe. The Armenian community in Europe, even if away from Motherland by thousands of miles, undoubtedly can benefit from relationships with Armenians elsewhere. One of the major mediums for those relationships is the press which, by spreading information on the ideas, activities, and lifestyles of Armenians, can help build union and solidarity among them.[41]

The geographic scope of this coverage portrayed the dispersion of Armenians around the globe. It rendered the Armenian identity as historically and essentially transnational and the concept of homeland, 'Motherland', as vital for its survival.

Along with lengthy reports of ongoing news, the journals covered long historical articles on Armenian traditions and legends. The editors were unhappy about their readers' knowledge of their own history. It was believed that 'the duty of every Armenian [is to] better know one's Fatherland'.[42] However, the knowledge of the 'Fatherland' was often limited to myths, legends and historical events and was seen as blocking the nation's intellectual and moral progress. According to Chobanian, those 'educated on the legends of Paradise . . . and Hayk[43] look down on all nations of the world and do not sense the need to overcome their own mediocrity'.[44] The imperative was to scrutinize the relevance and workability of the past models of survival for the present. Chobanian did exactly this in an article entitled 'The Heroes' published in 1898 following the massacres of Armenians in the provinces.[45] Dedicating a good part of the article to the heroism of the fifth-century iconic warrior-hero Vardan Mamikonian, much praised in the Armenian historical narratives, Chobanian addressed the failure of Armenians to renew their notions of heroism along with the demands of the time:

> Long live Vardan! Without the feeling of self-devotion a nation is dead. The role of the hero is to shake life and open new paths. Then a long struggle for progress should start. It is the law of history that after revolution and blood-shed, the Hero is replaced by the Sage. Great is the nation that has both types [of heroes].[46]

Without underestimating the weight of Vardan in Armenian history, Chobanian believed that national liberation through bloody encounters meant 'pushing the nation to suicide'[47] and 'chanting patriotism' was to lead to 'straining death'.[48] Like Chobanian, Arpiarian too supported a fresh, more realistic look at liberation:

[O]ne needs to be convinced that a nation cannot be liberated only through bloodshed. That is not the case. . . . At least the possible warranty of liberation is in the understanding of this.[49]

Both Chobanian and Arpiarian implied that the unchanging models of heroism had held Armenians captive to the past. 'People chanting "Fatherland"' was a thing of the past.[50]

The profound limitation of clinging to past models and mechanisms of governance was pointed out and critiqued also during peaceful times. One such model rendered obsolete was the organization of welfare for the less privileged members of the community. Gift-giving, whether through pious endowment funds (*waqf*) or through donations to the Patriarchate or the National Treasury, was a common practice among the Armenians of the Ottoman Empire. Poverty-relief funds, orphanages and schools were founded thanks to the generous donations of the wealthy of the Armenian *millet*.[51] In the new cultural setting, this homeland practice of taking care of the needy was denounced by the editors. While the giver rejoiced at the glorification they received thanks to their benevolence,[52] these acts had 'disastrous outcomes in the mentality of the recipient'.[53] Instead of 'feeling intimidated' by the help, the recipient accepted the gift as if 'they owed it to them . . . and [it] is being returned to them'.[54] Those benefiting from charity were referred to as 'victims of mercifulness' and the act of charity was referred to as 'dated love for the nation'.[55]

'True patriotism' would help make those in need financially self-sufficient.[56] Educating the poor and advancing education were seen as the true expression of love for co-nationals and 'a sign of national unity and sacrifice'.[57] Money had to be directed towards education. Chobanian criticized prominent Russian Armenian oil magnate Alexander Mantashev for purchasing expensive land near the Champs-Élysées avenue in Paris for the construction of a church:[58]

> [Although] a nationally valuable endeavor . . . the church alone will bring in no change in the well-being of the community. A church and a school, side by side – this is the real wholeness. And of the two – all Armenians are convinced today – the most important is the school.[59]

Valuing the school above the church was consistent with the belief of the progressive elements in the Ottoman Empire who saw progress through the establishment of schools and secularization of education. Referring to the religiosity of Armenians in Constantinople, Arpiar Arpiarian wrote:

> Those huge crowds hurrying to the church in Galata, [Constantinople]! I am not criticizing, I am just saying. In their personal life though, an Armenian, who is in the anticipation of the Supernatural cannot have a serious, thoughtful and critical mind in real life.[60]

The discussions cited above meant to explore whether the past was viable for the present. Even though the editors had led similar cultural negotiations in the homeland too, in their new settings the debates pursued the clear goal of moulding a workable, cohesive and united collective identity out of multiple cultural references and contexts. Collective identities, as Tölölyan puts it, look united not because of the continuity with the original culture and tradition but because 'they produce new collective identities and repress the memory of old ones even while they celebrate memory and roots'.[61] The negotiations were to result in this outcome.

Recognition by the host country: Establishing the present

In addition to promoting the emergence of a cohesive collective identity, these debates served another purpose. The negotiations of the past with an advocacy for renewed historic and cultural models marked the writers' own transitions from editor-in-homeland to editor-in-exile status. According to Vahé Oshagan, in the course of the nineteenth and twentieth centuries, Armenian writers often transcended the national context through integration of what was perceived to be a higher culture, most notably French and English. This 'frequent rejection' of tradition in favour of cosmopolitanism 'was reinforced by exile, which plunged Armenians directly into foreign cultures'.[62]

Prior to their exile, the editors viewed Europe as a source of economic, philosophical, intellectual and literary inspiration. Similar to their progressive peers in the Ottoman Empire, identification with Christian Europe and the European culture had served the means through which they dissociated themselves from Ottoman rule and culture, thus rendering themselves more progressive vis-à-vis the 'backward' Muslims. The national identity and the Armenian culture were rendered as compatible with Europe.[63] Adoption of Europe as a cultural model, however, was much criticized by the traditionalists in the homeland, turning these contestations into an intra-community fight between the 'benighted' and the 'enlightened'.[64] In this respect, the exile brought about a sense of liberation from the cultural pressures in the homeland. Arpiar Apriarian eloquently describes this liberation:

> There was a time when the periodical press in Constantinople was mocked for being too pro-European which was believed to have nothing in common with a religious nation like the Armenians. Experience, however, showed that the situation of the Armenian nation is strongly connected with the European politics and interests.[65]

In the periodical press in the diaspora, European was rendered not only as compatible but at times, superior to the Armenian culture. *Patani* considered its readers to be 'lucky enough to live in a civilized country like England'.[66] Arshak Chobanian believed that the foundation of 'our education must always be the French education'.[67] He referred to the 'spirit of West . . . as a new, healthy, beautiful element . . . compatible with Armenians' and saw salvation in Europe for the 'spirit of Armenians which had been buried in the deep darkness of Islam'.[68] Having settled in Paris, for him this 'spirit' was also undoubtedly French: 'Whatever anglophiles or germanophiles say, the Armenian is the French of the Orient, and must remain so . . .'.[69] European superiority was praised also with the understanding that Armenia's 'salvation' had to come from Europe. Analysing Europe's role in the Berlin Congress of 1878 bringing together the Great Powers to decide the fate of the Ottoman subjects, *Nor Keank'* concluded that 'the Armenian nation was not mistaken in counting on the intervention of Europe'.[70] Moreover,

> The salvation of not only Armenians but also other ethnic groups within the Ottoman Empire is only possible through European administration. . . . Even if the most good-willed and smart Sultan comes to power, state reform, that is to say, survival of a state, would still be impossible only under the Islamic people.[71]

The proper assessment and appreciation of Europe's role for Armenians both in the homeland and in the diasporic space, and efforts directed at creating a better, improved image of Armenia and Armenians were on the agendas of the editors. The editors were unhappy about the image of a 'helpless' people that Armenians had earned themselves in seeking Europe's protection from the physical threat they were subjected to in the Ottoman Empire. *Nor Keank'* was concerned that the main sentiment that the Europeans felt for Armenians was 'empathy and pity'.[72] This was an issue of unease for Chobanian too. Like Apriarian, he too believed that 'to enjoy the deep and effective admiration of Europe, we should have presented ourselves to them not with proof for our misery, but power, [we should have] appeared not as wretched but as respectable'.[73] Both authors blamed the Armenians for not having earned themselves more fame like 'the Persian, the Arab and the Jew [who] are known worldwide'.[74] This failure was attributed to the lack of 'a practical vision for the future' of Armenia and Armenians which was contrasted to the 'practicability' that the Jews had demonstrated.[75] All along, the Jews had had a clear vision for progress and had founded 'Zionism as an entity that aims returning the Jews to their ancestral homeland'.[76] A Patriot, for Chobanian, would, then, be 'the person who sees this bitter truth' of failure to make the world know about the Armenian people, and 'tries to find ways for our recognition . . .'.[77] The journals and papers that were founded in Europe, thus, aimed to repair this failure.

Being in a diasporic space required efforts to appear more 'exemplary' as misconduct could damage the collective identity and the good fame that the 'old community' had already earned itself prior to the arrival of the 'new community' after 1890s. *Nor Keank'* printed a long report of crimes committed by the 'newcomers' and asked rhetorically:

> The groups of Armenians, which after the calamities [of 1890s], became dispersed around the globe and came to add to the already-formed communities, what impressions are they starting to make on the locals (*odars*) with their norms and behavior?[78]

Arpiarian called on his readers to submit similar stories, perhaps with the intent of shaming to prevent similar incidents in the future.[79] On the other hand, every occasion of coverage of Armenians in the local press brought forth feelings of national pride in editors. The printing of Arshak Chobanian's speech on the conditions of Armenians in the Ottoman Empire in *Revue de Paris* brought 'unspeakable joy to the community'.[80]

Nor Keank' proudly covered the review of the piano concert of Vahram Svajian emphasizing that 'the audience was entirely composed of Europeans, and this is exactly why Svajian's success is significant and joyful – our co-national is appreciated by the foreigners (*odars*)'.[81] Following the death of Egypt's first prime minister Nubar Pasha in 1899, *Nor Keank'* took pride in his Armenian origin and observed with satisfaction that 'European and especially English papers' covered biographical accounts of him.

Nor Keank' offered lengthy translations of the reviews in its pages, and concluded that Nubar Pasha was 'indeed, an individual of whom any nation could be proud'.[82] These moments of pride were seen as the means through which the Armenians, as a diasporic group and as a cultural collectivity, could break away from the image of the 'helpless' and the 'unknown' and present themselves to the host culture in a positive and admirable light.

Preservation of culture: Ensuring the future

As illustrated in the discussions above, the past with its history, myths and acclaimed cultural values, as well as self-criticism was at the heart of the editors' definitions of Armenian identity in the diasporic space. While negotiations for internal group cohesion and external recognition of the group continued on the pages of the Armenian periodical press, the editors were aware that their efforts would be wasted without an intergenerational transmission of the emerging new meanings and definitions of national identity. Diaspora culture, as has been argued, contains an awareness of the links that unite its members despite dispersion, and ensures that exchanges, whether real or symbolic, continue to occur in the place of dispersion.[83] The editors sought to establish mechanisms of transmission of cultural codes, values and knowledge from one generation to another aimed at the continual existence of the diasporic community.

What were these mechanisms of transmission of culture and how were they selected? Literature on the history of nationalism illustrates that family was central to the nationalist agendas both for colonizing and the colonized states.[84] The family, and especially the women in the family, had dual roles in this discourse. As an institution, the family had to embody the change that was in the making on the one hand and become the transmitters of this change to the younger generations on the other.[85] The Armenian journals published in Constantinople illustrated the centrality of family to the definitions of new nationhood. All major journals of the time period, such as *Masis, Biwzandion*, and *Hayrenik'*, covered extensive articles and studies on the status of the families and the role of women in the families. They advocated the modernization of the family to meet the new images of the nation, whether existing or in the making. Articles calling on emancipation of and new social roles for women were on the front pages of these journals. Curiously, the family as a thematic platform for identity negotiations was abandoned in exile during the period covered by this chapter at least up until the post-genocide period when themes of family became intertwined with, and fundamental to the discourse of survival. Even Arshak Chobanian, who had been instrumental in the early writing career of prominent author and feminist Zabel Yesayan by encouraging her to contribute to his magazine *Tsaghik* in Constantinople,[86] went through years of silence on the topic in Paris. Apparently, dispersed and embedded in a new cultural milieu, family could not have been as easily subjected to social discipline and control as it was in the homeland.

It is evident from the periodicals that for the editors of the journals discussed especially for Chobanian and Arpirarian, students as a demographic group came to replace the institution of family as the intergenerational transmitters of culture. The journals considered students to be the carriers of national ideals and culture and had the responsibility 'to accomplish the huge work of reconstruction and restoration for the devastated, semi-dead nation, and prepare themselves for this [responsibility] with courage and consciousness'.[87] Students were 'the Armenians of tomorrow' and 'the Armenians of tomorrow starts from students'.[88] Any initiative by students aiming to advance education among Armenians was literally seen as a chance of 'rebirth' for the nation.[89]

It is noteworthy that rather than concentrating on their local communities, the editors comfortably made cross-European references. The cross-cultural upward or downward comparisons served the purpose of either encouraging or condemning similar activism in the local community. This was especially true of coverage of the operation of Armenian student unions in European big cities. Events and initiatives of the unions, for example, the founding of reading halls, libraries and public lectures, were covered in the journals with a sense of admiration and pride attached to them. In 1899, the students of Leipzig initiated the establishment of a transnational union – the Union of European Armenian Students. In 1900, the union published the first annual report, leaving the Armenian editors in awe. Inspired by the union's report, Arshak Chobanian published a lengthy article entitled 'Our Students'.[90] Praising the initiative of the students of Leipzig, Chobanian condemningly remarked that 'there are Armenian students in Paris, but there is no [Armenian] studentship'. For him, while acting independently was important to the development of individualism, bonds and organized group actions by students were key to the building and preservation of a collective identity. Both had to be practised:

> Dealing with public problems and collective activity too much is harmful for the individual development of an Armenian student, yet, staying completely in isolation is equally harmful for the formation of a social and national character. Lectures twice a month, a party once a year where the students and the immigrants can meet; a club-library open a few days a week at certain hours . . . which can be frequented by students to hold discussions, get to know each other, have tea together, read the newspapers – all of these are essential needs for the students just as heart is an essential organ for the body.[91]

Chobanian celebrated the fact that the members of the European Armenian Students' Union had no political affiliation: 'These are a group of young Armenians who do not belong to any party and are purely Armenian. *Still*.'[92] Chobanian feared that students were easily manipulated by the political parties and regarded political affiliation as narrowing and limiting for the scope of the students' activism. Moreover, it was harmful for the sense of collectivity that the community so desperately strove to forge. The students were the chance 'to start afresh and engage in collaboration devoid of personal offense and party clashes'.[93]

What was most expected from the Armenian students was 'to prepare themselves *to be capable to act*'[94] with no specifics of the spheres of activity. Such an open-ended definition of the scope of activities was deliberate, and in essence, a call for the acknowledgement of a transnational identity that the Armenian youth carried. Return to the homeland was to be part of this transnational identity. According to Chobanian, 'students must, above everything else, understand that they are destined to return to Russia or Turkey, where they must play individual and social roles'.[95] The students had to have a full awareness of their transnational existence and that 'their duties are much more multidimensional, much more compulsory and much more emotionally stirring than the duties of students of big and happy nations'.[96] Thus, students, as the young, educated politically informed and yet, politically unbound segment of the community, were attributed a unique status. On the one hand, such a status was empowering, since the students were seen as the most potent segment of the community with a 'multidimensional' space for operation and activism. On the other hand, this activism was inherently limited by the students' transnational existence unlike in the case of their peers in 'big and happier' nations.

Conclusion

In the late nineteenth century, the editors of the Armenian journals in Europe utilized the periodical press to define 'Armenianness' in the new diasporic public sphere and construct cultural cohesiveness away from the homeland. They repeatedly negotiated for themselves, and for the community at large, the need to preserve internal group cohesion under the pressures of cultural preservation, on the one hand, and local European cultural accommodation on the other. The periodical press allowed the editors of journals to appropriate and assert a cultural identity that they viewed as 'practical', 'workable' and modern in the new political and cultural setting. Through a public discourse, the editors strove to ensure the intergenerational transmission of new understandings of the diasporic identity by placing the local Armenian students under a microscope. In the process, they projected their authority over the communities and asserted themselves as ambitious and competitive leaders in matters pertaining to the nation and the diaspora. In so doing, the editors did not draw their models from unchanging notions of culture. Rather, their definitions revealed that diasporas, as Vahé Oshagan puts it, are, indeed, 'mobile, ever-changing reality, a kaleidoscope of mentalities and life-styles fashioned partly by the culture of the host countries and partly by national traditions'.[97]

Notes

1 *Anahit* 11–12 (March–April 1909), 211.
2 The term is from Benedict Anderson's landmark book in which he refers to nations as 'imagined communities' because well-designed policies and agendas entail a sense of 'horizontal comradeship' among people who have never met, and yet claim a

common identity. See, *Imagined Communities: Reflections on the Origins and Spread of Nationalism* (London: Verso, 1983).

3   The following titles are discussed: Arshak Chobanian's *Anahit*, Paris: references are to the issues published between 1898 and 1904; Arpiar Apriarian's *Nor Keank'* (New Life), London: references are to the issues published between 1898 and 1902;Yervand Otian's *Azat Khōsk'* (Free Speech), Paris later Alexandria: references are to the issues published between 1901 and 1903; K. Basmadjian's *Banasēr* (Philologist), Paris: references are to the issues published between 1899 and 1903; Mkrtich Portugalian's *Armenia*, Marseille: references are to the issues published between 1885 and 1905; *Patani* (Youngster), London: references are to issues published between 1902 and 1903; S. Hakhumian's *Zhamanak* (Time), Paris: references are to the issues published between 1901 and 1902. Of all editors, only Hakhumian was of Russian Armenian origin. The journals were not consistent in the numbering and publication data. These inconsistencies are reflected in source referencing in this article.

4   The term 'diasporic public sphere' is borrowed from Khachig Tölölyan's article 'Elites and Institutions in the Armenian Transnation', *Diaspora: A Journal of Transnational Studies* 9, no. 1 (2000): 107–36. Tölölyan draws the notion of diasporic public sphere from Jurgen Habermas's popular formulation of 'public sphere'.

5   This scope derives from the frequency of the repeated themes in selected periodicals published between 1895 and 1905 and the discursive analysis of these themes. It is by no means a complete and comprehensive analysis of the complexities of the construction and preservation of the Armenian diasporic identity in Europe.

6   For the reforms, see, Nyazi Berkes, *The Development of Secularism in Turkey* (Montreal: McGill University Press, 1964); Roderic H. Davison, *Reform in the Ottoman Empire, 1856–1876* (Princeton: Princeton University Press, 1963).

7   The word *amira* derived from Arabic word *emir* denoting prince and was a title given by the sultan to wealthy Armenians who were the bankers directly employed by the Ottoman government.

8   See, Vahé Oshagan, 'Cultural and Literary Awakening of Western Armenians, 1789–1915', *Armenian Review* (Autumn 1983): 57–70. For the struggle for the vernacularization of the Armenian language, see Hakob Sirouni, *Constantinople and its Role*, v. IV (Antilias: Tparan Katoghikosutean Hayots Metsi Tann Kilikioy, 1987), 1–90. For the passage to a standardized and vernacular language as an essential phase for nationalist agendas, see, Anderson, *Imagined Communities*; E. Ernest Gellner, *Nations and Nationalism*, 2nd ed. (New York: Cornell University Press, 2008).

9   Benedict Anderson, 'Nationalism, Identity, and the World-in-Motion: On the Logistics of Seriality', in *Cosmopolitics: Thinking and Feeling Beyond the Nation*, ed. Peng Cheah and Bruce Robbins (Minneapolis: University of Minnesota Press, 1998), 117–33; Benedict Anderson, *The Specter of Comparisons: Nationalism, Southeast Asia and the World* (London: Verso, 1998).

10 Michael Billig, *Banal Nationalism* (Los Angeles: Sage Publication, 1995).

11 Oshagan, 'Cultural and Literary Awakening of Western Armenians', 60.

12 Ibid., 70. My emphasis.

13 Khachig Tölölyan, 'Exile Government in The Armenian Polity', *Journal of Political Science* 18, no. 1 (1990): 124–47.

14 Ibid.

15 Tölölyan's term. Ibid.

16 For example, the institution of Patriarchate which despite its weakening power, remained the mediator between the state and the Armenian *millet* up until the fall of the Empire; the National Assembly with its multiple committees that legally and administratively handled matters and problems defined as 'cultural' by the Ottoman state, such as education (with variations across time), marital and property rights, welfare and so on.
17 *Nor Keank'*, 1 January 1898, 1.
18 Khachig Tölölyan, 'Rethinking Diaspora(s): Stateless Power in the Transnational Moment', *Diaspora* 5, no. 1 (1996): 3–35.
19 *Zhamanak*, 1 July 1901.
20 *Hayastan*, 1 November 1888.
21 *Patani*, January 1902.
22 *Azat Khōsk'*, August 1901.
23 *Azat Khōsk'*, October 1901.
24 *Azat Khōsk'*, November 1901.
25 *Banasēr*, v. 3, 1901.
26 *Azat Khōsk'*, October 1901.
27 Arshag Chobanian, *Mer Grakanut'iwnĕ* (Our Literature) (Paris, 1926).
28 *Zhamanak*, January 1902.
29 *Azat Khōsk'*, September 1902.
30 *Azat Khōsk'*, October 1902.
31 *Banasēr*, January 1902.
32 *Zhamanak*, January 1902.
33 *Armenia*, 8 January 1902.
34 Pnina Werbner, *Imagined Diasporas among Manchester Muslims: The Public Performance of Pakistani Transnational Identity Politics* (Oxford: James Currey Pub., 2002).
35 Ronald Suny, *Looking Toward Ararat: Armenia in Modern History* (Bloomington: Indiana University Press, 1993), 11.
36 Anthony D. Smith, *The Ethnic Origins of Nations* (Cambridge: Blackwell Publishers, 1986).
37 Eric J. Hobsbawm, *The Invention of Tradition* (Cambridge: Cambridge University Press, 1983).
38 Eric J. Hobsbawm, 'Ethnicity and Nationalism in Europe Today', *Anthropology Today* VIII, no. 1 (February 1992): 81.
39 Khachig Tölölyan, 'Contemporary Discourse of Diaspora Studies', *Comparative Studies of South Asia, Africa and the Middle East* 27, no. 3 (2007): 650.
40 Khachig Tölölyan, 'Diaspora Studies: Past, Present, and Promise', *IMI Working Papers* 55 (2012): 13.
41 *Armenia*, Issue 1, 1885.
42 *Armenia*, 12 August 1885.
43 Hayk, known as Hayk Nahapet (Patriarch), is the legendary founder of the Armenian nation through a glorious victory against Bel of, presumably, Gutian dynasty of Sumer.
44 *Nor Keank'*, 15 April 1898.
45 For the analysis of the events referred to as Hamidian massacres, see Ronald Grigor Suny, 'The Hamidian Massacres, 1894–1897: Disinterring a Buried History', *Études arméniennes contemporaines* 11 (2018): 125–34.
46 *Nor Keank'*, 15 February 1898.
47 *Nor Keank'*, 1 March 1898.

48 *Nor Keank'*, 1 January 1898. Chobanian refers to the seizure of the European-managed Ottoman Bank by a group of ARF party members in Constantinople on 26 August 1896, to push for the intervention of Europe to stop the massacres in the provinces. The takeover of the Bank resulted in the killings of over 6,000 Armenians in the capital city.
49 *Nor Keank'*, 1 September 1898.
50 *Nor Keank'*, 15 April 1898.
51 For the discussion of organization of philanthropy and charity in the Ottoman Empire, see Hasmik Khalapyan, 'Nationalism and Armenian Women's Movement in the Ottoman Empire, 1875–1914' (PhD diss., Central European University, Budapest, Hungary, 2008), 67–92.
52 Ibid.
53 *Nor Keank'*, 15 March 1900. The journal refers to the shelter for elderly in Paris built through donations where 'healthy men' who could have earned their own leaving and support others, spent nights at the shelter and 'none of who ever felt humiliated, none of who ever blushed when a piece of bread was thrown on them'. Ibid.
54 *Nor Keank'*, 15 March 1900.
55 *Nor Keank'*, 19, 1901.
56 *Nor Keank'*, 15 March 1900.
57 *Anahit*, 1 January 1901.
58 The first stone of the church, St. John the Baptist, was laid in 1902, and the construction was concluded in 1904.
59 *Anahit*, 1 January 1901.
60 *Nor Keank'*, 1 September 1898.
61 Tölölyan, 'Rethinking Diaspora(s): Stateless Power in the Transnational Moment', 28–9.
62 Vahé Oshagan, 'Literature of the Armenian Diaspora', *World Literature Today* Spring 60, no. 2 (1986): 224. My emphasis.
63 This sense of ease with European cultural superiority and compatibility European culture was in contrast to the crisis in cultural identity and contestations in preserving 'the authentic culture' that one can see in postcolonial histories. In struggles for national liberation, anti-colonial nationalists and reformers employed what Partha Chatterjee calls an 'ideological sieve' through which the European ideas were filtered in order to fashion a national identity that was modern, but nonetheless not Western. While accepting the economic superiority of Europe, the reformers demonstrated their resistance and power in the protection of the culture which was believed to be superior to the European culture. In these cultural debates, references were made to the 'authentic' culture which was rendered as fully capable to accept the social and political transformations caused by European economic penetration. See Partha Chatterjee, *The Nation and its Fragments* (Princeton: Princeton University Press, 1993). See also Ania Loomba, *Colonialism, Postcolonialism*, 2nd ed. (London: Routledge, 2005).
64 Khalapyan, 'Nationalism and Armenian Women's Movement in the Ottoman Empire', 31–43.
65 *Nor Keank'*, 1 January 1898.
66 *Patani*, January 1902.
67 *Anahit*, March–April 1900.
68 *Anahit*, November 1898.
69 *Anahit,* March–April 1900.

70　*Nor Keank'*, 15 January 1900.
71　*Nor Keank'*, 15 February 1898.
72　*Nor Keank'*, 1 April 1900.
73　*Nor Keank'*, 15 April 1898.
74　Ibid.
75　*Nor Keank'*, 15 October 1898.
76　Ibid.
77　*Nor Keank'*, 15 April 1898.
78　*Nor Keank'*, 1 April 1900.
79　Ibid.
80　*Nor Keank'*, 15 February 1898.
81　*Nor Keank'*, 15 June 1898.
82　*Nor Keank'*, 1 February 1899.
83　Chantal Bordes-Benayoun and Dominique Schnapper, *Diasporas et Nations* (Paris: Odile Jacob, 2006), 222.
84　Eric Hobsbawm, *The Age of Empire, 1875–1914* (New York: Vintage Books, 1987), 192–218; Kumari Jayawardena, *Feminism and Nationalism in the Third World* (London: Zed Press, 1986); Chatterjee, *The Nation and Its Fragments*.
85　For this discussion in the late Ottoman Armenian context, see Khalapyan, 'Nationalism and Women's Movement in the Ottoman Empire'.
86　Zabel Yessayan, 'Autobiography', Zabel Yessayan Fund, Folder 6, National Museum of Literature and Art, Yerevan, Armenia.
87　*Anahit*, February–March, 1900.
88　Ibid.
89　*Nor Keank'*, 1 February 1900.
90　*Anahit*, February–March, 1900.
91　Ibid.
92　Ibid.
93　Ibid.
94　Ibid. My emphasis.
95　Ibid.
96　Ibid.
97　Oshagan, 'Literature of the Armenian Diaspora', 224.

5

Transnational Politics and Governmental Strategies in the Formative Years of the Post-genocide Armenian Diaspora (1920s–1930s)

Vahe Sahakyan

In 1924, the American Central Committee of the Armenian Revolutionary Federation (ARF) published a volume by Simon Vratsian – a former prime minister of the Republic of Armenia and a prominent leader of the Armenian Revolutionary Federation – that provided detailed justifications as to why the ARF should continue operating among the dispersed Armenian masses following the fall of the short-lived Republic of Armenia (1918–20). Written in response to the pessimistic account of his former comrade, Hovhannes Kajaznuni – the first prime minister of the Republic of Armenia – who concluded that the ARF had no reason to exist after the Sovietization of Armenia, Vratsian stated in this book: 'Bolshevism is not an Armenian regime. . . . Armenian Bolshevism is the continuation and a small part of the Russian bolshevism.'[1] Knowing well that the 'fate of the Soviet government in Armenia' was decided in Moscow and that overthrowing the Bolshevik government would be impossible, Vratsian, nevertheless, believed that the Bolshevik regime in Armenia would not last long and that the ARF, therefore, had a mission to continue among the dispersed Armenian populations:

> We have more than 700,000 Armenians in the colonies – that is one third of the Armenian people. Should we not tell them the truth about the current situation and the role of the Bolsheviks in Armenia?
>
> A dictatorship cannot last very long: it will either explode or turn into another regime, even if it becomes something similar to the tsarist dictatorship. . . . We are convinced the Bolsheviks will disappear in the former way, but we don't deny the possibility of the latter. In either case, the masses should be ready, and therefore, they must know and understand the events happening around them.[2]

Vratsian was not alone in his opposition to Kajaznuni. Several other former leaders of Armenia also denounced Kajaznuni's verdict that the ARF had lost its 'raison d'être'.[3]

Ruben Darbinian, former Minister of Defense; Arshak Jamalian, former Minister of Communications; and Vahan Navasardian, former mayor and ARF MP in the Republic of Armenia, also published responses, all three of them justifying the continuation of the ARF.[4] It should be noted also that their accounts were published outside of Armenia, in places like Boston, Vienna and Cairo, where the ARF had been able to develop an extended network of chapters, clubs and publishing houses and maintain Armenian-language periodicals.[5]

Founded in 1890 in Tiflis in the Russian Transcaucasia, the Armenian Revolutionary Federation had fought for decades for the liberation of Armenians in the Ottoman Empire. In the aftermath of the First World War, the ARF became the dominant political party in the short-lived Republic of Armenia.[6] Following the Sovietization of Armenia in 1920 and the unsuccessful revolt the ARF had led against the Bolshevik regime in Armenia in February–April 1921, most of its leaders escaped the country using the party's transnational network and settled among the dispersed Armenians in various countries.

This chapter examines the governmental efforts of these ARF leaders as they aspired to consolidate the ARF ranks around an anti-Bolshevik discourse and to project their power over the dispersed Armenian populations transnationally in the 1920s and 1930s. The anti-Bolshevik discourse, not widely shared within the ARF in the 1920s, nevertheless, became defining by the end of the 1930s. By then the party's influential periodicals and Central Committees in the diaspora had come under the dominant influence of these former leaders of the Republic of Armenia and their staunch anti-Bolshevik and anti-Soviet rhetoric.

If governmentality implies the ensemble of institutions, procedures, calculations and tactics that allow the exercise of power and regulate the conduct of people, the actions of these ARF leaders in the 1920s and 1930s can be characterized as governmental.[7] If governmentality or the art of 'governing men', in the Foucauldian perception, is also an art of 'conducting, directing, leading, guiding, taking in hand, and manipulating men, an art of monitoring them and urging them on step by step',[8] the actions of the ARF leaders were governmental in this sense as well: these leaders employed the institutional leverages of the party (the administrative network of the party in various countries), the periodicals under their control (such as *Droshak* – the official organ, *Harach* in Paris, *Husaber* in Cairo (Egypt), the *Hayrenik'* daily and the *Hayrenik'* monthly in Boston, Massachusetts and others) and social discipline in order to promote the anti-Bolshevik discourse; maintain and consolidate their ranks; and conduct, direct, lead and guide their followers. The ARF leaders were able to do so transnationally, in the diaspora, while lacking the extensive and coercive apparatus of a state.

Governmentality, according to Foucault, emerges in the modern age when population becomes 'the ultimate end of the government', when 'government has as its purpose not the act of government itself, but the welfare of the population'.[9] State and population were the primary areas of focus in Foucault's lectures on governmentality.[10] But if diasporas are the 'paradigmatic others' of nation-states,[11] and in essence trans-state and transnational formations, how did a diasporic organization, such as the ARF, establish transnational governmentality over populations that were residents and, in some cases, citizens of various states? In what ways were the dispersed populations of

Armenians incorporated into the transnational governmental domains of the ARF? And in what specific ways did the exercise of governmentality become possible over the dispersed masses of Armenian populations transnationally?

Recent studies of governmentality and diasporas do not have readily available answers to these questions. These studies have primarily focused on the governmental policies of a sending state towards its emigrant populations, or, in some cases, on the policies of the exiled elites and institutions.[12] Concerned primarily with issues of 'managing distance' either from the vantage points of a sending-state or expatriate populations, these approaches provide limited analytical frameworks when applied to the cases of diasporas – and the Armenian case, in particular – that predate the emergence of nation-states. Emigration of Armenians from the Ottoman Empire had started earlier in the nineteenth century, intensified in the 1890s and sharply increased as a result of the genocide and deportations during the First World War, predating the foundation of the Republic of Armenia in 1918. By the time the Republic of Armenia became an independent state, Armenian immigrants from the Ottoman Empire had formed diasporic communities in many places across the United States.[13] Many other Armenian Genocide survivors who had settled in Europe or the Middle East, who never went to what became the Republic of Armenia, also formed communities not originating from an Armenian nation-state.

This chapter, therefore, examines the establishment of ARF transnational governmentality in the context of the transnational power struggles with the Bolshevik government of Armenia to explain the governmental strategies that the ARF leaders and their opponents employed to construct governable populations among the dispersed Armenian populations. I look more closely at the events that unfolded primarily in France and the United States for reasons that will become apparent in the later sections. More than focusing on those localities, however, I examine the transnational aspect of the governmental power struggles because the activities of the ARF leaders and their affiliates or the Soviet Armenian officials and their supporters were not limited to certain localities or countries.

Elites and institutions play an important role in the construction of diasporic discourses and cultural production, as Khachig Tölölyan reminds us. By emphasizing the role of diasporic elites and institutions, Tölölyan argues that 'organized, institutionally mobilized and sustained connections, combining material and cultural exchange among diasporic communities as well as between the diaspora and the homeland, are key components of a specifically "diasporic" social formation'.[14] In this chapter, I focus on the governmental efforts of the ARF leaders to explain the particular ways in which they were able to develop, institutionally mobilize and sustain connections among their followers in the diaspora in their opposition to and struggles against the Soviet government of Armenia. By examining the transnational politics and governmental efforts of the Bolshevik regime of Soviet Armenia and the ARF leaders, this chapter argues that their governmental strategies involved three parallel processes which included: (a) the discursive construction of Armenian collective needs,[15] (b) the creation of spaces of socialization, in which the dispersed Armenians and their diaspora-born descendants would be exposed to these discourses on a regular basis and (c) the expansion of their governmental efforts over the organized and established

Armenian spaces in the diaspora. In addition to these three strategies, as the Armenian 'government-in-exile' aspiring to become the 'government of exiles',[16] the ARF leaders also employed social discipline and exclusion to deal with dissenting voices and to consolidate the party's ranks around the anti-Soviet discourse. The success of the anti-Soviet rhetoric of the ARF leaders – as I argue throughout the chapter – owed in significant part to the exclusionary governmental policies of the Soviet Armenian elites and their supporters against the ARF transnationally.

While the focus of this chapter is limited to the governmental efforts and activities of the ARF leaders and the Soviet Armenian elites in the period after the Sovietization of Armenia until the 1930s, it may provide some insights for further comparative studies on diaspora and governmentality. Contrary to many contemporary studies of diaspora and governmentality that either focus on state policies or the policies of an exiled diasporic group, diasporic governmentality, as I show in this chapter, may involve many different actors, both state- and diaspora-based, with incompatible ideologies and governmental aspirations. The transnational activities of these state and non-state actors, as the Armenian case suggests, may end up fractioning diasporic spaces locally, nationally and transnationally, rather than integrating the dispersed populations into a singular governable and governmental space. In the Armenian case, moreover, it should be noted that some other diasporic Armenian institutions and populations – such as the Armenian Catholic or Protestant churches and congregations in various countries – remained institutionally uninvolved in the transnational governmental struggles of the Soviet Armenian elites and the ARF leaders for reasons the analysis of which falls beyond the scope of this chapter. Yet these institutions – one may argue – also developed independent governmental spaces within the Armenian diaspora, with strategies, calculations and tactics that regulated the conduct of their respective congregations. By closely examining the governmental efforts of both state- and diaspora-based actors in the formative years of the post-genocide Armenian diaspora, this chapter, thus, problematizes both state-centric approaches and those focusing on the governmental strategies of a single diasporic institution, suggesting a conception of diaspora that comprises multiple conflicting and overlapping governmental spaces and offers a more nuanced approach to diasporic governmentality.

Discursive construction of Armenian collective needs

In September 1921 the Bolshevik government of Armenia established *Hayastani ōgnut'yan komite* (Committee to Aid Armenia, hereafter the HOK), and launched the policy of gathering the dispersed Armenians in the Soviet Armenian homeland. On 16 September 1921, the HOK issued an appeal to the displaced Armenian populations that read in part:

> *To the Armenian People dispersed in four corners of the world*
>
> The free and independent Armenia is finally rising . . . [t]oday the Committee to Aid Armenia comes to announce to all the Armenians everywhere that peace

has been established in our homeland, and [she is] in peaceful and harmonious relations with her old neighboring peoples. She is now attending to healing her wounds and recovery. The government has mobilized all its resources to help people survive the prevailing and the anticipated famine in particular and to rebuild the destroyed country.

At a time, when the neighboring proletarian peoples have extended their hand of brotherly assistance to the Armenian workers today . . .; when the American people continue their aid with greater effort, is it possible for you to remain indifferent to her sufferings and efforts of construction – you, her migrant exiled brother, you, who are far from the homeland, with all your thoughts harking back to the homeland? It is impossible!

Yes, the HOK realizes full well that you too are divided along various political party affiliations, just as any people in a political and civil society. The HOK itself is made up of people with various political persuasions, but it is fully aware that saving the Armenians from starvation and the rebuilding of the destroyed Armenia stand above all political disagreements. And [it is with such] reasoning [that] they have all rallied around this noble cause, have formed an independent and a non-partisan public body and invite everyone to action. Of like mind is the government of Armenia's Soviet republic, which not only gives full rights to act, but also supports everybody and every organization, all those who want to help – to come in person, witness and supervise their assistance. Now, listen, Armenians, wherever you are – from Europe to America, Egypt to India and anywhere else. Hear the call of the homeland and hasten to help anyway you can, so that you may achieve what you have dreamed of for centuries – a free and prosperous homeland.[17]

Even though the appeal was largely addressed to the scattered Armenian populations whose homes remained outside Soviet Armenia, the appeal promoted Soviet Armenia as the homeland of all the Armenians, and defined their collective needs: to rebuild the 'destroyed' homeland and to 'save the Armenians from starvation'. In order to mobilize the Armenians around these needs and to bring them to the homeland, the Soviet Armenian officials began extending their influence over the dispersed Armenian populations by establishing HOK chapters in various countries.

The rivalry with the ARF and the fear of counter-revolutionary activists, however, made the Bolshevik leaders of Soviet Armenia extremely cautious of including any ARF affiliates in local HOK chapters that began emerging in Europe and the Americas from the mid-1920s. The exclusion of the ARF was introduced into the political agenda by the top officials of Soviet Armenia. Aleksander Miasnikyan, the first chairman of the Council of People's Commissars of Soviet Armenia, wrote in 1924:

There are two [opposing] social poles in Armenian life – communism and nationalism, or Bolshevism and Dashnakism. The former is the new Armenia; the latter is the old Armenia. The former is our revolution, our present and, moreover, our future; the latter is the regressive life of Armenians, the bad past, which is breathing its last.[18]

In the official propaganda of Armenia's Bolshevik leaders the ARF embodied the regressive nationalist bourgeois ideologies. The word 'Dashnak' became increasingly associated with all kinds of subversive anti-communist elements and the servants of imperialist interests.[19] In 1925, Ashot Hovhannisyan, the secretary of the Communist Party of Armenia, instructed:

> The HOK should stop serving as an arena for the consolidation of the 'living forces', national classes and political parties of the [Armenian] people. It should turn into an organ for organizing the masses of the proletariat, which should contribute to the class stratification of the nation by putting an end to the barren mentality of cooperation between incompatible classes.[20]

The exclusion of the ARF affiliates, those suspected of having connections with the ARF and all other 'incompatible classes' of Armenians, turned the HOK into a de-facto political organization.[21] By politicizing the HOK mission, the Bolshevik leadership attempted to extend their governmental efforts beyond the state boundaries. In order to disseminate and shape the needs of the 'masses of proletariat' among Armenian populations abroad, as the HOK leadership envisioned in their discourses, a delegation appointed by the HOK Central Committee spent thirteen months between November 1925 and December 1926 among Armenians in various parts of Europe and the United States, recruiting supporters and establishing local HOK chapters.[22]

In this period HOK chapters began emerging in France, Greece, Egypt, the United States and elsewhere.[23] Within less than a decade, the HOK established about 200 chapters outside the Soviet Union with more than 10,000 members, most of them in France and the United States[24] These local chapters subsequently established cultural unions, libraries, clubs, theatrical and dance groups. The discursive construction of the collective needs of Armenians was accomplished in these emerging spaces of socialization, through individual meetings, public lectures and addresses and also through extensively produced and disseminated propaganda materials about Soviet Armenia. These included bulletins, films, albums, postcards and exhibitions, and also some periodicals, that reached the Armenian communities in various countries, promoting Soviet Armenia as the homeland of all Armenian workers, and inviting them either to immigrate to the homeland or to contribute to its reconstruction.[25]

The extension of 'state power' beyond the boundaries of Soviet Armenia was in sharp conflict with the aspirations of some prominent leaders of the ARF. In their mind, the ARF was the Armenian government-in-exile after the Bolshevik takeover of Armenia. In addition, the party also represented the interests of displaced Armenians in various countries. The Delegation of the Republic of Armenia – led by Avetis Aharonian and comprised solely of the ARF members, which had been active in Paris since 1919 and was one of the signatories of the Treaty of Sévres in 1920 – continued representing Armenian interests in France even after the Sovietization of Armenia. Among other services, the delegation issued passports of the Republic of Armenia to Armenians from their office in Paris. After France established diplomatic relations with the Soviet Union in October 1924, the French government stopped recognizing the Armenian government-in-exile and the passports issued by the Delegation of the Republic of

Armenia. The ARF, however, continued promoting the party as the government-in-exile through the affiliated periodicals and party networks.[26] The active exclusion of the ARF affiliates from the HOK chapters and the lists of potential immigrants to Soviet Armenia prepared a fertile ground on which the anti-Bolshevik rhetoric of some influential ARF leaders would take root in the following years. In sharp contrast to the discourse promoted by the Soviet Armenian leadership and the HOK chapters in various countries, in their discursive construction of the Armenian collective needs, many prominent ARF leaders – Simon Vratsian, Ruben Darbinian, Vahan Navasardian and Arshak Jamalian more importantly – denounced Bolshevism by framing it as alien, anti-Armenian and dictatorial, and aspired to mobilize Armenians in various countries around the goal of restoring the independence of Armenia.

Since the foundation of the party in 1890, the transnational network of the ARF had developed a decentralized administrative system that had allowed the party chapters to exercise considerable flexibility in addressing the local needs of their followers in various countries. Decisions taken at the General Assemblies or the Bureau came down through the party network to the rank-and-file and supporters mainly through the ARF-affiliated periodicals published in various countries and through public events and lectures delivered by ARF leaders.[27] The decentralized administrative network made possible the publication of reports in the ARF-affiliated periodicals at the discretion of their editors, which sometimes acknowledged the achievements of Armenia's Soviet government, even if indirectly, and at times encouraged their readers to contribute to projects in Armenia. On 30 August 1929, the *Hayrenik'* daily in Boston, for example, published a report by a representative of the *Union of Arabkir Armenians of America*, who had visited Soviet Armenia and recorded the progress made in the construction of *New Arabkir* quarter near Yerevan, the capital of Soviet Armenia.[28] On 20 September 1929, the same paper advertised the fundraising campaign in Worcester, Massachusetts, for the construction of *Nubarashēn* quarter again near Yerevan.[29] *Ḥaṛach* in France, whose editor, Shavarsh Missakian, was an ARF Bureau member at the time, would also occasionally highlight various developments in Soviet Armenia. The ARF, thus, represented a dynamic transnational organization with members and supporters living in various countries outside Armenia, with varying expectations from the party's affiliated periodicals. The anti-Soviet rhetoric of its leaders published in these periodicals, therefore, was occasionally accompanied by reports that would portray Soviet Armenia in a positive light.

The period following the ARF Tenth General Assembly (1924–5), however, was the most critical for the decentralized administrative network of the party as it faced challenges both externally – by the activities of the HOK and their various supporters – and internally – by the growing opposition to the anti-Bolshevik discourse promoted by some of its influential leaders. The ARF Bureau, elected at the Tenth General Assembly, was represented by three members of the former Republic of Armenia – Simon Vratsian, Arshak Jamalian and Ruben Ter-Minasian (former Minister of Defense) – and two members from the diaspora – Shavarsh Missakian and Shahan Natalie. Shahan Natalie became the vocal opponent of the extreme anti-Bolshevik orientation, which, in his assessment, influenced his colleagues' thinking on possible cooperation with Turkey.[30] In his book *Turkism from Angora to Baku and Turkish Orientation* published in 1928, Natalie alluded to a decision of the ARF Bureau in 1926 to join efforts with the Promethean movement – an anti-Bolshevik alliance of some expatriate political groups from the Caucasus supported by Poland, Ukraine and Turkey.[31] Natalie's intention was to expose the true nature of the alliance – its 'Turkish orientation' – and to speak against the ARF's possible involvement as the representative of Armenians. 'Let it be decisively clear that the [Armenian Revolutionary] Federation's orientation, at least until the Eleventh General Assembly – and we believe also after it – is not Turkish', he wrote, and continued regretfully: 'It is also clear that unfortunately there are in the Federation leaders, who have Turkish orientation.'[32] Natalie quoted excerpts from various articles penned by Vratsian and Ter-Minasian – two of his Bureau colleagues – and Vahan Navasardian and Ruben Darbinian, who entertained the ideas of reconciliation with Turkey, as evidence of their 'Turkish orientation'. Vahan Navasardian at the time served as the editor of *Husaber* in Cairo, and Ruben Darbinian served as the editor of the *Hayrenik'* daily and *Hayrenik'* monthly in Boston.[33] Both were also quite influential in their local ARF Central Committees. Russian dominance was also unacceptable for Natalie. However, in his mind, it was the lesser evil for the Armenians compared to the Turkish alternative. 'If the purpose of the Caucasian People's Union is to change masters, replacing Russians with Turks', he concluded, 'our position must also be clear – *we are against changing masters*'.[34]

Natalie's discourse, however, was suppressed, and apparently he resigned from the ARF Bureau before the expiration of his term.[35] The ARF Eleventh General Assembly, held in Paris in March–May 1929, re-elected Simon Vratsian, Ruben Ter-Minasian, Arshak Jamalian and Shavarsh Missakian in the Bureau, alongside two other new members – Abraham Gyulkhandanian and Vahan Papazian – both also former officials in the Republic of Armenia. Two years later, in March 1931, *Droshak*, the official organ of the ARF, announced the expulsion of Shahan Natalie from the ARF ranks. Natalie was just another name in the list of the expelled individuals between 1928 and 1932, the time around the ARF Eleventh and Twelfth General Assemblies. In this period *Droshak* published twenty-three names of expelled individuals, mostly from among the party ranks in France, Greece and Egypt. These included, among others, five members of the ARF Western European Central Committee, expelled in September 1932.[36] Most of these expulsions were happening because of the opposition of some prominent members of the party to the anti-Soviet discourse promoted by former leaders of the Republic of Armenia among the ranks. The ousted five members of the Western European Central Committee launched a new periodical in Paris – *Martkots'* (Bastion) – claiming to be the new organ of the ARF. They believed the real mission of the ARF should have been the struggle against Turkey – the country which refused to take responsibility for destroying the Armenian populations in their native lands during the First World War and for being the real reason why scores of surviving Armenian refugees had to start a new life in other countries. Shahan Natalie also joined the *Martkots'* movement, continuing the harsh criticism of his former Bureau colleagues in the pages of *Martkots'*. The movement was short-lived and declined after the ARF Twelfth General Assembly (held in Paris in 1933), to which neither Natalie nor the former members of the Western European Central Committee were invited.[37]

In their governmental efforts, the former leaders of the Republic of Armenia employed social discipline and the leverages of the ARF Bureau to silence internal criticism and deal with the dissenting voices by expelling many individuals. The exercise of social discipline and expulsions contributed to the internal consolidation of the ARF ranks around an anti-Bolshevik discourse centred on the idea of restoring Armenia's independence. With the suppression of internal criticism, the opposition to the Bolshevik regime in Armenia and restoring Armenia's independence became consistently emerging themes in the ARF-affiliated periodicals in various countries. Editorials and analytical articles by Ruben Darbinian in *Hayrenik'*, Vahan Navasardian in *Husaber*, Shavarsh Missakian in *Ḥaṛach*, Simon Vratsian, Arshak Jamalian and other influential leaders continued shaping the collective needs of Armenians persistently around a political orientation that emphasized a free and independent Armenia. These themes received more prominent attention in the editorials and articles, especially in the issues dedicated to Armenia's independence day, celebrated by the ARF-affiliated circles on 28 May. The 'free and independent Armenia' and the associated tricolour flag of the Republic became increasingly more important in the ARF discourse. An editorial in *Hayrenik'* on 30 May 1929, most likely by Ruben Darbinian, illustrates this point very well: 'The Armenian tricolor was and still is the *national or state flag of the free and independent Armenia*, because an alien political regime that overthrew Armenia as a free and independent country and that enslaved it again could not and cannot impose its flag on the Armenian people as a national or state flag.'[38]

The consolidation of the ARF ranks around an anti-Bolshevik discourse followed the Twelfth General Assembly, held in February–March 1933, that issued a statement addressed to Armenians in various countries calling them to support the 'the only organized power' among Armenians:

> The ARF continues to remain united and of one mind, the only organized power of our scattered people. Let's unconditionally support the ARF, always keeping in mind that whatever we give to the ARF, we give to the homeland and the Armenian people.... Wherever we are, whether in Armenia or beyond its borders, in the places of torture in Siberia or on foreign shores, let's remain mindful of the high mission that history has bestowed on our party. Let's unite around its revolutionary flag that has endured many storms, let's hold it tightly, close our ranks firmly, remaining confident that the time of freedom is not far away.[39]

The ARF, thereby, constructed an image of itself as a party that represented the interests of all Armenians, whether in Armenia, exiled in Siberia or scattered outside Armenia. If the HOK and the Bolshevik propaganda first and foremost were addressed to the Armenian working class, the ARF message was more inclusive: it promoted an all-Armenian nationalist agenda, addressed to everyone, regardless of social class.

By the end of the 1920s the HOK and the ARF emerged as rival organizations in France and the United States, in particular, aspiring to rally the Armenian masses around their conflicting ideologies. In their discursive construction of Armenian collective needs, the HOK continued to promote Soviet Armenia as the homeland of Armenian workers and encouraged immigration to Armenia, excluding the ARF and its supporters in these calls. The ARF, by contrast, constructed transnational propaganda and activism around the goal of restoring Armenia's independence and aspired to organize dispersed and displaced Armenians for a future move to Armenia. In their attempts, they both sought to expand their governmental domains not only by creating new chapters and spaces of socialization but also by attempting to bring under their control established Armenian organizations in various localities.

Expansion of the HOK and ARF governmental domains

In contrast to the HOK, the ARF had been involved in Armenian political affairs transnationally for many decades and had established an extended network of chapters and affiliate organizations. In transnational politics, the ARF had also developed some complicated relations with other Armenian political parties – the Social-Democratic Hunchakian Party and the Armenian Democratic Liberal (Ramkavar) Party. This section discusses in the first part the orientations that the Armenian political parties adopted towards Soviet Armenia in order to explain how these orientations influenced the establishment and expansion of the HOK chapters. I then discuss the governmental efforts of the HOK and ARF leaders in France and the United States – countries where most of the HOK chapters emerged in the 1920s and 1930s – in order to describe the strategies they both employed and also to explain why the mutual exclusion and struggles became more intense, especially in the United States.

Established in 1887 in Geneva, the Social-Democratic Hunchakian Party (SDHP) adopted socialism as the party's distant goal to be pursued after the immediate goal of Armenia's independence was achieved. The SDHP, therefore, welcomed the Sovietization of Armenia as the realization of their immediate and distant goals. A few months after the Sovietization of Armenia, on 23 February 1921, the party's official organ *Eritasard Hayastan* wrote:

> The absolute safety of the Armenians is guaranteed thanks to the Sovietization of Armenia. The Armenian workers should no longer think that they don't have a homeland, they don't have a future. They have it all. Soviet Armenia is the homeland, the home, the future.[40]

Following the Sovietization of Armenia many Hunchakians, therefore, considered the mission of the party completed and joined the local Communist parties and workers' movements. SDHP members also made a significant contribution to the organization of the HOK chapters in various countries by joining them and supporting their activities.[41]

The orientation towards Soviet Armenia for the Armenian Democratic (Ramkavar) Liberal party (ADL) was a complicated matter of negotiations.[42] The liberal-democratic platform of the ADL placed them in opposition to the socialist ideology of the Bolsheviks. The ADL's orientation towards Soviet Armenia, however, developed in the context of their strained relations with the ARF. Many influential leaders of the ADL had been involved in the Armenian National Delegation that represented Armenian interests in Europe since before the foundation of the Republic of Armenia.[43] The relations between the Armenian National Delegation and the ARF leadership of the Republic of Armenia had deteriorated after May 1919, when the ARF leaders proclaimed themselves to be the government of the 'United Armenia' and sent a separate delegation to represent the Armenian interests in the Paris Peace Conference in 1919–20.[44] The presence of two Armenian political representations – the Armenian National Delegation and the Delegation of the Republic – influenced the adversarial relationships between their supporters transnationally, prior to the Sovietization of Armenia. For many ADL leaders, the Bolsheviks, unlike the ARF, had brought peace in the region and secured the physical existence of Armenia and the Armenians. ADL's support of the Bolshevik regime in Armenia, therefore, grew stronger after the Treaty of Lausanne in 1923 that put an end to the Armenian question.[45] The Second World Congress of the ADL, convened in Paris in January–February 1924, defined the party's orientation towards the ARF as follows: 'Any possible general collaboration [with the ARF] is conditioned on the positive orientation it will adopt towards the current government of Armenia and to the reconstruction of Armenia.'[46] Unlike the SDHP, however, while supporting the HOK in various countries, the ADL preserved independent chapters, periodicals and governmental spheres of influence that only partially overlapped with the emerging HOK governmental domains.

Despite the support the Bolshevik government of Armenia and the HOK chapters received from the SDHP and the ADL, their collaboration was tense and at times even conflictual. In the eyes of the Bolsheviks, the SDHP was not as influential as it used to be in the past, and the ADL was another 'bourgeois' party not to be fully trusted.[47] Both were seen as 'friendly' organizations, but the Bolshevik leaders of Armenia sought to expand their governmental domains mainly through the expansion of the HOK and the establishment of HOK-affiliated spaces of socialization. The HOK activists in various countries, therefore, often targeted the Armenian population and more organized segments of the community that had been less involved in Armenian politics.

Among non-political Armenian organizations, the Armenian General Benevolent Union (AGBU) was the largest philanthropic institution, established in Cairo, Egypt, in 1906 by Boghos Nubar Pasha.[48] Boghos Nubar was also the former leader of the Armenian National Delegation. Many of the AGBU influential leaders – some also members of the ADL – had developed complicated relations with the ARF. Following the Sovietization of Armenia, the AGBU developed a friendly attitude towards Soviet Armenia and began supporting construction projects and contributing to the organization of Armenian immigration to Soviet Armenia. The AGBU also continued supporting Armenian orphans and genocide survivors in Syria and Lebanon, splitting its financial and organizational resources between Soviet Armenia and the needs of the most desperate masses of Armenians in the Middle East. For this reason, the AGBU relations with the HOK and the Soviet Armenian leadership developed in a complicated and at times even antagonistic fashion.

Karen Mikayelyan – one of the members of the HOK delegation in France and the United States in 1925–6 – implied in a book published a few years after his return to Soviet Armenia that the funds raised by the AGBU in the name of Armenia were not entirely spent on Armenia's needs.⁴⁹ Aghasi Khanjian, the first secretary of the Communist Party of Armenia, was harsher in his criticism in October 1931 when he accused the AGBU leadership of collaborating with the 'Anglo-French imperialist circles' and sponsoring the ARF in their attempts to create a 'national home' (*azgayin ōjakh*) in Syria for an 'anti-Soviet imperialist intervention'.⁵⁰ The accusations and the unsuccessful attempt of the Soviet Armenian elites to extend their governmental control over the AGBU and to regulate the conduct of the AGBU leaders resulted in the resignation of the AGBU president Calouste Gulbenkian – the successor of Boghos Nubar – and the subsequent dissolution of the AGBU chapters in Soviet Armenia.⁵¹

Transnational Armenian politics, however, had not extended throughout the Armenian diasporic space. Many established Armenian communities in the United States or the emerging Armenian neighbourhoods and communal spaces in Europe or the Middle East remained disengaged from politics. As the Bolshevik government of Armenia aspired to expand their governmental influence through the HOK chapters among the dispersed Armenian workers, and as the former leaders of the ARF worked to organize the scattered Armenian populations and become the 'government of exiles', they faced different challenges in various countries. In France, for example, the HOK and the ARF competed more or less on equal grounds in order to attract Armenian immigrants and genocide survivors, whose numbers had significantly increased after 1922. The 'brutal proletarization' that had been turning Armenian peasants into hard labourers created more fertile ground for the HOK propaganda targeting the Armenian workers. Armenian workers had not been granted citizenship to France or any other country following the Treaty of Lausanne and held temporary passports named after Fridtjof Nansen – the high commissioner of the Refugees in the League of Nations (1921–30). The *Nansen* passports allowed the Armenians to stay and work in France, but as foreigners.⁵² The HOK was apparently more successful in operating in this context, among those Armenians who could not become French citizens and had nowhere to return. The relative proximity of France to Soviet Armenia, the occasional visits of the HOK Central Committee members to France and the establishment of the HOK official organ in Paris in 1933 provided extra impetus to the HOK activities in France. In April 1933, the HOK Fourth Regional Congress in Paris reported of fifty-one chapters operating in France with 1,756 members.⁵³

The ARF, by contrast, was less successful in France. In a series of instalments published in the *Hayrenikʻ* daily between 3 and 7 July 1928, Hay Gnduni expressed a harsh criticism of Simon Vratsian's views in general, which also included a passing mention of the lack of strong organization in France, with the exception of Marseille.⁵⁴ The expulsion of many comrades between 1928 and 1932, including Hay Gnduni and the five members of the France-based Western European Central Committee, further weakened the ARF in France. While many local ARF chapters and *Ḥaṛach* continued, the ARF Bureau subsequently moved from France to Cairo, in the mid-1930s.

In the United States, by contrast, the ARF remained more organized and strong and provided an extra challenge for the emerging HOK chapters. The ARF had developed a stronger presence among various Armenian communities since the late 1890s, while the HOK chapters began emerging only in the mid-1920s. The anti-Bolshevik propaganda of the ARF leaders found many supporters among the established Armenian communities in America – compatriotic societies, social clubs, women's groups, youth and athletic societies and other places of Armenian socialization. This support was in part gained during the period when the ARF was the government of the Republic of Armenia, when the Republic's symbolism had become integrated into the social and communal life of various segments of the established Armenian-American communities. For many years after the fall of the Republic of Armenia, the tricolour flag of Armenia alongside the ARF banner would often be on display in social clubs and during various community events. The Republic's national anthem would be performed at the celebrations of Armenia's independence day on 28 May, or at various other occasions and public events sponsored by the ARF or related organizations. The ARF-affiliated organizations, such as the Armenian Relief Corps[55] or the Armenian General Athletic Union,[56] disseminated the ARF message and helped in establishing the Republic's symbolism among Armenian Americans. The ARF's three influential periodicals, the *Hairenik'* daily (established in 1899) and the *Hairenik'* monthly (established in 1922) in Boston, and the *Asbarēz* weekly in Fresno (established in 1908), also played their part. The ARF used its extensive network of periodicals, chapters, social clubs and affiliate organizations to reach the dispersed Armenian populations throughout the United States.

The Sovietization of Armenia influenced this state of affairs in the Armenian-American communities. Benefiting from the friendly attitude of the ADL, the AGBU and other organizations towards Soviet Armenia, the emerging HOK chapters were successful in expanding their governmental influence over some Armenian-American hometown societies.[57] Comprised of Armenian immigrants originating from the same village, town or region in the Ottoman Empire, these societies had been capable of raising significant funds from among their compatriots to support various educational and charitable projects in their native villages or towns before the First World War. The genocide and displacement of their compatriots during and after the First World War had a significant impact on these societies in the United States as well. Some declined, while others redefined their missions to provide support to their surviving countrymen, women and orphans in the Middle East, or to engage in construction projects for their compatriots in Soviet Armenia. The conflicting perspectives and collective needs as they were constructed in the incompatible discourses promoted by the leaders of Soviet Armenia and the ARF influenced the decision of many such societies.

Grigor Vardanyan – a member of the HOK delegation who spent a few years abroad establishing chapters in the United States, France and elsewhere – reported that there were about 130 compatriotic societies in America in 1928. He commended the fruitful collaboration with some of them, singling out the Compatriotic Unions of Arabkir (New York) and Malatia (New York), who sponsored the construction of New Arabkir (1925) and New Malatia (1927) quarters near Yerevan. But he also regretfully noted that many other societies became 'tools in the hands of various political parties'.[58] As the HOK continued efforts to expand its governmental domains over the Armenian hometown societies, it faced challenges by the influential presence of the ARF. A correspondent from New York reported to the HOK official organ in Paris in March 1933:

We need to understand that the nationalist elements, led by the ARF are working at the moment not only to prevent new compatriotic societies from embarking on construction [projects] in Soviet Armenia, but also to openly fight, that those compatriotic societies, who have been involved in the construction [projects] stop all their assistance to the New Townships [in Soviet Armenia] and contribute [instead] to the educational work [among the Armenians] abroad.[59]

The dilemma of whether the funds and resources should be allocated to the construction of villages and quarters in Soviet Armenia or to the support of the surviving compatriots in the Middle East, exacerbated by the presence of members within compatriotic societies sympathetic to Soviet Armenia or with the ARF, often caused internal conflicts and schisms. *Sebastio verashinakan miut'iwn* (Sebastia Reconstruction Union) in New York, for example, after several years of internal disputes, disagreements and confrontations, eventually split. The ARF-sympathetic faction accused its opponents of being under the influence of the HOK and the Bolsheviks in their subversive attempt to destroy their union.[60] Their opponents accused the ARF-sympathetic circle of its reluctance to support the construction projects in Soviet Armenia.[61] By 1936, *Hama-sebastats'iakan shinarar miut'iwn* (Pan-Sebastian Construction Union) and *Sebastats'ineru hayrenakts'akan miut'iwn* (Sebastian's Compatriotic Union) had emerged as separate societies, sympathetic to the incompatible discourses and causes promoted by the HOK and the ARF.[62]

Expanding and popularizing the HOK among the diaspora Armenian workers became a matter of utmost priority in the 1930s, especially in the United States, where an American-born generation was coming of age, with English as their primary language of communication. The HOK competed with local chapters of the ARF and the ADL to reach the American-born generations and influence their conduct accordingly. Patrik Selian – one of the participants of the Sixth HOK Regional Congress of the American chapters in 1932 – underlined the popularization of the HOK among the Armenian workers as one of the 'most neglected issues'.[63] He praised the creation of twelve HOK youth chapters between 1932 and 1933, but these were apparently not enough, as he explained:

> The ARF, in particular, uses the Armenian General Athletic Union in order to bring the youth under its influence. The Ramkavars [ADL] publish *The Armenian Mirror* newspaper in the English language in order to reach out to the new generation of Armenian-Americans. The Dashnaks publish English language columns every day in their newspaper in order to poison the new generation with their anti-Soviet attacks.[64]

In addition to these, both the ADL and the ARF started youth organizations the same year – the ADL Junior League and the ARF youth group *Ts'eghakrōn* respectively.[65]

The governmental aspirations of the Soviet Armenian leadership and the HOK in the United States, thus, often required not only recruiting from among the 'friendly' groups in the Armenian-American diaspora but also confronting the ARF and challenging its longer-established presence in many communal and organizational spaces. The political struggles between the HOK and the ARF that began involving Armenian hometown societies, and the Armenian-American youth, expanded into other spheres of community life, eventually spreading into the parishes of the Armenian Apostolic Church.

Incompatible governmental efforts and the schism of the Armenian Church in America

The extensive network of parishes the Armenian Church in America had developed since the 1890s – stretching from New England, New York, to Midwest and California – had no parallel in France or any other country in Europe, where most Armenian churches emerged in the 1920s and 1930s with the influx of the Armenian Genocide survivors.[66] The Diocese of the Armenian Church in America, established in 1898 in Worcester, Massachusetts, integrated parishes in America into an administrative network, regulating the religious and communal affairs of the Apostolic Armenian community. The by-laws of the diocese allowed the election of lay persons in local parish councils of Armenian churches, members of which could be elected to participate in the Diocesan Assembly – the highest representative body of the Apostolic Armenian community in America. Usually convened every four years, among other rights, the Diocesan Assembly could elect or depose the primate of the Armenian Church of America.[67]

Several months before the Sovietization of Armenia, in July 1920, Bishop Tirayr Ter-Hovhannisian was elected primate at the Diocesan Assembly.[68] After his arrival to America from Ejmiatsin – the spiritual centre of the Armenian Church – Ter-Hovhannisian developed cordial relations with local chapters of the ARF. Even after the Sovietization of Armenia he continued permitting the celebrations of Armenia's independence day in the Armenian Church premises on 28 May and presided over many ARF-sponsored events outside the church. The Armenian clergy under his leadership also participated in community events, often held at church premises. The ARF benefited from the cordial relations with the primate as well, as its members remained represented in the parish councils and the Diocesan Assembly, and as the party used the community spaces provided by Armenian Apostolic parishes to reach wider audiences for the dissemination of the anti-Bolshevik discourse centred on the 'free and independent' Armenia. The Sovietization of Armenia, however, began having a significant impact on the established relations between the ARF and the primate.

As the Soviet government increased pressure on the Catholicosate of Ejmiatsin in Armenia – the supreme centre of the Armenian Apostolic Church – aspiring to bring the church and its transnational network under their governmental control, the relations between the Catholicosate and the Armenian Church primates outside of Armenia became strained. Pressured by Ejmiatsin, Ter-Hovhannesian resigned in September 1928.[69] In the summer of 1929, all Armenian Church primates received a circular from the Supreme Spiritual Council of the Holy See of Ejmiatsin that read in part:

Considering that there are partisans, particularly Tashnags, who are trying to turn the Church and Church assemblies into forums for political propaganda and making anti-Soviet speeches there ... and that our representatives, the clergy, have not prohibited the delivery of such speeches;

Also considering that there are individuals and groups who have intentionally spread, and are spreading, wicked slanders about Ejmiatsin for the sake of their personal or organizational monetary interests;

The Holy See hereby declares that [the Church] is far from adhering to any party nor will it protect the interest of any faction but ... she states her loyalty and friendship towards the Soviet regime and advises all the Diocesan Primates as well as the religious jurisdictions and the clergy subject to them to be likewise loyal and friendly towards the Soviet regime. Having as a guide the principle of division of church and state, they are asked not to allow speeches against the state or to permit the exploitation of Church functions and institutions for anti-Soviet propaganda. The Armenian faithful must be advised to follow the same course. It should be made known that the opposite course is and will hereafter be disapproved and subject to censure.[70]

The circular explicitly targeted the ARF and used the anti-ARF language of the Soviet leaders of Armenia. The *Hayrenik'* daily published the text of the circular on 16 August 1929, with several editorials and articles condemning the circular in the following issues. The ARF criticism of the circular did not deny the fact that celebrations of Armenia's independence day were held at various Armenian churches, nor that the Armenian clergy participated and often presided over such celebrations. Instead the ARF refused to accept that the celebration of Armenia's independence day was political propaganda, accusing the secret police of Soviet Armenia of coercing the Supreme Council to disseminate such a circular. The editorial in the *Hayrenik'* daily on 18 August 1929 speculated:

The Spiritual Council understood perfectly well that the celebration of the independence, which was the result of the exceptional struggle of the Armenian people, was far from being political propaganda. ... [They] knew that it was not a 'Dashnak' celebration, but involved the entire Armenian people. [They] knew that erecting a tricolor is a precious sanctity for all classes of the Armenian people without any discrimination, that also includes the church and the clergy of the same people. ... It is clear, therefore, that the Cheka[71] forced them to issue such a circular.[72]

In this period, the ARF even entertained the idea of transferring the Catholicos, the Supreme Spiritual Council and the Holy See out of Soviet Armenia.[73]

The implementation of the demands expressed in the circular remained at the discretion of the Armenian Church primates and local priests, creating further tensions. The Diocesan Assembly of 1931 elected Archbishop Leon Tourian (Ghewond Durean) as primate of the Diocese of the Armenian Church in America. Primate

Tourian began implementing the instructions of the Supreme Council, prohibiting any clergymen under his jurisdiction to participate in any celebration or commemoration event outside the church.[74] These new policies affected all the clergymen, even though some remained sympathetic with the ARF. Tensions between the primate and the ARF escalated further during and after the *Century of Progress International Exposition* World Fair in Chicago in July 1933. The primate was invited to preside over the Armenian Day festivities and give an opening address. At the sight of the Armenian tricolour flag of the Republic of Armenia, Tourian refused to take the stage until the flag was removed. The Armenian tricolour flag, which had become the political symbol of the ARF-propagated 'free and independent' Armenia, was rejected for the same reason by the HOK and the supporters of Soviet Armenia, including the ADL, SDHP and many others who wanted to remain politically neutral. The removal of the Armenian tricolour flag, therefore, led to escalating tensions, fistfights, police intervention and arrests. Following the incident, the ARF opposition to the primate grew increasingly more personal and intolerant. The *Hayrenik* daily called the primate an 'imposer, fraud and traitor' and urged the people to 'teach him a lesson'.[75] On 12 July 1933, an editorial, entitled 'An Undeserving Primate', demanded his impeachment:

> The American-Armenians cannot and should no longer tolerate an undeserving clergyman as Primate, who does not have respect for the greatest sanctities of his own flock, who constantly insults the precious feelings of his people publicly, who does not hesitate to discredit the Armenian people and the Armenian church in the presence of foreigners, making the honor and name of Armenians an object of mocking and contempt . . .
>
> By his disgusting conduct in Chicago, Archbishop Tourian sentenced himself to *moral death*. The Armenian-Americans have no recourse but to banish such a person from his exalted office. The Armenian-American communities must consider it their national responsibility to *morally boycott* this unworthy clergyman and must resort to all legal means to depose him.[76]

The forthcoming Diocesan Assembly could provide the 'legal means' to depose the primate. Scheduled to be held at the St. Illuminator Armenian Apostolic Church in New York on 2 September 1933, the assembly attracted a huge crowd, mostly ARF supporters, who demanded the deposition of the primate. To avoid the tense atmosphere at the St. Illuminator Armenian Church, Primate Tourian, who was absent reportedly because of illness, instructed the delegates to change the location of the assembly to Hotel Martinique. The ARF-sympathetic delegates refused to follow Tourian's instructions and continued the assembly at the St. Illuminator Armenian Apostolic Church. Their opponents – the supporters of the primate – attended the parallel assembly convened at Hotel Martinique. Both assemblies sent minutes to the Catholicosate of Ejmiatsin for approval. As expected, Ejmiatsin approved the minutes submitted by the supporters of Primate Tourian and considered the other assembly illegitimate and unconstitutional. The Catholicos then instructed Primate Tourian to 'summon a new Assembly at the proper time to meet under his presidency, and give the opportunity to the delegates to gather and come to an accord'.[77] The primate, however, did not have a chance to convene another Diocesan Assembly. On 24 December 1933, as he was proceeding to the altar through the single aisle in the centre of the Holy Cross Church in uptown Manhattan on Christmas Eve, six men surrounded him between the fifth and sixth pews and stabbed him to death with a butcher's knife. Nine ARF members were consequently convicted and two of them received life sentences, while the party denied any involvement and responsibility.[78]

The assassination of the primate sent shockwaves throughout the Armenian communities in the United States and beyond. Major American newspapers also made headlines of this incident. A front-page column in *The New York Times* announced in bold heading: 'ARCHBISHOP ASSASSINATED IN PROCESSION TO ALTAR; LAID TO OLD-WORLD FEUD.' The lengthy article further described the assassination and the arrests made afterwards, explained the tensions between the primate and the 'anti-Soviet faction', and provided the names of some arrested individuals without making any explicit reference to the ARF.[79] *The Washington Post* wrote on 28 December 1933: 'Tashnak – Armenian revolutionary society – was defended today by counsel for two of five members held in connection with the slaying of Archbishop Leon Tourian, head of the Armenian church in Western Hemisphere.'[80] While the accusations mounted, the ARF blamed the incident on Tourian's close connections with the Soviets and his supporters, as the editorial of the *Hayrenik'* daily of 28 December, which was published also in the English translation on 29 December, explained:

> [A]ll those who, consciously or unconsciously, became tools in the hands of the Soviet Cheka and tried to use the Armenian Church as a weapon to spread the propaganda of the Soviets and to fight those Armenians who staunchly stand for the freedom of Armenia, cannot escape the moral responsibility of the terrible event of last Sunday.[81]

As the investigation and arrests continued, tensions and hostilities grew within Armenian-American public spaces. Members, affiliates or sympathizers of the ARF were stigmatized and labelled as 'assassins' and 'priest killers'. Businesses owned by ARF sympathizers and members were boycotted, employees sympathetic to the ARF were fired, families broke apart, ARF affiliates were no longer welcome in Armenian churches across the country that remained loyal to the diocese and the Catholicosate in Ejmiatsin.[82] Correspondingly, several parishes of the Armenian Apostolic Church with dominant ARF member and affiliate presence in parish councils, supported by the ARF-sympathetic clergymen, were placed under the jurisdiction of a Central Executive Committee, formed during the Diocesan Assembly at the St. Illuminator Armenian Apostolic Church in September 1933. The Central Executive Committee and churches under its jurisdiction denied the authority of the primate and the Catholicosate of Ejmiatsin, forming an independent administrative system of the Armenian Apostolic Church.[83] The assassination of the primate made the disagreements and conflict that had originated in the controversial Diocesan Assembly of September 1933 irreconcilable, thereby becoming the catalyst of the schism within the Armenian Apostolic Church in the United States.

The governmental efforts of the Soviet leaders of Armenia to control the conduct of the Armenian clergy transnationally and the attempts of the ARF affiliates to maintain their influential presence within the Armenian Church Diocese resulted in the schism of the Armenian Church in America and in the emergence of an independent Armenian church administration alongside the Diocese.[84] The schism of the Armenian Church in America produced in the following years self-regulating and self-disciplined mutually exclusive communities of Armenian Americans. Parallel parishes began emerging within the same localities, creating two Armenian Apostolic churches in proximity, with separate congregations and church events, attended by rival factions of the supporters of the ARF and their opponents, who remained loyal to the diocese and the Catholicosate of Ejmiatsin. The church schism provided another institutional framework reinforcing the incompatible and independent spaces of Armenian socialization in the United States, which would produce American-born generations of Armenians with firmly established antagonistic ideological orientations, either centred on the Soviet Armenian homeland or the 'free and independent' Armenia.

Conclusion

This chapter explored the transnational politics and governmental strategies of the Armenian political elites among the displaced Armenian populations in the 1920s and 1930s to argue that these efforts, aspiring to create self-disciplined diasporic populations, resulted instead in the emergence of independent and mutually exclusive governmental domains, fragmenting the established and establishing Armenian diasporic communities. In pursuing their governmental efforts, both the ARF leaders of the former Republic of Armenia and the Bolshevik leaders of Soviet Armenia followed similar strategies and tactics, which included the discursive construction of Armenian collective needs centred on the incompatible ideologies of 'free and independent' Armenia and supporting the Soviet Armenian homeland; the establishment of spaces of socialization in which these incompatible discourses would be disseminated and reproduced; and the expansion of the spheres of influence – governmental domains – to incorporate the existing and emerging Armenian diasporic institutional, organizational and communal spaces. What began as a transnational political struggle between two incompatible ideologies and governmental efforts of the former and current Armenian governments, as I argued throughout this chapter, expanded into the social, educational and communal affairs of the dispersed Armenian populations, eventually involving the network of the Armenian Church in America.

In exploring the development of the incompatible governmental domains, this chapter also addressed the dynamic processes within the transnational network of the ARF, and between the HOK and its various supporters in the 1920s and 1930s. By discussing the disagreements and divergences among the ARF leaders within a decentralized transnational administrative network of the party and by examining the many factors that made the reluctant collaboration between the HOK, the SDHP, the ADL, the AGBU and others possible, this chapter recorded the complexity of both the ARF and the HOK as dynamic, living and developing transnational organizations, suggesting a more nuanced conceptualization of the governmental efforts of these non-state and state-backed actors. The transnational coherence around the discourse centred on the 'free and independent' Armenia constructed by the ARF leaders was achieved through propaganda, by employing the leverages of the party, by creating supporting and affiliated organizations, by exclusion and social discipline, but also, as importantly, due to the constant and ongoing exclusion of the ARF affiliates and sympathizers from projects benefiting Soviet Armenia, from spaces that came under the governmental control of the leaders of Soviet Armenian state through the chapters of the HOK and their supporting organizations.

By the end of the 1930s, the major ARF periodicals and Central Committees came under the dominant influence of the former leaders of the Republic of Armenia, who exercised governmental control over some established populations of Armenians in America, France and elsewhere. Even after the HOK was dissolved in Soviet Armenia, at the height of the Stalinist purges in 1937,[85] the mutually exclusive governmental domains between the ARF and the supporters of Soviet Armenia continued. The governmental strategies pursued by the ARF leaders and their political opponents examined in this chapter, while limited to the period between the 1920s and 1930s, can provide a useful framework for explaining the governmental struggles in the Armenian diaspora that continued in the following decades, during the Second World War and the years of the Cold War. The discussion in this chapter also contributes to more complex conceptualizations of diasporic governmentality as multi-agency, multi-locational and multidimensional processes, involving both state and non-state actors, transnational commitments and engagements, networks, populations and discourses, which may produce and reinforce parallel and often incompatible governmental spaces.

Notes

1 Simon Vratsian, *Kharkhapʻumner. H. Kʻajaznunu "H. H. Dashnaktsʻutʻiwnĕ anelikʻ chʻuni aylews" grkʻi artʻiw.* (Gropings. Regarding Kajaznuni's "The Dashnaktsutyun Has Nothing to Do Anymore" Book) (Boston: Hayrenikʻ tparan, 1924), 150; Hovhannēs Kajaznuni, *H. H. Dashnaktsʻutʻiwnĕ anelikʻ chʻuni ayl ews* (The Armenian Revolutionary Federation Has Nothing to Do Anymore) (Vienna: Mkhitʻarean Tparan, 1923). Translations of the quotations are the author's unless otherwise stated.
2 Vratsian, *Kharkhapʻumner*, 176–7.
3 Kajaznuni, *H. H. Dashnaktsʻutʻiwnĕ anelikʻ chʻuni*, 77.
4 Ruben Darbinian, *Mer pataskhanĕ H. Kʻajaznunii* (Our Response to H. Kajaznuni) (Boston: Hayrenikʻ tparan, 1923); Vahan Navasardian, *H.H. Dashnaktsʻutʻean anelikʻĕ* (What the ARF Has to Do) (Gahirē: Husaber, 1924); Arshak Jamalian, 'H. Kʻajaznunin ew H.H. Dashnaktsʻutʻiwnĕ' (H. Kajaznuni and the ARF), *Hayrenikʻ amsagir* (Hairenik Monthly) 2, no. 3–5, 8–9(1924).
5 Jamalian's response appeared in instalments in the *Hayrenikʻ* monthly, volumes 3–5, 8–9, between January and July 1924 in Boston. Navasardian's response was published in Cairo, Egypt. Ruben Darbinian's book was published by the *Hayrenikʻ* association that owned the *Hayrenikʻ* daily (1899–) and the *Hayrenikʻ* monthly (1922–). Darbinian was the editor of both publications.

6 Throughout the nineteenth century Armenians lived in the borderland regions of the Russian and Ottoman Empires, predominantly concentrated in what were known as the Armenian provinces of the Ottoman Empire. The Republic of Armenia emerged as an independent state in May 1918 in the Russian Transcaucasia. The independent Republic did not include the Armenian provinces of the former Ottoman Empire, which had become devoid of the native Armenian population following the genocide and deportations of Armenians during the First World War. For further details about the Armenians in the Russian Transcaucasia, see Stephen Badalyan Riegg, *Russia's Entangled Embrace: The Tsarist Empire and the Armenians, 1801–1914* (Ithaca [New York]: Cornell University Press, 2020); Ronald Grigor Suny, *Looking toward Ararat: Armenia in Modern History* (Bloomington: Indiana University Press, 1993); Lisa Khachaturian, *Cultivating Nationhood in Imperial Russia: The Periodical Press and the Formation of a Modern Armenian Identity* (New Brunswick: Transaction Publishers, 2009). For the Armenian provinces, Armenians in the Ottoman Empire and the Armenian genocide and deportations, see Ronald Grigor Suny, *'They Can Live in the Desert but Nowhere Else': A History of the Armenian Genocide* (Princeton and Oxford: Princeton University Press, 2015).

7 Michel Foucault attributes various meanings to the term 'governmentality'. Among others, he defines governmentality as 'the ensemble formed by the institutions, procedures, analyses and reflections, the calculations and tactics that allow the exercise of this very specific albeit complex form of power, which has as its target population, as its principal form of knowledge political economy, and as its essential technical means apparatuses of security'. Michel Foucault, 'Governmentality', in *The Foucault Effect: Studies in Governmentality: With Two Lectures by and an Interview with Michel Foucault*, ed. Graham Burchell, Colin Gordon, and Peter Miller (Chicago: The University of Chicago Press, 1991), 102.

8 Michel Foucault, *Security, Territory, Population: Lectures at the Collège de France, 1977–1978*, ed. Michel Senellart, François Ewald, and Alessandro Fontana, trans. Graham Burchell, 1. Picador ed, Lectures at the Collège de France (New York: Picador, 2009), 165.

9 Foucault, 'Governmentality', 100.

10 'Why should one want to study this insubstantial and vague domain covered by a notion as problematic and artificial as that of "governmentality"?' Foucault asked in one of his lectures at Collège de France, and continued, 'My immediate answer will be, of course in order to tackle the problem of the state and population' (Foucault, *Security, Territory, Population*, 116). Literature on governmentality has also mostly addressed it within the context of a state. See Fiona McConnell, 'Governmentality to Practise the State? Constructing a Tibetan Population in Exile', *Environment and Planning D: Society and Space* 30, no. 1 (February 2012): 80.

11 Khachig Tölölyan, 'Nation-State and Its Others: In Lieu of a Preface', *Diaspora: A Journal of Transnational Studies* 1, no. 1 (1991): 5.

12 See, for example, Stéphane Dufoix, *Diasporas* (Berkeley, Los Angeles, London: University of California Press, 2008), 81–92; Beverley Mullings, 'Governmentality, Diaspora Assemblages and the Ongoing Challenge of "Development"', *Antipode* 44, no. 2 (March 2012): 406–27; Francesco Ragazzi, 'A Comparative Analysis of Diaspora Policies', *Political Geography* 41 (2014): 74–89; Rahel Kunz, 'Mobilising Diasporas: A Governmentality Analysis of the Case of Mexico', in *Glocal Governance and Democracy Series Working Paper*, vol. 3 (Lucern: University of Lucerne, 2010); Alan Gamlen, 'Diaspora Institutions and Diaspora Governance', *International Migration*

Review 48, no. 1 (September 2014): 180–217; McConnell, 'Governmentality to Practise the State? Constructing a Tibetan Population in Exile', 78–95.
13 For a detailed history of Armenians in America between the 1890s and 1914, see Robert Mirak, *Torn Between Two Lands: Armenians in America, 1890 to World War I* (Cambridge, MA: Harvard University Press, 1983).
14 Khachig Tölölyan, 'Elites and Institutions in the Armenian Transnation', *Diaspora: A Journal of Transnational Studies* 9, no. 1 (2000): 108.
15 Fiona McConnell's account on the ways in which Tibetan Government-in-Exile (TGiE) 'constructed a population' in India in the 1960s suggested some insights for my analysis here. McConnell explores the ways in which the TGiE created a population 'to legitimize its governance', by learning about its population through census and statistics, imagining and normalizing the population through discourses and managing the population by regulating conduct (McConnell, 'Governmentality to Practise the State?'). I use 'discursive construction' to stress the role of discourses expressed in public appeals, published articles, monographs and by other written or spoken forms of communication, in promoting certain political agendas and creating certain needs among the dispersed Armenian populations.
16 Khachig Tölölyan, 'Exile Governments in the Armenian Polity', in *Governments-in-Exile in Contemporary World Politics*, ed. Yossi Shain (New York: Routledge, 1991), 166–85; Khachig Tölölyan, *Redefining Diasporas: Old Approaches, New Identities. The Armenian Diaspora in an International Context* (London: Armenian Institute, 2002).
17 Quoted in A. A. Sargsyan, 'Hayastani ōgnut'yan komitei himnadir p'astat'ght'erĕ' (Founding Documents of the Committee to Aid Armenia), *Lraber hasarakakan gitut'yunneri (Herald of Social Sciences)* 2 (2003): 185–6.
18 Aleksandr Martuni, *Kusakts'ut'yunnerĕ gaghut'ahayut'yan mej* (Political Parties Among Diaspora Armenians) (Tiflis: Petakan hratarakch'ut'yun, 1924), 125. The chairman of the Council of People's Commissars was the highest executive office in the Soviet republics.
19 'Dashnak' or 'Tashnag' in Western Armenian pronunciation is short from Dashnakts'ut'yun – Federation (Hay Heghap'okhakan Dashnakts'ut'yun – Armenian Revolutionary Federation).
20 Ashot Hovhannisyan, *Gaghut'ahay khndirner* (Diaspora-Armenian Issues) (Erevan: Petakan hratarakch'ut'yun, 1925), 23.
21 See also Karlen Dallakyan, *Hay sp'yurk'i patmut'yun (Hamarot aknark)* (A History of the Armenian Diaspora. Brief Outline) (Erevan: Zangak-97, 2004), 34.
22 Hovik Meliksetyan, 'Hayastani ōgnut'yan komiten ev nra derĕ hayrenik'i het sp'yurk'ahay ashkhatavorneri kaperi amrapndman gortsum' (The Committee to Aid Armenia and Its Role in Strengthening the Connections of Diaspora Armenian Workers with the Homeland), *Haykakan SSṚ Gitut'yunneri akademiayi teghekagir. Hasarakakan gitut'yunner* (Proceedings of the National Academy of the Armenian SSR, Social Sciences) 8 (1959): 39.
23 *Hayastani Koch'nak*, an Armenian-language periodical published in New York, reported on 4 July 1925 of the creation of the first HOK chapter in New York ('Hay gaght'akanut'iwnĕ' [Armenian Migrant Communities], *Hayastani Koch'nak (The Gotchnag)*, 4 July 1925, 852). *Ḥaṛach* reported on 30 October 1925 of the tensions the founding of HOK chapters in Greece and France had created among local Armenian populations. In Egypt HOK chapters emerged in 1926, the first chapter being founded on 8 February 1926 ('Hayastani ōgnut'ean komiten Gahirēi mēj' [Committee to Aid

Armenia in Cairo], *HŌK: Parberakan Prak* [HOK: Periodical Volume], 1 June 1926, 2).

24 See Meliksetyan, 'Hayastani ōgnut'yan komiten', 35; Levon Chormisian, *Hamapatker arevmtahayots' mēk daru patmut'ean* (Panorama of a Century Long History of the Western Armenians), vol. 4. Hay spiwṛk'ě. Fransahayeru patmut'iwně (Armenian Diaspora. History of the French-Armenians) (Pēyrut': Tp. Sewan, 1975), 117.

25 See Ashot Abrahamyan, *Hamaṛot urvagits hay gaght'avayreri patmut'yan* (Brief Outline of the History of Armenian Diaspora Communities), vol. 2 (Erevan: Hayastan, 1967), 385; Meliksetyan, 'Hayastani ōgnut'yan komiten', 35–6; Hovik Meliksetyan, *Hayrenik'-sp'yuṛk' aṛnch'ut'yunneṛě ev hayrenadardzut'yuně (1920–1980 t'.t'.)* (Homeland-Diaspora Relations and the Repatriation (1920s-1980s)) (Erevan: Erevani Hamalsarani hrat., 1985), 165.

26 Anahide Ter-Minassian, 'Salon Du Livre Arménien d'Alfortville: L'hommage à Hrant Samuel', *France Arménie*, no. 353 (2010): 24–6; Tölölyan, 'Exile Governments in the Armenian Polity', 181–2.

27 The ARF General Assembly (or World Congress) was the highest authority of the party, made up of elected and appointed representatives from various countries, which convened every four to five years. The Bureau was the highest executive body of the party, usually comprised of five to seven members, elected at the General Assembly. The bureau was responsible for the implementation of the decisions and the party's course taken at General Assemblies, and reported to the General Assembly. The ARF also established Central Committees in countries or regions, where the membership exceeded certain number of people (500 according to the by-laws adopted at the 1925 General Assembly). Central Committees were responsible for regional executive affairs, and reported to the Bureau. Central Committees were elected in regional assemblies of ARF delegates, and represented the ARF in certain countries (such as the United States) or regions (such as Western Europe). (See *Kazmakerpakan kanonner: hastatuats Zh. ěndh. zhoghovin koghmē* (By-Laws: Approved by the Tenth General Assembly) (Zhěnew [Geneva]: H. H. Dashnakts'ut'iwn, 1925); Hrach Dasnabedian, *H.H. Dashnakts'ut'ean kazmakerpakan kaṛoyts'i holowoytě* (The Evolution of the ARF Organizational Structure) (Pēyrut': Hamazgayini Vahē Sēt'ean tparan, 1974.)

28 'Teghekut'iwnner Nor Arabkirēn' (News from New Arabkir), *Hayrenik' ōrat'ert'* (Hairenik Daily), 20 August 1929, 2.

29 'H.B.Ě. Miut'iwn: Vustěr, Nuparashēni hanganakut'ean k'ěmp'ēyn' (A.G.B. Union: Worcester, A Fundraising Campaign for Nubarashen)], 20 September 1929, 4. The campaign was organized by the Armenian General Benevolent Union (AGBU). I discuss the details about the AGBU and its complicated relations with the HOK and the ARF in the next section.

30 Shahan Natalie was one of the leading minds and organizers of the 'Operation Nemesis' – the assassination campaign of the Turkish perpetrators of the Armenian genocide between 1920 and 1922, and could not tolerate the change of the party's course. For further details on the Operation Nemesis, the assassinations of the Turkish perpetrators of the Armenia Genocide and the internal struggles within the ARF, see Jacques Derogy, *Resistance and Revenge: The Armenian Assassination of the Turkish Leaders Responsible for the 1915 Massacres and Deportations* (New Brunswick, U.S.A: Transaction Publishers, 1990).

31 Shahan Natalie, *Turkism from Angora to Baku and Turkish Orientation ; The Turks and Us* ([Nagorno-Karabakh]: Punik Publishing, 2002), xvi, 102–3. Part of Natalie's

thoughts in this book were earlier published in the *Hairenik'* daily on 21, 22 May 1927. The ARF leaders had, indeed, some contacts with the leaders of the Promethean movement, but the ARF, as the representative of Armenians, did not join the movement. For further details, see Paweł Libera, 'Polish Authorities and the Attempt to Create the Caucasian Confederation (1917–1940)', *Studia z Dziejów Rosji i Europy Środkowo-Wschodniej* 52, no. 3 (19 August 2018): 231.

32 Natalie, *Turkism from Angora to Baku*, 102. This English translation includes two of Shahan Natalie's publications, *Turk'izmĕ Angorayēn Pak'u* (Turkism from Angora to Baku) and *Turk'erĕ ew menk'* (The Turks and Us), both initially published in Athens (Greece) in 1928.

33 Short biographies of these leaders can be found in Christopher J. Walker, *Armenia: The Survival of a Nation* (New York: St. Martin's Press, 1990), 409–58; George Mouradian, *Armenian InfoText* (Southgate, MI: Bookshelf Publishers, 1995).

34 Natalie, *Turkism from Angora to Baku*, 125.

35 Natalie complained in his 1928 publication that *Ḥaṛach* had refused to publish an article of his, written in 1927, when he was still 'an ARF Bureau member' (Natalie, *Turkism from Angora to Baku*, 113).

36 *Ḥaṛach* published a small announcement of the expulsion of these individuals, on 4 September 1932, on page 3. *Droshak* published the expulsion announcement in September-October joint issue of 1932.

37 I discuss the details of the conflict in Vahe Sahakyan, 'Between Host-Countries and Homeland: Institutions, Politics and Identities in the Post-Genocide Armenian Diaspora (1920s to 1980s)' (PhD diss., Department of Near Eastern Studies, University of Michigan, Ann Arbor, 2015), 167–71.

38 'Haykakan eṛagoyn droshakĕ' (The Armenian Tricolor Flag), *Hayrenik' ōrat'ert'* (Hairenik Daily), 30 May 1929, 4.

39 'H.Ḥ. Dashnakts'ut'ean 12-rd ĕndhanur zhoghovi haytararut'iwnĕ' (The Announcement of the ARF 12th General Congress), *Hayrenik' ōrat'ert'* (Hairenik Daily), 9 April 1933, 1.

40 Quoted in *K'arasnameak (1903–1943) Eritasard Hayastani.* (Fortieth Anniversary (1903–1943) of Eritasard Hayastan) (New York: s.n., 1944), 41–2.

41 Yeghia Djeredjian, 'SDHK-Komintern karaberut'iwnnerĕ' (Relations between SDHP and the Comintern), *Haigazian Armenological Review* (2002): 161–232; Chormisian, *Hamapatker*, 4. Hay spiwrk'ĕ. Fransahayeru patmut'iwnĕ (Armenian Diaspora. History of the French-Armenians): 111, 115; Arsen Kitur, *Patmut'iwn S. D. Hnch'akean Kusakts'ut'ean, 1887–1962* (History of the Social-Democratic Hunchakian Party), vol. 1 (Beirut: SDHP Press, 1962), 495–500.

42 The Armenian Democratic Liberal (Ramkavar) party was founded in October 1921, in Constantinople, of the merger of the Reformed Hunchakian and the Constitutional Democratic parties. The Reformed Hunchakian party had emerged as a result of the internal split within the SDHP in 1896. The Armenian Constitutional Democratic party was founded in Alexandria, Egypt, in 1908, a few months after the Young Turk revolution in the Ottoman Empire. For further details, see Karlen Dallakyan, *Ṛamkavar Azatakan Kusaktsut'yan patmut'yun* (History of the Democratic Liberal Party), vol. 1, 1921–1940, 2 vols. (Erevan: Gitut'yun, 1999).

43 The Armenian National Delegation was an Armenian representation in Europe, led by Boghos Nubar Pasha – the son of the former prime minister of Egypt, and the founder and president of the Armenian General Benevolent Union (1906). In 1912, the Supreme Patriarch of the Armenian Church, Catholicos Gevorg V, appointed

Boghos Nubar as a special envoy in Europe to negotiate autonomy for Armenians in the Ottoman Armenian provinces. The Armenian National Delegation under his leadership had represented the Armenian interests during and after the First World War, before the foundation of the Republic of Armenia (Richard G. Hovannisian, *The Republic of Armenia. Vol. 1: The First Year, 1918–1919*. (Berkeley: University of California Press, 1999), 257.

44 The Act of United Armenia, presented by Alexander Khatisian, the acting prime minister and minister of foreign affairs of the Republic of Armenia, on 28 May 1919 declared: 'To restore the integrity of Armenia and to secure the complete freedom and prosperity of her people, the Government of Armenia, abiding by the solid will and desire of the entire Armenian people, declares that from this day forward the divided parts of Armenia are everlastingly combined as an independent political entity . . . In promulgating this act of unification and independence of the ancestral Armenian lands located in Transcaucasia and the Ottoman Empire, the Government of Armenia declares that the political system of United Armenia is a democratic republic and that it has become the Government of this United Republic of Armenia' (quoted in Hovannisian, *Republic of Armenia. Vol. 1*, 461–2).

45 The Armenian question had emerged as an internal issue within the Ottoman Empire in the mid-nineteenth century that became internationalized after the Russo-Turkish war of 1877–8. The reforms that promised equality and administrative autonomy to the Armenians had since remained on the agenda of the European powers in their relations with the Ottoman Empire. The treaty of Lausanne signed between Turkey and the major European powers (French Republic and the British Empire including), however, made no reference to the Armenians or the Armenian question. For further details on the Armenian question see Richard G. Hovannisian, 'The Armenian Question in the Ottoman Empire 1876–1914', in *The Armenian People from Ancient to Modern Times*, vol. 2. *Foreign Domination to Statehood: The Fifteenth Century to the Twentieth Century* (Basingstoke: Macmillan, 1997), 203–39; Walker, *Armenia: The Survival of a Nation*.

46 'Ramk. Azat. Kusakts'ut'ean B. ěndh. patgm. zhoghovin art'iw' (On the Occasion of the 2nd General Congress of ADL), *Abakay*, 23 February 1924, 1–2.

47 In the same book where Aleksandr Miasnikyan condemned the ARF, he also wrote about the SDHP and the ADL. The ADL in his view was a 'peaceful party', compared to the militant ARF, but still a 'bourgeois' party, representing an opposite pole to the Bolsheviks (Martuni, *Kusakts'ut'yunnerě*, 61–2, 76).

48 Shortly after its foundation, the AGBU expanded in the emerging Armenian settlements in various parts of the Middle East, Europe and the Americas. The first AGBU chapter in the United States was established in 1908 by Vahan Kurkjian in Boston, then gradually the AGBU network of chapters expanded to include various parts of New England and New York. By 1914, the AGBU had fifty-four chapters in the United States (Mirak, *Torn Between Two Lands*, 175–6). The first AGBU chapters in France emerged in 1911. In 1921, the AGBU headquarters moved from Cairo, Egypt, to Paris, France, that was becoming the centre of Armenian social and political activism. In 1943, the AGBU headquarters moved to the United States (*Armenian General Benevolent Union: Historic Outline, 1906–1946* [New York: Published by the Central Committee of America, 1948]).

49 Karen Mikayelyan, *Hay zhoghovrdakan harstut'yunnern artasahmanum: ktakner, nviratvut'yunner yev hasarakakan gumarner* (Armenian National Wealth Abroad: Wills, Gifts, and Public Funds) (Moskva: Hratarakut'yun Hayastani ōgnut'yan komiteyi, 1928), 49–52.

50 Speech given on 14 October 1931, at the meeting of the propaganda department leaders of the Armenian Communist Party. Quoted in Karlen Dallakyan, *H.B.Ĕ Miut'yan nakhagah G. Kyulpenkyani hrazharakani harts'i shurj* (About the Resignation of the AGBU President C. Gulbenkian) (Erevan: Hratarakut'iwn Azg ōratert'i, 1996), 48.
51 Eduard Melkonyan, *Haykakan baregortsakan ĕndhanur miut'yan patmut'yun* (History of the Armenian General Benevolent Union) (Erevan: Mughni hratarakch'ut'yun, 2005), 203–308.
52 For the 'brutal proletarization', the Nansen passports, and the social-political contexts in France, see Aïda Boudjikanian-Keuroghlian, *Les Arméniens Dans La Région Rhône-Alpes: Essai Géographique Sur Les Rapports d'une Minorité Ethnique Avec Son Milieu d'accueil.* (Lyon: Association des Amis de la "Revue de géographie de Lyon", 1978); Clarisse Lauras, *Les Arméniens à Saint-Étienne: Une Escale Dans Un Parcours Migratoire?* (Saint-Étienne: Publications de l'Université de Saint-Étienne, 2006); Anahide Ter-Minassian, *Histoire Croisees: Diaspora, Arménie, Transcaucasie 1890–1990* (Marseille: Editions Parenthéses, 1997).
53 'HŌKi Fransayi shrjani 4-rd artakarg patgamaworakan zhoghovĕ' (HOK 4th Regional Emergency Congress of France), *HŌK: Ōrgan artasahmanean hōkeru (HOC: Revue Mensuelle)*, April 1933, 53.
54 Hay Gnduni, 'H.Ḥ.D. k'aghak'akanut'iwnĕ gaghut'ahayut'ean mēj' (The ARF Policy among Diaspora Armenians), *Hayrenik' ōrat'ert'* (Hairenik Daily), 4 July 1928, 1.
55 The Armenian Relief Corps was established in New York in 1910 as the Armenian Red Cross Society. Since its foundation the Armenian Red Cross had remained closely affiliated with the ARF. Between 1910 and 1920, the Armenian Red Cross had expanded with chapters in various countries. Following the Sovietization of Armenia, in parallel to the creation of HOK chapters, the Soviet authorities also began chapters of Armenia's Red Cross organization, that came into conflict with the ARF Red Cross. For a while, there were two Armenian Red Cross organizations operating within many Armenian-American communities. The ARF affiliated Armenian Red Cross was soon renamed into the Armenian Relief Corps, even though the name in Armenian remained *Hay Karmir Khach'* (Armenian Red Cross) for several more years. In the 1940s, the Armenian Relief Corps was renamed into the Armenian Relief Society. See Tatul Sonents-Papazian, ed., *Hariwrameay hushamatean Hay ōgnut'ean miut'ean (Centennial Memorial of the Armenian Relief Society)* (Boston: Armenian Relief Society, 2010), 3–9; Mirak, *Torn Between Two Lands*, 178–9.
56 The Armenian General Athletic Union (Hay marmnakrt'akan ĕndhanur miut'iwn, also known as *Homenĕt'men*) was founded in Istanbul in 1918. The athletic and scouting organization subsequently spread among the dispersed Armenian communities in many countries in part thanks to the support of the ARF.
57 Mirak, *Torn Between Two Lands*, 173–5.
58 Grigor Vardanyan, 'Hayrenakts'akan miut'yunnerĕ ev Khorhrdayin Hayastanĕ' (Compatriotic Societies and Soviet Armenia), *HŌK-i Teghekatu* (HOK Bulletin), 1928, 16.
59 Patrik Selian, 'HŌKi 6rd hamagumari oroshumnerĕ: dēpi noranor haght'anakner anonts' iragortsumov' (The Decisions of the HOK 6th General Congress: Towards the Newer Victories with Their Implementation), *HŌK: Ōrgan artasahmanean hōkeru (HOC: Revue Mensuelle)* 1, no. 2 (March 1933): 50.
60 'Hakaṛakordneru pōlshewik paraglukhnerĕ inch'u hamar k'andel kuzen mer miut'iwnĕ' (Why Do the Bolshevik Leaders of the Opponents Want to Destroy Our Union), *Alis* 15, no. 3–4 (1934): 3–5.

61 Arakel Patrik, *Patmagirkʻ-hushamatean Sebastioy ew gawaṛi hayutʻean (History of the Armenians of Sebastia and Neighboring Villages)*, vol. 2 (Pēyrutʻ, Niw Chĕrzi: Hratarakutʻiwn Hamasebastahay verashinatsʻ miutʻean, 1983), 441–6; *Hamaṛot patmutʻiwn Hama-Sebastatsʻiakan shinarar miutʻean* (Brief History of the Pan-Sebastian Construction Union) (New York: Hama-Sebastatsʻiakan shinarar miutʻiwn, 1945).
62 For further details on the conflict and the split in the Sebastia Reconstruction Union, see Sevan Yousefian, 'Picnics for Patriots: The Transnational Activism of an Armenian Hometown Association', *Journal of American Ethnic History* 34, no. 1 (2014): 34–8.
63 Patrik Selian, 'HŌKi 6rd hamagumari oroshumnerĕ: dēpi noranor haghtʻanakner anontsʻ iragortsumov' (The Decisions of the HOK 6th General Congress: Towards New Victories with Their Implementation), *HŌK: Ōrgan artasahmanean hōkeru (HOC: Revue Mensuelle)* 1, no. 3 (April 1933): 46.
64 Ibid., 48.
65 The *Tsʻeghakrōn* movement was founded by Garegin Nzhdeh in 1933 in Boston. The movement was later renamed the Armenian Youth Federation during the Second World War. See Sarkis Atamian, *The Armenian Community: The Historical Development of a Social and Ideological Conflict* (New York: Philosophical Library, 1955), 388–96.
66 By 1916, several Armenian communities in America had already constructed Armenian Church buildings, but many more parishes held Armenian religious services at rented halls of Episcopal and other churches (see Mirak, *Torn Between Two Lands*, 190).
67 Oshagan Minassian, *A History of the Armenian Holy Apostolic Orthodox Church in the United States (1888–1944)* (Monterey: Mayreni Publishing, 2010).
68 Arten Ashjian, *Vichakatsʻoytsʻ ew patmutʻiwn Aṛajnordakan Tʻemin Hayotsʻ Amerikayi, 1948* (Register and History of the Diocese of the Armenian Church in America, 1948), (New York: Hratarakutʻiwn Amerikayi Hayotsʻ Aṛajnordarani, 1949), 31–2.
69 Minassian, *History of Armenian Church*, 203.
70 *Documents on the Schism in the Armenian Church of America* (New York: Diocese of the Armenian Church of America, 1993), 20–1.
71 Cheka stood for the All-Russian Extraordinary Commission (chrezvychainaia komissiia – initialism ChK) for combating counter-revolution and sabotage, which acted as the Soviet secret police.
72 'Erewani kaṛavarutʻean nor ʻeloytʻĕ" (The Recent 'Address' of the Yerevan Government), *Hayrenikʻ ōratʻertʻ* (Hairenik Daily), 18 August 1929, 4.
73 A front-page article by Aris Ter Israyelian in the *Hayrenikʻ* daily, published on September 7, 1929, provided justifications of why the transfer of the Catholicos and the Supreme Council out of Soviet Armenia was necessary and how it could be organized (Aris Ter Israyelian, 'Khndir mĕ, or ir lutsman kĕ spasē' [A Problem That Needs to be Solved], *Hayrenikʻ ōratʻertʻ* [Hairenik Daily], 7 September 1929, 1).
74 *Documents on the Schism*, 23.
75 Ibid., 33.
76 'Khmbagrakan: Anarzhan aṛajnord mĕ' (Editorial: An Undeserving Primate), *Hayrenikʻ ōratʻertʻ* (Hairenik Daily), 12 July 1933, 4. See also Minassian, *History of Armenian Church*, 279.
77 *Documents on the Schism*, 44.
78 See Minassian, *History of Armenian Church*, 316–20; Atamian, *Armenian Community*, 369.

79 'Archbishop Assassinated in Procession to Altar; Laid to Old-World Feud', *The New York Times*, 25 December 1933, 1.
80 '1 Held in Death of Archbishop', *The Washington Post*, 28 December 1933, 2.
81 'The New York Murder', *Hayrenik' ōrat'ert'* (Hairenik Daily), 29 December 1933, 4.
82 Jenny Phillips, *Symbol, Myth, and Rhetoric: The Politics of Culture in an Armenian American Population* (New York: AMS Press, 1989), 130–4.
83 Minassian, *History of Armenian Church*, 321–35.
84 The Soviet policies towards the Armenian Apostolic or Georgian Orthodox churches in the early 1920s were ambiguous and often were left at the discretion of local Bolshevik leaders. In these early years, churches were often plundered and closed, and priests and clergymen were persecuted and arrested, causing much discontent among local populations. More consistent attempts to bring the Armenian Church under Soviet control began in the mid-1920s, more intensely after the death of Catholicos Gevorg V in 1930. For further details, see Jakub Osiecki, 'The Invigilation of Armenian Clergy (1920–1930) According to Documents in the Possession of the Armenian National Archive and the Georgian State Archive', *Journal of the Society for Armenian Studies* 21 (2012): 271–6; Jakub Osiecki, *The Armenian Church in Soviet Armenia: The Policies of the Armenian Bolsheviks and the Armenian Church, 1920–1932*, trans. Paweł Siemianowski and Artur Zwokski (New York: Peter Lang, 2020), 122–48.
85 The Soviet government found the HOK no longer serving a purpose, which in their mind had turned into an organization of 'foreign agencies and spies' (Meliksetyan, *Hayrenik'-sp'yurk'*, 170).

6

Defiant Adherence

Cultural critiques in late twentieth-century Armenian Diaspora literature

Lilit Keshishyan

In a 1991 interview for *AIM* magazine, Los Angeles-based writer and translator Ishkhan Jinbashian, acknowledging the prolific Western Armenian writer Vahé Oshagan's propensity to push boundaries in his writing, asks Oshagan about his views on conventional Armenian literary traditions carried on by contemporary writers. Oshagan answers that for Armenians, the traditional 'carries an idolatrous hue that is unacceptable in our day. And writers who perpetrate worship of this kind are dead weight upon our literature. [He] denounce[s] their stylistic shabbiness, their thematic limitation, their impotence to create as free and self-governing artists';[1] however, he then qualifies his critique in a defence of tradition, stating:

> That which I . . . accept is the traditional as the crystallization of the wisdom and experience of the ages – particularly in language and religious sensibility. I go to church in order to find the Armenian people and my spiritual fatherland; in the Armenian Revolutionary Federation, I live the identity, the quintessence of the Armenian being, something that touches me and kindles my imagination, I try to find the idea of roots, of fundament and archetype, the lessons of history, the basic aspects of the human spirit, which are all embodied in traditional art. Tradition becomes significant when it is taken as a point of departure towards the uncharted. In the search for identity, man is often pitted against tradition; he must challenge and confront it, but above all he must learn and absorb it utterly.[2]

Oshagan's answer, within the context of the breadth of his literary work, might seem contradictory, precisely because of his proclivity to challenge accepted narratives and his reluctance to overtly reference or accept the traditional in a majority of his literary works. His poetry, arguably his strongest form, can seem abstract and existential in nature. Oshagan's insistence on absorbing tradition while simultaneously challenging it illuminates his approach to his prose but also reveals a condition inherent in the diasporic experience. To be living as diasporan, by default, means adopting the traditional to some capacity – accepting and embodying foundations from outside the current space, whether that be language, history, customs, religion or political beliefs. The presence of the 'old world' or the space to which one has ties is encompassed in the duality or plurality inherent to the notion of a diaspora and thus, rejecting tradition completely can challenge the notion of diaspora altogether.

Furthermore, Oshagan's disposition towards the church and the Armenian Revolutionary Federation in his defence of the traditional amplifies the importance of institutions in his vision of diasporic identity and cultural production; institutional leadership and membership (both formal and informal) shape narratives of belonging and identity and provide a framework for achieving shared goals. Citing the difference between definitions of ethnic and diasporan communities, Khachig Tölölyan argues that '[t]he distinguishing diasporan feature tends to be the existence of a multitiered minority, consisting of the committed, the activists, and sometimes a handful of radical activists or militants. They constitute the "leadership elites" or, in another parlance, an "interest group," whose members staff and fund organizations that have specifically diasporan concerns'.[3] Acknowledging a more informal, yet integral form of participation in the cultivation of diasporic identity, Tölölyan adds that 'the ranks of the politically and *institutionally* engaged usually do not include some of the most important ethnodiasporic figures – the loosely connected scholars and intellectuals who produce a diasporist discourse, and above all the writers, musicians and other artists who produce high and low cultural commodities that underpin diasporic identity'.[4] The categorization of intellectual elites in the diaspora as a distinct group often separate from the institutional leadership elites both underpins the interdependent relationship between the groups as it pertains to diaspora building and signals potentially incompatible methods and visions. The intellectual elite is shaped by, but not bound to, the ideas of the leadership elites. In this chapter, I will discuss the select works of Armenian diasporic writers Hakob Karapents, Vahé Oshagan and Vahe Berberian; as writers and cultural figures, they along with many of their literary protagonists fall under Tölölyan's second category of ethnodiasporic figures, tangentially tied to formal organizations as they produce diasporic discourse through scholarship and the arts. These authors' identities as diasporans inform their work in many ways, as they push the boundaries, critiquing the institutions they are a part of, but never completely rejecting them in doing so.

Oshagan's insistence on the traditional invokes Tölölyan's categorization of institutional and intellectual elites and underscores the latter's reliance on the former. The aforementioned institutional elites rely on a historical narrative that explains the construction and existence of the diaspora and create a narrative that explains the connection and allegiance to the homeland or a larger diasporic body. While the writers themselves might not formally hold institutional power, their artistic output is both tangentially generated by what institutional bodies enable and consumed by the communities those institutions serve. Reflecting on the role of the diaspora writer, Hakob Karapents writes,

> Ultimately, Diaspora literature must reflect Armenian Diaspora life – our daily ups and downs, our individual and collective crises, the question of generational

changes, the perpetual predicament of preserving the Armenian identity, the dwindling of tradition, the transformation of morals and customs, the new man, the Armenian citizen of the world who suffers to establishes security amidst the increasingly disturbing echoes of his tribe.[5]

The literary works discussed in this chapter follow Karapents's call to reflect diasporic experiences. The focus on diaspora life produces and reflects the questions and challenges to institutions, both Armenian and non-Armenian. Like Oshagan, Karapents posits tradition in some forms as necessary and in other forms as something to reject, with the implication that the tradition that informs diasporic identity, while likely subjective, should be embraced to some degree. Maintaining this balance requires a challenge to the status quo, the production of literature that honestly reflects the current moment and the critique of the establishment while respecting the institutions that might have enabled the crises of the moment.

Often, even when being challenged, the weight of what Tölölyan terms 'stateless power', informs Karapents, Oshagan and Berberian's cultural output, leading to an acquiescence of sorts that acknowledges the limitations of diasporic narratives, without seeing a clear alternative. The texts and their central characters are conscious of how strongly language and cultural narratives script experience, and they repeatedly contemplate the powers and limitations of placing diasporic narratives at the centre of identity and belonging, especially amid more dominant, pluralistic spaces. Nonetheless, the characters, at times, completely accept the scripted narratives of identity in the absence of new narratives that might usurp the traditional and the proven. This acceptance implies the necessity of seeing these narratives as forms of cultural 'survival' even as they are repeatedly critiqued and questioned for their limitations. These texts, in both embracing and critiquing narratives of identity, provide their own revised narratives that acknowledge the limitations of fulfilling expectations of Armenian diasporic identity.

The inability to reconcile incompatible narratives places the contradiction, and the attempt at working through it, at the core of diasporic identity. The paradox also becomes a testament to the strengths of diaspora institutions, the narratives they bestow and their capital within the community. The texts challenge the constructed aspects of nation and origin, and resist traditional notions of identity, but are often unwilling to reject or replace that which is being challenged. This raises questions about the precarious position of the diaspora writer writing in Armenian, as the narratives and institutions being critiqued are also the ones that facilitate the spaces and culture that enable their literary content and output.

The presence of the past in Karapents's *Adam's Book*

Hakob Karapents's early upbringing was shaped by his family and by Armenian Iranian cultural and political institutions of his hometown of Tabriz, which, at the time, was home to the largest population of Armenians in Iran. Born in 1925, Karapents was the founder of the youth group 'Light and Mind' (Loys ev Mitk') in 1939 and later in

1944 was instrumental in establishing the Ararat Armenian Cultural Foundation (Hay Mshakutʻayin Ararat Miutʻiwn), of which he was the first president.[6] Strong Armenian cultural influence was accompanied by Karapents's formal education, which included Russian schooling, later Persian, French and Armenian. In 1947, Karapents moved to the United States to attend the University of Kansas in Missouri. He then relocated to New York where he received a graduate degree in journalism. A short move to California preceded a move back to New York and later to Massachusetts.[7]

Published by diaspora-based Armenian presses, Vosketar Publishing (Osketar Hratarakchʻakan) and Blue Crane Books, Karapents's literary works often touch on issues of the bifurcated identities and characters who navigate between different linguistic and cultural spaces and allegiances. The existential crises of Karapents's characters are often implanted on a male protagonist in search of the 'true self', as he navigates the physical world around him, his memories and fraught relationships. Most characteristic of this style is in Karapents's 1983 novel *Adami Girkʻë*, or *Adam's Book*.

The old and the new consistently clash in *Adam's Book*, not overtly between groups of people but within the protagonist Adam Nurian, who at the beginning of the novel has divorced his Armenian wife and quit his job as a respected English-language newspaper editor to focus on writing a book in English. Karapents's novel lacks a clear plot. Adam drives and walks around the city, makes a brief visit to his aunt's house in New York and eventually picks up his love interest Zelda, as they take a trip to Vermont. In the midst of these events, he reminisces about his past, recalling events from his childhood in Iran; composes editorials about the state of American capitalism and consumerism in his mind; contemplates his relationship with his ex-wife and children; and ruminates on his life as an Armenian American. The novel clearly places the past within Adam's present.

While the novel does not directly critique the diaspora or its institutions, the constant presence of the past, articulated through notions of loss, literal narratives of identity relayed through books and poetry and a sense of having failed at family, informs his confused state and inability to be at peace. Early in the novel, Adam goes to Harlem, New York, to visit his aunt, a teacher at an Armenian school. During this visit, lamenting the state of both the Armenian Diaspora and Adam's situation, the aunt refers to the Armenian experience as a 'black destiny' determined to disperse and isolate Armenians all over the world. Adam strongly disagrees with her ominous outlook, asserting that one's fate lies in one's own hands, to which his aunt responds:

> If that is the case, then why are you not controlling your own destiny? Your wife left you, your children are scattered here and there, and you go from one city to another. Is this what you call life? And it deeply pains me that you've moved away from your Armenianness. Why don't you write in Armenian?[8]

The aunt's comments point to the core issues of identity and belonging that the protagonist deals with throughout the novel. Adam's decision to write in English and the breakup of his family are equated to a loss of Armenianness and as something to be lamented. The aunt's commitment to Armenianness is represented through her home décor, described as an 'oasis of Armenianness'[9] in Harlem, her job as an Armenian teacher and her critique of Adam. Ironically, she relies on Adam to console her as she questions her own contributions, the state of diaspora and her decision to leave her birthplace, Iran. Adam's consolation and confident assertions about fate are later proven superficial as the attempts at reaching an 'ideal' standard of Armenian diasporic identity are unsuccessful and, melodramatically, result in personal tragedy.

Shortly after this interaction, the text moves to a first-person flashback of Adam's childhood, recounting the events that led to his young friend Gabo's death. Gabo is struck on the head with a rock and killed during a turf war between ethnic Armenian and ethnic Turk children in the Tabriz neighbourhood of Iran. As explained shortly thereafter, this battle becomes a manifestation of Adam and Gabo's fantasies of war, nationhood and patriotism. Karapents uses Armenian writer Raffi's seminal novel *The Madman (Khent'ě)* as the awakening of revolutionary fervour and nationalist sentiment in young Adam's life. Framing this awakening around the account of Gabo's untimely death, the text emphasizes the implications of historical events and narratives on succeeding generations. Adam recalls, 'Gabo had read Raffi's *Khent'ě* and had gone crazy. He gave the book to me, I read it, and went crazy as well. We decided to form an army, go to Armenia and free ourselves from the Turks. We decided to become pioneers.'[10]

The inclusion of *Khent'ě* as well as its impact on the children's sense of identity points to the impact of this particular text on the collective Armenian psyche. Raffi's writings are considered critical in shaping Armenian national identity, particularly for members of the Armenian Revolutionary Federation, with which Karapents, Berberian and Oshagan are affiliated in various degrees. The placement of this flashback immediately after the aunt's accusation that Adam has lost his Armenianness in a way legitimizes her critique of Adam. His forward-looking, non-Armenian-centred aspirations are just that, aspirations. The narratives of Armenianness – of duty – hold strong, even as Adam critiques Armenian nationalist sentiments, resisting them to a degree, by forcing himself to write in English, critiquing his aunt's fixation on the past and dating Zelda.

While Adam repeatedly composes scathing editorials about American capitalism and consumerism as he roams around the city, Armenians or their institutions are not outwardly critiqued in the novel. The critique of diaspora comes through in the protagonist's own sense of failure and lack of purpose. The ending of *Adam's Book* serves as critique of the diaspora experience as a whole, rendering the mission of successfully straddling two worlds as impossible, even as the impetus to do so remains inescapable. Ironically, at the urging of his English-speaking, 'American' lover, Adam gives up on his English-language text and begins writing a book in Armenian. This is the only brief point in the novel where the protagonist is content. He is in Vermont with Zelda. Unlike his Armenian ex-wife who referred to his Armenianness as suffocating, Zelda not only accepts his Armenianness but encourages its exploration. His two 'worlds', or identities, for a very brief moment, coexist in perfect harmony. In a sudden, dramatic turn, however, his vacation and sense of peace end when Zelda dies in a freak accident in the forest.

Zelda's death coincides with Adam's new commitment to write in Armenian and harkens back to his inability to reconcile his two worlds. By writing in Armenian, Adam makes his writing and thus himself, inaccessible to his love interest and his 'American' reality; his mode of communication is illegible to that world. This paradox at the centre of diasporic identity is emphasized through Zelda's encouragement of Adam to embrace his authentic self; however, the ensuing events imply that authenticity for Adam would be a seamless merging of his two worlds, linguistically, temporally and culturally. If we take his writing as a symbol of self, neither writing exclusively in Armenian nor writing in English would represent Adam's self. At the end of the novel, Adam is still unsettled, still roaming, but is now writing in Armenian. His past and the narratives that have shaped him are embodied in the act of writing in Armenian. His decision to write in Armenian fulfils his aunt's wishes and the vision in Raffi's *Khentʽĕ* and presents a more authentic vision of Adam to Zelda, but it ultimately eliminates a possibility for an 'American' or cosmopolitan experience. The novel suggests that one cannot harmoniously coexist with the other, and the past continues to be a burden on the present.

The readership for both Karapents and his protagonist, Adam, is the diasporic Armenian. Overt criticism against diaspora institutions or the narratives that lead Karapents's characters to this crisis of consciousness would perhaps be alienating to the readers and the institutions supporting the production of the texts, but more importantly to the identity of the writer and his characters. While it is not surprising to have an autobiographical character, Karapents has given his protagonist so much of his own biography that it is difficult to separate the real author from the fictional one. Karapents and Adam Nurian are writing the same book and facing similar crises. One could surmise that a complete critique of diaspora institutions and the experiences and crises they cause would be counter-intuitive for a writer using the diaspora institutions to propel their work,[11] but in this case, it seems a more honest exhortation of the power of these institutions in disabling the critique, not necessarily for fear of retaliation but for fear of losing the self and a sense of authenticity.

A categorical rejection of narratives and institutions that have shaped belonging and communal ties would implore an abandonment of that which shapes his world view and decision-making. In the case of Karapents's Adam, it would suggest that his childhood bonds, his familial and romantic relationships, his career choices, his relationship with places and more broadly his place in the world are without foundation. The alternative to rejection becomes the product of the text which is an exploration of the duality of the diasporic experience, one that is consistently dynamic, in flux and worked through rather than something conclusive and binding. The incompatibility of a harmonious ombined American and Armenian experience implies the necessity to reject one over the other, something neither Karapents nor his protagonist is willing to do. We see similar sentiments echoed in Vahé Oshagan and Vahe Berberian's texts, as their narratives, too, become a project of unravelling and working through rather than rejecting.

Interrogating spaces of belonging in Vahé Oshagan's 'Unction'

Notions of exile and displacement omnipresent in Vahé Oshagan's work mirror the reality of the author's experience, which involved constant relocation beginning at an early age. The son of prominent Armenian novelist, Hagop Oshagan, Vahé Oshagan was born in Plovdiv, Bulgaria, in 1922. Soon after, his family moved to Egypt. In 1926, they moved from Egypt to Cyprus and then from Cyprus to Jerusalem in 1934. Oshagan left for Paris in 1946 to study literature at the University of Sorbonne. From 1952 to 1975 he resided in Beirut, Lebanon, where he taught at the local Armenian schools and at the American University of Beirut. He moved to the United States in 1975, where he taught literature and culture at the University of Pennsylvania in Philadelphia. A brief move to Australia brought him back to the United States, where he died in June of 2000.[12]

In an article memorializing the death of Vahé Oshagan, literary critic Marc Nichanian writes, 'Vahé achieved the task of obliterating with this book [*The City*], once and for all, all habitual points of reference for Armenian readers ... the poetic oeuvre of Vahé Oshagan was a continuing process of *desacralization*, applied iconoclasm in progress'.[13] Nichanian reveals some of the main tenets of Oshagan's work. Oshagan's prose often challenges or interrogates traditional and accepted symbols of Armenian identity. In his poetry, he refrains from addressing directly national, diasporic and cultural signifiers altogether. Instead, through omission, Oshagan situates notions of exile and alienation within the everyday, applying these feelings to the contemporary experience in the modern world.

Oshagan's novella 'Unction' ('Otsumě'), published in 1988, centres on a small Armenian community in Philadelphia. It begins with a description of the early morning activities of Ter Avetis, the priest at Philadelphia's St. Sarkis Armenian Church and his assistant Sukias. As Ter Avetis prepares for the Sunday morning services, we are introduced one by one to the sixteen parishioners of the church, all Armenian. A second narrative runs somewhat parallel to the church narrative, intermittently interrupting the initial storyline. Sona, Jacques and Bruce, a trio of diaspora Armenian youth, are planning a sacrilegious attack on St. Sarkis Church and its parishioners. Sona has immigrated to the United States from Beirut, where she was a member of an Armenian terrorist organization. Jacques, a socialist originally from France, is the ringleader of the group; he is adamant and secure in his plans against the church. Highly knowledgeable about and involved in Armenian Diaspora politics and culture, Jacques feels the need for an abrupt change in the status quo, which he feels is stagnant and detrimental to the well-being of the Armenian Diaspora community. Bruce, the most passive member of the trio, is identified as half-Armenian and from Fresno, California. Having a newfound interest in Armenian cultural and political issues, he seeks guidance from Sona and Jacques.

Jacques's plan to shake up the Armenian community involves entering the church wearing black masks and blaring loud rock music while Bruce and Sona passionately kiss in the pews. He then plans on disrobing the priest, Ter Avetis, as a symbolic act of revealing the façade of not only the church but the Armenian Diaspora community as a whole. Despite continued hesitation by Bruce and Sona, the first part of the plan is enacted; however, much to Jacques's surprise, Bruce interrupts Jacques's attempt to physically harm the priest. We later learn that the youth are arrested and spend time in jail. A few years later they reconvene and begin discussing new plans of attack without acknowledging their actions in the church.

The complexity of Oshagan's novella lies in its refusal to assign fault either to the Armenian Church and its representation of the status quo or to the actions of the youth. The text interestingly presents the concerns and motivations of the youth, the churchgoers and Ter Avetis as valid and worthy even as it critiques nuances in their approach or characters. Though paradoxical, these concerns and motivations make up the Armenian diasporic experience, in that they again reflect the foundations of centuries-old cultural identity alongside reflections and new lived experiences detached from those foundations. At one point we learn that Ter Avetis has questioned his own faith, his role in the church and the devotion of the parishioners. Ter Avetis

> found himself guilty for his nation's and the world's suffering, for which he had stopped praying. So that with his small mind and with his kind heart he had gone beyond Christ and his family to an imaginary god, completely detached from the pains and hopes of life, a kind of idea and ideal of God, an abstract something equal to his love and longing for his homeland, that had no relation with this liturgy and prayers.[14]

His inner dialogue throughout the story confirms Jacques's criticism of the church and its role in Armenian national identity, however, this confirmation does not heroize Jacques or completely devalue Ter Avetis's contribution. Ter Avetis is doing the best that he can and living what seems like a crisis of consciousness, both Armenian and spiritual. The fault lies not in the institution of the church but in human injustice and the abstraction of belief.

As the space of the church is questioned as a false bearer of Armenian culture and identity, the space occupied by the youth is also critiqued both literally and ideologically. The youth lack unity and are reckless. Jacques, the ringleader, sees no redeeming qualities in Ter Avetis's work, and his plan to humiliate the unassuming priest seems unwarranted and cruel. Unlike the churchgoers, the three youths do not have concrete markers of Armenian identity on which they unite. Moreover, they are as uncomfortable outside of the church as they are in it. Lacking any connection with the church and its parishioners, Jacques, Sona and Bruce are in a way exiled into the streets of Philadelphia. Oshagan describes the backdrop of the trio's meeting spaces along with the alienation the youth feel within these spaces. The city is always present through mentions of highway and street names, names of restaurants, the smells of the harbour and the continued presence of non-Armenians. As Sona and Jacques discuss their attack plans, we read that 'Beyond the window one could see a part of Philadelphia's port. Cold, monotonous smell of the rain has probably captured the world and the echo of Warf's grey noise has banged the glasses like a suffering endless heart'.[15] Philadelphia's presence in Sona and Jacques's life is circumstantial and burdensome. The frigid description of the city bombarding the youth with pain and sorrow displaces both Sona and Jacques from Philadelphia's parameters, relegating them to the confines of their meeting spaces and their ideas. The churchgoers, although having emigrated from different parts of the world, agree that their ethnicity and the church, both ideologically and physically, bind them together. The attack on the church, the youth's reluctance to complete the entire plan, the lack of change in the parishioners and Ter

Avetis's shaky faith reveal stagnancy and instability but also a commitment to working through identity, however contradictory the negotiations might be.

Oshagan's novella solidifies neither the establishment nor the youth as the true bearers of identity or progress in the community, but it does not reject them either. The church and its representative, Ter Avetis, as traditional and historic bearers of identity, while reaching only a small fraction of the Armenians represented, are still working towards establishing community and belonging among the Armenians in Philadelphia, even as Ter Avetis questions and works through his faith in that same space. Towards the end of the novella, we learn that Jacques, Sona and Bruce reconvene to plan their next attack immediately after their release from jail. While the details of future plans are unclear, they have not given up despite their own reluctance to complete their task, at least symbolically, of replacing markers of Armenian identity. The paradox lies in this simultaneous reluctance and insistence to break from tradition and forge a new path towards Armenian identity in the diaspora.

The pull of obligation in Berberian's *Letters from Zaat'ar*

Vahe Berberian has a significant presence in the Armenian Diaspora community as a writer, an artist and an intellectual. Born and raised in Beirut, Lebanon, Berberian moved to Los Angeles in 1976. His paintings, plays, comedic monologues and novels create a hotchpotch of an artistic career effectively catering to different parts of the Armenian community while reaching an international one. Berberian's popularity among the Armenian community of the diaspora and the Republic of Armenia is due mainly to his plays and original comedic stand-up performances. Based on his life in Beirut and Los Angeles, and performed throughout the world, the monologues chronicle Berberian's experiences with family and the Armenian community. The narratives rely heavily on diasporic Armenian cultural markers, such as food, clothing and inter-ethnic stereotypes. Entertaining, culturally insightful and replete with self-critique, these performances contribute to the artistic milieu of the Armenian diaspora and reach a large audience. Proportionately less widely known, Berberian's novels expand on the issues presented in his monologues and plays and distinctively contribute to the intellectual debate over issues of diasporic identity, nationalism and diaspora–homeland relations. The novel *Letters from Zaat'ar* (*Namakner Zaat'arēn*) was published in Los Angeles in 1996 with a print run of 1,000 copies. The success of the book marked by its absence from local Armenian bookstores prompted a 2009 second edition. The publication of a second edition of an Armenian-language novel written by a diaspora writer is rather rare and points to both the popularity of the novel and its author.

In *Letters from Zaat'ar*, protagonist Zohrap Anmahuni, like Karapents's Adam Nurian, is disenchanted with life, overtly laying much of the blame on an emptiness he attributes to a culture-gnawing America. He is unhappy with his domestic life, has been cheating on his wife and finds his job as an architect in a large firm unfulfilling. At a dinner party honouring the foreign minister of a newly independent Armenia, Zohrap is offered a position as Armenian consul in a fictional Zaat'ar, a country with four Armenian residents. Much to the disappointment of his wife Alice, Zohrap leaves his architecture position in Los Angeles and relocates to Zaat'ar with Alice and their two children. His wife, like Adam's aunt, an Armenian teacher, eventually decides to move back to Los Angeles with their children, leaving Zohrap on his own.

Before accepting the position as head Armenian consul general in Zaat'ar, Armenian Foreign Ministry head Aramayis Mnakian challenges Zohrap's sense of duty to the Armenian nation. Zohrap recalls, 'Mnakian grabs my shoulders firmly, then, looking straight into my eyes, asks what my role is going to be in getting Armenia back up on its feet.'[16] Mnakian's question to Zohrap implies an obligatory relationship between the diaspora and the new homeland that has been ascribed to him. It is important to note that *Letters from Zaat'ar* is set in the immediate years following the establishment of the Republic of Armenia after the fall of the Soviet Union in 1991. As Soviet policies significantly limited contacts between institutions and individuals in and outside Armenia, independence marked a shift in the relationships and expectations between Armenia and its diaspora. Mnakian does not ask *if* Zohrap will have a role in Armenia's future but rather *what* that role is going to be.

This sense of duty permeates throughout the novel. His experiences in Zaat'ar are marked by inadequacy. Zohrap has nothing to do, and his attempts at understanding the country and its history are unsuccessful. When he begins writing a novel in Armenian he shares his frustrations with the process with his friend Madam Veronica, a French national living in Zaat'ar. She asks him why he is not writing the novel in English and he responds, 'The moment I begin writing in English, I think I'll feel defeated, and convinced that the Armenian language will cease to exist, will have no use in the diaspora. I still can't come to terms with that idea'. Madam Veronica responds, 'It seems like writing in Armenian is like opening a consulate in Zaat'ar. There wasn't a hint of irony in Madam Veronica's tone.'[17] Madam Veronica equates his usage of the Armenian language with his decision to become the Armenian representative in Zaat'ar, a job that really serves no productive purpose and is a means of Zohrap dealing with his Armenian identity and his sense of obligation to his culture and people. Furthermore, Zohrap's later assertion that only about 400 people will actually read his novel admits to the fact that his endeavours, both as a writer and an Armenian, are limited, almost obsolete, but he continues anyway.

Like Karapents's and Oshagan's characters, Berberian's Zohrap is unable to quell the drive to perform a form of Armenian duty, even when that performance is admittedly absurd or unsuccessful, thus calling into question the institutions that instil the drive but not the structures to enable success. Zohrap's failure can be seen as a failure of the aspirations in his diasporic mission. While the institutions and the narratives they embody have successfully planted the seeds of duty, the fulfilment of that duty, outside the narrow scope embodied by the status quo, seems fruitless; the frameworks, however, hold strong as the diasporic identity remains rooted in duty, regardless of its effectiveness. While institutions as a whole are critiqued, as we see through Zohrab's disenchantment with the government in Zaat'ar, the institution of marriage and the corporate world, it is the ineptitude of individuals who are unable to escape institutional confines that is often blamed.

Zaat'ar, as an imaginary space, represents the intersection of Armenia and the diaspora and provides a metaphorical space in which to resolve existential diasporic questions – of identity, belonging, purpose and persistence. Pointedly, despite his futility in Zaat'ar, Zohrap feels fulfilled and does not want to return to Los Angeles, to his wife, children and prior life, and is only forced to leave after a civil war breaks out in Zaat'ar. At the end of the novel, we learn that the entire narrative based in Zaat'ar is a figment of Zohrap Anmahuni's imagination, a result of a mental breakdown in Los Angeles. These revelations further solidify the critique of the diasporic condition and position the drive towards establishing diasporic identity, in its various forms, as ineffective, unavoidable and often psychologically debilitating.

Conclusion

All the main characters in these texts feel an inherited responsibility as diasporic Armenians to contribute to something of value, whether that be ideologically, spiritually or politically, to the Armenian people. The origins of this inheritance are identified through the Armenian Church, Armenian schools, narratives like Raffi's *Khent'ĕ* and more indirectly through the unnamed political and social institutions that reinforce these avenues. Karapents, Oshagan and Berberian are simultaneously embodying, critiquing and identifying these inherited responsibilities and the resulting burden and angst, while implying that without said responsibilities they would cease to be 'diasporic'. In 'Elites and Institutions in the Armenian Transnation', Tölölyan argues:

> Like any long-lived social formation, the Armenian diaspora is best understood as composed of those who passionately share the conflicts that divide it about the nature of their local, national, and transnational commitments and identities. The institutions of diasporic civil society provide material support to (and often try to censor or guide or 'direct', in Gramsci's sense) the public sphere that conducts these debates and conflicts, engaging in a range of cultural productions and political practices, defining, reproducing, and producing the diaspora in the process.[18]

Karapents's Adam Nurian, having fallen off the path of duty, reluctantly returns to it when he begins writing his novel in Armenian instead of English. Oshagan's Ter Avetis performs his duty by preaching in church and providing a social space for the Armenians, even as he questions his role while doing it. Berberian's Zohrap performs this duty when he accepts the futile job of Armenian consul in Zaat'ar until we learn that the entire ordeal was actually part of his imagination after a psychotic break in Los Angeles, thus pathologizing that sense of duty. It is important to note that these texts do not have 'happy' endings. Ultimately, the characters are as lost as, if not more than, they were at the beginning of the stories. Despite the consequences, however, the persistent presence of what Tölölyan calls their 'local, national, and transnational commitments and identities' is presented as testament to the strength and impact of 'stateless power'. The texts neither cast off that power nor completely accept it; rather, they hesitatingly concede to it as a means of potentially 'defining, reproducing, and producing, the diaspora' (Tölölyan 2000, 111).

Karapents, Oshagan and Berberian's texts grapple with the paradoxes of belonging, as they both critique and aim to embody the ruling assumptions. Completely rejecting previous models and ruling assumptions would come with self-inflicting consequences, as the writers and their characters are products of the institutions that confirm their existence and claims to Armenianness. A complete critique of the system would be a rejection of the self, not necessarily a consequence of the institutions and the narratives they espouse but of the diasporic condition itself. In a rare personal reflection, Khachig Tölölyan outlines what he calls some of the 'ruling assumptions' of his youth as a diasporan:

> I grew up within and out of them, but modified versions of these assumptions are ones I grapple with every day, both in my life as a diasporan intellectual who writes in Armenian and as a scholar of diasporas who writes in English. To wit: diasporas exist neither in necessary opposition to their homelands' nationalism nor in a servile relationship to them. . . . The stateless power of diasporas lies in their heightened awareness of both the perils and rewards of multiple belonging, and in their sometimes exemplary grappling with the paradoxes of such belonging, which is increasingly the condition that non-diasporan nationals also face in the transnational era.[19]

Tölölyan's reflections represent an ideal version of what a diaspora can be if a delicate balance between sometimes seemingly opposing forces is reached; essentially, there is no alternative to the paradoxes of belonging, as they embody the diasporic experience. Through their work, intellectuals and artists shape diasporic identity by engaging in and maintaining the fluctuating discourse of diaspora. The commitment of the 'leadership elite' provides many experiences, environments and resources to do so.

Notes

1 Vahé Oshagan, 'Poles Apart: Vahe Oshagan on the Habitat, Imagery, and Inner Reaches of the Diaspora', Interview by Ishkhan Jinbashian. *Armenian International Magazine (AIM)*, July 1991, 15.
2 Ibid.
3 Khachig Tölölyan, 'Rethinking *Diaspora(s)*: Stateless Power in the Transnational Moment', *Diaspora: A Journal of Transnational Studies* 5, no. 1 (Spring 1996): 18–19.
4 Ibid., 19.
5 Hakob Karapents, *Erku Ashkharh (Two Worlds)* (Watertown: Blue Crane Books, 1992), 76–7; All translations in this chapter are my own, unless otherwise noted.
6 Ara Ghazarian, ed., *Hakob Karapents: A Complete Bibliography* (Watertown: Blue Crane Books, 1999), 3.
7 Ibid., 10–16.

8 Hakob Karapents, *Adami Girk'ě* (*Adam's Book*) (New York: Osketaṛ Hratarakch'akan, 1983), 65.
9 Ibid., 49.
10 Ibid., 66.
11 Many diaspora publications and cultural centres have historically been affiliated with the diaspora churches, political parties, and the Armenian General Benevolent Union (AGBU). These institutions have been instrumental in shaping Armenian Diaspora communities and are often the avenues through which community members interact and become exposed to cultural content. Karapents, Oshagan and Berberian's works have been published and reviewed favourably by institutionally affiliated or adjacent publications, without which their Armenian-language texts would either remain unpublished or reach a much smaller audience.
12 Marc Nichanian, 'In Memoriam: Vahé Oshagan', *Armenian Review* 47, no. 1–2 (2001): 168.
13 Ibid., 167–8.
14 Vahé Oshagan, *'Otsumē'* (*'Unction'*) *T'akardin shurj* (*Around the Trap*) (New York: Osketaṛ Hratarakch'akan, 1988), 48.
15 Ibid., 69.
16 Vahe Berberian, *Namakner Zaat'arēn* (*Letters from Zaat'ar*) (Los Angeles: Arvest, 1996), 4.
17 Ibid., 68–9.
18 Khachig Tölölyan, 'Elites and Institutions in the Armenian Transnation', *Diaspora: A Journal of Transnational Studies* 9, no. 1 (2000): 111.
19 Tölölyan, 'Rethinking *Diaspora(s)*', 7–8.

7

The Liturgical Subject of the Armenian Apostolic Church

Recent waves of migration*

Christopher Sheklian

Introduction

Wafting in from the sanctuary, incense mixed with the smell of burning candles as I sat with the priest in his office. After touring the grounds and admiring the fine examples of Armenian icons, noting the saints adorning the walls, Der Hayr and I retired to his office, connected to the sanctuary of the St. Mary Armenian Apostolic Church in Décines, France. We began discussing the ubiquitous problem of *Hayabahbanum*, 'staying Armenian', while drinking the thick coffee common among Armenians worldwide. I had the distinct feeling I had been here before. I had not. Not only was it my first time in Décines, a commune of Lyon, it was my first trip to France. Yet the flimsy cups of *haygagan surj* were nearly identical to the ones served with *simit* in a little room across the courtyard from the *Surp Pırgiç* Armenian Hospital in Istanbul that I frequented while living in Turkey. Incense suffused both the church in Décines and the brick chapel in Istanbul with the same smell permanently singed in my nostrils from week after week of swinging the *purvar*, the censor, in another brick church in Yettem, California. Sensorially, from the lingering smell of incense to the tactile sensation of the little cups to the grit of one sip of coffee too many, the Armenian Apostolic Church and its attendant spaces seem to knit space-time together. The Divine Liturgy, the *Badarak* conducted everywhere in Classical Armenian, the unique architecture of Armenian Church buildings, the Mother-and-Child icon at the centre of every altar and all of the elements of the Armenian liturgy are shared across time and space. Such a sensory commonality extends beyond the sanctuary, to priests' offices and banquet halls. The same tastes, smells and sounds greet one, no matter where in the world geographically that may be.[1]

As a major institution of the Armenian Diaspora, the Armenian Apostolic Church's ability to foster such common sensorial and affective experiences is central to its role in forging a particular kind of diasporic Armenian subject. This subject, shaped in the crucible of the liturgical life of the Armenian Church,[2] is but one of many potential modes of being and belonging for a transnational Armenian in the twenty-first century.[3] Yet due to the omnipresence of the Armenian Church in the diaspora and its foundational place among Armenian institutions, this liturgical subject of the Armenian Apostolic Church holds a prominent place in the national imagination. While the liturgical subject, the faithful, regular churchgoer that is the church's ideal, is but one potential mode of belonging to the Armenian Diaspora and (trans)nation in the twenty-first century, it is the ideal mode of belonging specific to one of the largest subsets of the Armenian Diaspora. Exploring the mode of subjectivation of the liturgical subject sheds light on the continued power and place of the church in broader diasporan life. Through the continued influence of the liturgical subject in diaspora life and in the place the figure has in the national imagination, the liturgical subject serves as a prime example of the non-state governmental power of institutions in diaspora.

In this chapter, I argue that the affective experience and the institutional role of the Armenian Apostolic Church encourage the formation of this particular kind of *liturgical subject*.[4] This liturgical subject, formed through what I will call *ecclesial governmentality*, is a diasporan Armenian subject grounded in the Armenian Apostolic Church. Drawing heavily on the ideas of influential French philosopher Michel Foucault and his work on power, governmentality and formation of subjects, I develop ecclesial governmentality as a mode of power specific to the institution of the church. To do so, I engage the work of more recent scholars who have found Foucault's inquiries useful for thinking about Christianity, including Talal Asad's discussion of discipline in Western Medieval monastic discipline and two earlier uses of the term 'liturgical subject' in the Byzantine and Eastern Orthodox contexts, one by Derek Krueger and another by Sergey S. Horujy.[5] Taken together, these concepts of liturgical subject and ecclesial governmentality help clarify the specific mode of belonging of the Armenian Church, delineate the place and power of the Armenian Church in Diaspora and offer a fine-grained description of an important form of non-state governmental power.

Ecclesial governmentality across the transnation

Ecclesial governmentality, while anchored in the liturgical life of the church, is limited neither to the liturgy nor even to the church itself. Through expressions of institutional influence including the instantiation of the liturgical subject as a normative figure in the Armenian Diaspora, the ecclesial governmentality of the Armenian Apostolic Church extends beyond the doors of the church itself. The Armenian Apostolic Church secures a central role in transnational Armenian life by encouraging the emergence of the liturgical subject as a pan-diasporan norm. In the workings of the ecclesial governmentality of the Armenian Church, a decidedly transnational institution, we have a prime example of non-state governmental power that elucidates the role of religious institutions in diaspora.

The exploration of this form of power, and the place of the Armenian Apostolic Church as an institution within the Armenian Diaspora in this chapter, owes much to the pioneering work of Khachig Tölölyan. In his argument that the Armenian Diaspora in the late twentieth century began a movement from 'exilic nationalism to diasporic transnationalism', he offers a profound take on the shifts still occurring and locates them in a broader argument about the role of stateless power.[6] His careful elucidation of the concepts of diaspora and transnation inform my use of the two terms.

Tölölyan distinguishes between diaspora and transnation, even while noting that they can be used together to describe the current state of Armenian dispersion worldwide.[7] 'Diasporas', he notes, 'are emblems of transnationalism because they embody the question of borders, which is at the heart of any adequate definition of the Others of the nation-state'.[8] Diaspora, in Tölölyan's lucid exposition, might not be as conceptually stringent as in an earlier understanding of the term grounded in a 'Jewish-centered definition that prevailed from the second century CE until circa 1968'.[9] Yet, he insists on some specificity, suggesting that 'a diaspora is never merely an accident of birth, a clump of individuals living outside their ancestral homeland, each with a hybrid subjectivity, lacking collective practices that underscore (not just) their difference from others, but also their similarity to each other, and their links to the people on the homeland'.[10] Transnation, on the other hand, 'includes all diasporic communities *and* the homeland'. In the Armenian case, 'the populations of the diaspora, of the Republic of Armenia, and of the Republic of (Nagorno- or Nagorny-) Karabagh [. . .] are together considered the Armenian transnation'.[11] Following Tölölyan, I deploy both diaspora and transnation throughout. In general, I use 'diaspora' to emphasize the population outside the 'homeland' and also to highlight the relationship between the homeland and these other communities. That is, I prefer diaspora in the instances either where the homeland is not invoked at all or in those where the connection between a community and the homeland is emphasized. Diaspora, then, in this usage, emphasizes that a given community or set of communities is outside the homeland. On the other hand, I use 'transnation' to emphasize any number of relationships between individual communities (including those in the Republic of Armenia) and to highlight the work across communities. Transnation, then, includes the 'homeland', but also focuses less on the fact that a given community is or is not in or out of the 'historic homeland', instead stressing the many and varied connections between communities.

In addition to these foundational conceptual distinctions, Tölöyan points us in the direction of non-state institutional power, especially in his 'Elites and Institutions in the Armenian Transnation'.[12] Finally, he has penned one of the clearest articulations of the place of the Armenian Church in Diaspora, 'The Role of the Armenian Apostolic Church in the Diaspora'.[13] Though this particular essay is now thirty years old and also more prescriptive than what follows, I lean heavily on Tölölyan's insights about the Armenian Apostolic Church. Thus, Tölölyan's keen analysis of the role of the church, the idea of diaspora and non-state institutional power provides an important springboard for my own reflections here on the role of the Armenian Church and its ecclesial power.

Ecclesial governmentality is how I will describe this form of ecclesial power, following Michel Foucault's understanding of governmentality as the specific art or technique of government.[14] In what follows, we will see the broad workings of ecclesial governmentality aimed at creating and securing the unique form of Christian collectivity, the church understood as *ecclesia*. In addition to the focus of ecclesial governmentality on the collective, the level of population, ecclesial governmentality also works at the level of the individual. It shapes a specific form of Armenian Christian subject, what I will call the liturgical subject.

In the case of the Armenian Apostolic Church, it is particularly important to attend to liturgy as a mode of subjectivation. The liturgy cultivates a certain moral subject. Several authors have drawn on the work of Foucault concerning both governmentality and the disciplinary formation of subjects to explore the Christian context. Talal Asad has argued in the case of medieval Christian monasticism that 'the formation/transformation of moral dispositions (Christian virtues) depended on more than the capacity to imagine, to perceive, to imitate'. Rather, it 'required a particular program of disciplinary practices' and these practices aimed at the formation of a distinctive Christian self by 'contruct[ing] and reorganize[ing] distinctive emotions'.[15] Following Asad, Saba Mahmood has shown how these disciplinary practices are fundamentally productive of an embodied subject with agency through a 'mode of subjectivation', that is, 'how people are incited or called up on to recognize their moral obligations'.[16]

Derek Krueger and Sergey S. Horujy likewise draw on Foucault's insights about subject formation in their respective deployments of the concept of the liturgical subject in the Byzantine and Eastern Orthodox Christian contexts. Derek Krueger argues that while 'the liturgical self was only one of many contending in the broader culture', 'it arguably had the greatest impact on Byzantine Christian self-conceptions across society'.[17] 'Liturgy was the place where Christians learned to apply the Bible to themselves', and ultimately, liturgy was a form of 'ritualization to produce subjectivity'.[18] Similarly, Sergey S. Horujy compares Eastern Christian practices to Foucault's 'practices of the self', describing how Eastern Christianity inculcates a subject through a wide variety of Christian practices whose ultimate aim or *telos* is communion with God.[19] Both Krueger and Horujy encourage attention to the techniques of the body cultivated in and through liturgy, influencing my description of a liturgical subject enmeshed in and produced through an ecclesial governmentality.

This chapter develops these two ideas of ecclesial governmentality and the liturgical subject as a way of describing the non-state governmental power of the Armenian Church across the Armenian transnation. As Tölölyan and other scholars including Hratch Tchilingirian have noted, the Armenian Church is a central institution for Armenian life.[20] This remains the case, especially at the institutional level, despite reduced church attendance and large numbers of parishioners who only attend services on special occasions.[21] In part, as this chapter demonstrates, the continued centrality of the church derives from the normative force of the liturgical subject. Despite this continued centrality of the church as an institution and the form of life specific to the church, its mode of power and subject formation and its precise role across the transnation remain vastly undertheorized. By attending to two specific cases, Baku Armenians in Detroit and Syrian Armenians in Décines, France, this chapter explores the role of the Armenian Church transnationally through the waves of migration from different nodes of the diaspora.

Continued waves of Armenian migration to previously established communities of the Armenian Diaspora offer one of the clearest dynamics through which to see the role of the church. While ecclesial governmentality operates wherever the church does, and the liturgical subject functions as a transnational norm, the movement of individuals from one community to another offers a particularly sharp heuristic into the workings of the disciplinary power of the Armenian Apostolic Church. Susan Paul Pattie, in her now-classic ethnographic study of Cypriot Armenians in both Cyprus and London, discerned the extent to which the church 'provide[s] an infrastructure that links communities on a more formal level'.[22] Moreover, she is one of the first to describe how both successive waves of migration and 'succeeding generations occupying the same territory have been known to accuse each of not understanding the other's world'.[23] Pattie's careful multi-sited ethnography – a methodological innovation at the time and still one of the few examples in the study of Armenians – is an important discussion of the 'waves of migration' that make up the overlapping populations of the modern Armenian Diaspora.[24]

Anny Bakalian's pioneering work *Armenian-Americans: From Being to Feeling Armenian* is one of the few texts to explicitly use the phrase 'waves of Armenian migration' to describe the phases of Armenian migration to America throughout the twentieth century.[25] Sensitively, she argues that not just the contours of the community but 'Armenianness in the United States' itself 'continues to be shaped and reshaped with the influx of new immigrants', often through conflicts over language use or the role of institutions.[26] Work on the vitality of Western Armenian in the United States has demonstrated that the language's viability has depended heavily on teachers and literati who have come to America from other diasporan nodes.[27] Ethnographic work such as my ongoing project with recent Armenian migrants and refugees is well suited to take up such dynamics that arise from the fact of waves of migration.

What we might term the modern Armenian Diaspora, formed after the catastrophe of the 1915 Armenian Genocide and in distinction to earlier Armenian dispersions, has been shaped by these 'waves of migration', mostly the movement from the Middle Eastern centres of the diaspora, such as Turkey, Lebanon and Iran, to countries further West.[28] Since the fall of the Soviet Union, an additional wave of migration came from the Republic of Armenia and other post-Soviet countries. A more recent wave has fled ongoing violence in the Middle East stemming from the US-led invasion of Iraq in 2003, the ongoing civil war in Syria and the rise of the Islamic State. Early in the twenty-first century, then, the modern Armenian Diaspora in Europe and the Americas is a complex patchwork of different Armenian populations and experiences grounded in locations associated with previous strata of migration.

Taking recent Armenian migration from Azerbaijan (Baku) to Detroit and Syria (Aleppo) to Décines, France, two established Armenian communities in America and Europe, this chapter demonstrates how the non-state ecclesial governmentality of an institutional church inculcates a normative diasporic subject, disciplining new arrivals and encouraging their formation as an ideal member of a new community according to the norms of church hierarchs and other community leaders. In particular, the case of the Baku Armenians in Detroit will be used to develop the broader workings of ecclesial governmentality. Church formation *qua ecclesia*, the body of Christ, is the primary object of ecclesial governmentality. Syrian Armenians in Décines, coming from a very different social milieu in Aleppo, provide ethnographic evidence to develop the concept of the liturgical subject. Taken together and in contrast, the two cases clarify the concepts of ecclesial governmentality and the liturgical subject.

Both concepts have a broader applicability outside of the Armenian case. Any church with an understanding of the church as the body of Christ can deploy ecclesial governmentality. Likewise, the liturgical subject emerges as a possible subjectivity among the liturgically oriented denominations. While the central ideas of this chapter are especially helpful in analysing the Armenian case, they have a potentially wider applicability. In particular, by looking at the waves of Armenian migration, the chapter suggests how this form of power and subject formation addresses the timely question of migration and refugees.[29]

Discussing the ways integration has been framed by both academics and policymakers, anthropologist Liisa Malkki describes 'the bureaucratic UN model of the three "durable solutions" to refugee problems – repatriation, integration, and resettlement'.[30] Often, the discussion around the integration of the migrant or refugee into a new country of residence describes the assimilation of the migrant as a problem, the burden of which falls heavily on the migrant herself. While Malkki is referring to the legal category of the refugee, one very distinct subset of the broader category of the migrant, the question of integration or assimilation is a common theme in discussions of migration. Clearly, there are practical and ethical, as well as theoretical, issues arising from the dramatic movement of people around the globe.[31] The current refugee crisis makes these questions all the more immediate.[32] Research on religion and migration has often noted the role of churches in facilitating movement.[33] This chapter adds to this literature by developing ecclesial governmentality as a conceptual tool to analyse the dynamics by which this occurs.

Thus, I offer the notion of ecclesial governmentality as a framework for understanding the subject formation of transnational migrants through a non-state but nonetheless dominant institution in a diasporic setting. Through the existing transnational networks of the church and the formative power of the church as an institution, migrants are incorporated into existing diasporic communities and inculcated in a normative subjecthood. The chapter develops the concepts of ecclesial governmentality and the liturgical subject in dialogue with ethnographic examples of waves of Armenian migration. In doing so, it addresses concerns unique to the Armenian case, such as the place of the Armenian Apostolic Church in the Armenian Diaspora, while also offering a broader theoretical framework for thinking about how transnational institutions influence the transition experienced by refugees and migrants.

The Armenian Apostolic Church: A 'National Home' in diaspora?

Diasporic institutions like the Armenian Apostolic Church strive to create a transferable sense of space grounded in a developed sensorium that feels like a common home. At the most immediate felt level, that of affect, even before feelings are processed into nameable emotions, sensations such as the lingering smell of incense evoke other times and spaces.[34] By cultivating experiences and sensations that harness such an affective response and by developing a sensorium that recognizes connections across time and space, diasporic institutions work to stitch individual sites together into a transnational network.[35] To the extent that they are successful in creating an affective sense of transferability their sites and spaces make claim on the nation itself, to be a site of 'home' outside the homeland.[36]

In the specific case of the Armenian Apostolic Church, this transferability is both a built-in feature of its organization *qua* church and the product of concerted ideological effort. It is an inherent feature of the understanding of church as *ecclesia*, the assembly gathered together as a single body that thus has a single experience. According to the liturgical self-understanding of the Armenian Apostolic Church, it invites worshippers to enter into God's time and to become the *ecclesia*, in Armenian *egeghets'i*, the church as the body of Christ that encompasses the living and the dead, all true worshippers of Christ across time and space.[37] Architecturally, an ornate neo-Gothic or concrete Brutalist structure can become an Armenian Apostolic Church through certain interior orientations and characteristics.[38] In these ways, experiential transferability is a built-in feature of the Armenian Apostolic Church.

At the same time, there is a history of concerted ideological claims by the church to be not only one among many institutions of the Armenian Diaspora but *the* institution, the national home for all Armenians. Historically, as Tölölyan notes, the church often did achieve institutional primacy, for instance in the Ottoman context when 'the Church had become *the* most important institution in Armenian life, *de jure* as well as *de facto* in the Ottoman Empire, and *de facto* beyond the boundaries of the Empire'.[39] Under the discourse of modern nationalism, the Armenian Apostolic Church asserted its claim not only to institutional primacy but to be coextensive with the nation.[40] Of course, there have often been Armenians who existed outside the purview of the church.[41] By the early twentieth century non-Apostolic Christian Armenians were a numerous, established and persistent reality. From that point forward, the institutional centrality of the Armenian Church in the construction of the ideal Armenian subject would necessarily be an ideological assertion and tenuous achievement. From this perspective, the Armenian Apostolic Church today must offer the transferability of experience as part of its claim to be a uniquely central institution.

Therefore, the Armenian Church mobilizes its inherent transferability of sensation and experience constitutive of it as *ecclesia* to make, in today's modern Armenian Diaspora, an ideological argument about its central institutional role in the life of the Armenian nation. Grounded in historical experience and built on the unique features of the *ecclesia*, the centrality of the Armenian Church remains a tenuous and continuous achievement. To assert that it is the 'national home' for all Armenians not only proffers its institutional centrality but also makes the normative assertion about who the 'proper' Armenian (diasporic) subject is.[42] As with many other diasporic institutions, it hopes to claim an indispensable importance in the life of all Armenians in the transnation. Like other institutions, it too puts forward a normative mode of belonging in the Armenian nation, its vision of what the ideal, active, engaged Armenian acts like. Political parties, philanthropic organizations, lobbying groups, artists and academics all truck in such normative figurations of the ideal Armenian subject, and different institutions have been more or less successful in asserting that their vision of a proper Armenian is *the* proper Armenian. The normative liturgical subject, even if not achieved by everyone who steps foot in a church, stands as the church's teleological goal of subject formation. The power that shapes such a subject, forms the church as such and exerts a sizeable influence throughout the Armenian transnation is what I call ecclesial governmentality.

It is through this ecclesial governmentality that the Armenian Apostolic Church continues to make its claim as the 'national home' for Armenians in diaspora. Such a claim depends on a fundamental identification of Armenian with Armenian Apostolic Christian. If this was ever true, it is certainly no longer the empirical reality of the Armenian Diaspora in the twenty-first century. Yet the liturgical subject inculcated through an ecclesial governmentality, the well-disciplined liturgical subject of the Armenian Apostolic Church, remains a powerful force in diasporan life, especially as a normative mode of belonging to the Armenian nation. This productive disciplinary power of the Armenian Apostolic Church is deployed precisely in and through spaces that feel like the common home of the nation.

Bringing them in: Ecclesial governmentality and Baku Armenians in Detroit

Governmentality refers to the specific art or technique of government. It is a neologism by the influential philosopher Michel Foucault, who distinguished the concept from sovereignty.[43] In Foucault's telling, a specific art or series of tactics of government emerges with the decline of absolute sovereignty and is co-emergent with a notion of population, which government manages through 'a range of absolutely new tactics and techniques'.[44] Governmentality has as its object both the individual subject – the disciplined body – and an emergent object – population, the body politic.[45] If governmentality as Foucault conceives it arranges, substantiates and works upon the population, the body politic, what I call ecclesial governmentality, works upon the ecclesial population, the church conceived as the body of Christ.[46] This disciplinary power, the ecclesial governmentality of the church, should not be seen in a negative valence but is inherently productive: of desires, subjects and populations, for instance.[47]

It is worth noting that much of Foucault's elaboration of the notion of governmentality, of 'the government of self and others', draws its genealogy and its insights from pastoral care and the disciplinarity of the church to begin with.[48]

Foucault's genealogical inquiries trace the emergence of modern forms of power in part out of specifically Christian contexts like the monastery or practices of confession. While 'pastoral care' and ascetic discipline are not the only antecedents to Foucault's notion of governmentality, the Christian context is central to its emergence. In a way, then, to discuss the formative disciplinary power of the Armenian Apostolic Church is to return to ecclesiology and the role of the church in subject formation through a Foucauldian lens.

Baku Armenians in Detroit, the first ethnographic example, exemplify the workings of such an ecclesial governmental rationality. Due both to broader Soviet policies and the specifics of life in the capital of the Soviet Republic of Azerbaijan, Baku Armenians had not been previously accustomed to acting as part of the body of Christ.[49] Disciplinary ecclesial power fostered their incorporation into the *egeghets'i* of the St. John's Armenian Apostolic Church in Detroit. This integration demonstrates the efficacy of ecclesial governmentality as a mode of power that forms the ecclesial population with a particular clarity, in large part because Baku Armenians were previously rather unfamiliar with the life of the church. As a new wave of migration across the transnation, ecclesial governmentality needed to bring them in to the body of the *ecclesia*, the first object of such pastoral power. Ecclesial governmentality, in this first ethnographic example, acts on the *egeghets'i* conceived as the body of Christ, that is, at the level of the ecclesial population.

Armenians from Azerbaijan, mostly Baku, are some of the most recent Armenian immigrants in several waves of migration to this established Detroit community. Baku Armenians started coming to Detroit as early as 1988, before the fall of the Soviet Union. Armenians in the ethnically Armenian enclave of Nagorno-Karabakh, also known as Artsakh, had been under the administration of the Soviet Republic of Azerbaijan since the early years of the Soviet Union. In the context of the political opening of Glasnost in the 1980s, Armenians advocated to be detached from the Soviet Republic of Azerbaijan and attached to the Soviet Republic of Armenia. In this context, anti-Armenian pogroms, notably the Sumgait Massacres in 1988, took place within Azerbaijan. With the breakup of the Soviet Union in 1991, war broke out over the status of Artsakh (Nagorno-Karabakh), lasting until a tenuous ceasefire in 1994 established a self-declared and internationally unrecognized Armenian Republic in Artsakh.[50] Fleeing this violence, a sizeable population of Baku Armenians arrived in the Detroit area.

Detroit is a major centre of Armenian life in the United States dating to the late nineteenth century. As Robert Mirak writes in his history of Armenians in America until the First World War, 'with impetus from Henry Ford's 1911 broadcast of 5$ per day wages and the city's rapid industrial spurt after World War I, Detroit's 337 member Armenian colony of 1910 increased five-fold to 1,692 by 1920'.[51] After the Armenian Genocide of 1915 and the establishment of the Republic of Turkey in 1923, the population of Armenians in Detroit grew further and the community built up infrastructure, including churches. 'On November 22, 1931, with Archbishop Leon Tourian officiating, the church was consecrated St. John the Baptist Armenian Apostolic Church.'[52] It moved to its current location in Southfield, with the new church consecrated on Sunday, 20 November 1966. In addition to St. John's Armenian Church, there are other Armenian churches, as well as an Armenian school and other Armenian spaces and institutions. Today, collective, institutional Armenian life in Detroit – one of the largest and most vibrant Armenian communities in the United States – is heavily weighted towards churches, and the Armenian Apostolic Church specifically.[53]

In interviews with Fr Garabed Kochakian, the former pastor of the St. John's Armenian Church in Detroit, I discussed the incorporation of Baku Armenians into the Armenian community of Detroit. Baku Armenians are often non-Armenian-speaking and, not only because of Soviet pressure but because of the specifics of life in Baku, are often not regular churchgoers. Fr Garabed described his pastoral desire to integrate the Baku Armenians into the church community. He asked himself what he and the existing community could do to 'bring them in', to support and incorporate those refugees and migrants beyond the few who came occasionally to St. John's. Eventually, he pushed to have a memorial to the Sumgait Massacres built alongside the 1915 Armenian Genocide Memorial at the church. Crucially, he advocated not only for the building of the monument but also of the inclusion of Baku Armenians in the process of planning and building the memorial. Despite the fact that the Sumgait memorial marked Baku Armenians as a unique subset of the Detroit Armenian community, the process of including them in the governance and decision-making structures of the church incorporated them into the active ecclesial body. More than the literal emplacing of the monument, it was the incorporation into committees and parish council boards that brought them into the ecclesial population.[54] In Fr Garabed's telling, this inclusive endeavour had the desired effect, and to this day, Baku Armenians remain an integral part of the St. John Armenian Church community.

Fr Garabed's narrative of the incorporation of Baku Armenians is a model of pastoral care.[55] It also helps to subvert a narrative wherein it is the refugee or migrant's job 'to integrate', and instead asks what the already established community can do. Finally, it deviates from common concerns over Armenian waves of immigration about the potentially destabilizing presence of another wave of migration to a community in equilibrium but rather asks the community in question to do the work of incorporation. Nonetheless, Fr Garabed's narrative upholds the idea of the Armenian Apostolic Church as the natural home for all Armenians discussed above. This means that it is the job of the church as an institution, the priest engaging in pastoral care, and all of the parishioners in a community to help bring newcomers into the life of the church and to instruct and inculcate those who are not used to the life of the church. In Fr Garabed's narrative, this included Armenian-American forms of parish governance including active participation in the decision-making, financial health and planning of a church community. To be a good member of the Armenian community in this context means to be appropriately conditioned to forms of behaviour both in the liturgical life of the church itself and in adjacent church activities.

Not only did these Baku Armenians need training in liturgical life, but they were addressed as a population of Baku Armenians who needed to be brought into the larger ecclesial population. The health of the whole body of Christ depended on the coordinated activity of all its parts, and for this to happen, Baku Armenians had to be properly trained in the functioning of Armenian ecclesial activity. It is this training, undertaken by many different members of the church body, the *egeghets'i*, that is precisely the working of a non-state form of power to which Tölölyan's work has pointed. Ecclesial governmentality forms the church as such and supports its claim to be the 'national home' for all Armenians, actively creating an affective experience that stitches the transnation together. 'Ecclesial governmentality', then, is a specific mechanism whereby the Armenian Apostolic Church does this transnational work at the level of individual Armenian communities around the world.

From ecclesial governmentality to the liturgical subject: Syrian Armenians in Décines, France

Through the first ethnographic example of the migrant and refugee Baku Armenians as a recent wave of migration to Detroit, an established Armenian community, we clearly see the ecclesial governmental action of the Armenian Apostolic Church operating at the collective level of the *ecclesia*. Yet ecclesial governmentality works not only on the level of group or population, on the church as a whole. It also works on the level of the individual, producing well-formed liturgical subjects. The aim of ecclesial governmentality is not mere membership but the emergence of a robust liturgical subject.

The liturgical subject, like an expert piano player, is formed through constant care and attention to the body through specific practices. To become a proper subject, one aims at a *telos* – whether that be virtuoso piano playing or spiritual comportment towards God – by working on the self through what Foucault called 'technologies of the self'.[56] Such practices constitute the fundamentally productive disciplinary process of subjectivation, 'how people are incited or called upon to recognize their moral obligations'.[57] In the specific case of the liturgical subject, this work of subjectivation occurs in large part through the context of the liturgy, the public collective worship of the Christian *ecclesia*.

The work of Sergey S. Horujy and Derek Krueger develops this concept of the liturgical subject in conversation with Foucault's insights. Horujy describes the *telos* that is specific to the liturgical subject, namely communion with God.[58] While this *telos* transcends worldly communal life, in the Eastern Christian understanding shared between the Armenian case and the Eastern Orthodox one Horujy describes, it cannot be accomplished outside the *ecclesia*, the body of Christ. Thus, individual liturgical subjectivation works through the collective and communal practice of the liturgy which is simultaneously the fullest expression of *ecclesia* itself. Taken together with Derek Krueger's description of liturgy in the Byzantine context as a form of 'ritualization to produce subjectivity',[59] Horujy's discussion clarifies the connection between the liturgical subject and ecclesial governmentality. Such a liturgical subject is not merely a member of the church, coming and sitting in the pews, but has a sensorium cultivated in and through liturgy. Possibilities for moral action, bodily comportment in and out of the church building and many other aspects of self all characterize this well-formed liturgical subject. My use of the term 'liturgical subject' differs slightly from both Horujy's and Krueger's – through the incorporation of Asad and Mahmood's insights into subject formation as well as through the grounding in the Armenian rather than Eastern Orthodox case. Yet, their earlier use of the term demonstrates the connection between the disciplinary power at the heart of ecclesial governmentality and the subject formed in the crucible of the liturgical life of the church.

Aleppo Armenians who have found refuge from the violence in Syria in Décines, France, offer a particularly instructive ethnographic example to help uncover the content and centrality of the liturgical subject that is inculcated through this ecclesial governmentality. In part because these Armenians come from communities with a robust communal life, where – unlike in Azerbaijan – both the church and other institutions such as schools play a major part, we can see ethnographically the contours of the embodied liturgical subject of the Armenian Apostolic Church and its role as a pan-diasporic norm in the Armenian transnation. Aleppo Armenians were often already incorporated into the *ecclesia* and had liturgical training before their arrival in Décines. Therefore, they shed light on a further dynamic of ecclesial governmentality and exemplify how the liturgical subject as transnational diasporic norm facilitates waves of migration and even encourages the integration of the migrant into new nodes of the transnation.

Syria in general and Aleppo in particular have long been important centres of the Armenian world. Aleppo, an important early pilgrimage stop,[60] grew into the largest city of a sizeable regional population by the late Ottoman period.[61] Following the catastrophe of the 1915 Armenian Genocide, especially after the French signed the Accord of Ankara on 20 October 1921, the Armenian population swelled with survivors.[62] Through the French Mandate period lasting from 1923 to 1946 and into post-Mandate independence, Aleppo, with its ancient cathedral, became the focal point of a robust Armenian life in Syria confident 'that their organized community life [. . .] would continue undisturbed under the new circumstances of national independence'.[63]

In that community of Aleppo, 'Armenian religious and communal institutions', especially the Armenian Apostolic Church, maintained significant control over 'internal organization' in the post-Mandate period.[64] Confessional difference, as in the related case of Lebanon, was 'coproduced by French Mandate officials, Armenian political parties and town associations, and the newly formed confessional state'.[65] Though one institution in a robust community, the Armenian Apostolic Church gained prominence through the confessional policies of the independent Syrian state. During the Hafiz al-Assad regime, Armenian churches became even more important in the communal life of Syrian Armenians, since 'less exposed to closures and expropriations than parties and associations, [the churches] had become, for instance, the custodians of communal property'.[66]

Until the crushing response of the Bashar al-Assad regime that transformed peaceful protests in 2011 into an ongoing multifaceted civil war and upended the lives of Armenians in Syria alongside the rest of the country, this situation largely held.[67] Aleppo was the site of some of the fiercest fighting of the conflict. Many Armenians fled, both initially after Assad's crackdown and in the phase of the war in 2014 marked by the rise of Islamist groups.[68] They have sought refuge wherever they could find it. Some were able to secure refugee status, while others fled without the legal underpinning of that status, including some who relocated to the Republic of Armenia[69] (Kasbarian 2020). Others moved from Syria to Lebanon. Of those Syrian Armenians who left the region entirely, some made their way to France, adding a new layer to the waves of Armenian migration to one of the largest and most important nodes of the Armenian transnation.[70]

Most of the Syrian Armenians who fled to France settled in Décines-Charpieu, today a suburb of Lyon. Décines, as it is commonly known, has been home to Armenians since the early twentieth century, part of the corridor between Paris and Marseilles where many Armenians settled. Bishop Grigoris Balakian consecrated the first Armenian Apostolic Church in Décines in 1932.[71] On 27 April 1947, after delays caused by the Second World War, the current St. Mary's Church was consecrated. In addition to the Armenian Apostolic Church, the same neighbourhood where Armenians have historically lived hosts an Armenian Evangelical Church,[72] an Armenian Genocide Memorial at a roundabout on the Rue de 24 avril 1915 (named on the fiftieth anniversary of the Armenian Genocide), and the recently opened National Center of Armenian Memory (Centre National de la Mémoire Arménienne, CNMA).[73] Together, these institutions anchor a vibrant and historic Armenian community in this Lyon suburb.

Syrian Armenians, mostly from Aleppo, came to this established Armenian community as the most recent wave of migration. Several characteristics of this wave of migration make it an ideal ethnographic case from which to develop the place of the liturgical subject in the Armenian transnation and to evaluate its role in the process of migration. Recently arrived Syrian Armenians form a dense population relative to the overall community, marked by a Facebook group dedicated to Syrian Armenians in Lyon.[74] The increased centrality of the church in Syria before migration meant that many Aleppo Armenians coming to Décines were already enmeshed in the ecclesial governmentality of the Armenian Church. As Décines is likewise anchored in the church while retaining other Armenian collective offerings, it allows us to see the choices made by individual Aleppo Armenians. We can thus evaluate the efficacy of ecclesial governmentality not just in forming an ecclesial body (as in the Baku Armenian example earlier), but in its ability to produce and highlight the liturgical subject as *the* ideal Armenian diasporic subject. The suburb of Lyon, then, offers a compelling ethnographic site from which to flesh out the idea of the liturgical subject.

To develop the contours of the liturgical subject and her place within the Armenian transnation, in this chapter I provisionally rely on one individual, a deacon from Aleppo we'll call Harout.[75] I met Deacon Harout shortly after the moment of sensorial familiarity I described at the outset of the chapter. Harout had joined us on Der Hayr's invitation after learning about my research interests. The three of us, from different locations of the Armenian transnation, having never met before, were quite at ease, a keen reminder of the spatial and affective work of ecclesial governmentality that clearly stitched us together as the *ecclesia*, the *egeghets'i*. In one of the first interviews of this still-new ethnographic project, Harout set out the ways in which a group of Syrian Armenians had reconstituted themselves in this suburb of Lyon. They had set up a Syrian Armenians of Lyon Facebook group and a *miut'iwn*, an organization on the order of the old Compatriotic Societies that flourished after the Genocide.[76] For Harout, the existence of other Armenians in Décines had certainly been a pull. At the same time, he emphasized the more mundane realities of the cost of living. He noted that while he was a deacon and that the church in Décines had supported the Syrian Armenians, other Armenian institutions in the suburb, like the CNMA, were also places of communal gathering and collective support.

A deacon like Harout, who described to me his long association with the church in Aleppo before his arrival in France, is already an ideal liturgical subject. When I asked Der Hayr about Syrian Armenians in Décines, he immediately thought of Harout, whom he held up as a communal exemplar. Over the course of our conversation it became clear that Deacon Harout not only served the broader community but he also helped other Aleppo Armenians in their transition to live in Décines. Thus Harout, as a well-trained liturgical subject, easily found a role and a purpose in the church after his migration to France and was able to help others make the same transition he had. He demonstrates that the well-formed liturgical subject, enmeshed in the ecclesial governmentality of the Armenian Apostolic Church brings in others to the body of Christ, serves as a broader communal exemplar of a form of life, and is at ease across diasporic spaces, making the migratory transition easier. I hypothesize further ethnographic research will show that someone less connected, less 'disciplined' by the ecclesial governmentality of the Armenian Church, will not move so seamlessly across diasporic spaces, especially when arriving to communities where the church is so central to collective Armenian life.

Further ethnographic work with the Aleppo Armenians in Décines will clarify the ways the pastoral government of the church encourages the subjectivation, especially through the liturgy, of a Syrian Armenian in a largely church-oriented community. Moreover, as the initial discussions with Deacon Harout demonstrate, a well-formed liturgical subject moves with ease across the nodes of the transnation, in ways that other migrants might not. Harout, precisely as a deacon who has been enmeshed in the liturgy for much of his life, comports himself with the embodied subjectivity specific to the liturgical subject: trained in chanting, responding to the smells of incense, making the sign of the cross. His communal expression, while not limited to the church, is certainly focused on it. Thus, the well-disciplined liturgical subject and the church as institution reproduce each other.

Crucially, this bodily comportment and moral disposition of the liturgical subject is formed in the practice of liturgy but extends beyond the liturgy itself. This liturgical subject is not only comfortable in the liturgical setting itself but practices Christian charity, serves the church joyfully and places God at the centre of their lives. Deacon Harout has internalized both the physicality and mentality of liturgical subjectivity such that it operates in his daily life. If Horujy's insights remind us that there is a genuine Christian *telos* to ecclesial governmentality and that the ultimate goal of the liturgical subject is communion with God, I would also insist that the liturgical subject, necessarily living outside the walls of the church, emerges as a transformed and properly disciplined subject of the broader Christian community.

Conclusion

In this fundamental connection between the collective operation of ecclesial governmentality and the individual subjectivation process of the liturgical subject the analytical purchase of these concepts emerges. We have offered, with some precision, a description of the place of the Armenian Apostolic Church in the Armenian 'diasporic transnation' and its particular form of productive pastoral power. At the same time, through the specific case of the movement of Armenians in the 'waves of migration' across the transnation, we have demonstrated more broadly how a church might facilitate the migrant movement.

Through the ecclesial governmentality of the Armenian Church and its attendant ideal liturgical subject, the Armenian Church secures its place in the Armenian transnation. First, as in the case of Baku Armenians, the pastoral power of the church forms the *eccleisa* itself, acting on the level of population. Then, through the individual process of subjectivation, a well-trained liturgical subject who embodies the Christian norms at the heart of the church's teachings emerges. Through her actions and opinions, she reinforces the now-precarious identification of Armenian and Christian. The isomorphism of Armenian and Christian embodied in the liturgical subject bolsters the Armenian Church's vision for Armenianness in the twenty-first century. Working tirelessly for the Armenian Church, both locally and in different nodes of the transnation, as we saw with Deacon Harout and his support for other Aleppo Armenians in Décines, the liturgical subject secures the material continuity and ideological centrality of the Armenian Church. Subject and institution constantly reproduce each other. Taken together, this coproduction of ecclesial governmentality and the liturgical subject describe the mechanism by which the Armenian Church secures its place in the Armenian Diaspora.

As we have seen, the Armenian Church has features that create spaces that feel the same in different locations while making the ideological argument that it is the 'national home' for all Armenians in diaspora. Incense, the Classical Armenian and the cadence of the chanting of the psalms all build an affective, sensorial space that reproduces sameness across geographic distance. The liturgical subject like Deacon Harout, cultivated in the rich sensorial experience of liturgy that creates the experience of sameness across localities and well formed by the ecclesial governmentality of the church, navigates these common spaces most effectively. A migrant who moves between discrete localities of the Armenian transnation will feel 'at home' in the church to the extent that they have been shaped by the ecclesial governmentality of the church into a liturgical subject. A well-formed liturgical subject is precisely the migrant who will most easily integrate into an existing community where the church is central.

Ecclesial governmentality, as we have seen with the case of the Baku Armenians, operates first and foremost at the level of population, bringing people into the collectivity of the *ecclesia*. As Deacon Harout and the Syrian Armenians of Décines remind us, ecclesial governmentality also shapes humans through the Armenian Christian liturgy itself. This slow process, aimed at the total transformation of the human in a Christian context, nonetheless has consequences for the broader Armenian community, shaping a liturgical subject as a lodestar for Armenian belonging in general. Such a liturgical subject, though anchored in specific countries and communities as distant as Detroit and Décines, also shares certain fundamental characteristics across the globe. Such a subject may therefore find integration into new nodes of the transnation easier. The ecclesial governmentality of the Armenian Church, diffracted through diasporic conditions, happily shapes liturgical subjects and shepherds refugees and migrants into individual Armenian communities. In this way, the Armenian Apostolic Church exerts a profound non-state influence on the subjectivity of the entire Armenian transnation.

Notes

* Thank you to the fabulous and careful editors of this volume, Talar Chahinian, Sossie Kasbarian and Tsolin Nalbantian, who have greatly improved this chapter. This work was first presented at the 'Diaspora and "Stateless Power"' conference and I thank the organizers and participants for that initial opportunity to develop this project. Khachig Tölölyan's comments at the conference, his written work, and his generous engagement with my research suffuse both this chapter and my broader thinking, for which I am deeply grateful.

    The ethnographic research that undergirds this chapter has been supported by my time as a Manoogian Postdoctoral Fellow in Armenian Studies at the University of Michigan and as part of my current participation in the 'Rewriting Global Orthodoxy: Oriental Orthodox Christians in Europe, 1970–2020' research project. The project has received funding from the European Research Council (ERC) under the European Union's Horizon 2020 research and innovation programme (grant agreement No. 834441 GlobalOrthodoxy). My thanks to the members of the wonderful research team under the direction of Heleen Murre-van den Berg, who read an earlier version of this chapter. My long-time collaborators and friends, Shefali Jha and Xiao-bo Yuan, also offered invaluable comments on an earlier version of the chapter. All errors and omissions are, of course, mine.

1. Though the social life around churches looks different to some extent in the Republic of Armenia than in various parts of the Armenian Diaspora, there is still a strong sensorial continuity. Coffee is still served during a visit with a priest in offices or small rooms adjoining a church. Festal events especially warrant banquet tables (as for instance, during the consecration of three bishops in May 2019 at Etchmiadzin).

2. The Armenian Church, or Church of Armenia, in Armenian *Hayasdaneayts' Egeghets'i*, often called the Armenian Apostolic Church, refers to the autocephalous Christian church that traditionally traces its roots to the apostles St Thaddeus and St Bartholomew (hence 'apostolic') and held the main ecclesial jurisdiction over the territories historically known as Armenia. Names such as 'Apostolic', 'Orthodox' or 'Gregorian' (after the patriarch who converted the Armenian king) distinguish this Armenian Church from Armenian Catholic and Protestant churches as well as other Orthodox churches. Throughout, both for brevity and following this self-naming, I most often use 'Armenian Church', though I also use 'Armenian Apostolic Church' for emphasis or distinguishing clarity.

3. Transnational refers to the complex interconnectivity of people across nations, and transnationalism has emerged as a major area of academic study. See, for instance, Handel Kashope Wright and Meaghan Morris, eds., *Cultural Studies of Transnationalism* (Milton Park: Routledge, 2012).

4. Susan Paul Pattie has also noted the highly sensorial elements of the Armenian Apostolic Church and their role in connecting Armenians to the church and each other across time and space. She writes that 'the feeling of being in a completely Armenian environment, entirely cut off from contemporary distractions, provides a link with past generations of Armenians, giving both a sense of comfort and a sense of duty'. Susan Paul Pattie, *Faith in History: Armenians Building Community* (Washington and London: Smithsonian Institute Press, 1997), 221. Later, she connects the 'heavily sensuous atmosphere of the church' to the Armenian believer's sense of the 'reality

of the supernatural order', arguing that 'the liturgy and the pageant of the Armenian Mass is clearly directed toward portraying the mystery, the awe-inspiring nature, and the otherness of God'. Ibid., 239.

5 Talal Asad, *Genealogies of Religion: Discipline and Reasons of Power in Christianity and Islam* (Baltimore and London: The Johns Hopkins University Press, 1993); Derek Krueger, *Liturgical Subjects: Christian Ritual, Biblical Narrative, and the Formation of Self in Byzantium* (Philadelphia: University of Pennsylvania Press, 2014); Sergey S. Horujy, *Practices of the Self and Spiritual Practices: Michel Foucault and the Eastern Christian Discourse*, trans. Boris Jakim (Grand Rapids and Cambridge: William B. Eerdmans Publishing Company, 2015).

6 Khachig Tölölyan, 'Elites and Institutions in the Armenian Transnation', *Diaspora: A Journal of Transnational Studies* 9, no. 1 (2000): 107.

7 In some bodies of work, diaspora and transnation(al/ism) are used in opposition. Thomas Faist describes them as 'awkward dance partners' that 'reflect different intellectual genealogies'. Thomas Fiast, 'Diaspora and Transnationalism: What Kind of Dance Partners', in *Diaspora and Transnationalism: Concepts, Theories and Methods*, ed. Rainer Baubök and Thomas Faist (Amsterdam: Amsterdam University Press, 2010), 9. We can see that in Tölölyan's use they have some overlap. The centrality of this interaction between these two concepts of diaspora and transnation(al/ism) in Tölölyan's careful work is marked by the fact that the journal he founded in 1991 is called *Diaspora: A Journal of Transnational Studies*.

8 Khachig Tölölyan, 'The Nation-State and Its Others: In Lieu of a Preface', *Diaspora: A Journal of Transnational Studies* 1, no. 1 (1991): 6.

9 Khachig Tölölyan, 'Rethinking *Diaspora*(s): Stateless Power in the Transnational Moment', *Diaspora: A Journal of Transnational Studies* 5, no. 1 (1996): 12.

10 Tölölyan, 'Rethinking *Diaspora*(s)', 30. Diaspora, for its part, has become one of those fraught academic concepts that seems to proliferate definitions beyond any use. As Khachig Tölölyan notes, quoting Walter Connors, diaspora for many theorists means simply 'that segment of a people living outside the homeland' (1996, 15). Such a capacious definition leads thinkers like Stéphane Dufoix to argue for the abandonment of the term, preferring instead 'the establishment of a broader, more complex analytical framework that takes into account the structuring of the collective experience abroad based on the link maintained with the referent-origin and the community stance this creates'. Stéphane Dufoix, *Diasporas*, trans. William Roadarmor (Berkeley and Los Angeles: University of California Press, 2008), 3. Tölölyan and others like him, on the other hand, continue to see value in the term, though laying out a framework that would have it designate something more specific than simply any community living in dispersion.

    Scholarly study of Armenians has been so bound up with the concept of diaspora that Tsolin Nalbantian has recently argued that 'situating Armenians exclusively within Diaspora Studies almost by necessity ignores, or at least smoothens, differences amongst Armenians within a particular location'. Nalbantian's important intervention invites careful consideration of when and how diaspora is deployed in the study of Armenian communities. Tsolin Nalbantian, *Armenians Beyond Diaspora: Making Lebanon Their Own* (Edinburgh: Edinburgh University Press, 2020), 24.

11 Tölölyan, 'Elites and Institutions in the Armenian Transnation', 130–1.
12 Ibid., 107–36.
13 Khachig Tölölyan, 'The Role of the Armenian Apostolic Church in the Diaspora', *Armenian Review* 41, no. 1 (1988): 55–68.

14 Michel Foucault, 'Governmentality', in *The Foucault Effect: Studies in Governmentality with Two Lectures by and an Interview with Michel Foucault*, ed. Graham Burchell, Colin Gordon, and Peter Miller (Chicago: University of Chicago Press, 1991): 94.
15 Asad, *Genealogies of Religion*, 134.
16 Saba Mahmood, *Politics of Piety: The Islamic Revival and the Feminist Subject* (Princeton: Princeton University Press, 2005), 29–30.
17 Krueger, *Liturgical Subjects*, 7.
18 Ibid., 8, 12.
19 Horujy, *Practices of the Self and Spiritual Practices*, 56.
20 Tchilingirian has written some of the most careful social scientific analyses of the Armenian Apostolic Church and the role of Christianity and the church in Armenian life more broadly. His rich oeuvre undergirds much of the discussion here. On the institutional role of the Armenian Apostolic Church, for instance, he writes that 'as the largest national institutional after the Armenian state, the Armenian Church remains the most institutionalized (and "bureaucratic" in the Weberian sense) Armenian establishment anywhere in the world'. Note that he connects this institutional priority precisely to its transnational character. Hratch Tchilingirian, 'Modern "Believers" in an Ancient Church: The Armenian Apostolic Church', in *Arméniens et Grecs en diaspora: approches comparatives*, ed. Michel Bruneau, Ioannis Hassiotis, Martin Hovanessian, and Claire Mouradian (Athens: École Française d'Athènes, 2007), 492–3.
21 See, for instance, the ongoing work of the 'Armenian Diaspora Survey', which is in the process of providing important data regarding Armenian communities around the world. The survey has a section dedicated to the 'religion and spirituality' of the individual taking the survey, including asking about an 'active spiritual life'. See the 2019 survey results, available at https://www.armeniandiasporasurvey.com/. Additionally, see the ethnographic and sociological work of Sara Kärkkäinen Terian, 'Sanctuary, Community or Museum? The Apostolic Church in the Life-Worlds of a Sample of Armenian Americans', in *Armenian Christianity Today: Identity Politics and Popular Practice*, ed. Alexander Agadjanian (Oxfordshire and New York: Ashgate, 2014), 253–72.
22 Pattie, *Faith in History*, 8.
23 Ibid., 5.
24 Since then, other studies of the Armenian Diaspora have taken up both the idea of 'waves of migration' and careful, often multi-sited ethnographic approaches. See, for example, Sossie Kasbarian, 'The Armenian Community in Cyprus at the Beginning of the 21st Century: From Insecurity to Integration', in *The Minorities of Cyprus: Development Patterns and the Identity of Internal-Exclusion*, ed. A. Varnavas, N. Coureas and M. Elia (Newcastle upon Tyne: Cambridge Scholars Publishing, 2009), 175–91. On the method of multi-sited ethnography, see the foundational essay by George Marcus, 'Ethnography in/of the World System: The Emergence of Multi-Sited Ethnography', *Annual Review of Anthropology* 24 (1995): 95–117.
25 Anny Bakalian, *Armenian-Americans: From Being to Feeling Armenian*, 2nd ed. (New York: Routledge, 2017), 23.
26 Ibid., 19.
27 Hagop Gulludjian, 'Language Vitality Through "Creative Literacy"', in *Western Armenian in The 21st Century: Challenges and New Approaches*, ed. Bedross Der Matossian and Barlow Der Mugrdechian (Fresno: The Press at California State University, Fresno, 2018), 103–32.

28 Often, these migrations followed significant upheaval or political change: in Turkey the 'Wealth Tax' during the Second World War and pogroms directed largely against the Greek community in 1955, the 1975–90 Lebanese Civil War and the 1979 Islamic Revolution in Iran. See Ayhan Aktar, *Varklık Vergisi ve 'Türkleştirme' Politikaları* (*The Wealth Tax and the Politics of 'Becoming Turkish'*) (Istanbul: İlteşim, 2000), 135–214; Ali Tuna Kuyucu, 'Ethno-religious "Unmixing" of "Turkey": 6–7 September Riots as a Case in Turkish Nationalism', *Nations and Nationalism* 11, no. 3 (2005): 361–80; Nicola Migliorino, (*Re*)*Constructing Armenia in Lebanon and Syria: Ethno-Cultural Diversity and the State in the Aftermath of a Refugee Crisis* (New York and Oxford: Berghahn Books, 2008); Joanna Randa Nucho, *Everyday Sectarianism in Urban Lebanon: Infrastructures, Public Public Services, and Power* (Princeton: Princeton University Press, 2016); James Barry, *Armenian Christians in Iran: Ethnicity, Religion, and Identity in the Islamic Republic* (Cambridge: Cambridge University Press, 2018).

29 Daniel Sack offers a fascinating look at the role of food among American Protestant Christians in *Whitebread Protestants* that also points to the role of ecclesial subject formation among migrant communities. Regarding the St. Pauls Church in Chicago founded by German immigrants in 1843, he notes that the church 'served as their community center, where people could both feel at home and experiment with assimilation. It preserved ethnic solidarity and tradition against the homogenizing forces of the larger culture. And it provided opportunities for young people to meet and court, encouraging marriage within the community'. Daniel Sack, *Whitebread Protestants: Food and Religion in American Culture* (New York: Palgrave, 2000), 66.

30 Liisa H. Malkki, 'Refugees and Exile: From 'Refugee Studies' to the National Order of Things', *Annual Review of Anthropology* 24 (1995): 505.

31 According to the most recent data of the United Nations High Commissioner for Refugees, there were 84 million forcibly displaced people worldwide in the middle of 2021. Of these, some 26.6 million were classified as refugees. See https://www.unhcr.org/refugee-statistics/. Of course, the stark rise in global mobility extends beyond the question of forcible displacement and is the subject of a huge body of literature on globalization and mobility.

32 The number of forcibly displaced persons and refugees is now more than those displaced during the Second World War. See Nick Cumming-Bruce, 'Number of People Fleeing Conflict Is Highest Since World War II, U.N. Says', *New York Times,* 19 June 2019, https://www.nytimes.com/2019/06/19/world/refugees-record-un.html. The numbers of forcibly displaced increased dramatically in the last decade or so, as noted in the UNHCR report from 2017, when the then-high number reached 68.5 million: 'The past decade has seen a substantial increase in the world's forcibly displaced population, with the number standing at 42.7 million in 2007.' See the 2017 report here: https://www.unhcr.org/globaltrends2017/#:~:text=In%202017%2016.2%20million%20people,new%20high%20of%2068.5%20million. The most recent report, cited in the footnote above, does not yet account for the dramatic rise of displaced persons resulting from Russia's invasion of Ukraine. Already before the release of their 2022 report, the UNHCR has said that the number of forcibly displaced persons has surpassed 100 million for the first time, a 'staggering milestone'. Diane Taylor, 'Number of Displaced Passes 100m for the First Time, Says UN', *The Guardian,* 23 May 2022. https://www.theguardian.com/globaldevelopment/2022/may/23/total-displaced-people-now-at-staggering-milestone-of-100msays-un. Accessed 24 May 2022.

33 Much of this work on religion and migration focuses on the United States-Mexico border, for instance Kristin E. Heyer, *Kinship Across Borders: A Christian Ethic of Immigration* (Washington, DC: Georgetown University Press, 2012). For a nice

overview of the literature on theology and migration that simultaneously offers a constructive theology of migration, see Ilsup Ahn, 'Theology and Migration', *Theology* 3, no. 2 (2019): 1–108. For work that explores the European refugee crisis after the Syrian War with an eye to Orthodox Christian responses, see Lucian N. Leustean, 'Summary Report of the British Academy Project on "Forced Migration, Religious Diplomacy and Human Security in the Eastern Orthodox World"', *International Journal for the Study of the Christian Church* 19, no. 1 (2019): 72–6.

34 For discussions of the affective sense of 'what does it feel like to be in diaspora', see Lauren Wagner, 'Feeling Diasporic', *Tilburg Papers in Culture Studies* 21 (2012). Svetlana Boym offers an important discussion of nostalgia, often a central element in the discussion of the emotional aspect of diaspora. Svetlana Boym, *The Future of Nostalgia* (New York: Basic Books, 2001).

35 Like the work on affect, there is a rich body of literature concerning senses and the sensorium. For a careful and sensitive ethnographic account of how an ethical sensorium is produced, see Charles Hirschkind, *The Ethical Soundscape: Cassette Sermons and Islamic Counterpublics* (New York: Columbia University Press, 2006).

36 Perhaps the most compelling discussion of the capacity of sites outside the 'historic homeland' to make a claim to be a home or even an alternative homeland is Tsolin Nalbantian's recent *Armenians Beyond Diaspora: Making Lebanon Their Own*.

37 There is a growing theological discourse, especially in the Eastern Orthodox churches, on the centrality of liturgy in the 'construction' of the *ecclesia*. A long line of Orthodox theologian/philosophers dating to the late nineteenth century have entered contemporary debates on community through re-readings of patristic writings about the church. In an author like Christos Yannaras, these discussions take a decidedly phenomenological character, emphasizing how the Christian experience of space and time, especially in liturgy, finds its fulfilment in the church understood as the body of Christ, as in this characteristic passage: 'The dynamic ec-stasy of nature *outside-of-nature*, the existential discovery and recognition of the *presence* of the Logos in the world, as the experiential content and work of ecclesiastical *askesis*, finds its "final" realization in the Church as a fact of *eucharistic thanksgiving*.' Christos Yannaras, *Person and Eros*, trans. Norman Russell (Brookline: Holy Cross Orthodox Press, 2007), 150, emphasis in original. The present chapter, while not engaging explicitly with this theological literature, owes much of the conceptualization of *ecclesia* and the liturgical subject to these theological-philosophical inquiries. This becomes explicit in the engagement with the work of Hourujy.

38 In addition to these physical characteristics that convert the interior of any space into an Armenian church, there is also a necessary *sacramental* transformation. Though any space, through the use of a consecrated *vemkar*, the central stone altarpiece, may function as a church, for a building to become a permanent Armenian Apostolic Church it must be sacramentally consecrated by a bishop. This service can be found in the *Mayr Mashtots*, the service book of the Armenian Church for use by a bishop. Gēorg Tēr-Vardanean, ed., *Mayr Mashtots'*, vol. I/1 (Holy Etchmiadzin: Holy See of Etchmiadzin Publications, 2012).

39 Tölölyan, 'The Role of the Armenian Apostolic Church in the Diaspora', 56.

40 Grappling with the vast literature on nationalism is well beyond the scope of this chapter. For important discussions of the Armenian case, see Ronald Grigor Suny, *Looking toward Ararat: Armenia in Modern History* (Bloomington: Indiana University Press, 1993) and Razmik Panossian, *The Armenians: From Kings and Priests to Merchants and Commissars* (London: Hurst & Company, 2006). If at times the church

served as a connecting institution, the assertion that the Armenian Apostolic Church is coextensive with the Armenian nation rests on a particular reading of Armenian history coupled with the dubious teleology of nationalism that assumes that all divisions of people find their ultimate fulfilment in the modern concept of the nation as a group of people bound by land and language, whose political fulfilment is one nation-one state. Modern nationalism assumes the conceptual separability of ethno-national and religious identities, while the earlier articulations of the centrality of the Armenian Apostolic Church depended entirely on a conceptual universe where no such distinction was possible. Once such a separation is conceptually thinkable, the institutional centrality of the Armenian Apostolic Church depends not just on an ecclesial claim but also a national one.

41   The absolute impossibility of a non-Apostolic Armenian was never the case, as early Chalcedonians, fourteenth century converts of Dominican friars residing at the Monastery of Corcor, or nineteenth and twentieth century Armenian Evangelicals and Catholics all make clear. For example, the Monastery of the Holy Mother of God at Corcor in the region of Siunik, founded around 1314 by Archbishop Zak'aria Cocorec'i, was one of the major centres of pro-Latin Christianity in medieval Armenia. Sergio La Porta, 'Armeno-Latin Intellectual Exchange in the Fourteenth Century: Scholarly Traditions in Conversation and Competition', *Medieval Encounters* 21 (2015): 276–7. On the Propaganda Fide and its Latin Catholic influence in relation to the Armenian Church, see Sebouh Aslanian, *Dispersion History and the Polycentric Nation: The Role of Simeon Yerevantsi's Girkʻ or Koči Partavčar in the 18th Century National Revival* (Venice: S. Lazarus, 2004), 23–5. For more on the relations between the Armenian Apostolic Church and Armenian Catholicism and Protestantism, in addition to forthcoming work by Daniel Ohanian, see Vartan Artinian, *The Armenian Constitutional System in the Ottoman Empire, 1839–1863: A Study of Its Historical Development* (Istanbul: Isis Press, 1988) and H. J. Siruni, *Bolisě ew ir terě, Aṛachin Hador (1453–1800) [Constantinople and its Role, Volume 1 (1453–1800)]*. (Beirut: Dbaran Mesrob, 1969).

42   For instance, this is how Archbishop Karekin Hovespian (who went on to become the Catholicos of the Great House of Cilicia) described his vision for the Armenian Church in America when he served as primate of the Diocese in New York. Eventually, this vision materialized into the St. Vartan Armenian Cathedral, which Bishop Daniel Findikyan, Primate from 2018 to 2022, echoing Hovespian, has also called the 'national home'. https://armenianchurch.us/2017/10/19/october-armenian-cultural-month/ and https://armenianchurch.us/2018/09/26/primate-welcomes-armenias-prime-minister-to-cathedral./

43   Foucault, 'Governmentality', 94.

44   Ibid., 100.

45   'Modern governmental rationality, Foucault has said, is simultaneously about individualizing and totalizing: that is, about finding answers to the question of what it is for an individual, and for a society or population of individuals, to be governed or governable'. Colin Gordon, 'Governmental Rationality: An Introduction', in *The Foucault Effect: Studies in Governmentality with Two Lectures by and an Interview with Michel Foucault*, ed. Graham Burchell, Colin Gordon, and Peter Miller (Chicago: University of Chicago Press, 1991), 36. On the emergence of this new object of population and its relation to the new science of statistics, see Ian Hacking, 'How Should We Do the History of Statistics?', in *The Foucault Effect: Studies in Governmentality with Two*

Lectures by and an Interview with Michel Foucault, ed. Graham Burchell, Colin Gordon, and Peter Miller (Chicago: University of Chicago Press,1991), 181–96.
46 *Ecclesia* as the body of Christ is not exactly the same kind of collectivity as a population, as Shefali Jha and Xiao-bo Yuan helpfully reminded me. While the modern emergence of population with its attendant practice, statistics, is indeed quite a different object from the *ecclesia*, today many practitioners and leaders engage the church as exactly a kind of population. Anxious about declining numbers in the pews, they deploy tools like the census and modern social science to manage the church as a population. Yet, the divergence between *ecclesia* and population, how they are apprehended and the practices they entail, all deserve closer attention.
47 Michel Foucault, *The History of Sexuality, Volume I* (New York: Vintage, 1990). For the discussion of the productive element of power, see, especially, Chapter Two, 'Method', 92–102.
48 Michel Foucault, *Omnes et Singulatim: Towards a Criticism of 'Political Reason'*, Tanner Lectures on Human Values at Stanford (SC1047), Dept. of Special Collections and University Archives (Stanford: Stanford University Libraries, 1979). These Tanner Lectures are Foucault's most explicit discussion of pastoral power and the Christian genealogy of 'the government of self and others'. See also Colin Gordon's introduction to the volume that first published Foucault's governmentality lecture in English translation, 'Governmental Rationality: An Introduction.'
49 There is considerable work on the Armenians of Baku and Azerbaijan, especially given the turbulent context of the tenuous position of the autonomous Republic of Artsakh. See, for instance, Levon Chorbajian, ed., *The Making of Nagorno-Karabagh: From Secession to Republic* (London: Palgrave Macmillan, 2001). While there are also several works on the earlier history of the region, less work is available on the everyday lives and experiences of Baku Armenians in the Soviet period leading up to massacre and war.
50 In addition to the works on Artsakh cited above, on the Sumgait Massacres specifically, see Samuel Shahmuratian, ed., *The Sumgait Tragedy: Pogroms Against Armenians in Soviet Azerbaijan: Eyewitness Accounts* (New Rochelle, NY: Aristide D. Caratzas, 1990). In 2016, and most devastatingly, at the end of 2020, hostilities resumed. The most recent 'Forty-Four Day War' led to a significant loss of territory by the autonomous Republic of Artsakh to the Republic of Azerbaijan. These recent events are outside the scope of this chapter, whose ethnographic work was conducted prior to 2020. New loss of life and territory has wrought human tragedy including new refugees, but those refugees and migrants mentioned in this chapter fled during the previous war in the 1990s.
51 Robert Mirak, *Torn Between Two Lands: Armenians in America, 1890 to World War I* (Cambridge, MA: Harvard University Press, 1988), 129.
52 Ashod Rhaffi Aprahamian, *Remarkable Rebirth: The Early History of the Armenians in Detroit* (East Lansing: Michigan State University Press, 2005), 47.
53 This is at least partially a characteristic of the United States and perhaps the Midwest region within the United States. A common refrain among scholars and political observers alike is that the United States is 'more religious' than Europe. See, for instance, Thomas A. Howard's description of 'secular Europe' and 'religious America'. Thomas A. Howard, *God and the Atlantic: America, Europe, and the Religious Divide* (Oxford: Oxford University Press, 2011), 2–4. However, Armenian Apostolic churches are to be found in nearly every sizeable Armenian community in the world. The recent work of the 'Armenian Diaspora Survey' makes clear that while there are

certainly communities – Detroit among them – where there are other institutions than the church, there are almost no communities where there is not a church (https://www.armeniandiasporasurvey.com/). Of course, the presence of a church itself reveals very little about the 'religiosity' of a people. However, it does demonstrate the continued institutional power and relevance of the Armenian Apostolic Church. In part, this chapter explores the 'gap' between the pervasive institutional presence of the church and the full realization of a 'properly trained' liturgical subject.

54 I explore the dynamic of emplacement, specifically what I call 'hagiographic emplacement', in a different context with the Armenian community of Maastricht in the Netherlands. See Christopher Sheklian, '"Their Compatriot St. Servatius": Armenian Emplacement in Maastricht', in *Europe and the Migration of Christian Communities from the Middle East,* ed. Martin Tamcke (Wiesbaden: Harrassowitz Verlag, 2022), 111–24 and 'Hagiographic Emplacement: St. Servatius, the Armenian Community of Maastricht, and Oriental Orthodox Christians in Europe', in *Anthropologies of Orthodox Christianity*, eds. Candace Lukasik and Sarah Riccardi-Swartz (New York: Fordham University Press, forthcoming).

55 Such pastoral care, as with the 'ecclesial governmentality' I am outlining here, is not limited to Armenians or the Armenian Apostolic Church. Any Christian church that operates with the understanding of church as the body of Christ, which has a truly ecclesial vision and structure, deploys ecclesial governmentality. The incorporation of individuals into the body of Christ, a feature of Christian churches and effect of ecclesial governmentality generally, is especially pronounced in the Armenian Apostolic Church because of its ecclesiology, its centrality to the larger community and the phenomenon of movement across the transnation. Yet the theoretical concept of ecclesial governmentality I am advancing in this chapter should be visible in any ecclesially grounded Christian church.

56 Michel Foucault, 'Technologies of the Self', in *Technologies of the Self, a Seminar with Michel Foucault,* ed. Luther H. Martin, Huck Gutman, and Patrick H. Hutton (Amherst: University of Massachusetts Press, 1988), 16–49.

57 Mahmood, *Politics of Piety,* 30.

58 Horujy, *Practices of the Self and Spiritual Practices,* 56.

59 Krueger, *Liturgical Subjects,* 12.

60 Artawazd Siwrmēean, *Patmutʿiwn Halēpi Hayotsʿ: teghagrakan, vichakagrakan, patmagrakan* (*The History of Armenian Aleppo: topographical, statistical, historical*) (Beirut: Tparan M. Magsutean, 1946), 2.

61 Avedis Sanjian, 'The Armenian Minority Experience in the Modern Arab World', *Bulletin of the Royal Institute for Inter-Faith Studies* 3, no. 1 (2001): 151.

62 Migliorino, *(Re)Constructing Armenia in Lebanon and Syria,* 31.

63 Sanjian, 'The Armenian Minority Experience', 162.

64 Migliorino, *(Re)Constructing Armenia in Lebanon and Syria,* 48.

65 Nucho, *Everyday Sectarianism in Urban Lebanon,* 14.

66 Migliorino, *(Re)Constructing Armenia in Lebanon and Syria,* 160.

67 While Armenian outmigration from Syria occurred throughout the second half of the twentieth century, the population was still robust after the transition of power from Hafez al-Assad, ruling since 1970, to his son Bashar al-Assad in 2000. The ongoing violence in Syria since 2011 stemming from al-Assad's violent crackdown has severely affected Armenians in the country. Some Armenian centres, like Qamishli, after being on the shifting front lines of the war against ISIS, are in (at the time of writing) Kurdish-held territories. Armenian monuments such as the Armenian

Genocide Martyrs' Memorial in Deir ez-Zor, the infamous endpoint of the genocidal deportations, was destroyed by ISIS in 2014. Heghnar Zeitlian Watenpaugh, 'Cultural Heritage and the Arab Spring: War over Cultur, Culture of War and Culture War', *International Journal of Islamic Architecture* 5, no. 2 (2016): 245–63; Sam Hardy, 'Who Blew Up the Armenian Genocide Memorial Church in Deir el-Zour?', *Hyperallergic*, 11 November 2014, https://hyperallergic.com/162080/who-blew-up-the-armenian-genocide-memorial-church-in-deir-el-zour/. Damascus, the capital, was largely spared the widespread destruction of other spaces, and many of the Armenians of Damascus remain.

68 While Armenians remain in the city, this current violence and wave of Armenians leaving as refugees to seek safety abroad will dramatically transform the ancient Armenian community of Aleppo.

69 Sossie Kasbarian, 'Refuge in the "Homeland" – the Syrians in Armenia', in *Aid to Armenia: Humanitarianism and intervention from the 1890s to the present. Humanitarianism: Key Debates and Approaches*, ed. Joanne Laycock and Francesca Piana (Manchester: Manchester University Press, 2020), 164–80; Uğur Ümit Üngor, 'Syrian Restaurants in Armenia: A Pinch of Home, a Taste of Exile', *The Armenian Mirror-Spectator,* 12 June 2019. https://mirrorspectator.com/2019/06/12/syrian-restaurants-in-armenia-a-pinch-of-home-a-taste-of-exile/.

70 The Armenian presence in France dates back centuries, with medieval contacts and later with the major port city of Marseille hosting Armenian merchants by the early modern period. Some of the earliest printed Armenian books were produced in Marseille. N. A. Oskanyan, A. Korgotyan, and A. M. Savalyan, *Hay girkʻě 1512–1800 tʻvakannerin: hay hnatip grkʻi matenagitutʻyun* (*The Armenian Book in the Years 1512–1800: Early-Printed Armenian Book Bibliography*) (Erevan: Haykakan SSH Kulturayi Ministrutʻyun, Al. Myasnikyani Anvan Zhoghovurdneri Barekamutʻyan Shkʻanshanakir HSSH Petakan Gradaran, 1988). Later, Paris played a major role in the Armenian cultural renaissance of the eighteenth and nineteenth centuries, with Armenian students from Istanbul sent to France to study. James Etmekjian, *The French Influence on the Western Armenian Renaissance, 1843–1915* (New York: Twayne Publishers, Inc., 1964), 94–6. In the region between Marseilles and Paris, France's third-largest city of Lyons, the town of Valence (about halfway between Marseille and Lyons), and Décines all host Armenian churches and cultural institutions. All of these places in the south of France grew in their Armenian population following the Armenian Genocide. Boris Adjemian, *Les petites Arménies de la vallée du Rhône: Histoire et mémoires des immigrations arméniennes en France* (Lyon/impr. en Serbie: Lieux Dits, 2020).

71 Bishop Balakian was an influential clergyman in the south of France in the early years after the Armenian Genocide. He was one of the few survivors of those deported from Istanbul on 24 April 1915, the traditional date of remembrance of the Armenian Genocide. In addition to his pastoral work, he authored of a well-known genocide memoir, *Armenian Golgotha*, translated into English through the efforts of his great-grandnephew, noted author Peter Balakian. Grigoris Balakian, *Armenian Golgotha: A Memoir of the Armenian Genocide, 1915–1918*, trans. Peter Balakian and Aris Sevag (New York: Vintage Books, 2010). L'Association des dames chrétiennes arméniennes had bought the property for the church shortly after it was founded in 1927 by Serpouhie Halepian. Association Culturelle Arménienne de Marne-la-Vallée (France), 'Église apostolique arménienne Sainte-Marie', http://www.acam-france.org/contacts/contact_eglise.php?cle=161. Accessed 8 April 2021.

72 Little Armenias, https://www.littlearmenias.com/listings/armenian-evangelical-church-20/. Accessed 8 April 2021.

73 Opened on 20 October 2013, the Center houses within its black stone walls with engraved Armenian letters an educational/community center and a library. An Armenian restaurant is on the lower floor. Aram Arkun, 'National Center of Armenian Memory in Décines, France Promotes Armenian Studies and Culture', *The Armenian Mirror-Spectator*, 7 December 2017, https://mirrorspectator.com/2017/12/07/national-center-armenian-memory-decines-france-promotes-armenian-studies-culture/. Accessed 8 April 2021. The memorial and Center were both the recent target of vandalism during the 2020 Artsakh War. PanArmenian.net, 'Armenian Genocide Memorial Vandalized in France', *Pan-Armenian.net*, 1 November 2020, https://www.panarmenian.net/eng/news/287292/Armenian_Genocide_memorial_vandalized_in_France. Accessed 16 June 2022. In addition to these churches and institutions, Lyons, connected by a short tram ride, has many additional institutions.

74 While the Facebook group extends to Syrian Armenians beyond just the suburb of Décines, the densest population is in Décines. According to Harout, with whom I conducted an interview in July 2018, there were forty Syrian Armenian families living in the suburb (Personal Interview, 2018). The Facebook group *Lioni Suria Hayer*, 'Syrian-Armenians of Lyon' still exists, though has very little activity since 2019: https://www.facebook.com/people/%D4%BC%D5%AB%D6%85%D5%B6%D5%AB-%D5%8D%D5%B8%D6%82%D6%80%D5%AB%D5%A1-%D5%B0%D5%A1%D5%B5%D5%A5%D6%80/100024732434121/.

75 The idea of an individual 'ethnographic subject' has a fraught methodological history in the discipline of anthropology. Further research will surely add to the single figure on whom I rely here. Within anthropology, the idea of an ethnographic or anthropological text dependent on a single person is most closely associated with João Biehl, *Vita: Life in a Zone of Social Abandonment,* photo. Torben Eskerod (Berkeley, Los Angeles, London: University of California, Press, 2005).

76 Compatriotic unions/societies were first formed in the late nineteenth and early twentieth centuries when the *pandukht*s, the temporary economic migrants who first went from the eastern Armenian provinces of the Ottoman Empire to Istanbul, began going further afield and working in America. Dzovinar Derderian, 'Nation-Making and the Language of Colonialism: Voices from Ottoman Van in Armenian Print and Handwritten Petitions (1820s to 1870s)' (PhD diss., University of Michigan, 2019), 201–45. Formed by 'compatriots' of cities, towns and villages in historic Armenia, the societies fostered connection in dispersion and organized aid to be sent home for families and to support schools. After the genocide, the organizations helped the scattered members of families and villages reconnect and published 'Houshamadyans', 'Memory-Books' that documented the lost worlds of their villages and cities in Armenia. On the *houshamadyan* genre, see Jennifer Gurahian, 'In the Mind's Eye: Collective Memory and Armenian Village Ethnographies', *Armenian Review* 43, no. 1 (1990): 19–29; Mihran Minassian, 'Tracking Down the Past: The Memory Book ("Houshamadyan") Genre – A Preliminary Bibligoraphy', https://www.houshamadyan.org/themes/bibliography.html. Accessed 9 April 2021. Minassian offers a short introduction to the genre and some texts of the 'houshamadyan' books on the excellent website that takes its name from these heavily utilized but understudied texts.

III

'The Social Text of Diaspora'

Diasporic becoming and legibility in diaspora's semantic domain

8

Sounding Armenian

The contours of the diasporic musical imaginary

Sylvia Angelique Alajaji

If I say 'Armenian music', what do you hear?*
If I say 'Armenian music', why do you hear what you hear?

"Armenian music" and its discontents

Perhaps it was my mistake. After all, I would contact potential interviewees and ask if I could speak with them with what, in hindsight, was a rather vague and clunky explanation of my work: 'I'm doing a project on the relationship between music and diasporic Armenian identity after the genocide.' Looking back, it is no surprise that in the game of telephone that would often transpire – one person introducing me to another, helping me widen my network – my research became summed up in a manner far pithier than my own: 'Meet Sylvia. She's doing a project on Armenian music.' Yet in that crucial switching of the modifier from 'identity' to 'music', my project, vague as it was to begin with, entered a discursive minefield that I had not prepared to contend with. Suddenly, my project was about 'Armenian music', a shorthand that given its seeming efficiency, I adopted perhaps a little too readily.

But how tempting it was to deploy this beguilingly self-evident phrase, its inherent absurdities so easily concealed, just as they are with any essentializing descriptions of the other. A phrase that like so many, manages simultaneously to say everything and nothing at all: 'I love Middle Eastern music!' 'I don't feel like Indian tonight, let's go out for Chinese.' Those of us in diaspora hear these phrases and know what they are meant to communicate. We know that they are meant for the world outside our own and yet also know that in many ways, they are among our few ways to be known. And so, they become a sort of take-it-or-leave-it opportunity: deploy them yourself and claim the narrative to the extent that the gaze will allow (there are limits, after all), making yourself palatable and understandable and still, somehow, you. They are phrases and discursive worlds that exist in and for diaspora: simplifying, stabilizing and legitimizing.

At first, it was not so much the contours of 'Armenian music' that interested me, for I thought I knew what it was. My Armenian family's route had been circuitous but hardly atypical – from the villages of the Ottoman Empire to Aleppo and the orphanages of Beirut, and eventually landing in Tulsa, Oklahoma, where I was raised (perhaps the Tulsa part was a bit atypical). My understanding of Armenian-ness emerged from the cacophony of this multilocality. And if the isolation in Tulsa afforded me anything, it was the assumption that this, indeed, was what it was to be Armenian.

And so it was when I began work on what was to become my dissertation. But very quickly, in my first few interviews, a recurring pattern began to emerge. In I would come, all smiles and nerves, there they would sit, patient, perhaps a bit uncertain, and I would begin:

'Can you tell me about X?' I would ask.
'Why do you want to know about that?' they would reply.
'Well, my project . . .'
'Yes, your project on Armenian music.'
'Yes, my project on Armenian music.'
'That's not Armenian music.'
'But . . .'

The first time, I tried switching the conversation to Armenian, blushing at the realization that 'Armenian music' was a phrase I had never spoken in Armenian; it seemed only to exist in English. Quickly, I uttered the closest approximation I could think of off the top of my head: 'Haygagan musique?' (I could feel my grandmother giving me the same look she would give me when I would say 'merci' instead of the multi-syllabic 'shnorhagal em'.) It was almost as if the topic existed in two different discursive worlds: Armenian and English. And depending on who I was speaking to, even our Armenians broke down differently: my Armenian, a mix of Turkish, Arabic, English and French loanwords, transparent in its diasporic journey; their Armenian – their journeys – sometimes like mine, sometimes not. My Armenian – my conceptions of 'Armenian music' – betraying the cacophony of my diasporic world; their Armenian – their conceptions of 'Armenian music' – betraying theirs.

Complicating matters even more, this was a work to be written in English. And in every conversation was the tacit acknowledgement of the implications embedded in whatever carried the mantle of 'Armenian music'. After all, this work would be for the world outside our own – a world in which being Armenian means being read and understood through modalities unique to the United States: its geopolitical alignments and motivations, its histories and its understandings of and relationships to race and its various ethnic and religious minorities. How would the cacophonies of the Armenian diasporic reality translate into these modalities? The swirling, dizzying mass of histories, homelands, needs and priorities that make up the Armenian communities in the United States – communities so varied in when they came, where they came from and why they came – how are they made into one? What of ourselves would I articulate in English and attempt to make legible and what would stay within?

And so it went, moving in and out of that which could be said and that which never could – those things that existed beyond Diaspora, outside the textbooks, off the stage. In English: 'That's not Armenian music.' In Armenian: 'Sylvia, menk nakhants enk' ('we are jealous'). Had not Edward Said once written something similar? 'Exile is a jealous state.'[1] A sentence that haunted me when I read it years before beginning my work was eerily reappearing before me. Jealous: vigilant over one's possessions, demanding of loyalty, possessing of envy. Slowly it became clear that hidden in 'That's not Armenian music' was something more than an easily dismissed, shallow claim to authenticity. Read in the context of the diasporic cacophony we seemed to inhabit, it seemed also to embed a plea: for clarity and for care; for the retention of something knowable, for something certain; and for an awareness of what was at stake. For what happens to the Diaspora when the borders so delicately stitched together collapse? Who do we become without them? (Who have we become and who have we lost because of them?)

'Armenian music', in these conversations, functioned as synecdoche – a stand-in for something larger than itself, a part made to stand in for the whole. It was so clearly a site guarded with vigilance and care, both for its promise and for what (and who) it sonically enacts into being. So what, then, is the sound of this Armenia made whole? What are its contours, textures and limits? What is the beginning – the home – that it embeds and the subsequent becoming? And what is the meaning of that sound for a diaspora marked by its multiplicities, in-betweens born of disparate elsewheres, and varied (dis)connections to the nation-state of Armenia? In this chapter, I reflect on what it means for a diaspora to sonically articulate itself as an entity – what I will be referring to as Diaspora – and subsume its cacophonies and incommensurabilities into a legible whole. It is a wholeness necessitated by a desire for survival but one that ironically, necessitates and bears its own fragmentations. In examining the implicit elisions, alignments, orientations and histories that attend such articulations, it becomes apparent that Diaspora, with its promises of clarity, stability and knowability, is a construction that both maintains and needs maintaining and one that finds its legibility in the expanse of the Western gaze.

Central to this exploration will be the work of the beloved Armenian composer and folklorist Komitas Vardapet (1869–1935). There is perhaps no name more ubiquitous or discursively powerful in Armenian musical culture than his.[2] He is a figure who has not only come to represent the very possibility of an Armenian music – a music that today functions as a sonic metonym for Armenianness – but, through the ways he has been written about, memorialized and made central to the Armenian musical imaginary, has come to represent the possibility of an Armenia made whole. Through an engagement with the discourses surrounding his life and work, I explore the implications of Komitas's centrality to the Armenian diasporic musical imaginary and how, through this centrality, the Armenian Diaspora sonically comes to be.

D/diaspora

Being in diaspora is often understood as encompassing various forms of belonging, with those in diaspora navigating varying hybrid identities and attachments. While those multiplicities were abundantly clear in the many conversations I had in the course of my fieldwork, so were the multiple ways there were of being diasporic – multiplicities that those with whom I interacted navigated with awareness. Here, I draw a distinction between these various forms of belonging by alternately referring to diaspora, which embeds the pluralities of the diasporic condition, and Diaspora, which embeds the discursive wholeness that diaspora belies. This distinction is vastly imperfect and should by no means be taken to infer an easily distinguishable dichotomy. Rather, I employ it as a way to distinguish between these multiplicities and to highlight not only the fluidities of the hybrid space but to see it as something sustained and maintained through complex relationships to and negotiations with sociopolitical forces both outside *and* within the diasporic community.

As Khatchig Tölölyan, Rogers Brubaker, Lily Cho and others have written, diaspora is both subjective and objective – as much a deliberate stance or positioning as it is a description.[3] Tölölyan's identification, for example, of three 'formative binaries' that can be found in the field of diaspora studies – dispersion and diaspora, objective and subjective, and home and homeland – speaks to the multiple ways 'diaspora' can be discursively wielded, structured, and structuring. Lily Cho's work sits squarely in the latter pole of the second set of binaries, as it advocates for a move away from the 'definitional tendency' within the field of diaspora studies that only reduces 'diasporic communities to the status of objects' and a turn towards an understanding of diaspora as a 'condition of subjectivity' – a turn that insists upon an interrogation into the complex relationships to power that exist both internally and externally and the ways these relationships give way to the formation of a diasporic subject.[4] As she writes, 'Diasporic subjectivity calls attention to the conditions of its formation. Contrary to studies of diasporas as objects of analysis where race or religion might be considered a defining feature, I have been arguing that no one is born diasporic. Rather, one *becomes* diasporic through a complex process of memory and emergence.'[5]

While Tölölyan takes issue with Cho's seeming dismissal of diaspora as an 'object of analysis', it is critical to note that even in its most 'objective' and disciplinary usage (perhaps especially in its most objective usage), diaspora belies an implicit positionality. To be sure, there is diaspora, used to refer in its most general sense to the dispersion and scattering of a people from a 'point of origin'. But even there, in that phrase ubiquitous to any discussion of diaspora, is an invitation to a positioning that betrays itself as such under the slightest of interrogations: *Whose* point of origin? *What* point of origin? *When* is this origin? *Who* decides? And the further diaspora becomes refined and articulated into legibility – as its contours and alignments begin to take shape – something emerges that can no longer be serviced by deceptively objective, seemingly descriptive terms. There is then also Diaspora, an entity in and of the world(s) in which it exists: studied, represented, maintained and made into being by forces within and without.

Too often there can be slippage between the descriptive and prescriptive possibilities of the term, making one synonymous with the other and thus foreclosing ways of being in diaspora that do not align with popular, institutional and/or disciplinary understandings of the term. In his seminal article, 'The "Diaspora" Diaspora', Brubaker grapples with the idea that one can be considered a 'dormant' member of a diaspora.

He writes, 'The very notion of "dormant members" of a diaspora is problematic; if they are really dormant – if they have "assimilated or fully integrated" into a host society (Sheffer 2003: 100) and merely "know or feel that their roots are in the diaspora group" – then why should they count, and be counted, as "members" of the diaspora at all?'[6] While the distinction I draw here between diaspora and Diaspora owes greatly to Brubaker's article, this passage necessitates some follow-up questions, asked in earnest: why should they *not* be counted? By what/whose metrics is inclusion in the diaspora being determined? Brubaker goes on to note that while 'diaspora can be seen as an *alternative* to the essentialization of belonging', it can also 'represent a non-territorial *form* of essentialized belonging' (emphases in original).[7] However, the idea that so-called dormant members of the diaspora are being read as having assimilated despite 'know[ing] or feel[ing] that their roots are in the diaspora group' implies that there is a certain form of diaspora that they are to claim in order to be counted, whether by scholars or state and/or institutional actors. Brubaker's later statement that 'we can explore to what extent, and in what circumstances, those claimed as members of putative diasporas actively adopt or at least passively sympathize with the diasporic stance' implicitly acknowledges that the power of the 'diasporic stance' is that it becomes an ontological tether – the prism through which the diaspora is understood and, I would add, the prism through which the diaspora comes to know itself.[8]

This Diaspora that I speak of emerges partly – and somewhat ironically – from the limits placed around the term itself and which, ontologically, allow it to emerge as an object of knowledge. In other words, embedded in the definition itself is a stance. Tölölyan, in his influential writings urging scholars for a use of the term that is more intentional and deliberate, often reminds us that at the core of this now widely utilized concept is a set of three distinctions that distinguish it from what would more generally be described as a dispersion: a diaspora is born of a collective trauma; it maintains a sense of collective identity tethered to a homeland; and it remains connected to the homeland, whether through 'a rhetoric of restoration and return', 'sustained and organized commitment to maintain relations with kin community' or other means.[9] With every distinction, the 'semantic domain' of the term becomes necessarily clearer and more refined, but so do the boundaries around what constitutes the diasporic community.[10]

So then, when we speak of 'the Armenian diaspora' in the United States, for example, what are we speaking of? The 'homelands' from which the Armenians in the United States have arrived and the collective traumas which compelled their departures are varied and, for many, multiple. There are those whose familial routes took them from the villages of the Ottoman Empire (where the 1915 genocide took place), to Lebanon, and then, amid the civil war, to the United States; those whose families came directly from the Ottoman Empire before the genocide; and those whose families remained in the Ottoman Empire and became citizens of present-day Turkey then eventually made their way to the United States. And then there are those whose familial roots cannot be found in the Ottoman Empire and for whom the genocide factors only tangentially into their cultural and familial histories (if at all): those with generational roots in Iran who arrived amid the overthrow of the Shah and, crucially, those who came from Armenia amid grave economic crises and political upheavals – those with a lived connection to the nation-state that the others perhaps have never known, have known only through purposefully and deliberately cultivated links, or know only in imagination.

These examples are by no means comprehensive and hardly begin to encompass the widely varying roots and complicated routes of Armenians who came to the United States.[11] And complicating matters further are the varying temporal relationships to the various traumas and homelands. For some, the connections to the traumas and homelands are immediate and lived, while for others they are distant, existing in realms that cannot quite be described as memory but as abstractions or something else altogether.[12] As Anny Bakalian's pioneering work on Armenians in the United States demonstrated, what 'being' and 'feeling' Armenian mean – that is, the ways Armenian-ness is understood, lived, read and recognized – varies widely.[13] And so, again: when we speak of 'the Armenian diaspora', of whom do we speak? What were to happen if the distinctions described earlier were to be applied? What (or who) would remain?

To be able to discursively create Diaspora out of the multiplicities that have been described – to make it knowable as an entity – inevitably entails and necessitates a positioning and centring of narratives that come to speak for the whole. While Tölölyan points to 'the difference between the emic discourse that diasporas use to talk about themselves to themselves . . . and the more recent etic scholarly activity called diaspora studies', I would add that it is not so much about the difference between the 'emic' and 'etic' but about the complex dialogue, manoeuvrings and negotiations between the two.[14] After all, not only can the Diaspora 'talk back', as Tölölyan writes, but it can make *itself* knowable. To put it bluntly, not everything that is discussed within makes it out. The Diaspora, while an articulation of existence born of a desire for survival, legibility and political salience, is also quite strategic, as the legitimacy it seeks is one for the time and places in which it exists.

'That's not Armenian music': a statement spoken by Armenians navigating the multiplicities of their diasporic belongings and the multiple ways in which Armenian-ness is read and understood, and made to me, an Armenian who grew up in the United States and who had access to an institutional world in which very little on Armenian music had been written; writing a dissertation that I wished to have approved, cited and read; and set with the task of translating what Armenian music is (and implicitly what it is not) into a world and a language where 'being Armenian' entailed, if known at all, a questionable genocide, contingent whiteness, Kardashians and cartoonish gangsters, and existed within empire-serving narratives of the clash of civilizations, with the phenotypically ambiguous Armenians as the hapless Christian victims of Islam, the perennial Western Other.[15] In our conversations was the implicit knowledge of the Armenian Diaspora as understood without, and the Diaspora as articulated from within, each belying the lived multiplicities, consciousnesses and narratives of contradiction from which I and my interlocutors had emerged.

What is the price we pay to speak so that we are heard? To speak so that we become one? Marc Nichanian writes,

> I have felt shame every time we spoke of ourselves. For, each time we spoke of ourselves, we did not speak to ourselves. Each time, an appeal was made to a third party, to the West, to the observer, to what Hagop Oshagan called 'civilized

humanity.' And, thus, I have felt shame continuously. As survivors, we have never ceased, in fact, to appeal to the external gaze. In the moment of this appeal, it is testimony that was constituting me. It was constituting me by the shame I was feeling, by my belonging to this 'we' I have just uttered, under the gaze of the civilized other, by this gaze itself.[16]

In my conversations, the external gaze often took the form of the Diaspora. For as much as the enunciations within the diasporic realm are a constitutive act, so too is Diaspora constitutive of the people within: we create diaspora, but diaspora also creates us. We are aware of its borders, its needs and its limits of belonging. We are aware of its need for legitimacy and its need for stability. We speak of diaspora but it is Diaspora – as a commitment – that speaks us into being.

Hearing Komitas in Diaspora

In those first few interviews, it did not take long to realize that my pre-prepared questions would have to undergo some revision as I could no longer take 'Armenian music' as a categorical known. Rather than make excuses for why I was asking about the things I was asking about and trying to find ways to fit these teleologically disruptive genres into narratives of Diaspora, I prepared for some detours, asking some version of, 'If this is not Armenian music, what is?' I relented, curious to see where the conversation would go – to see what, in fact, was 'Armenian music'.[17] I was eager to understand this thing that was being presented as a known: an ostensibly fixed unit of analysis, immutable, certain and somehow incommensurable with the private realm of memory, family and of history. I wanted to understand what 'Armenian music' was shorthand for – the discourses of nation, self and Armenianness that it embedded as well as the belongings it delineated and enabled. To put it more simply, we needed to establish a starting point.

Oddly enough, more often than not, the conversation would relax. This was far more comfortable. Here we were, finally, talking about what we should be talking about: that which we could more safely claim in the Diaspora's gaze. Not those genres that lay bare our contrapuntal existence and force a reckoning with the ways Armenians had become parts of the many worlds they inhabited (and how those worlds had inhabited them) – that is, the Turkish-language songs of our grandparents and great-grandparents; the pop songs that Armenians had created, listened to and loved in the various points on their diasporic journeys; and the folk songs that spoke to our diverging elsewheres – but those things that embed a beginning and subsequent teleology of particularity. Those genres that once established as a starting point, simultaneously stabilize, legitimize and determine all that was, is and is to follow.

Often, there would be talk of the *badarak* (the Armenian mass), of medieval *khaz* notation, sacred music, choral songs or various village folk songs from the Armenian highlands – genres that matched the relics, collectables and decorations that filled and adorned the many homes that I was graciously invited into and that spoke to the symbology of the 'Armenia' that has come to speak for Armenians the world over:

the biblical Armenia, where the story of the Diaspora begins; the majestic, historic Armenia, with its storied kings and saints who fought valiantly for the lands that would eventually be lost to enemies that exist to this day; the 'Armenia' in which present-day needs and circumstances and past struggles and victories collapse into a simultaneity from which a future can be imagined.[18] And attached to each of these was always one name, over and over. The very reason we had these songs and the very reason we could even speak of an 'Armenian music', they would say. One name, on which all the conversations would converge: Komitas. Always, Komitas. Komitas, our saviour. Komitas, the father of our music. In these conversations, it was clear: Komitas is Armenian music. Armenian music is Komitas.

He often gazed down upon us from paintings hanging on living room walls. Forever immortalized. In many of these paintings, he sits in the bright daylight alone under a tree, surrounded by nature and endless valleys and fields that stretch into the distance. He is often holding something – perhaps a pen and notebook, a book, a bird or a small reed instrument such as the duduk. In the background is some combination of symbols evoking an Armenia of the imagination: Mount Ararat, Etchmiadzin or apparitions of the mountain villagers whose songs he so diligently and lovingly transcribed.[19] It is not the Armenia that is, but the Armenia that was and the Armenia that should be. Komitas's face in these paintings is kindly, serene and pensive. We look at him, but he does not meet our gaze. We look at him, knowing what he does not know. Of 24 April 1915. Of his arrest. Of his eventual undoing – and ours. He remains ever so, blissfully unaware.

I had my own memories too, of course: the reverential tones with which my beloved Boston-born Armenian piano teacher used to speak of him, the tears in my mother's eyes when she first told me his story, and the first time I heard his setting of 'Grung' ('Crane'), perhaps the most iconic, ubiquitous and widely known of Armenian songs. Its lyrics, versions of which date from the seventeenth century, are a plea for news from a distant homeland:[20]

> Grung, usdi gukas?
> Dzaray em tsaynit.
> Grung, mer ashkharēn khabrig mĕ ch' unis?
> Inch badaskhan, ch'duir, elar knatsir.
> Grung, mer ashkharēn, de kna, herats'ir.
> [Crane, from where do you come?
> I am a servant to your voice.
> Crane, have you any news from our land?
> You gave me no answer, you left.
> Crane, leave my land, go away.]

I first heard it at the age of ten or eleven, while attending our small Tulsa community's annual commemoration of the genocide. As it played from a recording, I saw my parents and the adults around me – my makeshift family of aunties and uncles, my *tantig*s and *amo*s – begin to cry. I fought back my tears as I watched my parents' own pour forth, their pain and sadness rendered in a way I could only escape by closing my eyes. But doing so did not allow me to escape the song. Its pleading ascents and heart-rending descents sunk into my soul, each word drawn out so that they became, to my ears, a series of nonsensical syllables – ay, oos, ees.

There in that room, enveloped by the song, our small community in Tulsa – some from Iran, some from Syria, some from Massachusetts, some from California, all of us from our various elsewheres – became one. The *tantig*s who only spoke English and would mischievously share with me the naughty Armenian words they knew, the *tantig*s whose Armenian sounded like mine and the *tantig*s, whose Armenian I could not understand. There was no church that enabled our coming together, no organization functioning 'under the auspices' of X, Y or Z – just a living room, a record player and the sheer force of whatever it was that made us all Armenian. There, in that room, within the sonic borders of the song and its pleas, we became.

On the way back to our house, I asked my parents about the song and they told me about the bird and about pleading with it for news from home. 'Beirut?' I asked. I do not remember the answer or even if one was given. It was a question left hanging in the air – there, in the car; there, in my interviews; there, always, over us all. *Oosdi gookank*? From where do we come? In diaspora, it remains a question; in Diaspora – in Komitas – there is an answer.

Komitas was born Soghomon Soghomonian in 1869 in Kütahya, a city in what was then the Ottoman Empire. He was orphaned at a young age: his mother, Takuhi Hovhanessian, died in 1870 when Soghomonian was only six months old while his father, Kevork, died ten years later. The Western Anatolian town of Kütahya was renowned for its ceramics and around the time of Soghomonian's birth was home to approximately 3,000 Armenians.[21] Soghomonian's primary language was Turkish, just as it was for all the Armenians and various ethnic minorities who lived in the town. As Sato Moughalian writes, 'no one in Kutahya dared utter any language in public but Turkish, except while singing hymns in church. After several generations, many inhabitants knew no other language or spoke Armenian only within the seclusion of their homes'.[22]

In 1881, Soghomonian's life was changed when Kevork Vartabed Tertsagian, the bishop of the Armenian Apostolic Church in the nearby Ottoman city of Bursa, took him to be enrolled in the Kevorkian Seminary at the Holy See of Etchmiadzin, a school founded only seven years prior by Catholicos Kevork IV. Located in Vagharshapat, Armenia (which was then part of the Russian Empire), Etchmiadzin serves as the seat of the Armenian Apostolic Church and has been considered the holiest site for Armenians since at least the fourth century. Here, Soghomonian learned Armenian and caught the attention of the Catholicos. As biographer Rita Soulahian Kuyumjian describes it,

> Although Kevork IV seemed annoyed at first that the orphan from Kütahya could only speak Turkish, he quickly recognized Komitas's great natural talent for music. After addressing the boy in Armenian (Komitas later remembered being 'stupefied' by this), the Catholicos asked him to sing the hymn 'Luys Zwart' ['Joyful Light']. The voice that the old man then heard ringing from the walls of the chamber was so clear and subtle that it seemed to illuminate the Armenian words from within,

even though the little singer understood none of them. As Komitas would describe the occasion, the voice moved Kevork IV to tears, which 'tumbled down [his] face and . . . white beard . . . [and were] lost in the folds of his habit.' From then on, a deeply nurturing relationship grew between Kevork IV and the fatherless child. The Catholicos gave Komitas a seat near his own chair and often asked him to sing the solos during celebrations of the Mass.[23]

During his time at the seminary, Soghomonian received a musical education that introduced him to Western music theory, polyphonic composition, medieval Armenian musical systems and notation (known as *khaz*), and the musical and liturgical traditions of the Armenian Orthodox church.[24] It was also during this time that he first began collecting and notating the folk songs of villagers from the areas surrounding Vagharshapat (including, notably, love songs – a fact that did not endear him to the more conservative members of the clergy), publishing his first collection in 1891.[25] In 1894, the year following his graduation, Soghomonian was ordained into the priesthood and given the name Komitas (after the seventh-century Catholicos Komitas I) and in 1895 was officially ordained a celibate priest, earning the appellation Komitas Vardapet.

In the following years, Komitas would make his way to Tiflis (Tblisi), where he studied European harmony with Makar Yekmalian, and then to Berlin, where he enrolled at the prestigious Friedrich-Wilhelms-Universität and was invited to join the nascent Internationale Musikgesellschaft (International Musical Society) by its co-founder Oskar Fleischer. In addition to advancing his technical musical abilities and deepening his fluency in Western compositional methods, Komitas also became part of a circle of academic folklorists who encouraged and nurtured his work with Armenian folk and liturgical music – not only collecting, analysing and transcribing it but understanding it in terms of an Armenian essence – that is something that is *uniquely* Armenian. This discursive framework was consistent with the rising nationalist consciousness of the nineteenth century, a movement that at that time had taken particular hold in Europe and elements of which were embodied even in Komitas's earliest work.[26] Note, for example, his comment in a review published in 1898 that 'our music in its national spirit and style is as *Eastern* as is the Persian-Arabic, but that the Persian-Arabic is not our music, nor is our music a branch of theirs. The situation is that ours has been subjected to their influence' or the summation of a talk that he gave at the inaugural meeting of the IMS: 'Armenian church music – he [Komitas] explained – has remained the same from the beginning of Christianity to this day. It has its origins in ancient pagan chant, which in turn, emerged from folk music. The commonality between church and folk music can be seen in many ways in the analysis of the melodies. The church has only enriched with ornamentation what the people preserved.'[27] In Komitas's work it was clear: Armenia began and lived in the songs of the people – the people, of course, being those most closely connected to the land: the rural villagers of the valleys and mountains who preserved Armenian music in its unsullied form.[28] And, as he made clear in a blistering review of a book of Armenian folk songs (published shortly after his return to Etchmiadzin), any misrepresentation of the music surmounts to a misrepresentation of 'our moral and intellectual life, our past and our present'.[29]

In the years between Komitas's return to Etchmiadzin in 1899 and his eventual move to Constantinople in 1910, Komitas continued to actively collect, transcribe, publish, give lectures on and write about – with remarkable precision and detail – Armenian folk and religious music. Most significantly, however, he began to harmonize these works for choirs that he organized, thus ensuring their dissemination beyond intellectual circles and incorporating the melodies of the folk songs he collected into his own compositions. By the time he moved to Constantinople, his reputation was well established and his choirs would go on to tour Ottoman Turkey, Egypt and Europe to great acclaim. To the middle- and upper-class Armenians attending these concerts, the music was a revelation. And to the European scholars attending Komitas's lectures, the music was evidence of the unique 'Oriental spirit' embodied by the Armenians.

Significantly, the height of Komitas's career was taking place amid the rising nationalism of Armenians in the Ottoman Empire and the broader diaspora. Komitas's intellectual circle in Constantinople consisted of leading Armenian writers, artists and revolutionaries and he himself published or was interviewed in literary and political journals such as *Nawasard*, *Azatamart* and *Anahit*.[30] As the situation for Armenians in the Ottoman Empire began to worsen, the symbolic significance of Komitas's work became clear: the music that he was collecting, transcribing, preserving and introducing to the world was the music of the lands that had long ago been lost to the Ottomans. This music, in its unsullied form, was evidence not only of an Armenian essence or authenticity, but as the music was inextricably associated with the land – its lakes, valleys and streams – it was also proof of belonging to and being of the very land that was no longer theirs.

Given Komitas's visibility and increasing prominence, it was only inevitable that he would be among the more than 250 Armenian intellectual and political figures who were arrested by Ottoman authorities on 24 April 1915 – a date that has come to mark the formal beginning of the genocide. Although those arrested were officially designated to be deported and subsequently relocated within the Ottoman Empire as authorized by the Relocation and Resettlement Law ('Sevk ve İskân Kanunu') passed in May 1915, the majority were eventually killed. While Komitas was initially deported to the city of Çankırı, he was spared death and granted release thanks to the intervention of friends who had connections to Talaat Pasha and other Ottoman authorities. The ordeal, however, forever altered his mental state and Komitas spent the rest of his life in and out of various hospitals. He died in 1935, while at a psychiatric clinic in Villejuif, a suburb outside Paris. The following year, his ashes were transferred to Armenia, where he was laid to rest.

Hearing Diaspora in Komitas

It is not difficult to see in this biographical overview the tenor of what would become a sort of hagiography. Little Soghomon: orphaned, destitute and born outside the historic homeland, then rescued by the church and, in a sense, returned home. Although at first speaking only Turkish, his Armenianness lived in him through the holy melodies of the church. In the move from his Ottoman world to Armenia – at least the little bit that remained of the historic, storied kingdoms that existed centuries ago – there is a becoming that takes place: Soghomon to Komitas. And just as Catholicos Kevork IV was to see how Armenia survived in Soghomon despite it all, Komitas was to show Armenians and the rest of the world how 'Armenia' survived despite it all.

Since his lifetime, Komitas has been venerated by numerous Armenian scholars, writers and artists, forever immortalized in their paintings, poems and memoirs. In 'Requiem Aeternam in Memory of Komitas', a poem written shortly after Komitas's death, Yeghishé Charents characterizes him as 'the song of the homeland', making one synonymous with the other, while

Paruyr Sevak's epic narrative poem 'Anlṛeli Zangakatun' ('The Unsilenceable Belfry'), published in 1959, captures in heart-rending, intimate detail, the life of Komitas, using it as the basis of an anguished examination of the genocide. He is embedded in the Armenian consciousness like no other. Monuments have been erected in his honour all over the world, from the Armenian cities of Yerevan and Vagharshapat to Paris, Detroit, Istanbul, St. Petersburg, Montreal and Quebec City.[31] In Armenia, where there are no less than five landmarks and countless streets named after him, his name graces not only the country's state music conservatory but the pantheon where leading artistic figures from Armenia and the diaspora are buried. In London, there is the Gomidas Institute, an academic research institution and publishing house; in 1965, the Soviet Union released a stamp in his honour; and in 2019 UNESCO included his 150th birthday on its official Calendar of Anniversaries.[32]

The discourses employed in speaking of Komitas and his significance have been (largely) remarkably consistent over the past hundred years, such that we are able to have a discussion about who Komitas *was* and who Komitas *is*. As Aram Kerovpyan notes in an interview, 'Icons are venerated but not necessarily understood. Consequently, his [Komitas's] name often trespasses his person'.[33] For in some ways, what he has come to represent and what he has discursively made possible have taken on a life of their own, proxies through which the present-day Diaspora can articulate its borders and alignments. For example, an article in the California-based *Asbarēz* newspaper publicizing the North American concert tour of world-renowned soprano Isabel Bayrakdarian and pianist Serouj Kradjian (a tour that included a performance at Carnegie Hall) quotes Kradjian's description of Komitas as having 'laid the foundations of a national music culture, purifying Armenian music of all foreign influences', while Sirvart Poladian, in one of the earliest English-language publications on Komitas's work notes that

> Komitas discovered that the Armenian peasant carried the historic traditional idioms of Armenian music. This musical style was heretofore practically unknown to urban Armenians, particularly those in Turkey. In the course of centuries of subjugation to Islamic culture, not only the folk song and popular music of urban Armenians, but also the music of the church had been thoroughly impregnated with foreign influences-Turkish, Arabic and Persian musical styles. The native, traditional musical style all but disappeared.[34]

While the notions of 'purging' and 'purifying' speak at least superficially to what Komitas is perceived to have accomplished, there is something else at play here as well.

He was not merely a stenographer, but an *interpreter* of this music – both academically and musically. It was through his compositional settings and harmonizations that this music was made knowable. As Burcu Yıldız asks in an examination of the notion of authenticity as it has been made to apply to Komitas's music,

> does the arrangement of folk songs according to the principle of polyphony in accordance with the modernism of the period, the presentation in an aestheticized form, and popularization in society in this form not mean the 'reconstruction of tradition?' . . . Is not the 'harmony' that forms the base of piano-accompanied folk song or polyphonic choral performances of folk songs itself a 'foreign' element in the aforementioned Armenian authenticity?[35]

Yıldız's queries build on Nichanian's assertion that Komitas's work elevated the music of the peasantry to Art – an aestheticization that in Nichanian's words, 'creates the nation' and, I would add, makes it both locatable and legible – not just to Armenians, but to others as well.[36] He writes, 'Art is that which has the power of revelation and manifestation. [...] These popular "sources" include not only the people's "tragic songs," but also its narratives, tales and myths, which resemble an "undreamed dream."'[37] As Nichanian writes, for this aestheticization Komitas was venerated by intellectuals, revolutionaries, poets and writers, including Daniel Varuzhan, Hagop Oshaghan and Yeghishé Charents. As can be seen in their writings, it is clear that the ethnographic pursuit of 'authenticity', hidden and buried in the countryside and discovered and elevated to an Art by Komitas, was fundamental to the manifestation of nation. In a 1914 essay titled 'The Heart of the Fatherland', Constant Zarian wrote,

> When, from an extensive fatherland's every corner – from its mountain-peaks, from the depths of its fields, from atop its boulders – the voices and songs of those who live by creating rise up, when they feel an imperative need to express, as destiny commands, their souls' secret and eyes' light, the Heart of the Fatherland shall, amazingly, vibrate with miraculous life. [. . .] And then – o, I know this past all doubting – then the choral song of the new *ashoughs* shall rise joyous and clear, declaiming the new Mythology. For the Style will have been discovered. Style is the race's image, its coat of arms, its crown, studded with gems charged with meaning.[38]

In the same journal, just a few pages later, Hagop Oshagan writes, 'A Priest of Labor [Komitas] has *transformed our songs into music* as a revelation for us, for whom they had become something foreign' (emphasis mine).[39] In making these songs into something knowable and legible – taking them into concert halls and the pages of European academic journals – an aesthetic claim is made that embodies, through Komitas, the possibility of Armenia. Not the one bounded by the confines of the nation-state, but the sonically reterritorialized homeland of the Diaspora.

Diaspora, whether as description or prescription, is a concept ontologically tethered to a question of origin. By definition, there is no 'diaspora' without an elsewhere. And to be in diaspora is not only to have an elsewhere but to be at least somewhat oriented and determined by it. Scholars may argue about the importance that should be ascribed to this elsewhere – whether it can rightfully be viewed as a 'home' or 'homeland', whether it overdetermines understandings of diasporic identity, where/if/how 'it' exists and so on – but those arguments aside, diaspora conceptually necessitates a reckoning with that elsewhere, as it determines how the diaspora, as an object of study, is understood and approached from within and without.

Too often, this supposed 'point of origin', as it is commonly referred to, is taken as assumed or as a given when treating it as such only serves to obscure the positioning that it embeds – an obscuration that Diaspora, in many ways, is dependent upon. There is a choice to be made as to where one begins the story of the Diaspora. There are the places from which those in diaspora have come (i.e. the literal journeys that can be traced) and the abstract elsewhere(s) that exist in a different plane.[40] Just as there are multiple ways of being diasporic, there are multiple 'homes' that factor into the possible elsewheres of those in diaspora – there are diasporic elsewheres and Diasporic elsewheres. For example, a Syrian Armenian in the United States who traces their family lineage to the villages of the Ottoman Empire (present-day Turkey) and who has no immediate or lived connection to the physical country of Armenia may still have a sense of an 'Armenia' that factors into and orients their diasporic consciousness.[41]

It is this latter sense of an elsewhere on which the Diaspora largely depends in order for it to become so. In other words, Diaspora is not so much dependent on an origin as it is on a beginning that masquerades as an origin. Asking 'where is the beginning of the diaspora?' allows for a very different intervention than asking 'where is the origin of the diaspora?' In the former, there is something that comes next. It *leads*. As Edward Said writes, beginnings, unlike origins, are chosen and intentional. They are 'points of departure' that allow one to proceed along a 'given course' – points of departure, in other words, that simultaneously enable, determine, embed and frame the subsequent becoming. This 'transitive beginning', as Said calls it, 'foresees a continuity that flows from it. This kind of beginning . . . allows us to initiate, to direct, to measure time to construct work, to discover, to produce knowledge'.[42] In Komitas – or at least the Komitas that exists today – there is an aestheticization of that beginning. His music, in other words, has become a point of departure.

It is a beginning that narrativizes an ironic sort of particularity, proclaiming itself free of 'foreign influences' but dependent on them as well (demanding the question what, or who, counts as 'foreign'). It is an irony that shows itself in the booklet accompanying the 1978 conference of the London-based Institute of Armenian music, where, in its overview of 'Armenian Music', Komitas is described as having taken care to 'purge [Armenian sacred and secular music] of Islamic and occidental overtones, of Arabic, Kurdish and Turkish influences' yet opens and closes with quotes about Armenian music from a Russian symbolist poet and an English writer.[43] As the latter notes, 'The musical culture of Armenia is one of the most ancient in Europe. Its richness is nowhere more clearly manifested than in its abundant wealth of folk material'.[44] It is an irony apparent when Komitas's significance is articulated through Western perceptions of his work, such as, for example, the oft-repeated anecdote of Claude Debussy's reaction to hearing a performance of Komitas's choir in Paris: 'If Komitas had written only "Antuni," it would be sufficient to place him among the world's best musicians'.[45] Or when his absence from the 'garden of western classical music' is bemoaned in the pages of *the Guardian* (in an article that also includes the Debussy anecdote).[46]

In this discursive world, not only can 'Armenian music' be said to be purged of 'foreign influences' but can simultaneously be placed into a framework legible to a world outside the Armenians' own – so that it can be played in Carnegie Hall, taught in the Western world's leading conservatories and be published in its academic journals. Thus, it is not so much that Komitas himself made the music European – a claim far too simplistic and dependent on its own facile essentializations – but that it has been *discursively* made fit for its gaze. In the discursive emphasis on the purging that allowed for Armenianness to emerge unsullied and pure, there emerges the possibility of a West-ward orientation and form of belonging – an orientation and belonging that has simultaneously served as a vector through which Armenians throughout the world have been enabled to come together as a whole.

But to poke at the borders of this sonic world and to interrogate the alignments it facilitates is, in many ways, to interrogate the very Home that has made wholeness possible – to see it for its possibilities and impossibilities, its inclusions and exclusions. For what happens when we speak of Diaspora's limits when the stakes are what they are?

Komitas, *usdi gukas*?

Fittingly, the very first commercially recorded composition of Komitas's work was 'Grung', recorded in 1901.[47] The singer's pleading opening question, 'Grung, usdi gukas?' ('Crane, from where do you come?'), speaks profoundly to the diasporic condition and of that desperate desire for a connection to the homeland. But there is perhaps an interpretation of this question that is a bit more literal: Crane, from *where* do you come? Where is the home for which the singer pleads?

Those answers can perhaps be articulated in the realm of the aesthetic. In world-renowned Beirut-born, California-based Isabel Bayrakdarian's Grammy-winning version – a rendition heard at opera houses across the United States and Europe – her soprano voice soars, lifted by the string ensemble that accompanies her.[48] In this version, recorded at the Aram Khachaturian Concert Hall in Armenia's capital city of Yerevan, where is the singer's home? And where is it in New York City-born George Mgrditchian's lesser-known version?[49] It is still Komitas's setting but rendered wordlessly on the oud, with ornamentations and microtones evocative of those 'foreign influences' supposedly purged (but *are* they foreign influences?). Each setting traces its own contours of 'Armenian music', narrativizing forms of diasporic belonging. In which is there the promise, or the possibility, of wholeness?

There is a painting of Komitas by his friend Panos Terlemezyan that at first glance seems to be the prototype for the paintings that were to come: Komitas in nature sitting pensively under a tree. In many of these paintings, the setting is ambiguous enough that it seems to be the 'Armenia' made possible in Komitas's work. But look more closely at this painting, and see the beautiful leather shoes peeking from under his cassock while he reads under the tree. See the beautiful rug upon which he sits, the pottery displayed to his left and what appears to be a saz leaning against the tree. Komitas's father was a shoemaker. His mother, a carpet weaver. Kütahya, his place of birth, a town renowned for its ceramic pottery. And the saz, an instrument as Turkish, Iranian, Syrian, Azerbaijani and Kurdish, as it is Armenian.[50] Komitas came from Kütahya. Perhaps it was his beginning, perhaps it was not. Perhaps it was his elsewhere, perhaps it was not.

I look at this painting and I wonder: Komitas, *usdi gukas*?

Notes

* My sincerest gratitude to Talar Chahinian, Sossie Kasbarian and Tsolin Nalbantian for their insights, suggestions and reserves of patience. Many thanks also to the organizers and participants of the Society for Armenian Studies conference, 'Diaspora and "Stateless Power"', where this work was first presented. Philip Bohlman and the participants of the EthNoise! workshop at the University of Chicago also provided invaluable feedback. And thank you also to my friends and esteemed colleagues Sato Moughalian and Karen Leistra-Jones for their help and insights at various stages of this project. And finally, my utmost gratitude to Khachig Tölölyan, to whom my work owes so very much. Any errors are mine alone.
1 Edward W. Said, 'Reflections on Exile', in *Reflections on Exile and Other Essays* (Cambridge, MA: Harvard University Press, 2000), 141.
2 There is perhaps no figure in Armenian music as widely researched as Komitas. Jonathan McCollum and Nercessian's bibliography provides an impressively comprehensive overview of existent work up to the book's time of publication. For a detailed bibliography of Komitas's works (and biographic overview), see Armineh Grigorian, Robert Atayan, and Aram Kerovpyan, 'Komitas Vardapet', *Grove Music Online* (2001), https://doi.org/10.1093/gmo/9781561592630.article.51868. Accessed 2 November 2020, Select reproductions and translations of Komitas's work can be found in Komitas, *Armenian Sacred and Folk Music*, trans. Edward Gulbenkian (Surrey: Curzon Press, 1998); Komitas, *Komitas: Essays and Articles*, trans. Vatsche Barsoumian (Pasadena: Drazark Press, 2001); and Melissa Bilal and Burcu Yıldız, *Kalbim o viran evlere benzer: Gomidas Vartabed'in müzik mirası* (Istanbul: Birzamanlar Yayıncılık, 2019). See also sources cited in footnote 27.
3 See in particular Brubaker, 'The "Diaspora" Diaspora', *Ethnic and Racial Studies* 28, no. 1 (2005): 1–19; Tölölyan, 'Diaspora: Past, Present, and Promise', IMI Working Papers Series, no. 55 (2011): 4–14; and Cho, 'The Turn to Diaspora', *Topia* 17, no. 4 (2007): 11–30.
4 Cho, 'The Turn to Diaspora', 14.
5 Ibid., 21.
6 Brubaker, 'The "Diaspora" Diaspora', 11. Brubaker cites Gabriel Sheffer, *Diaspora Politics: At Home Abroad* (Cambridge: Cambridge University Press, 2003), 100.
7 Brubaker, 'The "Diaspora" Diaspora', 12.
8 Ibid., 13.
9 Tölölyan, 'The Contemporary Discourse of Diaspora Studies', *Comparative Studies of South Asia, Africa and the Middle East* 27, no. 3 (2007): 649.

10　Tölölyan, 'The Nation-State and Its Others: In Lieu of a Preface', *Diaspora* 1, no. 1 (1991): 4.
11　On roots and routes and their significance to identity formation in the Black diaspora see Paul Gilroy, *The Black Atlantic* (Cambridge, MA: Harvard University Press, 1993). The examples of Armenian diasporic routes mentioned here are by no means meant to be exhaustive but serve as a mere sampling of some of the different possibilities. They also focus on examples of diasporic communities found in the United States.
12　For a discussion of generational differences in diasporic identifications see Tölölyan, 'The Contemporary Discourse of Diaspora Studies'.
13　Anny P. Bakalian, *Armenian-Americans: From Being to Feeling Armenian* (New Brunswick: Transaction Publishers, 1993).
14　Tölölyan, 'The Contemporary Discourse of Diaspora Studies', 654.
15　Since 2000, English-language work on Armenian music has increased considerably. However, there is critical early work that set the foundation for the later work that was to come. For an overview on published work on Armenian music, in numerous languages, see Jonathan McCollum and Andy Nercessian, *Armenian Music: A Comprehensive Bibliography and Discography* (Lanham: Scarecrow Press, 2004).
16　Marc Nichanian, *The Historiographic Perversion* (New York: Columbia University Press, 2009), 120.
17　See also Sylvia Alajaji, 'California', in *Music and the Armenian Diaspora: Searching for Home in Exile* (Bloomington: Indiana University Press, 2015), 133–66.
18　See also Bakalian, *Armenian-Americans*, 310 and Alajaji, *Music and the Armenian Diaspora*, 137.
19　Mount Ararat and Etchmiadzin are both iconic symbols of Armenian identity. Etchmiadzin, described later in the chapter, is in present-day Armenia, while Mount Ararat is in present-day Turkey.
20　See Michael Pifer, 'The Diasporic Crane: Discursive Migration Across the Armenian-Turkish Divide', *Diaspora* 18, no. 3 (2009): 229–52.
21　For further information on Kütahya and the role of Armenians in its storied ceramics tradition, see, among others, Dickran Kouymjian, 'The Role of Armenian Potters of Kutahia in the Ottoman Ceramic Industry', in *Armenian Communities in Asia Minor*, ed. Richard G. Hovannisian (Costa Mesa: Mazda Publishers, 2014), 107–30 and Sato Moughalian, *Feast of Ashes: The Life and Art of David Ohannessian* (Stanford: Stanford University Press, 2019). For the musical culture of Kütahya, see Arpi Vardumyan, 'Komitas Vardapet and the Armenian Musical Culture of Kutahia', in *Armenian Communities in Asia Minor*, 195–208.
22　Moughalian, *Feast of Ashes*, 57–8.
23　Rita Soulahian Kuyumjian, *The Archeology of Madness: Komitas, Portrait of an Armenian Icon* (Princeton: Gomidas Institute, 2001), 23–4. Kuyumjian cites Komitas, Autobiographical Papers, June 1908, Komitas Archives, doc. 71, Charents Museum of Literature and Art, Yerevan:12.
24　For work on Armenian modal and liturgical traditions generally and khaz notation specifically, see, among others, Robert At'ayan, *The Armenian Neume System of Notation*, trans. V. N. Nersessian (Surrey: Curzon Press, 1999); Aram Kerovpyan, 'Les *charakan* (*troparia*) et l'octoéchos arménien selon le *charaknots* (*tropologion* arménien) édité en 1875', in *Aspects de la musique liturgique au Moyen-Age*, ed. Christian Meyer (Paris: Creaphis, 1991), 93–123; Aram Kerovpyan, *Manuel de notation musicale arménienne moderne* (Tutzing: Hans Schneider, 2001); Jonathan McCollum, 'Analysis of Notation in Music Historiography: Armenian Neumatic

Khaz From the Ninth Through Early Twentieth Centuries', in *Theory and Method in Historical Ethnomusicology*, ed. Jonathan McCollum and David G. Hebert (Lanham: Lexington Books, 2014), 197–256; and Haig Utidjian, *Tntesean and the Music of the Armenian Hymnal* (Červený Kostelec: Pavel Mervart, 2018).

25 For a detailed examination of Komitas's relationship with the upper ranks and more conservative members of the clergy, see Kuyumjian, *The Archaeology of Madness*.
26 For in-depth analyses of Komitas's work and discourses of musical authenticity (particularly within an Ottoman/Turkish context, as seen in Bilal, Olley and Yıldız), see Melissa Bilal, 'Thou Need'st Not Weep, For I Have Wept Full Sore: An Affective Genealogy of the Armenian Lullaby in Turkey', (Ph.D. diss., University of Chicago, 2013); Bilal, 'Gomidas Vartabed ve Müzikolojinin Siyaseti', in *Kalbim o viran evlere benzer: Gomidas Vartabed'in müzik mirası* (Istanbul: Birzamanlar Yayıncılık, 2019), 167–219; Brigitta Davidjants, 'Identity Construction in Armenian Music on the Example of Early Folklore Movement', *Folklore: Electronic Journal of Folklore* 62 (2015): 175–200; Jacob Olley, 'Remembering Armenian Music in Bolis: Komitas Vardapet in Transcultural Perspective', *Memory Studies* 12, no. 5 (2019): 547–64; and Burcu Yıldız, *Experiencing Armenian Music in Turkey: An Ethnography of Musicultural Memory* (Würzburg: Ergon-Verlag, 2016), 101–23.
27 Komitas, 'The Singing of the Holy Liturgy', in *Armenian Sacred and Folk Music*, 126–7. Summary of Komitas's talk in Max Seiffert, 'Mitteilungen der Internationalen Musik-Gesellschaft: 1. Berlin', *Zeitschrift der Internationalen Musik Gesellschaft: Erster Jahrgang 1899-1900* 1, no. 2 (1899): 46. Original text: "Die armenische Kirchenmusik – so etwa führte er aus – ist sich von Anbeginn des Christentums bis heute gleich geblieben. Ihren Ursprung hat sie im älteren, heidnischen Tempelgesang gehabt, der seinerseits wieder aus der Volksmusik hervorgegangen ist. Die Gemeinsamkeit von Kirchen- und Volksmusik läßt sich noch vielfach durch Analyse der Melodien feststellen. Nur hat die Kirche durch Ornamente reicher ausgestaltet, was im Volke einfach geblieben."
28 See, for example, Komitas, 'Hayn uni ink'nuroyn yerazhshtout'yunner' ('Armenians Have a Unique Music'), *Azatamart* (Constantinople, 1913); and Komitas, 'Hay Zhoghovertagan ew Yegehets'agan Yerkerě' ('Armenian Folk and Religious Music'), in *Komitas Vartabed: Hotvadzner ew Usumnasirut'yunner* (Yerevan: Haybedhrad, 1941). Both translated into English in Komitas, *Komitas: Essays and Articles*, 206–9 and 163–7.
29 Komitas, Review of *Recueil des Chants Populaires Arméniens, no. 1*, in *Armenian Sacred and Folk Music*, 162 (originally published 1900).
30 According to Hayk Demoyan, Komitas was even asked to preside over the third Armenian Olympic Games in Constantinople. See Demoyan, 'Patriotism, Competitive Nationalism and Minority's Successes: Armenian Sports in the Ottoman Empire in the Pre-1915 Period', *International Journal of Armenian Genocide Studies* 1, no. 1 (2014): 25.
31 In August of 2020, the Komitas statue in Paris, which also serves as a memorial to the victims of the Armenian Genocide, was graffitied with the words "c'est faux" ("it's false").
32 The Gomidas Institute was founded in 1992 at the University of Michigan and has since been headquartered in London. It operates as an independent academic institution and among its many activities, serves as a publishing house for scholarship on Armenian studies. See http://gomidas.org/.
33 Nairi Khachadourian, 'Aram Kerovpyan: "Komitas's Name Often Trespasses His Person"', *Regional Post* (n.d.), https://regionalpost.org/en/articles/aram-kerovpyan-komitass-name-often-trespasses-his-person.html. Accessed 31 March 2002.

34 Kradjian's comment is cited in 'Bayrakdarian Dedicates Tour to Victims of Genocide', *Asbarez* (19 September 2008), https://asbarez.com/bayrakdarian-dedicates-tour-to-victims-of-genocide/. Accessed 31 March 2022. Sirvart Poladian, 'Komitas Vardapet and His Contribution to Ethnomusicology', *Ethnomusicology* 16, no. 1 (1972): 88.
35 Yıldız, 'Gomidas Vartabed and the Debate of Authenticity in "Armenian Music"', 122.
36 Nichanian, *Mourning Philology: Art and Religion at the Margins of the Ottoman Empire*, translated by G. M. Goshgarian and Jeff Fort (New York: Fordham University Press, 2014), 127.
37 Ibid., 30.
38 Constant Zarian, 'The Heart of the Fatherland', *Mehean*, no. 3 (March 1914): 36–7. Cited and translated in Nichanian, *Mourning Philology*, 278.
39 Hagop Oshagan, 'The Literature of All Armenians', *Mehean*, no. 3 (March 1914): 40. Cited and translated in Nichanian, *Mourning Philology*, 281.
40 In my previous work, I distinguish home from Home in order to expand the complex orientations towards elsewheres that exist for those in diaspora. Again, however, I offer these distinctions, imperfect as they are, as a means of adding texture to, expanding understandings of and troubling any suppositions of singular understandings or embodiments of the concepts. There are multiple homes to people in diaspora, just as there are many ways of embodying *being* diasporic. See Alajaji, *Music and the Armenian Diaspora*.
41 See Bakalian, *Armenian-Americans*.
42 Said, *Beginnings: Intention and Method* (1975; New York: Columbia University Press, 1985), 76.
43 Conference program for 'Music Armenia' 78: An International Celebration of Armenian Music', The Institute of Armenian Music, London, 6–13 August 1978, 42.
44 Ibid.
45 See, for example, 'One Nation, One Music! The Uniqueness of Komitas', *Armenian News Network/Groong*, 31 October 2014), http://www.groong.org/tcc/tcc-20141031.html. Accessed 2 November 2020. The Debussy anecdote is also referenced in Meline Toumani, 'Songs Lifted in Praise of an Armenian Hero', *New York Times*, 17 October 2008, https://www.nytimes.com/2008/10/19/arts/music/19toum.html.
46 Michael Church, 'Komitas Vardapet, Forgotten Folk Hero', *Guardian*, 21 April 2011, https://www.theguardian.com/music/2011/apr/21/komitas-vardapet-folk-music-armenia.
47 My sincerest gratitude to Yektan Türkyılmaz for this information. According to Türkyılmaz, this recording session took place in St. Petersburg in 1901 and featured a performer named N. Shakhlamian. See also the review of a talk given by Türkyılmaz at Columbia University: Taleen Babayan, 'Musical Records: The Beat of Armenian Hearts Around the World', *Armenian Mirror-Spectator*, 5 April 2018, https://mirrorspectator.com/2018/04/05/musical-records-the-beat-of-armenian-hearts-around-the-world/.
48 Isabel Bayrakdarian, 'Groong', on *Gomidas Songs*, with the Armenian Philharmonic Orchestra Chamber Players, conducted by Edvard Topchian (Nonesuch, 2008). See https://www.nonesuch.com/albums/gomidas-songs.
49 George Mgrditchian, 'Groong', on *Armenian Oud Masters in USA: Recordings from 40s, 50s, & 60s* (Vintage Music, 2012).
50 My sincerest gratitude to Sato Moughalian for her insights into this painting. As she writes in *Feast of Ashes*, Komitas sat for this painting in 1912 while he and Terlemezian were visiting the thermal baths of Ilija, outside of Kütahya (96).

9

'Toward the Diaspora'

The performative powers of Vahé Oshagan's poetry[1]

Karen Jallatyan

Declarations of independence

The early 1990s were a period of distinct declarations of independence affecting Armenian life. In December 1990, Vahé Oshagan (1922–2000), the prominent poet and critic writing in Western Armenian, penned a 'Literary Manifesto',[2] in which he declared and called for the independence of Armenian thought particularly in the diaspora. In the spring of 1991, the English-language journal *Diaspora: A Journal of Transnational Studies* was established by Khachig Tölölyan, Kourken Sarkissian and Gerard Libaridian, with the support of the Zoryan Institute, the Armenian-North American research centre at the time, based in Boston. The scope of this periodical was diaspora(s) in general, including but going far beyond matters concerning Armenians. In the fall of the same year, the Republic of Armenia declared independence. In the winter, the autonomous region of Artsakh (Nagorno-Karabakh), populated mostly by Armenians, declared independence from Azerbaijan.

Diaspora legitimized as well as shaped interdisciplinary academic inquiry around diaspora. One can get a sense of this from Tölölyan's 'The Nation-State and Its Others: In Lieu of Preface', which opens the journal's first volume, explicitly casts itself as a manifesto and calls for exploring the complexities of diasporic alterity in relation to the nation-state. Tölölyan's 1996 essay 'Rethinking Diaspora(s): Stateless Power in the Transnational Moment', also published in *Diaspora*, formulated by now the well-known call to explore transnational stateless power, on one occasion stating that the latter's 'particular strength in the transnational era lies in part in its nonconfrontational quality as a form of decentered power-knowledge . . . [which] works many of its effects by osmosis across porous boundaries'.[3] Despite its innovative intentions, the essay echoes humanist attitudes by relying too comfortably on concepts like identity, belonging and collective subjectivity characteristic of the discourse of 'identity politics' prevalent in the Anglophone world in the second half of the twentieth century and subjected to radical critique by the 1990s.[4] The essay also manifests disciplinary conservatism when protesting against what it considers as the privileging of 'theory-inflected investigation of texts' drawn from 'literary and theoretical discourse' in analysing 'the *social* text of diaspora life'.⁵ This begs the question of how we are to analyse and interpret the '*social* text' of diaspora if not by drawing from critical theory. Inversely, is it not necessarily the case that the 'literary and theoretical discourse' also has social – socio-textual – dimensions? This chapter will challenge the binary opposition in Tölölyan's essay between 'literary and theoretical discourse' and 'social text' by developing a notion of diasporic performance that falls within but cannot be contained by these categories. In doing so, my aim is to avoid essentializing modes of treating identity, something that still plagues Armenian life in the diaspora and in the state. Oshagan's texts, especially his poetry, will serve as the crucible for a specifically Armenian diasporic performance.

Oshagan's call for an independent Armenian diaspora was self-consciously and explicitly made in contradistinction to Armenia moving towards independence in the early 1990s. Armenian society of the time, particularly in the Republic of Armenia, but also in the diaspora, was swayed by calls for national unity, exacerbated by the first Artsakh (Nagorno-Karabakh) war.⁶ Oshagan reiterated the call for an independent Armenian Diaspora in the interview that he gave to the *Armenian International Magazine* (*AIM*) published mostly in English from Los Angeles between 1990 and 2004.⁷ The interview, 'Poles Apart: Vahé Oshagan on the Habitat, Imagery, and Inner Reaches of the Diaspora' (July 1991) was conducted by Ishkhan Jinbashian, a Los Angeles-based Western Armenian writer and translator, who first asked: 'Although functioning under often uneven sociopolitical climates, the main centers of the Diaspora still share a set of collective symbols, and continue to react to similar obstacles. But can we speak of a Diasporan spirit, a *zeitgeist*?'⁸ Oshagan replied in this manner:

> No. Such a spirit seems to be extraneous to the Diaspora. An ideal at best. Throughout our history, we've been caught between centripetal and centrifugal urges – toward the roots and the land, and toward the outer dimension, the free world. To this is added the working of a novel construct – *toward the Diaspora*, which is an altogether different identity than that of a traditional, half-conscious Diaspora of the last millennium.⁹

As we can see, Oshagan historicized the Armenian Diaspora by interpreting its past with the help of the centripetal/centrifugal dichotomy, which relies on a notion of centre as the proper site of identity and certainly constitutes the essence of modern nation-state-centred world order. Oshagan's next gesture decentres this dichotomy by introducing a third 'urge' – '*toward the Diaspora*'. To have a more nuanced sense of what he might mean, let us turn to the question that is posed to him next. To Jinbashian's subsequent inquiry pertaining to the overbearing politicization of the Armenian diaspora, Oshagan answered: 'Increasingly, however, it becomes essential that the Diaspora consider itself a sovereign political reality. It is time that the Diaspora shape a new political self-definition, a genuinely organic model that is consistent with the needs and strengths of a cultural entity, like ours, whose significance does not rest on statehood or a territorial base.' And a sentence later, he stated: 'So it is already possible to speak of a Diasporan declaration of independence, parallel to that of Armenia but irrespective of it. . . . As we are left to our own devices, we cannot but become self-reliant – in every respect.'[10] As we can see, Oshagan conceived the Armenian Diaspora as a 'cultural entity' that is not only irreducible to 'statehood or a territorial base' in general but also particularly to Armenia as a state and territory.

Given the earlier explicit arguments away from state-centred world order, Oshagan's views were met with hostility. For example, the 3 February 1992 number of Montreal's *Horizon Weekly*,[11] the official press of the Armenian Revolutionary Federation (ARF),[12] published the Armenian version of Oshagan's *AIM* interview as well as four op-eds by outspoken members of the ARF, Hraztan Zeitlian, Haiduk Shamlian, Vrej-Armen and Mher Karakashian.[13] Three of these opinions, taking most of the writing space, expressed vehement and even personally insulting opposition to Oshagan; only one offered some tepid support. The first op-ed *Sp'iwṛk'i ṛazmavaragan sgzpunk'ner* (Diaspora's Strategic Principles) by Hraztan Zeitlian began by stating that Oshagan had probably coined the phrase 'toward the Diaspora' in a provocative contradistinction to the motto 'toward the country' (*Tēbi Yergir*), which the ARF had adopted as its strategic orientation during its latest general meeting. It then condemned Oshagan for arguing that the Armenian Diaspora should focus its forces on itself when Armenia has just gained independence. Ironically, Zeitlian went on to defend a culturally and politically differentiated view of the Armenian Diaspora, which rather agreed with Oshagan's views.

Haiduk Shamlian's *Khent' gaydzer* (Mad Sparks), the mildest among the three, dwelt on the 'cultural' dimension of the issue as if the latter were separate from the economic-political one. Shamlian's article tried to deconstruct the question of art proper to the diaspora posed to Oshagan by Jinbashian, while also eventually stating that it had already begun producing such works. The most ardent rebuke was expressed by the third op-ed, Vrej-Armen's *Gizagēdē Hayasdan* (Focus on Armenia), which openly expounded a 'one people, one nation' ideology and stated that in the wake of the independence of the Republic of Armenia '[. . .] today we are the Abroad, we can see ourselves as the Abroad and our nature can be determined by our Country'.[14] While Zeitlian and Shamlian also preferred the term 'diaspora' over 'the abroad', Vrej-Armen appeared to be the most zealous by seeing the diaspora as temporary and Armenia as necessary to be prioritized in every way. All three negated, pathologized and/or repressed, from within and in the name of national ideology, the experience of alterity at the heart of diasporic becoming. Lastly, Mher Karakashian's op-ed 'Imagination's emancipation' – a phrase taken from Oshagan's *AIM* interview – carefully defended Oshagan's views by stating that now that Armenia was independent, diaspora's pre-existing ideology of preserving Armenianness could be thrown aside and the new reality of diasporic dispersion could be engaged more fully. The challenge in embracing that reality for Oshagan consisted of creatively sustaining a diasporic sensibility across languages and cultures.

It should be made clear that Oshagan himself had joined the ranks of the ARF in 1943, when living in Haifa, and was a member until the end of his life. The aforementioned thinly veiled attack against him by fellow ARF members could thus be seen as a quarrel internal to that political party. And yet, beyond political party and ideology, on a discursive level, the publication of these four op-eds gives us an idea of the resistance that Oshagan's contemporary readership perhaps could not but mount in the face of his vision and practice of diaspora.[15] Furthermore, the discourse from the 1990s ARF press deployed the binary 'abroad' and 'country' within a nation-state-centred ideological framework to privilege the latter. One may get the impression that Oshagan's intervention merely turned it on its head by privileging the 'abroad' over the 'country' while in this manner perpetuating the binary. Yet, the third formulation, 'toward the Diaspora', suggests emphatically that Oshagan sought to deconstruct the hegemony of the discourse of nationhood to create a space in which diaspora could legitimately coexist.

Diasporizing Armenian life

Deconstructing the ARF

Vahé Oshagan was born in Plovdiv, Bulgaria. He spent his childhood in Egypt, Cyprus and Palestine, where his father, the great Western Armenian novelist and critic Hagop Oshagan (1883–1948), who had narrowly survived the 1915 Armenian Catastrophe,[16] wrote and taught. Vahé Oshagan later studied in Paris, to then move to Beirut, where he taught at various universities and wrote some of his most influential works of poetry and literary criticism. With the outbreak of the Lebanese Civil War, Oshagan moved to Philadelphia, then San Francisco, Stepanakert (in Artsakh/Nagorno-Karabakh) and Sydney. He passed away in Philadelphia. The spatiotemporal trajectory of his life in many ways is a reflection of the Armenian Diaspora that his literary and critical works tried to embrace.

Oshagan's contribution not only consists of making deconstructive gestures from within institutions operating in the diaspora – for example, the ARF – but in performing diaspora across a poetic production stretching over some four decades. Methodologically speaking, theme-centred interpretations of poetry (and literature in general) problematically imply a respective pre-existent entity and/or reality that can be adequately captured through representation, in this case, poetic language. By contrast, an interpretation that tracks the twists and turns of recurring tropes in poetry safeguards against the inadequacy of merely relying on representation by treating the latter as performatively opening towards inherently emergent entities and/or realities. It is this kind of interpretation that I will attempt in what follows.

In theorizing diasporic performance, let us attempt to think of the Armenian Diaspora as an extrinsically relating assemblage. Taking up Gilles Deleuze and Félix Guattari's work, Manuel DeLanda, a philosopher writing on urban history and architecture, formulates an intrinsic relation thus: 'if a relation constitutes the very identity of what it relates it cannot respect the heterogeneity of the components, but rather it tends to fuse them together into a homogeneous whole.'[17] Extrinsic relations, by contrast, cannot be reduced either to the relations or to the elements in relation. Extrinsically conceived, diasporic 'cultural entities' – to use Oshagan's phrase – are irreducible singularities that participate in larger diasporic becoming while generating their independent singularity.[18] Independence here has to be understood and developed in the precise sense of independence from nation-state sovereignty, as independent from independence. To do so, while paying attention to the particularities of Armenian diasporic becoming, let us note DeLanda's beneficial elaboration of Deleuze and Guattari's conception of assemblage:

In their exposition of assemblage theory Deleuze and Guattari tend to use a series of oppositions: tree/rhizome, striated/smooth, molar/molecular, and stratum/assemblage. But they constantly remind us that the opposites can be transformed into one another. In particular, the kinds of ensembles designated as 'assemblages' can be obtained from strata by a decoding operation. [Endnote 3: 'Deleuze and Guattari, *A Thousand Plateaus*, p. 503. "Assemblages are already different from strata. They are produced in the strata, but operate in zones where milieus become decoded"', p. 17.] But if one member of these dichotomies can be transformed into the other then the oppositions can be replaced with a single parametrised term capable of existing in two different states. This yields a different version of the concept of assemblage, *a concept with knobs* that can be set to different values to yield either strata or assemblages (in the original sense). The coding parameter is one of the knobs we must build into the concept.[19]

By stating above that a stratum can be decoded into an assemblage, DeLanda allows us to think that intrinsically and extrinsically relating entities can themselves (extrinsically) relate to one another. In light of this, I find it beneficial to think of the diaspora and the nation-state as different states of Armenian life. The nation-state relies on and reproduces the codes of a modern nation-state-centred world order inherited from the nineteenth century. Given its strong tendency towards forming intrinsic relations, the nation-state-centred world order behaves more like a stratum. The diaspora's difference lies in opening to the possibility of decoding the nation-state-centred world order through various singular experiences of interacting with other cultures and economical, political and technological (media included) regimes. Such decoding operations should not be seen as merely negating the nation but also need to be considered more affirmatively as performing diaspora.

Theorizing Armenian life as consisting of both national stratum and diasporic assemblage can help overcome essentializing modes of thinking of its simultaneously diasporic and nation-state-centred existence.[20] It can also address the more serious critique of communalism that diaspora studies has received. Nanor Kebranian has argued that advocates of diasporas, faced with the anxiety of being excluded from humanity, keep trying to formulate modes of conceiving diasporic communal belonging.[21] This is not only contrary to the genealogy of the term 'diaspora', as it has mostly designated the breaking down of community, but also constrains diasporic creative freedom. After this diagnosis, Kebranian evokes the Paris-based interwar Armenian writers known as the *Menk'* (We) generation, to propose an ethics of strangers as a way out of modern nation-statist communalism. Despite its critical incisiveness, Kebranian's essay, as it itself acknowledges, does not elaborate as to how such ethics could lead, and has already led with the *Menk* generation as well as arguably with Oshagan, to diasporizing Armenian life. Hence, the present chapter's reading of diasporas as performing extrinsically relating assemblages is an attempt to account for the generative aspects of diasporic becoming.

Oshagan's poetry opens to diasporic becoming by decoding the nation-state-centred world order hegemonic in post-catastrophic Western Armenian literature.[22] One can find striking instances of this in his highly energetic and courageous 1971 volume *K'arughi*

(Crossroad), published in Beirut.[23] It contains texts that subject to diasporic becoming not only (epic) lyric poetry but also historical fiction and dramaturgy. The poem 'Beirut Paris' is set to rhythm partially through the repetition of the rather vulgar applauding sound 'Clap clap clap', much to the outrage of the refined Beirut Armenian readership expecting 'high cultured' poetry. The poem offers poignant images (narrative fragments) set in Paris and Beirut to react against, through much caustic sarcasm and provocation, the stagnation of Armenian life, stranded in endless lament and traditionalism. Here is an excerpt: 'The road from Beirut to Paris does not pass through Armenia / through the rotten and clammy longing for Armenia / but cuts across the grand highway of world's struggles / of dry-eyed and callous [dry-nerved], evil impatient and irritated / humanity'. Accordingly, Armenia is no longer the privileged site of Armenian life. The poem's ending performs a diasporic readership through the interpellative 'you':

> In Beirut [and] Paris you are destroyed every minute by your pleasure
> get lost from the world already
> if you have no gift to give to humanity,
> let your memory die too
> if you are going to live only with it, if having gotten used to yourself
> you are going to play brother and sister under the whorehouse's wall,
> if all you know is clapping when the world is disturbed
> no longer able to clap.
>   Clap clap clap clap clap.

The figure of the 'you' in the lines above is both individual and communal since it addresses a readership. In doing so, it creates and performs a diasporic communal sensibility. The latter consists of being able to give a 'gift to humanity'. The poem overall links two prominent diaspora Armenian locales through the explicit call and implicit promise of a creative relationship with 'humanity' – a figure of diasporic spatiality escaping that of the nation-state-centred world order. Signed 'March 1968' – a critical moment at least in the 'West', when France was experiencing anti-capitalist, anti-traditionalist uprisings and the United States was at the peak of the Civil Rights Movement while being in the middle of an increasingly unpopular war in Vietnam – 'Beirut Paris' constitutes a gesture of open-ended, translocal diasporic becoming that challenges the hegemony of nation-centred spatiality. Such translocal spatiality in many ways reflects Oshagan's own itinerant life.

Early traces of opening to diasporic becoming are inscribed in Oshagan's first published volume of poetry, *Baduhan* (Window), appearing in Beirut in 1956, about four decades before his 'Literary Manifesto'. In *Window*, amid the existentialist, prose-induced language occasionally taking highly provocative turns, one can read the following:

> We Armenians
> without revenge and faith and consolation
> but with great patience, non-resistance,
> not conformed, but anticipating the others,

the asphalt steel and glass nations,
anticipating their defeat and anger's
outcry,
especially the last one, without even having descended into the pit, but already
feeling:
(s)he, the Armenian, knowing this last outcry's
not the meaning or cause
but value.[24]

These lines – from the poem *Srjaranĕ (Usumnasirut'iwn)* (The Cafe (Study)), the penultimate of the volume's fifteen pieces – convey a sense of Armenian nationhood that survives 'defeat' and 'anger' and is thus different from ordinary nationalist triumphalism. This sense of difference appears in the volume's first poem *Tashnagts'ut'iwn* (Federation) referring to the ARF. While at places seeming to rather conventionally heap praise on the largest political party active in the Armenian Diaspora, it also offers the following remarkable lines: 'And if you are really Armenian, / having reached there / and with greatness, beauty / armed / in the gazes of every one / you will recognize yourself. / And with recognition, maybe, who knows . . ./that you will break into pieces the cast / of your flesh's basin, / and become free / from the smell of the earth, taste of the water, / from the uniform of your nothingness'.[25] Echoing (anti-)nihilistic attitudes, this excerpt recasts the ARF – a modern, national political party in its historical emergence and role – as more than a territorially bound, nation-state-centred entity. The liminality of the figure of the window, the title of this volume of poetry, can also be read as inscribing the possibility of post-national diasporic becoming.[26] Just as Oshagan's 'toward the Diaspora' does not negate the nation by reproducing a diaspora/nation binary opposition but strives to deconstruct it, post-national in this case does not mean negating the nation but situating it within an Armenian life that overflows it. It should also be noted that there is a deeper connection between post-War existentialism and Oshagan's performance of diaspora in poetry written in Western Armenian. Just as the Western Armenian literary language is alienated from itself due to the catastrophic dispersion that it has been undergoing since 1915, post-war existentialism – and arguably modernity more broadly – inscribes the alienation of the West from structures of meaning and value (e.g. Christianity, monarchy and/or certain currents of philosophy) that were crucial for it.

Armenian Christianity in a renewed exile

Oshagan's poetry performs diaspora not only through the most influential Armenian national political party, the ARF, operative in the diaspora during and after the Soviet Period, but also through the arguably most influential national mode of Armenian existence, Armenian Christianity.[27] It does so by sustaining a long-lasting and widely interspersed preoccupation with Christian theology. The latter as a result is seen as acquiring post-national diasporic qualities. To give an example, in the last section of his groundbreaking 1963 volume *K'aghak'* (The City), titled 'Church', these lines stand out:

'religion / which like the shadow of God / has fallen on the Human / to spare, probably, our eyes / from the truth's radioactive / ray'.[28] A church, among other city sites, is where the absurd ('the truth') dwells but is denied and concealed. Oshagan's preoccupation with Christian theology is powerfully present already in the 1953 play *Mernoghner* (Mortals), published in Beirut's *Agos* in the March–April 1955 number (3-4), on the fortieth anniversary of the Armenian Catastrophe, as well as in the novella *Ōdzumĕ* (The Unction), the historical fiction *Avarayr 80* (Avarayr 80), both published in 1988 in the volume *T'akartin shurch* (Around the Snare), in the 1996 volume *Hampuyr* (Embrace) and in the posthumously published play *Badkam* (The Oracle) dated from 1990.[29]

In January 1962, the inaugural issue of the literary and artistic monthly (at the time) review *Pakine*, founded in Beirut and active to this day – for which Oshagan was part of the initial editorial committee – published a short poem titled *P'okhan aghōt'k'i* (In Place of Prayer) which is included in the 2017 Oshagan anthology *Stations*.[30] The first-person voice of the 'In Place of Prayer' addresses god by rejecting any of the usual modes of expressing deference for him. After this desanctifying gesture – pervasive and crucial in Oshagan's work, as it is noted and reflected on by both Nichanian and Beledian – the voice acknowledges that god must exist and refers to him in a manner that alludes to negative mystical theology: 'you adjectiveless and adverbless, lowercase [uncapitalized] / contemporary'.[31] Both critics have written extensively on the ways in which Oshagan, who lived in Paris from 1946 to 1952 and was influenced by post-war French existentialism that renders religion and language absurd, created a highly original modernist poetry.[32] The voice of the poem then expresses the desire to speak with god as equal to equal and asserts himself as being in the present, isolated, including when relating to church and religion, and uncertain of his existence. The poem ends with the following fragment:

> So let's walk together,
> contemporary,
> you who are, I who am or am not . . .?
> At least understand why my person deteriorates
> when it desires to be like you,
> To be!
> doesn't matter if a stone on a road, a raindrop, a love, a pain
> or simply nothing,
> but to be.
> Haven't both of us fallen into the same trap? –
> you cannot not be, I cannot be,
> for ever and ever,
> Amen.[33]

The intertextuality of Oshagan's lines – alluding to the Lord's Prayer and evoking its form and gestures – gives rise to a notion of god as the mere ontological opposite of the human: 'Haven't both of us fallen into the same trap?– / you cannot not be, I cannot be'. Man and god in an ontological double bind, both 'trapped' and not free, recasts them as existentially alienated. The impossibility of becoming god as deterioration, also seen in the lines quoted above, is arguably another instance of existentialist decoding of Christian mystic theology. Namely, the 'prayer' of the poem 'fails' in existentialist terms as deterioration. Overall, the poem affirms elements from inherited Christian mystical discourse by maintaining the possibility of addressing god, no matter how paradoxical this can be in its negative mystical theological form.[34] And yet, as we saw, 'In Place of Prayer' decodes Christian mystic theology through modern/ist ('contemporary') existentialist terms.

A notion of anthropomorphized god figures even more prominently in the larger work *The Oracle* from the late 1980s. *The Oracle*'s first part, the fifteen-poem series 'But Those Who Say', opens with a brief text titled *Arwesdi sahmannerun (nakhapan)* (At the Borders of Art (Prelude)), where one finds a distinction between a god 'about whom we can assume absolutely nothing' and another, the 'uppercase [capitalized] God, humanity's personal god'.[35] By contrast, it is interesting to note that in the poem 'In place of prayer', the god is described as 'lowercase [uncapitalized]'. It seems that from one work to the next, Oshagan's poetry deploys a distinction between an absolutely incommunicable god and an anthropomorphic God. Ultimately, this distinction seems to emerge from the problematic of the existentialist absurd, as the notion of an absolutely incommunicable, unreachable god can be interpreted as deifying the chaos underlying an absurdist world view, while the anthropomorphic god refers to the fallen (hitherto meaningless and powerless) gods created by humanity in its image.

To get a further idea of Oshagan's decoding of Christian theology as a mode of performing diaspora, let us take a look at the first part of *The Oracle*. As Oshagan notes in the 'At the Borders of Art (Prelude)', the first part, titled *Isg ork῾ asen* (But Those Who Say) is meant to 'set the mood' for the second and main part called *Nor badarak* (New Mass), but can also stand on its own. 'But Those Who Say' consists of fifteen poems, each beginning with a clause from the Lord's Prayer 'as a kind of modern prayer'.[36] These poems were first exhibited in San Francisco in 1985, in an Armenian community centre, along with visuals from the Paris-based Armenian painter Archak and were first published in the July, August, October and November 1987 issues of *Asbarez' Literary Supplement*, along with renditions of Archak's visuals.

'But Those Who Say' is in Classical Armenian and alludes to the First Council of Nicaea (AD 325) in which the Christian world declared that Jesus Christ is 'consubstantial' with his Father, and decreed as heresy the view propagated by Arius, a churchman from Alexandria, that Jesus did not have divine nature and therefore was temporal ('contemporary', as Oshagan might say). This refutation can be found at the end of the Nicene Creed, declared following the council, and begins with the phrase 'But those who say'. The Armenian Church, which between 301 and 314 had become the officially recognized church of the Armenian Kingdom, was represented at the First Council of Nicaea and incorporated the Nicene Creed into its liturgy. The actual phrase of Oshagan's title must have been written down not very long after the creation of the Armenian alphabet in AD 405. The dualism refuted, but also reaffirmed, by the Nicene Creed re-emerges through Oshagan's existentialist discourse as the absolutely unknowable god and the anthropomorphic god. Oshagan's reactivation of this early Christian controversy is a modernist gesture of heretic desanctification.

However, 'But Those Who Say' goes further than this. In the third poem of the series, the first-person voice poses the following question to god, presumably to the anthropomorphic one: 'are you a bastard like us, too? / without surname without address vagabond, wandering / the universe's inhospitable burrows roads of longing / in your own Diaspora you too stranger and superfluous / you too the victim of illiterate orphan words which have abandoned language'.[37] Only once more does the term 'Diaspora', uppercase, appear in the fifteen poems of the series. In the passage cited above, this term partakes in a remarkable gesture. Through it the fallen anthropomorphic Christian god is subjected to diasporic decoding. Furthermore, the last clause of the citation – 'the victim of illiterate orphan words which have abandoned language' – inscribes the reciprocal diasporizing of two events, the advent of modernity (with its existentialist absurdist conception of language) with the accompanying 'death of god' and the Armenian Catastrophe. For diaspora Armenians, the Western Armenian standard literary language is their inheritance only in a post-catastrophic, alienated mode. Oshagan's decoding operations of Western Armenian literature orient the former towards diasporic becoming. An analogous experience of diasporic becoming is inscribed to some extent by modernity since it too is undergoing a series of creative existential(ist) crises. Lastly, Oshagan's modernist decoding of Christian theology amounts to diasporizing Armenian Christianity as no longer a merely national but also a post-national religion.

Diasporizing modernist narrativity

Above, we glimpsed the strong modernist inclinations of Oshagan's poetry concerning matters that are explicitly Armenian. Here, I set out to demonstrate that through a fine-grained web of tropes, Oshagan's poetry extends beyond strictly Armenian themes. In doing so, it undermines broader narrative structures crucial for subtending modern identitarian discourses of belonging to – loving, killing and dying for – a territorially bound, linguistic (if not monolingual) nation inherited from early nineteenth-century romantic nationalism.[38]

Oshagan's poetry decodes modern narrativity by drawing from post-war existentialist absurdist sensibility (e.g. Jean-Paul Sartre, Albert Camus) as well as high-modernist poetry and theatre (e.g. T. S. Eliot, Antonin Artaud, Samuel Beckett, Allen Ginsberg). To see how this plays out, let us look at another major volume of poetry by Oshagan titled *Ahazank* (Alarm), as it offers a mature articulation of the above. Published in Philadelphia in 1980, *Alarm* opens with a homonymous piece in which the 'I' of the poem states: 'I am the only one who hears the alarm and wakes up / I chase after the unseen, unbridled plotter or angel? / the lives that we are to live [...]'. The poem is set in Philadelphia; the 'I' walks its streets, has a meal in a restaurant alone and so on, while sounding the alarm of meaninglessness. Philadelphia in this case is thus not just a foundational city in the imagination of the US national myth but also the site of the breakdown of such myths. Towards the end of this piece, the following lines appear: 'life must be one of the masks of death / which slowly becomes identical, probably, to the face and / melts in it / leaving us with a ridiculous stupid question, without questioner and answer. / I will come / to say all of this to you [. . .].' The questioning and questioned 'I', as we can see, is intimately tied to the closely interlinked tropes of life and death. Only after 'ringing the alarm' in this manner does the volume proceed to the next section, a relatively short, three-page-long poem titled *Nakhapan* (Preface). By setting the piece 'Alarm' before the 'Preface', *Alarm* subverts the implicit narrative sequentiality of the revelation of meaning inscribed within modern genre conventions. This is just one gesture of decoding narrativity enacted by the volume.

Alarm decodes modern narrativity across the key tropes of love, mourning and exile, as well as myth, language and image. For instance, in the piece titled *Niw York'i Met'ron* (New York's Metro), one can find these lines: 'outside, under the *radioactive* blanket, love its secret / has hidden, / life, having barely touched light, is already flame and ash'. Here, the possibility of forming a narrative with the help of the figures of life and love, inspired by modern romantic or even premodern Christian tropes, is exploded with a disturbing image of a nuclear disaster. This absurdist devastation also subverts romantic national narratives that appropriate life, death and love, oftentimes through a sacrificial logic, for the sustainment of national myths. In the next piece, *Antin* (Beyond), where the trope of love appears frequently, these lines are striking: 'atoms holding candles nose to nose requiem for whom? / I am still alive'. Here, it is life that persists death, rendering mourning untimely. 'Beyond' ends in a performative gesture that rejects common narratives of life and death by linking the latter with language through the trope of pronoun, a metonymy for language: 'we neither die nor are buried in our body nor we are / but a decomposed myth of the naked and abandoned pronoun / having come and fallen into this dungeon to remember and long for / beyond the wall . . .'.[39] The Armenian word for pronoun, *deranun*, is composed of the prefix *der* and the root *anun*, meaning both name and (grammatical) noun. And since the prefix also means 'role', *deranun* connotes that words play roles and thus are not what they seem.

In the piece *Aṛantsnut'iwn* (Solitude), where one encounters the metonymic trope of the word often, these lines are particularly striking in their way of decoding expected grammatically coherent meaning:

> faded mist of seed [sperm] inside the gigantic wet flashing eye socket
> and outside at the myth's first breath's threshold confused
>   and self-enclosed waiting
> being looked at the absurd's *noumenon* life's rocket in your palm
> ray atomic bomb put on the top you tremble
>   from the horror
> we are going to explode when the inevitable excessive arrow comes
> of degradation and impossible to endure crawling
>   life[40]

In the last two citations, the hope of grounding myths, romantic national ones, for example, on language – the staple of linguistic if not monolingual nationalism with the known schema of the people speaking a national language and the national language sustaining the people in return – is also subverted. Above, the inscriptions of the impossibilities of grounding life and myth on sound meaning are extended to the visual trope of the eye and are once again decoded with nuclear imagery. Skipping a few pieces, in *T'agart* (Snare) we come across these lines:

> light sprinkles tale on the back of desolation and passes–
> past present and future
> there is and is not a corpse
> but which lives by unwillingly eating itself
> immortality and its fraud at the same time.
> but somewhere there must be a *negative*
> at least one
> if only we could slip inside it and take our place
> one person one position
> authentic eternal.[41]

With the above text as an instance, the decoding of romantic modes of interlinking life and death, among other tropes, explicitly touches upon the trope of image. If all that life, death and language do is inscribe the absurd, perhaps there is an elusive image that could capture this 'truth' and thus serve as a ground for meaning. Yet, even this is not possible, as the piece *Lusangar* (Photograph) in the same volume, indicates. A little longer than two pages, it evokes again the figure of the negative of a photograph by opening with the following line: 'It is the last negative.' The piece continues agrammatically by not capitalizing the first letter of what would have to be a new sentence both in Armenian and English. It relates a brief narrative dialogue of an ageing couple who are tourists, another recurring transient figure in Oshagan's works. The man stops to take a photo with the camera to his eye, but the camera does not work. The following lines close the section:

> It was probably the only image that was taken
> but towards inside, behind the eye this time
> there
> where the inhabitants of the world, living and dead, wet and limping,
> from roads and roofs have poured and heaped
> in the venomous sticky mist of suffering and pleasure
> of consciousness,
> where the tourist
> naked hungry and astonished roams
> and searches.[42]

Accordingly, the possibility of taking a photograph, of forming an image, is increasingly elusive. The next section relates the various ways in which this search is futile and impossible, a condition that, according to the poem, undermines history and ideals. The third and last section of the piece is the following: 'In the beginning / there was the man, past sixty and a bachelor, bald and with a cold / who turns around the pile / still. / *Tourist*'. The tourist is the figure – perhaps that of humanity – that is obsessed with taking images but is trapped in their absurd superficiality. In this manner, images

– photographic but not only – as purported representations of pre-existent truths, like modern national myth, are decoded through Oshagan's poetry.

Alarm closes with a longer and much more narrativistic work titled *Ojir ev badizh* (Crime and Punishment). Echoing Dostoevsky's imposing work, it is a rare and daring take on the Lebanese Civil War (1975–90) in Western Armenian letters. With it, Oshagan deploys a panoply of poetic gestures familiar to his reader to approach a disaster that was ongoing at the time of the piece's publication in 1980 and was deeply personal for the poet since he lived in Beirut from 1952 to 1975. Beyond the strictly personal, Oshagan's decoding operations in 'Crime and Punishment' struggle against modern, all too convenient confessional and ethno-national modes of generating and justifying collective violence. These decoding operations challenge the political, legal and theological discourses that ground modern national forms of collective violence.

Taking epic proportions, 'Crime and Punishment' weaves distinctly recognizable narrative strands involving urban and rural Lebanese people from all walks of life and of different ethno-religious backgrounds. The short prelude 'Entry' is followed by 'Crime', a section in which one can read the following:

> under this un-identity disguise
> another person, another stage are still hiding
> where an unthinkable tragedy is happening
> and is celebrated the hideous scandal of the universe's
>   abortion,
> but this time there are neither actors nor a *scenario*
> only the catastrophe untellable, horrid, dreadful
> from the inside of which is seen
> the black colossal womb of Crime –[43]

By qualifying the notion of crime as 'unthinkable' and 'untellable', these lines suggest that the violence of the Lebanese Civil War is absurd. What follows, on the same page of the verses cited above, is an implication that renders absurd presumably all of humanity or at least everyone linked with the disaster engulfing Lebanon: 'all of us are the victim and witness of this crime / which looks for an accomplice, hires terrorist and agent / bribes us with free *seven up* to the third floor of Azariyah / and pits us against each other'. Azariyah is an important building in the central commercial district of Beirut with a significant Armenian communal and business presence. During the war, this area turned into a battleground. In Oshagan's poem, Azariyah becomes one of the specific sites of the absurd violence of the civil war. Azariyah is by far not the only proper name encountered in the poem. Street names, neighbourhoods and, of course, character names are also deployed. Here, proper toponyms, just like with 'Philadelphia' in the volumes *Alarm* and *Khujab* (Panic) (1983), no longer merely and tacitly perpetuate national territorial referentiality but decode them with an absurdist diasporic spatiality. We can see what this amounts to by reading the closing lines of the section 'Crime':

> From the entrails of extensive delight and panic
> rose at that time, from the court's, parliament's and prison's cesspool,

generations of man-hunters
and each one of them having bitten a spark of truth
hopped from roof to roof
to spread the good news of liberation from crossroad to crossroad
groups of criminals
came out of the stages of mosques and temples
and with the impersonal and unfailing technic of angels
spread the delight of death.
It was so that until noon
Lebanon already was beginning to atone for the sin of its crime and carry the burden of its
punishment
and was tensing its nerves, muscles to live
the suffering, the recompense
of truth.[44]

Reverberating with the Homeric narrative of the fall of Troy, the cataclysms undergone by Lebanon, however, cannot easily be attributed to an external political force destroying it through conniving and/or divine wrath. The catastrophic violence enveloping Lebanon is the trace of the tragic absurdity of existence ('the recompense / of truth'). What gives the above lines an epic quality is the larger-than-life, all-encompassing nature of the violence. In this way, 'Crime and Punishment' echoes Oshagan's seminal volume of poetry *The City*. Most of the sections of this volume – organized under the headings 'Entrance', 'Mind', 'Street' 'Cafe', 'Cinema', 'Cabaret', 'Room' and 'Church', in that order, too – point to sites in the city where the absurd dwells but is denied recognition. With 'Crime and Punishment', Oshagan continues to decode the traditional epic (myth) powerfully initiated with *The City* and continued with the volume *Panic*, by reinscribing an absurdist diasporic spatiality over the epic's nationalizing mode of configuring time and space.

'Crime and Punishment' is followed by three sections respectively and matter-of-factly titled 'Punishment 1', 'Punishment 2' and 'Punishment 3'. Each of the three 'punishment' sections decodes one constitutive aspect of the normalizing binary of punishment. 'Punishment 1' does so with the ethical binary economy between crime and punishment; 'Punishment 2' with the law and religion which are called for to repair and regulate these matters; 'Punishment 3' with the appropriating modes of closure (e.g. mourning and its desired or implied effect, forgetting) that efface the nature of violence. Consequently, the political, legal and theological discourses subtending modern national forms of collective violence are decoded by 'Crime and Punishment'.

Coda

Oshagan's decoding gestures, which as I argued above extend beyond strictly Armenian concerns, create the possibility of diasporizing Armenian life away from its essentializing tendencies of privileging the national strata – relying on the term from DeLanda mentioned earlier. As we saw, Oshagan's poetry performs diaspora across decades, locales, institutional and ideological contexts, with and against influential tropes that tend to ground a nation-state-centred world order. The extrinsic mode, in which I insist on approaching them, furnishes us with a theoretical model for thinking of diasporic becoming in general and diasporic transnational power in particular. The latter's independence from nation-state-centred independence is the possibility of generating a different kind of difference from within and across ideological, representational and organizational landscapes that comprise Armenian life. This process is striking in Oshagan's poetry and literature in general but is also definitely not confined to it. Diasporic differentiation can take place and can be read across other interrelated Armenian cultural and disciplinary spheres, such as architecture, music or even patterns of economic behaviour.[45] What is particularly fascinating is that such processes of becoming can and have been, as we see for example through Oshagan's poetry, inscribed through the standardized Western Armenian literary language. The latter has arguably led a diasporic existence for the past millennium under different epistemic and technological regimes involving the Armenian Kingdom of Cilicia, Istanbul, Venice, Calcutta, Beirut, Paris and Los Angeles, to name only a few privileged locales, and continues to generate an historicizable diasporic archive.

Notes

1 Early versions of parts of this chapter appeared in *GAM Analytical and Critical Review* 8, no. 2 (2020).
2 In Armenian *Kragan Hrch'agakir*, signed 'December 18, 1990, San Francisco'. It was first published in the literary supplement of the Armenian newspaper *Horizon Weekly*, appearing from Montreal and was republished in the anthology *Stations* (*Gayanner*, Yerevan: Sargis Khachents, Printinfo, 2017) on Oshagan's poetry, prepared and edited by Krikor Beledian. I will cite this and other Oshagan texts from *Stations* because it is more readily available to the public.
3 Khachig Tölölyan, 'Rethinking Diaspora(s): Stateless Power in the Transnational Moment', *Diaspora: A Journal of Transnational Studies* 5, no. 1 (1996): 22.
4 For a nuanced discussion of 'identity politics' see *Multiculturalism: A Critical Reader*, ed. David Theo Goldberg (Malden, Oxford: Blackwell Publishers Ltd, 1994). In the introduction, Goldberg gives a genealogy of multiculturalism, with a particular focus on the United States and, inspired by Homi Bhabha's theorization of heterogeneity, takes issue with the positivist attitudes that treat identity as pre-given and ahistorical, and consequently envision 'identity politics' as a predictable process in a predetermined field dominated by an imperial (sexist and racist) hegemony not subjected to radical critique.
5 Tölölyan, 'Rethinking Diaspora(s): Stateless Power in the Transnational Moment', 28–9.
6 As I was writing these lines, the second Artsakh war went on. Most recently, the Armenian state itself is gravely endangered by threats of war. I cannot help but wonder how this essay will be received, or rather resisted.

7 One can freely access the complete archive of the journal online here: http://armenia ninternationalmagazine.com/.
8 Vahé Oshagan, 'Poles Apart: Vahé Oshagan on the Habitat, Imagery, and the Inner Reaches of the Diaspora', interview by Ishkhan Jinbashian, *Armenian International Magazine*, July 1991, 13.
9 Ibid.
10 Ibid.
11 I thank Sonia Kiledjian and Raffi Ajemian for making this source available to me. If memory serves, it is through them that I gained access to it.
12 ARF, a democratic socialist political party, is the strongest political party active in the Armenian diaspora. It was formed in 1890 in Tbilisi, at the time part of the Russian Empire. From 1918 to 1920, the ARF was the governing political force of the short-lived First Republic of Armenia. After the fall of the Republic and during the entire existence of Soviet Armenia (1920–91), the party had no official presence in Armenia and so existed only in the diaspora, mostly in the Middle East, in Europe and in the Americas. For a profitably recontextualized discussion of the ARF and other Armenian modern national revolutionary parties and activities in the late nineteenth and early twentieth centuries, see Houri Berberian's *Armenians and the Connected Revolutions in the Russian, Iranian, and Ottoman Worlds* (Los Angeles: University of California Press, 2019).
13 In *GAM* 8, partly devoted to Oshagan, the editor Marc Nichanian states that Oshagan apparently had sent the Armenian version of the interview to the *Horizon Weekly* without realizing that its publication would be accompanied by hostile reactions (34).
14 Hraztan Zeitlian, 'Spʻiwṛkʻi razmavaragan sgzpunkʻner' (Diaspora's Strategic Principles), *Horizon Weekly*, 3 February 1992, 11. Here and elsewhere, all quotations from Armenian are my translations, unless otherwise noted.
15 Oshagan reiterates the need for the Armenian Diaspora, in particular its intellectuals, to see itself and act independently in a slightly later interview that he gave to no other than the same Vrej-Armen. See 'Spʻiwṛkʻē ardyergir chē, yergir ē' ('Diaspora is not an Abroad [outside the country], it is a Country!'), *Horizon Literary Supplement* 8, no. 95 (August 1992): 1–3. See also *GAM* 8, mentioned in an earlier endnote, for further relevant texts and discussions. Last but not least, in 1994, Oshagan gave an interview in Western Armenia to the multimedia artist Hrayr Anmahouni Eulmessekian, which was video recorded in Los Angeles and during which Oshagan reiterated the call to declare and think of the Armenian Diaspora as independent. Eulmessekian recently made the interview available on YouTube: https://www.youtube.com/watch?v=zQ1xklZpCso.
16 The phrase 'Armenian Catastrophe', capitalized, is critically more robust since it does not reduce the 1915 event into a juridico-political discourse centred on proof and recognition which the term 'Armenian Genocide' does. In choosing to use the phrase 'Armenian Catastrophe', I follow Marc Nichanian, who in his turn takes into consideration Hagop Oshagan's use of the Armenian word *Aghēd* (Catastrophe). See Marc Nichanian's *The Historiographic Perversion*, trans. Gil Anidjar (New York, Chichester, West Sussex: Columbia University Press, 2009).
17 Manuel DeLanda, *Assemblage Theory* (Edinburgh: Edinburgh University Press, 2016), 'Introduction', 2.
18 The ontological status of this whole is the same as that of its parts or other assemblages: 'the whole exists alongside the parts in the same ontological plane. In

other words, the whole is immanent, not transcendent' (22). This is why they are all 'historically unique', DeLanda specifies in the same paragraph.
19 DeLanda, *Assemblage Theory*, 3.
20 Every once in a while, there are enthusiastic and accusatory calls to think the Armenian dispersion as a homogenous if not single Network. Too often, however, the conception and 'content' of such calls are naively conceived in an intrinsically national mode with no thought given to the diaspora's generative difference. For an example see *The Armenian Mirror-Spectator*'s 24 February 2021 publication of the 'Network State: The New Armenia Vision' by Vahram Ayvazyan. It proposes an 'All for Armenia' approach and offers a structure for a global network 'state'.
21 Nanor Kebranian, 'Dispersing Community: Diaspora and the Ethics of Estrangement', in *Manifestos for World Thought*, ed. Lucian Stone and Jason Bahbak Mohaghegh (London, New York: Rowman & Littlefield International, Ltd., 2017), 83–98.
22 For an elaboration of the notion of post-catastrophic Western Armenian literature, see Nichanian's 'Melancholia Philologica', in *Anywhere but Now: Landscapes of Belonging in the Eastern Mediterranean*, ed. Samar Kanafani, Munira Khayyat, Rasha Salti and Layla Al-Zubaidi (Beirut: Heinrich Böll Foundation, Middle East Office, 2012), 253–69.
23 The intense and daring paintings on the cover of the volume and before every new piece in it are by V. Barsoumian.
24 Vahé Oshagan, *Srjaraně (Usumnasirut'iwn)* (The Cafe (Study)), *Baduhan* (Window) (Beirut: Olympic Press, 1956), 74–5.
25 Oshagan, *Tashnagts'ut'iwn* (Federation), *Baduhan* (Window) (Beirut: Olympic Press, 1956), 7.
26 Beledian, referring to the way in which the figure of the window is closely linked with that of the author in Oshagan's *K'aghak'* (The City), has interpreted this figure as a spatial schema that is both inside and outside, is a kind of 'foreignness' where the author is ('Vahé Oshagan and Contemporary Poetry', in *Darm* (Flock) [Beirut; Yerevan: Sargis Khachents-PrintInfo, 2015], 153–69, 154–5).
27 Having adopted Christianity as a state religion in the beginning of the fourth century, the vast majority of Armenians belong to the Armenian Apostolic Church, even though it has two Sees, each one associated more closely with (post-)Soviet Armenia and the post-catastrophic Armenian diaspora particularly in the Middle East. There are also a significant number of Catholic Armenians, along with Christian Armenians of other denominations.
28 Vahé Oshagan, *K'aghak': Tiwts'aznerkut'iwn mě* (The City: An Epic), Volume 1, (Beirut, 1963), 167.
29 I will not analyse these works here, except for the first part of *The Oracle*.
30 In *Stations*, Beledian places the 'In Place of Prayer' right before the 'But those who say' and *The Oracle*, I rely on the association that is made in this way between these texts.
31 Vahé Oshagan, *P'okhan aghōt'k'i* (In Place of Prayer), *Stations*, ed. Krikor Beledian (Yerevan: Sargis Khachents, Printinfo, 2017), 317. First published in *Pakine* 1, no. 1 (1962): 41–3.
32 From Nichanian, see 'Whispers from Vahé Oshagan', *Hasg Armenological Annals* 6 (1995): 137–62, for a philosophically well-grounded discussion of Oshagan's poetic gestures. From Beledian, 'Vahé Oshagan and the Contemporary Poetry', in *Darm* (Flock) (Beirut, Yerevan: Sargis Khachents, Printinfo, 2015), 153–69.
33 Vahé Oshagan, *P'okhan aghōt'k'i* (In Place of Prayer), *Stations*, 320.

34 A prominent instance of such a discourse among Armenians is the work of the tenth–eleventh-century mystic poet Gregory of Narek. In Oshagan's prose-poetic volume *Embrace* (Sydney: Momjian Press, 1996) this mystic poet figures prominently.
35 See *Stations*.
36 Vahé Oshagan, *Isg ork' asen* (But Those Who Say), *Stations*, ed. Krikor Beledian (Yerevan: Sargis Khachents, Printinfo, 2017), 324. First published in *Asbarez' Literary Supplement* in July, August, October and November 1987.
37 Ibid., 329.
38 Not that there is another, non-romantic kind of nationalism; for two definitive studies on the matter, see Marc Nichanian's *Mourning Philology: Art and Religion at the Margins of the Ottoman Empire*, trans. G. M. Goshgarian and Jeff Fort (New York: Fordham University Press, 2014) and Stathis Gourgouris's *Dream Nation: Enlightenment, Colonization and the Institution of Modern Greece* (Stanford: Stanford University Press, 1996).
39 Vahé Oshagan, *Antin* (Beyond), *Ahazank* (Alarm) (Philadelphia: Vosketar, 1980). This work is without pagination.
40 Vahé Oshagan, *Aṛantsnut'iwn* (Solitude), *Ahazank* (Alarm) (Philadelphia: Vosketar, 1980). This work is without pagination.
41 Vahé Oshagan, *T'akart* (Snare), *Ahazank* (Alarm) (Philadelphia: Vosketar, 1980). This work is without pagination.
42 Vahé Oshagan, *Lusangar* (Photograph), *Ahazank* (Alarm), (Philadelphia: Vosketar, 1980). This work is without pagination.
43 Vahé Oshagan, *Ojir ew badizh* (Crime and Punishment), *Ahazank* (Alarm) (Philadelphia: Vosketar, 1980). This work is without pagination.
44 Ibid.
45 Already in the 1960s, Pascal Paboudjian defended the modernization of Armenian religious architecture in the diaspora. I am grateful to Vahé Tachjian and Joseph Rostum for pointing out this to me in a recent conference. In music, the work of the composer Ohannes Salibian, who happens to have engineered sound recordings of Oshagan reading from his poetry, is another moment of embracing modernization. Both arguably engage in diasporizing decoding. One can read their views for instance in the Beirut-based periodical *Ahegan* (1966–70).

10

The Armenians in Turkey

From autochthonous people to diaspora

Talin Suciyan

This chapter will demonstrate the historical lines of divisions, discrepancies and controversies which were created and reproduced throughout the nineteenth and twentieth centuries in the Ottoman Empire, Turkey and later among Armenians remaining in Turkey and those abroad. By doing so, it will show the process over the twentieth century by which Armenians as an autochthonous population were turned into a diaspora community on their historic lands and within the same nation-state in which they lived.

This article regards the concept of genocide as central and will refer to a process of structuring the structure, that is, the emergence of the Ottoman Armenian diaspora and their realities around the world. It will detail the series of divisions and discrepant experiences which lie at the heart of the unevenness created among Armenians, both during the Ottoman Empire and later in Turkey, resulting in a condition known as non-contemporaneous contemporaries regarding the divergent experiences of their populations in Istanbul and the provinces, along with those in diaspora communities spread around the world. The Armenians living in the capital of the Ottoman Empire and later Turkey and those in the provinces experienced different historical contexts and politico-economic conditions. The former had always been an institutionally defined diaspora community, while the latter lived in their autochthonous lands. However, their differences became accentuated throughout the nineteenth century, when economic conditions and violence in the provinces increased, a reality unlike that lived or even able to be understood by the Armenians in Istanbul. Genocide was the peak of this unevenness and its denial embodied the primary and most durable structures to continue exacerbating that unevenness throughout the twentieth century for Armenians both in Turkey and abroad. Further, this chapter will focus on Aram Pehlivanian and Zaven Biberyan, whose works reflect the peak of marginalization brought against the surviving Armenian intellectuals in Turkey. The sheer scale of their exclusion by other diaspora communities and the oppression they faced from their Turkish peers and the state made them some of the most uneven and non-contemporaneous intellectuals of their time.

In the case of the Ottoman Armenians, the structuring carried out by the government through genocidal policies and genocide itself is integral to their becoming diaspora.[1] The primary reason for the decision to annihilate the Armenians in 1915 was to sever the connection between this autochthonous people and their land, which included eradicating their knowledge of living on those lands and their history of ever having lived on those lands. Further, I will argue the methods by which the remaining Armenians were forced to live only in Istanbul during the post-genocide decades, where they had recourse to Armenian institutions but no roots. Hence, they were pushed out of their autochthonous lands and encapsulated in the panopticon of Istanbul as a perpetually exiled diaspora community, one that was also marginalized and isolated throughout the twentieth century from the rest of the global Armenian diaspora communities.

Turning autochthonous populations into survivor *kaght'agan*s

If the Ottoman government's decision to annihilate its Armenian population in 1915 was a turning point in history, the end of 1922 marked the institutionalization of a new Turkey without its autochthonous Christian populations – namely the Armenians, Assyrians, Syriacs, Chaldeans as well as exiled Rum populations.[2] For the Armenian survivors after 1915, neither Istanbul nor anywhere else was 'home', hence they existed in a diaspora regardless of their location. Safety and security, concepts which had already been alien to Ottoman Armenians since at least the mid-nineteenth century, were and still are non-existent for those remaining in Turkey. Whether the Armenians in Turkey after 1915 managed to remain in the provinces or were forced to Istanbul, they all had to live under the constant threats posed not just by the local and central authorities but their own neighbours as well. This made their lives almost impossible to sustain, especially in the geography of genocide, diminishing their existence to that of day-to-day survival.[3] This engineered situation increasingly turned one of the oldest autochthonous populations living under Ottoman and later Turkish rule into the paradoxical-sounding situation of living as a diaspora community while still on their historic lands. For survivors of a genocide, life became unrecognizable, often with no home to return to, perhaps no family members to relate to or neighbours to count on. Even if they returned to the place where they had lived, their roots had been severed and the landscape permanently altered. The knowledge of living within the geography of a genocide rendered them into a diaspora community in their own land. Many Armenian survivors could never return to their places of origin, and those who did found their properties destroyed or soon to be confiscated if they had not been already. The survivors were unable to claim their rights to their properties, and were gradually pushed out over the following years and decades as threats against them mounted and life became impossible.[4] Istanbul was one of the most common destinations for these exiles, even decades after 1915, as it had increasingly become the centre of Armenian administration throughout the nineteenth century and had various

Armenian institutions, including the central Armenian administration, the Armenian Patriarchate, the two Armenian Hospitals (Surp Prgich and Surp Hagop), along with churches and schools. It was the only place left for Armenians in Turkey, one where they had support structures, but no roots. The first step for these Armenians who remained in the villages and towns across Anatolia was to move to the nearest cities, especially if it still had an Armenian community such as Kayseri, Yozgat, Amasya, Tokat, Ordu, Diyarbekir and Kastamonu. From there they mainly continued on to Istanbul, before often being forced even further into exile yet again to destinations abroad like Europe, the United States or Canada.

Historical background

Diaspora communities are by nature uneven, as their institutionalization is directly linked to the countries in which they are established. The institutionalization of the Armenian diaspora in Istanbul was a historically well-established one. The Armenian Patriarchate and the Armenian administration in the empire's capital became pivotal only in the nineteenth century as the Armenian administration was centralized in tandem with that of the Ottoman administration.[5] This centralization in Istanbul meant a decrease in the authority and entitlements of important monasteries and other religious and administrative centres in the provinces, particularly the Catholicosate of Aghtamar and that of Sis in Cilicia.[6] This was a process which preceded the institutionalization of the Armenian Constitution (*Nizamname*) in 1863. Although Armenians were not autochthonous to Istanbul, Armenians in Turkey have rarely thought of themselves as diasporic as Khachig Tölölyan has stated:

> It is worth nothing that what was for a couple of centuries the largest and the most important Armenian diasporic community, that of Istanbul, rarely thought of itself as diasporic; except when persecuted by the Turkish state, it regarded itself 'at home' in an ancient, superbly organized, and institutionally saturated community (*hamaynkʻ*) that was accommodated by the composite society of Istanbul.[7]

Tölölyan's statement holds true and resonates with the statements of most Armenian public intellectuals.[8] I read Tölölyan's approach of seeing the Armenian community at 'home' in Istanbul as a part of an unevenness created over the course of history during both the Byzantine and Ottoman Empires, since Istanbul as a capital has held a position of privilege vis-à-vis the rest for well over 1,000 years. Especially during the nineteenth century but also even before, Armenians in Istanbul had well-established institutions and enjoyed the privileges of living in the capital as did all other co-habitants of the city. Unlike Armenians in the provinces, who were exiled and annihilated en masse, the Armenians of Istanbul except for intellectuals were generally allowed to remain in place, a strategy which lies at the heart of the discrepant experiences of genocide and survival between these two groups.

While Armenians in Istanbul during the nineteenth century considered themselves at home, those in the provinces, *yergir* or *kawaṛ*, both in the historic lands of Armenians and the empire's other provinces suffered from oppressions which created a growing unevenness between them and those in Istanbul. Thus, these two parties increasingly became non-contemporaneous contemporaries.[9] For Armenians, provincial oppressions had become a part of everyday life, in which their labour was seized, their natural resources hijacked and they were terrorized in ways that jeopardized their lives and families. Unfair and abusive taxation, forced labour, monopolization of water away from the Armenian peasants, rampant discrimination and maltreatment, kidnapping of Armenian women and forcing men into leaving to become migrant workers, and subjugation to precarious living conditions, along with many other forms of unevenness in all their relations, resulted in waves of famine and starvation in the provinces. This in turn rendered Armenian life in the provinces of the Ottoman Empire nearly unsustainable.[10] Despite their constant efforts, Armenians were unable to make their voices heard, and even if/when they were heard, their living conditions were not ameliorated and their issues remained unresolved. This situation reached its peak in 1915, when the provinces were emptied of Armenians and Istanbul lost its Armenian intelligentsia. In other words, Ottoman methods of governance throughout the nineteenth-century centralization process maintained different treatment regarding the capital and the rest of the empire and thus reproduced the non-contemporaneity of the contemporaries onto the lives of Armenians in each place, creating discrepant and conflicting realities in which people belonging to the same group could not understand the magnitude of the problems of their co-ethnics and were unable to support each other. By exiling the provincial Armenians in 1915 while keeping the community in Istanbul mostly intact, the Ottoman government created yet another layer of unevenness, a method that made the gap between the surviving Armenians of the provinces and the ones in Istanbul unbridgeable for at least a century to come.

During the post-genocide decades, as Tölölyan argues, the reason why thousands of Armenian *kaghtʻagans*[11] continued to come to Istanbul was that it was the only city in which Armenian survivors could get access to the institutional support they desperately required. Especially in the first decades after 1915, Armenian community life in Istanbul was primarily preoccupied with the *kaghtʻagan* waves pouring tens of thousands of survivors from the provinces into the city as a result of the violence they continued to endure there. Persecution and violent expulsion continued to be decisive in the provinces, which transformed the historic Armenian homeland into the most insecure place for the few who survived and remained there. Hence, genocide, the annihilation of one's own home with its social, cultural and economic relations, and continuing persecutions were pivotal in the transformation of what was home into the most insecure of diasporas. Meanwhile, it was also the state's strategy to keep the Armenian community in Istanbul and its institutions intact to a certain degree in order to maintain the unevenness of the genocidal experiences faced by the Armenians in the Ottoman Empire. The state used Istanbul as a panopticon, a well-surveilled, open-air prison for the remaining survivors to empty into throughout the twentieth century.

Post-1923 Armenians in Turkey: Immense unevenness between Istanbul and Armenians in the provinces

Armenians in post–First World War Istanbul, especially the *kaght'agan* survivors, were the most uneven group of people. They were unwanted, had no place to return to, were landless, penniless and were the most vulnerable group in Istanbul at that time. Almost all Armenian institutions, representatives and administrative structures were undermined to the extent that their functioning was only permitted arbitrarily.[12] There were no authorities the survivors in need could turn to in the provinces. De facto there was an Armenian Patriarchate and an Armenian administration in Istanbul, however, their members were either murdered or exiled. Armenian Patriarch Zaven Der Yeghiayan had to leave the city nearly incognito in December 1922, along with the Armenian administration's second most important person Madteos M. Eblighatean.[13] The task of supporting the *kaght'agan* survivors in the capital became the duty of the remaining Armenians of Istanbul.

The knowledge and experience gathered by the Ottoman state and transmitted to the Turkish ruling elite throughout the process of committing a genocide regarded the durability and effectiveness of creating unevenness both temporally and territorially, not just between different groups but within a single group. Therefore, the Turkish ruling elite continued the determination of their Ottoman predecessors to end the existence of Armenians in the provinces. Rıza Nur, who represented Turkey during the Lausanne negotiations, cheerfully reported back to the parliamentarians in Turkey that:

> there will be no minorities left. Only Istanbul will be an exception. (Voices shouting: 'Armenians'). However, how many Armenians are there? (Voices shouting: 'Jews'). There are thirty thousand Jews in Istanbul. They have not created problems. (Noises.) Jews, as everybody knows, are people who go where one moves them [*Museviler malum, nereye çekilirse oraya giden insanlardır*]. Of course it would have been much better had they too not existed.[14]

This statement should be considered as the first signal that the Treaty of Lausanne would not be applicable in the provinces. Looking back, it is clear that indeed Lausanne was not enforced in the provinces, as not a single Armenian church, monastery or local institution was allowed to exist there to serve them. Hence, this international treaty, which is said to guarantee the rights of the Armenians along with Greeks and Jews, was only to be enacted in Istanbul. Non-enforcement of Lausanne was utilized as a method of creating further unevenness, not just on the national level but the international one as well, while no attention was drawn to the issue. It was clear to the Turkish ruling elites that by suppressing these institutions, coupled with the hostile attitude locally against Armenians in the provinces, it was only a matter of time until these regions would be completely emptied of them. The peak of unevenness created by the genocidal policies during 1915 and 1916 was reproduced throughout the twentieth century, criminalizing Armenian existence in Turkey, forcing the remaining Armenians out of the provinces to Istanbul, and finally annihilating the living knowledge of the autochthonous people on their land with their only remnants in perpetual exile.

Uneven worlds: Armenians in Turkey and diaspora communities

There was yet another layer of unevenness to be created: the unevenness between the remaining Armenians in Turkey and the Armenian diaspora communities around the world. This official policy of Turkey remains in place until today. The daily violence that Armenians both in the provinces and in Istanbul had to endure throughout the twentieth century was of an unimaginable magnitude.[15] If disconnecting the Armenian survivor communities in the provinces from Istanbul was one of the state's major policies in the post-1923 decades, separating the Armenian survivors in Turkey from other diaspora communities around the world was the second most important component to this strategy of sustaining unevenness. Denial of genocide was the main tool for fuelling the policy of unevenness among Armenians. This denial targeted all Armenians around the world, and their responses to it reproduced unevenness among them as Armenians in Turkey naturally had a different response to the denial than those abroad. Armenians in Turkey were pushed to the edge, as they did not have any means to struggle for genocide recognition and were constantly terrorized and criminalized for being Armenian. Hence, the more violent state denial became, the more the Armenian community squeezed to Istanbul was forcibly co-opted into this denial in order to survive. While almost every Armenian family in Turkey had and has relatives in other diaspora communities, they had to distance themselves from their relatives as the state policies and public opinion makers in Turkey constantly used the term 'diaspora' as a smear.[16] For instance, during the global commemoration in 1965 of the fiftieth anniversary of the genocide, Armenians in Turkey had to organize a denialist ceremony in order to show their loyalty to the state and distance from their own relatives.[17] Every aspect of Armenian existence outside Turkey, including publications, political demands and cultural activities, could be instrumentalized by the Turkish state in order to criminalize diaspora Armenians.

One of the most striking early cases showing the extent of the perversion of denial forced upon Armenians is the book-burning ceremony of Franz Werfel's *The 40 Days of Musa Dagh* held in 1935 by Armenians in the backyard of Pangaltı Armenian School.[18] The Turkish press had begun its campaign the previous year against the novel which dramatized the resistance and survival of Musa Dagh Armenians during the genocide, first by urging the German authorities to stop dissemination of the book, which Minister of Propaganda Goebbels immediately did as it was widely read in the Jewish community.[19] Within a very short period of time, *The 40 Days of Musa Dagh* had become a bestseller in the United States and a film based on the novel was planned. Turkish authorities were alarmed by the situation and forced Armenians in Turkey into the self-destructive and self-denialistic act of a book-burning ceremony. Almost all Turkish newspapers furiously attacked both Armenians and Jews over the issue.[20] Compelled to imitate the Nazi party's book-burning campaigns, the Armenians of Istanbul prepared an altar upon which they burnt copies of the book along with the author's portrait.[21] By this perverse act of violence, they would not only denounce the author but also the book's content, thereby denouncing themselves and denying their own history, separating themselves from the survivor Armenians of Musa Dagh as well as from all genocide survivors around the world, thus forcefully becoming part of denial.

Isolating and criminalizing Armenian existence both in Turkey and around the world is one of the most persistent state policies of the republic period and manifested through various methods. One of these methods was to scrutinize Armenian newspapers and publications both in Turkey and all over the world, criminalizing their existence and readership. The Turkish State Archives are full of reports on Armenian publications from abroad that they investigated and banned.[22] For Armenian newspapers published in Istanbul, one of the criteria demonstrating their allegiance to the state was whether they contained news items and reports on the diaspora communities.[23] An important figure in this process was the reporter Mithat Akdora, who was the translator of Armenian newspapers for the state's 'Armenian Department' (*Ermeni Masası*), a special office that monitored Armenian activities both in Turkey and abroad. Akdora was a useful operative as he had graduated from an Armenian school in Istanbul, as non-Armenians still attended Armenian schools in the early twentieth century. He found the difference between the publication policies of the *Zhamanag* and *Marmara* daily Armenian newspapers to be worth noting. While the former published very little news related to other Armenian communities and their activities abroad, never commenting on those news items, *Marmara* systematically followed the activities of Armenians abroad and visibly reported on Armenian life outside Turkey. Considering the fact that this difference was the first thing mentioned in his report, it was clearly a decisive criterion for the state. Another important criterion regarded news items related to the Armenian administration, for which once again *Zhamanag* was highly praised by the state for not reporting about nearly as much as other daily newspapers. *Zhamanag* seemed to be the state's ideal Armenian newspaper as it did not publish news on diaspora communities, did not devote much space to Armenian communal life, and last but not least, praised the ruling party. Essentially, the state envisaged Armenian newspapers as well as Armenian intellectuals to increasingly become Armenian-language carbon copies of Turkish newspapers, complicit with Turkish public opinion makers, distanced from the global Armenian diaspora and alienated from themselves, actively denying who they were and are.

The government's control and scrutiny of Armenian publications, the banning of their publication and the criminalization of their existence within personal and institutional libraries, forced Armenians into annihilating their own libraries over the course of twentieth century. Mihran Dabag, the director of Diaspora and Genocide Studies at Bochum University who was born in Diyarbekir in 1944 and later lived in Istanbul, related an oral historical account about the level of terrorization that Armenian institutions endured:

> We didn't have the right to keep Armenian books at school [Surp Haç Tıbrevank in Istanbul]. That is, it wasn't possible to keep books published before 1923 or outside

of Turkey. The administration didn't know where to keep them. First they were hidden up in the Surp Haç bell – they sneaked them right up to the bell tower. Then the church administration started to become afraid. So they brought them back down to the school again, and then the school administration started to get afraid. Finally, because they just didn't know what else to do with the books, they had to throw them straight into Tıbrevank's heating boiler: I was there, right in front of it, and that moment will always remain before my eyes. [...] The Patriarch's library was also going to be relocated in Tıbrevank; that's what he said in his will, but for the same reason, it couldn't be done.[24]

During my doctoral research, each and every Armenian I conducted oral history with told me similar stories of annihilating their Armenian books as random house raids were common practices and finding any Armenian book could have been a reason to be prosecuted. Hence, Armenians themselves were forced to annihilate their own libraries, their own cultural heritage and, ultimately, their own selves throughout the twentieth century. A forceful and perpetual self-destruction on this level should be considered the perpetuation of the genocidal policies by the victims and their descendants, a systematic practice specific to the Armenians remaining in Turkey. While there were direct, outright attacks and cases of systematic violence against Armenians in the provinces, this type of subtle, unspoken, perpetual annihilating violence has been the fuel of unevenness which marked the difference between Armenians remaining in Turkey and those scattered around the world, a very specific distinction that still continues. Hence, the genocidal policies of direct and subtle violence continued to shape the structures, both within Armenian communities in Turkey and outside, in ways that forced these communities to be unable to reach, hear or understand each other's conditions, needs and fears, but most importantly to be unable to remember their common destiny.

Being an Armenian intellectual in Turkey in the twentieth century

While the Armenians in the provinces had to face the violent denialist policies of both their neighbours and the state, resulting in their displacement as *kaght'agan*s to Istanbul, Armenian intellectuals in Istanbul had a *mission impossible*: to reproduce the state's and society's habitus of denial. They were the intellectuals of a surviving, isolated community, one which lacked functioning administrative bodies and had almost no contact with the tens of thousands of Armenians remaining in the provinces who were in need of shelter, money or any kind of support to survive. Armenian institutions and intellectuals were required to be part of the denial under these circumstances; it was the price they had to pay for their undesired existence.

Self-destruction as well as self-denial is the most effective form of denial, even more so than official denial. Therefore, the state expected full-fledged complicity from Armenian survivors and their descendants, both individually and institutionally, in order to show the whole world that the position of official denial was indeed supported and reproduced by Armenians themselves. Survivors remaining in Turkey were not allowed to have a past or a future, their existence was defined merely by surviving anew every day. While the survivor Armenians in the diaspora could live within their own circles in a present-past, as Harry Harootunian puts it,[25] Armenians in Turkey had only the moment to survive, with no past, no future and no memory permitted for themselves or their families. Their lives were simply squeezed into their moment of existence; the more performative their denial was, the longer their lives might last.

Armenian intellectuals of the first post-genocide generation were confronted with the task of perpetuating denial, as were the Armenian institutions and even the survivors themselves. This confrontation and their struggle against denial created a unique situation for Armenian intellectuals in Turkey over the decades following 1915, especially with the emergence of a new generation of Armenian intellectuals in the 1940s. The existential threats they endured can only be compared with that of the Jewish intellectuals in Europe during the same period.[26] Their publications could easily be banned, as befell *Aztarar* published by Manuk Aslanyan,[27] *Hay Gin*, a women's magazine published by Hayganush Mark,[28] *Nor Ōr* by Aram Pehlivanian and others. These publishers were survivors who, through their articles and newspapers, were in daily confrontation with the perpetrators. There was a deep line of separation, an unbridgeable gap, by which the legacy of the genocide divided Armenian intellectuals from Turkish public opinion makers. There was also a dimension of political power associated with these relations, as Turkish public opinion makers and publishers were often parliamentarians as well. Just being in parliament meant being complicit in the crime, either by the silent approval it reflected or because the office was a provision granted for their active involvement in the crime.

Born into the aftermath of the genocide, Armenian intellectuals of this generation devoted their lives to a cause already lost, and thus shared the destiny of the survivors. Nobody was interested in their intellectual struggle because nobody was interested in the survivors' experiences due to the fact that the survivors never *existed* since there had been *no crime*. The rage, despair and self-defeating struggle of the Armenian intellectuals in Turkey remained completely unknown to their peers globally. Similarly, the continued struggles of Armenians in Turkey remained unknown to the other Armenian communities around the world due to the policy of forced estrangement. The unevenness between the Armenians in Turkey and those around the world successfully and effectively shaped the landscape of Armenian diaspora in a way that until the murder of Hrant Dink in 2007, diaspora communities largely kept silent regarding the existence of Armenians in Turkey. While state policies and the denialist habitus in Turkey turned the Armenian community into a marginalized, isolated and completely subjugated group, their struggle to exist and survive did not matter much to the outside world. The community's existence finally attracted attention from the global diaspora not because of its relentless struggle for justice and equality, but because of further violence – the murders of Dink and later Sevag Balıkçı.[29] One of the most important experiences, namely being survivors of a genocide in one's autochthonous lands, needed a hundred years until it was finally heard by the great-grandchildren of the survivors.

Zaven Biberyan: A life between two catastrophes, a life stolen from time

One of the windows we have into the mechanism and consequences of the state's habitus of denial is the life and works of one of the most ostracized groups in Turkey during the mid-twentieth century, Armenian intellectuals such as Zaven Biberyan and Aram Pehlivanian.[30] They directly opposed the denialist interpellations of the state and did not surrender to its oppressive and insistent demands to reproduce that denial. That meant living a life under close scrutiny and surveillance; every word they wrote, every step they took was followed. A series of reports can be found at the Prime Ministry Archives in Istanbul, one of which was written in February 1946 after *Nor Lur*'s publication of Zaven Biberyan's article 'Badmagan Nshmarner' (translated as: '*Tarihten İşaretler*'/Signs from History). Biberyan's articles were closely scrutinized, especially because of his famous article 'Enough is Enough' (*'Al Gě Pavē'*) that was published in January 1946.[31] In this powerful and very insightful article, Biberyan not only criticized state policies but also targeted all public intellectuals and editors-in-chief who were outright racist and systematically anti-Armenian. The best tool with which to attack Armenians by the end of the Second World War was to accuse them of being communists, as many Armenians from Turkey were looking to emigrate and settle in Soviet Armenia. As such, one of the earliest instances of anti-communist propaganda in Turkey launched by the state was focused on the emigration call made by Stalin to the Armenian Diaspora. Biberyan wrote a series of articles in those days including one entitled '*Badmagan Nshmarner*',[32] which fulfilled all the state's criteria to be flagged as problematic. The article not only provided a summary of Armenian history, but also advocated for the very right to emigrate to Soviet Armenia which was being maligned by the Turkish state. Turkish opinion makers targeted all Armenians in Turkey, arguing that they were traitors, portraying their desire to emigrate to what was left of an Armenian state in the communist Soviet Union as evidence of a deep belief in communism.

In those days, Armenians in Turkey were indeed trying to emigrate to Soviet Armenia, but merely in hopes of a safe and secure life.[33] The Soviet consular report from the same period described the forces creating public opinion in Turkey as follows:

> In Turkey in general and in Asia Minor particularly, religion still plays a big role. The population remains fanatically religious.. . . One can encounter the worst manifestations of racial and religious intolerance in Constantinople and all over Asia Minor. The populace, in its backwardness, ignorance and bigotry, cannot tolerate another ethnic group professing a different faith. And the so-called 'intelligentsia' is even more chauvinistic and encourages people's fanaticism.[34]

According to the consul, Armenians applying to emigrate were not just from Istanbul but also 'from faraway provinces of Anatolia such as Sivas, Samsun, Kayseri, Eskişehir and other regions'.[35] There were long queues in front of the Soviet consular building in Istanbul.

Consular reports prove that Armenians were taking enormous risks in travelling from the provinces to Istanbul in order to register themselves, their relatives and fellow villagers to emigrate. As a result, they were accused of 'being communists', a dreaded accusation right after the Second World War, and consequently their right to live in a 'new homeland' was criminalized. Biberyan wrote in response: 'Just like there is a Jewish Question, there has been an Armenian Question, since half of the Armenian population lives away from their homeland.'[36] Biberyan keenly followed and commented on political developments happening all over the world. In drawing this parallel between Jews and Armenians with an emphasis on their diasporic lives, he implied without specifically mentioning the similar fate Jews and Armenians shared. For an intellectual of his calibre, it is simply impossible to imagine that his only concern was the diasporic fate of both, making an undeniable reference to the recent fate of European Jewry.

Zaven Biberyan was born in 1921 in Çengelköy, Istanbul, and spent his childhood in Moda attending Dibar Grtaran Armenian Elementary School. He continued his education at Saint-Joseph College and graduated from the Academy of Trade (*Ticari İlimler Akademisi*).[37] He wrote his first novel at the age of ten in French, which remained the language of his writing until he was twenty. In a letter he wrote in 1962 to his friend Hrant Paluyan in Paris, he confessed the heavy burden of having become an Armenian intellectual writing exclusively in the Western Armenian language: 'I regret that I wrote in [Western] Armenian. Had I known what it meant to be an Armenian writer when I was 20, and had I not thought "being an Armenian, I should be writing in Armenian", I would have never ever stopped writing in French'.[38] He changed his literary language to Armenian during the forty-two-month period of his military service between 1941 and 1945. After three and a half years under tents from the western-most to eastern-most parts of Turkey in both the north and south, struggling against malaria while learning to write in perfect Armenian, he returned to Istanbul and became actively involved in the Armenian press at the editorial level. By this choice, he also chose his readership, that is Western Armenian readers, mostly confined to a certain circle found in Middle Eastern Armenian cultural centres such as Aleppo and Beirut or those in Europe such as Paris and Marseille. The choice of becoming an Armenian intellectual by writing in Western Armenian became a burden of increasing heaviness over the decades, resulting in a number of consequences which he had to bear; primarily that by writing for a survivor community, he was destined to be silenced just like his readers.

Isolation and marginalization were also tools of deep and unbridgeable unevenness in the case of Armenian intellectuals. 'Zaven Biberyan is never mentioned among the most prominent Armenian novelists of the diaspora', wrote Sevan Değirmenciyan in his foreword to Biberyan's masterpiece, the novel *Mrchiwnneru Verchaluysě* (The Sunset of the Ants),[39] which is probably one of the best novels of the twentieth century written in the Western Armenian language as well as one of the best novels in Turkish literature.[40] Değirmenciyan pointed out the rather marginal position of Istanbul in the diaspora's geography to be a reason for the disregarding of Biberyan's genius or his outright exclusion.[41] In his review of the same novel, Marc Nichanian pointed out the exclusion that Biberyan went through, noting that while reading the novel he felt a grudge against all those who knew Biberyan and denied his literary talent, never valuing his work because of their personal issues. Nichanian concluded that Biberyan endured a great deal of marginalization which resulted in bitterness he had to endure all alone.[42] This bitterness mentioned by Nichanian had multiple layers of reasons, none of which Biberyan bore any blame for. What remains to an intellectual if his largest audience, his fellow countrymen, see him as an enemy, and if his primary target group, Western Armenian readers and writers, ignore him? The two communities he addressed in his writing, the Armenians in Turkey and those around the world, either distanced themselves from him or pronounced him a *persona non grata*, leaving his work unknown in diaspora communities. Moreover, his courageous and radically oppositional political position made him increasingly marginalized within his own community. An intellectual who made one of the most valuable contributions of his time to literature and history, Biberyan was silenced both by his fellow Armenians around the world as well as his countrymen in Turkey.

Biberyan worked in Istanbul and Beirut as a publisher or editor for many Armenian periodicals such as *Zhamanag, Nor Lur, Nor Ōr, Aysōr, Zart'ōnk'* and *Ararat* (the last two in Beirut). He also published a monthly literary journal, *Tēbi Luys*. *Nor Ōr* in particular was a short-lived but influential newspaper that was ahead of its time and probably the most intellectually outstanding and critical one in Turkey's printing history. Not surprisingly, it was considered by the state to be the most dangerous of them all. Its criticism of state policies included articles about the unequal treatment of non-Muslims, the arbitrary drafting of non-Muslim men (Yirmi Kura Askerlik),[43] the implementation of the Wealth Tax, an oppressive and abusive tax based on the Ottoman policies of taxation and the physical and verbal harassment of Armenians in the streets. *Nor Ōr* strove for equality for all, criticizing the racist attacks against Armenians, devoting columns on post–Second World War global politics and advocating for the right to emigrate to Soviet Armenia. The administrative problems for Armenians in the Turkish Republic and the issue of not having elected representatives who prevented Armenians from administering their institutions were themes problematized and constantly discussed in the columns of *Nor Ōr*.

Both Biberyan and Pehlivanian spent time in Beirut. During Biberyan's three years there, besides his time publishing periodicals, he also had periods of unemployment or jobs below his expertise such as a typesetter or construction worker. He returned to Istanbul frustrated. As he told his friend Paluyan: 'Finally I came to think that the diaspora exploited yet another Istanbulite perfectly, that diaspora which sincerely hates the Istanbulite. I returned to Istanbul, thinking that nobody would leave me without daily bread, like an abandoned alien, or that I would not be thrown onto the streets.'[44] In fact, by the 1970s he was even more isolated by his own community due to his sharp criticism of the Turkish state and Armenian religious and hierarchical structures. 'I do not know how many jobs I've had to change. They all had their contribution to me in some ways, apart from bringing wealth.'[45]

Effectively shunned by Armenians, the larger society of Turkey's intellectuals of which he was also part, did not want to hear from him either as he was a vocal Armenian. After all, it was easier to marginalize a person who had already been marginalized within his own community. Perhaps the magnitude of state scrutiny, censorship and constant threats aimed at Biberyan and his inability to move elsewhere except for his difficult time in Beirut led to seclusion and despair far deeper than that faced by most Armenian or non-Armenian intellectuals of his time. His experience mirrored those of his peers of the previous 1915 generation and is only comparable – with a few exceptions – to the Jewish intellectuals of this period like Walter Benjamin. Thus the translator of Jack London, Maxim Gorki, Aram Andonian and many others, as well as the author of several groundbreaking novels, and probably one of the most brilliant minds of the post-genocide period, Zaven Biberyan, was forced to live and die marginalized in extreme poverty in Istanbul.

Aram Pehlivanian: A high-ranking Armenian socialist politician and intellectual

Aram Pehlivanian's life took a different trajectory. He described his early years in this autobiography written and submitted to the Communist Party:

> I was born in 1919 in Istanbul. Attended Getronagan Armenian High School and Istanbul University Faculty of Law. I graduated in 1943. I was already following the activities of the Turkish Communist Party in 1935. I became a member of T.C.P. in 1938. I was arrested along with Reşad Fuad and anti-fascists in 1943, imprisoned for 8.5 months. After the trial I was acquitted. (...) In the same year I established the Armenian political and literary weekly newspaper Nor Or. I had previously already published periodicals in Armenian, such as Ashkhadank and Badger literary and sociological magazines. In 1946 I took part in the establishment of Turkey's Party for Labourers and Peasants (Türkiye Emekçi ve Köylü Partisi). I served in its Istanbul branch as its head of office. I started publishing the weekly Nor Or as a daily and became the editor-in-chief. I participated actively in the establishment of trade unions in Turkey (...). 16 December 1946, just like the Turkey's Party for Labourers and Peasants was shut down, so was my newspaper Nor Or too banned under the Martial Law and I was arrested for claims of having committed communist activities. I was sentenced to 3 years of imprisonment. ... 22.4.1955 Aram B.[üyük] Pehlivanian[46]

Shortly after being released from prison in 1950, he was drafted into the military with the rank of a private. As a university graduate, Pehlivanian should have been drafted as a junior officer. Knowing this, he felt his life was being threatened and he fled the country, first to Aleppo and then to Beirut. He continued his activities as a member of the Turkish Communist Party during his approximately eight years in those cities.[47] The photographs in his personal archives from this period seem to reflect an intellectually and socially fulfilling time, during which he published literary and art critiques in the Armenian periodical *Mshaguyt'*. He spent his years in Beirut actively involved in Armenian intellectual life, while continuing his engagement in the Turkish Communist Party (TKP). In hopes of realizing his political ideals on a higher level, Pehlivanian eventually left Beirut for East Germany to be involved in international party politics and became active at the party's highest echelons. He served the party for twenty years under the assumed Turkish name of A. (Ahmet) Saydan(m). Members of the Communist Party had code names in order to avoid criminalization and detection, and having been given a Turkish code name, his Armenian identity was simply erased on the initiative of his party. For about two decades he was the international face of the Communist Party in Europe and attended congresses in Paris, Moscow, Prague, Rome and elsewhere. While the party made full use of his intellectual and personal skills for two decades, it confined him to being an interface, an interface which denied his identity as an Armenian intellectual. In the last years of his life he became marginalized within the party, his dedication to which had almost completely erased him from Armenian intellectual life.[48] In the official announcement of his death in 1979, the Turkish Communist Party (TKP) hardly utilized the autobiography Pehlivanian had submitted to them in 1955, not even using his real name. It only included a few sentences regarding his activities in the establishment of Turkey's Party for Labourers and Peasants and his engagement with the TKP. Reading this text, one would think that his belief in communism, equality, national liberation and peace solely stemmed from the fact he came from a 'poor [Turkish] peasant family'. Apparently for his comrades, his Armenianness, his birth into a genocidal state and society, his persistent struggle until being forced to leave Turkey, and his complete intellectual investment in Western Armenian writing and publication were in no way relevant to the political movement he believed in and served for years.[49] While it may be suggested that he was given a Turkish name in order to not criminalize the whole Armenian community in Istanbul, this does not hold up as the very existence of Armenians was enough to be criminalized, and more importantly, he became a high-ranking party officer in East Germany, not in Istanbul, so there was no need to Turkify him, especially after his death.

Like Zaven Biberyan, Aram Pehlivanian was one of the foremost Armenian intellectuals in Turkey. The newspaper he published with his best friend Avedis Aleksanyan, *Nor Ōr*, was a platform for many Armenian intellectuals of the survivor generation to express themselves. Pehlivanian had this to say about anti-Armenianism, racism and the complete consensus between the state and public intellectuals on the matter:

> If this anti-Armenian attitude were just the specialty of a newspaper, it would not be worth talking about. However, there is a mentality in the country, racist and especially anti-Armenian, which denies the existence of the other ... The press and the government are hooked on the same mentality, complementing each other. If the state changed its mentality, the press would not have the same courage to do so. Shall we be hopeful or not? History cautions us not to be.[50]

To see such lines in any periodical or publication in those days, especially in such a clearly formulated manner, was simply unthinkable. Pehlivanian was targeting the state and its fully complicit tool, the press, by challenging the system as a whole. The abandonment, the marginalization, the fear and the threats he and his colleagues had to endure to publish an oppositional Armenian newspaper meant imprisonment and later exile for Pehlivanian.

Aram Pehlivanian wrote his autobiography in 1955, in which he emphasized his identity as an Armenian intellectual by mentioning the Armenian high school he attended and the Armenian periodicals he published along with his political activities as a communist. I read his autobiography as an intervention against the Turkish Communist Party's policy of refusing to acknowledge the immediate connection between his communist persuasions and his identity as an Armenian intellectual. In 1978, his name was mentioned in a secret correspondence as the one 'to be gotten rid of'.[51] He was pulled back from his high-profile political engagement and instead given the task to write a history of the party. He passed away not long afterwards in Leipzig at the age of sixty-two.

The Armenian intellectuals in the circles of *Nor Ōr* and *Nor Lur* found themselves in exile, either at home or abroad. The post-genocide Armenian intellectuals of Turkey were not simply oppositional figures challenging their state. The state they opposed was responsible for the annihilation of their families, confiscation of their properties and destruction of their culture. Thus, they knew what the consequences of their opposition might be. They were the carriers of historical knowledge: the knowledge of annihilation as well as survival. This was the very reason why the state scrutinized these intellectuals so closely, having them repeatedly arrested, imprisoned and forced into exile. Indeed, we are reminded of the quote from Pehlivanian's autobiography: '16 December 1946, just as the Turkey's Party for Labourers and Peasants was shut down, so too was my newspaper Nor Or banned under the Martial Law and I was arrested for claims of involvement in communist activities.' He could not have been arrested for 'claims' of communist activities, as he was already a leading communist within Turkey's Labourers and Peasants Party. Pehlivanian, an intellectual who could write skilfully, precisely and powerfully in several languages, who knew that it was regular practice in those days to arrest communists for their political activities, might have been implying that his position as editor-in-chief at *Nor Ōr* must have played an important role in his conviction, at least as important as his membership in the party. The amount and content of reports in the Turkish State Archives written about Pehlivanian and *Nor Ōr* should be regarded as supporting evidence for this argument.[52]

Conclusion: Uneven diasporas

Walter Benjamin in his *Theses on History* draws our attention to the fact that 'the tradition of the oppressed teaches us that the "state of emergency" in which we live is not the exception but the rule'.[53] Taking Benjamin's point on the oppressed one step further, we may think of the histories of annihilated peoples as the key to understanding the world we live in: a world of multiple, parallel processes of unevenness. The major reason for the creation of the Ottoman Armenian diaspora was the provincial oppressions of the nineteenth century followed by the genocide. The annihilation left Armenians with various layers of unevenness, including the limits, constrictions and discrepancies among the diaspora communities. Hence, genocide, survival and denial delineated the structures of unevenness among Armenians, and in the case of Armenians in Turkey, silenced histories of continuing survival.

In the case of the Armenian diaspora, the way the various communities responded to the Armenian genocide shaped their relations with each other. Struggling for justice and recognition of genocide was a duty taken on by the diaspora communities around the world especially after 1965, a response which was absolutely necessary, and yet had immediate repercussions in the further marginalizing and criminalizing of the Armenians in Turkey. The discrepancies, differences and unevenness between the global diaspora and the one in Turkey were further reproduced, since the more Armenians globally raised their voices for justice, the more negative consequences befell those in Turkey. Thus, the structures that initially created the diaspora – provincial oppressions, the genocide and denial – have also been catalysers in making relations more uneven and in perpetuating conflicting relations among Armenian diaspora communities.

Though the classical definition of diaspora is a group dispersed to communities away from the homeland, I propose that even those remaining in their physical homeland can be rendered into a diaspora through massive violence such as genocide. If the main aim of a genocide is to irreversibly disrupt the connection between people and their lands, such a process unequivocally includes the complete erasure of those autochthonous groups and their cultural heritage on those lands, which in turn alienates survivors from their lands and their own history.[54] Considering the remaining Armenians in Turkey as a part of diaspora enhances our understanding of the concept of diaspora, as it forces us to reflect upon the historical conditions that led to the establishment of this specific type of diaspora. I consider home as a conglomeration of one's life with all means of production, networks (family, friends and foes and others), relations to nature and to geography as well as relations with other groups, all of which generate a knowledge of living on a given land. Genocide, as an act of intervention, restructures all of these and replaces the autochthonous knowledge of living on the land with the knowledge of annihilation; that is, living without institutions, without land and without one's own temporality. This is the moment of becoming diaspora, which persists for Armenians in Turkey.[55]

The Armenian intellectuals were completely isolated and marginalized, causing them to lose touch with the global intellectual world to which they deserved to be a part. Zaven Biberyan, with his conscious choice of becoming an Armenian critic and leftist intellectual, was marginalized both by the intellectual circles of the Armenian diaspora and in the end by his own community. For Aram Pehlivanian, the only way to fulfil his ideals of having a politically active life was under an assumed name which allowed him access to the highest echelons of the Turkish Communist Party, at the expense of his identity as an Armenian intellectual. Despite their different paths, the result was not very different for either Biberyan or Pehlivanian. The price they paid as intellectuals, as people of struggle, as survivor intellectuals, was the same. They were both destined to be silenced; the former within the Western Armenian world, the latter within the political movement he fought for. In the final analysis, it was the burden of being born into the catastrophe which followed them all their lives, both within Armenian communities as well as outside them. Their intellectual heritage, courage and resistance are unique contributions to the intellectual history of the twentieth century, as their struggle was against a state which annihilated the people to which they belonged. Even if it has come quite late, acknowledging the conditions under which they survived and contributed to the intellectual heritage of their time is a powerful intervention and inspiration for those Armenians and non-Armenians alike who make the difficult choice of insisting upon what they believe in. A struggle that was self-defeating, relentless and inspiring all at the same time.

Notes

1 Khachig Tölölyan and Taline Papazian, 'Armenian Diasporas and Armenia: Issues of Identity and Mobilization: An Interview with Khachig Tölölyan', *EAC* 3 (2014): 83–101, https://doi.org/10.4000/eac.565.
2 Turkey's *Rum* population was exiled, and Assyrians were massacred along with Armenians. For more, see David Gaunt, *Let Them Not Return: Sayfo – The Genocide of the Assyrian, Syriac, and Chaldean Christians in the Ottoman Empire* (New York: Berghahn Books, 2017); David Gaunt, *Massacres, Resistance, Protectors: Muslim-Christian Relations in Eastern Anatolia during World War I* (Piscataway: Gorgias Press, 2006); George Shirinian, *Genocide in the Ottoman Empire: Armenians, Assyrians and Greeks* (New York: Berghahn Books, 2017).
3 On diminished lives, see Harry Harootunian, *The Unspoken as Heritage: The Armenian Genocide and its Unaccounted Lives* (Durham: Duke University Press, 2019), 114–48.
4 On the confiscations of properties, see Nevzat Onaran, *Emval-i Metruke Olayı: Osmanlı'da ve Cumhuriyette Ermeni ve Rum Mallarının Türkleştirilmesi* (Istanbul: Belge Yayınları, 2010); Nevzat Onaran, *Osmanlı'da Rum ve Ermeni Mallarının Türkleştirilmesi (1914–19)* (Istanbul: Evrensel Basım Yayın, 2013) and Nevzat Onaran, *Cumhuriyet'te Ermeni ve Rum Mallarının Türkleştirilmesi (1920–1930)* (Istanbul: Evrensel Basım Yayın, 2013); Taner Akçam and Ümit Kurt, *The Spirit of Laws: The Plunder of Wealth in the Armenian Genocide* (New York: Berghahn Books, 2017); Uğur Ümit Üngör and Mehmet Polatel, *Confiscation and Destruction: Young Turk Seizure of Armenian Property* (London: Continuum, 2011); Sait Çetinoğlu, 'Diyarbakır'da Ermeni Mallarını Kim Aldı?' in *Diyarbakır Tebliğleri, Diyarbakır ve Çevresi Toplumsal ve Ekonomik Tarihi Konferansı*, ed. Bülent Doğan (Istanbul: Hrant Dink Vakfı Yayınları, 2013), 376–84.
5 Raymond Kevorkian and Paul Paboudjian, *1915 Öncesinde Osmanlı İmparatorluğu'nda Ermeniler* (Istanbul: Aras Yay, 2012), 11.
6 For the centralization of Armenian administration in Istanbul and the Armenian *Nizamname*, see Vartan Artinian, ed., *Osmanlı Devleti'nde Ermeni Anayasası'nın Doğuşu* (Istanbul: Aras Yay, 2004). For the Armenian administration during the Tanzimat period, see Suciyan, 'Contesting the Authority of Armenian Administration at the Height of Tanzimat: A Case of Incest, Adultery and Abortion', *Reflektif Journal of Social Sciences* 2, no. 1 (2021): 29–47, https://dergi.bilgi.edu.tr/index.php/reflektif/article/view/20/19. Accessed 15 February 2021.
7 Khatchig Tölölyan, 'Elites and Institutions in the Armenian Transnation', *Diaspora: A Journal of Transnational Studies* 9, no. 1 (2000): 120, doi:10.1353/dsp.2000.0004.
8 For instance, see the statement of Rober Haddeciyan given to Ulf Björklund in Ulf Björklund, 'Armenians of Athens and Istanbul: The Armenian Diaspora and the "Transnational" Nation', *Global Networks* 3, no. 3 (2003): 345.

9   Talin Suciyan, 'Hagop Mnts'uri's The Second Marriage: Armenian Realities in the Pre- and Post-Genocide Ottoman Empire and Turkey', *British Journal of Middle Eastern Studies*, doi:10.1080/13530194.2022.2069085. On non-contemporaneity of the contemporaries, see Ernst Bloch, *Heritage of Our Times* (Cambridge: Polity Press, 1991); Harry Harootunian, '"In the Zone of Occult Instability": Some Reflections on Unevenness, Discordant Temporalities and the Logic of Historical Practice', in *Archaism and Anachrony: Reflections on the Question of Historical Time and Uneven Development* (Durham: Duke University Press, forthcoming).

10 On provincial oppressions, see Kiwd Aghanyants', ed., *Tiwan Hayots' Badmut'ean Kirk' 18: Harsdaharut'iwnner Dajgahayasdanum (Vawerakrer 1801–1888)* (Tblisi: Dbaran N. Aghanyants'I, 1915); Yasar Tolga Cora, Dzovinar Derderian and Ali Sipahi, eds., *The Ottoman East in the 19th Century: Societies, Identities and Politics* (London: I.B. Tauris, 2016); Talin Suciyan, *Ya derdimize derman, ya katlimize ferman (Either Save Us from This Misery or Order Our Death: Tanzimat of the Provinces* (Syracuse: Syracuse University Press, forthcoming); Richard Antaramian, *Brokers of Faith, Brokers of Empire: Armenians and the Politics of Reform in the Ottoman Empire* (Stanford: Stanford University Press, 2020).

11 *Kaghat'agan*s are those survivor Armenians who were perpetually exiled from one village to the other or from the provinces to Istanbul and in many cases emigrated abroad. The repeated displacements, exiles and survivals are all encapsulated in the term *kaght'agan*, which has no direct translation, and so is rendered in the original, the way all Armenian periodicals and publications referred to these survivors, particularly in the 1920s and 1930s.

12 For instance, gatherings of the Armenian National Assembly were not permitted. The members of the Religious and Civil Assemblies were either killed or exiled but new elections were not permitted to replace them. The Patriarchate's authorities were undermined to a great extent, with its agency and authority squeezed into the realm of religion. Yet Armenians' issues were mostly political in nature rather than religious, especially after 1915, as being an Armenian survivor in itself was a political issue. Changes undertaken in the Law on Pious Foundations turned the administration of properties belonging to pious foundations into a matter of arbitration too. Talin Suciyan, *The Armenians in Modern Turkey: Post-Genocide Society, Politics and History* (London: I.B. Tauris, 2016), 91–126.

13 Madtēos M. Êblighatean, *Geank mĕ azkis geank'in mēch: Aganadesi ew masnagts'oghi Vgayut'iwnner 1903–1923* (Antelias: Dbaran Gatoghigosut'ean Medzi Dann Giligioy, 1987), 15.

14 Rıza Nur in secret hearings in the Turkish Parliament. See *TBMM Gizli Celse Zabıtları*, Vol. 4 (Ankara: İşbankası Yayınları, 1985), 8. For its English translation, see Suciyan, *The Armenians in Modern Turkey*, 41.

15 Ibid., 127–32.

16 Ayda Erbal and Talin Suciyan, 'One Hundred Years of Abandonment', *Armenian Weekly* (2011), https://armenianweekly.com/2011/04/29/erbal-and-suciyan-one-hundred-years-of-abandonment/. Accessed September 2022.

17 Kersam Aharonyan, *Khoher Hisnameagi Awardin* (Beirut: Atlas Publ., 1966), 149.

18 Rıfat Bali, *Musa'nın Evlatları Cumhuriyet'in Yurttaşları* (İstanbul: İletişim Yayıncılık, 2001), 133.

19 Ayşe Hür, 'Franz Werfel ve Musa Dağ'da Kırk Gün', *Taraf*, 18 December 2011, https://www.marmarayerelhaber.com/Ayse-HUR-Taraf-yazilari/5349-Franz-Werfel-ve-Musa-Dagda-Kirk-Gun. Accessed 8 September 2022.

20 Edward Minassian, 'The Forthy Days of Musa Dagh: The Film That Was Denied', *Journal of Armenian Studies* 3, no.1–2 (1985/6): 121–31.
21 For more see Erbal and Suciyan, 'One Hundred Years of Abandonment'.
22 Suciyan, *The Armenians in Modern Turkey*, 127–42.
23 Ibid., 135.
24 Talin Suciyan, 'Dört nesil: Kurtarılamayan son', *Toplum Bilim*, no. 132 (2015): 128–9. For more on oral history with Mihran Dabağ, see Suciyan, *The Armenians in Modern Turkey*, 132–49.
25 Haroutunian, *The Unspoken as Heritage*, 82.
26 Walter Benjamin committed suicide as a result of the oppression and exile he endured; Franz Werfel's book was banned before publication by the Nazi party.
27 Ara Koçunyan, *Voğçuyn Amenkin* (Istanbul: Aras Yay, 2008), 78–9.
28 For more, see Melissa Bilal and Lerna Ekmekçioğlu, *Bir Adalet Feryadı* (Istanbul: Aras Publishing, 2006) and Lerna Ekmekçioğlu, *Recovering Armenia: The Limits of Belonging in the Post-Genocide Turkey* (Stanford: Stanford University Press, 2016).
29 For articles published on the murder and commemoration of Sevag Balıkçı, see 'Murderer of Armenian Soldier in Turkey Sentenced to 17 Years of Prison', 13 June 2020. https://horizonweekly.ca/am/murderer-of-armenian-soldier-in-turkey-sentenced-to-17-years-in-prison/, Hrag Avedanian, 'Songs of Comfort', in *Armenian Weekly*, April 2020. https://armenianweekly.com/2020/04/24/songs-of-comfort/, Fiona Guitard, 'Remembering Sevag Balıkçı on April 24 in Istanbul', in *Armenian Weekly*, June, 2015, https://armenianweekly.com/2015/06/15/balikci-istanbul/, 'Sevag Balıkçı Case Update: Two Murder Witnesses Sentenced to Imprisonment', in *Civilnet*, 23 December 2015, https://www.civilnet.am/en/news/385901/sevag-balikci-case-update-two-murder-witnesses-sentenced-to-imprisonment/. Accessed 15 October 2022.
30 Others who bear mentioning include Adrine Dadrian, Araksi Babikyan, Armenuhi Özer, Avedik Aleksanyan, Lilit Koç, Garbis Cancikyan, Hagop Mntzuri, Jak İhmalyan, Roz Vartanyan, Sirvart Gülbenkyan, Malvine Valideyan, Manişak Giragosyan, Sarkis Keçyan, Sona Der Markaryan, Vahan Toşikyan, Vartan Ihmalyan, and Verjin Hacınlıyan. For Armenian women writers of the 1940s, see Pakarat Tevyan, *Erchanig Darekirkʻ 1946* (Istanbul: Ak-Ün Basımevi, 1945), 12–17.
31 *Nor Lur*, 5 January 1946.
32 *Nor Lur*, 22 January 1946.
33 For more on *repatriation*, see Vahé Tachjian, '"Repatriation": A New Chapter, Studded with New Obstacles, in the History of AGBU's Cooperation in Soviet Armenia', in *The Armenian General Benevolent Union: A Hundred Years of History (1906–2006)*, vol. 2 (1941–2006), ed. Raymond H. Kevorkian and Vahé Tachjian (Cairo, Paris, New York: AGBU, 2006), 291–309.
34 National Archives of Armenia, File No. 326.1.72. More on Stalin's 'repatriation call' and the Armenians' responses to it in the forthcoming article by Talin Suciyan, 'The Repatriation Never Took Place: The Soviet Armenian Call for Immigration of 1946 and Its Impact on Turkey', in *After the Ottomans. The Long Shadow of Genocide, and Armenian Resilience*, ed. Hans Lukas Kieser, Seyhan Bayraktar and Khatchig Mouradian (London: I.B. Tauris, 2023).
35 NAA, File No. 326.1.102.0002.
36 *Nor Lur*, 22 January 1946. All translations are mine.
37 Zaben Biberyan, *Mrchiwnneru Verchaluysě* (Istanbul: Aras Yayıncılık, 2007), 7.

38 Biberyan, 'Namag Hrant Paluyan'i', in *Mrchiwnneru Verchaluysĕ*, 553. Unless otherwise noted, all translations are mine.
39 Sevan Değirmenciyan, 'Haṛachapan' (Foreword), in *Mrchiwnneru Verchaluysĕ*, 10. See also Marc Nichanian, 'Zavēn Bibēryanin Mrchiwnnerĕ' (Ants of Zaven Biberyan), in *Mrchiwnneru Verchaluysĕ*, 560.
40 Zaven Biberyan, *Babam Aşkaleye gitmedi*, trans. Sirvart Malkhasyan (Istanbul: Aras Publ., 1999). The Turkish translation of *The Sunset of the Ants* was first published under the title *Babam Aşkale'ye Gitmedi* (My Father Did Not Go to Aşkale) and in 2019 as *Karıncaların Günbatımı*, with the exact translation into Turkish of its original title.
41 Değirmenciyan, 'Haṛachapan', 10. Marc Nichanian also notes that Biberyan's name is barely known to Armenian diaspora communities and his work has not been mentioned in the anthologies of Armenian literature. For more, see Nichanian, 'Zavēn Bibēryanin Mrchiwnnerĕ', 559–60.
42 Ibid., 559.
43 For more on the random draft of non-Muslim men during the Second World War, see Rıfat N. Bali, *Yirmi Kur'a Nafıa Askerleri: II. Dünya Savaşında Gayrimüslimlerin Askerlik Serüveni* (Istanbul: Kitabevi Yayınları, 2008).
44 Biberyan, 'Namag Hrant Palueani', 551.
45 Ibid., 552.
46 Aram Pehlivanian, autobiography written on 22 April 1955. I thank Aram Pehlivanian's daughter Meliné Pehlivanian for making his archive available to me. The autobiography was written in Turkish, the English translation is mine. It was first published in *Agos* weekly on 14 December 2019. See Talin Suciyan, 'Eşitlik bir Lütuf değil Haktır', *Agos,* 14 December 2019, available on the *Agos* website at: http://www.agos.com.tr/tr/yazi/23342/esitlik-bir-lutuf-degil-haktir. Accessed 25 May 2020.
47 Aram Pehlivanian under his penname A. Şavarş contributed to Armenian periodicals including *Mshaguyt* for which he wrote articles on literature and dialectic materialism or literature and painting. See Aram Pehlivanian, 'Kragan Shrchanagi Ngarchagan Tsutsahantese', in *Mshaguyt* (Beirut, April 1955), 91–8. See http://tert.nla.am/archive/NLA%20AMSAGIR/mshakuytB/1955(4).pdf. Accessed 2 July 2021.
48 For more, see Suciyan, 'Eşitlik bir Lütuf değil Haktır'.
49 See 'Duyuru' in Aram Pehlivanian, *Özgürlük İki Adım Ötede Değil* (Istanbul: Aras Yayıncılık, 1999), 104–5.
50 Aram Pehlivanian, 'Mamul ew garavarut'iwni', *Nor Or*, 30 August 1946. For its English translation, see Suciyan, *The Armenians in Modern Turkey*, 161.
51 Document dated 23 August 1978 signed by Ismail Bilen. For more, see Suciyan, 'Eşitlik bir Lütuf değil Haktır'.
52 See the report on Pehlivanian and *Nor Ōr* in the Turkish State Archives, BCA, 030.01.101.623.6.
53 Walter Benjamin, 'On the Concept of History', in *Illuminations*, ed. Hanna Arends, trans. Harry Zohn (New York: Schocken Books, 1969), 253–64.
54 Aylin Vartanyan, "Broken memory and natal alienation" in Agos Weekly, June 9, 2023. https://www.agos.com.tr/en/article/28751/broken-memory-and-natal-alienation?fbclid=IwAR1yS0tlQb-9ZMh3tTgrY-MVo_fUzI5Z3kbGNueqHqU2pmJ2AH0hQL7geks.
55 The process which turns autochthonous peoples into diaspora communities upon their historical geography can also be understood through the experiences of the indigenous populations of the Americas.

11

Are Istanbul Armenians Diasporic? Unpacking the famous debate

Hrag Papazian

Since 2014, when I first embarked upon my research on Armenians in Istanbul, the question of whether the people I study constitute a diasporic community or not has been stubbornly following me. It is not only a topic that I lengthily thought over in university libraries or when strolling the streets of Istanbul but a question that I was often asked by fellow Armenians. 'Are they *spʻiwrk*ʻ?', acquaintances have asked me with sincere curiosity on multiple occasions, using the Armenian word for 'diaspora'.[1] In Armenian scholarly circles, at academic workshops, or semi-academic meetings, the issue has also been raised on several occasions, even if often dropping the question mark in favour of rather assertive statements: 'But *Bolsahayutʻiwn* (Armenian community of Istanbul) is not really a diaspora', 'Their diasporicity is debatable', 'But/even if/although they don't perceive themselves as a diaspora . . .' and the like. This interest in and sensitivity towards the issue of Istanbul Armenians being diasporic or not has been a growing phenomenon in the Armenian transnation especially after the turn of the twenty-first century when Armenians of *Bolis* (Armenian for Constantinople/Istanbul) started intensifying their connections with the wider Armenian world, including with Armenia,[2] thus attracting attention towards them and their issues.

In 2011 this question turned into a public, transnational, virtual debate with several op-eds and statements arguing against one another. During a visit to Istanbul, Hranush Hakobyan, Armenia's then Minister of Diaspora, honoured fifteen Istanbul Armenian intellectuals with medals on the part of the Republic of Armenia. Istanbul Armenian journalist Vercihan Ziflioğlu soon published an article in *Hürriyet Daily News* in which several of the awarded intellectuals voiced discontent with the fact that it was particularly Armenia's Minister of *Diaspora* that had visited and honoured them and vehemently argued against being classified as members of a 'diasporic' community.[3] Their stance was supported by a couple of diaspora Armenians from Canada and London featured in the same article, while only one interviewee from Aleppo argued that 'Istanbul Armenians are a de facto diaspora'.[4] The article was just the first episode of a debate that went on over the next few weeks, attracting various voices from different corners of the Armenian transnation.[5] Representatives from Armenia were among the first to respond, complaining about the public criticism against their ministry but essentially agreeing, even in a statement by the Minister of Diaspora herself, that Istanbul Armenians are 'not considered diaspora'.[6] Soon, however, opposing views started to emerge arguing that *Bolis* Armenians *do* constitute 'a diaspora'.[7]

However, none of the articles taking part in this public debate, nor the very few scholarly texts addressing the issue of Istanbul Armenians' (non)diasporicity,[8] base their analyses and arguments on the rich body of literature in the field of diaspora studies which has produced pages of theoretical discussions on what diasporas are and what factors characterize them in contrast to other social formations (and in which, Khachig Tölölyan, an Armenian scholar with family roots in Istanbul, has played a prominent role). This chapter aims to undertake that very task: approaching the question of whether Istanbul Armenians are diasporic or not through an application of established scholarly theories on diaspora. I start by closely analysing and critiquing the arguments of the two opposing theses – 'Istanbul Armenians *are* diasporic' versus 'Istanbul Armenians are *not* diasporic' – which paves the way for me to address the oft-asked question myself. Discussing the logic and argumentation behind each of the two views in the debate, I will point at some of their methodological problems and inaccuracies.

For my analysis of the debate, I draw from two sources: first, publications participating in the debate; second, ethnographic material from my fieldwork conducted in Istanbul in two phases (July 2014 and September 2015 to May 2017). In my interviews and informal conversations with Istanbul Armenians, I have often asked their opinion on the matter. Contrary to conventional views, not all *Bolis* Armenians reject being categorized as diasporic – though most of my interlocutors did so. The debate, thus, belongs also to the community itself. Since some of the arguments there repeat those voiced in the public debates that include outsiders to the community as well, I find it productive to conduct a combined analysis of the two fields: the field of emic 'study of diasporas', an expression that Tölölyan uses to account for the discourse that communities employ 'to talk about themselves to themselves' and the 'etic field of diaspora studies',[9] in which scholars study diasporic communities.[10]

Problems within the 'Diaspora' thesis

I begin by critiquing what might seem, to many, as the more commonsensical among the two theses. Those maintaining that *Bolsahayut'iwn* is a 'diaspora' often limit their argument to the assertion that Istanbul Armenians reside *outside* their 'true homeland'. This approach can be found in texts from the 'diaspora' side of the 2011 debate which meticulously argue and explicate that the city of Istanbul does not lie within the territorial boundaries of Armenians' (hence, the argument's logic goes, also Istanbul Armenians') homeland as they conceive it.

For instance, Uruguay-born Armenian scholar Vartan Matiossian maintains that the Istanbul Armenian community is diasporic because *Bolis* is 'historically and geographically speaking' not part of Historical Armenia, the Western boundary of which is considered to be the Euphrates River.[11] Kurken Berksanlar, this time an Istanbul-born Armenian, hence an *emic* voice in the debate, also constructs his argument on the territorial positionality of Istanbul vis-à-vis the 'Armenian homeland'.[12] Referring to a 'very simple dictionary definition' of diaspora, which reads 'people living outside the homeland/country/native country' (*Yurt dışında yaşayanlar*, in Turkish), he argues that to be able to decide whether Istanbul Armenians are diasporic or not the 'Armenian homeland' should first be defined. He suggests two possible definitions for it, from which he deduces two possible definitions of the 'Armenian diaspora': (1) every Armenian living outside the borders of contemporary Armenia is part of the diaspora (he finds this definition as the most logical), and (2) those living outside the boundaries of Historical Armenia constitute the diaspora. He then discusses the borders of Historical Armenia, the most encompassing option being that of Armenian King Tigranes (95–55 BCE), even embeds the corresponding map of it in his article, and concludes that 'Istanbul has never been within these borders [of the Armenian homeland]' from which he deduces the 'diasporicity' of Istanbul Armenians.[13]

A related argument within this approach consists of drawing attention to the fact that most Istanbul Armenians today are either primary or second/third-generation internal migrants who have left their hometowns in the eastern provinces of Turkey for Istanbul during the Turkish Republican period (1923–present). Coming as a response to arguments about *Bolsahayut'iwn* being a centuries-old community and hence being 'at home' rather than 'a diaspora' (to be discussed later), this line of thought maintains, referring to historical facts,[14] that the majority of contemporary Istanbul Armenians are in any case not direct descendants of the old 'settled' community, from which it deduces, again, their diasporicity. Matiossian, for instance, asks: 'What are the contemporary residents of *Bolis* – who have been uprooted from this or that corner of Historical Armenia and transplanted into the once Ottoman capital – if not emigrants (*bantukhd*, in Armenian), to use the old word, [or] diasporised offshoots, to use the new word?'[15] He then concludes that although those people have not left Turkey, 'they have nevertheless left [Historical] *Western Armenia*' (emphasis in original). In a 2009 op-ed entitled 'Diaspora Kim' ('Who is the diaspora'), historian Talin Suciyan (herself an Istanbul Armenian) similarly argues that 'almost all' of Turkey's Armenians 'are diasporic' because 'the true country/homeland of the Armenians who were forced to come to Istanbul is not Istanbul'.[16] She also takes up this issue in her book on the history of Armenians in modern Turkey, describing the 'perpetual exodus from [Turkey's eastern] provinces to Istanbul', as a 'process of becoming diaspora'.[17]

Some of my interviewees in Istanbul have also explained their self-identification as diasporic based on a similar logic of being outside, and/or of having left, the homeland. An editor of one of the Istanbul Armenian newspapers, for instance, criticized those in the community rejecting the 'diaspora' label as follows: 'Why aren't we a diaspora? Istanbul has never been Armenia in history, nor it has been part of the Armenian Plateau.[18] Scientifically speaking, it's a diaspora.'[19] Another prominent journalist shared a similar stance:

> Of course, it is a diaspora. Primarily because it is outside the homeland. Whether you consider the homeland to be contemporary Armenia or the territories of the Historical Greater Armenia, Istanbul remains outside those in any case. Besides,

my people's ancestors have not come to this city of their own free will; they have often been forced to come . . .

The problem with these arguments is not in the veracity of the historical and geographical facts that they present. Nor is the 'diaspora' argument necessarily and completely wrong in and of itself, as I will further elaborate on in the last section. The problem is methodological: it belongs to the realm of argumentation, and it is twofold. First, being (forced) outside one's homeland does not *automatically* and *necessarily* make someone, let alone a whole community, diasporic. In other words, that mere fact cannot serve as evidence for the 'diaspora' argument. Second, the 'Armenian homeland' as conceived by voices in the 'diaspora' side of the debate is not necessarily and not always congruent with the 'homeland (of Armenians)' imagined by all Istanbul Armenians whom those voices hasten to categorize as 'diasporic'.

Confusing 'diaspora' with 'dispersion'

Even if, for the time being, we leave unquestioned the assertion that Istanbul lies *outside* the homeland of Armenians living in the city today, this does not, according to well-established diaspora theories, in and of itself serve as evidence of Istanbul Armenians' diasporicity. In fact, in the academic literature of diaspora studies, one notices a persistent effort, especially on the part of the more theoretically and conceptually stringent scholars in the field, to save the concept of 'diaspora' from losing its *analytical value and relevance* by getting merged with other sociological categories that might share with it the characteristic of territorial dispersion or displacement, such as migrants, exiles, refugees and the like. The theoretical core of diaspora studies, in other words, maintains that not all dispersions, whether coerced or voluntary, and not all collectivities outside homelands should casually be treated as 'diasporas' or 'diasporic'. Prominent scholars have criticized the casual use of the notion of diaspora 'in an untheorized or undertheorized way',[20] and the 'over-use and under-theorization of the notion of "diaspora" [that] threatens the term's descriptive usefulness'.[21] They warned about the 'danger of ["diaspora"] becoming a promiscuously capacious category',[22] about the risk of 'the term los[ing] its discriminating power, its ability to pick out phenomena, to make distinctions'[23] or even the risk of 'los[ing] all meaning' through overstretched and loose definitions,[24] of which 'that segment of a people living outside the homeland' is an oft-critiqued example.[25]

Instead, they have always emphasized the importance of *translocal connections* and *relationships* fostered and maintained after dispersion as *fundamental conditions* for diaspora and diasporicity. In his prominent article in the first-ever publication of *Diaspora*, the leading journal in the field, William Safran had already laid down a list of six characteristics that members of expatriate communities should share for the concept of 'diaspora' to apply to them. Whereas 'dispers[ion] from a specific original "center"' is the first of these, Safran certainly does not find it sufficient, unlike what seems to commonly be the case in the 'diaspora' front of the debate concerning the Istanbul Armenians. Four of the other characteristics he cites have to do with connectedness with and orientation towards the 'original homeland': retention of a collective memory, vision or myth about it; perception of it as the ideal home to which the dispersed or their descendants must eventually return; collective commitment to its maintenance or restoration; and a continuous relationship with it that serves as a basis for the ethnocommunal collective consciousness.[26] Whereas Safran does not expect diasporic communities to meet *all* six characteristics, he clearly emphasizes connectedness with the homeland in this or that of the four ways, and openly rejects qualifying people as diasporic based *solely* on the first characteristic of dispersion from the original 'center'. He brings the example of Polish immigrants in the United States after the 1880s who 'were not a diaspora', he argues, because they were quick to take the path of assimilation and 'were not much concerned with the political fortunes of their progenitors' homeland'.[27]

In a similar vein, Khachig Tölölyan, founding editor of *Diaspora*, finds using the concept simply 'for any combination of mobility, scattering beyond a territory of origin, and resettlement elsewhere' to be 'conceptually untidy' and 'problematic'.[28] He stresses the importance of differentiating between 'dispersion', on the one hand, and 'diaspora', on the other, for the sake of maintaining the analytical usefulness of the latter concept. '"Dispersion" was [originally] a very large category of which diaspora was a specific subset, a part not identical with the whole', he writes and argues that 'the extension of the term diaspora to old and new dispersions . . . blurs several distinctions that should continue to matter'.[29] He writes critically,[30] for instance, about historian George Shepperson's argument that people of African origin constitute a diaspora merely because of a coerced departure from the original lands, a resulting suffering and a continuing distinctness of identity perpetuated by racism[31] – an argumentation quite similar to that of some thinkers on the 'diaspora' side of the debate concerning the Istanbul Armenians.[32] Tölölyan emphasizes maintained connections, whether real or imaginary, with the homeland, and treats these as a condition for 'diaspora' in contrast to, for instance, simply 'ethnic communities', which 'are not characterized by such sustained contact with the homeland'.[33] He describes this 'salient characteristic of diasporas' as follows:

> a rhetoric of restoration and return that, in practice, takes the form of a sustained and organized commitment to maintaining relations with kin communities elsewhere, and with the homeland, to which diasporans either return literally or, more commonly, 're-turn' without actual repatriation: that is, they turn again and again toward the homeland through travel, remittances, cultural exchange, and political lobbying and by various contingent efforts to maintain other links with the homeland.[34]

These connections are 'key components of a specifically "diasporic" social formation, one that is not only a renamed ethnic group', he writes on another occasion.[35] Diasporas are thus 'a *special category* of ethnicized dispersion', not simply any dispersed ethnic formation, Tölölyan argues,[36] concurring with others, like Brubaker, who similarly think that 'there is no reason to speak of the diasporization of every more or less dispersed population'.[37]

Even arguments about a possible absence of ties with the homeland among some diasporas have nevertheless stressed *multilocal connectedness across dispersion* as a defining factor. Whereas links with the original point of dispersion might have waned and disappeared in the case of such 'deterritorialized diasporas', connections and a shared consciousness with dispersed people and communities of the same origin in *other* localities are necessarily maintained.[38] Revising and expanding Safran's list, Robin Cohen includes also 'a sense of empathy and solidarity with co-ethnic members in other countries' among the nine strands of his 'diasporic rope' (of which three still relate to links with the ancestral home/homeland).[39] Examples of such de-territorialized diasporas are the Caribbean peoples whose links are across communities in distant places in the 'Black Atlantic' rather than with Africa,[40] or the Roma that 'exist as a diaspora across borders *because* their leaders recognize themselves as dispersed and oppressed fragments of a people, fragments that they increasingly work to *reconnect*'.[41]

Thus, whether 'radial', that is directed towards an original centre or homeland, or 'lateral' and 'decentered', *connections* are central and indispensable for the phenomenon scholars call 'diaspora'.[42] Diasporas, as social forms, are 'identified group[s] characterized by their relationship-despite-dispersal', which maintain 'a variety of explicit and implicit ties with their homelands' and/or develop 'solidarity with co-ethnic members in other countries of settlement'.[43] Diaspora's 'empowering paradox . . . is that dwelling *here* assumes a solidarity and connection *there*'.[44]

The diasporicity of any displaced person or dispersed community, hence, cannot be assumed a priori. Being outside one's homeland is a precondition for diasporic existence, but not a sufficient factor for it. Defenders of the 'diaspora' argument in the debate concerning Istanbul Armenians thus often make the methodological mistake of conflating dispersion with diaspora, of presenting the history of exile and the condition of being outside the 'real homeland' as *evidences* of 'diaspora', whereas they are not – at least not if we were to follow these long-established scholarly definitions of the concept aiming to maintain its analytical relevance.

It is interesting, for instance, to notice the difference between how the idea of 'becoming diaspora' is defined, on the one hand, in Suciyan's study of Turkey's Armenians,[45] and, on the other hand, by Tölölyan in his conceptual-theoretical discussion of the phenomenon. Whereas the former perceives a process of 'becoming diaspora' in the 'ongoing flow of the Armenians from the Provinces', that is in the process of dispersion itself,[46] Tölölyan defines the same expression, and its synonym 'diasporization', as the process through which 'dispersions . . . successfully transform themselves into diasporas'. Importantly, that transformation happens not at the moment of dispersion or because of it per se but at a later stage, during 'transitional periods, which come no earlier than the second and third generations [of the dispersed] . . . thanks to the collective work of memory and commemoration, the performance of difference, the cultivation of ideologies of identity, and the institutionalization of practices of connection to the homeland'.[47] This important point is also raised by Cohen, who, drawing on Marienstras's argument that 'time has to pass' before it is possible to assess whether a migrant community 'is really a diaspora', maintains that 'one does not announce the formation of the diaspora the moment the representatives of a people first get off the boat at Ellis Island (or wherever)'.[48]

Of course, such work of forging links and relations with the 'original homeland' and/or with other dispersed Armenian communities *might* have taken place among

Armenians arriving in Istanbul from the eastern provinces during the Turkish Republican period. But a solid argumentation about their 'diasporicity' should focus on these processes, rather than neglect them or just assume their occurrence. Because those radial or lateral connections, whether mental, social or practical, do not naturally and passively occur on their own. Instead, they, and hence diasporicity itself, should be actively exercised and performed through social and cultural means.[49] Any diaspora is 'in the first instance ... a category of *practice*' and is 'held together or re-created through the mind, through cultural artefacts and through a shared imagination'.[50] Scholars have already cautioned against 'assuming a common sense of attachment to place of origin among dispersed communities', instead inviting 'investigation of the ways in which attachment is *variously* felt and constructed within differently constituted spaces, institutional arrangements and material conditions'.[51]

My interview material suggests that at least some contemporary Istanbul Armenians show *no sign* of practices of connection to, hence no sign of practices of diasporicity towards, the old Anatolian hometowns which their parents or grandparents had to leave. When I asked Hagop, a musician in his forties, whether 'Anadolu' (Turkish for Anatolia) and particularly Yozgat and *Gessaria* (Kayseri), where his parents had come from, meant anything special to him, he responded in a somewhat dispassionate tone that he has never been there nor ever really desired to visit, adding that he does *not* hold a feeling of belonging, 'a feeling of this place is my place' as he put it, towards those regions. Artin, a thirty-year-old political activist and student of history, gave an even more telling response:

> My origins are from *Gessaria*, Yozgat, and Adana, but there is nothing [that I have inherited] from those places. . . . I have not heard stories about them . . . hence I don't have any emotional connection to them. To call a place a 'homeland', you should mentally imagine it as historically related to you, you should think 'I used to be from there', you should [visualize] the village's fountain, and so on. . . . I know nothing; hence I don't have these [connections].

Hagop and Artin's words seem to portray a *disconnect* rather than a connectedness with those lands they are told to be a 'diaspora' of.

Thus, without attending to the cultivation of connections and links between the new 'here' and old 'there', without an analysis of the diasporic relationships-despite-dispersal – or even if referring to such links but failing to present them as *evidence* for diasporicity and instead focusing on the mere fact of 'living outside the homeland'[52], arguments on the 'diaspora' side of the debate ultimately fall short of proving that Istanbul Armenians are diasporic. Being dispersed from and outside of the homeland does not necessarily entail diasporicity. This is the first, but not the only, methodological problem.

The problem with 'the homeland'

The 'outside the homeland' argument often comes as a response to assertions maintaining that Armenians in Istanbul 'have not left our/their lands, hence are not diasporic'. Such assertions were very often voiced during my conversations or interviews with Istanbul Armenians and appeared in the 2011 public debate as well.[53] The counter-argument discussed above, singling out *Istanbul* and showing that the city has always been outside the 'Armenian homeland', might at first glance seem a reasonable and legitimate response. However, the emic perspective on the matter challenges taken-for-granted conceptions of what the 'homeland of Armenians' could be.

Thus, a second problem with the 'diaspora because of being outside the homeland' argument is that it applies its own understanding of the 'Armenian(s')' homeland' without questioning its validity for the people whose diasporicity it attempts to assess. To what extent are the *etic* and *emic* perspectives on 'homeland' congruent? Is 'their homeland', as conceived by the analyst, and 'our homeland', as conceived by the analysed, the same? Lest we fall into the trap of essentializing and naturalizing 'homelands' as bounded and substantial entities, we should keep in mind that it is people themselves who subjectively construct, remember and lay claim to particular territories as 'homelands'.[54] Homelands are not fixed and tangible entities agreeable upon in unison but products of context-specific sociocultural construction, and variably 'imagine[d] domain[s] of the nation'.[55] Hence, they might be objects of contestation and disagreement as well.

My analysis of Istanbul Armenians' own thoughts about homeland and diasporicity, reflected in informal conversations as well as dozens of semi-structured interviews that I have conducted since 2014, allows me to differentiate between two approaches within the widely used 'we have not gone anywhere' or 'we live on our lands' discourse in the community. The first of these, as I will elaborate in this section, stands in firm and genuine opposition to the definition of a homeland that leaves Istanbul outside its boundaries, thus legitimately countering the 'diaspora' argument. The second version, as I will detail in the next section, is based on either confusion or manipulation.

The 'homeland of Armenians', as perceived by several, though not all, of my Istanbul Armenian interlocutors of different ages, socioeconomic classes, genders and political orientations, is not geographically congruent with the 'Armenian homeland' defined in terms of either the contemporary Republic of Armenia or the territories ruled by historical Armenian Kingdoms to which some in the 'diaspora' side of the debate refer. When these interlocutors talk about not having left 'these lands', which also gets voiced as '*our* lands' or 'Armenians' lands', they speak of a larger territory to which Armenians, in their understanding and imagination, unequivocally belong. This imagined geography is loosely bounded, and it includes not only the eastern regions of contemporary Turkey coinciding with territories where Kingdoms of Armenia had ruled in Antiquity but also more Western parts of the Anatolian plateau and, importantly, also Istanbul 'where there has been an Armenian presence for centuries' and which has been, as they would often remind me, the centre of Ottoman Armenian cultural and sociopolitical life.[56] This conception of a 'land of Armenians', perhaps partly at odds with an 'Armenian homeland' imagined by others, emphasizes *temporality* instead of *polity*. It imagines Kütahya, for example, where there has been an Armenian presence since as old as the Byzantine era,[57] and where renowned Armenian musician Father Komitas was born in 1869, to be *part* of the 'lands where we belong', rather than being outside of them. It does not see it, nor Istanbul, as a 'foreign' land for Armenians only because these have not come under Armenian sovereign rule.

When a young man named Aren argued that 'we are not a diaspora here because these are our lands', I asked, then naively thinking that I was challenging him, 'but *Bolis* is not in that "our lands", right?' 'Bolis was not in the old Armenian Kingdoms like Van and Mush were, but in Ottoman times there used to be Bolis Armenians, Adapazarı Armenians, etc . . . I'm not sure how to name it, but . . . I *don't feel to be outside* [of it] here', he replied. Garabed, a publisher in his mid-sixties, is a third-generation Istanbulite whose grandfathers have come to the city from Tekirdağ and Çorlu, both located further to the West of Istanbul (hence even farther from the territories others would consider to be the 'Armenian homeland'). He shares the feeling of 'living on my native lands, on the lands of my great-great-grandfathers', with many other Istanbul Armenians I met. When he stated that he has 'never, ever, never since my young ages felt to be diasporic here', and explained that feeling by the fact that 'we have a past here, come, let me show you our centuries-old cemeteries', I asked, thinking that I had understood him, whether it was 'the antiquity of the community *despite being outside the homeland*' that made him feel a local. 'But where is the homeland? That's not that clear either . . . ', he said rejecting my exclusion of Istanbul from the 'homeland'.

Thus, when Istanbul Armenians deny being diasporic, they might do so based on a genuine feeling of belonging to the territories in which they currently live and which they consider to be their – in fact all Armenians' – homeland. Importantly, this homeland is not a *Turkish* homeland, in which case Matiossian's counter-argument about a confusion between 'Turkish diaspora' and 'Armenian diaspora' would be analytically well placed.[58] When I asked Sibil, a woman of the same generation as Garabed, herself born in the eastern province of Erzurum but living in Istanbul for decades, whether she meant Turkey by 'my country' in her 'I am still living in my country', she countered: 'Not Turkey. These lands. When I say these lands, I don't limit myself to the times of the Turkish Republic.' This homeland, thus, is precisely about the *lands of Armenians* – not (to be) understood in a nationalist and exclusivist sense – about which Sarkis, a rock musician in his early thirties, was perhaps the most explicit: 'If you think about the old times, in Istanbul, in Van, everywhere here, Armenians used to live . . . hence, *we don't see Bolis to be outside the land of Armenians.*'[59]

Whereas other Armenians in Armenia, in the diaspora or even in Istanbul itself, might have a different geographical imagination of what constitutes the 'homeland of Armenians', they can surely not deny or overlook the subjective conception of that 'homeland' among Istanbul Armenians such as Aren, Garabed, Sibil, Sarkis and many others. Belonging to the subjective realm, homelands cannot be a matter of externally imposed definition. In this sense, 'not [to] feel to be outside [the homeland]', in the words of Aren, is empirically equivalent to *not* being outside the homeland. It means, in other words, being in one's homeland. How, then, can Aren and the others be diasporic Armenians? In these cases, even evidence of connections with the Republic of Armenia, with Historical Armenia or with Armenian diasporic communities in different corners of the world would not entail diasporicity.

Problems within the 'not diaspora' thesis

Though I do not intend to attend to all reasonings behind the 'not diaspora' argument (especially to ones that are already duly addressed elsewhere[60]), I will address a few commonly voiced rationalizations of it that are problematic in contrast to the legitimate 'homeland' justification discussed above. Not everyone on the 'not diaspora' side of the debate perceives Istanbul to be (part of) a homeland of Armenians. Some of my Istanbul Armenian interlocutors have openly rejected to include the city within their imagined 'our lands', while vehemently rejecting to be categorized as diasporic.

One rationalization goes as follows: although Istanbul is not a homeland and Istanbul Armenians have left the 'real homeland' in the eastern part of Turkey, it would be incorrect to use the word 'diaspora' for people who have not crossed state boundaries. When I asked whether they thought of themselves as being diasporic Armenians, the Arık couple answered negatively, explaining that they 'have not left the historical lands'. When I wondered about the definition of those 'historical lands', Janet replied with a telling smile, 'not Istanbul, of course', as if correcting her previous statement. 'But you're in Istanbul', I replied. Sahag, her husband, intervened to respond that 'but Istanbul is still within the boundaries of the same government [*sic*]', and let Janet continue: 'My mother left Sivas and came to Istanbul, my father came out of Malatya . . . but they stayed in the same country, they did not go elsewhere'. Unlike in the case of people discussed in the previous section, the reference point for this couple was not a loosely defined '(home)land of Armenians', including Istanbul, but the 'country', the 'government', that is the Turkish state. A similar conversation occurred with a high-ranking priest in the Armenian Apostolic Church who was quick to correct his 'Turkey is our lands' to 'rather, some regions in Turkey used to be our lands'. 'You mean not *Bolis*?' – I was keen not to misinterpret the distinction he made. 'Yes, of course. That's separate. And we always say that if an Armenian tells you that they're Istanbulite, they are lying. Armenians are not Istanbulites. Though there has been an Armenian presence here since the 5th century, [it] has developed only with time', he replied, confirming that he excludes Istanbul from his vision of 'our [historical] lands'. Soon, however, he argued that they are not diasporic because 'diaspora means being dispersed, whereas we now live in our lands', thus contradicting himself. Responding to my request for clarification, he explained, 'it's because our roots and this place [Istanbul] are within the boundaries of the same country . . . therefore we are not dispersed. Even if we are dispersed, we are dispersed within the same land. The country has not changed'.

What appears in these examples is a confusion between two spatial-conceptual categories: 'our (historical) lands' and 'the country'. For the Arık couple, the priest and several others among my interlocutors, the two categories are, importantly, distinct. Unlike the others for whom Istanbul is unequivocally part of a larger, perhaps abstract, homeland of Armenians, they do not perceive their city of residence as a 'homeland' or as part of 'our lands', and they express this quite explicitly. In practice, however, and especially when thinking about being diasporic or not – or, in fact, reacting to the existing debates or questions concerning the issue – they find it difficult to distinguish between the two categories, which apparently alternate, intersect and even blend, thus leading them to confusion when it comes to questions of territorial boundaries, dispersion and diasporicity. Although they have left 'our lands' for Istanbul, they have not left any tangible 'country' in the sense of a nation-state. And it is the (Turkish) nation-state framework that eventually dominates in their self-analysis of being diasporic Armenians or not, even though the question of dispersion and diasporicity is, in reality, independent of it and is rather situated, as they are aware, within the context of their *Armenian* identities and their 'homeland' *as Armenians*. Their high awareness of a 'here' defined in terms of the country's political borders, perhaps resulting from the nation-state's long-term 'spatialization effect',[61] leads them to adopt a methodological nationalism when trying to make sense of their (non-)movement, (non-)dispersion and (non-)diasporicity as Armenians, as they reproduce and apply the nation-state as a primary unit of analysis and limit their analytical focus to its boundaries.[62] Some, like Vahe, are more conscious of the internal contradiction in their thoughts. 'Real Armenia is in Turkey now', he tried to explain his rejection of the 'diasporic' label, 'it's Kars, it's Van . . . *Bolis* not really . . . but since *Bolis* is also in Turkey, we're letting it pass!', he explained himself laughingly. Matiossian's critique maintaining that 'we are speaking about the Armenian diaspora, not the Turkish diaspora',[63] is surely pertinent in the case of this line of reasoning which, incidentally, is not restricted to the *emic* field. For instance, in a passing remark in the conclusion of his book, Armenian author Ruben Melkonyan finds Istanbul Armenians' assertion about 'residing in a country in which a large part of historical Armenia is situated' to be a 'well-grounded justification' for their rejection of being categorized as 'diasporic Armenians'.[64]

Commonly voiced variants of this rationalization focus on the experiential dimensions of remaining within the boundaries of the same nation-state in which the perceived 'original homeland' is also located. Some Istanbul Armenian interlocutors, for instance, bring up the fact of 'still living in a more or less similar environment' due to linguistic, cultural and sociopolitical continuities between the 'here' of Istanbul and the 'there' of their Anatolian hometowns belonging to the same Turkish national space. Whereas some of them voiced this in parallel to considering Istanbul as (part of) the 'homeland', others employed it as an argument for non-diasporicity while *not* including Istanbul in their vision of 'homeland', which made their argumentation problematic, again. Yet others argued that they are not diasporic because they have stayed 'very close' to the original lands which, though elsewhere, always remain very easily accessible for them. Hermine, a middle-aged woman working in an Armenian organization in Istanbul, perceived contemporary Armenia and her parents' hometowns *Kharpert* (Harput) and Tokat as her 'homelands', whereas Istanbul merely as 'the place where I was born and raised due to circumstances, that's it'. Nevertheless, she argued against being diasporic because 'we have remained within the borders of the same country and, being its citizens, we can go to Kharpert and Tokat whenever we want'. Mr Arık similarly argued, 'I can easily and freely go to my homeland, I mean to Gürün, *Sepasdia* (Sivas), Kars, etc . . . unlike you or others in the diaspora, I don't go there as a tourist, I go there as a local! So maybe this is what gives me that feeling [of not having left the homeland/of not being diasporic].' Mari, a documentary filmmaker in her late twenties at the time, defined her expression 'our lands' as 'Diyarbakır, Kars, Gessaria . . . no, Istanbul has never been our land in that sense', but was nevertheless stating that 'we are not a diaspora'. When I asked to elaborate, she explained: 'because we're in the same state today ... I can go to Diyarbakır, rent a house and reside there whenever I want, whereas you can't ... or you would need a visa and so on ... but in my case, since I am a citizen of Turkey, that is still *my land* in a way'.

These arguments, whether asserting that 'we have not gone anywhere' based on the cognitive-geographic framework of the Turkish nation-state or referring to experiential continuities and the practical accessibility of the 'old lands' resulting from remaining within the same polity, fall short of proving the non-diasporicity of the people who voice them. In fact, the literature in diaspora studies has developed a particular term for diasporas who live within the boundaries of the same polity in which the place they consider to be their original homeland remains: 'intrastate diasporas'.[65] That concept could well apply to these individuals who *themselves* exclude Istanbul from the geography *they* consider to be their homeland – in case, importantly, they also meet the other core characteristics of diasporicity discussed above. In this sense, their *self-categorization* as 'non-diasporic' (independently of the subjective/political motivations that it may also have, as discussed elsewhere[66]) does not suffice for us to accept their 'non-diasporicity' as an analytical category – all the more so if/when they hold at least a mental link with those distant (though accessible) lands which they consider to be their 'real homelands' in contrast to their city of residence.

Are Istanbul Armenians diasporic? Concluding remarks and directions for future research

Having dissected and analysed the main existing arguments in the debate, I can now address the troubled question myself. A methodologically rigorous approach lets us identify at least two[67] categories of people in the community: *diasporic Armenians of Istanbul* and *non-diasporic Armenians of Istanbul*. Lest we get drawn into a 'groupist' approach dismissing internal heterogeneity,[68] we should avoid seeking totalizing answers for the whole of the *Bolsahayut'iwn*, and instead make a case-by-case assessment of individual Istanbul Armenians.

The diasporic category consists of all those who – independently of whether they self-identify as 'diasporic' or not – meet *both* of the following conditions. First, they perceive Istanbul, hence themselves, as being *outside* the '(home)land of Armenians' however conceived and defined; second, they foster and maintain active links and connections, whether mental, emotional or practical, with localities they consider to be (parts of) the homeland and/or with other Armenian communities and individuals in the broader Armenian diaspora. Those among the Armenians of Istanbul who 're-turn' to the 'real homeland' in the eastern parts of Turkey,[69] or are engaged with the Republic of Armenia – whether as a 'homeland' or a more abstract 'center for Armenians' as some of them prefer to say – through regular visits, commercial, educational, cultural activities, temporary residence or more recently citizenship acquisition, and/or participate in various activities in the Armenian diasporic network or otherwise in the 'cultural production in the contemporary Armenian diaspora',[70] all this *while also* considering themselves to be *outside* 'the homeland' (even if 'feeling close to it') in Istanbul, belong to this analytical category of diasporic Istanbul Armenians.[71] The non-diasporic category consists of all those Istanbul Armenians who do not meet either of those two preconditions. As much as it is analytically difficult to categorize as 'diasporic' those who perceive themselves as living in a '(home)land of Armenians', however vaguely defined but unequivocally including Istanbul as well, it is equally problematic to do so for those who do not manifest active diasporic stances towards and connections with a homeland elsewhere nor with other dispersed Armenian communities whatsoever, even if they do not consider Istanbul, perhaps nor any other place, to be (part of) their homeland.

Much as indefinite and theoretical this answer might be, it stands, I hope, analytically and methodologically coherent. As such, it could perhaps serve as a guiding model or framework for further research and discussion that goes beyond the question of *whether* Istanbul Armenians are diasporic Armenians (as some of them surely are, but some others are surely not), and studies the specificities and characteristics of, and changes and developments in, their being or not being diasporic. I thus end my discussion by suggesting a few alternative questions or directions for such research on Armenians in Istanbul (and beyond).

First, I suggest bringing temporality and history into the discussion. As diasporicity is a matter of stance, awareness and practice,[72] rather than essence predetermined merely by one's territorial location vis-à-vis the 'homeland', it can develop, mutate, increase or decrease among individuals and, hence, within communities with time. Tölölyan describes this process as follows:

> The diasporic category both loses adherents (to ethnicization and assimilation) and gains them from several sources: from the ranks of recent immigrants who begin to settle in the new country; or from ethnics who respond to the stimulation of increasingly facilitated transnational connections with the homelands; or, indeed, from among those who respond to the work of the transnational institutions whose mission is explicitly theorized as diasporic rather than only ethnic and local-communal.[73]

It is thus worth studying the evolution of the level of diasporicity within the Istanbul Armenian community *across time*. The recent decades, for instance, have been witnessing an increase in connections between Istanbul Armenians, the Republic of Armenia and Armenian communities elsewhere.[74] In earlier times, in contrast, Turkish state policies had resulted in 'the distancing of the Armenian community in Istanbul from the rest of the Armenian communities in the world and from the Republic of Armenia',[75] hence perhaps securing a condition of *not* becoming or *un*-becoming diasporic for a long time – at least in relation to the Armenian Republic and the worldwide Armenian communities. But it would be interesting to study the evolution of stances and feelings towards the old hometowns left in the eastern provinces of Turkey as well. Has there been, with time, a change of imagination or attitude towards 'our historical lands' in eastern Anatolia among Istanbul Armenians originating from there? The recent burgeoning of hometown associations of Armenians of Sivas,

Armenians of Malatya, Armenians of Sassoon, and the like in Istanbul and the increase in visits/pilgrimage trips from Istanbul to those parts of the country come to mind.[76] Whether this suggests a process of 'becoming diaspora' vis-à-vis the 'old homeland',[77] perhaps in parallel to a similar process towards contemporary Armenia considering increasing links and connections with it as well, might be a question for scholars to take up.

A second research strand could focus on what we can now call the '*Bolsahay* diaspora'. To be discerned from Armenians *in* Istanbul (whether diasporic or not), this consists of what has become, during the past decades, a transnational network of Armenians who have emigrated from Istanbul to different countries such as the United States, Canada and France. People and organizations in this network, like the 'Organization of Istanbul Armenians' in Los Angeles or the 'Cultural Association of Armenians from Istanbul' in Canada, build their local and translocal connections on the *Istanbul Armenian* dimension of their identities, anchoring their diaspora in Istanbul, which serves as a diasporic centre this time. Studying this diaspora, perhaps comparing it with Armenians (still) *in* Istanbul, could lead to further revelations and nuances about Istanbul Armenians' self-positioning in the wider Armenian world as well as their conceptions of home, homeland and 'diaspora'. It would also be worthwhile to examine whether and how this new process of diasporisation vis-à-vis Istanbul has impacted and/or relates to processes of diasporisation *in* Istanbul vis-à-vis one of the other possible Armenian homelands.

Finally, there is certainly much room for comparative work in which the characteristics, manifestations and evolution of Istanbul Armenians' diasporicity-or-not could be studied in juxtaposition with that of other Armenian communities elsewhere.[78] In this regard, comparing the (non-)diasporic stances and practices of Istanbul Armenians with those of other Armenians also residing 'close to the homeland' or in places that they might perceive to be part of the 'historical homeland', such as in various regions of Georgia and Iran, could be especially revealing. Another case of particular comparative relevance is the rather new community of post-Soviet Armenian migrants in Istanbul already showing signs of a process of diasporisation vis-à-vis Armenia.[79] Such comparative work could perhaps help overcome some of the methodological inaccuracies and a priori assumptions that might exist in conventional perceptions and depictions of yet other 'Armenian diaspora communities' that surely have their own complexities, specificities, internal diversities and contradictions.

Notes

1 All citations from Armenian or Turkish sources in this chapter are translated by the author.
2 Hrag Papazian and S. Aykut Öztürk, 'Between Passports and Belongings: Armenian Citizenship Acquisition among Armenians of Turkey', *Citizenship Studies* 27, no. 4 (2022): 481–97. doi:10.1080/13621025.2022.2151571
3 Verichan Ziflioğlu, 'Armenians Split Over Who Belongs to the "diaspora"', *Hürriyet Daily News*, 9 May 2011.

4 Ibid.
5 Khachig Tölölyan, 'Elites and Institutions in the Armenian Transnation', *Diaspora: A Journal of Transnational Studies* 9, no. 1 (2000): 107–36.
6 See 'H. Hakobyan Considers Hürriyet's Misinformation about her Speech to be a Provocation' [translated title], *Armenpress*, 12 May 2011. https://armenpress.am/arm/news/652197; and Ruben Melkonyan, 'Shark'ayin T'urk'agan abadeghegadvut'yun', *Hayern Aysor*, 11 May 2011. https://old.hayernaysor.am/archives/2944; for other Istanbul Armenian voices rejecting the "diaspora" classification, see Gayane Abrahamyan, 'Are Turkish-Armenians a Diaspora?: Istanbul Journalist Says Turkey's Armenians Live in Their Historical Lands', *Armenia Now*, 19 May 2011; and Rober Haddeciyan, 'Diaspora bakanlığı tarafından bana verilen madalya hakkında', *HyeTert*, 26 January 2011. https://hyetert.org/2011/01/26/diaspora-bakanligi-tarafindan-bana-verilen-madalya-hakkinda/.
7 Vartan Matiossian, 'Is Bolis Diaspora or not?' [translated title], *Armeniaca*, 2 July 2011. http://armeniaca-haygagank.blogspot.com/2011/07/blog-post.html?utm_source=feedburner&utm_medium=email&utm_campaign=Feed%3A+Armeniaca-+%28ARMENIACA+-+%D5%80%D4%B1%D5%85%D4%BF%D4%B1%D4%BF%D4%B1%D5%86%D5%94%29; Kurken Berksanlar, 'Are Armenians of Turkey a Diaspora?', *HyeTert*, 23 May 2011. https://hyetert.org/2011/05/23/turkiye-ermenileri-diaspora-mi/
8 See for example, Ulf Björklund, 'Armenians of Athens and Istanbul: The Armenian Diaspora and the "Transnational" Nation', *Global Networks* 3, no. 3 (2003): 337–54; Ruben Melkonyan, *Review of History of the Armenian Community in Istanbul* (Yerevan: VMV-Print, 2010); Talin Suciyan, *The Armenians in Modern Turkey: Post-Genocide Society, Politics and History* (London, New York: I.B. Tauris, 2016).
9 Khachig Tölölyan, 'The Contemporary Discourse of Diaspora Studies', *Comparative Studies of South Asia, Africa and the Middle East* 27, no. 3 (2007): 647–55.
10 The two fields have also some overlaps, as some of the voices who participate in the discussion on the scholarly, hence 'etic', level, are Armenians from Istanbul themselves. See for example Suciyan, 'Diaspora Kim', *Taraf*, 20 October 2009. https://hyetert.org/2009/10/20/diaspora-kim-talin-sucuyan/ and *The Armenians in Modern Turkey*.
11 Matiossian, 'Is Bolis Diaspora or not?'; See also Razmik Panossian, *The Armenians: From Priests and Kings to Merchants and Commissars* (New York: Columbia University Press, 2006), 34.
12 Berksanlar, 'Are Armenians of Turkey a Diaspora?'.
13 Ibid.
14 See Hakem Al-Rustom, 'Rethinking the "Post-Ottoman": Anatolian Armenians as an Ethnographic Perspective', in *A Companion to the Anthropology of the Middle East*, ed. Soraya Altorki (Hoboken, NJ: Wiley-Blackwell, 2015), 452–79; and Suciyan, *The Armenians of Modern Turkey*.
15 Matiossian, 'Is Bolis Diaspora or not?'.
16 Suciyan, 'Diaspora Kim'.
17 Suciyan, *The Armenians in Modern Turkey*, 15.
18 For more on the Armenian Plateau, see Robert H. Hewsen, 'The Geography of Armenia', in *The Armenian People from Ancient to Modern Times*, ed. Richard G. Hovannissian (New York: St. Martin's Press, 1997), 1–17.
19 All interview excerpts in this chapter are translated from the original Western Armenian to English by the author.

20 Robin Cohen, *Global Diasporas: An Introduction* (Seattle: University of Washington Press, 1997), x.
21 Steven Vertovec, 'Three Meanings of "Diaspora", Exemplified among South Asian Religions', *Diaspora: A Journal of Transnational Studies* 6, no. 3 (Winter 1997): 277.
22 Khachig Tölölyan, 'Rethinking *Diaspora*(s): Stateless Power in the Transnational Moment', *Diaspora: A Journal of Transnational Studies* 5, no. 1 (1996): 8.
23 Rogers Brubaker, 'The "Diaspora" Diaspora', *Ethnic and Racial Studies* 28, no. 1 (2005): 1–19.
24 William Safran, 'Diasporas in Modern Societies: Myths of Homeland and Return', *Diaspora: A Journal of Transnational Studies* 1, no. 1 (1991): 83.
25 Walker Connor, 'The Impact of Homelands Upon Diasporas', in *Modern Diasporas in International Politics,* ed. Gabriel Sheffer (London: Croom Helm, 1986), 16.
26 Safran, 'Diasporas in Modern Societies', 83–4.
27 Ibid., 85; For a similar argument about the Parsees being *non*-diasporic despite their dispersal see Cohen, *Global Diasporas*, 188–9.
28 Tölölyan, 'The Contemporary Discourse of Diaspora Studies', 648.
29 Ibid; see also Tölölyan, 'Diaspora Studies: Past, Present, and Promise', IMI Working Papers Series, No. 55 (University of Oxford, UK, June 2012), 5–8.
30 Tölölyan, 'The Contemporary Discourse of Diaspora Studies', 648.
31 See George Shepperson, 'The African Abroad or the African Diaspora', in *Emerging Themes of African History*, ed. T. O. Ranger (London: Heinemann, 1968), 152–76.
32 See, for an example, Suciyan, *The Armenians in Modern Turkey*.
33 Tölölyan, 'The Contemporary Discourse of Diaspora Studies', 649.
34 Ibid.
35 Tölölyan, 'Elites and Institutions in the Armenian Transnation', 108.
36 Tölölyan, 'Diaspora Studies', 212 (emphasis mine).
37 Brubaker, 'The "Diaspora" Diaspora', 4.
38 Robin Cohen, 'Solid, Ductile and Liquid: Changing Notions of Homeland and Home in Diaspora Studies', QEH Working Paper Series, No. 156 (University of Oxford, UK, October 2007).
39 Cohen, *Global Diasporas*, 25–6.
40 See Paul Gilroy, *The Black Atlantic: Modernity and Double Consciousness* (London: Verso, 1993).
41 Tölölyan, 'Diaspora Studies', 9 (Emphases mine).
42 'Radial' taken from Andrea Klimt and Stephen Lubkemann, 'Argument across the Portuguese-Speaking World: A Discursive Approach to Diaspora', *Diaspora: A Journal of Transnational Studies* 11, no. 2 (2002): 158; "Lateral" and "Decentered" from James Clifford, 'Diasporas', *Cultural Anthropology* 9, no. 3 (1994): 302–38.
43 Vertovec, 'Three Meanings of "Diaspora", Exemplified among South Asian Religions', 278–9.
44 Clifford, 'Diasporas', 322. (Original emphasis.)
45 Suciyan, *The Armenians in Modern Turkey*.
46 Ibid., 33. In addition to the phenomenon of 'perpetual exodus', she considers 'the loss of institutional and legal basis as a community' also to be a manifestation or evidence of Turkey's Armenians' 'becoming diaspora' (ibid., 15). This seems to echo her suggestion to 'build a more comprehensive conceptualization of the diaspora that includes the social, legal, institutional, cultural and economic experiences of Armenians remaining in Turkey after 1923' (ibid., 31). A consideration of those

post-genocidal conditions of Armenians makes Suciyan question 'to what extent "homeland" could have remained a homeland for survivors' and maintain that 'it is difficult to assume that the survivor generation felt at home in Istanbul or even in the provinces' (ibid., 31–2). This argument focuses, once again, merely on the aspect of not feeling to be in one's home/homeland – a supposition in this case – and does not attend to the forging of ties and connections that are fundamental to diasporicity and discussions thereof.

47 Tölölyan, 'The Contemporary Discourse of Diaspora Studies', 649–50.
48 Cohen, *Global Diasporas,* 24–5.
49 See Klimt and Lubkemann, 'Argument across the Portuguese-Speaking World', 151.
50 Brubaker, 'The "Diaspora" Diaspora', 12 (Emphasis mine); Robin Cohen, 'Diasporas and the Nation-State: From Victims to Challengers', *International Affairs* 72 (1996): 516.
51 See Klimt and Lubkemann, 'Argument across the Portuguese-Speaking World', 150. (Emphasis mine).
52 See Björklund, 'Armenian of Athens and Istanbul'.
53 See, for example, Ziflioğlu, 'Armenians Split over Who Belongs to the "diaspora"'; Haddeciyan, 'Diaspora bakanlığı tarafından bana verilen madalya hakkında'. See also Melissa Bilal, 'Longing for Home at Home: Armenians in Istanbul', *Thamyris/Intersecting,* no. 13 (2006): 55.
54 Liisa Malkki, 'National Geographic: The Rooting of Peoples and the Territorialization of National Identity among Scholars and Refugees', *Cultural Anthropology* 7, no. 1 (1992): 25.
55 Al-Rustom, 'Rethinking the "Post-Ottoman"', 464; See also Benedict Anderson, *Imagined Communities: Reflections on the Origin and Spread of Nationalism* (London: Verso, 1999).
56 See also Bilal, 'Longing for Home at Home', 56; and Panossian, *The Armenians,* 83–6.
57 Richard Hovannisian, and Armen Manuk-Khaloyan, 'The Armenian Communities of Asia Minor', in *Armenian Communities of Asia Minor,* ed. Richard G. Hovannisian (Costa Mesa, CA: Mazda Publishers, 2014).
58 Matiossian, 'Is Bolis Diaspora or Not?'.
59 Emphasis mine.
60 One such argument, duly criticized by Matiossian, 'Is Bolis Diaspora or not?', merely draws attention to the cultural importance of *Bolis* in Western Armenian history while not necessarily sharing – or at least not expressing – the view in which the perceived homeland of Armenians is not limited to current or historical Armenias and encompasses the city of Istanbul as well.
61 Michel-Rolph Trouillot, 'The Anthropology of the State in the Age of Globalization: Close Encounters of the Deceptive Kind', *Current Anthropology* 42, no. 1 (2001): 133.
62 Andreas Wimmer and Nina Glick Schiller, 'Methodological Nationalism and Beyond: Nation-State Building, Migration, and the Social Sciences', *Global Networks* 2, no. 4 (2002): 301–34.
63 Matiossian, 'Is Bolis Diaspora or not?'.
64 Melkonyan, *Review of History of the Armenian Community in Istanbul,* 95; See also 'H. Hakobyan Considers Hürriyet's Misinformation about her Speech to be a Provocation'.
65 Khachig Tölölyan, 'Exile Government in the Armenian Polity', *Journal of Political Science* 18, no. 1 (1990): 128, and 'Rethinking *Diaspora*(s)', 6.
66 Although the matter lies outside the scope of this chapter, which is concerned not as much with *subjective motivations* behind the (self-)categorization of Istanbul

Armenians as "diasporic" or "not diasporic" as much as with the *content and logic of arguments* behind such (self-)categorization, a comprehensive analysis of the range of possible reasons behind many Istanbul Armenians' *self-identification as* – not to equate with *state of* – being "non-diasporic" should certainly take into consideration their political motivations as well. Scholars have already pointed at some of the structural conditions encouraging such discourse that proactively denies "diaspora" or "diasporic" as descriptive labels, including issues of exclusion, marginalization and invisibility that push Istanbul Armenians to react with a constant affirmation of belonging to and of having roots within their place/country of residence (see Bilal, 'Longing for Home at Home', 59), and Turkey's long-term dehumanization of the 'Armenian diaspora' which would naturally discourage the country's Armenians from adopting such self-categorisation (Suciyan, *The Armenians in Modern Turkey*, 31–2).

67 A third potential category might be composed of those occupying a liminal position, that is being in a process of either becoming or ceasing to be diasporic.
68 Rogers Brubaker, 'Ethnicity Without Groups', *Archives Européennes de Sociologie* 43, no. 2 (2002): 163–89.
69 See Tölölyan, 'The Contemporary Discourse of Diaspora Studies', 649.
70 Tölölyan, 'Elites and Institutions in the Armenian Transnation', 125.
71 See, for example, Melis Solakoğlu, 'Hamahaygagan'da hazırlıklar tamam', *Agos*, 30 June 2015; Papazian and Öztürk, 'Between Passports and Belongings'; Miran Manukyan, 'Euro Armenian Games'te İstanbul da var', *Agos*, 24 February 2016; and Björklund, 'Armenians of Athens and Istanbul'.
72 Brubaker, 'The "Diaspora" Diaspora'.
73 Tölölyan, 'Elites and Institutions in the Armenian Transnation', 113.
74 See Bilal, 'Longing for Home at Home', 61; Björklund, 'Armenians of Athens and Istanbul', 436; and Papazian and Öztürk, 'Between Passports and Belongings'.
75 Suciyan, *The Armenians in Modern Turkey*, 32.
76 See, for example, Siranush Ghazanchyan, '1,100-year-old Armenian church in Van holds 10th Holy Mass since Reopening', *Public Radio of Armenia*, 5 September 2022.
77 Tölölyan, 'The Contemporary Discourse of Diaspora Studies', 649.
78 See for example Björklund, 'Armenians of Athens and Istanbul'.
79 See Hrag Papazian, 'Contesting Armenianness: Plurality, Segregation, and Multilateral Boundary Making among Armenians in Contemporary Turkey' (PhD diss., University of Oxford, 2020), 190–207; see also Lülüfer Körükmez, 'Ulus-ötesi göç ağları ve sosyal alanların oluşumu: Ermenistan'dan Türkiye'ye işgücü göçü üzerine sosyolojik bir araştırma' (PhD diss., Ege University, 2012); and S. Aykut Öztürk, 'En Route to Unity: Armenian Travelers and Dwellers in Twenty-First-Century Turkey' (PhD diss., University College London, 2019).

Afterword

Armenian diaspora studies and its transformative supplement, the study of diasporas

Khachig Tölölyan

This essay originates from a talk I gave at the conference celebrating the forty-fifth anniversary of the Society for Armenian Studies, held at UCLA on 12–13 October 2019. It proposes a reorientation of Armenian diaspora studies and a recalibration of our thoughts and practices for thinking about the past, current practices, and the future of the Armenian diaspora.

To begin: it is critical to affirm the relevance of not just the scholarly study of the Armenian (or indeed any other) diaspora but also the serious investigation of *what that diaspora says about itself*. This emic discourse, as I shall call it, appears in a variety of media; it produces debate, performs culture, tinkers with, adjusts and ultimately reconstructs the differences that distinguish the diaspora from the larger society in which it is embedded and so constructs itself anew – reconstructs its 'identity', as some scholars of diaspora would put it.

The second issue has to do with 'power'. Scholars of diaspora acknowledge that the larger, sometimes hostile, 'host' society in which a diaspora is embedded, and above all the state that regulates the life of that society, are endowed with power: diasporas only flourish to the extent that state power permits. Broadly speaking, this is always true. But what too habitually follows this assertion is the conclusion that lacking state power, diasporas are therefore powerless. Among some scholars on the cultural Left, the powerlessness attributed to diasporas makes them virtuous, exempting them from the kinds of wrongs committed by the nation-state. Given the complex conceptions of power now available in the larger scholarly discourse, my own view is that the simple binary of state power and diasporic powerlessness is inadequate. Starting in the mid-1990s, I named 'stateless power'[1] as a diasporic issue; this umbrella term embraces multiple forms of diasporic power *and* powerlessness. Diasporas can negotiate within the constraints of state power and diasporic elites can exercise power within their own communities. The stateless society of diasporas is not necessarily apolitical or exempt from the operations of power.[2]

There is also a third issue that *should* be engaged: the changing vocabulary in Armenian and English of the simplifying binary of 'diaspora' and 'homeland'. Home, homeland and nation have not always designated a fixed territory or a consistent concept and state of collective being; neither have the terms designating diaspora, exile, mobility, hybridity and transnationalism. Though this complexity is generally acknowledged, its implications for both the scholarly and lay studies of the contemporary Armenian diaspora have not received consistent attention. This essay cannot address that evasion as an independent topic. But some of the changing meanings of homeland, pre-diasporic scattering and post-genocide diaspora are dealt with in my discussion of the diaspora's reflections of itself.

To be clear: I do not summarily dismiss the binary oppositions I name and intend to query – diaspora studies versus study of diasporas, power and powerlessness, diaspora and homeland – as useless. Each is useful in certain contexts. Nevertheless, I aspire in each case to question and rethink a polarized duality that has structured, even dominated, an aspect of Armenian diasporic discourse, because representations framed under the influence of those binaries can hinder collective thought and action.

I.

The first opposition I want to address contrasts multidisciplinary diaspora *studies*, which has fully emerged in academic contexts since 1991 and is conducted with scholarly rigour, with the *study* of diasporas, variously conducted for centuries by literate members of diasporic communities, such as religious leaders, intellectuals, teachers, columnists and essayists. Such cultural workers are in the category Jeff Perl names 'civilian scholars'[3]: they are not quite academics, are not university-based, do not publish research in professional, refereed journals, and so in the strictest sense are not 'scholars' at all. But Perl (who is not writing about diasporas) believes their discourse has specific intellectual value and social efficacy. As do I. In this essay, the thought of such people, developed in the study of diasporas, matters a great deal. Furthermore, those who '*study* diaspora' in my sense of the verb include two other categories of cultural workers that are usually excluded from the scholarly, yet in this matter are connected. One includes performers and artists; the other is comprised of rhetoric-wielding aspirants to institutional positions and political leadership within the diaspora.[4] While these cultural and political workers are distinct in their varied practices, all contribute to the 'study' of diasporas. In this context, 'study' refers to the self-conscious cultivation of and play with diasporic language, tropes, behaviours and representations, unchecked by scholarly or disciplinary procedures. Such practices qualify as 'study' in that they require a deep understanding of, and fluency in, a diaspora's self-constitutive use of language and the quotidian arts as well as the practice of everyday life.[5]

I have been convinced for some time that we as scholars of diaspora studies in general and of Armenian diaspora studies in particular have not sufficiently scrutinized the work of either 'civilian scholars' or non-academic, diasporic citizens who write articles and books – some quite thoughtful, others risible – and who make speeches at commemorative events, deliver non-scholarly but nonetheless serious lectures, present talks at Zoomed seminars and conferences, and generally offer ideas, analyses and often partisan arguments in the context of popular discourse in print and pixel. In other words, we have declined to attend sufficiently to a particular kind of Armenian public sphere.

There is an enormous range of knowledge and learning among those who participate in this group: some are presentist, barely versed in the history and cultural heritage of the community, while others possess a detailed knowledge of their own diaspora community and know a great deal about aspects, at least, of the entire Armenian diaspora. For example, any reader of Sisag H. Varjabedian's multivolume *Hayerě Lipanani mēch, 1925-1980*[6] (The Armenians in Lebanon, 1925-1980) will be impressed by its combination of the objective presentation of events, mixed with more partisan recollections depicting his own role in the collective debate. Varjabedian represents, interprets, criticizes, prescribes and moralizes – in all but this last function, he is a memoirist functioning as a civilian scholar.

Similarly, figures as diverse as H. J. Siruni, Arshag Alboyajian and Mesrovp Jacob Seth, writing respectively on the Armenian community of Istanbul (whose status as a diaspora is disputed), the history of Armenian diasporas, and India's Armenian diaspora,[7] have not only contributed to our knowledge about these diasporas, but also, even in their shortcomings, have raised productive questions about if and how highly localized and sedentary diaspora communities together, additively, constitute a real Armenian Diaspora with distinct properties of its own; what the role and value of the concept of 'diaspora' is within the daily life of any specific diasporic 'community'; and how secondary diasporas orient themselves towards originating sites of migration, whether a primary diasporic community, a homeland region or the homeland. Does Seth represent the Indian Armenian diasporic community as a dispersion from Armenia? Old Jugha? Nor Jugha? Works like Seth's act as ripostes (whether or not fully intended) to the tendency of those scholars who see diasporas as dispersions from a central homeland, 'a *supposed* centre', as Boris Adjemian cautions (in this volume, p. 29).

One way of domesticating my dissident emphasis on the binary of study/studies is to turn to the more familiar distinction between emic and etic in the social sciences. This terminology first emerged within linguistics in the 1950s. A native speaker of her language, say Kessab Armenian, speaks her dialect fluently, but she may not be able to articulate a single grammatical rule underpinning it; she does not need that knowledge or metalanguage in order to speak. It is the linguist who uncovers and maps the unconsciously operating machinery of a native language. I use *emic* to designate the ways in which people perform and understand the meanings of their performances within their diasporic language and culture, and *etic* to indicate how external observers, ranging from scholars to dissident intellectuals, perceive an order and attribute meanings within the emic sphere that are not obvious to members of the community under study.

Both the emic and etic practices and understandings have validity and value. Scholars of the Armenian diaspora must acknowledge the need for a challenging conversation between the emic understanding of diasporans and what we as scholars may interpret differently. When scientists work on, for example, atoms or bacteria, there is no consciousness in those objects of knowledge that can respond to them and express dissent. But the diaspora is an *object* of scholarly knowledge that yet consists of speaking *subjects* who through their own study and performance of diaspora can talk back, report different perceptions and experienced meanings, and contest our interpretations. Indeed, in the Armenian instance, their existence is a precondition for our own work and interventions. Hence the need for scholars to engage more directly with the ways in which the citizen scholars and cultural workers experience, understand and perform their diasporicity in texts and performances they produce, now and in the past.

I am aware that there are ongoing debates over the value of emic research versus etic research.[8] If here I emphasize emic study, it is because I believe that with the possible exception of anthropology, scholarly research in the social sciences consistently underestimates the thoughtful work of culture conducted by members of the diaspora communities they study. This includes Armenian scholars. We do not yet know how to incorporate into our research the quotidian cultural production of diasporic Armenians, production that is not merely automatic repetition but entails thought and brings change. (Even the dismissal of repetition is itself problematic. Much repetition is unself-conscious, but thoughtful repetition – along with the recovery of lost or forgotten texts and practices – can also function as consequential cultural and intellectual practice.)

Before turning to the emic formulations and understandings of pre-genocide Armenians' understanding of their lives as 'pre-diasporic' (*Nakha- sp'iwrk'ean*, in Father Karnig Koyounian's words[9]), I offer one example of the usefulness of thinking in terms of the emic. In discussion and argument with me (between 1983 and 1985), the late Armenian philosopher Garbis Kortian repeatedly argued, as he also did at an inaugural conference of the Zoryan Institute), that 'Armenians have no philosophy'. He was right in the sense that if philosophy is the Western discipline first elaborated by Socrates, Plato and Aristotle, altered yet sustained by Descartes, Spinoza, Kant, Hegel, Sellars and Singer, the Armenian cultural tradition has virtually no philosophy. Yet it's worth remembering that professional philosophers are usually focused on their particular genre of rigorous thought, which is disciplined and disciplinary in its questions and the forms that answers must take; they find most popular thought inadequate *as thought*, full of faulty premises and invalid arguments. Certainly, Professor Kortian affirmed the contrast of philosophical as against unsystematic popular *thought* and did not properly evaluate the latter.

In fact diasporic and other lives are daily thought about and discussed in public by both civilian scholars and ordinary Armenians, albeit without philosophical precision and its specialized vocabulary; this does not make such thought irrelevant or *inconsequential* either to diasporic studies or to diasporic life. Canny politicians do not make that error of judgement; good analysts of culture shouldn't, either. Faulty, or merely extra-disciplinary thought is also and still thought, and it is often consequential, particularly in diasporic societies where neither the state nor academia can authorize and regulate thought. Within Armenian studies, both Vartan Matiossian and I have stressed that understanding the thought practice inherent in many kinds of cultural productions is essential. Armenians have studied and thought about their situation of dispersion in poetry and song, pre-professional historical writings and memoirs, in journalism and comedy. Poems also think, films think, music lyrics think and arguably all cultural performers and products think, not just about how and what they make but often also for whom. Their specific audience and their larger society overlap; both are rethought and reworked by their production and consumption of cultural products.

I would further argue that we do not yet have a proper grasp of the ways in which, starting in the eleventh century, Armenians – while thinking of the dispersion precipitated by the attacks of the Seljuk Turks, the end of the Bagratuni dynasty and the destruction of Ani – developed in self-study their consciousness of themselves as a kind of proto-diaspora, a Diaspora in the making. Their aristocratic leaders, artists and the organic intellectuals (in Gramsci's sense) attached to them – scribes, monks and poets – were pressed to formulate a vocabulary and give an account of their new collective situation. Almost a millennium before *sp'iwṛk'* became a standard designation of 'diaspora', Armenians had begun to think anxiously about their dispersion in a variety of *emic* locutions, vocabularies and texts. It is almost impossible to exaggerate the extent of this, as Vartan Matiossian's brief but rich study of *bantukhd*s demonstrates.[10] I will mention a few examples, to both suggest the omnipresence of the topic and the way in which Armenians – who were dispersed from and remembered a conquered homeland – saw themselves in danger of becoming like the Jewish people, whose dispersal they knew both from biblical texts and from observation in Mesopotamia, Persia and the Crimea.

Once Armenians were Christianized, the Jewish experience of exile and dispersion became a constant example and indispensable resource for thinking about their own situation. Matiossian tells us that the word *bantukhd* permeates the *Asdwadzashunch'*, the classic translation of the Bible achieved by 438 CE, where it is used sixty-one times. The thought of expulsion, and consequently of having to live in a strange land, emerges astonishingly early. From the perspective of the Hebrew Bible, human life begins with the punitive expulsion of Adam and Eve from Paradise, and the Jewish people are formed in homelessness. In Genesis 15.13, the Lord says unto Abram, who will become Abraham: 'Know of a surety that thy seed shall be a stranger in land that is not theirs, and shall serve them', meaning that Abraham's people will live in dispersion, exile, *galut*, subjugation, in what we now call diaspora, serving Egyptians and perhaps others. And again, in Genesis 23.4 the issue is raised when Abraham says to the people of Hebron, 'I am a stranger and a sojourner with you'. The *Asdwadzashunch'* renders these words as: Bantukhd ew nzhteh em i mich' tserum; the two words *bantukhd/pandukht* and *nzhteh/nzhdeh* are prominent in medieval Armenian self-description, and signify respectively one who dwells in a foreign *home* and a sojourner in a foreign *land* (Ajaryan). In a highly significant inversion of customary thought, Nation and Homeland do not simply precede Diaspora. The Jewish people are as yet unsettled; they consolidate their covenantal identity over time, both with Abraham, before the collective exile to Egypt, and again in the Sinai desert, on the way to the land that they would conquer, settle and call Homeland. The vocabulary of dispersion and wondering, derived from the Torah, persists in the Greek version of the Alexandrian Septuagint, where the word 'diaspora' is used twelve times (though not as a synonym to *galut/gaghut* or exile but rather to 'scattering'), and then in the New Testament. There is a long history of the use of 'diaspora' in succeeding early Christian texts that I will not engage; Bishop Arowele's account of that tradition is unmatched and does not bear repetition.[11] I have lingered on these details to underscore that the semantic domain of diaspora emerges in religious and then popular discourse two millennia before scholars get around to it, just as I am arguing that Armenians think about their diasporicity for a near-millennium before they come to routinely use the word *sp'iwṛk'* in their discourse. It is important to note that a people can form by self-consolidation in a state of enforced mobility before they settle in territory they will eventually know as their Homeland.

Around 440 CE, Pavsdos Byuzant attributes to Bishop Daniel an accusation directed at King Diran in which he charges the king with '. . . ew ts'ruests'ik sahmank' tser orbēs ew Israel' (scattering your/across borders, like Israel/the Jews). Centuries later, Aristakes Lastivertsi writes, 'Zi gamnets'aw dēr ardak'sel . . . ts'ruel ew heṛats'ust'anel zmez ent azks awdars . . . iprew Israel hawurs Eghiayi ew zSamaria hawurs Eghishēyi.' (For the Lord willed our expulsion . . . [deciding to] scatter us to distant places in the land of odars, of strangers . . . as he did to Israel in the days of Yeghia and to Samaria as in the days of Elijah.)[12] Lastivertsi speaks of *bantkhdanal* and *darakruil* from 'hayots' ashkharh', the Armenian world, starting at the very beginning of Book I. In two sentences he sums up the situational awareness and self-consciousness of his contemporaries: '. . . hasdadunk' hashkharhi i bantkhdut'ean iwreants' bandtkhdets'an ergrort ankam, ew eghen vdarantik' i tseṛanē *bantkhdots'* absdampats'. I sireleats' k'agdealk' zors och' sur sadageats' ts'ruets'an zōrēn asdeghats' moloragan goch'elots'.' (They became established as bantukhds for a second time [the first on the occasion of the expulsion from Eden], expelled by other rebellious bantukhds. Unlinked from those they loved, those [Armenians] not killed by the sword were scattered, wondering as if by the law of those meandering stars we call planets.) [Strikingly, he sees the Seljuk Turkish invaders who expel many Armenians from their homeland as "rebellious *bantukhds*", no longer residing in their homeland of West Central Asia].

As late as 1792, the early Armenian nationalist Joseph Emin said that he grieved 'for my religion and my country, [living] . . . like Jews, vagabonds upon the Earth'.[13] Elsewhere, in the fifteenth and sixteenth centuries, the *gharib* (from the Arabic, the 'estranged', usually in the West) and the *bantukhd* continued to be a theme in the poetic work of Mgrdich Naghash and Nahabed Kouchag. In the Cilician interlude of the eleventh to the fourteenth centuries, the Armenians of Cilicia appear to have had the Armenian homeland and their expulsion from it in mind even as they settled as a territorialized people. The precariousness of the position of the Cilician kingdom was a persistent issue. Grigor Skevratsi (1246–1301), addressing the military elite of the region in the late thirteenth century, writes that '. . . tadasdanaw darakrets'ak' i pun hayots' ashkharhēn ew ĕnt ldzov mdak' dērants' aylaserits' . . . i khnamots' Asdudzoy huyl hazadats'n hayots' pakhsdealk' egeal amrats'an i kawaṛn ...ew t'akawork' erewts'an hayots' azkis'. (By divine judgement you were expelled from the true land of the Armenians and passing under the yoke entered the territories of non-Armenians. By the grace of God the host of fleeing, free [non-serf] Armenians came and fortified these regions . . . and kings [literally crown-bearers] of the Armenian nation appeared.) Cilicia – which I have elsewhere called the first territorialized diaspora state; the second is Chinese-dominated Singapore – was ruled by elites that knew just where they came from in the abandoned homeland, knew they were defeated and dispersed and, even in their moment of Cilician victory, feared the precariousness that characterizes newly territorialized diasporas. Both Levon Ter Petrosyan and S. Peter Cowe have written of the constant, anxious efforts needed to secure a place among kingdoms for the Cilician principality. Cowe writes that 'the emerging principality sought to mold itself into a fixture on the Levantine geopolitical scene . . . the Cilician state's acceptance into the Western hierarchical structure afforded it much desired recognition and status'.[14] Such acceptance afforded an anxious elite an occasional sense of security, the kind diasporics often seek and rarely find.

It is from this same period that the most quoted use of passages concerning dispersion occurs. It comes in an encyclical by the Catholicos Nerses Shnorhali (served 1166–73), which marks the official recognition by the head of the Armenian Church that his flock now lives not only in Eastern Armenia and Cilicia but in regions outside even the largest extent of Historical Armenia.[15] He writes:

> Nersēs, servant of Christ, and by His mercy the Catholicos of the Armenians. To all the faithful of the Armenian nation, those in the East who inhabit our homeland Armenia, those who have *emigrated* to the regions of the West, and those in the Middle lands who were taken among foreign peoples, and who for our sins are *scattered* in cities, castles, villages and farms in every corner of the earth.

The word 'emigrated' does not fully render Nerses's *sahealk' nzhtehut'eamp*. 'Sahil' can designate either a controlled sliding or an unintended and uncontrolled stumbling into foreign lands.

I have lingered on these examples in order to stress that while lacking the modern Armenian word *sp'iwrk'* for diaspora, the medieval Armenian scribes, clergymen and poets conducted a sustained interpretation of Armenian history as dangerously parallel to those of the Jews and insistently pointed to scattering beyond the borders of Medz Hayk and the absence from an established home as a catastrophe. The latent diasporicity of the Armenian situation – never far from either the popular mind or the thought of the secular scribes – seems to have seen catastrophe as always pending; they were reminded of it by both the fall of Jerusalem and the laments or *Oghp*-s of the poets for other cities lost to Muslim powers by Christians in general and Armenians in particular, from medieval Jerusalem and Edessa to early modern Constantinople.

The post-genocide diaspora, like Cilicia, has repeatedly relived a conceptual, geopolitical and psychological version of the Cilician episode: not states but prosperous centres of sedentary Armenian diasporic life, of 'home', emerged in Haleb and Beirut and Iran, only to be shaken, dismantled or destroyed. Whereas diasporic life in the West avoids precariousness in the old sense, of course anxiety over the loss of collective identity and assimilation has taken its place in the emic imagination.

Between 1375 (the end of the Cilician state) and 1918, Armenians repeatedly formulated their understanding of both their state-deprived, borderless homeland (for 'border' is the construct of an operating state) and the episodically emerging stateless diaspora. As best as I can determine in conversation with specialists in the first half of that period, 'Hayots' Ashkharh' (The World of the Armenians) was used much more frequently to designate the old homeland than 'Hayastan' (Armenia), while 'Hayrenik'' was an eighteenth-century addition, a translation of the European 'Fatherland'.[16] I concur with the perhaps-counterintuitive hypothesis that 'the homeland is not necessarily a place that had existed prior to the being of a diaspora' (Boris Adjemian, in this volume, p. 32).[17]

This does not mean that some notion of a *place of origin* was altogether lost but that place, that 'home', was variously named, imagined and in some sense indeterminate. As Sebouh Aslanian has established in his indispensable oeuvre,[18] how the residents of Nor Jugha/Isfahan defined their homeland changed over the generations. Between 1605 and 1650, Old Jugha, from which they had been forcibly removed, was still identified as their home, but already by 1650, the children and grandchildren of the uprooted had come to enjoy the benefits of life as a prosperous and un-persecuted minority near Isfahan. Aslanian locates a reluctant admission of this attitude in Arakel Davrijetsi's *Book of Histories (1662, 1669)*, in which he notes that as New Julfans expanded their trade networks in Europe and Asia, especially India, they began to refer to New Julfa as 'home' and even homeland. As New Julfa declined further in the eighteenth century under the assaults of Afghans (*c*. 1722–49) and subsequent shifts in commercial travel, the Primate of the town asked wealthy merchants in India, Russia and the Netherlands for financial assistance to repair 'their' devastated town. He did so in terms that leave little doubt about where 'home' was – *not* in Armenia. He addressed those who 'orkʻ i spʻiwr̄kʻ ēk hamatarats ĕnd amenayn teghis ew terutʻiwns' (who are in dispersion and widespread in many states) for help. The encyclical appeals to their patriotic self-interest by reminding them that, 'at least after repairing it [Nor Jugha] and making it firm, you may also be able with God's help to return to your *fatherland*'. ('. . . te astutsov shineloyn yev hastateloyn hetĕ dukʻ ews dar̄naykʻ i hayrenis dser.') The 'fatherland' is emphatically Nor Jugha.

Aslanian additionally notes that two years later, in 1751, Khwaja Petros di Woskan, 'the most eminent Armenian merchant in Madras during the early part of the eighteenth century', left a substantial sum in his will to be used in New Julfa for the repair of homes, the payment of 'the town's tribute' (i.e. future taxes) and even for the building of a school to train students in the arts of theology, philosophy and the study of European languages. Woskan's patriotism – his profound attachment to New Julfa as his homeland can be seen in the way he narrates his life as a merchant travelling and trading throughout the network as far as Manila. As he puts it, 'from the time of my setting out from my own Country, I was desirous to spend the money I should get for the Good of *our People and Town*, which desire I have obtained, and thanks be to God for the Gift he has given me'. This Madras-based New Julfan stipulated in his will

> That after my Death according to the Pleasure of God and the Delivery of My Soul to Christ, they shall immediately send for a Physician and take My heart out of my body and prepare it with necessary Ingredients that it should not be corrupted and Shut it up in a Box . . . and [be] carried unto Julpha *to his own Country* for the sake of the Love thereof and the said heart is to be buried in 'the Great *town* of his Birth Place'.

Nor Jugha was, so to speak, his *polis* as Athens was Socrates's; Hellas and Armenia did not come before Athens and New Julfa.

It was not scholars of diaspora studies but clerics like Davrizhetsi, along with literate merchants, who wrote in various texts about where home and homeland were. They constituted and then reconstituted it in their words above all and in their actions, often. Only in the second half of the eighteenth century, when New Julfa declined irreversibly, did the great Armenian merchants of India begin to refer to a vaguely defined 'Armenia/Hayastan' as their homeland; eighteenth-century nationalism took hold not only in the Mkhitarist Father Chamchian's *History* but in the public sphere of Madras merchants. By the early 1800s, that sphere included literature.[19]

To continue to paraphrase Aslanian's invaluable account: fifty years or two generations later, by the 1770s, the idea that Julfa was a 'fatherland' to which the exiled merchants were expected to return, as anticipated in the encyclical, had 'all but faded from memory'. Indeed, a small group of Julfan merchants residing in the network's last surviving 'peripheral node' at British-administered Madras redefined the meaning of 'homeland/fatherland' (*hayrenikʻ*) and patriotism (*hayrenasirutʻiwn*). Under the influence of Enlightenment ideas concerning nation and nationalism surfacing in Europe and the Americas, these merchants displayed a new kind of nostalgic longing, no longer for their small mercantile suburb near Isfahan but for the lost 'original' homeland in 'historic Armenia', the site of their first dispersion inflicted on them in 1603–05 that led to the founding of New Julfa. This nostalgia for the original national homeland in 'Historic Armenia', and 'the corresponding erasure of Julfa as their fatherland and nodal center of their coalition and the network that once sustained it, became more acute as Julfan trade in India and particularly in Madras failed to show signs of recovery'.[20] The names and meanings attached to both places of origin and sites of dwelling were demonstrably mobile, fluctuating within a lexicon of exile and resettlement. None of these geographies of attachment took shape under or were guided by the scrutiny of diaspora scholars.

Earlier, I included 'performers and artists' in the provisional category of intellectuals and civilian scholars. Perhaps artists cannot be said to 'study' their medium and craft in the traditional scholarly sense, but prepare and study they do, and both their study and their performances are consequential intellectually, aesthetically and culturally. Even if this claim elicits considerable scepticism, it must be made and considered. Cultural forms have to be studied, whether in order to repeat and preserve or to alter them; artists and performers are continually engaged in this task. As scholars, we must take seriously and attend to the work of those who present and re-present a diasporic social formation's culture to itself; the paradox of such performance is that it both perpetuates and transforms tradition over time, because repetition is not perfect replication. Whether cementing loyalty to traditional forms or performing differently and so eliciting criticism or support, the repetition through performance of traditional culture acts as study if not always as scholarly analysis, and leads to energetic commentary. The alterations that traditional forms undergo during these not-quite-perfect repetitions lead to innovations that revise, reshape and sustain a culture in the long run.

Historically, diasporic music, literature, theatre and dance, along with other popular arts, both enabled preservation and occasioned small but cumulative change, and in these performances of change invited audiences to express and enact new ways of being Armenian in diaspora, doing Armenian things and interpreting Armenian meanings while also signifying their collective being to other citizens of the host land. Of course, literature sometimes does this magisterially, though usually in that form it reaches a small number of people. But at least one text, Shahnour's novel *Nahanchĕ arants' erki* (Retreat Without Song, Haratch Press, Paris, 1929), shaped the literate post-genocide diaspora's thinking about itself even before the word '*sp'iwṛk'*/diaspora' had begun to attain its current prominence in the Armenian lexicon for the scattering.[21] Antranig Dzarougian's *T'ught' aṛ Erevan*, Epistle to Yerevan (1946), a triumph of rhetorical performance, had a less long-lasting but major impact on diasporic discourse at a crucial moment when return migration to Armenia was being effected. In recent decades, in the US diaspora above all, as 'creative writing' and 'non-fiction' poetry and prose (and to a much lesser extent drama) have expanded, attracting many students and producing at least a dozen Armenian-American writers working in English; these modern scribes of culture have altered the spaces of expression and exploration in which a younger generation creates new challenges to (and more rarely endorsements of) diasporic Armenian norms. These authors do not always set out to address the diaspora explicitly or exclusively, but in so far as their narratives and analyses formulate views of ethnic and diasporic Armenian norms of 'belonging' – a crucial if misguided term – they are to be inscribed among the ranks of those who study diasporas in the sense that term has here. Whether they are as well known as William Saroyan and Michael Arlen were known at one time and Peter Balakian is known now, they are engaged in the interrogation and articulation of new ways of Armenian being.

I will not endeavour to address in any detail music, painting, theatre and dance as forms of the self-conscious study and reformulation of diasporic being, not because they are less important but for lack of space and because these are new Armenian practices and genres to which I have not been exposed as much as I would like to be. However, since music and video have become the apex of contemporary cultural practices, it is essential at the very least to acknowledge diasporic artists who experiment with American and global musical genres. In particular, contemporary 'rock', very broadly understood, has been a site for an exceptional degree of interaction between Western and Eastern Armenian diasporic elements, something that simply has not happened in literature. *System of a Down* and Gor Mkhitarian have fashioned a deeply hybridized music that speaks to Western Armenians in an idiom that melds together global rock and Eastern Armenian musical tastes and sensibilities.

Finally, the emergence of new spaces, first of the internet (1983), then the Web (1991) and finally of social media (c. 2000–4), has created a digital public sphere in which the genres engaged in the study of diaspora as defined above are evolving ever more rapidly. While the swift growth of the circulation on media of music and images and dance is well known, diaspora scholars have not yet analysed sufficiently the proliferation of *writing* and rhetoric-laden lay study, disputation and debate that has both changed and exploded online and in social media. This proliferation has enabled, on and off social media sites, the reiteration of ageing concepts in traditional rhetoric characteristic of the once-vibrant, now-fading Armenian print media to the digital universe. The sheer number of those who now write on social media (mostly in anger, cajoling and hectoring their audience) has grown to the point where we must invoke the difficult Hegelian concept concerning the relation of quantity and quality, to wit. Whereas at first an increase in quantity alters only proportion, within a given conceptual space, a spurt of large quantitative growth results in the emergence of a qualitatively different entity emerges, and we enter a new state. Today, the Armenian digital public sphere demands new conceptions of diasporicity.

Crucially, the digital spaces of diaspora and homeland remain distinct but not altogether separate. Diaspora Armenian figures, some well informed, others merely rhetorically skilled, are now interviewed endlessly by homeland television programmes that are circulated and followed on YouTube by thousands in the diasporic audience. The novelty and impact of this borderless discourse between diaspora and homeland audiences have not yet been assessed by media scholars, just as the hybridization of Armenian rock music by performers like Gor Mkhitarian has not been. Whether such contact will increase and alter the discourse of diasporic study remains to be seen – it must be seen. Certainly, much more homeland vocabulary penetrates the diasporic lexicon than the reverse. I do not know whether the flow is a productively interactive, two-way circulation, or a more amorphous, multi-modal dispersal. For example, we know that the writings and interviews of Jirair Libaridian are viewed by audiences in the Republic of Armenia and in the diaspora – yet he is a special case, a diasporan who held major posts in Armenia for years. To the best of my knowledge, we have no data as to whether highly popular Western Armenian writers and performers, like Vahe Berberian, are viewed either by recent emigrants from Armenia to Los Angeles or by audiences in the homeland; the barriers of language and un-shared experience and memory may be too great, for now. In this vein, the most hopeful development is, curiously, not in the study of diasporas, whose relevance I have been advocating, but in diaspora studies and related forms of Armenological scholarship. The barriers that separated the two were broken by the diasporic Richard Hovannisian's books four decades ago, and since then a trickle that has grown to a stream of exchange has developed.

II.

The questions of circulation and inter-action lead inevitably to the question of power.[22] I turn now to the possible meanings of 'power' in the diasporic condition of statelessness. The success or failure of old forms of stateless power and the innovation of new modes of deploying such power is highly uncertain, depending above all on permissiveness or indifference by the dominant state or society, and reliant on collective imagination and will, scarce and unpredictable resources for any polity – no outcomes can be guaranteed. I begin by stressing how extraordinary it is that *any* diaspora emerges and endures, reproducing some version of itself generation after generation instead of wholly assimilating to the dominant context. Consider what a state, or a nation-state secure in its homeland has that the diaspora lacks. The traditional nation may come into being as Benedict Anderson's 'imagined community', but its assets, therefore its powers, are not at all imaginary. It is endowed with concrete assets, such as a contiguous territory. It endures on the basis of both real and fictional kinship, through generally endogamous marriage and generational *filiation*, whereas diasporas are threatened by exogamy and shaped through voluntary, elective *affiliation*. Nations share land, language, history and collective memory, inculcated by means of state-supervised education and culture;

they often also share a religion, observe national holidays, live in a society of their own, work in an economy that binds them to each other, are united by service in an army and above all through necessary obedience to the laws of their state, which both enables and dominates them as its citizens and draws on their resources, gathering and augmenting the state's power. In modern times, Foucault argues, such a state produces and functions with what he called governmentality.[23]

What do diasporas have? They have no land of their own, though they sometimes have for a generation or three their territorialization in places like Beirut's Bourj Hammoud, Aleppo's Nor Kyugh, Isfahan's Nor Jugha, Istanbul's Kurtulus and perhaps Hollywood's Little Armenia. They do not live in one society or a single culture but in at least two. Diasporas also lack an economy they can call their own, even though many of their members may occupy an economic niche, be it as silk merchants in Persia in the seventeenth century or as the prominent artisans, machinists and mechanics of old Aleppo, who kept the tractors and trucks running during the crucial Jazira harvest. But niches do not add up, or measure up, to a national economy. A few Swiss and Canadian scholars have attempted to explore the notion of a diaspora economy, but I am not aware of any strong results. When it comes to non-state law, despite Mkhitar Gosh's *Datastanagirk'* and its importance in dispute settlement, the Armenian diaspora has generally lacked its own law courts. We might ask what can it possibly mean to speak of stateless power under such circumstances? Certainly, as one of the contributors in this volume, Vahe Sahakyan, has argued, 'diasporas are inherently ungovernmental'.[24] Yet some have existed and functioned with kinds of self-regulation and self-reproduction that invite us to think about what *un*governmental power might be. This requires a rethinking of power, especially in diasporic contexts. How does power work when diasporas are permitted to administer, supervise and even govern themselves to a large extent? And can diasporas exercise stateless power in the form of influencing the government of the state?

Over the past century, a heterogeneous lot of theorists have mused about the existence and efficacy of something other than the undisputed hard power exercised by nation-states. In international politics, they take into consideration the role of non-governmental organizations, ethical arguments, diasporas and transnational communities. In interstate situations, they consider the soft challenge of minorities, corporations and lobbies that can redirect or moderate the exercise of state power. The emergence of "soft" power in its cultural dimension is a by-now familiar addition to the conceptual deliberation concerning what I have called "stateless" power. Of course, all concerned understand that sovereign power, the power to monopolize violence, to jail, to take life either by execution or by drafting young men to go and die for their country, the power to tax people, all these and more belong to certain hegemonic elites and institutions. Decades ago, C. W. Mills invited passionate rebuttals by arguing[25] that the United States was a sovereign power whose state was operated by a tiny percentage of the population, by elites whose varieties he detailed. The sovereign hard power of the state, he argued, was subservient to the skilful exercise of the softer financial power of three or four kinds of elites who, if they did not control, certainly guided the state apparatus to serve their interests. State capture by bourgeois elites is an insight Marx already had by 1848. Mills was a professional sociologist, on the Left, and a fine popularizer. He and Gramsci shared a vision of most modern industrial societies as ultimately ruled by hegemonic economic and cultural elites possessed of overt and covert – what we might now call hard and soft – forms of power; the elites alter in composition over time but nevertheless perpetuate their hold on the state and civil society both. In various versions of his *Who Rules America?* (Oxford UP, 1967, 1983, 1998), William Domhoff updated and elaborated this version into a theory of overlapping elites (among which the economy predominates). Such formulations leave room for the possibility that socially consolidated, wealthy *diasporic* economic elites, including the Jewish in Europe, the Armenians in the Ottoman Empire and the Chinese in Southeast Asia,[26] might attain some sort of influence if not direct power (and thus elicit persecution from national majorities).

By contrast, Fritz Stern's portrayal of the relationship between Bismarck and the banker on whom he relied, Gerson von Bleichröder, challenges and successfully contradicts the notion that diasporic Jewish economic power could ever command or even reliably guide the German state power.[27] Whether certain 'middleman minority' (Zenner)[28] diasporas can ever attain state power remains questionable. But that they can acquire multiple softer forms of power in the economy, society and culture is demonstrable. Furthermore, that diasporic elites have in many times and places exercised mainly soft but sometimes even hard power *within* their own tightly bound communities is clear. Such power was exercised at certain moments by the church, the *amira* economic elite, the bourgeois authorities of Istanbul and Armenian political parties in Lebanon.[29]

We know that at various times the heads of Armenian church in the Ottoman Empire had the power to fine and even imprison dissenting and troublesome individuals, just as in the sixteenth and seventeenth centuries, the Jewish courts and councils of Venice and Amsterdam also had the authority to do the same, even excommunicating and stripping away religious identity in a place and time when such identity was crucial. Elsewhere, diasporic Armenians have even been known to kill fellow Armenians when institutional power struggles opened up a space for interpersonal violence.[30] But such displays of coercive power are the exception. Hitherto, the post-genocide modern Armenian diaspora has been sustained by elites, the institutions they controlled, the loyalties of ordinary Armenians they attracted and by their ability to mobilize the early communalism of the survivor generation. While of course every survivor needed to earn a living, she or he also yearned for collective goods – a functioning church, school, social clubs, charitable organizations, medical care – *social goods*, not primarily identitarian in nature, that did not require hard power to sustain them. Soft power was the rule, largely directing individual aspirations so that they were effectively channelled through social institutions. As a result, what emerged in the post-genocide Armenian Middle East for at least fifty years were communities that renewed themselves by recruiting new generations to dominant and elite-governed institutions that possessed the prerequisites of stateless power: links to state power, financial resources (meagre in many cases, substantial in others), a regulatory apparatus acknowledged by the community, social and cultural services, and resonating rhetoric that was able to reinvigorate popular consent for over two, sometimes three generations.

Such institutions never fully attracted the population of the displaced Armenians who were being organized as diasporic. In France, after the first generation, it's doubtful if more than a quarter of the diaspora worked through diasporic institutions. By contrast, in Aleppo, when I was a child there in the 1950s, virtually the entire community was involved in the functioning of its institutions. My own sense that we were not just individuals but a collective, a people, was inculcated not just by the church and school and culture and the political party now referred to as the ARF, but by the Armenian boy scout movement and athletic competition managed by the HMEM. An event like the annual football game between the Beirut and Aleppo HMEM athletic organizations filled the municipal stadium of Aleppo with 25,000–35,000 Armenians, most of the adult male Armenian population of the town and unusually many women as well, screaming support for and advice at their team while cursing the opposition – often in Turkish and Arabic. I mention this not as a personal indulgence but because, at that place and time, the HMEM's management of soccer exemplified soft power. Under the aegis of the ARF, it prospered without coercion, recruited on the basis of enabling both communal and individual achievement, and endowed us with a sense that we belonged to an entity that could organize and stage manageable, enticing competition. Rival athletic organizations also functioned along similar lines. To play against is still and always to play with; in the end, certain kinds of competition sustain and bind the competitors to each other within the diasporic enclave. Armenian diaspora scholarship must acknowledge and explore the diverse forms of stateless, soft power have functioned in such communities, where they have shaped diasporic subjectivity and achieved communal aims. It must also ask how such soft power is being challenged by the aspirational turn to individualism in recent public life.

The aspirational turn requires expansion here but above all in essays and scholarship to come. Until recently, stateless power was pursued within countries in the name of diasporas and other ethnic and cultural communities. But in the era of global capitalism and social media, at least in the West, serious communal political effort is proving less attractive to many in emerging generations; the very real idealism of recent social movements like Occupy in 2011 or the LGBTQ movement is nevertheless less institutional, more social and personal than was the case earlier, even during the marches of the Sixties. I am inclined to agree with Pankaj Mishra that the communal ideal – including the diasporic ideal – has weakened, and that what he calls 'selfie individualism' has taken its place. He argues that there has been 'a massive and under-appreciated shift worldwide, [such that] people understand themselves in public life primarily as individuals'.[31] If he is right that people enter *public* life solely to further the claims of their *private*, individual concerns, often having to do with identity, then societies in general and diasporic social formations in particular face a double dilemma: stateless power will find it harder to elicit and maintain communal and institutional commitments as individuals either avoid public life or, when they become active in it, increasingly want to bend public life to their own personal aspirations and individual satisfaction. In such circumstances, stateless power exercised through communal institutions and organizations will be less effective than it has been.

Faced with a new generation of young Armenians everywhere but especially in the West, our institutions and practices of stateless power are confronted by ABCs, Armenians By Choice; they inevitably become what I have elsewhere called 'part-time Armenians', who will conditionally and partially participate in communal life only when an issue that matters to them as individuals comes up. In such conditions, diasporicity in tolerant societies will naturally culminate in hybrid identities and part-time commitments. It is virtually impossible to function effectively as a 'full-time' American and also a 'full-time Armenian'. Consequently, commitment to a general and sustained diasporic struggle guided by diasporic institutions is likely to be replaced by engagement with narrower, specific issues. Loyalties now have 'Use-by' dates, embodying conditional and temporary commitments to specific efforts. This is the case not just in the Armenian diaspora but it is emphatically true there.[32]

The new Armenians of the contemporary Western diasporas increasingly feel at home in their societies and, even when declining to be fully assimilated, have limited commitment to diasporic communal aims elaborated under elite institutional direction. Life was easier for the leaders of both nations and diasporas when there was sustained, long-term commitment to the single entity of the *azg*, the nation in diaspora, rather than some still important but more fragmented issues of the day. New, inventive forms of the practice of stateless power are needed to formulate inviting, multiple, segmented issues and occasions that can attract real though partial commitments from younger diasporic generations, in particular. Whether, if attracted and recruited, they will seek to reshape the communal institutions that have hitherto sustained the Armenian diaspora or to bypass them in order to work through ad hoc groups and task forces focused on specific communal projects and objectives, I cannot say, but I am inclined to believe that institutions will continue to lose the ability to attract and retain loyal members over the long term. As I write this, I am respectfully aware of the number of my college students and young Armenians who would protest that they are fully committed to a specific issue, say Black Lives Matter or fighting climate change. Still, there is reason to be disheartened by the brevity and conditionality of youthful diasporic Armenian commitments. I suspect the future is one of sporadic, segmented, piecemeal activism and commitment by the young, taking the form of episodic narrative rather than a lifelong Bildungsroman, so to speak. How the elites of the diaspora will reshape the practices of soft power that sustained the post-genocide diaspora until recently is a matter that requires experimental, innovative re-imagining and pooling of resources and information. I hope that the Armenian Diaspora Survey[33] now being conducted will give us a better sense of where we are and how the geography of passivity, engagement and commitment can be mapped and perhaps altered.

To sum up: the Armenian Diaspora and its practice of soft, stateless institutional power is now challenged by a series of factors. One set of challenges consists of the new individualist aspirations and hybrid identities I have sketched, which lead the young to make most commitments outside the family partial, conditional, voluntary and therefore revocable. Another challenge has to do with the rapid and unpredictable transformation of some of the core pillars of identity formation and maintenance, namely difference and memory. Where identity is based on the difference from a threatening other, Armenian identity is ironically easier to maintain. Whereas where the host state accepts one as a citizen and the host society is not antagonistic, as in Canada or the United States, and instead offers opportunities to participate fully, there institutionalized diasporic commitments – whether political, religious, charitable or cultural, say to Hamazkayin and the Tekeyan – become harder to sustain. Where older diasporic or homeland institutions falter and show themselves to be mired in old conflicts, unable to change fast enough and above all unable to offer young people experiences that enable them to do what they want, they lose institutional loyalty.

I do not mean by these words to imply that all youthful aspiration is selfish, by no means – but it is self-oriented. The young are drawn to experiences and institutional settings where they can not only be Armenian but act as and make new as Armenians.

Being is made by becoming, by making, by engagement with similarly minded others, doing specific work that addresses issues the young care about not just in Armenian but also in non-Armenian settings – nature, the climate, support for victimized people towards whose well-being the young want to direct their efforts. These diasporan Armenians cannot successfully be invited to help the nation by serving its needs as identified by an institution. But they can be recruited to help for a time certain issues, especially those facing the homeland of the diasporic nation – a forest here, a lake there, an orphanage elsewhere or a faltering community of new refugees needing to learn a dominant language. They will serve the national homeland and the diaspora for a narrowly defined period of time, through projects that respond to their own aspirations and preferences. In the 1980s, a movement like *Land and Culture* was exemplary, creating work that interested the young, and work sites that offered intense but temporary social environments where friendships were established that continue to enrich the lives of former participants.

I have not spoken about the challenges and seductions, the massive power of social media, whose effects I observe but am too technically inept to describe. I cannot analyse the predispositions of the young who live by handheld screen, by earbud and ear pod, by text and Instagram. They become accustomed early to a world that solicits their attention in many ways and that challenges their ability to be attentive and focused on larger, longer projects, with the possible exception of long-running video games. It is now repeatedly observed that social media erode the authority of older institutions, elites, community leaders and of course older media. In the new attention economy, individuals can either become isolates or members of new communities. How will the older diasporic elites learn to draw in this cohort formed by new, digital experiences? I don't know, but I know that this is one of the venues that must be worked hard. I wish I could believe that Kim Kardashian and Alexis Ohanian can show our leadership the way, but do not believe it's likely.

I also wish I could believe that the homeland will facilitate the task of reanimating the diaspora. It can do much, but by its very nature, it cannot do all that is needed. Certainly for the generation born after 1988, Karabagh and the Republic of Armenia have created a significant reorientation – when the young think of Armenian community, they may still be drawn to HMEM and the Lark Society and the AYF, but many orient themselves to a variety of ways of imagining Armenia and their connection to it. As the government of Armenia works to draw the older diasporic elites into its orbit, the leaderless young re-orient themselves towards Armenia in their own way. Only a new inventiveness in politics, especially Armenian-American politics, and in cultural production, including Western Armenian and new forms of education, can revive and reanimate the Western diaspora.

Notes

1. Khachig Tölölyan, 'Rethinking Diasporas: Stateless Power in the Transnational Moment', *Diaspora* 5, no. 1 (1996): 3–36; 'Exile Government in the Armenian Polity', in *Governments-in-Exile in Contemporary World Politics*, ed. Yossi Shain (London: Routledge, 1991), 166–87.
2. Compare with: '[Early medieval Iceland] was not quite a stateless society; nor is a stateless society apolitical.' Richard A. Posner, 'Medieval Iceland and Modern Scholarship' (review of William Ian Miller, 'Bloodtaking and Peacemaking: Feud, Law and Society in Saga Iceland', *Michigan Law Review* 90, no. 1495 (1992): 1495–511, 1496. Settled by a 'diaspora' of Scandinavian Vikings *c.* 930–1200 CE, Iceland acknowledged no state, had no army or bureaucracy; it was stateless.
3. Jeff Perl, 'Civilian Scholarship', *Common Knowledge* 8, no. 1 (2002): 1–6, 1.
4. My views on diasporic entrepreneurs aspiring for leadership positions are influenced by Paul Brass's extensive work on the ways in which leaders of territorialized ethnic groups have acted to re-formulate, alter and utilize existing ethnic identities and reshape them. See Brass, *Ethnicity and Nationalism* (Newbury Park: Sage, 1991), 1–17. Brass's larger work on the formation, persistence and transformation of ethnic identities over time offers suggestive analogies for diasporic work.
5. While my view of these quotidian students and innovators of culture is influenced by Michel de Certeau, my categories are not identical to his. Those who engage in the *study* of diasporas in my sense can in some circumstances be ordinary people who are 'mere consumers' of their official culture; in actuality they tend to be drawn mostly from the ranks of those who *self-consciously* 'practice' their cultures. Cf. Michel de Certeau, *The Practice of Everyday Life*, trans. Steven Rendall (Berkeley: University of California Press, 1984).
6. Beirut: Sevan Publishers, 1981.
7. H. J. Siruni, *Bolisĕ ew ir terĕ*, 4 Vols (Beirut: Lebanon, 1965, 1970, 1987, 1988); Alboyajian, *Badmutʻiwn hay kaghtʻaganutʻean* (Cairo, Egypt, Vol. 1, 1941, Vol. 2, 1955, Vol. 3, 1961); Mesrovb Jacob Seth, *Armenians in India*, Co-published by the Holy Church of Nazareth, Calcutta, Gulab Promlani (Oxford: IBH Publishing, 1937 [1983]).
8. Punnett, Betty Jane, David Ford, Bella Galperin, and Terri Lituchy, 'The Emic-Etic Research Cycle', *AIB Insights*, 17, no. 1 (2017). http://documents.aib.msu.edu/publications/insights/v17n1/v17n1_Article1.pdf.
9. Fr Karnig Koyounian, 'Sʻpʻiwṛkʻĕ anun ew erevoyt'', *Horizon Weekly* (in Armenian), Montreal, 17 October 2022, 4.
10. Vartan Matiossian, 'Bantukhdĕ hay kraganutʻean mēch', *Horizon-Kragan*, November 2011, 4–12. The word *bantukhd* has had a range of meanings, from homeless wanderer to someone who journeys to labour beyond his home place, at some considerable distance, either within or across state borders.
11. Bishop Aiyenakun P. J. Arowele, 'Diaspora-Concept in the New Testament: Studies on the Idea of Christian Sojourn, Pilgrimage and Dispersion', Inaugural-Dissertation

zur Erlangung der Doktorwurde der Theologischen Fakultat der Bayerischen Julius-Maximilians-Universitat, Worzburg, 17 January 1977.

12 Aristakes Lastivertsi, *History Regarding the Sufferings Occasioned by Foreign Peoples Living Around Us*, written between 1072 and 1079, translated online http://www.attalus.org/armenian/altoc.htm by Robert Bedrossian. There is a confusion here I cannot resolve, for the names of Elijah and Elias, Yeghishe and Yeghia, distinct in Armenian, are usually taken to refer to the same Prophet in Hebrew.

13 Quoted in Ronald Suny, *Looking toward Ararat* (Bloomington: Indiana University Press, 1993), 38.

14 Peter Cowe, 'Theology of Kingship in 13th C Armenian Cilicia', Hask Hayakidagan Hantes, Nor Shrchan/New Series 11, 2009, 417–30, 418. Levon Ter Petrosyan, *Khachagirnerě ew Hayerě* [Crusaders and Armenians], Armenian Library of the Gulbenkian Foundation, 2007, esp. Foreword if Volume II.

15 'Nersēs dzaṛay Krisdosi ew oghormadzutʻeamp norin gatʻughigos Hayotsʻ. Ěnthanur hawadatsʻelotsʻ haygaganatsʻt seṛitsʻ, orkʻ harewls i sepʻhagan ashkharht Hayasdaneaytsʻ pnagealkʻ, ew orkʻ harewmdean goghmanst sahealkʻ nzhtehutʻeamp ew orkʻ i michergreays i mēch aylalezu azkantsʻ darperealkʻ, ew orkʻ hiwrakʻanchʻiwr hezers ashkharhatsʻ ěsd mehgatsʻ *tsʻruealk*ʻ i kʻaghakʻs ew i tgheags, i kiwghs ew i harkaragatsʻ . . .'. From Nerses Shnorhali, *Tʻughtʻěnthanragan* (Erevan: HH KAA "Science" Publishing, 1995), 53. In that text, the Encyclical is titled, Nersēsi Gatʻughigosi Hayotsʻ aṛ Hamōrēn Hayaseṛ Azins (Oroy Deschʻutʻiwn Hawadatsʻaw Nma i Deaṛnē). The translation is from St. Nersēs Šnorhali, *General Epistle*, trans. and intro. Fr. Arakel Aljalian (New Rochelle, New York: St. Nersess Armenian Seminary, 1996), 13.

16 Sebouh Aslanian notes that the word 'Hayastan' was not unknown before the work of M'khitarist historians. He points to the colophon of Hovannes Jughayetsi's 1647 *Girkʻ tumaratsʻ or ew parzatumar kochi* (*Book of Calendars, also called a Simplified Calendar*) in which a sentence referring to the work of moving a printing press from Italy to 'Hayastan' occurs: 'Tʻ [9] ami ashkhadutʻean meroy or Idaliay aṛeal zkordzaran dbakrotʻean pazum neghutʻeamp adzakʻ i Hayasdan.'

17 Shelly Chan's *Diaspora's Homeland: Modern China in the Age of Global Migration* (Durham: Duke University Press, 2018) comes tantalizingly close to discussing the extent to which the changing status and issues of massive Chinese emigration in the nineteenth century were linked to changes in the self-conception of the Chinese state and its bureaucracy. She does not explicitly and exclusively attribute changes in one to changes in the other, but rather depicts each (waves of migration, rules and roles of the state) continually responding to the other.

18 Starting with his dissertation: Sebouh D. Aslanian, 'From the Indian Ocean to the Mediterranean: Circulation and the Global Trade Networks of Armenian Merchants from New Julfa/Isfahan, 1605–1747', Doctoral dissertation, Columbia University, 2007, particularly the second half of chapter 8.

19 Khachig Tölölyan, 'Textual Nation: Poetry and Nationalism in Armenian Political Culture', in *Intellectuals and the Articulation of the Nation*, ed. Ronald G. Suny and Michael D. Kennedy (Ann Arbor: University of Michigan Press, 1999), 79–105.

20 Aslanian, Sebouh D. "From the Indian Ocean to the Mediterranean: Circulation and the Global Trade Networks of Armenian Merchants from New Julfa/Isfahan, 1606-1747." Doctoral Dissertation, Columbia University, 2007. p. 377

21 For a helpful recent attempt to track the vocabulary of the semantic domain of 'diaspora' or Sʻpʻiwṛkʻ in Armenian, see Karnig Koyounian, 'Spʻiwṛkʻě anun ew erevoytʻ', *Horizon Weekly* (Montreal), 14 October 2022.

22 While I reference power primarily in its broadly political sense, I think it is helpful to recall that electric power emerges as a flow, an interchange between two poles of difference (of charge).
23 A topic ably discussed in this volume by Vahe Sahakian, so I will not elaborate its meanings here.
24 In his talk at the conference where a first draft of this essay was also presented: 'State(less) Power and Beyond: The (Im)possibility of Governmentality in the Armenian Diaspora', 12 October 2019.
25 *The Power Elite* (New York: Oxford University Press, 1956).
26 Cf. Walter P. Zenner, *Minorities in the Middle: A Cross-Cultural Analysis* (New York: SUNY Press, 1991).
27 Fritz Stern, *Gold & Iron: Bismarck, Bleicherodr and the Building of the German Empire* (London: Allen & Unwin, 1977).
28 Zenner, *Minorities in the Middle*.
29 Khachig Tölölyan, 'Exile Governments in the Armenian Polity', *Journal of Politial Science* 18 (1990): 124–45; 'Exile Government in the Armenian Diaspora', in *Governments-in-Exile in Contemporary World Politics*, ed. Yossi Shain (London: Routledge, 1991), 166–87. Currently, Maroush Nahhas-Yeramian is editing hitherto unknown reports and letters in the AGBU archives in Cairo in which Simon Zavarian reports to the Istanbul Patriarch the results of his mission to study the state of Armenian education in the schools of Giligia Z. in 1909–10, essentially performing the function of a governmentally empowered inspector.
30 Professor Ara Sanjian has an authoritative, as-yet unpublished study, with names and figures, of Armenians who fell victim to other Armenians in Lebanon in the 1958 clashes. It is mentioned in the fourth instalment of an extensive interview with *Nor Ḥaṙach*, 21 June 1996, 4.
31 *Age of Anger: A History of the Present* (New York: Farrar, Straus and Giroux, 2017), 12.
32 Here we must keep in mind the porous but real boundary between Armenians who are ethnic, the majority, and that minority whose identity and behaviour are consistently centred on bilocal and multilocal diasporic commitments. Ethnics are on occasion recruited to diasporic views and behaviours, but are rarely permanently converted to them. For details, see Tölölyan, 'Rethinking Diaspora(s)', 3–36, particularly the section titled 'The Ethnic and the Diasporic', 16–19.
33 https://www.armeniandiasporasurvey.com/.

Epilogue

Sebouh Aslanian

In 2019, to celebrate and honour the singularly important work of one of the leading scholars of diaspora studies in the world, Khachig Tölölyan, I was asked by the Society of Armenian Studies (SAS) to organize a conference called 'Diaspora and Stateless Power: Social Discipline and Identity Formation in the Armenian Diaspora during the Long Twentieth Century'. What I offered there as opening remarks to the conference, I revisit here as concluding thoughts to the volume. In both instances, my aim has been to offer a glance into his inspiring life history and begin with a brief backdrop on his intellectual trajectory, and conclude with how the 2019 conference theme and this subsequent volume relate to his remarkable corpus of work on diasporas, both global and Armenian and sometimes together.

Ever since I had the good fortune of meeting Khachig Tölölyan over drinks at a New York City hotel after a conference in 1997 or 1998, he has been a dear friend, mentor, colleague and often coerced recipient of email communications from me about this or that new archival discovery that I thought I had made while travelling across Europe or Asia. His fame and reputation as a connoisseur and concierge of knowledge (both of the Armenian and non-Armenian variety) usually precedes him; however, it bears repetition and exposition.

Fortunately, my task in drawing a vignette of Tölölyan's life is made all the easier because Khachig has already published a beautifully crafted intellectual biography titled 'Memoirs of a Diasporan Nationalist' appended to what remains my favourite of his works and the one that has had the most influence on me. I am referring to his essay 'Textual Nation: Poetry and Nationalism in Armenian Political Culture', a razor-sharp hermeneutical exegesis of the ideological work of a tiny group of eighteenth-century diasporan intellectuals in Madras, India, a work that creatively blends his expertise in three adjacent fields of intellectual inquiry: literature, nationalism and diaspora studies.

Khachig Tölölyan was born in 1944 in the Armenian diaspora community of Aleppo to parents who were genocide survivors and refugees from the Ottoman Empire. Both his mother (née Kohar Chobanian) and father were highly educated diasporans and members of that *archetypical* political party of the diaspora, the Armenian Revolutionary Federation (ARF), whose networks and activities as a 'government in exile' helped shape much of what we take for granted in the 'core' Middle Eastern diasporas of the twentieth century. His father, Minas Tölölyan, a native of Bardizag outside of Istanbul, was a well-known literary critic, writer, educator and public intellectual; some of his influential two-volume anthology *Tar mě Kraganut'iwn* (A Century of Literature, 1850–1950), I remember reading as a graduate student at Columbia.

'My mother taught me to read Armenian and French when I was four from an illustrated dictionary of science and an even more excitingly illustrated zoology textbook, both published by the Armenian Catholic Mekhitarist monks of Venice: the perfect diasporan multidisciplinary texts', Tölölyan notes in his memoirs.[1] A year later, he learnt the elements of anatomy and dissection, and by six had started to study Arabic. 'Mine was largely an indoor and sickly life of reading', he writes poignantly, adding that it was 'punctuated by periods of relative robustness, dominated by soccer and occasional hunting'.[2] At twelve (1956), the Tölölyans experienced the first of several geographic displacements that many of us have all too easily come to associate as a conspicuous hallmark of being diasporan and Armenian during the twentieth century: they moved from one cultural hub of the diaspora (Aleppo) to another – (Cairo) Egypt.[3] There Khachig began to learn English, which he continued in Beirut a short while later when he attended the 'International College', a high school affiliated with the American University of Beirut. Fluency in the English language opened up new worlds and new genres of reading to the young scholar and aesthete: detective novels, science fiction, comic books and so forth now became part of his intellectual diet. Hardly had he entered this new world, however, when the Lebanese Civil War of 1958 broke out. His father's prominent role as an intellectual affiliated with the ARF earned him two attempts on his life and prompted the family to uproot and transplant once again. Arriving in Watertown (America) in 1960, the sixteen-year-old Tölölyan was well positioned to 'live the immigrant dream'.[4] He was worldly beyond his youthful age, and unlike many monolingual Americans, he was a polyglot who already possessed a well-rounded education (he knew who the Roman generals Lucullus and Pompey were when he was only nine!). At eighteen, he enrolled in Harvard with a full scholarship. Oddly, he chose to do his BA in molecular biology (perhaps as a consequence of reading all those illustrated Mekhitarist books on science) and decided to pursue a doctorate in marine biology and oceanography. Finding the world of the laboratory too confining, especially at a time when much of the world was experiencing the creative cultural upheaval of the 1960s, Tölölyan deftly changed tracks and pursued his graduate studies in English literature, 'reading voraciously and, through Roman Jacobson and Levi-Strauss, "finding" theory and myself'.[5] In 1970, at Brown University's famed Department of Comparative Literature, he wrote a dissertation on 'cosmographic narrative', which is on epic narratives that try to give cultural confusion a shape. He worked on texts by Homer, Virgil, Joyce and Faulkner and later added the American novelist Thomas Pynchon.

From 1974 until his retirement in 2020, Khachig taught literature, theory and the humanities at Wesleyan, where he had a cult-like following among his students. I recently met two of them, a married couple, now teaching at UCI and UCLA, who were still reminiscing over how great a mentor 'Katch' was to them. You know when you are in the presence of a great professor and mentor when their students still remember the comments they received on an undergraduate paper written more than twenty years ago.

In addition to being a polymath and exceptionally gifted scholar and educator, Khachig has also been a very devoted editor. In 1979, he founded a small journal

Pynchon Notes and worked as a contributor in Armenian to the Armenian literary periodical in Paris, *Haṛach*. His columns in that paper were published in 1980 in a volume titled *Sp'iwṛk'i Mēch* (In the Diaspora), which is his main book to date. In the 1980s, no doubt unbeknownst to many, Khachig wrote a series of trailblazing essays on the culture of Armenian political terrorism where he honed his innate skills as a discerning reader and interpreter of literary texts to decode contemporary history and politics in the diaspora. For example, in his 'Cultural Narrative and the Motivation of a Terrorist', a work that retains much of its value thirty odd years later, he provided a deeply stimulating reading of how certain master narratives from the Armenian past (the story of Vardanants', for instance) can operate like filters or templates that allow groups or individuals belonging to such groups to perceive or make sense of the complex world around them. Perhaps the most important turning point in Tölölyan's intellectual trajectory came in 1991 when he became the founding editor of the Zoryan Institute-sponsored *Diaspora: A Journal of Transnational Studies*. The publication of the celebrated 'Preface' to the inaugural issue of this trailblazing journal and numerous essays both here and elsewhere have made Tölölyan a household name among those who study diasporas as a profession.

You may be asking yourself, where does all this bring us as far as the theme of this edited volume is concerned? Perhaps this quotation will help clarify. 'Man is not fitted for Society by nature but by discipline.'[6] Before you think that Tölölyan wrote this passage in the memoir from which I have already quoted or paraphrased copiously, let me disabuse you of that notion. The passage I quoted was written in the second half of the seventeenth century by the English political philosopher Thomas Hobbes in his posthumously published work on the art of modern government titled *De Cive*. Upon reading it, one thinks of how a myriad of state and non-state institutions operate in subtle and not-so-subtle ways in shaping and moulding human beings into docile and compliant members of society. This process of shaping individuals is omnipresent and operates at all levels of any given community. Philosophers and theorists after Hobbes have called it 'social discipline' and the process giving shape to it, in a manner of speaking, as 'governmentality'.

These two notions were the central concerns for the French philosopher Michel Foucault in the final decade of his life and can be traced to his lectures on power and biopolitics that he delivered at the *College de France* in the 1970s. In a 1978 talk on governmentality he defined this elusive concept as 'the manner in which the conduct of an ensemble of individuals becomes implicated to a greater and greater degree in the exercise of state power'.[7] To help flesh out this abstruse yet increasingly popular way of approaching state formation, Foucault also introduced the notion of 'social discipline' to explain how populations came to be simultaneously the subjects and objects of governance. Social discipline in this sense is the imposition of group conformity to a norm, usually enforced by the levers of state institutions and apparatuses with the purpose of creating greater and greater conformity to the religious and social codes of society and stricter moral behaviour. For Foucault, both governmentality and social discipline were coeval. Both have their origins in the early modern period, the same period that saw the flourishing of Hobbes's writings on the state, and specifically with the Protestant Reformation and Catholic counter-reformation that historians now call the era of confessionalization.[8] Over the last few decades, governmentality and social discipline have been used by scholars mostly to examine the exercise of power in its diverse forms by nation-states in the nineteenth and twentieth centuries. Dedicated to the work of Khachig Tölölyan, the leading theorist and scholar of the Armenian diaspora, the chapters in this volume focus on the exercise of what Tölölyan calls 'stateless power', and indeed of governmentality, in the formation of the Armenian diaspora during the long twentieth century. The chapters explore the nexus of diaspora and stateless power in the making of Armenian communities outside the 'homeland'. They privilege the study of forms of 'social discipline' and community organizations as well as elites and cultural production in far-flung sites of the Armenian diaspora such as Addis Ababa, Aleppo, Décines, Detroit, Kiev, Leipzig, Los Angeles and Tulsa, to name a few.

Let me conclude by highlighting two hallmarks that stand out from Tölölyan's life as a scholar, editor and educator. First, Khachig's enduring legacy should *not* be limited to his scholarly contributions and accomplishments, some of which I have attempted to exemplify here. More than publishing journals and influencing an entire field of scholarly inquiry known as diaspora studies, Khachig has also been a remarkable mentor to scholars whose essays he has remoulded and published. I can speak from personal experience here. Though I am a historian and not a literary scholar or theorist like Khachig, and though we have disagreed almost as often as we have seen things through a similar lens, I can say unequivocally that I know of no other Armenian scholar who is as well-read and nimble in his thinking and who has helped me become the scholar I am today than Khachig. Khachig is someone who can quote a passage from the seventeenth-century English political theorist John Locke and the more contemporary and much more enigmatic, not to say unfathomable, Slovenian philosopher Slavoj Žižek and compellingly find a way to make both resonant and relevant to Armenian studies.

The second takeaway from our brief microhistory of Khachig's life and works is that, like all good microhistories, his story is both singular and resonant at the same time. It is unique because it has many quirky details and brims with intellectual talent that sparkle on its surface and render it a unique work of art, a life in short that only Khachig Tölölyan could have lived. It is also, however, doubly significant because it is quite representative of a more general pattern of a twentieth-century diaspora condition that binds many of us, whether we like it or not, together as accomplices in the same history of displacement, transplantation, rebirth, of being in-between and of living in difference and creative hybridity – a life, in short, that is punctuated by civil wars and revolutions. This is the very same diaspora condition the study of which Tölölyan has long interrogated, made sense of and helped shape in profound ways.

Notes

1 Khachig Tölölyan, 'Memoirs of a Diasporan Nationalist', in *Intellectuals and the Articulation of the Nation*, ed. Ronald Grigor Suny and Michael D. Kennedy (Ann Arbor: The University of Michigan Press, 1999), 104.

2 Ibid.
3 For the Middle Eastern 'core' diasporas, see the useful treatments in Ara Sanjian, 'The Armenian Minority Experience in the Modern Arab World', Bulletin of the Royal Institute for Inter-Faith Studies 1 (2001): 149-179, and Razmik Panossian, The Armenians: From Kings and Priests to Merchants and Commissars (New York: Columbia University Press, 2006), 291-318.
4 Ibid., 105.
5 Ibid., 106.
6 Quoted in Philip Gorski, *The Disciplinary Revolution: Calvinism and the Rise of the Rise of the State in Early Modern Europe* (Chicago: The University of Chicago Press, 2003), 24.
7 Michel Foucault, 'Sécurité, territoire, et population', in *Resume des cours, 1970–1982* (Paris: Julliard, 1989), quoted in Gorski, *The Disciplinary Revolution*.
8 For a discussion on confessionalization and social discipline, see Sebouh David Aslanian, *Early Modernity and Mobility: Port Cities and Printers across the Armenian Diaspora, 1512-1800* (New Haven: Yale University Press, 2023), especially chapters 2 and 5.

Bibliography

Unpublished Primary Sources

Aram Pehlivanian, autobiography written on April 22, 1955 in family archive of Pehlivanian.
National Archives of Armenia, File No. 326.1.72.

Periodical Press

Anahit (Paris), 1898–1904.
Armenia (Marseille), 1885–1905.
Armenian Weekly (Watertown, MA), 2022.
Asbarēz (Los Angeles), 2016.
Azat Khōsk' (Paris, Alexandria), 1901–1903.
Banasēr (Paris), 1899–1903.
Hairenik' Daily (Watertown, MA), 1925–1933.
Horizon Weekly (Montreal), 1992.
Hürriyet Daily (Istanbul), 2011.
Nor Keank' (London), 1898–1902.
Nor Lur (Istanbul), 1946, 2007.
Patani (London), 1902–1903.
The Armenian Mirror-Spectator (Watertown, MA), 2017.
The New York Times (New York), 2019.
The Washington Post, 1933.
Zhamanak (Paris), 1901–1902.
Abakay. 'Ṛamk. Azat. Kusakts'ut'ean B. ĕndh. patgm. zhoghovin aṛt'iw' [On the Occasion of the 2nd General Congress of the ADL]. 23 February 1924, 1–2.
Abrahamyan, Ashot. *Hamaṛot urvagits hay gaght'avayreri patmut'yan* [Brief Outline of the History of Armenian Diaspora Communities]. Vol. 2. 2 Vols. Erevan: Hayastan, 1967.
Abrahamyan, Gayane. 'Are Turkish-Armenians a Diaspora?: Istanbul Journalist Says Turkey's Armenians Live in Their Historical Lands'. *Armenia Now*, 19 May 2011.
Abramson, Yehonatan. 'Making a Homeland, Constructing a Diaspora: The Case of Taglit-Birthright Israel'. *Political Geography* 58, no. 1 (2017): 14–23. https://doi.org/10.1016/j.polgeo.2017.01.002.
Adalian, Rouben. 'The Armenian Colony of Egypt During the Reign of Muhammad Ali (1805–1848)'. *Armenian Review* 33 (June 1980): 115–44.
Adjemian, Boris. 'Archives, exil et politique: Aram Andonian et la Bibliothèque arménienne de Paris (1927–1951)'. *Mémoire inédit pour l'habilitation à diriger des recherches, École normale supérieure*, 2022.

Adjemian, Boris. 'De l'expérience migratoire au Grand Récit de la migration: Le mythe de l'adoption dans la mémoire des Arméniens d'Éthiopie'. *L'Homme. Revue française d'anthropologie* 211 (2014): 97–116.

Adjemian, Boris. 'Du récit de soi à l'écriture d'un Grand Récit: Une autobiographie collective arménienne en Éthiopie'. *Diasporas. Histoire et sociétés* 22 (1 September 2013): 139–53.

Adjemian, Boris. 'Immigrants arméniens, représentations de l'étranger et construction du national en Éthiopie (XIXe - XXe siècle): Socio-histoire d'un espace interstitiel de sociabilités'. Thèse de doctorat, École des hautes études en sciences sociales, 2011.

Adjemian, Boris. 'La fanfare arménienne du négus. Représentations des étrangers, usages du passé et politique étrangère des rois d'Éthiopie au début du 20e siècle'. *Vingtième Siècle. Revue d'histoire* 119, no. 3 (2013): 85–97.

Adjemian, Boris. *La fanfare du négus. Les Arméniens en Éthiopie (XIXe-XXe siècles)*. Paris: Éditions de l'EHESS, 2013.

Adjemian, Boris. *Les Petites Arménies de la vallée du Rhône: Histoire et mémoires des immigrations arméniennes en France*. Lyon: Lieux dits éditions, 2020.

Adjemian, Boris. 'Stateless Armenians in Ethiopia Under Fascist Occupation (1936–1941): Foreignness and Integration, From Local to Colonial Subject'. In *Citizens and Subjects of the Italian Colonies: Legal Constructions and Social Practices, 1882–1943*, edited by Simona Berhe and Olindo De Napoli, 223–44. London: Routledge, 2021.

Adjemian, Boris and Talin Suciyan. 'Making Space and Community through Memory: Orphans and Armenian Jerusalem in the Nubar Library's Photographic Archive'. *Études arméniennes contemporaines* 9 (2017): 75–113.

Aghanyants', Kiwd, ed. *Tiwan Hayots' Badmut'ean Kirk' 18: Harsdaharut'iwnner Dajgahayasdanum (Vawerakrer 1801–1888)*. Tblisi: Dbaran N. Aghanyants'i, 1915.

Aharonyan, Kersam. *Khoher Hisnameagi Awardin*. Beirut: Atlas Publ., 1966.

Ahn, Ilsup. 'Theology and Migration'. *Theology* 3, no. 2 (2019): 1–108.

Aktar, Ayhan. *Varklık Vergisi ve 'Türkleştirme' Politikaları [The Wealth Tax and the Politics of "Becoming Turkish"]*. Istanbul: İltşim, 2000.

Aktokmakyan, Maral. 'So, Did We Really Find Yesayan?', *Journal of the Society for Armenian Studies* 28, no. 2 (2021): 212–19.

Al-Rustom, Hakem. 'Rethinking the "Post-Ottoman": Anatolian Armenians as an Ethnographic Perspective'. In *A Companion to the Anthropology of the Middle East* (First edition), edited by Soraya Altorki, 479–552. Hoboken, NJ: Wiley-Blackwell, 2015.

Alajaji, Sylvia. *Music and the Armenian Diaspora: Searching for Home in Exile*. Bloomington, IN: Indiana University Press, 2015.

Alboyadjian, Archag [Albōyajyan, Arshag]. *Badmut'iwn Malatioy Hayots': Deghakragan, badmagan ew azkakragan* [Histoire des Arméniens de Malatia]. Beirut: Sevan, 1961.

Alis: Orkan Sebastioy Verashinats' Miut'ean [Alis: Organ of the Sivas Reconstruction Union]. 'Hakarakordneru pōlshewik paraglukhnerě inch'u hamar k'andel kuzen mer miut'iwně' [Why Do the Bolshevik Leaders of the Opponents Want to Destroy Our Union]. January–October, no. 3–4, 1934, 3–5.

Ambrosini, Maurizio. *Irregular Immigration in Southern Europe*. New York: Springer International Publishing, 2018.

Ambrosini, Maurizio. 'Why Irregular Migrants Arrive and Remain: The Role of Intermediaries'. *Journal of Ethnic and Migration Studies* 43, no. 11 (2017): 1813–30. https://doi.org/10.1080/1369183X.2016.1260442.

Anderson, Benedict. *Imagined Communities: Reflections on the Origin and Spread of Nationalism*. London: Verso, 1999.

Anderson, Benedict. 'Nationalism, Identity, and the World-in-Motion: On the Logistics of Seriality'. In *Cosmopolitics: Thinking and Feeling Beyond the Nation*, edited by Pheng Cheah and Bruce Robbins, 117–33. Minneapolis, MN: University of Minnesota Press, 1998.

Anderson, Benedict. *The Specter of Comparisons: Nationalism, Southeast Asia and the World*. London: Verso, 1998.

Andézian, Sossie. 'Des pèlerins sédentaires. Formation d'une diaspora arménienne à Jérusalem'. In *Les pèlerinages au Maghreb et au Moyen-Orient*, edited by Sylvia Chiffoleau and Anna Madœuf, 47–69. Damas: Presses de l'Ifpo, 2010.

Antaramian, Richard. *Brokers of Faith, Brokers of Empire: Armenians and the Politics of Reform in the Ottoman Empire*. Stanford, CA: Stanford University Press, 2021.

Anteby-Yemini, Lisa. *Les juifs éthiopiens en Israël: Les paradoxes du paradis*. Paris: CNRS éditions, 2004.

Aprahamian, Ashod Rhaffi. *Remarkable Rebirth: The Early History of the Armenians in Detroit*. East Lansing, MI: Michigan State University Press, 2005.

Arkun, Aram. 'National Center of Armenian Memory in Décines, France Promotes Armenian Studies and Culture'. *The Armenian Mirror-Spectator*, 7 December 2017. https://mirrorspectator.com/2017/12/07/national-center-armenian-memory-decines-france-promotes-armenian-studies-culture/.

Armenian Diaspora Survey. 'Armenia Diaspora Survey'. armeniandiasporasurvey.com, accessed 8 April 2019.

Armenian General Benevolent Union: Historic Outline, 1906–1946. New York: Published by the Central Committee of America, 1948.

Armenpress. 'Our Compatriots That Continue to Live in Syria are Heroes'. *Armenpress*, 21 November 2016. https://www.armenpress.am/arm/news/868647/

Armstrong, John A. 'Mobilized and Proletarian Diasporas'. *American Political Science Review* 70, no. 2 (1976): 393–408. https://doi.org/10.2307/1959646.

Arsan, Andrew. *Interlopers of Empire: The Lebanese Diaspora in Colonial French West Africa*. London: Hurst & Company, 2014.

Artinian, Vartan. 'A Study of the Historical Development of the Armenian Constitutional System in the Ottoman Empire, 1839–1863'. Ph.D. diss., Brandeis University, 1970.

Artinian, Vartan, ed. *Osmanlı Devleti'nde Ermeni Anayasası'nın Doğuşu*. Istanbul: Aras Yay., 2004.

Artinian, Vartan. *The Armenian Constitutional System in the Ottoman Empire, 1839–1863: A Study of its Historical Development*. Istanbul: Isis Press, 1988.

Asad, Talal. *Genealogies of Religion: Discipline and Reasons of Power in Christianity and Islam*. Baltimore and London: The Johns Hopkins University Press, 1993.

Ashjian, Arten. *Vichakats'oyts' ew patmut'iwn Aṛajnordakan T'emin Hayots' Amerikayi, 1948* [Register and History of the Diocese of the Armenian Church in America, 1948]. New York: Hratarakut'iwn Amerikayi Hayots' Aṛajnordarani, 1949.

Aslanian, Sebouh David. 'From "Autonomous" to 'Interactive" Histories: World History's Challenge to Armenian Studies'. In *An Armenian Mediterranean: Words and Worlds in Motion*, edited by Kathryn Babayan and Michael Pifer, 81–125. London: Palgrave Macmillan, 2018.

Aslanian, Sebouh David. *Early Modernity and Mobility: Port Cities and Printers across the Armenian Diaspora, 1512-1800*. New Haven: Yale University Press, 202.

Aslanian, Sebouh David. *From the Indian Ocean to the Mediterranean: The Global Trade Networks of Armenian Merchants from New Julfa*. The California World History Library 17. Berkeley, CA: University of California Press, 2011.

Association Culturelle Arménienne de Marne-la-Vallée (France). 'Église apostolique arménienne Sainte-Marie'. http://www.acam-france.org/contacts/contact_eglise.php?cle=16, accessed 8 April 2021.

'Asylum Trends. Language Selection Nederlands'. *IND Naturalisatiedienst*, https://ind.nl/en/about-ind/figures-and-publications/Pages/Asylum-Trends.aspx, accessed 24 April 2020.

Atamian, Sarkis. *The Armenian Community: The Historical Development of a Social and Ideological Conflict*. New York: Philosophical Library, 1955.

Atayan, Robert. *The Armenian Neume System of Notation*. Translated by V. N. Nersessian. Surrey: Curzon Press, 1999.

Ayanian, Jean. *Le kemp: Une enfance intra-muros*. Marseille: Éditions Parenthèses, 2001.

Bakalian, Anny. *Armenian-Americans: From Being to Feeling Armenian*, 2nd ed. 1993. Reprint, New York: Routledge, 2017.

Bakalian, Anny and Zeynep Turan. 'Diaspora Tourism and Identity: Subversion and Consolation in Armenian Pilgrimages to Eastern Turkey'. In *Diasporas of the Modern Middle East*, ed. Sossie Kasbarian and Anthony Gorman. Edinburgh: Edinburgh University Press, 2015, 173–212

Balakian, Grigoris. *Armenian Golgotha: A Memoir of the Armenian Genocide, 1915–1918*. Translated by Peter Balakian and Aris Sevag. New York: Vintage Books, 2010.

Bali, N. Rıfat. *Yirmi Kur'a Nafıa Askerleri: II. Dünya Savaşında Gayrimüslimlerin Askerlik Serüveni*. Istanbul: Kitabevi Yayınları, 2008.

Barry, James. *Armenian Christians in Iran: Ethnicity, Religion, and Identity in the Islamic Republic*. Cambridge: Cambridge University Press, 2018.

Basch, Linda, Nina Glick Schiller, and Cristina Szanton Blanc (1994), *Nations Unbound: Transnational Projects, Postcolonial Predicaments and De-Territorialized Nation-States*. Langhorne, PA: Gordon and Breach, 1994.

Baser, Bahar and Mari Toivanen. 'Diasporic Homecomings to the Kurdistan Region of Iraq: Pre-and Post-Return Experiences Shaping Motivations to Re-return'. *Ethnicities* 19, no. 5 (2019): 901–24. https://doi.org/10.1177/1468796818757265.

Bastide, Roger. 'Les Arméniens de Valence'. *Revue Internationale de Sociologie* 1–2 (February 1931): 17–42.

Bayrakdarian, Isabel. 'Groong'. On *Gomidas Songs*. With the Armenian Philharmonic Orchestra Chamber Players, conducted by Edvard Topchian. Nonesuch, 2008.

Belli, Meriam. 'Zabel Yesayan, "Chronicle – The Role of the Armenian Woman during the War"'. *Journal of the Society for Armenian Studies* 28, no. 2 (2021): 220–34.

Benjamin, Walter. 'On the Concept of History'. In *Illuminations*, 253–64. New York: Schocken Books, edited by Hannah Arendt. Translated by Harry Zohn. 1969.

Berberian, Houri. *Armenians and the Iranian Constitutional Revolution of 1905–1911: "The Love for Freedom Has No Fatherland"*. Boulder, CO: Westview Press, 2001.

Berberian, Houri. *Roving Revolutionaries Armenians and the Connections Revolutions in the Russian, Iranian and Ottoman Worlds*. Los Angeles: University of California Press, 2019.

Berberian, Vahe. *Namakner Zaat'arēn [Letter from Zaat'ar]*. Los Angeles: Arvest, 1996.

Berkes, Nyazi. *The Development of Secularism in Turkey*. Montreal: McGill University Press, 1964.

Berksanlar, Kurken. 'Are Armenians of Turkey a Diaspora?', *HyeTert*, 23 May 2011. https://hyetert.org/2011/05/23/turkiye-ermenileri-diaspora-mi/

Biberyan, Zaven. 'Al Gě pave'. *Nor Lur*, 5 January 1946.
Biberyan, Zaven. *Babam Aşkale'ye gitmedi*. Translated by Sirvart Malkhasyan. Istanbul: Aras Yay., 1999.
Biberyan, Zaven. 'Badmagan Nshmarner'. *Nor Lur*, 22 January 1946.
Biberyan, Zaven. *Zaben Biberyan, Mrchiwnneru Verchaluysě*. Istanbul: Aras Yay, 2007.
Biehl, João. *Vita: Life in a Zone of Social Abandonment*. Photographs by Torben Eskerod. Berkeley, CA, Los Angeles and London: University of California Press, 2005.
Bilal, Melissa. 'Gomidas Vartabed ve Müzikolojinin Siyaseti'. In *Kalbim o viran evlere benzer: Gomidas Vartabed'in müzik mirası*, 167–219, edited by Melissa Bilal and Burcu Yıldız. Istanbul: Birzamanlar Yayıncılık, 2019.
Bilal, Melissa. 'Longing for Home at Home: Armenians in Istanbul'. *Thamyris/Intersecting* 13 (2006): 55–66.
Bilal, Melissa. 'Thou Need'st Not Weep, For I Have Wept Full Sore: An Affective Genealogy of the Armenian Lullaby in Turkey'. Ph.D. diss., University of Chicago, 2013.
Bilal, Melissa and Burcu Yıldız. *Kalbim o viran evlere benzer: Gomidas Vartabed'in müzik mirası*. Istanbul: Birzamanlar Yayıncılık, 2019.
Billig, Michael. *Banal Nationalism*. Newbury Park, CA: Sage Publication, 1995.
Biswas, Shampa. 'W(h)ither the Nation-state? National and State Identity in the Face of Fragmentation and Globalisation'. *Global Society: Journal of Interdisciplinary International Relations* 16, no. 2 (2002): 175–98.
Björklund, Ulf. 'Armenians of Athens and Istanbul: The Armenian Diaspora and the "transnational" Nation'. *Global Networks* 3, no. 3 (2003): 337–54.
Bloch, Ernst. *Heritage of Our Times*. Cambridge: Polity Press, 1991.
Bonacci, Giulia. *Exodus !: L'histoire du retour des rastafariens en Ethiopie*. Paris: Scali, 2007.
Bonacich, Edna. 'A Theory of Middleman Minorities'. *American Sociological Review* 38, no. 5 (1973): 583–94.
Bordes-Benayoun, Chantal and Dominique Schnapper. *Diasporas et nations*. Paris: Odile Jacob, 2006.
Bordes-Benayoun, Chantal and Dominique Schnapper. 'Revisiter les Diasporas'. *Diasporas. Histoire et sociétés* 1, no. 1 (2002): 11–21.
Boudjikanian-Keuroghlian, Aïda. *Les Arméniens Dans La Région Rhône-Alpes: Essai Géographique Sur Les Rapports d'une Minorité Ethnique Avec Son Milieu d'accueil*. Lyon: Association des Amis de la "Revue de géographie de Lyon", 1978.
Boym, Svetlana. *The Future of Nostalgia*. New York: Basic Books, 2001.
Brah, Avtar. *Cartographies of Diaspora: Contesting Identities*. New York: Routledge, 2005.
Braudel, Fernand. *Civilisation, économie et capitalisme: XVe-XVIIIe siècle*. Paris: Librairie générale française, 1993.
Braudel, Fernand. *La Méditerranée et le monde méditerranéen à l'époque de Philippe II*. Paris: Armand Colin, 1949.
Brinkerhoff, Jennifer M. 'Creating an Enabling Environment for Diasporas' Participation in Homeland Development'. *International Migration* 50, no. 1 (2012): 75–95. https://doi.org/10.1111/j.1468-2435.2009.00542.x.
Brubaker, Rogers. 'Ethnicity Without Groups'. *Archives Européennes de Sociologie* 43, no. 2 (2002): 163–89.
Brubaker, Rogers. 'The 'Diaspora' Diaspora'. *Ethnic and Racial Studies* 28, no. 1 (2005): 1–19.
Bruneau, Michel. *Diasporas*. Montpellier: GIP Reclus, 1995.

Bruneau, Michel. *Diasporas et espaces transnationaux*. Paris: Anthropos/Economica, 2004.
Bruneau, Michel, ed. *Les Grecs Pontiques: Diaspora, identité, territoires*. Paris: CNRS éditions, 1998.
Bruneau, Michel. 'Les monastères pontiques de Macédoine, marqueurs territoriaux de la Diaspora'. In *Les Grecs Pontiques: Diaspora, identité, territoires*, edited by Michel Bruneau, 213–28. Paris: CNRS éditions, 1998.
Burgess, Katrina. 'Collective Remittances and Migrant-State Collaboration in Mexico and El Salvador'. *Latin American Politics and Society* 54, no. 4 (2012): 119–46. https://doi.org/10.1111/j.1548-2456.2012.00175.x.
'By the Community, For the Community'. *Asbarez*, 18 February 2016.
Carlson, John Roy. 'The Armenian Displaced Persons: A First Hand Report on Conditions in Europe'. *Armenian Affairs* 1, no. 1 (1949–1950): 26.
Cerulli, Enrico. *Etiopi in Palestina: Storia della comunità etiopica di Gerusalemme*. 2 Vols. Rome: Libreria dello Stato, 1943.
Chahinian, Talar. *Stateless: The Politics of the Armenian Language in Exile*. Syracuse: Syracuse University Press, 2023.
Chahinian, Talar. 'The Making of a Diasporic Literary Center: Post WWII Armenian Intellectual Life in Beirut'. In *Armenians in Lebanon*, edited by Carla Edde, Levon Nordiguian, and Vahé Tachjian, 284–303. Beirut: University of Saint Joseph Press, 2017.
Chahinian, Talar. 'Zabel Yesayan: The Myth of the Armenian Transnational Moment'. *Journal for the Society of Armenian Studies* 28, no. 2 (2021): 203–11.
Chatterjee, Partha. *The Nation and its Fragments*. Princeton, NJ: Princeton University Press, 1993.
Chivallon, Christine. 'Du territoire au réseau: Comment penser l'identité antillaise'. *Cahiers d'Études africaines* 37, no. 148 (1997): 767–94.
Chivallon, Christine. *La diaspora noire des Amériques: Expériences et théories à partir de la Caraïbe*. Paris: CNRS Éditions, 2016.
Chivallon, Christine. 'La Diaspora noire des Amériques. Réflexions sur le modèle de l'hybridité de Paul Gilroy'. *L'Homme. Revue française d'anthropologie* 161, no. 1 (2002): 51–73.
Cho, Lily. 'The Turn to Diaspora'. *Topia* 17, no. 4 (2007): 11–30.
Chobanian, Arshak. *Mer Kraganut'iwnĕ* [Our Literature]. Paris, 1926.
Chorbajian, Levon. *Hamapatker arevmtahayots' mēk daru patmut'ean* [Panorama of a Century Long History of the Western Armenians]. Vol. 4. Hay spiwrk'ĕ. Fransahayeru patmut'iwnĕ [Armenian Diaspora. History of the French-Armenians]. 4 Vols. Pēyrut': Tp. Sewan, 1975.
Chorbajian, Levon, ed. *The Making of Nagorno-Karabagh: From Secession to Republic*. London: PalgraveMacmillan, 2001.
Clifford, James. 'Diasporas'. *Cultural Anthropology* 9, no. 3 (1994): 302–38.
Clifford, James. *Routes: Travel and Translation in the Late Twentieth Century*. Cambridge, MA: Harvard University Press, 1997.
Cohen, Robin. 'Diasporas and the Nation-State: From Victims to Challengers'. *International Affairs* 72 (1996): 507–20.
Cohen, Robin. *Global Diasporas: An Introduction*. London: University College London Press, 2001.
Cohen, Robin. 'Solid, Ductile and Liquid: Changing Notions of Homeland and Home in Diaspora Studies'. QEH Working Paper Series, no. 156, University of Oxford,

UK, October 2007. https://www.qeh.ox.ac.uk/publications/solid-ductile-and-liquid-changing-notions-homeland-and-home-diaspora-studies.

Connor, Walker. 'The Impact of Homelands Upon Diasporas'. In *Modern Diasporas in International Politics*, edited by Gabriel Sheffer, 16–46. London: Croom Helm, 1986.

Cora, Yaşar Tolga, Dzovinar Derderian, and Ali Sipahi, eds. *The Ottoman East in the Nineteenth Century: Societies, Identities and Politics*. New York: I.B. Tauris, 2016.

Cora, Yaşar Tolga and Laurent Dissard. *Home(Land)s: Place, Loss and Return in Contemporary Turkey*. Special issue of *Études Arméniennes Contemporaines* 13 (2021).

'Court of The Hague'. *Uitspraken.rechtspraak.nl*. https://uitspraken.rechtspraak.nl/inziendocument?id=ECLI%3ANL%3ARBDHA%3A2020%3A8018, accessed 21 August 2020.

Craven, Catherine Ruth. 'Critical Realism, Assemblages and Practices Beyond the State: A New Framework for Analysing Global Diaspora Engagement'. *The SOAS Journal of Postgraduate Research* 11, no. 11 (2018): 100–16. https://eprints.soas.ac.uk/26314/.

Cumming-Bruce, Nick. 'Number of People Fleeing Conflict Is Highest Since World War II, U.N. Says'. *New York Times*, 19 June 2019. https://www.nytimes.com/2019/06/19/world/refugees-record-un.html.

Curtin, Philip D. *Cross-Cultural Trade in World History*. Studies in Comparative World History. Cambridge and New York: Cambridge University Press, 1984.

Dabag, Mihran and Kristin Platt, eds. *Identitaet der Fremde*. Bochum: Brockmeyer, 1993.

Dallakyan, Karlen. *H.B.Ē Miutʻyan Nakhagah G. Kyulpenkyani hrazharakani hartsʻi shurj* [About the Resignation of the AGBU President C. Gulbenkian]. Erevan: Hratarakutʻiwn Azg ōratertʻi, 1996.

Dallakyan, Karlen. *Hay spʻyurkʻi patmutʻyun (Hamaṟot aknark)* [A History of the Armenian Diaspora. Brief Outline]. Erevan: Zangak-97, 2004.

Dallakyan, Karlen. *Ṟamkavar Azatakan Kusaktsutʻyan patmutʻyun* [History of the Democratic Liberal Party]. Vol. 1, 1921–1940. 2 Vols. Erevan: Gitutʻyun, 1999.

Dallin, Alexander. *German Rule In Russia, 1941–1945: A Study of Occupation Policies*. Boulder, CO: Westview Press, 1981.

Darbinian, Ruben. *Mer pataskhanē H. Kʻajaznunii* [Our Response to H. Kajaznuni]. Boston: Hayrenikʻ tparan, 1923.

Darieva, Tsypylma. 'Rethinking Homecoming: Diasporic Cosmopolitanism in Post-Soviet Armenia'. *Ethnic and Racial Studies* 34, no. 3 (2011): 490–508. https://doi.org/10.1080/01419870.2011.535546.

Dasnabedian, Hrach. *H.H. Dashnaktsʻutʻean kazmakerpakan kaṟoytsʻi holowoytě* [The Evolution of the ARF Organizational Structure]. Beirut: Hamazgayini Vahē Sētʻean tparan, 1974.

Davidjants, Brigitta. 'Identity Construction in Armenian Music on the Example of Early Folklore Movement'. *Folklore: Electronic Journal of Folklore* 62 (2015): 175–200.

Davison, Roderic H. *Reform in the Ottoman Empire, 1856–1876*. Princeton, NJ: Princeton University Press, 1963.

DeLanda, Manuel. *Assemblage Theory*. Edinburgh: Edinburgh University Press, 2016.

Della Gatta, Marisa. 'A "Nation in Exile": The Renewed Diaspora of Syrian Armenian Repatriates'. *British Journal of Middle Eastern Studies* 46, no. 3 (2019): 339–57. https://doi.org/10.1080/13530194.2017.1403308.

Demoyan, Hayk. 'Patriotism, Competitive Nationalism and Minority's Successes: Armenian Sports in the Ottoman Empire in the Pre-1915 Period'. *International Journal of Armenian Genocide Studies* 1, no. 1 (2014): 7–38.

Der Alexanian, Jacques. *Les héritiers du pays oublié: 1922–1987*. Paris: R. Laffont, 1991.

Derderian, Dzovinar. 'Nation-Making and the Language of Colonialism: Voices from Ottoman Van in Armenian Print and Handwritten Petitions (1820s to 1870s)'. PhD diss., University of Michigan, Ann Arbor, MI, 2019.

Derogy, Jacques. *Resistance and Revenge: The Armenian Assassination of the Turkish Leaders Responsible for the 1915 Massacres and Deportations*. New Brunswick, NJ: Transaction Publishers, 1990.

Der Matossian, Bedross. 'Explaining the Unexplainable: Recent Trends in the Armenian Genocide Historiography'. *Journal of Levantine Studies* 5, no. 2 (Winter 2015): 143–66.

Der Matossian, Bedross. 'The Armenians of Jerusalem in the Modern Period: The Rise and Decline of a Community'. In *Routledge Handbook on Jerusalem*, edited by Suleiman A. Mourad, Naomi Koltun-Fromm, and Bedross Der Matossian, 396–407. London and New York: Routledge, 2019.

Der Sarkissian, Jean and Lucie Der Sarkissian. *Les pommes rouges d'Arménie*. Paris: Flammarion, 1987.

Diocese of the Armenian Church of America (Eastern). 'Primate's Words of Welcome to Catholicos and Prime Minister'. https://armenianchurch.us/2018/09/26/primate-welcomes-armenias-prime-minister-to-cathedral/, accessed 8 April 2021.

Diocese of the Armenian Church of America (Eastern). 'Why is October "Armenian Cultural Month"?'. https://armenianchurch.us/2017/10/19/october-armenian-cultural-month/, accessed 8 April 2021.

Djeredjian, Yeghia. 'SDHK-Kominteṙn Haraberutʻiwnnerě' [Relations between SDHP and the Comintern], *Haigazian Armenological Review*, 2002, 161–232.

Documents on the Schism in the Armenian Church of America. New York: Diocese of the Armenian Church of America, 1993.

Douglas, Daniel and Anny Bakalian. 'Sub-ethnic Diversity: Armenians in the United States'. *Journal of the Society of Armenian Studies* 18, no. 2 (2009): 55–70.

Dubnow, Simon. 'Diaspora'. In *Encyclopaedia of the Social Sciences*, edited by Edwin R. Seligman and Alvin Johnson, 126–30. New York: Macmillan, 1931.

Dufoix, Stéphane. *Les Diasporas*. Paris: Presses Universitaires de France, 2003.

Eblighatian, Madteos. *Geankʻ mě azkis geankʻin měch: Aganadesi ew masnagtsʻoghi Vgayutʻiwnner 1903–1923*. Antelias: Dbaran Gatoghigosutian Medzi Dann Giligio, 1987.

Ekmekcioglu, Lerna. *Recovering Armenia: The Limits of Belonging in Post-Genocide Turkey*. Stanford, CA: Stanford University Press, 2016.

Etmekjian, James. *The French Influence on the Western Armenian Renaissance, 1843–1915*. New York: Twayne Publishers, Inc., 1964.

Faist, Thomas. 'Diaspora and Transnationalism: What Kind of Dance Partners'. In *Diaspora and Transnationalism: Concepts, Theories and Methods*, edited by Rainer Baubök and Thomas Faist, 9–34. Amsterdam: Amsterdam University Press, 2010.

Fittante, Daniel. 'Connection Without Engagement: Paradoxes of North American Armenian Return Migration'. *Diaspora* 19, no. 2–3 (2017): 147–69. https://doi.org/10.3138/diaspora.19.2-3.147.

Flanner, Janet. 'Letter from Aschaffenburg'. *The New Yorker*, 22 October 1948, 98–101.

Flores-Yeffal, Nadia Y. 'Migration-Trust Networks: Unveiling the Social Networks of International Migration'. In *Immigration and Categorical Inequality*, edited by in Castañeda Eva, 83–98. London: Routledge, 2017.

Fortier, Anne-Marie. 'Community, Belonging and Intimate Ethnicity'. *Modern Italy* 11, no. 1 (2006): 63–77. https://doi.org/10.1080/13532940500492308.

Fortier, Anne-Marie. *Migrant Belongings: Memory, Space, Identity*. London: Routledge, 2000.
Foucault, Michel. *Discipline and Punish: The Birth of the Prison*. Translated by Alan Sheridan. New York: Random House, Inc, 1995.
Foucault, Michel. 'Governmentality'. In *The Foucault Effect: Studies in Governmentality: With Two Lectures by and an Interview with Michel Foucault*, edited by Graham Burchell, Colin Gordon, and Peter Miller, 87–104. Chicago, IL: The University of Chicago Press, 1991.
Foucault, Michel. *Omnes et Singulatim: Towards a Criticism of 'Political Reason'*. Tanner Lectures on Human Values at Stanford (SC1047), Dept. of Special Collections and University Archives. Stanford, CA: Stanford University Libraries, 1979.
Foucault, Michel. *Security, Territory, Population: Lectures at the Collège de France, 1977–1978*. Edited by Michel Senellart, François Ewald, and Alessandro Fontana. Translated by Graham Burchell. 1. Picador ed. Lectures at the Collège de France. New York: Picador, 2009.
Foucault, Michel. 'Technologies of the Self'. In *Technologies of the Self, a Seminar with Michel Foucault*, edited by Luther H. Martin, Huck Gutman, and Patrick H. Hutton, 16–49. Amherst, MA: University of Massachusetts Press, 1988.
Foucault, Michel. *The History of Sexuality, Volume I*. New York: Vintage, 1990.
Galstyan, Mihran, Ruben Ohanjanyan, Tamara Zaqaryan, Gayane Hakobyan. *Contemporary Armenian Family in Transformative Society*. Yerevan: NAS RA, Gitutyun, 2017.
Galstyan, Nare. 'Engaging Stateless and State-Linked Diasporas: Assyrians and Armenians in the Netherlands'. Ph.D. diss., University of Milan and University of Turin, 2019.
Gamlen, Alan. 'Diaspora Engagement Policies: What are They and What Kinds of States Use Them?'. *Centre on Migration, Policy and Society Working Paper Series 32*, 2006. www.compas.ox.ac.uk/publications/Working%20papers/WP0632-Gamlen.pdf.
Gamlen, Alan. 'Diaspora Institutions and Diaspora Governance'. *International Migration Review* 48, no. 1 (September 2014): 180–217.
Gamlen, Alan. 'The Emigration State and the Modern Geopolitical Imagination'. *Political Geography* 27, no. 8 (2008): 840–56. https://doi.org/10.1016/j.polgeo.2008.10.004.
Gellner, Ernest E. *Nations and Nationalism*. 2nd ed. New York: Cornell University Press, 2008.
Genizi, Haim. *America's Fair Share: The Admission and Resettlement of Displaced Persons, 1945–1952*. Detroit: Wayne State University Press, 1993.
Ghanalanyan, Tigran. 'Transportation of Displaced Armenians to America after the Second World War' (in Armenian). *Etchmiadzin* 12 (2015): 69–89.
Ghazanchyan, Siranush. '1,100-year-old Armenian Church in Van Holds 10th Holy Mass Since Reopening'. *Public Radio of Armenia*, 5 September 2022. https://en.armradio.am/2022/09/05/1100-year-old-armenian-church-in-van-holds-10th-holy-mass-since-reopening/
Ghazarian, Ara, ed., *Hakob Karapents: A Complete Bibliography*. Watertown: Blue Crane Books, 1999.
Ghorashi, Halleh. 'Agents of Change or Passive Victims: The Impact of Welfare States (The Case of the Netherlands) on Refugees'. *Journal of Refugee Studies* 18, no. 2 (2005): 181–98. https://doi.org/10.1093/refuge/fei020.
Gilroy, Paul. *Against Race: Imagining Political Culture Beyond the Color Line*. Cambridge, MA: Harvard University Press, 2000.

Gilroy, Paul. 'Diaspora and the Detours of Identity'. In *Identity and Difference*, edited by K. Woodward, 299–346. Newbury Park, CA: Sage Publications, 1997.
Gilroy, Paul. *The Black Atlantic: Modernity and Double Consciousness*. London: Verso, 1993.
Goldschmidt, Henry. '"Crown Heights is the Center of the World": Reterritorializing a Jewish Diaspora'. *Diaspora: A Journal of Transnational Studies* 9 (1) 2000: 83–106.
Gordon, Colin. 'Governmental Rationality: An Introduction'. In *The Foucault Effect: Studies in Governmentality with Two Lectures by and an Interview with Michel Foucault*, edited by Graham Burchell, Colin Gordon, and Peter Miller, 1–52. Chicago, IL: University of Chicago Press, 1991.
Greenspoon, Leonard J., ed. *Next Year in Jerusalem: Exile and Return in Jewish History*. West Lafayette: Purdue University Press, 2019.
Grenet, Mathieu. 'Appartenances régionales, expérience diasporique et fabrique communautaire: Le cas grec, fin XVIe-début XIXe siècle'. *Tracés. Revue de Sciences humaines* 23 (2012): 21–40.
Grenet, Mathieu. *La fabrique communautaire. Les Grecs à Venise, Livourne et Marseille 1770–1840*. Athènes: École française d'Athènes, 2016.
Grigorian, Armineh, Robert Atayan, and Aram Kerovpyan. 'Komitas Vardapet'. *Grove Music Online* (2001). https://www.oxfordmusiconline.com/grovemusic/view/10.1093/gmo/9781561592630.001.0001/omo-9781561592630-e-0000051868, accessed 3 November 2020.
Gulludjian, Hagop. 'Language Vitality through "Creative Literacy"'. In *Western Armenian in the 21st Century: Challenges and New Approaches*, edited by Bedross Der Matossian and Barlow Der Mugrdechian, 103–32. Fresno, CA: The Press at California State University, Fresno, 2018.
Gurahian, Jennifer. 'In the Mind's Eye: Collective Memory and Armenian Village Ethnographies'. *Armenian Review* 43, no. 1 (1990): 19–29.
Gutman, David. *The Politics of Armenian Migration to North America, 1885–1915: Sojourners, Smugglers and Dubious Citizens*. Edinburgh Studies on the Ottoman Empire. Edinburgh: Edinburgh University Press, 2019.
'H. Hakobyan Considers Hürriyet's Misinformation About her Speech to be a Provocation'. [translated title], *Armenpress*, 12 May 2011. https://armenpress.am/arm/news/652197.
Hacking, Ian. 'How Should We Do the History of Statistics?'. In *The Foucault Effect: Studies in Governmentality with Two Lectures by and an Interview with Michel Foucault*, edited by Graham Burchell, Colin Gordon, and Peter Miller, 181–96. Chicago, IL: University of Chicago Press, 1991.
Haddeciyan, Rober. 'Diaspora bakanlığı tarafından bana verilen madalya hakkında'. *HyeTert*, 26 January 2011. https://hyetert.org/2011/01/26/diaspora-bakanligi-tarafindan-bana-verilen-madalya-hakkinda/.
Hakobyan, Arsen. 'From Aleppo to Yerevan: The War and Migration from the Window of the Bus'. *Tbilisi in Fundamentalism Ethnographies on Minorities, Discrimination and Transnationalism* 44 (2016): 21–41.
Halbwachs, Maurice. *La topographie légendaire des Évangiles en Terre Sainte. Étude de mémoire Collective*. Paris: Gallimard, 1941.
Hall, Stuart. 'Cultural Identity and Diaspora'. In *Identity: Community, Culture, Difference*, edited by J. Rutherford, 222–37. London: Lawrence & Wishart, 1990.
Hamaṛot patmut'iwn Hama-Sebastats'iakan shinarar miut'ean [Brief History of the Pan-Sebastian Construction Union]. New York: Hama-Sebastats'iakan shinarar miut'iwn, 1945.

Hardy, Sam. 'Who Blew Up the Armenian Genocide Memorial Church in Deir el-Zour?'. *Hyperallergic*, 11 November 2014. https://hyperallergic.com/162080/who-blew-up-the-armenian-genocide-memorial-church-in-deir-el-zour/.

Harootunian, Harry. *The Unspoken as Heritage: The Armenian Genocide and its Unaccounted Lives*. Durham, NC: Duke University Press, 2019.

Harootunian, Harry. '"In the Zone of Occult Instability": Some Reflections on Unevenness, Discordant Temporalities and the Logic of Historical Practice'. In *Archaism and Anachrony: Reflections on the Question of Historical Time and Uneven Development*. Durham, NC: Duke University Press, forthcoming.

Hay, Gnduni. 'H.Ḥ.D. k'aghak'akanut'iwně gaghut'ahayut'ean mēj' [The ARF Policy among Diaspora Armenians]. *Hayrenik' ōrat'ert'* [Hairenik Daily], 4 July 1928, 1.

Hayastani Koch'nak [The Gotchnag]. 'Hay gaght'akanut'iwně [Armenian Migrant Communities]. 4 July 1925, 852.

Hayrenik' ōrat'ert' [Hairenik Daily]. 'Erewani kařavarut'ean nor "eloyt'ě"' [The Recent "Address" of the Yerevan Government]. 18 August 1929, 4.

Hayrenik' ōrat'ert' [Hairenik Daily], 'H.B.Ē. Miut'iwn: Vustěr, Nuparashēni hanganakut'ean k'ēmp'ēyn' [A.G.B. Union: Worcester, A Fundraising Campaign for Nubarashen]. 20 September 1929, 4.

Hayrenik' ōrat'ert' [Hairenik Daily]. 'H.Ḥ. Dashnakts'ut'ean 12-rd ěndhanur zhoghovi haytararut'iwně' [The Announcement of the ARF 12th General Congress]. 9 April 1933, 1.

Hayrenik' ōrat'ert' [Hairenik Daily]. 'Haykakan eřagoyn droshakě' [The Armenian Tricolor Flag]. 30 May 1929, 4.

Hayrenik' ōrat'ert' [Hairenik Daily]. 'Khmbagrakan: Anarzhan ařajnord mě' [Editorial: An Undeserving Primate]. 12 July 1933, 4.

Hayrenik' ōrat'ert' [Hairenik Daily], 'Teghekut'iwnner Nor Arabkirēn' [News from New Arabkir]. 20 August 1929, 2.

Hayrenik' ōrat'ert' [Hairenik Daily]. 'The New York Murder'. 29 December 1933, 4.

Haytoug. Displaced Person Strengthening Communities: The Story of the Montebello DPs. June 2011. https://ayfwest.org/news/displaced-person-strengthening-communities/, accessed May 10, 2022.

Hewsen, Robert H. 'The Geography of Armenia'. In *The Armenian People from Ancient to Modern Times*, edited by Richard G. Hovannissian, 1–17. New York: St. Martin's Press, 1997.

Heyer, Kristin E. *Kinship across Borders: A Christian Ethic of Immigration*. Washington, DC: Georgetown University Press, 2012.

Hirschkind, Charles. *The Ethical Soundscape: Cassette Sermons and Islamic Counterpublics*. New York: Columbia University Press, 2006.

Hobsbawm, Eric J. 'Ethnicity and Nationalism in Europe Today'. *Anthropology Today* 8, no. 1 (February 1992): 3–8.

Hobsbawm, Eric J.. *The Age of Empire, 1875–1914*. New York: Vintage Books,1987.

Hobsbawm, Eric J. *The Invention of Tradition*. Cambridge: Cambridge University Press, 1983.

HŌK: Ōrgan artasahmanean hōkeru (HOC: Revue Mensuelle). 'HŌKi Fransayi shrjani 4-rd artakarg patgamaworakan zhoghově' [The HOK 4th Regional Emergency Congress of France]. April 1933, 51–64.

HŌK: Parberakan Prak [HOK: Periodical Volume]. 'Hayastani ōgnut'ean komiten Gahirēi mēj' [Committee for Aid to Armenia in Cairo]. 1 June 1926, 2–4.

Holian, Anna Marta. *Between National Socialism and Soviet Communism: Displaced Persons in Postwar Germany*. Ann Arbor, MI: University of Michigan Press, 2011.

Horujy, Sergey S. *Practices of the Self and Spiritual Practices: Michel Foucault and the Eastern Christian Discourse*. Translated by Boris Jakim. Grand Rapids, MI and Cambridge: William B. Eerdmans Publishing Company, 2015.

Hovanessian, Martine. 'Diaspora arménienne et patrimonialisation d'une mémoire collective: L'impossible lieu du témoignage ?'. *Les Cahiers de Framespa* 3 (2007). https://journals.openedition.org/framespa/314.

Hovanessian, Martine, ed. *Diaspora arménienne et territorialités*. Special issue of *Hommes et migrations* 1265 (2007).

Hovanessian, Martine. 'Diasporas et identités collectives'. *Hommes et migrations* 1265 (2007): 9–21.

Hovanessian, Martine. 'La notion de diaspora'. *Journal des anthropologues* 72–73, no. 1 (1998): 11–30.

Hovanessian, Martine. 'La notion de diaspora: Les évolutions d'une conscience de la dispersion à travers l'ensemble arménien'. In *Les diasporas: 2000 ans d'histoire*, edited by Lisa Anteby-Yemini, William Berthomière and Gabriel Sheffer (2005): 65–78.

Hovanessian, Martine. *Le lien communautaire: Trois générations d'Arméniens*. Paris: Armand Colin, 1992.

Hovanessian, Martine. 'Le religieux et la reconnaissance: Formes symboliques et diaspora arménienne en France'. *Les Annales de la Recherche Urbaine* 96, no. 1 (2004): 125–34.

Hovanessian, Martine. 'Récits de vie et mémoire(s) de l'exil: Les enjeux à l'œuvre dans l'histoire orale'. *Revue du monde arménien moderne et contemporain* 6 (2001): 75–96.

Hovannisian, Richard G. and Armen Manuk-Khaloyan. 'The Armenian Communities of Asia Minor: A Pictorial Essay'. In *Armenian Communities of Asia Minor*, edited by Richard G. Hovannisian, 9–88. Costa Mesa, CA: Mazda Publishers, 2014.

Hovannisian, Richard G. and David N. Myers, eds. *Enlightenment and Diaspora: The Armenian and Jewish Cases*. Atlanta: Scholars Press, 1999.

Hovannisian, Richard G. and David N. Myers. 'The Armenian Question in the Ottoman Empire 1876–1914'. In *The Armenian People from Ancient to Modern Times, 2. Foreign Domination to Statehood: The Fifteenth Century to the Twentieth Century*, 203–39. Basingstoke: Macmillan, 1997.

Hovannisian, Richard G. and David N. Myers. *The Republic of Armenia. Vol. 1: The First Year, 1918–1919*. Berkeley, CA: University of California Press, 1999.

Hovhannisyan, Ashot. *Gaghut'ahay khndirner* [Diaspora-Armenian Issues]. Erevan: Petakan hratarakch'ut'yun, 1925.

Howard, Thomas A. *God and the Atlantic: America, Europe, and the Religious Divide*. Oxford: Oxford University Press, 2011.

Hür, Ayşe. 'Franz Werfel ve Musa Dağ'da Kırk Gün'. *Taraf*, 18 December 2011. https://www.marmarayerelhaber.com/Ayse-HUR-Taraf-yazilari/5349-Franz-Werfel-ve-Musa-Dagda-Kirk-Gun, accessed 8 September 2022.

Jacoby, Tami Amanda. 'A Theory of Victimhood: Politics, Conflict and the Construction of Victim-Based Identity'. *Millennium* 43, no. 2 (2015): 511–30. https://doi.org/10.1177/03058298145502.

Jamalian, Arshak. 'H. K'ajaznunin ew H.H. Dashnakts'ut'yunĕ' [H. Kajaznuni and the ARF]. *Hayrenik' amsagir* [Hairenik Monthly] 2, no. 3–5 (1924): 8–9.

Jayawardena, Kumari. *Feminism and Nationalism in the Third World*. London: Zed Press, 1986.

Kaiser, Robert J. In *The Geography of Nationalism in Russia and the USSR*, 94–148. Princeton, NJ: Princeton University Press, 1994.

Kajaznuni, Hovhannes. *H.H. Dashnakts'ut'iwnĕ anelik' ch'uni ayl ews* [The Armenian Revolutionary Federation Has Nothing to Do Anymore]. Vienna: Mkhit'arean Tparan, 1923.
Kanaiaupuni, Shawn Malia. 'Reframing the Migration Question: An Analysis of Men, Women, and Gender in Mexico'. *Social Forces* 78, no. 4 (2000): 1311–47. https://doi.org/10.1093/sf/78.4.1311.
Karakashian, Mher. 'Yerevagayut'ean azatakrumĕ' [Imagination's emancipation]. *Horizon Weekly*, 3 February 1992.
Karapents, Hakob. *Adami Girk'ĕ* [Adam's Book]. New York: Osketaṛ Hratarakch'akan, 1983.
Karapents, Hakob. *Erku Ashkharh* [Two Worlds]. Watertown: Blue Crane Books, 1992.
K'arasnameak (1903–1943) Eritasard Hayastani [Fortieth Anniversary (1903–1943) of Eritasard Hayastan]. New York: s.n., 1944.
Kasbarian, Sossie. 'Refuge in the "Homeland: The Syrians in Armenia"'. In *Aid to Armenia: Humanitarianism and Intervention from the 1890s to the Present*, edited by Jo Laycock and Francesca Piana. 164–80. Manchester: Manchester University Press, 2020.
Kasbarian, Sossie. 'Rooted and Routed: The Contemporary Armenian Diaspora in Cyprus and Lebanon'. Ph.D. diss., School of Oriental and African Studies (University of London), 2006.
Kasbarian, Sossie. 'The Armenian Community in Cyprus at the Beginning of the 21st Century: From Insecurity to Integration'. In *The Minorities of Cyprus: Development Patterns and the Identity of Internal-Exclusion*, edited by A. Varnavas, N. Coureas, and M. Elia, 175–91. Newcastle upon Tyne: Cambridge Scholars Publishing, 2009.
Kasbarian, Sossie. 'The Armenian Middle East – Boundaries, Pathways and Horizons'. In *The Routledge Handbook on Middle Eastern Diasporas*, edited by Dalia Abdelhady and Ramy Aly. 405–19. New York: Routledge, 2022.
Kasbarian, Sossie. 'The Myth and Reality of "Return"—Diaspora in the "Homeland"'. *Diaspora: A Journal of Transnational Studies* 18, no. 3 (Fall 2009): 358–81.
Kasbarian, Sossie. 'The "Others" Within: The Armenian Community in Cyprus'. In *Diasporas of the Modern Middle East: Contextualising Community*, edited by Anthony Gorman and Sossie Kasbarian, 241–73. Edinburgh: Edinburgh University Press, 2015.
Kasbarian, Sossie. 'The Politics of Memory and Commemoration: Armenian Diasporic Reflections on 2015'. *Nationalities Papers* 46, no. 1 (2018): 123–43.
Kazazian, Anne. 'Les Arméniens au Caire dans la première moitié du XIXe siècle: L'implantation d'une communauté en diaspora'. In *Arméniens et Grecs en diaspora: Approches comparatives*, edited by Michel Bruneau, Ioannis Hassiotis, Claire Mouradian, and Martine Hovanessian, 133–49. Athènes: École française d'Athènes, 2007.
Kazmakerpakan kanonner: Hastatuats Zh. ĕndh. zhoghovin koghmē [By-Laws: Approved by the 10th General Assembly]. Zhĕnew [Geneva]: H.H. Dashnakts'ut'iwn [A.R. Federation], 1925.
Kebranian, Nanor. 'Dispersing Community: Diaspora and the Ethics of Estrangement'. In *Manifestos for World Thought*, edited by Lucian Stone and Jason Bahbak Mohaghegh, 83–98. London: Rowman & Littlefield International, Ltd., 2017.
Keck, Margaret and Kathryn Sikkink. 'Transnational Advocacy Networks in International and Regional Politics'. *International Social Science Journal* 51 (1999): 89–101.
Keles, Janroj Yilmaz, Eugenia Markova, and Rebwar Fatah. 'Migrants with Insecure Legal Status and Access to Work: The Role of Ethnic Solidarity Networks'. *Equality, Diversity*

and Inclusion: An International Journal (2019). https://doi.org/10.1108/EDI-10-2018-0203.

Kerovpyan, Aram. 'Les *charakan* (*troparia*) et l'octoéchos arménien selon le *charaknots* (*tropologion* arménien) édité en 1875'. In *Aspects de la musique liturgique au Moyen-Age*, edited by Christian Meyer, 93–123. Paris: Creaphis, 1991.

Kerovpyan, Aram. *Manuel de notation musicale arménienne Modern*. Tutzing: Hans Schneider, 2001.

Kevorkian, Raymond. *The Armenian Genocide: A Complete History*. London: I.B. Tauris, 2011.

Kevorkian, Raymond and B. Paul Paboudjian. *1915 Öncesinde Osmanlı İmparatorluğu'nda Ermeniler*. Istanbul: Aras Yay, 2012.

Khachaturian, Lisa. *Cultivating Nationhood in Imperial Russia: The Periodical Press and the Formation of a Modern Armenian Identity*. New Brunswick, NJ: Transaction Publishers, 2009.

Khalapyan, Hasmik. 'Nationalism and Armenian Women's Movement in the Ottoman Empire, 1875–1914'. PhD diss. Central European University, 2008.

Kitur, Arsen. *Patmut'iwn S. D. Hnch'akean Kusakts'ut'ean, 1887–1962* [History of the Social-Democratic Hunchakian Party]. Vol. 1. 2 Vols. Beirut: SDHP Press, 1962.

Klimt, Andrea and Stephen Lubkemann. 'Argument across the Portuguese-Speaking World: A Discursive Approach to Diaspora'. *Diaspora: A Journal of Transnational Studies* 11, no. 2 (2002): 145–62.

Koçunyan, Ara. *Voğçuyn Amenkin*. Istanbul: Aras Yay., 2008.

Koinova, Maria and Gerasimos Tsourapas. 'How Do Countries of Origin Engage Migrants and Diasporas? Multiple Actors and Comparative Perspectives'. *International Political Science Review* 39, no. 3 (2018): 311–21. https://doi.org/10.1177/0192512118755584.

Komitas. *Armenian Sacred and Folk Music*. Translated by Edward Gulbenkian. Surrey: Curzon Press, 1998.

Komitas. *Armenian Sacred and Folk Music*. Translated by Edward Gulbenkian. Surrey: CurzonPress, 1998. Originally published in *Ararat* (Etchmiadzin, 1898): 111–17.

Komitas. *Komitas: Essays and Articles*. Translated by Vatsche Barsoumian. Pasadena, CA: Drazark Press, 2001.

Komitas. 'The Singing of the Holy Liturgy'. Review of *Ergets'oghut'iwnk' Srboy Pataragi* [*The Singing of the Holy Liturgy*], by Makar Ekmalian. Leipzig: Breitkopf and Hertel, 1896.

Körükmez, Lülüfer. 'Ulus-ötesi göç ağları ve sosyal alanların oluşumu: Ermenistan'dan Türkiye'ye işgücü göçü üzerine sosyolojik bir araştırma'. PhD diss., Ege University, 2012.

Kouymjian, Dickran. 'Cilicia and its Catholicosate from the Fall of the Armenian Kingdom to 1915'. In *Armenian Cilicia*, edited by Richard Hovannisian and Simon Payaslian, 297–308. Costa Mesa, CA: Mazda Publishers, 2008.

Kouymjian, Dickran. 'The Role of Armenian Potters of Kutahia in the Ottoman Ceramic Industry'. In *Armenian Communities in Asia Minor*, 107–30, edited by Richard G. Hovannisian. Costa Mesa, CA: Mazda Publishers, 2014.

Kredian, Armin. 'The Armenian Community of Egypt: World War I and Genocide 1914–1919'. *Haigazian Armenological Review* 35 (2015): 201–48.

Krikorian, Michael. 'A Reunion of the Displaced'. *Los Angeles Times*, 15 September 1997.

Krueger, Derek. *Liturgical Subjects: Christian Ritual, Biblical Narrative, and the Formation of Self in Byzantium*. Philadelphia: University of Pennsylvania Press, 2014.

Kunth, Anouche. *Exils arméniens: Du Caucase à Paris, 1920–1945*. Paris: Belin, 2016.
Kunz, Rahel. 'The Discovery of the Diaspora'. *International Political Sociology* 6, no. 1 (2012): 103–7. https://doi.org/10.1111/j.1749-5687.2011.00152_4.x.
Kuyucu, Ali Tuna. 'Ethno-religious "unmixing" of "Turkey": 6–7 September Riots as a Case in Turkish Nationalism'. *Nations and Nationalism* 11, no. 3 (2005): 361–80.
Kuyumjian, Rita Souahian. *The Archeology of Madness: Komitas, Portrait of an Armenian Icon*. Princeton, NJ: Gomidas Institute, 2001.
La Porta, Sergio. 'Armeno-Latin Intellectual Exchange in the Fourteenth Century: Scholarly Traditions in Conversation and Competition'. *Medieval Encounters* 21 (2015): 269–94.
Larner, Wendy. 'Expatriate Experts and Globalising Governmentalities: The New Zealand Diaspora Strategy'. *Transactions of the Institute of British Geographers* 32, no. 3 (2007): 331–45. https://doi.org/10.1111/j.1475-5661.2007.00261.x.
Lauras, Clarisse. *Les Arméniens à Saint-Étienne: Une Escale Dans Un Parcours Migratoire?* Saint-Étienne: Publications de l'Université de Saint-Étienne, 2006.
Laycock, Jo. 'Armenian Homelands and Homecomings, 1945–9'. *Cultural and Social History* 9, no. 1 (2012): 103–23.
Laycock, Jo. 'Armenian Homelands and Homecomings, 1945–9. The Repatriation of Diaspora Armenians to the Soviet Union'. *Cultural and Social History* 9, no. 1 (2012): 103–23.
Laycock, Jo. 'The Repatriation of Armenians to Soviet Armenia, 1945–1949'. In *Warlands Population Resettlement and State Reconstruction in the Soviet-East European Borderlands, 1945–1950*, edited by Peter Gattrell and Nick Baron. London: Palgrave MacMillan, 2009.
Leslau, Wolf. *Concise Amharic Dictionary*. Wiesbaden: Harrassowitz, 1976.
Leustean, Lucian N. 'Summary Report of the British Academy Project on "Forced Migration, Religious Diplomacy and Human Security in the Eastern Orthodox World"'. *International Journal for the Study of the Christian Church* 19, no. 1 (2019): 72–6.
Levy, André, ed. 'A Community That is Both a Center and a Diaspora: Jews in Late Twentieth Century Morocco'. In *Homelands and Diasporas: Holy Lands and Other Places*, 68–96. Stanford, CA: Stanford University Press, 2005.
Libera, Paweł. 'Polish Authorities and the Attempt to Create the Caucasian Confederation (1917–1940)'. *Studia z Dziejów Rosji i Europy Środkowo-Wschodniej* 52, no. 3 (August 19, 2018): 231.
Little Armenias. 'Armenian Evangelical Church'. https://www.littlearmenias.com/listings/armenian-evangelical-church-20/, accessed 8 April 2021.
Loomba, Ania. *Colonialism/Postcolonialism*. 2nd ed. London: Routledge, 2005.
Loqmakeozyan, Dzovinar. 'Best in Baghramyan Avenue'. *Agos*, 7 March 2015, https://www.agos.com.tr/am/hvotvadzi/12052/lawakvohnnyeri-paghramyean-bvoghvodahi-vrah.
Macdonald, Sharon. *Memorylands: Heritage and Identity in Europe Today*. London: Routledge, 2013.
Mahmood, Saba. *Politics of Piety: The Islamic Revival and the Feminist Subject*. Princeton, NJ: Princeton University Press, 2005.
Malkki, Liisa H.. 'National Geographic: The Rooting of Peoples and the Territorialization of National Identity among Scholars and Refugees'. *Cultural Anthropology* 7, no. 1 (1992): 24–44.
Malkki, Liisa H. 'Refugees and Exile: From "Refugee Studies" to the National Order of Things'. *Annual Review of Anthropology* 24 (1995): 495–523.

Ma Mung, Emmanuel. 'Non-lieu et utopie: La diaspora chinoise et le territoire'. In *Les réseaux des diasporas*, edited by Georges Prévélakis, 205–14. Paris: KYREM, L'Harmattan, 1996.

Mandel, Maud. *In the Aftermath of Genocide: Armenians and Jews in Twentieth-Century France*. Durham, NC: Duke University Press, 2003.

Manjikian, Lalai. 'Collective Memory and Diasporic Articulations of Imagined Homes: Armenian Community Centres in Montréal'. PhD diss., McGill University, 2005.

Manukyan, Miran. 'Euro Armenian Games'te İstanbul da var'. *Agos*, 24 February 2016. https://www.agos.com.tr/tr/yazi/14458/euro-armenian-gameste-istanbul-da-var.

Marashlyan, Vardan, Galstyan Nare, and Hovhannisyan Irena. *Integration Practices of Repatriates in Armenia*. Yerevan: Ministry of Diaspora of the Republic of Armenia, 2015.

Marcus, George E. 'Ethnography in/of the World System: The Emergence of Multi-Sited Ethnography'. *Annual Review of Anthropology* 24 (1995): 95–117.

Mardikian, George M. *Song of America*. New York: McGraw-Hill, 1956.

Martuni, Aleksandr. *Kusakts'ut'yunnerě gaghut'ahayut'yan mej* [Political Parties Among Diaspora Armenians]. Tiflis: Petakan hratarakch'ut'yun, 1924.

Matiossian, Vartan. 'Bolisĕ sp'iwṛk' ē t'ē och''. *Armeniaca*, 2 July 2011. http://armeniaca-haygagank.blogspot.com/2011/07/blog-post.html?utm_source=feedburner&utm_medium=email&utm_campaign=Feed%3A+Armeniaca-+%28ARMENIACA+-+%D5%80%D4%B1%D5%85%D4%BF%D4%B1%D4%BF%D4%B1%D5%86%D5%94%29.

Matossian, Bedross Der. 'The Armenians of Palestine 1918-48'. *Journal of Palestine Studies* 41, no. 1 (November 2011): 24–44.

McCollum, Jonathan. 'Analysis of Notation in Music Historiography: Armenian Neumatic *Khaz* From the Ninth Through Early Twentieth Centuries'. In *Theory and Method in Historical Ethnomusicology*, edited by Jonathan McCollum and David G. Hebert, 197–256. Lanham, MD: Lexington Books, 2014.

McCollum, Jonathan and Andy Nercessian. *Armenian Music: A Comprehensive Bibliography and Discography*. Lanham, MD: Scarecrow Press, 2004.

McConnell, Fiona. 'Governmentality to Practise the State? Constructing a Tibetan Population in Exile'. *Environment and Planning D: Society and Space* 30, no. 1 (February 2012): 78–95.

Médam, Alain. 'Diaspora/Diasporas. Archétype et typologie'. *Revue européenne des migrations internationales* 9, no. 1 (1993): 59–66.

Meliksetyan, Hovik. 'Hayastani ōgnut'yan komiten ev nra derě hayrenik'i het sp'yuṛk'ahay ashkhatavorneri kaperi amrapndman gortsum' [The Committee for Aid to Armenia and Its Role in Strengthening the Connections of Diaspora Armenian Workers with the Homeland]. *Haykakan SSṚ Gitut'yunneri akademiayi teghekagir. Hasarakakan gitut'yunner* [Proceedings of the National Academy of the Armenian SSR, Social Sciences] 8 (1959): 31–48.

Meliksetyan, Hovik. *Hayrenik'-sp'yuṛk' aṛnch'ut'yunnerě ev hayrenadardzut'yuně (1920–1980 t'.t'.)* [Homeland-Diaspora Relations and the Repatriation (1920s-1980s)]. Erevan: Erevani Hamalsarani hrat., 1985.

Melkonyan, Eduard. *Haykakan baregortsakan ěndhanur miut'yan patmut'yun* [History of the Armenian General Benevolent Union]. Erevan: Mughni hratarakch'ut'yun, 2005.

Melkonyan, Ruben. *Review of History of the Armenian Community in Istanbul*. Yerevan: VMV-Print, 2010.

Melkonyan, Ruben. 'Shark'ayin Turk'agan abadeghegadvut'yun'. *Hayern Aysor*, 11 May 2011. https://old.hayernaysor.am/archives/2944.

Mey, Elyda. 'Cambodian Diaspora Communities in Transitional Justice'. *Briefing Paper*. New York: International Center for Transitional Justice, 2008. www. ictj. org/sites/default/files/ICTJ-Cambodia-Diaspora-Justice-2008-English. pdf.

Mgrditchian, George. 'Groong'. On *Armenian Oud Masters in USA: Recordings from 40s, 50s, & 60s*. Vintage Music, 2012.

Migliorino, Nicola. '"Kulna Suriyyin"? The Armenian Community and the State in Contemporary Syria'. *Revue des Mondes Musulmans et de la Méditerranée* 1 (2006): 115–16. https://doi.org/10.4000/remmm.3020.

Migliorino, Nicola. *Re)Constructing Armenia in Lebanon and Syria: Ethno-Cultural Diversity and the State in the Aftermath of a Refugee Crisis*. New York and Oxford: Berghahn Books, 2008.

Mikayelyan, Karen. *Hay zhoghovrdakan harstut'yunnern artasahmanum: ktakner, nviratvut'yunner ev hasarakakan gumarner* [Armenian National Wealth Abroad: Wills, Gifts, and Public Funds]. Moskva: Hratarakut'yun Hayastani ōgnut'yan komiteyi, 1928.

Minassian, Edward. 'The Forthy Days of Musa Dagh: The Film That Was Denied'. *Journal of Armenian Studies* 3, no.1–2 (1985/6): 63–73.

Minassian, Mihran. 'Tracking Down the Past: The Memory Book ("Houshamadyan") Genre- A Preliminiary Bibligoraphy'. https://www.houshamadyan.org/themes/bibliography.html, accessed 9 April 2021.

Minassian, Oshagan. *A History of the Armenian Holy Apostolic Orthodox Church in the United States (1888–1944)*. Monterey, CA: Mayreni Publishing, 2010.

Mirak, Robert. *Torn Between Two Lands: Armenians in America, 1890 to World War I*. Cambridge, MA: Harvard University Press, 1983.

Monge, Mathilde and Natalia Muchnik. *L'Europe des diasporas: XVIe-XVIIIe siècle*. Paris: Presses universitaires de France / Humensis, 2019.

Moughalian, Sato. *Feast of Ashes: The Life and Art of David Ohannessian*. Stanford, CA: Stanford University Press, 2019.

Mouradian, George. *Armenian InfoText*. Southgate, MI: Bookshelf Publishers, 1995.

Muchnik, Natalia. 'La terre d'origine dans les diasporas des XVIe-XVIIIe siècles. " S'attacher à des pierres comme à une religion locale . . .''. *Annales. Histoire, Sciences Sociales* 66ᵉ année, no. 2 (2011): 481–512.

Mullings, Beverley. 'Governmentality, Diaspora Assemblages and the Ongoing Challenge of "Development"'. *Antipode* 44, no. 2 (March 2012): 406–27.

Nalbantian, Tsolin. *Armenians beyond Diaspora: Making Lebanon Their Own*. Edinburgh: Edinburgh University Press, 2020.

Nalbantian, Tsolin. 'From Murder in New York to Salvation from Beirut: Armenian Intra-Sectarianism'. In *Practicing Sectarianism: Ethnographic and Archival Interventions on Lebanon*, edited by Lara Deeb, Tsolin Nalbantian, and Nadya Sbaiti, 116–37. Stanford, CA: Stanford University Press, 2022.

Nalbantian, Tsolin. 'Going Beyond Overlooked Populations in Lebanese Historiography: The Armenian Case'. *History Compass* 11, no. 10 (2013): 821–32.

Natalie, Shahan. *Turkism from Angora to Baku and Turkish Orientation; The Turks and Us*. [Nagorno-Karabakh]: Punik Publishing, 2002.

Navasardian, Vahan. *H.H. Dashnakts'ut'ean anelik'ě* [What the ARF Has to Do]. Gahirē: Ḥusaber, 1924.

Nercessian, Y. T. *A Short History of Armenian Martyrs Memorial Monument in Montebello, California Montebello*. Montebello, CA: Armenian Monument Council, 2007.

The New York Times. 'Archbishop Assassinated in Procession to Altar; Laid to Old-World Feud'. 25 December 1933, 1.
Nichanian, Marc. 'In Memoriam: Vahé Oshagan'. *Armenian Review* 47, no. 1–2 (2001): 168.
Nichanian, Marc. *Mourning Philology: Art and Religion at the Margins of the Ottoman Empire.* Translated by G.M. Goshgarian and Jeff Fort. New York: Fordham University Press, 2014.
Nichanian, Marc. *The Historiographic Perversion.* New York: Columbia University Press, 2009.
Nichanian, Marc. *Writers of Disaster: Armenian Literature in the Twentieth Century.* Vol. 1. The National Revolution. Princeton, NJ and London: Gomidas Institute, 2002.
Nichanian, Marc. 'Zavēn Bibēryanin Mrchiwnnerě' (Ants of Zaven Biberyan). In *Mrchiwnneru Verchaluysě,* edited by Sevan Değirmenciyan, 557–71. Istanbul: Aras Yay, 2007.
Noiriel, Gérard. *Immigration, antisémitisme et racisme en France, XIXe-XXe siècle: discours publics, humiliations privées.* Paris: Fayard, 2007.
Noiriel, Gérard. *Le Creuset français. Histoire de l'immigration XIXe- XXe Siècle.* Folio Histoire, Paris: Gallimard, 2006.
Nucho, Joanne. 'Becoming Armenian in Lebanon'. *Middle East Report* 267 (Summer 2013): 32–6.
Nucho, Joanne. *Everyday Sectarianism in Urban Lebanon: Infrastructures, Public Services, and Power.* Princeton Studies in Culture and Technology. Princeton, NJ: Princeton University Press, 2016.
Olley, Jacob. 'Remembering Armenian Music in Bolis: Komitas Vardapet in Transcultural Perspective'. *Memory Studies* 12, no. 5 (2019): 547–64.
Orjuela, Camilla. 'Divides and Dialogue in the Diaspora During Sri Lanka's Civil War'. *South Asian Diaspora* 9, no. 1 (2017): 67–82. https://doi.org/10.1080/19438192.2016.1236469.
Orozco, Manuel and Michelle Lapointe. 'Mexican Hometown Associations and Development Opportunities'. *Journal of International Affairs* 2 (2004): 31–51. https://www.jstor.org/stable/24357864.
Oshagan, Hagop. 'Sp'iwřk'i K'raganut'ean Abak'an' [The Future of Diaspora Literature]. *Nayiri* 4, no. 1 (1948): 78.
Oshagan, Vahé. *Ahazank (Alarm).* Philadelphia: Vosketar, 1980.
Oshagan, Vahé. *'Baduhan' Window.* Beirut: Olympic Press, 1956.
Oshagan, Vahé. 'Cultural and Literary Awakening of Western Armenians, 1789–1915'. *Armenian Review* 36, no. 3 (Autumn 1983): 57–70.
Oshagan, Vahé. 'Grakan Hrch'agakir' (Literary manifesto). In *Stations,* edited by Krikor Beledian, 5–16. Yerevan: Sargis Khachents, Printinfo, 1990/2017.
Oshagan, Vahé. 'Isg ork' asen' (But those who say). In *Stations,* edited by Krikor Beledian, 321–49. Yerevan: Sargis Khachents, Printinfo. First published in *Asbarez' Literary Supplement,* July, August, October and November 1987, 1987/2017.
Oshagan, Vahé. *K'aghak': Tyuts'aznergut'iwn mě (The City: An Epic).* Vol. 1. Beirut, 1963.
Oshagan, Vahé. *K'aṙughi (Crossroad).* Beirut, 1971.
Oshagan, Vahé. *Khujab (Panic).* New York: Vosketar, 1983.
Oshagan, Vahé. 'Literature of the Armenian Diaspora'. *World Literature Today* 60, no. 2 (Spring 1986), 224–8.
Oshagan, Vahé. 'Nor Badarak' (New Mass). In *Stations,* edited by Krikor Beledian, 351–417. Yerevan: Sargis Khachents, Printinfo, 1990/2017.

Oshagan, Vahé. 'Otsumë' ['Unction'] *T'akardin shurj* [Around the Trap]. New York: Osketar Hratarakch'akan, 1988.

Oshagan, Vahé. 'P'okhan aghōt'k'i' (In Place of prayer). In *Stations*, edited by Krikor Beledian, 315–20. Yerevan: Sargis Khachents, Printinfo. First published in *Pakine* 1. no 1 (January 1962): 41–43, 1962/2017.

Oshagan, Vahé. 'Poles Apart: Vahé Oshagan on the Habitat, Imagery, and the Inner Reaches of the Diaspora', interview by Ishkhan Jinbashian, *Armenian International Magazine*, July 1991. www.armenianinternationalmagazine.com/1991-2/.

Osiecki, Jakub. *The Armenian Church in Soviet Armenia: The Policies of the Armenian Bolsheviks and the Armenian Church, 1920–1932*. Translated by Paweł Siemianowski and Artur Zwokski. New York: Peter Lang, 2020.

Osiecki, Jakub. 'The Invigilation of Armenian Clergy (1920–1930) According to Documents in the Possession of the Armenian National Archive and the Georgian State Archive'. *Journal of the Society for Armenian Studies* 21 (2012): 271–6.

Oskanyan, N. A., A. Korgotyan, and A. M. Savalyan. *Hay girk'ë 1512-1800 t'vakannerin: hayhnatip grk'i matenagitut'yun [The Armenian Book in the Years 1512-1800: Early-Printed Armenian Book Bibliography]*. Erevan: Haykakan SSH Kulturayi Ministrut'yun, Al. Myasnikyani Anvan Zhoghovurdneri Barekamut'yan Shk'anshanakir HSSH Petakan Gradaran, 1988.

Østergaard-Nielsen, Eva. 'The Democratic Deficit of Diaspora Politics: Turkish Cypriots in Britain and the Cyprus Issue'. *Journal of Ethnic and Migration Studies* 29, no. 4 (2003): 683–700. https://doi.org/10.1080/1369183032000123459.

Öztürk, S. Aykut. 'En Route to Unity: Armenian Travelers and Dwellers in Twenty-First-Century Turkey'. Ph.D. diss., UCL, 2019.

PanArmenian.net. 'Armenian Genocide Memorial Vandalized in France'. *PanArmenian .net*, 1 November 2020, https://www.panarmenian.net/eng/news/287292/Armenian _Genocide_memorial_vandalized_in_France, accessed 16 June 2022.

Pankhurst, Richard. 'The History of Ethiopian-Armenian Relations (I)'. *Revue des études arméniennes (nouvelle série)* 12 (1977): 273–345.

Pankhurst, Richard. 'The History of Ethiopian-Armenian Relations (II)'. *Revue des études arméniennes (nouvelle série)* 13 (1978–79): 259–312.

Panossian, Razmik. 'Between Ambivalence and Intrusion: Politics and Identity in Armenia-Diaspora Relations'. *Diaspora: A Journal of Transnational Studies* 7, no. 2 (Fall 1998): 149–96.

Panossian, Razmik. 'Courting a Diaspora: Armenia-diaspora Relations since 1998'. In *International Migration and Sending Countries*, edited by Eva Østergaard-Nielsen, 140–68. London: Palgrave Macmillan, 2003.

Panossian, Razmik. *The Armenians: From Kings and Priests to Merchants and Commissars*. New York: University of Columbia Press, 2006.

Papazian, Hrag. 'Contesting Armenianness: Plurality, Segregation, and Multilateral Boundary Making among Armenian in Contemporary Turkey'. Ph.D. diss., University of Oxford, 2020.

Papazian, Hrag and S. Aykut Öztürk. 'Between Passports and Belongings: Armenian Citizenship Acquisition among Armenians of Turkey'. Forthcoming 2023.

Pashayan, Araks and Lilit Harutyunyan. *Siriaji hay hamajnqe: Ardi himnakhndirner [The Armenian Community of Syria: Actual Issues]*. Yerevan: Institute of Oriental Studies National Academy of Sciences of the Republic of Armenia, 2011.

Patapan, Hayg. *Arti Et'owbia ew Hay Kaghoutë* [Modern Ethiopia and the Armenian Colony]. Venice: Mekhitarist Congregation of St. Lazare, 1930.

Patrik, Arakel. *Patmagirkʻ-hushamatean Sebastioy ew gawaṛi hayutʻean (History of the Armenians of Sebastia and Neighboring Villages)*. Vol. 2. 2 Vols. Beirut and New Jersey: Hratarakutʻiwn Hamasebastahay verashinatsʻ miutʻean, 1983.

Pattie, Susan. *Faith in History: Armenians Rebuilding Community*. Smithsonian Series in Ethnographic Inquiry. Washington, DC: Smithsonian Institution Press, 1997.

Pattie, Susan. 'Refugees and Citizens: The Armenians of Cyprus'. *The Cyprus Review* 25, no. 1 (2013): 133–45.

Pawłowska, Karolina. 'Ethnic Return of Armenian Americans: Perspectives'. *Anthropological notebooks* 23, no. 1 (2017): 93–109.

Pehlivanian, Aram. *Özgürlük İki Adım Ötede Değil*. Istanbul: Aras Yay, 1999.

Pehlivanian, Aram. 'Kragan Shrchanagi Ngarchʻagan Tsʻutsahantēsē'. *Mshaguytʻ*, Beirut, April 1955.

Pehlivanian, Aram. 'Mamul ew garavarutʻiwn'. *Nor Ōr*, 30 August 1946.

Phillips, Jenny. *Symbol, Myth, and Rhetoric: The Politic of Culture in an Armenian American Population*. New York: AMS Press, 1989.

Pifer, Michael. 'The Diasporic Crane: Discursive Migration Across the Armenian-Turkish Divide'. *Diaspora* 18, no. 3 (2009): 229–52.

Poladian, Sirvart. 'Komitas Vardapet and His Contribution to Ethnomusicology'. *Ethnomusicology* 16, no. 1 (1972): 82–97.

Portes, Alejandro. 'Economic Sociology: A Systematic Inquiry'. NJ: Princeton University Press, 2010.

Portes, Alejandro and Julia Sensenbrenner. 'Embeddedness and Immigration: Notes on the Social Determinants of Economic Action'. In *The Sociology of Economic Life*, edited by Mark Granovetter, Richard Swedberg. 93–115. London: Routledge, 2018.

Prévélakis, Georges. 'Les diasporas comme négation de l' "idéologie géographique"'. In *Les diasporas: 2000 ans d'histoire*, edited by Lisa Anteby-Yemini, William Berthomière, and Gabriel Sheffer, 113–24. Rennes: Presses universitaires de Rennes, 2005.

Prévélakis, Georges, ed. *Les réseaux des diasporas*. Nicosia: Kykem, 1996.

Ragazzi, Francesco. 'A Comparative Analysis of Diaspora Policies'. *Political Geography* 41 (2014): 74–89.

Reis, Michele. 'Theorizing Diaspora: Perspectives on "Classical" and "Contemporary" Diaspora'. *International Migration* 42, no. 2 (2004): 41–60. https://doi.org/10.1111/j.0020-7985.2004.00280.x.

Riegg, Stephen Badalyan. *Russia's Entangled Embrace: The Tsarist Empire and the Armenians, 1801–1914*. Ithaca, NY: Cornell University Press, 2020.

Rose, John H. Melkon. *Armenians of Jerusalem: Memories of Life in Palestine*. London: Radcliffe press, 1993.

Rubchak, Marian J. '"God Made me a Lithuanian": Nationalist Ideology and the Construction of a North American Diaspora'. *Diaspora: A Journal of Transnational Studies* 2, no. 1 (1992): 117–30.

Sack, Daniel. *Whitebread Protestants: Food and Religion in American Culture*. New York: Palgrave, 2006.

Safran, William. 'Diasporas in Modern Societies: Myths of Homeland and Return'. *Diaspora: A Journal of Transnational Studies* 1, no. 1 (1991): 83–99.

Safran, William. 'The Jewish Diaspora in a Comparative and Theoretical Perspective'. *Israel Studies* 10, no. 1 (2005): 36–60.

Sahakyan, Vahe. 'Between Host-Countries and Homeland: Institutions, Politics and Identities in the Post-Genocide Armenian Diaspora (1920s to 1980s)'. Ph.D. diss., University of Michigan, 2015.

Said, Edward. *Beginnings: Intention and Method*. New York: Columbia University Press, 1985.
Said, Edward. 'Reflections on Exile'. In *Reflections on Exile and Other Essays*, 137–49. Cambridge, MA: Harvard University Press, 2000.
Salibi, Kamal. *A House of Many Mansions: The History of Lebanon Reconsidered*. Los Angeles: University of California Press, 1990.
Sanjian, Ara. 'The Armenian Minority Experience in the Modern Arab World'. *Bulletin of the Royal Institute for Inter-Faith Studies* 3, no. 1 (2001): 149–79.
Sargsyan, A. A. 'Hayastani ōgnutʻyan komitei himnadir pʻastatʻghtʻerě' [Founding Documents of the Committee For Aid to Armenia]. *Lraber hasarakakan gitutʻyunneri (Herald of Social Sciences)* 2 (2003): 184–99.
Schwalgin, Suzanne. 'Why Locality Matters: Diaspora Consciousness and Sedentariness in the Armenian Diaspora in Greece'. In *Diaspora, Identity and Religion*, edited by Waltraud Kokot, Khachig Tölölyan, and Carolin Alfonso, 72–92. London and New York: Routledge, 2004.
Scott, Erik. *Familiar Strangers: The Georgian Diaspora and the Evolution of Soviet Empire*. New York: Oxford University Press, 2016.
Seiffert, Max. 'Mitteilungen der Internationalen Musik-Gesellschaft: 1. Berlin'. *Zeitschrift der Internationalen Musik Gesellschaft: Erster Jahrgang 1899–1900* 1, no. 2 (1899): 46–47. Leipzig: Druck und Verlag von Beritkopf & Härtel.
Selian, Patrik. 'HŌKi 6rd hamagumari oroshumnerě: Dēpi noranor haghtʻanakner anontsʻ iragortsumov' [The Decisions of the HOK 6th General Congress: Towards New Victories with Their Implementation]. *HŌK: Ōrgan artasahmanean hōkeru (HOC: Revue Mensuelle)* 1, no. 2 (March 1933): 47–50.
Selian, Patrik. 'HŌKi 6rd hamagumari oroshumnerě: Dēpi noranor haghtʻanakner anontsʻ iragortsumov' [The Decisions of the HOK 6th General Congress: Towards New Victories with Their Implementation]. *HŌK: Ōrgan artasahmanean hōkeru (HOC: Revue Mensuelle)* 1, no. 3 (April 1933): 46–50.
Semerdjian, Elyse. 'The Liberation of non-Muslim Women and Children in Turkey'. *Journal of the Society for Armenian Studies* 28, no. 2 (2021): 235–48.
Shahmuratian, Shah, ed. *The Sumgait Tragedy: Pogroms Against Armenians in Soviet Azerbaijan: Eyewitness Accounts*. New Rochelle, NY: Aristide D. Caratzas, 1990.
Shain, Yossi. *Marketing the American Creed Abroad: Diasporas in the U.S. and Their Homelands*. New York: Cambridge University Press, 1999.
Shamlian, Haiduk. 'Khentʻ gaydzer' (Mad sparks). *Horizon Weekly*, 3 February 1992.
Sheffer, Gabriel. *Diaspora Politics: At Home Abroad*. New York: Cambridge University Press, 2003.
Sheffer, Gabriel, ed. *Modern Diasporas in International Politics*. London: Croom Helm, 1986.
Shepperson, George. 'The African Abroad or the African Diaspora'. In *Emerging Themes of African History*, edited by T. O. Ranger, 152–76. London: Heinemann, 1968.
Sigona, Nando, Alan John Gamlen, Giulia Liberatore, and Hélène Neveu Kringelbach, eds. *Diasporas Reimagined: Spaces, Practices and Belonging*. Oxford: Oxford Diasporas Programme, 2015.
Sirouni, Hakob. *Bolisě ew ir derě Constantinople and its Role*, v. IV. Antilias: Tparan Katoghikosutean Hayots Metsi Tann Kilikioy, 1987.
Siruni, H. J. *Bolisě ew ir terě, Arachin Hador (1453-1800) [Constantinople and its Role, Volume 1 (1453-1800)]*. Beirut: Dbaran Mesrob, 1969.

Siwrmēean, Artawazd. *Patmut'iwn Halēpi Hayots'*: *Teghagrakan, vichakagrakan, patmagrakan [The History of Armenian Aleppo: Topographical, Statistical, Historical].* Pēyrut': Tparan M. Magsutean, 1946.
Slezkine, Yuri. 'The USSR as a Communal Apartment, or How a Socialist State Promoted Ethnic Particularism'. *Slavic Review* 53, no. 2 (1994): 414–52.
Smith, Anthony D. *The Ethnic Origins of Nations.* Cambridge: Blackwell Publishers, 1986.
Smith, Hazel and Paul Stares, eds. *Diasporas in Conflict: Peace-Makers or Peace-Wreckers?* Tokyo: UNU Press, 2007.
Smith, Pamela Ann. 'The Palestinian Diaspora, 1948–1985'. *Journal of Palestine Studies* 15, no. 3 (1986): 90–108. https://doi.org/10.2307/2536751.
Solakoğlu, Melis. 'Hamahaygagan'da hazırlıklar tamam'. *Agos*, 30 June 2015. https://www.agos.com.tr/tr/yazi/12022/hamahaygaganda-hazirliklar-tamam.
Sonents-Papazian, Tatul, ed. *Hariwrameay hushamatean Hay ōgnut'ean miut'ean (Centennial Memorial of the Armenian Relief Society).* Boston: Armenian Relief Society, 2010.
Stepanyan, Armenuhi. *XX dari hayrenadardzut'yunĕ hayots' ink'nut'yan hamakargum [Repatriation of the XX century in the system of Armenian identity].* Yerevan: "Gitutyun" Publishing House, 2010.
Suciyan, Talin. 'Diaspora Kim'. *Taraf*, 20 October 2009. https://hyetert.org/2009/10/20/diaspora-kim-talin-sucuyan/.
Suciyan, Talin. 'Dört nesil: Kurtarılamayan son'. *Toplum Bilim* 132 (2015): 132–49.
Suciyan, Talin. *The Armenians in Modern Turkey: Post-Genocide Society, Politics and History.* London and New York: I.B. Tauris, 2016.
Suciyan, Talin. 'The Repatriation Never Took Place: The Soviet Armenian Call for Immigration of 1946 and Its Impact on Turkey'. In *After the Ottomans. The Long Shadow of Genocide*, edited by Hans Lukas Kieser, Seyhan Bayraktar, and Khatchig Mouradian. London: I.B. Tauris, forthcoming.
Suciyan, Talin and Ayda Erbal. 'One Hundred Years of Abandonment'. *Armenian Weekly*, 2011. https://armenianweekly.com/2011/04/29/erbal-and-suciyan-one-hundred-years-of-abandonment/, accessed September 2022
Suny, Ronald Grigor. *Looking Toward Ararat: Armenia in Modern History.* Bloomington, IN: Indiana University Press, 1993.
Suny, Ronald Grigor. 'The Hamidian Massacres, 1894–1897: Disinterring a Buried History'. *Études arméniennes contemporaines* 11 (2018): 125–34.
Suny, Ronald Grigor. *'They Can Live in the Desert but Nowhere Else': A History of the Armenian Genocide.* Princeton, NJ and Oxford: Princeton University Press, 2015.
Suny, Ronald Grigor, Fatma Muge Gocek, and Norman M. Naimark, eds. *Question of Genocide: Armenians and Turks at the End of the Ottoman Empire.* Oxford: Oxford University Press, 2011.
Tachjian, Vahé. '"Repatriation": A New Chapter, Studded with New Obstacles, in the History of AGBU's Cooperation in Soviet Armenia'. In *The Armenian General Benevolent Union: A Hundred Years of History (1906–2006), vol. 2 (1941–2006)*, edited by Raymond H. Kevorkian and Vahé Tachjian, 291–309. Cairo, Paris and New York: AGBU, 2006.
Tanajyan, Lusine. *The Experience of Integration of Syrian-Armenian in Armenia. Problem Solving Mechanisms.* Report for Open Society Foundation, 2018.
Taylor, Diane. 'Number of Displaced People Passes 100m for the First Time, Says UN'. *The Guardian*, 23 May 2022. https://www.theguardian.com/globaldevelopment/2022/may/23/total-displaced-people-now-at-staggering-milestone-of-100msays-un, accessed 24 May 2022.

TBMM Gizli Celse Zabıtları. Vol. 4. Ankara: İşbankası Yayınları, 1985.
Tchilingirian, Hratch. 'Modern "Believers" in an Ancient Church: The Armenian Apostolic Church'. In *Arméniens et Grecs en diaspora: Approches Comparatives*, edited by Michel Bruneau, Ioannis Hassiotis, Martin Hovanessian, and Claire Mouradian, 491–508. Athens: École Française d'Athènes, 2007.
Tchilingirian, Hratch. 'The Catholicos and the Hierarchal Sees of the Armenian Church'. In *Eastern Christianity: Studies in Modern History, Religion and Politics*, edited by Anthony O'Mahony, 140–59. London: Melisende, 2004.
Tchilingirian, Hratch. 'The "Other" Citizens: Armenians in Turkey between Isolation and (Dis)integration'. *Journal for the Society of Armenian Studies* 25, no. 4 (2017): 123–55.
Terian, Sara Kärkkäinen Terian. 'Sanctuary, Community or Museum? The Apostolic Church in the Life-Worlds of a Sample of Armenian Americans'. In *Armenian Christianity Today: Identity Politics and Popular Practice*, edited by Alexander Agadjanian, 253–72. Oxfordshire and New York: Ashgate, 2014.
Ter Israyelian, Aris. 'Khndir mě, or ir lutsman kě spasē' [A Problem That Needs to be Solved]. *Hayrenik' ōrat'ert'* [Hairenik Daily], 7 September 1929, 1, 3.
Ter-Minassian, Anahide. *Histoire Croisees: Diaspora, Arménie, Transcaucasie 1890–1990*. Marseille: Editions Parenthéses, 1997.
Ter-Minassian, Anahide. 'Salon Du Livre Arménien d'Alfortville: L'hommage à Hrant Samuel'. *France Arménie* 353 (2010): 24–6.
Ter-Vardanyan, Gēorg. *Mayr Mashtots'*. Vol. I/1. Holy Etchmiadzin: Holy See of Etchmiadzin Publications, 2012.
Terzibashian, Avedis [T'erzibashian, Avedis]. *Ergu Dari Adis Abēbayi mēch* [Two Years in Addis Ababa]. Paris: Imp. A. Der Agopian, 1944.
Tettey, Wisdom J. 'Regenerating Scholarly Capacity through Diaspora Engagement: The Case of a Ghana Diaspora Knowledge Network'. In *Diasporas, Development and Governance*, edited by Abel Chikanda, Jonathan Crush and Margaret Walton-Roberts, 171–86. Cham: Springer, 2016.
Tevyan, Pakarat. *Erchanig Darekirk'* 1946. Istanbul: Ak-Ün Basımevi, 1945.
The Washington Post. '1 Held in Death of Archbishop'. 28 December 1933, 2.
Thomassian, Levon. *Summer of '42: A Study of German-Armenian Relations During the Second World War*. Atglen: Schiffer, 2012.
Tint, Barbara, Vincent Chirimwami, and Caroline Sarkis. 'Diasporas in Dialogue: Lessons from Reconciliation Efforts in African Refugee Communities'. *Conflict Resolution Quarterly* 32, no. 2 (2014): 177–202. https://doi.org/10.1002/crq.21111.
Tolich, Martin. 'Internal Confidentiality: When Confidentiality Assurances Fail Relational Informants'. *Qualitative Sociology* 27, no. 1 (2004): 101–6. https://doi.org/10.1023/B:QUAS.0000015546.20441.4a.
Tölölyan, Khachig. 'Beyond the Homeland: From Exilic Nationalism to Diasporic Transnationalism'. In *The Call of the Homeland*, edited by Allon Gal, Athena S. Leoussi, and Anthony D. Smith, 27–45. Leiden: Brill, 2010.
Tölölyan, Khachig. 'Commentary'. *Diaspora: A Journal of Transnational Studies* 1, no. 2 (1991): 225–8.
Tölölyan, Khachig. 'Diaspora Studies: Past, Present, and Promise'. *IMI Working Papers Series, no. 55*, University of Oxford, UK, June 2012. https://www.migrationinstitute.org/publications/wp-55-12.
Tölölyan, Khachig. 'Elites and Institutions in the Armenian Transnation'. *Diaspora: A Journal of Transnational Studies* 9, no. 1 (2000): 107–36.

Tölölyan, Khachig. 'Exile Governments in the Armenian Polity'. In *Governments-in-Exile in Contemporary World Politics*, edited by Yossi Shain, 166–85. New York: Routledge, 1991.
Tölölyan, Khachig. 'Nation-State and Its Others: In Lieu of a Preface'. *Diaspora: A Journal of Transnational Studies* 1, no. 1 (1991): 3–7.
Tölölyan, Khachig. *Redefining Diasporas: Old Approaches, New Identities. The Armenian Diaspora in an International Context*. London: Armenian Institute, 2002.
Tölölyan, Khachig. 'Restoring the Logic of the Sedentary to Diaspora Studies'. In *Les Diasporas: 2000 Ans d'histoire*, edited by Lisa Anteby-Yemini, William Berthomière, and Gabriel Sheffer, 137–48. Rennes: Presses universitaires de Rennes, 2005.
Tölölyan, Khachig. 'Rethinking *Diaspora* (s): Stateless Power in the Transnational Moment'. *Diaspora: A Journal of Transnational Studies* 5, no. 1 (1996): 3–36.
Tölölyan, Khachig. *Spʻiwṛkʻi Mēch [In Diaspora]*. Paris: Ḥaṛach Series, 1980.
Tölölyan, Khachig. 'The Contemporary Discourse of Diaspora Studies'. *Comparative Studies of South Asia, Africa and the Middle East* 27, no. 3 (2007): 647–55.
Tölölyan, Khachig. 'The Role of the Armenian Apostolic Church in the Diaspora'. *Armenian Review* 41, no. 1 (1988): 55–68.
Tölölyan, Khachig and Taline Papazian. 'Armenian Diasporas and Armenia: Issues of Identity and Mobilization. An Interview with Khachig Tölölyan'. *Études arméniennes contemporaines* 3 (2014): 83–101. https://doi.org/10.4000/eac.565.
Traboulsi, Fawwaz. *A History of Modern Lebanon*. London: Pluto Press, 2012.
Trivellato, Francesca. *The Familiarity of Strangers: The Sephardic Diaspora, Livorno, and Cross-Cultural Trade in the Early Modern Period*. New Haven, CT: Yale University Press, 2009.
Trouillot, Michel-Rolph. 'The Anthropology of the State in the Age of Globalization: Close Encounters of the Deceptive Kind'. *Current Anthropology* 42, no. 1 (2001): 125–38.
Tsuda, Takeyuki. 'When the Diaspora Returns Home'. In *A Companion to Diaspora and Transnationalism*, edited by Ato Quayson and Girish Daswani, 172–89. New York: Wiley-Blackwell, 2003.
Üngör, Uğur Ümit. 'Syrian Restaurants in Armenia: A Pinch of Home, a Taste of Exile'. *The Armenian Mirror-Spectator*, 12 June 2019. https://mirrorspectator.com/2019/06/12/syrian-restaurants-in-armenia-a-pinch-of-home-a-taste-of-exile/.
United Nations High Commissioner on Refugees. 'Figures at a Glance'. https://www.unhcr.org/figures-at-a-glance.html, accessed 8 April 2021.
United Nations High Commissioner on Refugees. 'Global Trends: Forced Displacement in 2017'. https://www.unhcr.org/globaltrends2017/#:~:text=In%202017%2016.2%20million%20people,new%20high%20of%2068.5%20million, accessed 8 April 2021.
United Nations High Commissioner on Refugees. 'UNHCR Helps Displaced Syrian-Armenians Facing Hardship Amid Pandemic'. www.unhcr.org/news/stories/2020/5/5ecf78874/unhcr-helps-displaced-syrian-armenians-facing-hardship-amid-pandemic.html#:~:text=Around%2022%2C000%20Syrians%20have%20fled, accessed 31 March 2022.
Utidjian, Haig. *Tntesean and the Music of the Armenian Hymnal*. Červený Kostelec: Pavel Mervart, 2018.
Van der Laan, H. Laurens. *The Lebanese Traders in Sierra Leone*. The Hague: Mouton & Co., 1975.
Van Meeteren, Masja, Peter Mascini, and Devorah van den Berg. 'Trajectories of Economic Integration of Amnestied Immigrants in Rotterdam'. *Journal of Ethnic and*

Migration Studies 41, no. 3 (2015): 448–69. https://doi.org/10.1080/1369183X.2014.924846.

Van Reenan, Antanas J. *Lithuanian Diaspora: Königsberg to Chicago*. Lanham, MD: University Press of America, 1990.

Varadarajan, Latha. *The Domestic Abroad: Diasporas in International Relations*. Oxford: Oxford University Press, 2010.

Vardanyan, Grigor. 'Hayrenakts'akan miut'yunnerě ev Khorhrdayin Hayastaně' [Compatriotic Societies and Soviet Armenia]. *HÔK-i Teghekatu* [HOK Bulletin], 1928.

Vardumyan, Arpi. 'Komitas Vardapet and the Armenian Musical Culture of Kutahia'. In *Armenian Communities in Asia Minor*, edited by Richard G. Hovannisian, 195–208. Costa Mesa, CA: Mazda Publishers, 2014.

Vartkes, Nalbandian. *'I Want to Die with a Flag'. Ethiopia: My Delusions and Disillusionment*. Canada, 2019.

Vertovec, Steven. 'Three Meanings of "Diaspora," Exemplified among South Asian Religions'. *Diaspora: A Journal of Transnational Studies* 6, no. 3 (Winter 1997): 277–99.

Vezzoli, Simona and Thomas Lacroix. 'Building Bonds for Migration and Development. Diaspora Engagement Policies of Ghana, India and Serbia'. PhD diss., International Migration Institute, Gesellschaft für Technische Zusammenarbeit (GTZ), 2010.

Vratsian, Simon. *Kharkhap'umner. H. K'ajaznunu "H.H. Dashnakts'utyuně anelik' ch'uni aylews" grk'i aṛt'iw*. [Gropings. Regarding Kajaznuni's "The Armenian Revolutionary Federation Has Nothing to Do Anymore" Book]. Boston: Hayrenik' tparan, 1924.

Vrej-Armen. 'Gizageděh Hayastan'. *Horizon Weekly*, 3 February 1992.

Wagner, Lauren. 'Feeling Diasporic'. *Tilburg Papers in Culture Studies* 21 (2012).

Wahlbeck, Östen. 'The Concept of Diaspora as an Analytical Tool in the Study of Refugee Communities'. *Journal of Ethnic and Migration Studies* 28, no. 2 (2002): 221–38. https://doi.org/10.1080/13691830220124305.

Walker, Christopher J. *Armenia: The Survival of a Nation*. New York: St. Martin's Press, 1990.

Watenpaugh, Heghnar Zeitlian. 'Cultural Heritage and the Arab Spring: War over Culture, Culture of War and Culture War'. *International Journal of Islamic Architecture* 5, no. 2 (2012): 245–63.

Werbner, Pnina. *Imagined Diasporas among Manchester Muslims: The Public Performance of Pakistani Transnational Identity Politics*. Oxford: James Currey, 2002.

Wessendorf, Susanne. *Pathways of Settlement among Recent Migrants in Super-diverse Areas. No. 25*. IRIS Working Paper Series, 2018.

Wessendorf, Susanne. 'Pioneer Migrants and Their Social Relations in Super-Diverse London'. *Ethnic and Racial Studies* 42, no. 1 (2019): 17–34. https://doi.org/10.1080/01419870.2017.1406126.

Wiebelhaus-Brahm, Eric. 'Exploring Variation in Diasporas' Engagement with Transitional Justice Processes'. *Journal of Peacebuilding & Development* 11, no. 3 (2016): 23–36. https://doi.org/10.1080/15423166.2016.12269.

Wilcock, Cathy. 'Mobilising Towards and Imagining Homelands: Diaspora Formation among UK Sudanese'. *Journal of Ethnic and Migration Studies* 44, no. 3 (2018): 363–81. https://doi.org/10.1080/1369183X.2017.1313104.

Wimmer, Andreas and Nina Glick Schiller. 'Methodological Nationalism and Beyond: Nation-state Building, Migration, and the Social Sciences'. *Global Networks* 2, no. 4 (2002): 301–34.

Winland, Daphne N. '"We Are Now an Actual Nation": The Impact of National Independence of the Croatian Diaspora in Canada'. *Diaspora: A Journal of Transnational Studies* 4, no. 1 (1995): 3–30.

Wright, Handel Kashope and Meaghan Morris, eds. *Cultural Studies of Transnationalism*. Milton Park: Routledge, 2012.

Wyman, Mark. *DPs: Europe's Displaced Persons, 1945–1951*. Ithaca, NY: Cornell University Press, 1998.

Yannaras, Christos. *Person and Eros*. Translated by Norman Russell. Brookline, MA: Holy Cross Orthodox Press, 2007.

Yessayan, Zabel. 'Autobiography'. From National Museum of Literature and Art, *Zabel Yessayan Fund Folder 6*. accessed September 2002.

Yıldız, Burcu. *Experiencing Armenian Music in Turkey: An Ethnography of Musicultural Memory*. Würzburg: Ergon-Verlag, 2016.

Yousefian, Sevan. 'Picnics for Patriots: The Transnational Activism of an Armenian Hometown Association'. *Journal of American Ethnic History* 34, no. 1 (2014): 31–52.

Yousefian, Sevan. 'The Postwar Repatriation Movement of Armenians to Soviet Armenia, 1945–1948'. Ph.D. diss., University of California, Los Angeles, 2011.

Zadoian, Hratch. *Our Brothers' Keepers: The American National Committee to Aid Homeless Armenians (ANCHA)*. New York: SIS Publications, 2012.

Zeitlian, Hraztan. 'Sp'iwṛk'i ṛazmavaragan sgzpunk'ner' (Diaspora's strategic principles). *Horizon Weekly*, 3 February 1992.

Zekiyan, Boghos Levon. *The Armenian Way to Modernity*. Venice: Supernova, 1997, 23–6.

Ziflioğlu, Vercihan. 'Armenians Split over Who Belongs to the "Diaspora"'. *Hürriyet Daily News*, 9 May 2011.

Index

Abbysinia/Abbysinian 29, 33, 41 nn.12, 15
Abeghian, Artashes 49, 53
Abeghian, Manuk 49
Abovean, Khachatur 13
Accord of Ankara (1921) 159
Adam's Book (*Adami Girkʻē*, Karapents) 137–40, 145
Adana 10, 47, 238
Addis Ababa 29, 33, 34
African Diaspora 3
Aharonian, Avetis 112
Ahazank (Alarm, Oshagan) 203–4, 206
Akdora, Mithat 218
Alawis of Syria 262
Alboyajian, Arshag 252
Aleksanyan, Avedis 225
Aleppo 2, 29, 38, 73, 80, 152, 153, 159–62, 176, 222, 224, 232, 261–3, 269, 270, 272
Alexandrian Septuagint 254
Almelo 72, 75
Ambrosini, Maurizio 71–2
Amenun Darekirkʻē (Armenian Almanac, Kevorkian) 53
American Friends Service Committee 52
American immigration laws 45
American Jewish Joint Distribution Committee 52
American National Committee to Aid Homeless Armenians (ANCHA) 55
American Occupation Zone, Germany 50, 51
*amira*s 92
Anahit (journal) 91, 94
Anatolia 9, 12, 17, 214, 221, 238, 239, 242, 244
ancrage/enracinement 30, 39
Anderson, Benedict 92, 260
Andonian, Aram 38, 224
'Anlṛeli Zangakatun' ('The Unsilenceable Belfry,' poem, Sevak) 186

Antelias 11
anti-Bolshevik discourse 108, 113, 115, 121
Antin (Beyond, poem, Oshagan) 204
anti-Soviet discourse 110, 113, 114
Apostolic Christians 54
Aram Khachaturian Concert Hall 189
Aṛantsnutʻiwn (Solitude, poem, Oshagan) 204
Arapgir 29
Araradyan orphanage, Jerusalem 30
Ararat (mountain) 36, 182, 191 n.20
Ararat (periodical) 223
Ararat Armenian Cultural Foundation (Hay Mshakutʻayin Ararat Miutʻiwn) 138
Arba Lejoch (the 'forty children') 30, 31
Archak 202
Arlen, Michael 259
Armenia
   conflict with Azerbaijan 74
   government 77, 78, 81
   history 10
   homeland 35, 67, 215, 234, 238–40, 242, 245, 255
   independence day celebration in American Armenian Church 121, 122
   independence of 14, 46, 58, 70, 113, 115, 116, 119, 131 n.44, 144, 194–197, 208
   Republic of 6, 70, 71, 107, 108, 109, 112, 114, 115, 117, 119, 125, 126, 152, 159, 195, 239, 244, 260
   as step-homeland 70, 81
   socioeconomic and sociocultural conditions 70, 71, 74, 79, 80
   Soviet Armenia (*see* Armenian Soviet Socialist Republic)
   Sovietization of 107, 108, 110, 112, 116, 117, 119, 121

Armenia (journal) 94, 95
Armenian Apostolic Church 7, 37, 54, 75, 76, 121, 124, 148–63, 163–4 nn.2, 4, 20, 167 n.40, 169 n.53, 183, 241
   Armenian Church in America 121–5
   Armenian Patriarchate of Istanbul (Constantinople) 92, 214, 216
   Holy Cross Armenian Apostolic Cathedral 58–9
   Holy Cross Church 124
   as national home in diaspora 154–5
   St. Illuminator Armenian Apostolic Church 123, 124
   St. John's Armenian Apostolic Church 156
   St. John the Baptist Armenian Apostolic Church 156, 157
   St. Mary Armenian Apostolic Church 148
   St. Mary's Church 160
Armenian Constitution (*Nizamname*) 214
Armenian Democratic Liberal (Ramkavar) Party (ADL) 116, 117, 119, 120, 125
   Second World Congress 117
Armenian Diaspora/diaspora 1, 2, 3, 39, 47, 54, 149, 150, 152, 154, 155, 162, 163 n.1, 177, 180, 188, 195, 200, 227, 252. *See also individual entries*
   associations and institutions 38, 68, 218–20
   communities 6, 12, 37, 58, 59, 69, 70, 73, 77, 100, 109, 125, 141, 143, 153, 178, 213, 214, 217, 227, 232, 233, 236, 240, 251, 252
   as cultural entity 196
   definition 234
   discourse 250, 251
   Indian Armenian 252
   institutionalization of 6, 38, 214
   memorialization in 31, 34, 35, 38
   Ottoman 212, 226
   places and off-places in 28–32
   politicization of 75, 195
Armenian Diaspora literature 2, 5, 12, 27, 29, 31, 34, 40 n.4, 46, 67–9, 71, 72, 92, 100, 135–46, 153, 197, 198, 203, 208, 210 n.22, 223, 233, 235, 243, 258, 259, 269
Armenian Diaspora Survey 264
Armenian displaced persons (DPs)
   displacement and diaspora to America 54–8
   displacement to Germany 49–51
   Funkerkaserne 51–4
   oral histories 46
   post-genocide displacement and life in Soviet Union (USSR) 46–9, 70
Armenian Evangelical Church 160
Armenian General Athletic Union (HMEM) 119, 120, 262–3, 265
Armenian General Benevolent Union (AGBU) 37, 38, 117–19, 125
Armenian Genocide (1915) 1, 10, 11, 13, 14, 28, 30, 32, 33, 36–8, 45, 46, 58, 73, 109, 152, 156, 159, 179
   survivors 46, 109, 121, 213, 215, 217, 219–20
Armenian Genocide Memorial 160
Armenian hospitals 148, 214
Armenian immigration/migration/immigrants 27–34
   to Canada 12, 32, 78, 214, 232, 245, 264
   to Ethiopia 28–32, 34, 35, 38, 39
   experiences 35–9
   to France 35–6, 38, 39
   to Netherlands 15, 67, 68, 72–83
   to the United States of America 12, 32, 53, 55–58, 64 n.79, 70, 78, 109, 112, 118–21, 123–5, 138, 141, 152, 153, 155-8, 162, 176, 179, 180, 182, 183, 188, 245, 264, 272
   waves 34, 35, 38, 152, 153, 157, 160, 162
Armenian International Magazine (*AIM*) 135, 195, 196
Armenian language 74
   education 54
   linguistic diversity in 74
   schools 47
Armenian Mesrobian School 57–8
Armenian Mirror, The (newspaper) 120
Armenian music 175–90
   culture 177
   D/diaspora and 177–81

'Grung' (Komitas)   189–90
and Komitas   177, 181–9
and its discontents   175–7
Armenian National Assembly   92
Armenian National Committee of America   57
Armenian National Council   49, 53
Armenian National Delegation   116, 117
Armenian National Library of Paris (*P'arizi Haygagan Azkayin Madenatarane*)   38
Armenian Relief Society (Armenian Relief Corps)   52, 53, 57, 119, 132 n.55
Armenian Revolutionary Federation (ARF, Dashnaktsoutiun/Dashnak/Tashnag/Tashnak)   15, 17, 53, 55, 57, 59, 65 n.90, 75, 87 n.64, 105 n.48, 107–15, 117–26, 128 n.19, 129 nn.27, 30, 130 n.31, 131 n.47, 132 nn.55, 56, 135, 136, 139, 196, 197, 200, 209 n.12, 262, 263, 269, 270, 209 n.12, 262, 263, 269, 270
Armenian(s). *See also individual entries*
of Aleppo   159, 160–2
in Armenia   77, 81, 240
Baku Armenians in Detroit   155–8, 162
Catholics   47, 54
of Cilicia   255
compatriotic associations (*hayrenagts'agan miut'iwnner*)   36
criminalization   72, 216, 218, 225, 227
culture   75, 98, 100–2, 142
of Cyprus   14, 152
in Europe   96
in France   118
in Greece   74
homeland in Ethiopia   32–5
in Indonesia   74
in Iran (New Julfans)   8, 14, 257, 258
of Iraq   75, 76
in Istanbul   212, 214, 215, 217, 218
in Jerusalem   34, 35, 38
of Kessab   252
in Lebanon   11
life   198–200, 207, 208, 215
literary traditions   135
liturgy   148
in the Middle East   56, 74, 78, 79, 82, 117

of Musa Dagh   217, 218
in the Netherlands   74–5
refugees   34, 35, 46, 47, 52, 53
in Rhône valley   37
in Russia (*rusahay*)   10, 45–9, 51–8, 70, 74–6, 102, 156, 257
of Syria   158–61
in Turkey   74, 109, 212–28
in the United States   12, 32, 53, 55–58, 64 n.79, 70, 78, 109, 112, 118–21, 123–5, 138, 141, 152, 153, 155-8, 162, 176, 179, 180, 182, 183, 188, 245, 264, 272
Armenians By Choice (ABCs)   263
Armenian Soviet Socialist Republic (ASSR/Soviet Armenia)   36, 47–9, 53, 56, 59, 116, 119, 156, 221. *See also* transnational politics and governmental strategies of post-genocide Armenian diaspora (1920s–1930s)
ARF leaders against   109
Bolshevik regime in   107–13, 117 (*see also* Bolshevism)
compatriots societies in   119, 120
elites and institutions   53, 109, 110, 118
gathering dispersed Armenians in   110–11
as homeland of Armenians   110–12, 115, 125
Armenian Youth Federation (AYF)   57, 133 n.65, 265
Armeno-Turkish clashes (1918)   46
Armstrong, John A.   5, 73
Arpiarian, Arpiar   91, 93, 96–9, 101
Artaud, Antonin   203
artel   47
Artemis (magazine)   94
Artsakh (Nagorno-Karabakh)   156, 194
first Artsakh War   156, 195
Artvin   47, 51
Asad, Talal   149, 151, 158
Asbarēz (newspaper)   119, 186, 202
Askarian, Vahan   54
Aslanian, Sebouh   8, 14, 257, 258
Aslanyan, Manuk   220
al-Assad, Bashar   159
al-Assad, Hafiz   159

assemblage theory 197, 198
Assyrians 79
Ayanian, Jean 36
Ayntab 29
Aysōr (periodical) 223
Azat Khōsk' (newspaper) 94, 95
Azerbaijan
    Azerbaijan Soviet Socialist Republic or Soviet Azerbaijan 156
Aztarar (periodical) 220

badarak (the Armenian mass) 148, 181
Badkam (The Oracle, Oshagan) 201, 202
'Badmagan Nshmarner' (*'Tarihten İşaretler'*/Signs from History, Biberyan) 221
Baduhan (Window, poem, Oshagan) 199
Baghdasarian, Tigran 53
Baghdassarian, Hagop 33
Bakalian, Anny 12, 152, 180
Bakhtin, Mikhail 95
Baku 12
    Armenians in Detroit 152, 153, 155–158, 162
Balakian, Grigoris 160
Balakian, Peter 259
Balıkçı, Sevag 220
Banasēr (journal) 94, 95
Banber 54
*bantukhd*s 254, 255
Basmadjian, Karapet 94
Bayrakdarian, Isabel 186, 189
Beckett, Samuel 203
Beirut 2, 12, 38, 54, 141, 143, 176, 197, 199, 201, 206, 208, 222–4, 256, 261, 263, 270
Benjamin, Walter 224, 226
Berberian, Houri 10
Berberian, Vahe 136, 137, 139, 140, 143–6, 260
Berksanlar, Kurken 233
Berlin Congress (1878) 99
Biberyan, Zaven 212, 221–4, 222, 225, 227
Bismarck, Otto von 262
Black Lives Matter 264
Black Sea 46, 48, 52
blitzkrieg 48

Blue Crane Books 138
Bolsahayut'iwn 233, 234, 243
Bolshevism, Bolsheviks 107, 111, 113
Book of Histories (Davrijetsi) 257
Boston 2, 57, 108, 113, 114, 119, 131 n.48, 133 n.65, 194
Brown, Jerry 57
Brubaker, Rogers 69, 178–9, 236
Bulgaria 12, 56, 141, 197
'But Those Who Say' (*Isg ork' asen*, poem, Oshagan) 202, 203
Byuzant, Pavsdos 255
Byzantine Empire 214

Cairo 94, 108, 114, 117, 118, 131 n.48, 268 n.28, 270
California 15, 45, 55, 57, 63 n.49, 121, 138, 141, 148, 183, 186, 189
camps 36, 49–55, 61 n.27, 62 n.33, 64 n.65
Camus, Albert 203
Catholic Charities 52
Catholicosate of Aghtamar 214
Catholicosate of Cilicia 11, 21 n.61
Catholicosate of Ejmiatsin, Armenia 183, 121, 123–5
Caucasian People's Union 114
Central Executive Committee 124
Century of Progress International Exposition World Fair (1933) 123
Chahinian, Talar 12
Charents, Yeghishé 186, 187
Cheraz, Minas 94
Chernomorska Komuna 47
Cho, Lily 178
Chobanian, Arshak 91, 94, 96–102
Chobanian, Kohar 269
Christen Unie 79
Christian theology 17, 200–3
Christianity 200–3
Cilicia 11, 52, 208, 214, 255, 256
Cilician See. *See* Catholicosate of Cilicia
citizenship 32, 33, 48, 51, 56, 77–8, 81
civilian scholars 251
civil society
    actors 72
    organizations 76
Clifford, James 70
Cohen, Robin 5, 73, 237

collective farms   46-8
collective memory   30, 31, 35, 58
collective traumas   179, 180
Committee to Aid Armenia
   (HOK)   110-13, 115-21, 123, 125, 126, 134 n.85
commemoration   37, 58, 72
communalism   198
Communist Party of Armenia   112, 118
Compatriotic Unions of Arabkir   119
Council of Nicaea   202
Council of People's Commissars of Soviet Armenia   111
Cowe, S. Peter   255-6
Craven, Catherine Ruth   69
Crimea   7, 46-9, 54, 60 nn.8, 15, 254
Cultural Association of Armenians   245
cultural production   53, 109, 136

Dabag, Mihran   218
Darakir   54
Darbinian, Ruben   108, 113-15
Dashnak. *See* Armenian Revolutionary Federation (ARF)
Dashnaktsytyn. *See* Armenian Revolutionary Federation (ARF)
Datastanagirkʻ (Gosh)   261
Davitkhanian, Davit   53
Davrijetsi, Arakel   257
Debussy, Claude   188
Décines   35, 37, 38, 148, 152, 153, 158-62, 171 nn.70, 73, 172 n.74, 272
Değirmenciyan, Sevan   222
DeLanda, Manuel   197, 198, 208
Delegation of the Republic of Armenia   112-13, 117
Deleuze, Gilles   197, 198
Della Gatta, Marisa   70
Der Alexanian, Jacques   36
Der Matossian, Bedross   9, 10
Der Sarkissian, Jean   36
Der Yeghiayan, Zaven   216
Detroit   2, 55, 152, 153, 155-8, 162, 169 n.53, 186, 272
Deukmejian, George   57
Deutsch-Armenische Gesellschaft (German-Armenian Society)   49
dialogism   95

diaspora. *See also* Armenian Diaspora/diaspora
   Afro-Caribbean   29
   building mechanisms   69
   Chinese   30, 262, 267 n.17
   concept of   1, 3-5, 27, 29, 30, 47, 110, 150, 164 nn.7, 10, 179, 187, 188, 227, 235, 248 n.48, 252, 260
   culture   100
   definition   29, 34, 102, 164 n.10, 227, 234
   diaspora of   13-14
   and dispersion   34, 178, 235-8
   elites and institutions   2, 16, 53, 71, 72, 92, 93, 109, 110, 118, 125, 136, 146, 216, 250, 255, 256, 261, 262, 264, 265, 272
   Greek   29 n.14, 29
   internal   47, 60 n.17
   intrastate   93, 243
   Jewish   34, 68
   networks   6, 68, 73-7, 82, 243
   organizations   37, 68, 71-5, 77-9, 82, 83, 108
   public sphere   91, 102, 103 n.4
   relations with homeland   67-83, 143
   spaces   14, 93, 99, 100, 110, 118, 161
   state-generated   5-6
   studies   2-7, 9, 14, 17, 27, 29, 30, 32-4, 39, 69, 178, 180, 198, 233, 235, 243, 250-65, 269, 272
   territorializing ability of   30
   trade   5, 8
   vs. transnation   150, 163-4 n.7
   victim   5, 78, 87 n.60
Diaspora: A Journal of Transnational Studies (journal)   2, 3, 4, 194, 235, 236, 271
diasporic becoming   17, 196-200, 203, 208
diasporicity   260
diasporic public sphere   91, 102, 103 n.4
diasporic transnationalism   6-14, 83, 150
diasporization 1, 236, 237, 245
Dibar Grtaran Armenian Elementary School   222
digital public sphere   259, 260
digital spaces   259, 260
Dink, Hrant   220
Displaced Persons Act (1948)   45, 55

Displaced Persons Documentation
   Project   46
displacement   3, 45, 46, 50, 52, 54–8, 73, 78, 119, 140
   Armenian post-genocide   46–9
Diyarbakir   242–3
Domhoff, William   261
Donbas (Ukraine) war (2014)   71
Droshak (periodical)   108, 114
Dutch Armenian organizations   68, 74–5
Dzarougian, Antranig   259

Eastern Orthodox Christian/Christianity   149, 151, 158, 159
Eastern Orthodox churches   167 n.37
Eblighatean, Madteos M.   216
ecclesia   151, 153, 154, 158, 160, 162, 167 n.37, 168 n.46
ecclesial governmentality   149–53, 162, 170 n.55
   and Baku Armenians in Detroit   155–8
   and Syrian Armenians in Décines, France   158–61
Education Society of Malatia (*Malat'ioy Grt'asirats' Miut'iwnĕ*)   36
Egypt   43 n.34, 52, 56, 108, 111, 112, 114, 117, 128 n.23, 130 n.42, 131 n.48, 141, 185, 197, 254, 270
Ejmiatsin/Echmiadzin   11, 121–3. *See also* Catholicosate of Ejmiatsin, Armenia
Ekmekcioglu, Lerna   11
Emic/etic   252, 253
Emin, Joseph   255
endowment funds (*waqf*)   97
England   91, 98
'Enough is Enough' (*'Al Gĕ Pavē'*, Biberyan)   221
Eritasard Hayastan (periodical)   116
Erzurum   47, 51
Ethio-Armenians (*Habeshahay/ Et'ovbahay*)   29–34
Ethiopia(n)   28, 38
   Armenian immigration to   28–32, 34, 35, 38, 39
   government   30
   historiography of   31
   as homeland   33
   kings   31

Ethiopianization   31, 33
Ethiopian revolution (1974)   29, 32, 33
exile   28, 30–2, 39, 48, 70, 91, 140
exilic nationalism   150
exilic transnationalism   6

färänj   29, 31
Federal Republic of Germany   52
feminism   11
First Armenian Republic   53
First Council of Nicaea (AD 325)   202
First World War   29, 33, 34, 52, 108, 109, 119, 156
Fleischer, Oskar   184
Flores-Yeffal, Nadia Y.   71
folk music   184, 185
folk songs   181, 184, 185
Ford, Henry   156
Forty Days of Musa Dagh, The (Werfel)   217
Foucault, Michel   108, 149, 151, 155, 156, 158, 271. *See also* governmentality
France/French   28, 33, 35, 38, 39
   government   112
   historiography   27
French Mandate   159
Fuad, Reşad   224
Funkerkaserne   51–4, 56–8

Gamlen, Alan   69
Geneva   116
genocide   9–10, 78, 79, 109, 119, 212, 213, 215–20, 227. *See also* Armenian Genocide
Georgia   48, 245
Germany   49–51, 53, 55, 56
Gilroy, Paul   3, 70
Ginsberg, Allen   203
Gizagēdĕ Hayasdan (Focus on Armenia, Vrej-Armen)   196
Gnduni, Hay   118
Gomidas Institute   186
Gorki, Maxim   224
Gosh, Mkhitar   261
governmentality   3, 108, 155, 156, 271, 272
   diasporic   110
   studies   109
   transnational   108–9
government-in/of-exile   53, 69, 75, 110, 112, 113, 118, 269

Gramsci, Antonio 261
Great Repatriation (1946–8) 70
Greece 30, 56, 74, 112, 114, 128 n.23
'Gṛung' ('Crane,' song, Komitas) 182, 189–90
Guattari, Félix 197, 198
Gulbenkian, Calouste 118
Gutman, David 13, 14
Gyulkhandanian, Avetis 114

habäsha 29, 31. *See also* Ethio-Armenians
Hadjinian, Jack 59
The Hague 72
Hairenikʻ (periodical) 119
Hakobyan, Arsen 77
Hakobyan, Hranush 232
Halbwachs, Maurice 34, 35
Hamasebastatsʻiakan shinarar miutʻiwn (Pan-Sebastian Construction Union) 120
Hampuyr (Embrace, Oshagan) 201
Haṛach (periodical) 2, 38, 108, 113, 115, 118, 271
Harar 28
Harootunian, Harry 220
Hayabahbanum 148
hayaser (Armenophile) 58
hayashad (Armenian populated) 36
Hayastan (journal) 94
Hayastani ōgnutʻyan komite (Committee to Aid Armenia, HOK) 110–13, 115, 117, 121–5, 126
  Central Committee 112, 118
  expansion 116–21
  Fourth Regional Congress 118
  in France and United States 117, 118, 120
  governmental domains 116–21
Hay Gin (magazine) 11, 220
Haykakan Karmir Khachʻ (Armenian Red Cross). *See* Armenian Relief Society
Haylä Sellasē (Emperor) 33
Hayrenikʻ (periodical) 2, 108, 113–15, 118, 122–4
hayutʻyun (Armen-ity) 47
Hebrew Bible 254
'The Heroes' (Chobanian) 96

HMEM. *See* Armenian General Athletic Union
Hobbes, Thomas 271
Hobsbawn, Eric 95
homecoming 4, 28, 78
homeland 32–5, 36, 39, 67, 72, 95, 96, 110, 111, 118, 179, 180
  ancestral 67, 68, 70, 82, 99
Horizon Weekly (journal) 196
Horujy, Sergey S. 149, 151, 158, 161
Hovanessian, Martine 30, 33
Hovannisian, Richard 260
Hovhanessian, Takuhi 183
Hovhannisyan, Ashot 112
Hürriyet Daily News (newspaper) 232
Husaper (periodical) 108, 114, 115

identity
  Armenian 12, 45, 47, 49, 54, 59, 91, 96, 100, 137, 141–4, 175, 191 n.20, 225, 242, 264
  borders 28, 29
  collective 2, 91, 95, 98, 99, 101, 179, 256
  diasporic 1, 16, 68, 72, 81, 91–102, 103 n.5, 136, 137, 139, 140, 143–6, 188
  formation process 45, 47, 191 n.12, 264
  making 34
  national 28, 56, 75, 91–3, 95, 98, 100, 105 n.63, 139, 142
  politics 194, 208 n.4
  shaping 15, 53
  Soviet 54, 59
'Imagination's emancipation' (Karakashian) 196
imagined community 260
India 8, 111, 128 n.15, 252, 257, 258, 269
Institute of Armenian music 188
institutional and intellectual elites 136
integration 28, 38, 39, 69, 153
Internationale Musikgesellschaft (International Musical Society) 184
International Refugee Organization 52
Iran 7, 20 n.36, 51, 56, 74, 87 n.63, 137–9, 152, 179, 183, 245, 256
Iraq 20 n.36, 56, 74–6, 152
Iraq War (2003–11) 71
Istanbul 38, 212–15, 217

Istanbul Armenians   232–45
   diasporic   243–5
   problems within 'diaspora'
      thesis   233–40
   problems within 'not diaspora'
      thesis   241–3
Izvestia   47

Jacobson, Roman   270
Jalalian, Sedrak   53
Jamalian, Arshak   108, 113–15
Jerusalem   28, 34, 35, 38
   Armenian Quarter of   34
Jews   27, 35, 99, 222
Jinbashian, Ishkhan   135, 195, 196
Julfa. *See* New Julfans
justice-seeking mechanisms   72

kaghakats'i   34, 35
*kaght'agan*s   213–16, 219, 229 n.12
k'ahana-s (married priests)   37
Kajaznuni, Hovhannes   107
Kanayan, Drastamat (Dro)   53
Karakashian, Mher   196
Karapents, Hakob   136–40, 137, 145, 146
Kardashian, Kim   264
Kars   61 n.20, 242
Kasbarian, Sossie   14, 70, 81
kawaṛ   215
Kemp   36
Kempjis   36
Kerovpyan, Aram   186
Kessab   252
Kevorkian, Garo   53
Kevorkian Seminary   183
khach'k'ar-s   37
Khanjian, Aghasi   118
Kharkov   47, 51
Kharpert   29, 41 n.11, 242
Khent'ĕ (Raffi). *See* Madman
Khent' gaydzer (Mad Sparks, Shamlian, Haiduk)   196
Khujab (Panic, poem, Oshagan)   206, 207
K'aghak' (The City, poem, Oshagan)   200, 207
K'arughi (Crossroad, poem, Oshagan)   198–9
Kiev   47, 51
Kochakian, Garabed   156

Komitas (Soghomon Soghomonian)   177, 181–90, 239
Korenizatsiya (Indigenization)   47
Kortian, Garbis   253
Kouchag, Nahabed   255
Koyounian, Karnig   253
Kradjian, Serouj   186
Krueger, Derek   149, 151, 158
Kulischer, Eugene   45
Kuyumjian, Rita Soulahian   183

Lark Society   265
Lastivertsi, Aristakes   255
Lausanne Treaty (1923)   117, 118, 216
League of Nations   118
Lebanese Civil War
   1958   270
   1975–90   206
Lebanon   11, 71, 53–4, 159, 179, 207
Leipzig   101, 226, 272
Les pommes rouges d'Arménie (Sarkissian)   36
Letters from Zaat'ar (*Namakner Zaat'arēn*, Berberian)   143–5
Levi-Strauss, Claude   270
Lezginka   57
LGBTQ movement   263
Libaridian, Gerard   194, 260
Librairie Orientale   38
'Light and Mind' (Loys ev Mitk')   137
literary discourse   195
'Literary Manifesto' (Oshagan)   194, 199
Lithuanian displaced persons (DPs)   54
'Little Armenias' (*ayn p'ok'rig hayut'iwnĕ*)   38
liturgical music   184
liturgical subject   149, 151, 153, 155, 158–62
liturgy   142, 148, 149, 151, 158, 161, 162, 163 n.4, 167 n.37, 202
Locke, John   272
London, Jack   224
Los Angeles   57
Lusangar (Photograph, poem, Oshagan)   205
Lutheran World Federation   52
Lyon   35, 36

Maastricht   72, 75, 169 n.54
McCarthy, Joseph   56

Macdonald, Sharon   72
McNarney, Joseph T.   50
Madman, The (*Khentʿĕ*, Raffi)   139, 140, 145
Mahmood, Saba   151, 158
Maisons de la Culture arménienne (Center for Armenian Heritage)   38
Makarian, Jora   57
Malkki, Liisa   153
Ma Mung, Emmanuel   30
Mängestu Haylä Maryam   33
Mantashev, Alexander   97
Marash   47
Mardgotsʿ (periodical)   114
Mardikian, George   54–5
Mark, Haiganoush   11, 220
Marmara (newspaper)   218
Martial Law   224, 226
Marx, Karl   261
Matiossian, Vartan   233, 234, 240, 242, 253, 254
Mehyan movement   13
Mekhitarists   54, 270
Melkonyan, Ruben   242
Menelik II (emperor)   29
Menk (We) generation   13, 198
Meṛnoghner (Mortals, Oshagan)   200
Mersin   47
Mgrditchian, George   189
Miasnikyan, Aleksander   111
Migliorino, Nicola   73
migration, migrants. *See specific entries of migration, migrants and diaspora*
Mikayelyan, Karen   117
Mikoyan, Anastas   47
Mills, C. W.   261
Mirak, Robert   156
Mishra, Pankaj   263
Missakian, Shavarsh   38, 113–15
Mitterrand, François   38
miutʿiwn   160
Mkhitarian, Gor   259, 260
mobilization, diasporas as   68, 69
modernization   92–3, 100, 211 n.44
Montebello   57, 58
Moughalian, Sato   183
Mrchiwnneru Verchaluysĕ (The Sunset of the Ants, Biberyan)   222
Mshaguytʿ (periodical)   224

Musa Dagh   52, 217–18
Mush   240
music   12, 16, 29–31, 80, 141, 175–7, 180–9, 190 n.3, 191 n.16, 192 n.27, 208, 211 n.44, 253, 258–60

Naghash, Mgrdich   255
Nagorno-Karabakh   77, 156, 194, 195, 197. *See also* Artsakh
Nahanchĕ aṛantsʿ erki (Retreat Without Song, Shahnour)   259
Nakhapan (Preface, poem, Oshagan)   204
Nalbandian, Kevork   31
Nalbandian, Vartkes   33
Nalbantian, Tsolin   11, 164 n.10
Natalie, Shahan   113–14
National Assembly   92
National Center of Armenian Memory (Centre National de la Mémoire Arménienne, CNMA)   160
national home (*azgayin ōjakh*)   118
national identity   28, 75, 91–3, 95, 98, 100, 139, 142
nationalism   29, 33, 53, 55, 95, 100, 143, 154, 167 n.40, 197, 200, 203, 204
Nationalities Policy (1920s)   47
national liberation   96, 98
naturalization, politics of   48
Navasardian, Vahan   108, 113–15
Nazi Germany   49
Nazi party   217
Near East Relief refugee camps, Syria   36
negusä negest   29
nerkaght/nerkaghtʿtsʿi   17–18 n.1, 36
Netherlands, The   2, 15, 67, 68, 72–82, 87 n.62, 169 n.54, 257
New Arabkir quarter, Yerevan   113
New Julfans   8, 14, 257, 257-8
New York   12, 22 n.63, 119–21, 123, 128 n.23, 131 n.48, 132 n.55, 138, 168 n.42
New Yorker, The   50
New York Times, The   124
Nichanian, Marc   12, 141, 180, 187, 201, 222, 223
Niw Yorkʿi Metʿron (New York's Metro, poem, Oshagan)   204
non-state governmental power   3, 149, 150, 151

non-state institutional power 150
Nor badarak (New Mass, poem) 202
Nor Jugha/Isfahan 252, 257, 258, 261.
    See also New Julfa
Nor Keank' (journal) 93, 95, 99, 100
Nor Lur (periodical) 226
Nor Ōr (periodical) 220, 221, 223–6
Northern Greece 30
nostalgia 36, 39, 80
Nubarashēn quarter, Yerevan 113
Nubar Library. *See* Armenian National Library of Paris (*P'arizi Haygagan Azkayin Madenataranĕ*)
Nubar Pasha, Boghos 38, 100, 117
Nur, Rıza 216

Occupy movement (2011) 263
Ohanian, Alexis 264
Organization of Istanbul Armenians 245
Oshagan, Hagop 1, 94, 139–41, 180, 187
Oshagan, Vahé 92, 98, 102, 135–7, 140–3, 145, 146
Oshagan's (Vahé) poetry 194–208. *See also individual works*
    Armenian Christianity in renewed exile 200–3
    declarations of independence 194–7
    decoding gestures 207–8
    deconstructing ARF 197–200
    diasporizing modernist narrativity 203–7
Otian, Yervant 91, 94
Ottoman Armenians 29, 74, 91, 92, 93, 97. *See also* Armenians in Turkey
Ottoman Armenian literati 92, 93
Ottoman Empire 1, 10, 54, 56, 93, 97–9, 108, 109, 179, 185, 212, 215
Ottoman Revolution (1908) 9
'Our Students' (Chobanian) 101

Paboudjian, Pascal 211 n.44
Pakine (magazine) 201
Palestine 34, 35, 39
Paluyan, Hrant 222, 223
Pangaltı Armenian School 217
Panossian, Razmik 56
Papazian, Vahan (*Goms*) 53, 114
Paris 1, 3, 12–14, 38–9, 91, 95, 97–101, 105, 108, 112, 114, 117–19, 141, 160, 171 n.70, 185, 186, 188, 192 n.32, 197–9, 201, 208, 222, 225, 271
Paris Peace Conference (1919–20) 117
Party for Labourers and Peasants 225
Patani (journal) 94, 98
patriotism, 96, 97
    within the Ottoman Empire 96, 97
Pattie, Susan Paul 14, 47, 152, 163 n.4
Pawłowska, Karolina 71
Pehlivanian, Aram 212, 220, 221, 223, 224–7
periodicals, Armenian
    Anahit (journal) 91, 94
    Ararat (periodical) 223
    Armenia (journal) 94, 95
    Armenian International Magazine (AIM) 135, 195, 196
    Armenian Mirror, The (newspaper) 120
    Artemis (magazine) 94
    Asbarēz (newspaper) 119, 186, 202
    Aysōr (periodical) 223
    Azat Khōsk' (newspaper) 94, 95
    Aztarar (periodical) 220
    Banasēr (journal) 94, 95
    Biwzandion (journal) 100
    Diaspora: A Journal of Transnational Studies (journal) 2, 3, 4, 194, 235, 236, 271
    Droshak (periodical) 108, 114
    editors 2, 91, 93–102, 113, 114, 138, 209 n.13, 223, 234, 236, 270–2
    Eritasard Hayastan (periodical) 116
    Hairenik' (periodical) 119
    Harach (periodical) 2, 38, 108, 113, 115, 118, 271
    Hayastan (journal) 94
    Hay Gin (magazine) 11, 220
    Hayrenik' (journal) 2, 100, 108, 113–15, 118, 122–4
    Horizon Weekly (journal) 196
    Husaper (periodical) 108, 114, 115
    Mardgots' (periodical) 114
    Marmara (newspaper) 218
    Masis (journal) 100
    Mshaguyt' (periodical) 224
    Nor Keank' (journal) 93, 95, 99, 100
    Nor Lur (periodical) 226
    Nor Ōr (periodical) 220, 221, 223–6

Pakine (magazine) 201
Patani (journal) 94, 98
Tēbi Luys (journal) 223
Tsaghik (magazine) 100
Zartʻōnkʻ (periodical) 95, 223
Zhamanak (newspaper) 94, 95, 218, 223
Perl, Jeff 251
Pʻokhan aghōtʻkʻi (In Place of Prayer, poem, Oshagan) 201, 202
Poladian, Sirvart 186
Polish American Congress 52
Pontic Greeks 30
Portes, Alejandro 71
Port Said 52, 64 n.71
Portugalian, Mkrtich 91, 94, 95
'pre-diasporic' (*Nakha- spʻiwṛkʻean*) 253
Prisoners of War (POWs) 46, 50, 54, 55

Raffi 139, 140, 145
Red Cross 52, 132 n.55
Relocation and Resettlement Law ('Sevk ve İskân Kanunu,' 1915) 185
repatriation 17–18 n.1, 36, 50, 56, 59, 62 n.33, 65 n.90, 70, 71, 78, 86 n.38, 153, 236
'Requiem Aeternam in Memory of Komitas' (poem, Charents) 186
return, diasporic 70
Rhône Valley 35, 37, 38
Romania 50, 56, 62 n.42
Rome 50, 225
ṛusahay 10, 45–9, 51–8, 70, 74–6, 102, 156, 257
Russia, Republic of 46, 53, 56, 60 nn.8, 9, 76, 94, 102, 166 n.32, 257
ṛusahay 10, 45–9, 51–8, 70, 74–6, 102, 156, 257
Russian Soviet Federated Socialist Republic (RSFSR/Soviet Russia) 46
Russian Revolution 48
Russification 54
Russo-Turkish borderland 48

Safran, William 32, 68, 235–7
Sahakyan, Vahe 261
Said, Edward 177, 188
Samuel, Hrand 38
San Francisco 54, 197, 202

Sarkissian, Kourken 194
Saroyan, Suren 55
Saroyan, William 259
Sartre, Jean-Paul 203
Sebastatsʻineru hayrenaktsʻakan miutʻiwn (Sebastian's Compatriotic Union) 120
Sebastio verashinakan miutʻiwn (Sebastia Reconstruction Union) 120
Second World War 45, 46, 126, 160, 221, 222
sedentariness 27–8, 35, 38, 39
Selian, Patrik 120
Seth, Mesrovp Jacob 252
Sevak, Paruyr 186
Sevan Armenian Dance Ensemble 57
Shamlian, Haiduk 196
Shäwa 29, 33
Shepperson, George 236
Shnorhali, Nerses 256
Siruni, H. J. 252
Sis in Cilicia 214. *See also* Cilician See
Sivas 221, 241, 242, 245
Social Democratic Hunchakian Party (SDHP, Hnchak Party) 95, 116, 117, 123, 125, 130 n.42, 131 n.47
social media 259, 263
social text 195
Society of Armenian Studies (SAS) 250, 269
Soviet-American relations (1960s) 58
Soviet Armenia. *See* Armenian Soviet Socialist Republic
Soviet Ukraine. *See* Ukrainian Soviet Socialist Republic
Soviet Union. *See* Union of Soviet Socialist Republics (USSR)
Spʻiwṛkʻi ṛazmavaragan sgzpunkʻner (Diaspora's Strategic Principles, Zeitlian) 196
Srjaranĕ (*Usumnasirutʻiwn*) ('The Cafe (Study), poem, Oshagan) 200
Stalin, Joseph 70, 221
state-centric studies 5–6, 69, 81, 110
stateless power 3, 37, 137, 145, 146, 150, 194, 250, 261, 263, 272
Stern, Fritz 262
Stratton Bill 55
students' groups

activism 101, 102
　student unions 101–2
Sultan Abdul Hamid 13, 93
Sumgait Massacres (1988) 156, 157
Suny, Ronald 95
Surb Karapet Church, Maastricht 75
Svajian, Vahram 100
Syrian Armenians 73–4
　in Décines, France 158–61
Syrian Armenians in Netherlands 67–83
　Armenian citizenship to 67, 77–8, 81 vs. Armenians in Armenia 81
　collective problems and diaspora organizations 77–9, 82
　diaspora-homeland relations 67–71, 81, 83
　diaspora organizations and newly arrived migrants 71–2, 82
　and Dutch Armenian diasporic networks 73–7
　returning to Syria and Armenia 79–81
Syrian Civil War 71, 73, 77, 81

Täfäri Mäkonnen (Crown Prince) 30, 31
Talaat Pasha 185
Tanzimat 92
Tashnak. *See* Armenian Revolutionary Federation (ARF)
Tashnag. *See* Armenian Revolutionary Federation (ARF)
Tchilingirian, Hratch 151
Tēbi Luys (journal) 223
teghats'is (locals) 57, 65 n.93
Ter-Hovhannisian, Tirayr 121
Terlemezyan, Panos 189
Ter-Minasian, Ruben 113, 114
Ter Petrosyan, Levon 255
tertōn 94
Tertsagian, Kevork Vartabed 183
Terzian, Avedis 33
Terzibashian, Avedis 33
T'akart'in shurch (Around the Snare, Oshagan) 201, 205
T'ashnagts'ut'iwn (Federation, poem, Oshagan) 200
Tiflis/Tbilisi 46, 94, 108, 184
Tigranes (King) 234
Tokat 214, 242
Tölölyan, Khachig 2–4, 6–14, 27, 28, 31, 32, 34, 37, 53, 56, 67–70, 75, 81–3, 93, 95, 98, 109, 136, 137, 145, 146, 150–1, 154, 158, 178, 194, 214, 215, 233, 236, 237, 244, 269–72
Tölölyan, Minas 269, 272
Torah 254
Torlakian, Misak 53
Tourian, Leon 122–4, 156
trade unions 47
transimperial cosmopolitanism 5
transnational governmentality 69
transnationalism 2–4, 6–14, 83, 95, 150, 163 n.3, 251
transnational organizations 75–7, 82. *See also* Armenian Apostolic Church; Armenian Revolutionary Federation (ARF)
transnational politics and governmental strategies of post-genocide Armenian diaspora (1920s-1930s) 107–26
　ARF leaders and anti-Bolshevik discourse 107–10
　Armenian Church in America 121–5
　discursive construction of Armenian collective needs 110–16, 125
　HOK and ARF governmental domains 116–21
trauma 45
Treaty of Sévres (1920) 112
Tsaghik (magazine) 100
Ts'eghakrōn 120
T'ught' aṙ Erevan (Epistle to Yerevan, Dzarougian) 259
Tulsa 182, 183
Turkey, Republic of 1, 11, 61 n.20, 156
Turkey's Party for Labourers and Peasants (Türkiye Emekçi ve Köylü Partisi) 224, 226
Turkish Communist Party (TKP) 224–7
Turkish-language songs 181
Turkish State Archives 218, 226
Turkism from Angora to Baku and Turkish Orientation (Natalie) 113

Ukraine 53, 54, 56, 71, 114
　Soviet Ukraine 46–9, 59, 166 n.32
Ukrainian Soviet Socialist Republic (Soviet Ukraine) 46–9, 59, 166 n.32
Ukrainian American Relief Committee 52

Ukrainization 47
Unction (*Otsumĕ*, Oshagan) 140–3, 145, 201
Union of Arabkir Armenians of America 113
Union of European Armenian Students 101
Union of Soviet Socialist Republics (USSR) 1, 46–52, 54–6, 70, 221
   diplomatic relations with France 112
   USSR Citizenship law (1938) 48
United Nations Refugee Rehabilitation Authority (UNRRA) 51, 52
United States 2, 12, 16, 32, 45, 112, 141, 152, 156, 169 n.53, 176, 199, 208 n.4, 214, 261, 264
   AGBU in 131 n.48
   Armenians in 54–8, 64 n.80, 70, 78, 109, 118, 120, 124, 125, 157, 176, 179, 180, 188, 245
   government 55
   HOK and ARF 115–17, 119, 120
   Polish immigrants in 236
University of California, Los Angeles (UCLA) 250
University of Southern California (USC), Institute of Armenian Studies 46
Utrecht 72

Valence 35, 36, 38
Van 33, 60 n.9, 61 n.20, 240, 242
Varadarjan, Latha 6
Vardan Mamikonian 96
Vardanyan, Grigor 119
Vardapet, Komitas 177
Varjabedian, Sisag H. 252
Varuzhan, Daniel 12, 187
Vasbouragan 33
victimization 72, 79, 82
Vienna 38
Volksdeutsche 52
von Bleicheröder, Gerson 262
Vosketar Publishing (Osketaṛ Hratarakchʻakan) 138
Vratsian, Simon 107, 113–15, 118
Vrej-Armen 196

Washington Post, The 124
Wealth Tax 223
Werbner, Pnina 95
Werfel, Franz 217
Western Allies 50
Western Armenia 70
Western Armenian literature 203
   language 200, 208
   tradition 1
women, women's groups, periodicals 75, 119, 263
   Artemis (magazine) 94
   Biwzandion (journal) 100
   at camp 51
   in families 100
   Hay Gin (magazine) 11, 220
   Hayrenikʻ (journal) 100
   kidnapping 215
   Masis (journal) 100
   social roles 100
Woskan, Khwaja Petros di 257

Yalta Agreement 50
Yekmalian, Makar 184
Yerevan 12, 46, 48, 53, 62 n.42, 83, 87 n.63, 113, 119, 186, 189
yergir 215. *See also* homeland
Yesayan, Zabel 12, 100
Yıldız, Burcu 187
youth, youth groups and movements 75, 102, 119, 121, 141–3, 146
   Armenian Youth Federation (*Tsʻeghakrōn*) 57, 120, 133 n.65
   HOK youth chapters 120
   'Light and Mind' (Loys ev Mitkʻ) 137
Yozgat 214, 238

Zarian, Constant 187
Zartʻōnkʻ (periodical) 95, 223
Zeitlian, Hraztan 196
Zekiyan, Levon 1
Zhamanak (newspaper) 94, 95, 218, 223
Ziflioğlu, Vercihan 232
Zionism 99
Žižek, Slavoj 272
Zoryan Institute, the 3, 194